AdvancED Game Design with Flash

Rex van der Spuy

AdvancED Game Design with Flash

AdvancED Game Design with Flash

Copyright © 2010 by Rex van der Spuy

All rights reserved. No part of this work may be reproduced or transmitted in any form or by any means, electronic or mechanical, including photocopying, recording, or by any information storage or retrieval system, without the prior written permission of the copyright owner and the publisher.

ISBN-13 (pbk): 978-1-4302-2739-7

ISBN-13 (electronic): 978-1-4302-2740-3

Printed and bound in the United States of America 9 8 7 6 5 4 3 2 1

Trademarked names, logos, and images may appear in this book. Rather than use a trademark symbol with every occurrence of a trademarked name, logos, or image we use the names, logos, or images only in an editorial fashion and to the benefit of the trademark owner, with no intention of infringement of the trademark.

The use in this publication of trade names, service marks, and similar terms, even if they are not identified as such, is not to be taken as an expression of opinion as to whether or not they are subject to proprietary rights.

Distributed to the book trade worldwide by Springer Science+Business Media LLC., 233 Spring Street, 6th Floor, New York, NY 10013. Phone 1-800-SPRINGER, fax (201) 348-4505, e-mail orders-ny@springer-sbm.com, or visit www.springeronline.com.

For information on translations, please e-mail rights@apress.com or visit www.apress.com.

Apress and friends of ED books may be purchased in bulk for academic, corporate, or promotional use. eBook versions and licenses are also available for most titles. For more information, reference our Special Bulk Sales–eBook Licensing web page at www.apress.com/info/bulksales.

The information in this book is distributed on an "as is" basis, without warranty. Although every precaution has been taken in the preparation of this work, neither the author(s) nor Apress shall have any liability to any person or entity with respect to any loss or damage caused or alleged to be caused directly or indirectly by the information contained in this work.

The source code for this book is freely available to readers at www.friendsofed.com in the Downloads section.

Credits

President and Publisher:
Paul Manning

Lead Editor:
Ben Renow-Clarke

Technical Reviewer:
Joshua Freeney

Editorial Board:
Clay Andres, Steve Anglin, Mark Beckner, Ewan Buckingham, Gary Cornell, Jonathan Gennick, Jonathan Hassell, Michelle Lowman, Matthew Moodie, Duncan Parkes, Jeffrey Pepper, Frank Pohlmann, Douglas Pundick, Ben Renow-Clarke, Dominic Shakeshaft, Matt Wade, Tom Welsh

Coordinating Editor:
Kelly Moritz

Copy Editor:
Marilyn Smith

Compositor:
Lynn L'Heureux

Indexer:
Brenda Miller

Artist:
April Milne

Cover Designer:
Bruce Tang

For Mom and Jim, for all your love and support

Contents at a Glance

Contents

About the Author

Rex van der Spuy, author of *Foundation Game Design with Flash*, is a freelance interactive media designer specializing in Flash game design, interface design, and ActionScript programming.

Rex programmed his first adventure game at 10 years' old on his Commodore VIC-20. He went on to study film production, graduating with a BFA in Film/Video from York University (Toronto) in 1993, and spent a number of years working as an independent producer and freelance cameraman. He has designed Flash games and done interactive interface programming for clients such as Agency Interactive (Dallas), Scottish Power (Edinburgh), DC Interact (London), Draught Associates (London), and the Bank of Montreal (Canada). He also builds game engines and interactive museum installations for PixelProject (Cape Town). In addition, he taught advanced courses in Flash game design for the Canadian School of India (Bangalore).

In his spare time, Rex has done a considerable amount of technical and fiction writing, and maintains a semiprofessional musical career as a performer on the sitar. Rex currently divides his time equally between Canada, India, and South Africa, and works on consulting and software development projects for clients in India, North America, and the UK. He also maintains the game design learning and experimental lab, `www.kittykatattack.com`.

About the Technical Reviewer

Josh Freeney is currently a partner in a new Michigan-based interactive firm called YETi CGI. His focus at YETi is getting high-quality Flash content and infrastructure in place to serve both business and entertainment applications. He is also an instructor for the Digital Animation and Game Design program at Ferris State University in Grand Rapids, Michigan. Josh teaches Flash game development classes focused on rapid agile production with maximum reusability. He likes board games, camping, sleeping in, and anything LEGO.

About the Cover Image Designer

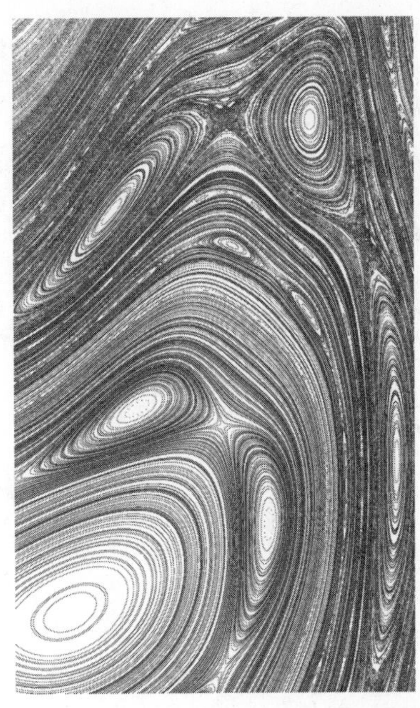

Bruce Tang is a freelance web designer, visual programmer, and author from Hong Kong. His main creative interest is generating stunning visual effects using Flash or Processing.

Bruce has been an avid Flash user since Flash 4, when he began using it to create games, websites, and other multimedia content. After several years of ActionScripting, he found himself increasingly drawn toward visual programming and computational art. He likes to integrate math and physics into his work, simulating 3D and other real-life experiences on the screen. His first Flash book was published in October 2005. Bruce's folio, featuring Flash and Processing pieces, can be found at `www.betaruce.com`. Visit his blog at `www.betaruce.com/blog`.

The cover image uses a high-resolution Henon phase diagram generated by Bruce with Processing, which he feels is an ideal tool for such experiments. Henon is a strange attractor created by iterating through some equations to calculate the coordinates of millions of points. The points are then plotted with an assigned color.

$x_{n+1} = x_n \cos(a) - (y_n - x_n^p) \sin(a)$

$y_{n+1} = x_n \sin(a) + (y_n - x_n^p) \cos(a)$

Acknowledgments

A great debt of gratitude to the phenomenally hard-working, dedicated, and talented team at friends of ED who made this book possible. You're the best bunch of people to work with, ever. Josh, Fran, Kelly, Marilyn, and Ben, we did it!

A particular note of gratitude to the lead editor, Ben Renow-Clarke. It was his vision for *Foundation Game Design* and *AdvancED Game Design* to be two books, and they exist thanks to his consistent vision and encouragement over the two years that it took to write them.

Introduction

Game design is unquestionably one of the most interesting and complex challenges that a programmer can take on. If you've ever tackled the design of even a simple game, you'll know that the questions you have and the problems you encounter while building it can often boggle the mind with their seemingly labyrinthine complexities. But like any labyrinth, it's not hard to navigate if you know the way.

Enter the labyrinth!

Most of the problems that arise in building a game can disappear with a just bit of understanding of some of the basic principles behind them. This book takes a detailed look at the classic problems of video-game design, and offers a clear path to understanding and solving them:

- Keeping your game data and logic separated from your visuals
- Managing big games with hundreds of objects and variables
- Using vectors for pinpoint accurate collision detection and physics simulation
- Handling collisions between circles ("billiard-ball physics") and collisions between circles and corners
- Handling multiple object collisions and collisions between irregularly shaped objects
- Creating game environments that can be interactively destroyed and modified
- Saving, loading, and sharing game data
- Streamlining your game design management and performance by using a tile-based model
- Pathfinding so that game objects can navigate their way around complex environments

This is a classic education in making video games and a compendium of all the important techniques you'll need to know to flourish as a professional game designer.

Labyrinthine complexities? Not anymore! Theseus had a giant ball of string to help him escape from the labyrinth of the Minotaur. You have this book.

Things you need to know

AdvancED Game Design with Flash is a direct follow-up of my book *Foundation Game Design with Flash* (friends of ED, 2009). If you've read that book, and have had a bit of practical experience making some of your own games, you have all the skills and knowledge you need to enjoy the fun we're going to have in this book.

If you haven't read *Foundation Game Design with Flash*, but have a solid practical experience programming with ActionScript 3.0 (AS3.0), this book is all you need to jump right in and start building games.

However, make sure you have a comfortable understanding of these topics:

- Creating, controlling, and modifying `Sprite` and `MovieClip` objects
- Making and programming buttons
- Generating random numbers
- Controlling objects with the mouse and keyboard
- Moving objects with acceleration and friction
- Implementing collision detection: `hitTestObject`, `hitTestPoint`, and distance-based systems
- Using `ADDED_TO_STAGE` and `REMOVED_FROM_STAGE` events to reliably initialize and remove display objects
- Changing the display object-stacking order
- Filtering display objects to add bevel and drop-shadow effects
- Using the `Point` class and converting local coordinates to global coordinates
- Object-oriented programming (OOP):
  - Inheritance (making new classes by extending other classes)
  - *Composition* (using instances of classes inside other classes)
  - Private properties
  - Getters and setters
  - Different classes for game construction
  - Dependency (building classes so that they can work without depending on other classes)
- Using static properties and methods
- Calculating distance and angles using the `Math` class
- Making drag-and-drop objects
- Using a `Timer` object
- Dispatching events and event bubbling

If you think you might be a bit hazy in any of areas, have a quick flip through *Foundation Game Design with Flash* and see if you can find the level at which you're comfortable working. If you need to do a little more reconnaissance work, don't worry—this book will still be here waiting for you when you're ready!

I've also assumed that you have some familiarity with the drawing API: AS3.0's classes that allow you to draw lines and shapes on the stage. If you haven't used the drawing API before, take a quick look at the chapter "Using the drawing API" in Adobe's AS3.0 documentation (`http://help.adobe.com/en_US/ActionScript/3.0_ProgrammingAS3/`). At the end of Chapter 1 in this book, there's also a quick-reference guide to common drawing API commands. That should be all you need to know to get started.

What about math?

"Don't I have to be math genius to be good at game design?"

Of course not! Like *Foundation Game Design with Flash*, this book has been written from a 100% certified math-friendly point of view. That means that if the mathematical part of your brain somehow went on a very long vacation somewhere between fourth and fifth grade, and hasn't even sent you as much as a postcard since, all the math you need to know is covered in this book.

And you don't necessarily need to fully understand the math that we do cover. All you need to know is how to apply it to achieve the effect you want. This book's source files also include some helpful custom classes that contain most of these formulae. Just drop them into your own projects, and you're good to go.

But you'll be surprised at how much of the math you actually understand and enjoy learning when you see it applied in a practical context. And really, if you're serious about game design, you should know the math. It will help you to see simple solutions to problems that might otherwise be completely baffling.

Chapter 2 is all about vector math, which is covered in detail from the ground up. As you'll see, vector math is just a codified way of describing the geometry of space. You'll be able to see the result of every formula on the stage, and I'm sure you'll enjoy the great control it gives you over your game environment.

Things you need to have

An **integrated development environment** (IDE) is the tool that you use to make Flash games. Adobe has two commercial IDEs, and you've probably already used at least one of them:

- **Flash Professional (also known as Flash CS3, CS4, or CS5)**: A big advantage to using the Flash IDE is that you can draw your game objects using its drawing tools, have access to the movie clip timeline for doing animation, and create game objects using library instances.
- **Flash Builder 4**: Flash Builder (formerly Flex Builder) is optimized for AS3.0 programming. It doesn't allow you to create game objects visually—there are no drawing tools and no library. But it's probably the best pure-code AS3.0 editor available. Flash Builder is free for students.

If you don't need or want all the bells and whistles of Flash Professional or Flash Builder, and don't need to do timeline animation or create symbols, you can use an alternative IDE:

- **Flash Develop**: A completely free AS3.0 programming IDE for Windows.
- **Eclipse**: A general IDE for any programming language, which can be customized for AS3.0. It's free and available for Windows, Linux, and Mac OS X. Flash Builder is actually based on Eclipse, and Adobe has a Flash Builder plug-in you can use with it.
- **Xcode**: A free IDE from Apple that can be customized to work with AS3.0.
- **Plain text editor**: You can compile your code into a SWF file by using the Flex SDK command-line interface.
- **TextMate**: It's not free, but if you're using Mac OS X, you may want to consider it as a leaner alternative to Flash Builder or Eclipse. You'll also need to install TextMate's ActionScript 3.0 bundle, which is a plug-in for writing and compiling AS3 programs.

To use any of these alternative IDEs, you also need the following:

- **Adobe's free Flex Software Development Kit (SDK)**: This is the core software that compiles SWF files from AS3.0 programs. Slightly confusingly, the Flex SDK is not just for creating Flex applications. It's used to compile *any* AS3.0 program into a SWF. You can download it for free from Adobe's website (`http://opensource.adobe.com`).
- **Debug version of Flash Player**: The debug version of Adobe Flash Player is for AS3.0 developers using the Flex SDK to compile their code. It allows you to see the output of trace commands and runtime errors. If you're unsure which version of Flash Player you currently have installed, or where you can find the debug version, point your browser to `http://playerversion.com`.

A bit of time set aside to learn how to install the SDK and make it work with your chosen IDE. *The Essential Guide to Open Source Flash Development*, by Chris Allen *et al.* (friends of ED, 2008) and *The Essential Guide to Flex 4* by Charles Brown (friends of ED, 2010) are excellent guides to getting started with the SDK.

None of these IDEs allow you to visually draw or animate movie clip symbols or do motion-path animation on the timeline, so they're used purely for programming. But if you make the effort to learn how to use any of them, you can write cutting-edge AS3.0 games and programs without spending a penny.

This book doesn't assume that you're using a particular IDE, so you can work through the examples and source files in any programming environment you like. If you've used only Adobe's Flash IDE, now might be the ideal time to try one of these alternatives.

What kind of games will we make?

The focus of this book is on 2D action games. We're going to look at game-design techniques from the perspective of two classic genres: space-shooters and platform games. We'll cover all the core problems and solutions to building these games from scratch.

I've kept the code and graphics as simple as possible to maintain clarity. I'll leave it up to you take these examples and turn them into spectacular games. Everything you need is all right here, and you'll find a large library of support code, working examples, and game prototypes you can use in your own projects. By the end of the book, you'll be able to apply these skills to any game idea you might have. There's little that you won't be able to approach with confidence.

"Hey, where's the 3D?"

Like *Foundation Game Design with Flash*, this book strategically omits discussing 3D games. The reason is depth (pun intended!). 2D game design is itself such a big topic that you'll be far better prepared for 3D games if you have a comprehensive understanding of 2D. 2D and 3D game design share the same fundamentals, but it's far easier to learn the craft of game design without the extra layers of complexity you would need to tackle to simultaneously learn a 3D engine. At the end of this book, you'll be a great game designer—in any dimension—and you'll find 3D games a snap to develop when you're ready for them. You'll also have advanced knowledge of AS3.0's OOP techniques, such as how to use abstract classes and build a Model-View-Controller system, which you'll need before you can start using 3D APIs like Papervision3D, Alternativa3D, and Away3D.

How to read this book

This is not a book of quick fixes. It's very unlikely that you'll be able to skim through it and pick and choose snippets of code to help you meet a pressing deadline. Instead, it's a book about learning and understanding. I've kept all the material very general and open-ended, so that it can be used for as wide an application as possible. The techniques in this book won't decide for you what kinds of games you're limited to making—that's entirely up to you.

I've also kept the material as nonspecific to AS3.0 and Flash as possible. That means that most of the concepts in this book can be applied to other platforms and programming languages. That's important because, if you you're working at this level, it's unlikely that AS3.0 is going to be the only language you learn in your game-design career. Most of these concepts and techniques will be just as applicable to Java, C++, and Objective-C as they are to AS3.0.

The content follows a very linear path. Most of the content in this book requires that you understand the Model-View-Controller model (covered in Chapter 1) and basic vector math (covered in Chapter 2). So you're not going to get very far unless you've read the first two chapters. They're must-reads. But with those two chapters under your belt, you have a bit more flexibility:

Chapters 3 and 4 deal with specific areas of collision detection involving circles and polygons. If you don't think you'll need to use that information right away, consider skipping ahead to Chapter 5. However, make sure you read the section on abstract classes in Chapter 3 and the section on game structure in Chapter 4.

Chapter 6 contains a very important section on how to do bit-block transfers (blitting). If you work though that section, you could skip ahead to Chapters 7 and 8, which depend on knowing that technique.

Chapters 8 and 9 are about a specific style of game design called tile-based games. You can combine a tile-based design style with any of the other techniques in this book. Chapter 10 covers how to load and save game data using some of AS3.0's built-in tools.

To get the most benefit from this material, you should set aside some time to write your own code based on the examples and concepts.

Here's how I suggest you go about learning each new topic:

- **Understand it**: Take as much time as you need to become fluent with the new code and new concepts. Resist the temptation to jump ahead until you achieve this fluency. If you're struggling with a concept or bit of code, visit the ActionScript discussion forum at the `http://friendsofed.com` website, or any of the other online discussion forums, and run through questions about the concepts with the many friendly and helpful contributors you'll find there. This book can help point the way, but only you can cement the understanding in your own mind.
- **Practice it**: Create your own example files, using your own code, written in your own way. It may be very tempting to copy and paste the code I've written, but you'll be doing yourself a disservice. The best way to learn is by trying, failing, and trying again. When you solve your own problems in your own way, you'll retain the knowledge far better than by reading any explanation in this book. Use the example files as a starting point, but think of how you can improve them or use the same concepts and techniques to solve a problem you're working on. It's very important that the solutions come from your own personal motivation to tackle problems that interest you.
- **Apply it**: Set yourself challenges. At the end of each major section or chapter, set yourself the task of building a simple game based on the new material. I've made some suggestions throughout the text, but there will be plenty of applications that I haven't thought of that I'm sure will be obvious to you while you're reading. This book is about making games, so make as many games as you can! It will become easier and quicker to do so with each mini-game you make, and you'll develop a fluent style. By the end of book, I'm expecting a really great game from you. (And please send me a link when you've completed it.)

I'm asking a lot from you! This book is a big commitment, and it might take you quite some time to work through the material if you follow it properly. We're going to look at some complex topics in depth, and I haven't shied away from tackling some difficult subjects in a lot of detail. Don't be afraid to take as much time as you need. I can assure you that the end result will be worth it: a complete, comprehensive understanding of game design with AS3.0 and Flash that will take you as far as you want to go.

The files you'll need

You can download this book's source files from `http://friendsofed.com`. When you extract the ZIP file, you'll find the following:

- A folder called `com`. This contains all the custom classes and diagnostic mini-apps that we'll use in examples. I'll explain how to install these in the next section.
- Folders titled `Chapter01` to `Chapter10`. These contain subfolders with the AS and SWF files for the examples in each chapter. The AS files are in a folder called `src`, and the SWFs are in a folder called `bin`. I'll refer to these example files throughout the book, and you can test, change, and play with the code as much as you like.

In the next section, I'll explain how these files and folders work together, and how you'll need to set up your IDE to open, change, and recompile them.

Setting up your work environment

Over the decades that programming has matured as a craft, programmers have developed some consistent conventions about where and how to store and organize different types of files. It's worth taking a bit of time to learn these conventions for a number of important reasons:

- It's common for even small game-design projects to involve hundreds of image, code, sound, text, and video files. If after working on a big project for a few weeks, you find that you spend more time looking for files than actually doing any work with them, you'll recognize how important it is to implement a consistent organization system.
- Following conventions that others use is a way of learning from the wisdom of the crowd. Widely adopted conventions evolve because a lot of people struggled with similar problems and, through trial and error, found a system that helps to avoid them. Some of the conventions may not make sense right away, but if you follow them, you'll likely preempt a lot of problems that you might never have considered could occur.
- If you do what everyone else is doing, you'll be able to read their code, and they'll be able to read yours. Working in a team, this is essential. But even if you're working alone, it can often be hard to remember where you kept which file or how you wrote your code if you return to a project after a holiday. Stick to standard conventions, and you'll have a consistent system you can drop your work into.

Organizing the project folder

The `Chapter01` folder in the source files contains a subfolder called `HelloWorld`. It's a model of the file and folder organization convention that we're going to follow in this book. If you open it and look at its structure, you'll see something like Figure 1.

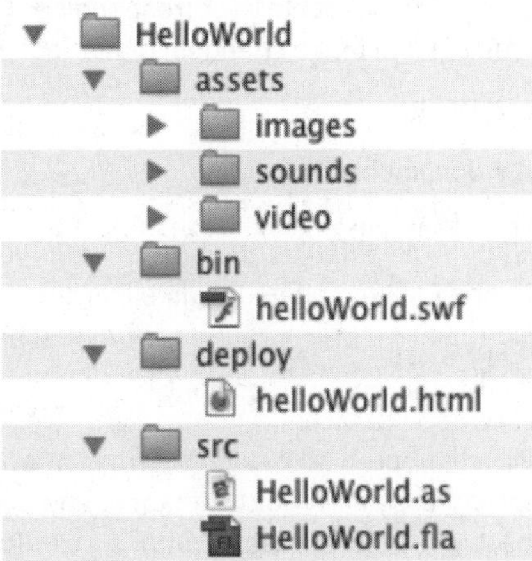

Figure 1. Folder and file conventions used in this book

The project folder, `HelloWorld`, contains all the project subfolders and files. You can give it any name you like, but the name shouldn't contain any spaces. `Hello_World` or `helloWorld` is fine, but not `Hello World`. This is to maintain compatibility with the Flex SDK, which can't compile files that have spaces in their names, or even spaces in the names of any folder in their directory path.

The project subfolders are organized as follows:

- `assets`: This folder contains the extra things that you use in your project, like images, video, and sound.
- `deploy`: This optional folder is used for the final published form that your game takes, such as part of an HTML file.
- `bin`: This is the destination folder for compiled SWFs. "bin" is short for "binary," which is another way of referring to finished, compiled programs. In this book, I use the lowerCamelCase naming convention for SWF names.
    - If you're using Flash Professional, you can specify this destination folder by navigating to **File ➤ Publish Settings ➤ Format** and setting the SWF file path to `../bin/fileName.swf`.
    - In Flash Builder, specify the output folder when you create a new ActionScript project. (By default, the output folder name is `bin-debug`, which is fine to use, too.)

`src`: This is the location of your project-specific AS source files. If you're using Flash Professional, it will also be the location of your main FLA file. (The AS file should be set as the FLA's document class.) You can add as many AS files and subfolders here as you like, including folders for project-specific class libraries.

FLAs and metadata for Flash Professional

Most of the source files in this book don't contain corresponding FLA files. If you're using Flash Professional, follow these steps if you want to make changes to and recompile the example SWFs:

1. Create a new FLA in the `src` folder.
2. Set the AS file as the FLA's document class.
3. Change your publish settings so that the SWF is created in the `bin` folder (this is optional).

The AS file will also contain at least one Flex metadata tag, like this one:

```
[SWF(backgroundColor = "0xFFFFFF",
frameRate = "60", width = "550", height = "400")]
```

Metadata tags are used to supply the compiler with extra information about how you want to publish the SWF. They can also be used to embed assets like fonts, images, and sounds that you want to use in the class. The `SWF` tag tells the compiler what the published SWF's size, frame rate, and background color should be.

Metadata tags are great because they allow you to tinker with your SWF settings and embedded assets directly in your AS code, without needing to depend on the IDE, like Flash's Properties panel. They help to keep all your code in one place, which means that your code is portable across all IDEs.

The only problem is that Flash Professional needs the help of the Flex SDK to use metadata. If you're using the Flash Professional IDE and try to publish AS code that contains a metadata tag, you'll receive a prompt asking you to tell Flash where it can find the SDK, as shown in Figure 2. If this happens, click the **`Update library path`** button. Flash Professional will link to the SDK, and the file will publish without problems. (Sometimes it doesn't publish on the very first attempt, but it will after you've updated the library path.) The Flex SDK is automatically installed when you install Flash Professional, so Flash will know where to find it.

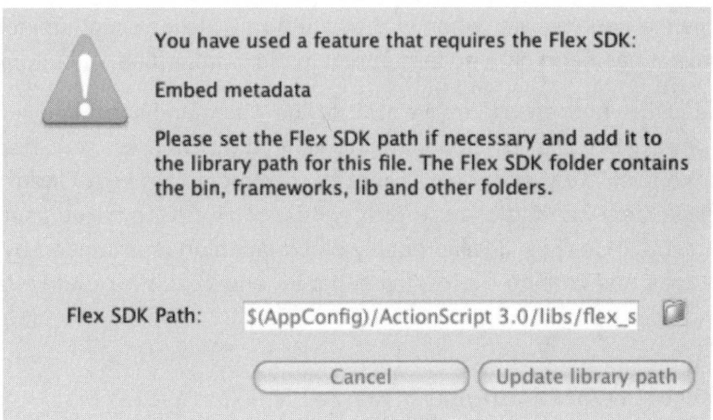

Figure 2. if you use metadata tags, Flash Professional will prompt you to update your library path to point to the Flex SDK.

Using the class library

This book's source files contain a folder called `com`. Open it, and you'll see that its path structure looks something like this: `com/friendsofed/lotsOfClassFolders`. Take a look in the `friendsofed` folder. There, you'll find a lot of different AS files and subfolders. This is a **class library**. The folders contain custom classes that are used by most of the examples and projects in this book. If you want to use them, they need to be available to *any* AS or program you write. This means you need to set up your IDE so that it can always find the class library, no matter where on your hard drive you're working.

Setting the path to the class library

If you're using Flash or Flash Builder, it's easy to set up the IDE to find the class library. In Flash Professional, follow these steps:

1. Open Flash's Preferences dialog box. In Windows, select **File ➤ Preferences**. In Mac OS X, select **Flash ➤ Preferences**.
2. Select **ActionScript ➤ ActionScript 3 Settings**. The Advanced Settings dialog box will open.
3. The first setting is **Source Path**. Click the folder icon, and browse to the location on your system where the com folder that you downloaded from the friends of ED website is located.

In Flash Builder, specify the source path when you create a new ActionScript project. You can change or modify this after the project has been created through the project properties.

If you're using the Flex SDK and an alternative IDE or the command-line compiler, you need to make changes to the flex-config.xml file. You can find this file in the SDK's frameworks folder. The path to it might look something like this: flex_sdk_4/frameworks/flex-config.xml. Open flex-config.xml. It contains all the settings that are used to compile your code. Look for a tag called <source-path>. If this is your first time modifying flex-config, it will probably be commented (surrounded by <!-- and --> tags). Remove the comment tags and change the <source-path> and <path-element> tags so that they look something like this:

```
<source-path append="true">
  <path-element>/absolute/path/to/your/classFolder</path-element>
</source-path>
```

The attribute append="true" means that the path you specify will be an **absolute path**—the complete path to the com folder from your hard drive's root. You'll generally want the path to your class libraries to be absolute so that the compiler can always find them. Let's imagine that you've saved the com folder in another folder called classes. The complete path to the classes folder might look something like this: /username/code/classes.

If you're using Windows, your <path-element> tag should look like this:

```
<path-element>C:\username\code\classes</path-element>
```

In Mac OS X, it should look like this:

```
<path-element>/username/code/classes</path-element>
```

You can add as many <path-element> tags for as many class libraries as you need.

Finally, save the flex-config.xml file.

Packages and namespaces

I've named this book's class library according to the very common reverse domain name convention. This convention came about as a reliable way to make sure that one developer's class names don't conflict with another developer's class names from a different library. Let's look at how this system works, and how it's used in the code examples in this book.

Imagine that you run a Flash game design website called www.kittykatattack.com. (Yes, I know, but all the good names were already taken!) You organize your class libraries in a folder structure that looks like this: `com/kittykatattack/classes`. The folders match your domain name, but in reverse order. The `com` folder is empty, but `kittykatattack` contains all your classes.

Let's say that in your next project, you want to use a class from your library called `GiantExplosion`. You need to give the class a **package name** that matches its position in the folder hierarchy, like this:

```
package com.kittykatattack
{
  public class GiantExplosion
  {
    //Class directives…
  }
}
```

You can now import the `GiantExplosion` class into another class with an `import` statement, like this:

```
import com.kittykatattack.GiantExplosion;
```

The class's prefix, `com.kittykatattack`, is known as the class's **namespace.** It should match the exact path to the `GiantExplosion` class: `com/kittykatattack/GiantExplosion.as`.

You can then use your new class like this:

```
private var _explosion:GiantExplosion = new GiantExplosion();
```

Makes sense, right?

Now suppose that you want to use a class from a library that you didn't develop. Maybe you have a friend working at `www.absolutelyimpossible.com` who has also coded some killer (figuratively, let's hope!) explosion classes that you would love to use in your game. But there's a problem. Your friend's class is also called `GiantExplosion`. How can you use it along with your own `GiantExplosion` class without causing a conflict? That's easy enough, as long as your friend has organized the class library following the format `com/absolutelyimpossible/`.

First, you'll need to copy the new library into your main classes directory and import it, like this:

```
import com.absolutelyimpossible.GiantExplosion;
```

Then you need to instantiate it in a way that lets the compiler know which `GiantExplosion` class you want to use. You can do this by specifying the class's namespace in the class name:

```
_explosion:com.absolutelyimpossible.GiantExplosion
 = new com.absolutelyimpossible.GiantExplosion();
```

If you want to instantiate your own `GiantExplosion` class, you can do it like this:

```
_explosionTwo:com.kittykatattack.GiantExplosion
 = new com.kittykatattack.GiantExplosion();
```

Yes, I know, it's certainly no fun to read, but it solved the problem!

You may be wondering why reverse domain names were chosen for this naming convention. Because domain names are guaranteed to be unique, you can be sure that a name you have registered isn't going to be registered by anyone else. It becomes a kind of digital signature.

Realize that using the reverse domain name convention is purely optional. You don't need to use it. You can use any system of your own that works for you. But it does work well and is widely employed by AS3.0 developers. And it doesn't matter at all whether the domain name you choose is real or even belongs to you. If you want to use `uk.co.google` or `me.whatever`, be my guest! As long as you're not doing any development work with a friend at Google, or your source code isn't publicly distributed, it's unlikely that there will ever be a class name conflict.

Using SWC Files

An alternative to reading class libraries from a directory is to read them from a SWC file. SWC files are archive files (like ZIP files) that contain all your classes. The advantage to using them is that if you have a complex class library with hundreds of classes and subfolders and you want to share that library with other developers, you can contain them in a single SWC file. If there's a library of classes that you want to use with any of your games, such as a physics or 3D library, it's very likely that they'll be distributed as a SWC file.

To use classes from a SWC file, link to it in the **Library path** section in your ActionScript 3.0 settings in Flash Professional.

In Flash Builder, add the path to the SWC in the library path when you create a new ActionScript project. If you need to change this after the project has been created, you can do so in the **ActionScript Build Path** option of the project properties.

If you're using the Flex SDK, paths to SWC files are described in the `<library-path>` tag. If you open `flex-config.xml`, you'll see a section of code that looks like this:

```
<!-- List of SWC files or directories that contain SWC files. -->
<library-path>
  <path-element>libs</path-element>
  <path-element>libs/player</path-element>
  <path-element>libs/player/{targetPlayerMajorVersion}</path-element>
  <path-element>locale/{locale}</path-element>
</library-path>
```

This is where the compiler goes to look for SWC files.

You might find it interesting that the classes that you commonly import, such as `flash.display.Sprite` and `flash.events.Event`, are listed in a SWC file called `playerglobal.swc`. You'll find it in the `framework/libs/player/10` directory of your Flex SDK installation. That file doesn't contain the classes themselves, but is a long list of class **interface definitions**. The actual code for the classes is part of Flash Player and is mostly written in C++, not ActionScript. (You'll find a quick primer on interfaces at the end of Chapter 1.)

To use a SWC class library with one of your own projects, you can link to the folder that contains it, like this:

```
<library-path append = "true">
  <path-element>/absolute/path/to/folder</path-element>
</library-path>
```

If you want to create your own SWC file, you can easily export it from Flash Professional and Flash Builder. Check your software documentation on how to do this.

Testing the class library installation

In this book's `Chapter01` source file folder, you'll find a folder called `HelloWorld`. Let's use this sample project to make sure that you have everything set up correctly and can use this book's class library.

Open the `HelloWorld.as` file that you'll find in the `src` folder. Notice that the `HelloWorld` class doesn't have a package name. Flash Builder and the Flex SDK require that the main **application class** *not* be part of a named package.

The application class is the main class that runs and imports the other classes. It's the same as Flash Professional's document class.

```
package
{
    import flash.display.Sprite;
    import com.friendsofed.utils.StatusBox;

    [SWF(backgroundColor="0xFFFFFF", frameRate="60",
    width="550", height="400")]

    public class HelloWorld extends Sprite
    {
        private var _status:StatusBox;

        public function HelloWorld():void
        {
            _status = new StatusBox("Hello World!");
            addChild(_status);
        }
    }
}
```

Compile the program as follows:

- If you're using Flash Professional, first open the `HelloWorld.fla` file. The FLA has `HelloWorld` linked as the document class. Select **`Control ➤ Test Movie`** (or **`Test Project`** if you've created a project using the Project panel). Because the `HelloWorld` class uses the SWF metatag, Flash may ask you to confirm the path to the Flex SDK.
- In Flash Builder, select the **`Run`** command.

If you're using the command-line compiler or an alternative IDE, refer to your software's documentation on how to compile the SWF.

View the published SWF. If you've set your IDE up as I've suggested, you'll find it in the `bin` folder. It should look like Figure 3 when you run it.

Figure 3. Import the custom StatusBox object to display text in box that you can drag around the stage.

You can drag the box containing the words "Hello World!" around the stage. Double-click to minimize it. If the SWF didn't compile properly, check all your settings and folder locations, and try again.

`StatusBox` objects are made from the custom `StatusBox` class that's in the `com.friendsofed` class library. Often in game-design projects, you'll need to track complex data while you build and test. You can use a `StatusBox` object as an on-stage console to display variable values or other properties. It's a slightly more usable alternative to AS3.0's `trace` command for quickly changing data. You can find the `StatusBox` class in the `com` folder here: `com\friendsofed\utils\StatusBox.as`.

The code itself is reasonably complex, but as you can see, it's easy to use. `StatusBox` objects have three public properties that you can set:

- `text`: Any `String`
- `fontSize`: A `uint` value that describes the size of the font
- `color`: A `uint` value that accepts any hexadecimal color code, such as 0x99CCFF (sky blue)

In Chapter 1, I'll explain the AS3.0 code that was used to draw the box around the text and apply filters.

I'll be introducing a few more useful diagnostic mini-apps and utilities, written exclusively for this book, in the chapters ahead. Feel free to use them with your own projects and change (and improve!) them as much as you like.

You're now all set up and ready to start working through the projects in this book.

Optimizing the code

The sample code in this book has been written for clarity, not optimal speed. This book is all about learning, and while you're learning, it's more important that you understand the code than that it runs as quickly as it possibly could. Code optimization is also quite a big art unto its own, and notoriously dependent on context. It would be unfair of me to burden you with obscure code that might be difficult to understand and then not actually amount to any speed benefit in your game.

So apart from some obvious and well-worn techniques, I've opted to leave the optimization of the code in this book up to you. But here are few tips that will always give your games a boost:

- **Bit-block transfer**: One of the biggest bottlenecks in Flash Player is displaying and moving objects on the stage. Using bit-block transfer, or **blitting**, will give you an immediate two to five times performance improvement and won't require much modification to the existing code. Chapter 6 has a detailed section on bit-block transfer, and you should use it at every opportunity. Chapters 8 and 9 show how to use it as the primary display system in a game engine.

- **Optimize the display**: Alpha transparencies, filter effects, scaling, and rotation are all beautiful effects, but they are also big CPU hogs. Cut them out or prerender them as bitmaps wherever you can.

- **Streamline your logic**: The other big bottleneck is logic. Reduce any unnecessary checking, and cut corners and approximate values wherever you can. Apart from display issues, optimizing logic is the biggest performance boost you can give your games.

- **Use the `Vector` class for arrays that contain the same data types**: Flash Player 10 introduced the `Vector` class. It's identical to the `Array` class, except that all the values it contains must be of the same data type. Use it for integers and floating-point (decimal) numbers. However, arrays can be faster than vectors if they contain classes or instances.

- **Use `uint` instead of `Math.floor`**: To round down a number, your first instinct might be to use `Math.floor`, like this: `Math.floor(9.3213);`. However, you can achieve the same effect by forcing the number to be typed as `uint` (for "unsigned integer," which is a whole number without a plus or minus sign): `uint(9.3213);`. This is much faster for Flash Player to process.

- **Multiplication is almost twice as fast as division**: Instead of writing a calculation like this: `x = (stage.stageWidth / 2);`, write it like this: `x = (stage.stageWidth * 0.5);`. The result is the same, but it's twice as fast to process.

- **Use lookup tables as much as possible**: Lookup tables are arrays that store precalculated values. It's much faster for Flash Player to read values from an array than it is to calculate them as needed in the middle of a game. Chapter 6 explains how to create and use lookup tables.

- **Avoid creating and destroying objects unnecessarily**: If you think you might need to use objects again, remove them from the game by setting their visibility to `false`, rather than removing them from the display list with `removeChild`. It's heavier on Flash Player to re-create the object than to just make the object visible again.
- **Consider object pooling**: When the game initializes, create the maximum number of objects that you think you'll need, and keep them in an array. If you need to destroy an object and create a new one, just assign a new value to an existing unused object in the array. That's much faster than creating a new object from scratch.
- **Bitwise operations are sometimes faster:** Bitwise operators allow you to do calculations in a format that matches the way calculations are done natively by the CPU. This cuts out some unnecessary conversion that it needs to do to handle base 10 numbers (the kinds of numbers we humans use every day). Reports from the field are that they're not necessarily faster than base 10 numbers, but again, context is everything and they're worth testing in your games. You can find out more about the bitwise operators in AS3.0's documentation.

And as always, test early and test often!

About the code

Adobe publishes an excellent document on preferred ways of writing AS3.0 code, called "Flex SDK coding conventions and best practices" (`http://opensource.adobe.com/wiki/display/flexsdk/Coding+Conventions`). It's worth reading this to see how it compares with your own style of coding. I've used these conventions for most of the code in this book. However, I've made adjustments to some of those formatting conventions to handle long lines of code. Also, in my code, I generally use public properties rather than public setters and getters if I don't need to validate any data.

Code format conventions

In this book, the page width limits the code line lengths to a maximum of 70 characters. Unfortunately, there are some aspects of AS3.0's syntax and its API that encourage writing really long lines of code that regularly exceed 80 or 90 characters. Rather than force you to endure messy and hard-to-read line breaks in the code, I've used formatting conventions so that they print in the most readable way possible.

The following is a typical long line of code. It adds up a lot of values and assigns the result to a variable.

```
explosion.x = _bulletModels[i].xPos - explosion.width * 0.5 , ➥
  + stage.stageWidth * 0.5;
```

It's too long to print without a line-break character to indicate that it continues on the next line. However, the line break makes it very difficult to read. So instead, I'll break the line at the operators, indent two spaces, and align each value under the previous one, like this:

```
explosion.x
  = _bulletModels[i].xPos
  - explosion.width * 0.5
  + stage.stageWidth * 0.5;
```

If there are fewer values, I'll keep them all on the second line:

```
explosion.x
  = _bulletModels[i].xPos - explosion.width * 0.5
```

I've used a similar format for creating new objects:

```
var explosion:BlitExplosion
  = new BlitExplosion(snapshotBitmapData, 4);
```

as well as methods with a lot of parameters:

```
snapshotBitmapData.copyPixels
  (_caveBitmapData, rectangle, point);
```

Object constructors with a lot of arguments are another area where I've used some creative formatting. Here's a typical example of a long object constructor:

```
var rect:Rectangle = new Rectangle(bullets[i].xPos ➥
  - 40, bullets[i].yPos - 40, 80, 80);
```

It's very hard to read those arguments. There's a lot of symmetry there that is much easier to understand if the arguments are properly aligned. Adobe's formatting conventions suggest formatting it something like this:

```
var rect:Rectangle = new Rectangle(bullets[i].xPos - 40,
                                   bullets[i].yPos - 40,
                                   80, 80);
```

That's much better, but it awkwardly pushes the arguments to the right side of the page. This format will also break down if the arguments or object names are too long. As a solution, I've formatted the values between aligned parentheses, like this:

```
var rect:Rectangle
  = new Rectangle
  (
    bullets[i].xPos - 40,
    bullets[i].yPos - 40,
    80, 80
  );
```

It's now much easier to see the meaning of that data, as well as to find and change it in your program. (Just keep in mind that the last arguments will not be followed by a comma.) Occasionally, I'll also format shorter lines of code like this to emphasize relationships in the arguments or to unclutter densely packed code.

Methods with lengthy arguments that won't fit on one line follow the same format, as in this example:

```
matrix.translate
  (
    _bulletModels[i].xPos + stage.stageWidth * 0.5,
    _bulletModels[i].yPos + stage.stage.Height * 0.5
  );
```

as do parameters in class constructor methods:

```
public function TurretAIView
  (
    model:AVerletModel,
    gameModel:Object,
    controller:TurretAIController,
    stage:Object
  ):void
```

This formatting also takes care of a lot of really unusual situations, like dealing with the infamously messy `BitmapData.hitTest` method. Here's what it looks like in the wild:

```
if(objectBitmap.bitmapData.hitTest(new Point(model.xPos, ➥
  model.yPos), 255, collisionBitmap, new Point(collisionBitmap.x, ➥
  collisionBitmap.y), 255))
{
```

It's virtually illegible. Aligning the values between parentheses cleans it up nicely:

```
if(objectBitmap.bitmapData.hitTest
   (
     new Point(model.xPos, model.yPos),
     255,
     collisionBitmap,
     new Point(collisionBitmap.x, collisionBitmap.y),
     255
   )
  )
{
```

In the case of long `if` statements, I've chosen to align them with the conditional operators:

```
if ((_bulletModels[i].yPos + height / 2 < 0)
|| (_bulletModels[i].yPos - height / 2 > stage.stageHeight)
|| (_bulletModels[i].xPos + width / 2 < 0)
|| (_bulletModels[i].xPos - width / 2 > stage.stageWidth))
{
```

In many instances in the examples, I've abridged sections of repetitive code. Abridged code is indicated like this:

```
//...
```

And finally, I've followed the convention of indicating private properties with an underscore character, like this:

```
_privateProperty
```

There are two nice side effects of sticking to a 70-character horizontal limit:

- Code becomes very easy to read and scan quickly.
- It makes it easy to compare programs if you open them in side-by-side windows.

Of course, you're entirely free to format the code however you wish.

Public properties or getters and setters?

I've also decided to keep all class properties public if they don't validate data. That means you can get or set public data from a class like this:

```
ClassA
{
  public var anyPublicProperty = 9.891;
}

ClassB
{
  classA = new classA();
  classA.anyPublicProperty;
}
```

The only time the code in this book uses public getters or setters is if the class needs to validate data or dispatch an event when the property changes, as in this example:

```
ClassA
{
  private var _anyPrivateProperty = 9.891;

  public function set anyPublicProperty(value:Number):void
  {
    if(the value isn't some crazy number)
    {
      _anyPrivateProperty = value;
    }
  }
}
```

The generally accepted OOP wisdom is to *always* route pubic data through getters and setters, whether or not they validate data. That means that code like this is recommended:

```
ClassA
{
  private var _anyPrivateProperty = 9.891;

  public function set anyPublicProperty(value:Number):void
  {
      _anyPrivateProperty = value;
  }
}
```

The setter doesn't validate anything—it just blindly assigns the value. So why not just use an ordinary public property? It seems like a lot of extra code to write for no reason.

If you're not writing code in AS3.0, there is good reason for this. It means that all properties have a common interface. If you're working on a big project and suddenly decide you to need validate some data, you can quickly add that validation to the getter or setter. It means you don't need to change what could possibly be hundreds of instances of that property across countless classes.

However, AS3.0 is little different from many other programming languages. Languages like Java and C++ don't have `get` and `set` functions. Their getters and setters are ordinary methods that change values:

```
ClassA
{
  private var _anyPrivateProperty = 9.891;

  public function setProperty(value):void
  {
    _anyPrivateProperty = value;
  }
}
```

To change a property in another class, you must access it through that method, like this:

```
ClassB
{
  classA = new classA();
  classA.setProperty(3.147);
}
```

That means that changing a public property into a getter or setter requires rewriting a whole line of code. In a big project, that could become a complex undertaking.

The `get` and `set` functions give AS3.0 programmers a big advantage. Using them makes getters and setters look identical to public properties. For example, can you tell whether the following is a getter or a simple public property?

```
classA.anyPublicProperty;
```

There's no way to tell, because the syntax is identical. This means that in AS3.0, you could decide you want to validate a property at the last moment and not need to change any code except to write the setter.

So, I've decided to always make unvalidated properties public for these reasons:

- It's logical, and doesn't make an AS3.0 project harder to maintain, manage, or debug.
- Public properties are faster to process than getters and setters. That's very important for games.
- The code becomes succinct and readable, especially for classes that store a lot of data.

However, make sure to follow the best practices of your work environment.

Layout conventions

To keep this book as clear and easy to follow as possible, the following text conventions are used throughout:

- Important words or concepts are normally highlighted on the first appearance in **bold type**.
- Code is presented in `fixed-width font`.
- New or changed code and comments are normally presented in **`bold fixed-width font`**.
- Pseudo code and variable input are written in *`italic fixed-width font`*.
- Menu commands are written in the form **Menu ➤ Submenu ➤ Submenu**.

Chapter 1

Modeling Game Data

Imagine this scenario: You're working on big, complex platform game. You have countless classes with complex physics and collision-detection systems. You've spent a month or two working on it, and it's running great. You're in the final stages of testing, and then you run into a problem. Sometimes your game character appears to get "stuck" inside a platform. It happens under certain conditions that are very hard to duplicate, but it happens frequently. You scour through your code, testing and changing, but it's impossible to pinpoint the problem. What could possibly be wrong?

This is by far the most common problem that novice Flash game designers face. It's the result of two factors:

- Not keeping the data that is used to make decisions in your game separated from the visuals on the stage
- Not centralizing the code that updates the positions of objects on the stage

It's common for game designers to write code that checks where objects are on the stage, and then use that information to figure out where other objects should be. Instead, your code should first create an abstract model of the game, and that game model should tell the objects where on the stage they should go. This allows you to resolve any conflicts before the result is displayed on the stage.

The other problem is that game designers will often write separate `ENTER_FRAME` events for each moving object. If you have three objects on the stage, each running its own `ENTER_FRAME` event, you have no control over the order in which these events run. Your collision checks might not resolve correctly because the game thinks two objects aren't colliding, when in fact they are. The result is that when the next frame swings by, two objects appear to be stuck together and can't be separated.

In this chapter, I'll show you how to solve these problems once and for all. We're going to look at two techniques that will become the foundation of the rest of the projects in this book:

- **Verlet integration**: A highly reliable game physics system
- **Model-View-Controller**: A design pattern that clearly separates the responsibilities of an object into three parts

With these two techniques under your belt, you'll be well on your way to building solid and easily configurable games.

This chapter also provides two quick primers: one on the drawing API and one on interfaces.

Verlet integration

If you've done any game design in the past, you've probably written sections of code that look a lot like this:

```
_vx += _accelerationX;
_vy += _accelerationY;
player.x += _vx;
player.y += _vy;
```

vx is the player object's horizontal velocity, and vy is its vertical velocity.

The player object is moved by adding its velocity to its current position. If you do this repeatedly through an ENTER_FRAME loop, the object appears to move.

This bit of code is essentially saying, "The object is here. It's moving at a certain speed and in a certain direction. So we know that in the next frame it should be over there."

This makes a lot of sense. If you're driving a car at 100 kilometers an hour, you know that in 10 minutes, you'll have covered 10 kilometers. Easy stuff!

This is a system for calculating an object's position called **Euler integration** (named after the eighteenth century mathematician Leohnard Euler). It predicts where an object will be based on its current position and its velocity. It's widely used because it doesn't put a lot strain on the processor and it's easy to implement. It's accurate if the velocity is constant, but if the velocity changes due to friction and acceleration, it can become wildly inaccurate. In complex physics scenarios with a lot of fast-moving objects, it also has a tendency to fall apart.

The problem with Euler integration

Imagine that you're driving that car at 100 kilometers an hour. Your friend, Leohnard Euler, has hatched a plan to predict where your car will be next by photographing your position every 10 minutes. He needs to figure out where you're going to be next, but all he has to work from is your velocity and position at the moment he takes each photograph.

It sounds reasonable enough, but the problem is that physical forces, like friction and wind resistance, are working on your car the *entire time,* and Leohnard has no idea how they're affecting you between those 10-minute snapshot intervals. That means there's no guarantee that your velocity will remain constant and that you'll actually end up at the spot that Leohnard thinks you will. And what happens if you decide to pull over for coffee and a doughnut?

So poor Leohnard is in a bit of a fix. He can improve his predictions of where you'll be if he takes snapshots more frequently, such as every minute. But there's still a huge gray area. He has no way of accounting for the unexpected, like the coffee-and-doughnut scenario. (And it tends to be those coffee-and-doughnut scenarios that cause game objects to stick together or get trapped in walls.) He would need to be taking photographs between intervals of close to infinity to account for all possible forces and events if he wants his predictions to be completely accurate.

You can think of each loop of an `ENTER_FRAME` event as a single photograph. In a practical Flash game design scenario, if our game is running at 60 frames per second, we're taking snapshots of our game 60 times each second. If we wanted to use absolutely accurate Euler integration, we would need to set our frame rate to infinity, which obviously is impossible!

This inaccuracy alone is not a huge problem in itself, because the trade-off that you get with Euler integration is increased game performance. That's worth it. And its inaccuracy isn't noticeable in the context of a game.

Its Achilles' heel for game design is that it calculates an object's position based on its acceleration and velocity. When combined with its inherent inaccuracy, it can sometimes lead to situations where it overshoots its mark, and an object's velocity will continue to increase without any apparent reason. In other words, crazy stuff starts happening on the stage, and you can't figure out why.

Sound familiar? Let's find a solution.

The first part of the solution removes velocity from the equation. Enter **Verlet integration**.

> *For deadly accurate, textbook-grade physics calculations, you may also want to consider an alternate game physics system called Runge-Kutta (RK). RK is a little more complex to implement than Verlet integration and puts quite a bit more load on the processor, so it's not a good general-purpose system for Flash game design like Verlet. But if you need precision physics, definitely look into this system. Keith Peter's* AdvancED ActionScript 3.0 Animation *(friends of ED, 2008) includes a good introduction to using RK with AS3.0.*

Understanding Verlet integration

Imagine now that you're out on the highway with your friend Loup Verlet. He is following you with his camera, taking a snapshot every 10 minutes. However, he doesn't actually know how fast you're driving. Instead, he uses a simple calculation to figure out your velocity.

He knows that in the first snapshot you were at the 30-kilometer mark. In the second snapshot, you were at the 40-kilometer mark. Loup subtracts 30 from 40, which is 10. That's your velocity: 10. If Loup takes six snapshots per hour, your speed is 60 kilometers per hour.

Verlet integration doesn't figure out your new position based on your velocity. Instead, it works out your velocity based on the difference between your current position and your previous position. Here's the basic Verlet formula:

```
velocity = currentPosition - previousPostion;
newPosition += velocity;
```

The most important thing to know about Verlet integration is that *when you change the position of an object, you also change its velocity*. This may sound like a small thing, but its implications are big:

- It means that if two or more objects are colliding, they just need to change their positions, and the Verlet formula will figure out their new velocities automatically.
- You still don't know what's happening to objects *between snapshots*. Because object-movement code is updated in fixed intervals, this is always going to be a limitation, no matter which physics system you implement. However, because Verlet integration isn't dependent on an unstable velocity variable, the inaccuracy doesn't result in unexpected changes in velocity.
- The positions of the objects are modeled in your code *before* they're applied to the positions of objects on the stage. That means that any conflicts regarding their positions in complex collision scenarios can be tested and fixed in advance of being displayed.

Figure 1-1 illustrates the difference between Euler and Verlet integration.

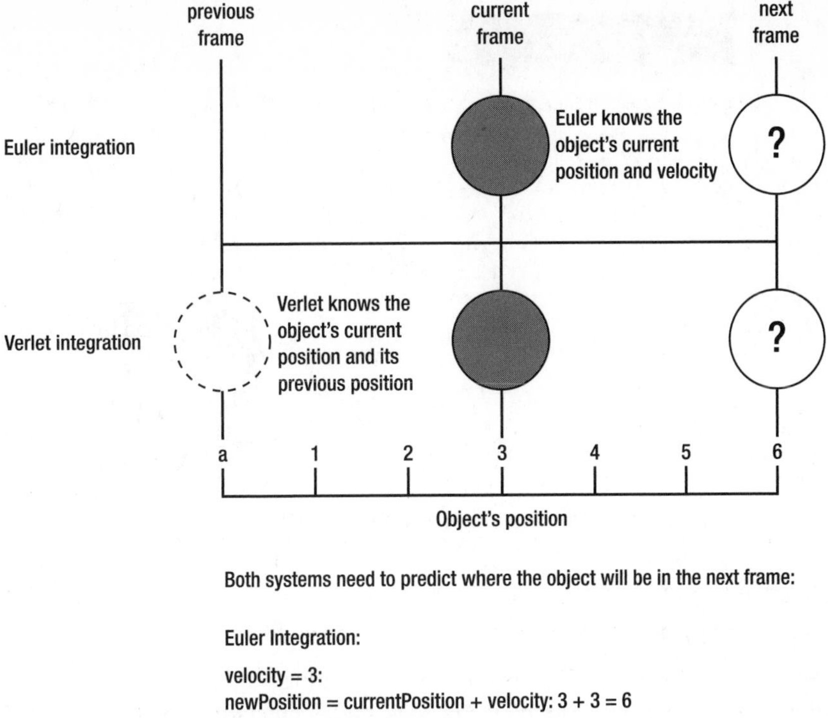
previous
frame
current
frame
next
frame
Euler integration
Euler knows the
object's current
position and velocity
?
Verlet integration
Verlet knows the
object's current
position and its
previous position
?
a
1
2
3
4
5
6
Object's position
Both systems need to predict where the object will be in the next frame:
Euler Integration:
velocity = 3:
newPosition = currentPosition + velocity: 3 + 3 = 6
Verlet Integration:
velocity = currentPosition - previousPosition : 3 - 0 = 3
newPosition = currentPosition + velocity: 3 + 3 = 6

Figure 1-1. How Euler and Verlet integration work

A small sacrifice that we need to make to use Verlet integration in our games is slightly more complex code. We need a system for keeping track of an object's previous position, as well as a way to calculate its velocity. This isn't hard to do, but it does require a bit more planning.

Using Verlet integration

In the `Chapter01` source files for this book, you'll find a folder called `VerletIntegration`. It's a practical example of how you can use Verlet integration for a game component: a keyboard-controlled character.

Run `VerletIntergration.swf`. A black square with a white circle will appear on the stage, as shown in Figure 1-2. You can move it with the arrow keys, and a status box displays its velocity. That itself is nothing to write home about, but what is important is the code that calculates the object's velocity.

Figure 1-2. Move the square around the stage with the arrow keys.

The code is composed of two parts:

- `Player`: This class contains the Verlet integration code.
- `VerletIntegration`: The main application class (also known as the document class). It adds the `_player` object to the stage, sets stage boundaries, and, most important, calls the player's `update` method that actually makes it move.

Let's look at the `Player` class first. If you've done any game design, you'll recognize most of this code, I've highlighted the core Verlet integration code in bold so you can clearly see how it's used in a practical context.

```
package
{
  import flash.display.*;
  import flash.events.Event;
  import flash.filters.*;
  import flash.events.Event;
  import flash.events.KeyboardEvent;
  import flash.ui.Keyboard;

  public class Player extends Sprite
  {
    private const SPEED:uint = 10;
    private var _shape:Shape;
    //Variables required for Verlet integration
    private var _previousX:Number = 0;
    private var _previousY:Number = 0;
```

```
private var _temporaryX:Number = 0;
private var _temporaryY:Number = 0;
public var xPos:Number = 0;
public var yPos:Number = 0;

public function Player():void
{
  addEventListener(Event.ADDED_TO_STAGE, onAddedToStage);
}

private function onAddedToStage(event:Event):void
{
  //Draw the player
  draw();

  //Add listeners
  addEventListener(Event.REMOVED_FROM_STAGE, onRemovedFromStage);
  stage.addEventListener(KeyboardEvent.KEY_DOWN, onKeyDown);
  stage.addEventListener(KeyboardEvent.KEY_UP, onKeyUp);

  //Remove the onAddedToStageHandler
  removeEventListener(Event.ADDED_TO_STAGE, onAddedToStage);
}

private function onRemovedFromStage(event:Event):void
{
  removeEventListener
    (Event.REMOVED_FROM_STAGE, onRemovedFromStage);
}

private function draw():void
{
  //Draw the outer shape
  var outerShape:Shape = new Shape();
  outerShape.graphics.beginFill(0x000000);
  outerShape.graphics.drawRoundRect(-25, -25, 50, 50, 10, 10);
  outerShape.graphics.endFill();
  addChild(outerShape);

  //Add a bevel and drop shadow and bevel filter
  var outerFilters:Array = outerShape.filters;

  //1. Bevel filter
  outerFilters.push
    (
      new BevelFilter
      (5, 135, 0xFFFFFF, 0.50, 0x999999, 0.50, 2, 2)
    );
```

```
    //2. Drop shadow filter
    outerFilters.push
      (
        new DropShadowFilter
        (5, 135, 0x000000, 0.60,10, 10)
      );

    //3. Apply the filters to the shape's filters array
    outerShape.filters = outerFilters;

    //Draw the inner shape
    var innerShape:Shape = new Shape();
    innerShape.graphics.beginFill(0xCCCCCC);
    innerShape.graphics.drawCircle(0, 0, 15);
    innerShape.graphics.endFill();
    addChild(innerShape);

    //Add a bevel filter to the inner shape
    var innerFilters:Array  = innerShape.filters;
    innerFilters.push
      (
        new BevelFilter
        (3, 315, 0xFFFFFF, 0.50, 0x999999, 0.50, 4, 4, 1, 1,"outer")
      );
    innerShape.filters = innerFilters;
  }

  private function onKeyDown(event:KeyboardEvent):void
  {
    if (event.keyCode == Keyboard.LEFT)
    {
      vx = -SPEED;
    }
    if (event.keyCode == Keyboard.RIGHT)
    {
      vx = SPEED;
    }
    if (event.keyCode == Keyboard.UP)
    {
      vy = -SPEED;
    }
    if (event.keyCode == Keyboard.DOWN)
    {
      vy = SPEED;
    }
  }
```

```
private function onKeyUp(event:KeyboardEvent):void
{
  if (event.keyCode == Keyboard.LEFT
  || event.keyCode == Keyboard.RIGHT)
  {
    vx = 0;
  }
  if (event.keyCode == Keyboard.UP
  || event.keyCode == Keyboard.DOWN)
  {
    vy = 0;
  }
}

//The update function is called by the application class's
//onEnterFrame event
public function update():void
{
  //Verlet integration in action:
  //1. Temporarily store the current x and y positions
  _temporaryX = xPos;
  _temporaryY = yPos;

  //2. Move the object
  xPos += vx;
  yPos += vy;

  //3. The position before the object was moved becomes the
  //previous position, which is used calculate velocity
  _previousX = _temporaryX;
  _previousY = _temporaryY;
}

//Getters and setters
//vx
public function get vx():Number
{
  return xPos - _previousX;
}
public function set vx(value:Number):void
{
  _previousX = xPos - value;
}

//vy
public function get vy():Number
{
  return yPos - _previousY;
}
```

```
    public function set vy(value:Number):void
    {
      _previousY = yPos - value;
    }

    //setX
   public function set setX(value:Number):void
    {
      _previousX = value - vx;
      xPos = value;
    }

    //setY
    public function set setY(value:Number):void
    {
      _previousY = value - vy;
      yPos = value;
    }
  }
}
```

You'll notice that nowhere does this code refer to the x and y sprite properties. The position of the object is being worked out abstractly. The object's current x and y positions are represented by these variables:

```
xPos;
yPos;
```

It's the job of the main application class, `VerletIntegration`, to actually move the object. It does this by calling the `Player`'s `update` method every frame. It then applies the `_xPos` and `_yPos` values to the `_player` sprite's actual x and y properties. You'll see how it does this in the pages ahead, but here's what the `Player` class's `update` method looks like:

```
public function update():void
{
  _temporaryX = xPos;
  _temporaryY = yPos;

  xPos += vx;
  yPos += vy;

  _previousX = _temporaryX;
  _previousY = _temporaryY;
}
```

Verlet integration works by comparing the difference between where the object is *now* with where it was in the *previous frame*. The first thing the code does is capture the object's *current* position:

```
_temporaryX = xPos;
_temporaryY = yPos;
```

The code temporarily stores the current position in its pristine state, before any changes are made to it.

Next, the object is moved according to the velocity.

```
xPos += vx;
yPos += vy;
```

Where are the vx and vy velocity values coming from? Not from a private variable, but from public getters:

```
public function get vx():Number
{
  return xPos - _previousX;
}
public function get vy():Number
{
  return yPos - _previousY;
}
```

Here's the key to understanding Verlet integration: *The velocity isn't stored as a variable. It's being dynamically calculated by subtracting the object's previous position from its current position.* That's the job of the vx and vy getters.

The velocity is set by pressing the arrow keys. But even then, its value isn't stored. It's calculated in real-time based on the current and previous positions:

```
public function set vx(value:Number):void
{
  _previousX = xPos - value;
}
public function set vy(value:Number):void
{
  _previousY = yPos - value;
}
```

So when the velocity is being set, it's actually just modifying the `_previousX` and `_previousY` variables, which in turn are used to calculate velocity.

The last thing the `update` method does is to copy the temporary positions, which record the position of the object before it was adjusted by velocity, into the `_previousX` and `_previousY` variables:

```
_previousX = _temporaryX;
_previousY = _temporaryY;
```

`_previousX` and `_previousY` will now be used in the *next frame* as the object's previous position.

Thanks to this bit of clever programming acrobatics, we can refer to the object's velocity without needing to store it as a variable. We've essentially taken velocity out of the equation, and this will make our physics code much more stable.

The benefits of this approach are not obvious in this simple example. In fact, if all you wanted to do was move an object around the stage with a keyboard, Euler integration would probably be a better choice, because the code would be much simpler. Using Verlet integration really pays off in physics simulations with multiple objects interacting, as you'll see in the chapters ahead. But it's important for you to understand how Verlet integration works in a simple example before we start building in more complexity.

As I mentioned earlier, an interesting feature of Verlet integration is that whenever you change the object's position, you're also going to change its velocity. This line of code, which changes the object's position, will also affect its velocity:

```
xPos = 10;
```

It will move the object to an x position of 10 on the stage, but it will also automatically set `vx` to `10`.

It may seem like a small thing, but the fact that you can reposition the object and affect its velocity simultaneously will greatly simplify your code and reduce the amount of debugging you'll need to do.

There is one drawback to this. Let's say you want to position an object in the center of the stage, like this:

```
xPos = 275;
yPos = 200;
```

This will also set the `vx` to 275 pixels per frame, and `vy` to 200 pixels per frame. Can you imagine what will happen? You'll see little more that a flicker of the object on the stage before it flies off at an impossible speed!

This means that we need to come up with way to reposition the object on the stage without changing its velocity. The `Player` class has setters called `setX` and `setY` that do just that.

```
public function set setX(value:Number):void
{
  _previousX = value - vx;
  xPos = value;
}
public function set setY(value:Number):void
{
  _previousY = value - vy;
  yPos = value;
}
```

`setX` and `setY` neutralize the `_previousX` and `_previousY` values so that the velocity isn't affected by a change of position. Use `setX` and `setY` to reposition objects on the stage.

Using the main application class

The `Player` class doesn't actually do the job of animating the object. It doesn't have an `ENTER_FRAME` event or even reference its x and y sprite positions. How does the player object actually move?

At the beginning of the chapter, I mentioned some very important things your code should do to be reliable and easy to debug:

- `ENTER_FRAME` events should be centralized. You should have only one that controls all the objects in the entire game.
- First, model the object's position abstractly. Then use that abstract model to apply it to the object's real position on the stage.

Here's how our two classes work together to do this:

- The `Player` class models its position with the `xPos` and `yPos` properties.
- The `VerletIntegration` class's `enterFrameHandler` calls the `_player`'s `update` method. This runs the Verlet motion engine and finds the `_player`'s new `xPos` and `yPos` properties.
- The `xPos` and `yPos` values are applied to the `_player`'s `x` and `y` sprite properties. This is what actually changes the position of the `_player` object on the stage.

Figure 1-3 illustrates how this works.

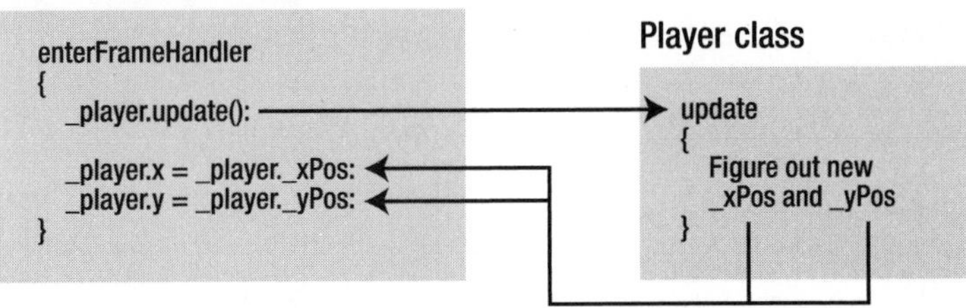

Figure 1-3. The main application class controls the Player class's update method.

The `VerletIntegration` class uses that model to move the object within its `ENTER_FRAME` event by calling the `_player` object's `update` method.

`VerletIntegration` is the **main application class**. If you're using Flash Professional, you'll recognize it right away as the beloved **document class**. It's the first class called by the program, and it's used to get the program running, instantiate the first objects, and import and coordinate all the other classes. Here's what it looks like:

```
package
{
  import flash.events.Event;
  import flash.display.Sprite;
  import com.friendsofed.utils.StatusBox;
  import com.friendsofed.utils.StageBoundaries;

  [SWF(backgroundColor="0xFFFFFF", frameRate="60",
  width="550", height="400")]

  public class Mainextends MovieClip
  {
    private var _player:Player;
    private var _status:StatusBox;

    public function VerletIntegration()
    {
      _player = new Player();
      addChild(_player);

      //Set the _player object's position on the
      //stage without affecting its velocity
      _player.setX = 275;
      _player.setY = 200;

      _status = new StatusBox();
      addChild(_status)

      addEventListener(Event.ENTER_FRAME,enterFrameHandler);
    }

    private function enterFrameHandler(event:Event):void
    {
      //1. Update the player position
      _player.update();

      //2. Check collisions (like stage boundaries)
      StageBoundaries.stop(_player, stage);

      //3. Move the player's position
      _player.x = _player.xPos;
      _player.y = _player.yPos;

      //4. Display player's velocity in the status box
      _status.text = "VX: " + _player.vx + " VY: " + _player.vy;
    }
  }
}
```

I've commented the most important bits of code, but let's take a close look at how all the pieces fit together.

Importing the classes

Two custom classes are imported: `StatusBox`, which displays the velocity, and `StageBoundaries`, which stops the player object at the edges of the stage. Both of these classes are imported from the `utils` folder in the `com/friendsofed` folder.

```
import com.friendsofed.utils.StatusBox;
import com.friendsofed.utils.StageBoundaries;
```

The compiler will look for the `com` folder based on the classpath you set in Flash Professional or Flash Builder, or the source path you included in the `flex-config.xml` file. If you followed my suggestion for setting this up (in this book's introduction), its location is *absolute*. The compiler will know where on your computer to look for these folders and classes.

Positioning the _player object

Next, the code creates the `_player` object from the `Player` class and uses `addChild` to display it on the stage. We want to set the `_player` object in the center of the stage when the SWF first runs. However, remember that, because we're using Verlet integration, as soon as we change the object's position, we also change its velocity.

We can't position the object like this:

```
_player.xPos = 275;
_player.yPos = 200;
```

This would give it an x velocity of 275 and a y velocity of 200. If the stage boundaries weren't set, we might just see a briefly flicker as it flashes of the edge of the stage at light speed toward the Planet X. If that sounds strangely appealing to you, however, go ahead and try it!

Instead, the code uses the `Player` class's special `setX` and `setY` setters to position it without affecting its velocity.

```
_player.setX = 275;
_player.setY = 200;
```

Figuring out the new velocity, checking collisions, and moving the player

The `enterFrameHandler` controls all the action. First, it calls the `_player`'s `update` method.

```
_player.update();
```

This does two things:

- The `_player` object calculates its new velocity.
- It sets the `_player`'s `xPos` and `yPos` properties, which tell the player where it should go next.

Before the code visually changes the position of the `_player` object on the stage, it's important to check to see whether its new `xPos` and `yPos` values cause it to collide with any other objects. This allows us to resolve any positioning conflicts before the result is displayed.

In this example, the collision we're checking for is with the edge of the stage. The custom `StageBoundaries` class has a static method called `stop` that does this for us.

```
static public function stop(object:Object, stage:Object):void
{
  if (object.xPos + (object.width* 0.5) > stage.stageWidth)
  {
    object.setX = stage.stageWidth - (object.width* 0.5);
    object.vx = 0;
  }
  else if (object.xPos - (object.width * 0.5) < 0)
  {
    object.setX = 0 + (object.width* 0.5);
    object.vx = 0;
  }
  if (object.yPos - (object.height* 0.5) < 0)
  {
    object.setY = 0 + (object.height* 0.5);
    object.vy = 0;
  }
  else if (object.yPos + (object.height* 0.5) > stage.stageHeight)
  {
    object.setY = stage.stageHeight - (object.height* 0.5);
    object.vy = 0;
 }
}
```

As you can see, it's pretty run-of-the-mill stage boundary code. But what's important to notice is that it's not changing the position of the object on the stage. It's just modifying the `_player` object's position and velocity properties. That means that if the code finds out that `_player` has actually overshot the stage boundaries, it can make a correction before any other collision code runs or the result is displayed. And because we're using Verlet integration, it also automatically adjusts velocity.

After fine-tuning the `_player` object's position, it's visually placed on the stage based on the final values of its `xPos` and `yPos` properties.

```
_player.x = _player.xPos;
_player.y = _player.yPos;
```

What you now have is a centralized system for deciding the order in which collisions are checked and resolved. In a complex game, this is vital in making sure that your system is stable.

Testing the system

Even in this simple example, you can see how important a centralized system is by making a small change to the code in the `enterFrameHandler`. Switch the code order so that the `StageBoundaries.stop` method runs *after* the `_player`'s x and y positions are adjusted.

```
_player.x = _player.xPos;
_player.y = _player.yPos;

StageBoundaries.stop(_player, stage);
```

Now compile and run the SWF. Use the arrow keys to move the `_player` object to the edge of the stage. It overshoots by 10 pixels, which is its velocity. Figure 1-4 shows what you'll see.

Figure 1-4. Every game designer's worst nightmare! If you change the order in which the code runs, the stage boundary collision appears to be off by one frame.

This is why collision objects get stuck together or collisions can seem maddeningly off by one frame. By running after the `_player` object's position changed, the stage boundary collision code is using the `_player`'s position data *for the next frame*.

If you have different `ENTER_FRAME` events running in different objects, you have no way of controlling the order that the code runs, and these kinds of problem crop up all the time. By centralizing the control system, as we've done in this example, you can test and fine-tune the order that objects should check collisions and correct their positions.

Over the course of the next few chapters, we're going to fine-tune and formalize this control system.

Onward to Planet X!

With Verlet integration, we have the physics equivalent of a Zonda or Lamborghini parked in our driveway, but so far haven't taken it for more than quick spin around the block. Let's take it onto the highway and rev the engine a bit.

Browse to the `VerletSpaceShip` folder in the chapter's source files and run the `spaceShip.swf` file in the `bin` folder. It's a spaceship that you can fly around the stage with the arrow keys, as shown in Figure 1-5. The ship wraps when it reaches the edges of the stage.

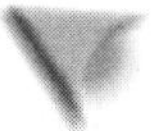

Figure 1-5. Use the arrow keys to fly the spaceship around the stage.

Unlike the simple square block in the previous example, this is a full-blown physics model, including acceleration and friction, based on Verlet integration. Most of the code is very similar to the spaceship code covered in Chapter 10 of *Foundation Game Design with Flash* (friends of ED, 2009). If you've read that book or done similar motion-based animation, much of it will be familiar. A very important change is that it has been adapted to run the same Verlet physics engine that we have been exploring here.

Revving the Verlet velocity engine

The `SpaceShip` class is quite long, but most of it is used for drawing the ship. We'll take a close look how the graphics for the ship were created in the "A crash course in the drawing API" section later in this chapter. Here, we're interested in how the spaceship speeds up and slows down using acceleration and friction.

When the player presses the up arrow key, the `_acceleration` variable is increased by `0.2`, and `_friction` gets a value of `1`, which means no friction. This allows the ship to accelerate freely, without additional drag. To slow down an object, you need to multiply an object's velocity by a value less than `1`. When the up key is released, acceleration is set to `0` and friction is set to `0.96`, which when multiplied by velocity will give us a number we can use to gradually slow down the spaceship.

```
private function keyDownHandler(event:KeyboardEvent):void
{
  if (event.keyCode == Keyboard.LEFT)
  {
    rotationSpeed = -10;
    }
    if (event.keyCode == Keyboard.RIGHT)
    {
      rotationSpeed = 10;
    }
    if (event.keyCode == Keyboard.UP)
    {
      acceleration = 0.2;
      friction = 1;
      thrusterFired = true;
      _thrusterShape.visible = true;
    }
  }

  private function keyUpHandler(event:KeyboardEvent):void
  {
    if (event.keyCode == Keyboard.UP)
    {
      acceleration = 0;
      friction = 0.96;
      thrusterFired = false;
      _thrusterShape.visible = false;
    }
    if(event.keyCode == Keyboard.LEFT
    || event.keyCode == Keyboard.RIGHT)
    {
      rotationSpeed = 0;
    }
  }
```

The `update` method takes those values and mixes them into the vx and vy velocity calculations:

```
public function update():void
{
  //Temporarily store the current x and y positions
  temporaryX = xPos;
  temporaryY = yPos;

  //Calculate the rotationValue
  rotationValue += rotationSpeed;
```

```
    //Calculate the angle and acceleration
    _angle = rotationValue * (Math.PI / 180);
    _accelerationX = Math.cos(_angle) * acceleration;
    _accelerationY = Math.sin(_angle) * acceleration;

    frictionX = vx * friction;
    frictionY = vy * friction;

    //Speed trap: Stop the object moving
    //if the up arrow isn't being pressed
    //and its speed falls below 0.1

    if(!thrusterFired)
    {
      if((Math.abs(vx) < 0.1) && (Math.abs(vy) < 0.1))
      {
        _accelerationX = 0;
        _accelerationY = 0;
        frictionX = 0;
        frictionY = 0;
      }
    }

    //Apply acceleration to the position
    xPos += _accelerationX + frictionX;
    yPos += _accelerationY + frictionY;

    //The temporary values become the
    //previous positions, which are used calculate velocity
    previousX = temporaryX;
    previousY = temporaryY;
}
```

This is a very good example of how Verlet integration is typically used. Physical forces, like friction and acceleration, are just *added to* the object's position:

```
xPos += _accelerationX + _frictionX;
yPos += _accelerationY + _frictionY;
```

It's very readable in a common-sense way. It says, "The object's position is the result of a combination of acceleration and friction."

If you had any more physical forces, you could simply add them in the same way.

```
xPos += _accelerationX + frictionX + wind;
yPos += _accelerationY + frictionY + gravity;
```

This is a very elegant way of dealing with physics. See, physics can be easy!

And nowhere is the object looking to its velocity to help it figure out where to move next. The only place velocity is explicitly referenced is to work out friction.

```
frictionX = vx * friction;
frictionY = vy * friction;
```

But even that's unnecessary. You could remove all references to vx and vy completely if you wanted to do that. You could just as easily use a line of code that looks like this:

```
frictionX = (xPos - previousX) * friction;
frictionY = (yPos - previousY) * friction;
```

Our little velocity engine is running quietly in the background, and the code really doesn't need to directly interact with it in any way.

Moving the spaceship

The main application class, `VerletSpaceShip`, makes the spaceship move. Its `enterFrameHandler` is almost identical to our first example. The only differences are that the ship's rotation is adjusted and that the code is using the `StageBoundaries.wrap` method to create the stage-wrapping effect. (Take a look at `com\friendsofed\StageBoundaries.as` if you're curious to see how it works.)

```
private function enterFrameHandler(event:Event):void
{
  //1. Update the player position
  _spaceShip.update();

  //2. Check collisions
  StageBoundaries.wrap(_spaceShip, stage);

  //3. Move the ship
  _spaceShip.x = _spaceShip.xPos;
  _spaceShip.y = _spaceShip.yPos;
  _spaceShip.rotation = _spaceShip.rotationValue;

  //4. Display the ship's velocity in the status box
  _status.text = "VX: " + _spaceShip.vx + " VY: " + _spaceShip.vy;
}
```

If this is the first time you've used Verlet integration, it's probably going take a bit of mental rewiring before you feel confident using it in your own games. Now might be a good time to take a short break from this chapter and see if you can rewrite one of your favorite player control systems using this technique. It works for any moving object and, as you'll see in the chapters ahead, it will become an essential part of a stable game physics system.

Introducing the Model-View-Controller Pattern

The simple system that we're using so far has actually brought us quite a long way in solving the two big game design pitfalls that I listed at the beginning of the chapter. Our game events are now centralized, and we're modeling and testing game data before displaying the result on the stage. "Yay! Programmers, one— bugs, zero!"

Not bad, but to keep our score up, we need to go one better.

A few pages earlier, I described a big problem that faces game animation: *We know where objects are and where they're going at specific snapshots in time, but we don't know what they're doing between each snapshot.*

To build a really robust system, we need our game objects to tell us if something happens to them between snapshots. So even if we're not watching them or expecting them to change, they should be able to tell us if they do.

We can do this by implementing a **design pattern** called **Model-View-Controller** (MVC). In addition to having a wonderfully thematic science-fiction sounding name, MVC is not only the great granddaddy of design patterns, but it's also probably the single most useful design pattern for games. If you take the time to learn only one pattern, then MVC should be it.

> *Design patterns are ways of organizing code into well-defined sections and responsibilities. The sections communicate with each other using the rules defined by the pattern they follow. Programmers love using them because each pattern has been bomb-proofed and battle-hardened by years of development and testing. If you choose the right pattern for the right problem and implement it correctly, your games and programs will be much easier to maintain and debug.*
>
> *There are loads of design patterns to choose from, and each is specialized for solving a particular type of problem. For example, if you need to make a lot of invading carnivorous dandelions sprouting from the ground in your platform game, you could use the Factory pattern. If you want a global control center for your game to manage the score and track all the dandelions that your game hero has trampled, you can use a Singleton pattern. If you are making a complex puzzle game with switches and levers that must be set in just the right position, the State pattern might work well for that. You need to have a fairly advanced understanding of OOP to be able to use design patterns confidently, but you'll surely have that confidence by the end of this book. Some excellent books on using patterns with AS3.0 are available, including* Object-Oriented ActionScript 3.0 *by Todd Yard, Peter Elst, and Sas Jacobs (friends of ED, 2007).*

Understanding MVC

If you think carefully about the spaceship we built in the previous example, you'll realize that what it does and how it behaves can be broken up into three parts:

- **Model**: All the data it contains, including acceleration, velocity, rotation speed, angle, and any nonvisual information that the spaceship needs to move. This would include all the getters and setters. It can also include the `update` method that processes that data internally.
- **View**: Anything you can see on the stage, as well as the keyboard controls you use to move the ship. It's anything that the player can directly interact with.
- **Controller**: All the logic that works out how user interaction should change the spaceship's data. For example, the controller deals with an issue like this: The player pressed the up arrow key, so let's set friction to 1 and the acceleration to 0.2.

MVC is a system that divides these responsibilities among three classes. (Often the view and controller can be part of the same class, but for learning purposes, it's better to separate them until you have a little more experience using MVC.)

In our spaceship example, all of these responsibilities have been jumbled up together in one class. There's nothing wrong with this, because it works perfectly. However, our design is completely rigid and will be very difficult to change or extend. If we want to add a feature, we'll need to navigate a tangled rats' nest of code and hope that our rewiring job doesn't mess up everything else.

For example, what if we decided that we actually want the ship to be controlled by the mouse instead of the keyboard? We would need to rewrite that section of the class, and then carefully recode the rest of the ship's properties. But if we had designed our ship according to the MVC framework, we could simply swap in a mouse-control system with one line of code. It would work with the rest of the ship's data automatically, without requiring us to rewrite any code. And we could also switch back to the original keyboard-control system at any time, if we decided that was the way to go.

Now let's imagine that after building this spaceship, we realize that we can use the same motion engine for our enemy ships as well. The enemy ships will behave the same way, but will look different and be controlled by an artificial intelligence (AI) script instead of the keyboard. The spaceship code is more than 300 lines long. It's going to be a tedious and complex job to extract the basic engine and rebuild it. But if we use an MVC framework, the ship's engine will be a completely separate component, and all we will need to do is snap on the ship's graphics to make a completely new type of ship. The AI system will be a separate system as well, so we can mix and match it with whatever different types of ships we have to see which combination we like best.

If we divide our objects between these three components—the model, the view, and the controller—how do they communicate with each other?

- The model dispatches a CHANGE event when its data changes.
- The view builds its visual display based on data from the model. The view also listens for changes in the model's data. When it detects that data changes, it automatically makes changes to its visual display to match those changes. For example, if the spaceship model tells the view that its rotation value has changed, the view rotates the spaceship to match the model's value. The view also captures user interaction, such as text input or mouse clicks, and sends that information to the controller.
- The controller processes the user input that is sent to it from the view, figures out what to do with it, and updates the model based on this analysis. For example, if the view tells the controller that the left arrow key is being pressed, the controller figures out that this means "rotate the ship to the left." It then tells the model to change its rotation value.

Figure 1-6 is a simple diagram of how an MVC system works.

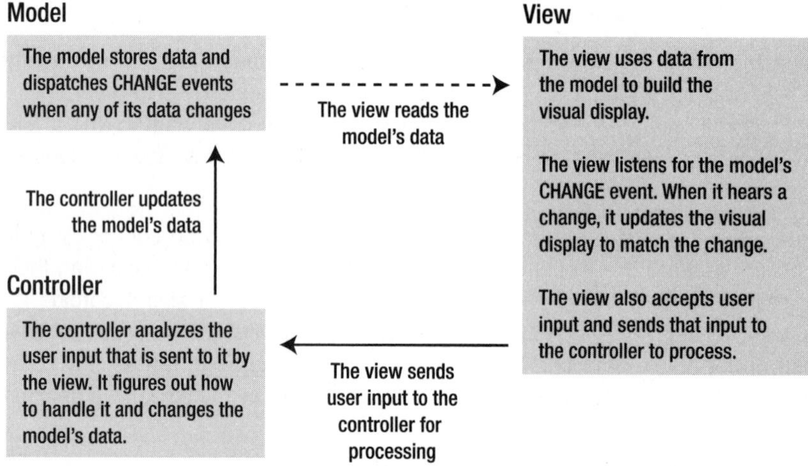
Model
The model stores data and dispatches CHANGE events when any of its data changes
The view reads the model's data
View
The view uses data from the model to build the visual display.
The view listens for the model's CHANGE event. When it hears a change, it updates the visual display to match the change.
The view also accepts user input and sends that input to the controller to process.
The controller updates the model's data
Controller
The controller analyzes the user input that is sent to it by the view. It figures out how to handle it and changes the model's data.
The view sends user input to the controller for processing

Figure 1-6. How the three building blocks of the MVC framework fit together

The MVC is programming's answer to Mr. Potato Head. You can mix and match views, models, and controllers in any combination. You're going to love using it when you see how much flexibility it will give your design.

MVC in action

Let's see how MVC works in a real ActionScript 3.0 (AS3.0) application. In the chapter's source files, you'll find a folder called `BasicMVC`. Run the SWF file and press the arrow keys. A status box displays the name of the key you've pressed, as shown in Figure 1-7. It's an example of what is just about the most basic MVC application that can be written.

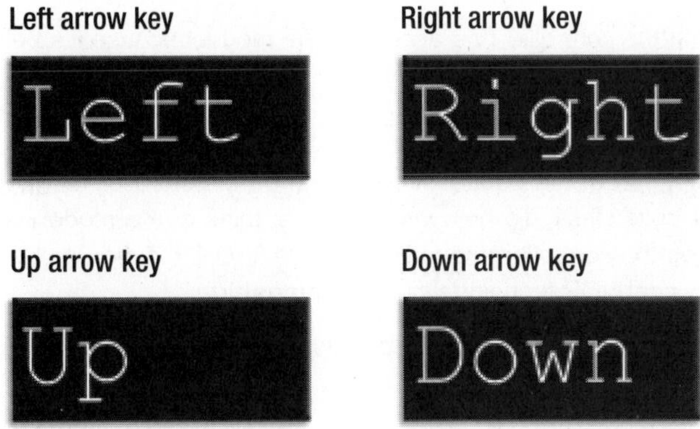

Figure 1-7. When you press an arrow key, the view informs the controller, the controller updates the model, and the view reads the new data from the model.

We're going to take a careful look at this simple application because if you understand it, you'll understand *all* MVC systems, no matter how much larger or more complex they appear.

Before we look at the code itself, let's see how the code is structured, as shown in Figure 1-8.

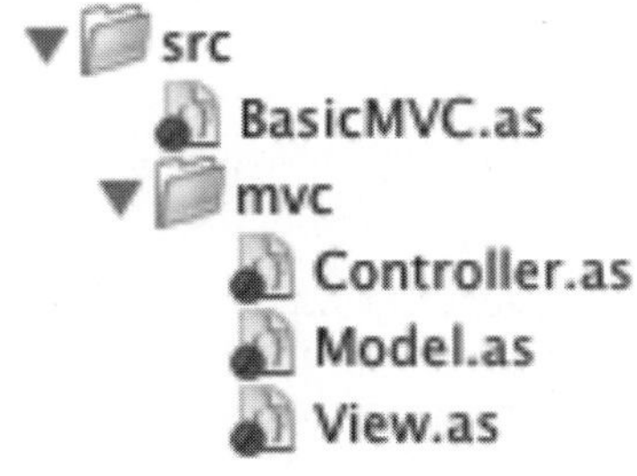

Figure 1-8. The main application class imports and composes the model, view, and controller.

BasicMVC is the main application class. It imports the model, view, and controller from the mvc package. It instantiates them and composes them in just the right way so that they work together. These are the most important lines of code in the BasicMVC class:

```
_model = new Model();
_controller = new Controller(_model);
_view = new View(_model, _controller);
addChild(_view);
```

You can see here that the controller has access to the model because it's being fed a reference to the model in its constructor argument:

```
_controller = new Controller(_model);
```

This makes the model part of the controller's DNA, and the controller can use this reference to the model anywhere in its class. To help visualize this, think of the model as a kind a parasitic worm that has infected the controller and is living inside it. OK, maybe don't visualize it then! But anyway, this is a very cool OOP technique called **composition**.

Composition is also used to feed the view references of the model and controller:

```
_view = new View(_model, _controller);
```

The view can now use the model and controller anywhere in its class.

If your mind is anything like mine, you might find it difficult to understand how the pieces of this puzzle all fit together, especially if the code is spread across three different classes. To help with what is the most crucial stage in the learning curve to understanding the MVC, take a look at Figure 1-9, also known as The Monster Diagram. It shows all the classes on one page and how they communicate with each other. You can follow the path the communication takes, from 1 to 5, to see how information flows through the system. (To save space, I've omitted the package block, import directives, variable declarations, and a few other small details, but the most important code from each class is shown.)

The best way to read this diagram is to have the BasicMVC.swf file running in front of you. Press one of the arrow keys, and then follow the information flow in the diagram. See if you can match up in your mind what you see on the stage with what you see in the diagram.

This diagram is the Rosetta Stone for understanding the MVC. Take as much time as you need to with it before continuing with this chapter. Really, I'm not going anywhere! When you get your "Aha!" moment, read on!

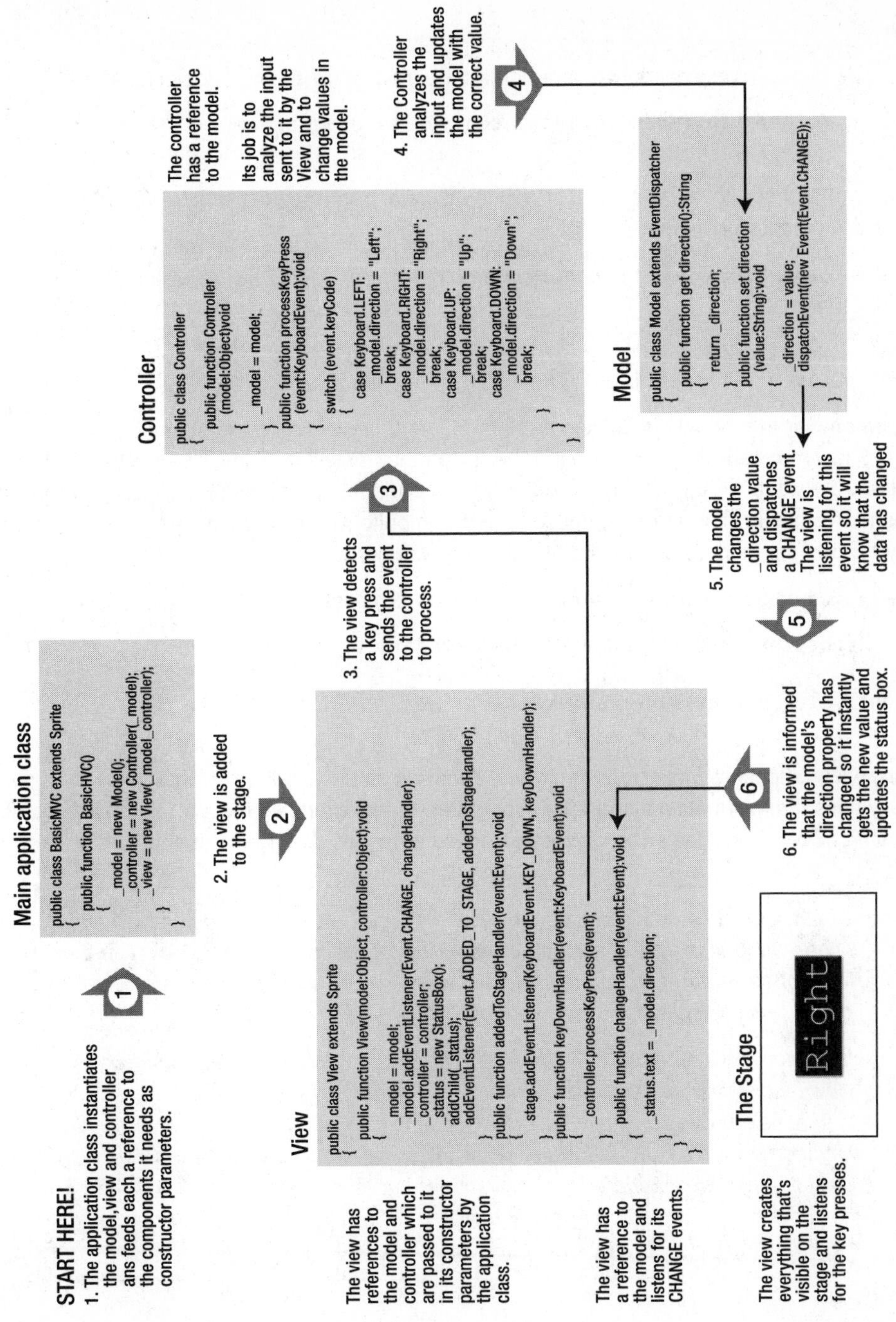

Main application class
public class BasicMVC extends Sprite
{
public function BasicHVC()
{
_model = new Model();
_controller = new Controller(_model);
_view = new View(_model_controller);
}
}
START HERE!
1. The application class instantiates the model,view and controller ans feeds each a reference to the components it needs as constructor parameters.
1
2. The view is added to the stage.
2
View
public class View extends Sprite
{
public function View(model:Object, controller:Object):void
{
_model = model;
_model.addEventListener(Event.CHANGE, changeHandler);
_controller = controller;
_status = new StatusBox();
addChild(_status);
addEventListener(Event.ADDED_TO_STAGE, addedToStageHandler);
}
public function addedToStageHandler(event:Event):void
{
stage.addEventListener(KeyboardEvent.KEY_DOWN, keyDownHandler);
}
public function keyDownHandler(event:KeyboardEvent):void
{
_controller.processKeyPress(event);
}
public function changeHandler(event:Event):void
{
_status.text = _model.direction;
}
}
}
The view has references to the model and controller which are passed to it in its constructor parameters by the application class.
The view has a reference to the model and listens for its CHANGE events.
3. The view detects a key press and sends the event to the controller to process.
3
Controller
public class Controller
{
public function Controller
(model:Object)void
{
_model = model;
}
public function processKeyPress
(event:KeyboardEvent):void
{
switch (event.keyCode)
{
case Keyboard.LEFT:
_model.direction = "Left";
break;
case Keyboard.RIGHT:
_model.direction = "Right";
break;
case Keyboard.UP:
_model.direction = "Up";
break;
case Keyboard.DOWN:
_model.direction = "Down";
break;
}
}
}
The controller has a reference to the model.
Its job is to analyze the input sent to it by the View and to change values in the model.
4. The Controller analyzes the input and updates the model with the correct value.
4
Model
public class Model extends EventDispatcher
{
public function get direction():String
{
return _direction;
}
public function set direction
(value:String):void
{
_direction = value;
dispatchEvent(new Event(Event.CHANGE));
}
}
5. The model changes the _direction value and dispatches a CHANGE event. The view is listening for this event so it will know that the data has changed
5
6. The view is informed that the model's direction property has changed so it instantly gets the new value and updates the status box.
6
The Stage
Right
The view creates everything that's visible on the stage and listens for the key presses.

Figure 1-9. The main application class imports and composes the model, view, and controller.

The view

The view's constructor accepts two parameters: the model and controller objects:

```
public function View(model:Object, controller:Object):void
{..
```

It needs references to them so that it can read data from the model and send the controller requests to process user input.

The view copies the value of the `model` parameter into its `_model` variable, and adds a `CHANGE` event listener to it.

```
_model = model;
_model.addEventListener(Event.CHANGE, changeHandler);
```

Now, whenever the model dispatches a `CHANGE` event, the view's `changeHandler` will be called. This is a key feature of MVC, and one of the things that makes it such a robust system. It means that the view will automatically synchronize with the model. This takes care of our "in-between-snapshots" problem. The program doesn't need to monitor or babysit the view, because the view always knows the model's current state and is able to update itself accordingly.

The view's other job is to accept user interaction, like key presses.

```
public function keyDownHandler(event:KeyboardEvent):void
{
  _controller.processKeyPress(event);
}
```

But the view shouldn't make any decisions about what to do with this input. Its job is just to dutifully pass the information along to the controller. In this example, the `event` property (which is a `KeyboardEvent`) is being passed to the controller's `processKeyPress` method.

> *Confusingly, user input, like key presses, is regarded as a type of "view." If you used sound in an MVC system, it would also be considered a view. You can think of the view as encompassing any sense that you use to interact with the game, such as sight, touch, and sound.*
>
> *It's also very common in an MVC system to divide these different types of views into separate classes. For example, you might have two view classes for a spaceship: one for the visual design of the ship and another view for the keyboard input. Even though the work would be distributed between two view classes, they would share the same model and same controller. You'll need to decide for each project how many views you'll have, depending on how much flexibility you'll want to mix and match them.*

It's very important that the view not make any logical decision about user input so that the MVC system remains modular. The view can, however use logic to help it display the model's data. If you were making a charting application, for example, the view would need to use some pretty complex logic to graph the model's data.

The controller

Although the controller accepts information from the view, it doesn't need to know any other information about it. It does need to know about the model, however, and so it's passed a reference to the model as a constructor parameter:

```
public function Controller(model:Object):void
{…
```

The controller has one method: `processKeyPress`. The view has been written so that when the user presses the keys, it sends the `KeyboardEvent` to the controller's `processKeyPress` method.

```
public function processKeyPress(event:KeyboardEvent):void
{…
```

The controller uses this event to figure out which key is being pressed.

```
public function processKeyPress(event:KeyboardEvent):void
{
  switch (event.keyCode)
  {
    case Keyboard.LEFT:
      _model.direction = "Left";
      break;

    case Keyboard.RIGHT:
      _model.direction = "Right";
      break;

    case Keyboard.UP:
      _model.direction = "Up";
      break;

   case Keyboard.DOWN:
     _model.direction = "Down";
     break;
  }
}
```

(Because the controller refers to keyboard events and key codes, it also needs to import `flash.events.KeyboardEvent` and `flash.ui.Keyboard`.)

The controller's job is to handle all the logic and to change the model's properties. And because the view is listening for CHANGE events on the model, the view is automatically updated as well.

The model

A feature of the Model class is that because it doesn't display anything on the stage, it doesn't need to extend Sprite or MovieClip. Instead, it extends EventDispatcher:

```
public class Model extends EventDispatcher
{...
```

The model's main job is to store data and dispatch events when the data changes.

The model doesn't need to know anything about the view or controller; it is completely independent from them. It isn't passed a reference to either of them in its constructor:

```
public function Model()
{...
```

It's this independence that that makes the MVC system so flexible. It means that other views can share this model, and other controllers can modify it. You can think of the model as a central hard drive full of data that other computers on a network can read.

When the controller sets any of the model's properties, the model dispatches a CHANGE event:

```
public function set direction(value:String):void
{
  _direction = value;
  dispatchEvent(new Event(Event.CHANGE));
}
```

This is like shouting out to the rest of the program, "Hey guys, I've updated one of my properties! If you're listening, you better make sure that you've got the right value!" However, the model doesn't know or care who is listening.

Because the view has subscribed to listen to CHANGE events in the model, the view knows about this change and calls its changeHandler. This keeps the view and model completely synchronized.

MVC your way

Is your brain feeling ready to explode yet? If you're new to using MVC or juggling data between many classes, this can be a lot to absorb all at once. Now might be a good time to take a short break from this chapter, and make some modifications to this example to help you get a better sense of how MVC works.

One simple change you can try to make on your own is to use the arrow keys to change the x and y position of the status box on the stage, as shown in Figure 1-10. Here's a hint: A well-placed switch statement in the view class might be all you need to make this work. You'll find the solution in the MoveKeyboardMVC folder.

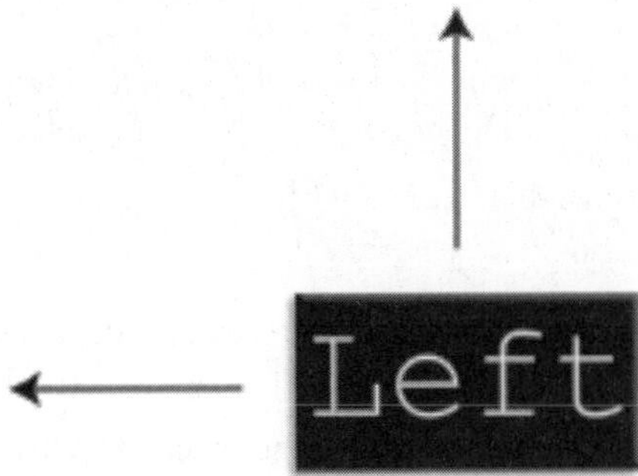

Figure 1-10. Challenge 1: Make the status box move in the direction of the arrow keys.

As a more challenging puzzle, you can try to make the status box display the x and y position of the mouse, as shown in Figure 1-11. You will need to import the flash.events.MouseEvent class and use the stage.mouseX and stage.mouseY properties to find the mouse's position. You will also need to import the flash.events.MouseEvent class into both the view and controller. The controller will need to use the stage.mouseX and stage.mouseY properties to find the mouse's position. The only problem is that mouseX and mouseY are properties of the stage. The only class that has access to the stage is the view. (The view has been added to the stage with addChild, by the application class, unlike the model and controller.) That means the view will need to send the controller a reference to the stage. Let's consider how to do that.

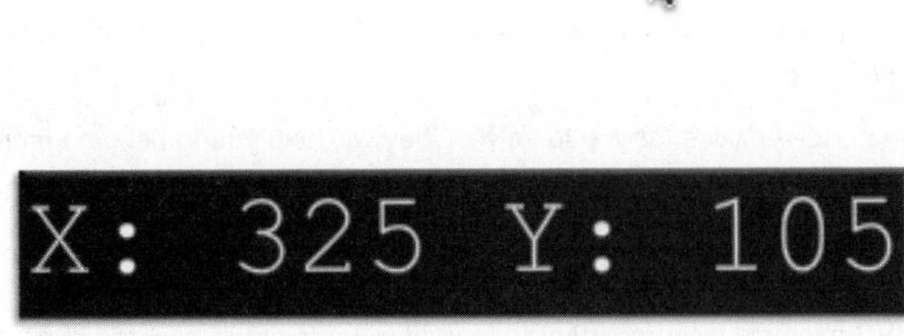

Figure 1-11. Challenge 2: Display the mouse's x and y position.

The view will first need to create a property called _stage so that it can store a local reference to the stage:

```
private var _stage:Object;
```

The view will need to initialize it to the value of stage in the addedToStageHandler:

```
public function addedToStageHandler(event:Event):void
{
  _stage = stage;
}
```

You'll need to add a MOUSE_MOVE event handler in the view to listen for changes to the mouse's position. This also needs to be added to the stage object in the addedToStageHandler:

```
public function addedToStageHandler(event:Event):void
{
  _stage = stage;
  stage.addEventListener(MouseEvent.MOUSE_MOVE, mouseMoveHandler);
}
```

The controller will need to have access to the stage object. But the controller is never added to the stage, so it can't access the stage object directly. That means the view must pass it a reference to stage when it asks the controller to figure out the mouse's position. You might end up with a method that looks like this:

```
public function mouseMoveHandler(event:MouseEvent):void
{
  _controller.processMouseMove(event, _stage);
}
```

Notice how the _stage is passed as a parameter to the controller's processMouseMove method. This will let the controller access the stage and all of its properties.

Make sure that the controller's processMouseMove method is set up to accept those parameters:

```
public function processMouseMove
  (event:MouseEvent, stage:Object):void
{…
```

That should be enough to get you started. If you get stuck, you'll find the solution in the DisplayMouseMVC folder.

These will be good little puzzles for you to solve. They will help you to become more comfortable using the MVC framework.

An MVC player and map view example

The previous MVC example was important to look at to understand how the MVC pattern works, but it's rather useless from a practical game design point of view. How can we take these MVC principles and apply them to a real-world problem, like building a keyboard-controlled player character?

Let's take the Verlet player control system that we started earlier in this chapter and fuse it with the MVC framework. And to show you just how easy it is to extend an MVC system, this next example uses two views that share the same model data.

Run `PlayerMVC.swf` in the `PlayerMVC` folder in the chapter's source files, and you'll see something like Figure 1-12. You can move the square around the stage with the keyboard, and the map in the top-right corner tracks the square's position at 1/15 scale. It's the kind of map display you've seen used in countless games, and it is especially useful for displaying the player's position in a large game world.

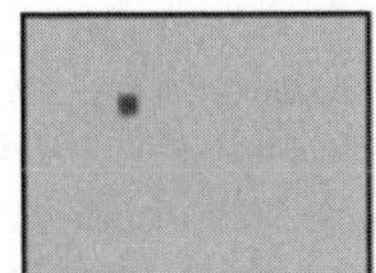

Figure 1-12. The map view tracks the player's position on the stage.

It was easy to add this map with MVC, because the map is just another view. It reads data from exactly the same model as the player's view. Take a look at the main application class, `PlayerMVC`, and you'll see the code that composes the objects:

```
_model = new PlayerModel();
_controller = new PlayerController(_model);
_view = new PlayerView(_model, _controller);
addChild(_view);

_map = new MapView(_model);
addChild(_map);
```

The model is just fed into the map's constructor. And that's all—it just works! The map is completely independent from the player's view and controller, and would work perfectly even if they didn't exist. This is why using an MVC framework makes it so easy to change and extend your game without breaking code that's already working. The map has no dependency on any other classes. And, in fact, you could feed it a *completely different model*, and it would work fine.

Let's look at the code that makes this example work. There's a lot code here, but don't let that scare you. The principals are exactly the same as the first MVC example. When you start building your own MVC-based control system, you'll find this a handy reference. You may want to just glance at Figure 1-9 (the Monster Diagram!) for a reminder of the way the classes communicate. Exactly the same communication is happening in this new example, except there are many more properties involved.

The PlayerModel

There are a few very important things you need to note about the model. One is that height and width are two of its properties. The view uses these to figure out what size to draw itself.

But aren't height and width visual things you see on the stage? Shouldn't they be part of the View class rather than the Model class?

Height and width are actually a kind of data, so they should be part of the model. The model doesn't make any decisions about how that data is displayed. The view's job is to decide how to use that data to make something visible on the stage. The model's job is to store this kind of "visual data." You'll see many more examples of this in the chapters ahead.

Also note that the update method, which figures out velocity based on the Verlet formula, is part of the model. In an MVC system, models can contain methods that process some of their internal data. For example, a model could contain a method that does a basic number conversion, like formatting a date.

The update method uses the public xPos and yPos properties, not the private ones (_xPos and _yPos). This is very important because it means that when those properties are set, the CHANGE event will be dispatched.

Apart from that, most of this class is just composed of getters and setters.

```
package player
{
  import flash.events.Event;
  import flash.events.EventDispatcher;

  public class PlayerModel extends EventDispatcher
  {
    private const SPEED:uint = 10;
    private var _xPos:Number = 0;
    private var _yPos:Number = 0;
    public var temporaryX:Number = 0;
    public var temporaryY:Number = 0;
    public var width:Number = 50;
    public var height:Number = 50;
    public var previousX:Number = 0;
    public var previousY:Number = 0;

    public function PlayerModel():void
    {
    }

    public function update():void
    {
      //Verlet integration
      temporaryX = xPos;
      temporaryY = yPos;
```

```
    xPos += vx;
    yPos += vy;

    previousX = temporaryX;
    previousY = temporaryY;
  }

  //Getters and setters
  //vx
  public function get vx():Number
  {
    return xPos - previousX;
  }
  public function set vx(value:Number):void
  {
    previousX = xPos - value;
  }

  //vy
  public function get vy():Number
  {
    return yPos - previousY;
  }
  public function set vy(value:Number):void
  {
    previousY = yPos - value;
  }

  //xPos
  public function get xPos():Number
  {
    return _xPos;
  }
  public function set xPos(value:Number):void
  {
    _xPos = value;
    dispatchEvent(new Event(Event.CHANGE));
  }

  //yPos
  public function get yPos():Number
  {
    return _yPos;
  }
```

```
    public function set yPos(value:Number):void
    {
      _yPos = value;
      dispatchEvent(new Event(Event.CHANGE));
    }

    //setX
    public function set setX(value:Number):void
    {
      previousX = value;

      //Sets the public xPos setter
      //which forces the CHANGE event
      //to be dispatched
      xPos = value;
    }

    //setY
    public function set setY(value:Number):void
    {
      previousY = value;

      //Sets the public yPos setter
      //which forces the CHANGE event
      //to be dispatched
      yPos = value;
    }

    //speed
    public function get speed():uint
    {
      return SPEED;
    }
  }
}
```

The PlayerView

The `PlayerView` uses the model's data to draw and position itself. The `PlayerModel` contains `height` and `width` properties that give the `PlayerView` its dimensions. The view uses these values to draw its outside rectangle shape in this line of code:

```
outerShape.graphics.drawRoundRect
  (
    -(_model.width * 0.5),
    -(_model.height * 0.5),
```

```
    _model.width, _model.height,
    10,
    10
  );
```

It also scales the inner circle shape to match:

```
innerShape.graphics.drawCircle(0, 0, _model.width * 0.25);
```

The rest of the PlayerView class is identical to the code earlier in the chapter. The only differences are the two lines highlighted in the preceding code.

The PlayerView also keeps its position synchronized to the model when the model dispatches a CHANGE event.

```
private function changeHandler(event:Event):void
{
  this.x = _model.xPos;
  this.y = _model.yPos;
}
```

Because it has subscribed to listen to changes in the model's values, any changes in the model will automatically affect the view.

Here's the PlayerView class:

```
package player
{
  import flash.display.*;
  import flash.events.Event;
  import flash.filters.*;
  import flash.events.Event;
  import flash.events.KeyboardEvent;
  import flash.ui.Keyboard;

  public class PlayerView extends Sprite
  {
    //Object that contains the player model
    private var _model:Object;

    //Object that contains the player controller
    private var _controller:Object;

    public function PlayerView(model:Object, controller:Object)
    {
      _model = model;
      _controller = controller;
```

```
    //Listen for changes on the model.
    //The event handler that reacts to changes
    //in the model's value is below
    _model.addEventListener(Event.CHANGE, changeHandler);

    addEventListener(Event.ADDED_TO_STAGE, onAddedToStage);
  }
  private function onAddedToStage(event:Event):void
  {
    //Draw the player
    draw();

    //Add listeners
    stage.addEventListener(KeyboardEvent.KEY_DOWN,onKeyDown);
    stage.addEventListener(KeyboardEvent.KEY_UP,onKeyUp);

    //Remove this listener
    removeEventListener
      (Event.ADDED_TO_STAGE, onAddedToStage);
  }
  private function onKeyDown(event:KeyboardEvent):void
  {
    _controller.processKeyDown(event);
  }
  private function onKeyUp(event:KeyboardEvent):void
  {
    _controller.processKeyUp(event);
  }
  private function draw():void
  {
    //Draw the outer shape
    var outerShape:Shape = new Shape();
    outerShape.graphics.beginFill(0x000000);
    outerShape.graphics.drawRoundRect
      (
        -(_model.width * 0.5),
        -(_model.height * 0.5),
        _model.width,
        _model.height,
        10,
        10
      );
    outerShape.graphics.endFill();
    addChild(outerShape);

    //Add a bevel and drop shadow and bevel filter
    var outerFilters:Array = new Array();
    outerFilters = outerShape.filters;
    outerFilters.push
```

```
        (
          new BevelFilter
          (
            5, 135, 0xFFFFFF, 0.50, 0x999999, 0.50, 2, 2
          )
        );
        outerFilters.push
        (
          new DropShadowFilter
          (
            5, 135, 0x000000, 0.60, 10, 10
          )
        );
      outerShape.filters = outerFilters;

      //Draw the inner shape
      var innerShape:Shape = new Shape();
      innerShape.graphics.beginFill(0xCCCCCC);
      innerShape.graphics.drawCircle(0, 0, _model.width * 0.25);
      innerShape.graphics.endFill();
      addChild(innerShape);

      //Add a bevel and drop shadow and bevel filter
      var innerFilters:Array = new Array();
      innerFilters = innerShape.filters;
      innerFilters.push
        (
          new BevelFilter
          (
            3, 315, 0xFFFFFF, 0.50, 0x999999,
            0.50, 4, 4, 1, 1, "outer"
          )
        );
      innerShape.filters = innerFilters;
      }

      //When the model changes its values,
      //it fires a CHANGE event which triggers
      //this changeHandler event handler
      private function changeHandler(event:Event):void
      {
        this.x = _model.xPos;
        this.y = _model.yPos;
      }
    }
  }
```

The PlayerController

The PlayerController analyzes the keyboard input and sets the PlayerModel's vx and vy based on its speed property. It doesn't display anything or dispatch events, so it doesn't need to extend any other class.

```
package player
{
  import flash.events.Event;
  import flash.events.EventDispatcher;
  import flash.events.KeyboardEvent;
  import flash.ui.Keyboard;

  public class PlayerController
  {
    private var _model:Object;

    public function PlayerController(model:Object):void
    {
      _model = model;
    }
    public function processKeyDown(event:KeyboardEvent):void
    {
      switch (event.keyCode)
      {
        case Keyboard.LEFT:
           _model.vx = -_model.speed;
           break;

        case Keyboard.RIGHT:
           _model.vx = _model.speed;
           break;

        case Keyboard.UP:
           _model.vy = -_model.speed;
           break;

        case Keyboard.DOWN:
           _model.vy = _model.speed;
           break;
      }
    }

    public function processKeyUp(event:KeyboardEvent):void
    {
      if (event.keyCode == Keyboard.LEFT
      ||  event.keyCode == Keyboard.RIGHT)
```

```
        {
          _model.vx = 0;
        }
        if (event.keyCode == Keyboard.UP
        ||  event.keyCode == Keyboard.DOWN)
        {
          _model.vy = 0;
        }
      }
    }
  }
```

The MapView

The `MapView` works almost identically to the `PlayerView`, but it's a little simpler because it doesn't need to send input to a controller. The `MapView` multiplies the model's data values by 0.15 (the value of its `_scaleFactor` property) to scale those values to a 1:15 ratio. The map boundary's size is found by taking the stage's height and width and multiplying it by the `_scaleFactor`.

```
_mapBoundary.graphics.drawRect
  (
    0, 0,
    stage.stageWidth *  _scaleFactor,
    stage.stageHeight * _scaleFactor
  );
```

This draws the map in exactly the correct dimensions. (Because the `MapView` is added to the stage by the application class, it can freely access the `stage` object and the `stage`'s properties.)

Because it's listening to the model's `CHANGE` events, the position of the red dot that represents the player (the `_positionMarker`) is also updated automatically whenever the model is updated.

```
private function changeHandler(event:Event):void
{
  _positionMarker.x = _model.xPos * _scaleFactor;
  _positionMarker.y = _model.yPos * _scaleFactor;
}
```

And because the values are multiplied by 0.15, the position is perfectly scaled.

```
package map
{
  import flash.display.*;
  import flash.events.Event;
```

```
public class MapView extends Sprite
{
  //Object that contains the player model
  private var _model:Object;

  private var _scaleFactor:Number;
  private var _mapBoundary:Shape;
  private var _positionMarker:Sprite;

  public function MapView(model:Object)
  {
    _model = model;
    _model.addEventListener(Event.CHANGE, changeHandler);

    addEventListener(Event.ADDED_TO_STAGE, onAddedToStage);
  }
  private function onAddedToStage(event:Event):void
  {
    _scaleFactor = 0.15;

    //Draw the map
    draw();

    //Remove this listener
    removeEventListener(Event.ADDED_TO_STAGE, onAddedToStage);
  }
  private function draw():void
  {
    //Draw the map boundary
    _mapBoundary = new Shape();
    _mapBoundary.graphics.lineStyle(1);
    _mapBoundary.graphics.moveTo(0, 0);
    _mapBoundary.graphics.beginFill(0xCCCCCC);
    _mapBoundary.graphics.drawRect
      (
        0, 0,
        stage.stageWidth * _scaleFactor,
        stage.stageHeight * _scaleFactor
      );
    _mapBoundary.graphics.endFill();
    addChild(_mapBoundary);
```

```
      //Draw the player position marker
      _positionMarker = new Sprite();
      _positionMarker.graphics.lineStyle();
      _positionMarker.graphics.moveTo(0, 0);
      _positionMarker.graphics.beginFill(0xFF0000);
      _positionMarker.graphics.drawRect(-2, -2, 4, 4);
      _positionMarker.graphics.endFill();
      addChild(_positionMarker);
    }

    private function changeHandler(event:Event):void
    {
      _positionMarker.x = _model.xPos * _scaleFactor;
      _positionMarker.y = _model.yPos * _scaleFactor;
    }
  }
}
```

The PlayerMVC application class

Finally, the last class that makes all of this work together is the application class, `PlayerMVC`. It works very much like the `BasicMVC` class you saw earlier, with one important addition: the `enterFrameHandler` that calls the model's `update` method and checks stage boundaries

```
private function enterFrameHandler (event:Event):void
{
  _model.update();
  StageBoundaries.stop(_model, stage);
}
```

It's the same kind of code that we needed for our Verlet engine.

You may be wondering how this bit of code fits into the whole MVC system? Technically, the application class is a controller. For now, let's call it the "game controller." This means that the model has two controllers: one for user-input events and the other for game events. In an MVC system, this is perfectly fine, Models can have numerous controllers and views. In future chapters, we'll look at how you can formally create a `GameController` class to centralize the game's events and logic.

Here's the full `PlayerMVC` application class:

```
package
{
  import flash.events.Event;
  import flash.display.Sprite;
  import com.friendsofed.utils.StageBoundaries;
```

```
  //Import the MVC components from subfolders
  import player.*;
  import map.MapView;

  [SWF(backgroundColor="0xFFFFFF", frameRate="60",
  width="550", height="400")]

  public class PlayerMVC extends Sprite
  {
    private var _model:PlayerModel;
    private var _view:PlayerView;
    private var _controller:PlayerController;
    private var _map:MapView;

    public function PlayerMVC()
    {
      _model = new PlayerModel();
      _controller = new PlayerController(_model);
      _view = new PlayerView(_model, _controller);
      addChild(_view);

      _map = new MapView(_model);
      addChild(_map);

      //Position the player in the center of the stage
      _model.setX = 275;
      _model.setY = 200;

       addEventListener(Event.ENTER_FRAME,enterFrameHandler);
    }

    private function enterFrameHandler(event:Event):void
    {
      _model.update();
      StageBoundaries.stop(_model, stage);
    }
  }
}
```

Verlet + MVC + physics = fun!

Wow, we've come a long way in this chapter, haven't we? I've walked you through all the building blocks of Verlet integration and the MVC design pattern in quite a bit of detail, so that you'll have all the resources you need to build these systems yourself from scratch. The last piece in this puzzle is to add some physics.

Run the `SpaceShipMVC.swf` file in the `SpaceShipMVC/src` folder of the chapter's source files. Figure 1-13 shows what you'll see: a keyboard-controlled spaceship with a map view and parallax scrolling background. This example includes all the techniques we've looked at so far in this chapter.

Figure 1-13. Physics-enabled space ship with a map view and parallax scrolling background

There's quite a bit of code here, so I'm going to let you dig around in the source files if you want to double-check any of the details. But there's absolutely nothing new going on here that we haven't already covered.

Here's how it works:

- I've applied the MVC framework to the Verlet-based spaceship we looked at earlier. The code is almost identical, but it has been broken down into three classes in exactly the same way that the previous MVC examples were organized. Take a look at the source code, and you'll see there are no surprises.
- I've added two additional views: the star field and the map. The map view uses *identical* code to the previous example. I didn't need to make modifications at all. All I did was drop it in and feed it the spaceship's model. Yay, MVC!
- The star field effect is made up of two classes: `Star` (which draws each star) and `StarFieldView`. `StarFieldView` is the view class. It randomly plots the stars on the stage and updates their positions based on the model.

Figure 1-14 shows how the files are organized.

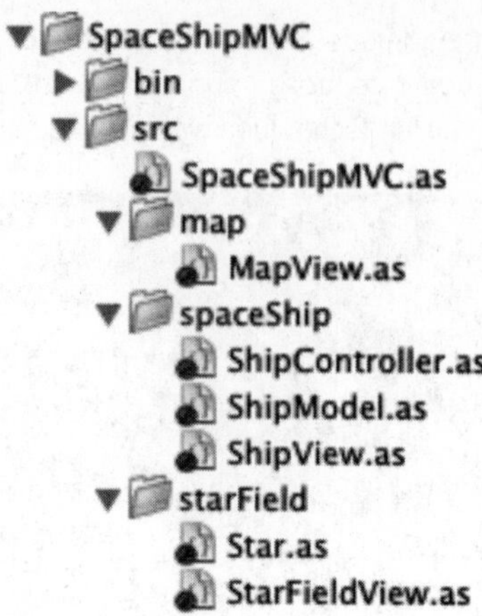

Figure 1-14. Objects organized into related packages

You can see that each view is organized into a separate folder and package. The application class, `SpaceShipMVC` imports these classes:

```
import spaceShip.*;
import starField.*;
import map.MapView;
```

It then elegantly composes them by feeding the ship's model into the three views

```
_model = new ShipModel();

_starField = new StarFieldView(_model);
addChild(_starField);

_map = new MapView(_model);
addChild(_map);

_controller = new ShipController(_model);
_shipView = new ShipView(_model, _controller);
addChild(_shipView);
```

You should be starting to recognize the MVC's signature in this code. And the entire system is thrown into action by this very simple `enterFrameHandler`:

```
private function enterFrameHandler(event:Event):void
{
  _model.update();
  StageBoundaries.wrap(_model, stage);
}
```

It's amazingly simple, but hides a whole lot of complexity going on behind the scenes. Fortunately, because I've implemented the MVC framework, that complexity is completely under control. If you're like me and looking at clean, neatly organized and bug-free code makes you really, really happy, then I have only one thing to say: use MVC!

Making stars

A fun feature of this example is the parallax scrolling star field. Sixty stars are plotted on the stage at various sizes, from 1 to 10. The smaller stars move more slowly, and the bigger stars move more quickly, which gives it very realistic sense of depth. There are also more stars in the background than in the foreground, which also adds to the effect. Take a look at the `StarFieldView` class to see how it all works. Here, we'll go over its major features.

First, an empty array is created to store the stars:

```
_starArray = [];
```

The code creates 60 stars (the default value of `_numberOfStars`) in a `for` loop. It gives them a random size and position on the stage, and pushes them into the `_starArray`.

```
for (var i:uint = 0; i < Math.round(_numberOfStars); i++)
{
  //Find a random star size. The random number will be weighted
  //to smaller sizes so that more stars appear in the background

  var starSize:uint = weightedRandomNumber(_starSize / 2);

  //Create a new star and position it randomly

  var star:Star = new Star(starSize, _starColor);
  star.x = Math.random() * stage.stageWidth;
  star.y = Math.random() * stage.stageHeight;

  //Push the star into the _starArray and add it to the stage

  _starArray.push(star);
  addChild(star);
}
```

The size of the stars is found by a method called `weightedRandomNumber`. It finds a value between 3 and 10, but weights the result so that it's far more likely for stars to be smaller size. This is important because for the star field effect to look realistic, there should be more small stars in the background than big stars in the foreground.

```
private function weightedRandomNumber(weight:uint):uint
{
  var randomNumber:int = Math.ceil(Math.random() * _starSize);
  var weightedNumber:int = randomNumber - (uint(Math.random() * weight));
  if(weightedNumber < 3)
```

```
  {
    weightedNumber = 3;
  }
 return weightedNumber;
}
```

The method first finds a random number between 1 and 10 (10 is the default value of _starSize).

```
var randomNumber:int = Math.ceil(Math.random() * _starSize);
```

It then finds another random number between 1 and 5 (the value of weight) and subtracts that from the first number.

```
var weightedNumber:int = randomNumber - (uint(Math.random() * weight));
```

For example, let's say the first random number (between 1 and 10) is 7. The second random number, (between 1 and 5) is 3. If you subtract 3 from 7, the result is 4.

Most of the numbers will be low, which is good, because it will give us a lot of small stars and only a few bigger ones. But the smallest size the stars should be is 3 pixels, so there's a check for that.

```
if(weightedNumber < 3)
{
  weightedNumber = 3;
}
```

This forces stars that are smaller than 3 up to a minimum size of 3.

This gives a good range of star sizes. There are certainly many more solutions to this problem, and maybe you can think of a better one.

Moving stars

The star field is a view of the spaceship's model, so I can use the model to move the stars. But, there's a problem: 60 stars to move! To do this, the changeHandler needs to loop through all the stars in the _starsArray and set their velocities and positions.

```
private function changeHandler(event:Event):void
{
  for (var i:uint = 0; i < _starArray.length; i++)
  {
    //Scale the velocity of the star based on its size
    var scale:Number = _starArray[i].size / _starSize;
```

```
      //Move stars
      _starArray[i].x -=  _model.vx * scale;
      _starArray[i].y -=  _model.vy * scale;

      //Screen wrapping
      StageBoundaries.wrap(_starArray[i], stage);
    }
  }
```

First, a `scale` value is worked out so big stars in the foreground will move faster than small stars in the background. This is done by dividing the star's size by 10 (the value of `_starSize`).

```
var scale:Number = _starArray[i].size / _starSize;
```

This `scale` value is then multiplied by the model's `vx` and `vy` properties. This gives them a unique velocity that proportionately matches their size. Small stars will move slowly, and big stars will move more quickly. This makes the stars appear to occupy different planes and creates the parallax perspective effect.

```
_starArray[i].x -=  _model.vx * scale;
_starArray[i].y -=  _model.vy * scale;
```

The new velocity is *subtracted* from the star's position so that the stars move in the opposite direction from the spaceship.

And finally, the stars are wrapped around the edges of the stage, which makes the background appear to scroll endlessly.

```
StageBoundaries.wrap(_starArray[i], stage);
```

And there we have a very convincing star field effect! Make sure you check out the complete `StarFieldView` class to see all this code in its complete context, and also take a look at the `Star` class, which draws the stars. Both of these classes are in the chapter's source files.

A crash course in the drawing API

The drawing API allows you to use AS3.0 code to draw lines, shapes, and colors on the stage. All the objects in this chapter were drawn using with the drawing API. If you've used it before but are a bit fuzzy on the details, I've put together this quick-reference guide. Check Adobe's documentation for detailed explanations and examples of the drawing methods. Keith Peter's *AdvancED ActionScript 3.0 Animation* is also an excellent introduction to the drawing API.

In the chapter's source files you'll find working examples of all this code in the `DrawingAPI` folder.

> *What is an API? It stands for application programming interface. It's essentially a set of custom classes that help you perform specific tasks, like drawing shapes.*

Drawing lines

The following code will draw the line shown in Figure 1-15.

```
var line:Shape = new Shape();
line.graphics.lineStyle(1);
line.graphics.moveTo(-40, -30);
line.graphics.lineTo(40, 20);
addChild(line);
```

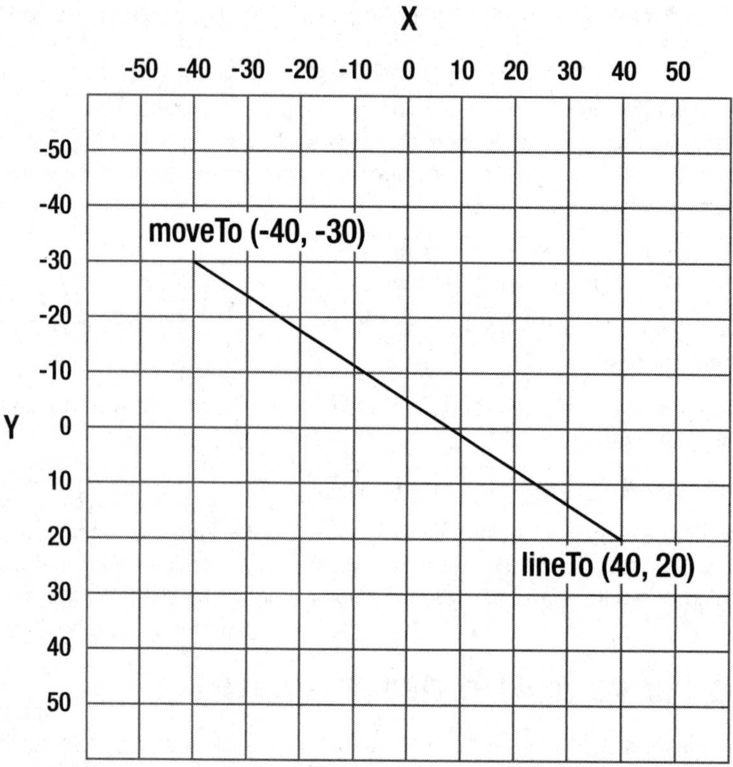

Figure 1-15. Drawing a line

Drawing squares

The square in Figure 1-16 is drawn so that its center point is at 0,0. This is useful for games where you often want your objects to be centered. (It makes collision-detection calculations a little simpler.)

```
var square:Shape = new Shape();
square.graphics.beginFill(0x000000);
square.graphics.drawRoundRect(-25, -25, 50, 50, 10, 10);
square.graphics.endFill();
addChild(square);
```

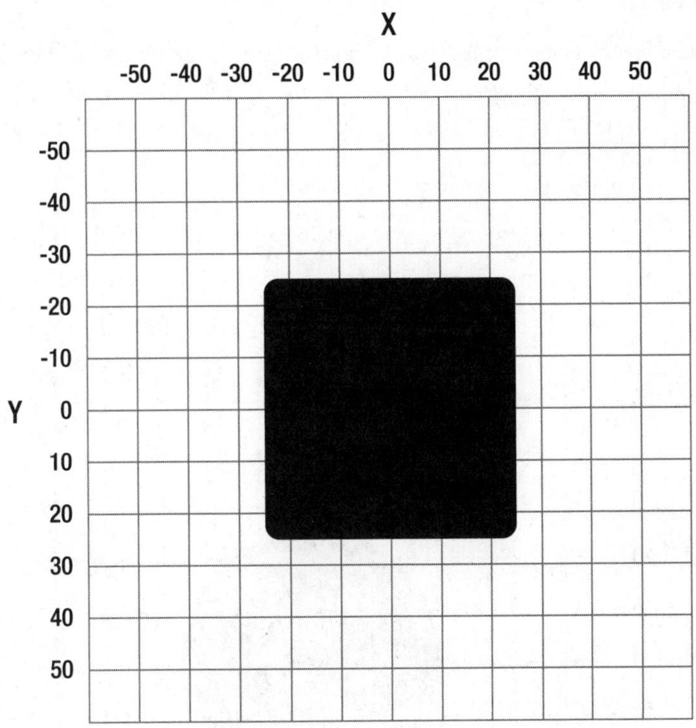

Figure 1-16. A square with rounded corners

To draw an outline around a square, add a `lineStyle` method.

```
var square:Shape = new Shape();
square.graphics.lineStyle(3, 0xCE1114);
square.graphics.beginFill(0x000000);
square.graphics.drawRoundRect(-25, -25, 50, 50, 10, 10);
square.graphics.endFill();
addChild(square);
```

This new code will draw a 3-pixel wide red line around the square.

When you draw a rectangle, the first four arguments represent x, y, `height`, and `width`.

```
drawRect(-25, -25, 50, 50);
```

With drawRoundRect, the last two arguments are the corner radius. They determine how rounded the corners are.

```
drawRoundRect(-25, -25, 50, 50, 10, 10);
```

Drawing circles

This code draws a black circle from 0,0 with a 25-pixel radius (see Figure 1-17):

```
var circle:Shape = new Shape();
circle.graphics.beginFill(0x000000);
circle.graphics.drawCircle(0, 0, 25);
circle.graphics.endFill();
addChild(circle);
```

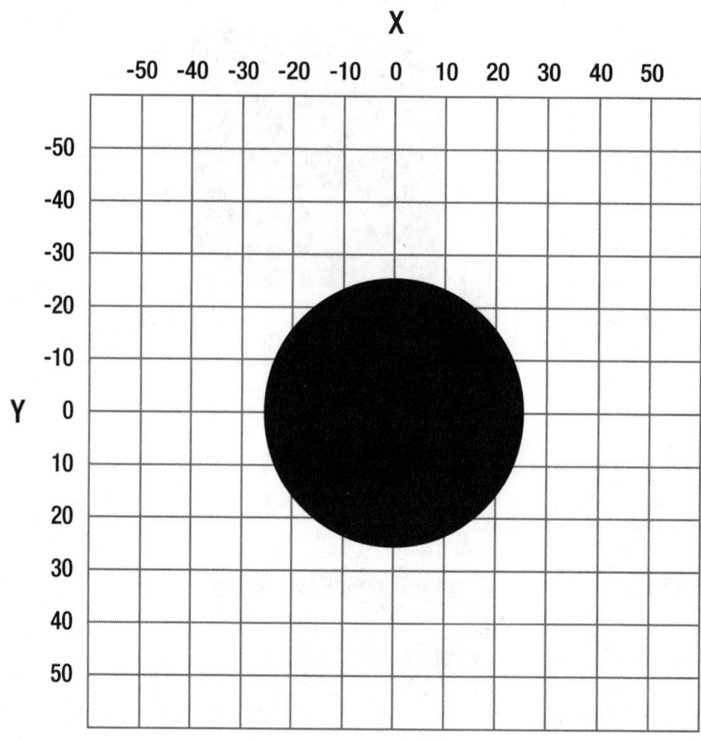

Figure 1-17. A circle positioned at 0,0 with a radius of 25

The drawCircle method takes three arguments: x, y, and radius

```
drawCircle(0, 0, 25);
```

Adding filters

All display objects have a property called `filters`. This is an array that stores all the filters that have been placed on an object. Use this strategy to apply a filter to an object:

- Remember to import the filter classes: `import flash.filters.*` .
- Make a copy of the object's `filters` property in a new array variable.
- Push the filters into the copy of the filter array.
- Give the original `filters` property the value of the copied array variable.

This is a confusing sequence of code to remember, but its actual application is very routine.

The following code shows how you can add a bevel and drop-shadow filter to a square shape (see Figure 1-18).

```
var squareFilters:Array = sqaure.filters;
squareFilters.push
  (
    new BevelFilter
    (
      5, 135, 0xFFFFFF, 0.50, 0x999999, 0.50, 2, 2
    )
  );
squareFilters.push
  (
    new DropShadowFilter
    (
      5, 135, 0x000000, 0.60, 10, 10
    )
  );
square.filters = squareFilters;
```

Figure 1-18. A rounded rectangle with bevel and drop-shadow filter

Gradient fills

Gradients are a big, complex subject. In the source files, you'll find a file called `GradientFill.as`, which you can use as a starting point for understanding and experimenting with gradient fills.

The following code draws a rectangle and fills it with a gradient, as shown in Figure 1-19.

Figure 1-19. A gradient fill

```
var matrix:Matrix = new Matrix();
matrix.createGradientBox(50, 50, 0, 0, 0);
var colors:Array = [0xCCCCCC, 0x333333];
var alphas:Array = [255, 255];
var ratios:Array = [0, 255];

var square:Shape = new Shape();
square.graphics.lineStyle(1)
square.graphics.beginGradientFill
  (GradientType.LINEAR, colors, alphas, ratios, matrix);
square.graphics.drawRect(0, 0, 50, 50);
square.graphics.endFill();
addChild(square);
```

Does it look confusing? Don't worry, even seasoned AS3.0 programmers need to look up this stuff before they use it! Let's break this down to see what's going on.

First, import the classes that you need for a gradient fill.

```
import flash.display.GradientType;
import flash.geom.Matrix;
```

Then you need to create a `Matrix` object. A matrix is used to help you control the math behind the way that objects are positioned on the stage (moved, scaled, skewed, or rotated). Matrices have many applications in AS3.0, including being necessary for adding gradient fills. The `createGradientBox` method belongs to the `Matrix` class.

```
var matrix:Matrix = new Matrix();
matrix.createGradientBox(50, 50, 0, 0, 0);
```

`createGradientBox` makes an invisible box that is used to contain the gradient. In this example, it has the same dimensions as the square, but you can make it larger or smaller if you want to. `createGradientBox` takes five arguments: height, width, rotation, x offset, and y offset. The rotation is the amount to rotate the gradient, in *radians*. If you have a number in *degrees*, convert it to radians first: `degrees = radians / (Math.PI / 180)`. x offset (referred to in Adobe's documentation as "translate x" or `tx`) is the amount by which you offset the start of the gradient on the x axis. In our example, if you change the x offset to 20, you'll see a result like the gradient shown in Figure 1-20.

```
matrix.createGradientBox(50, 50, 0, 20, 0);
```

The gradient only starts at an x position of 20. Similarly, the y offset (referred to in Adobe's documentation as "translate y" or `ty`) allows you to offset the start of the gradient on the y axis. (You'll be able to see this effect if you rotate the gradient 90 degrees.)

Figure 1-20. The tx parameter allows you to specify by how much you want to offset the start of the gradient.

Next, you need to create three arrays that store details about how you want the gradient to look. This is an example of a two-color gradient, but you can use as many colors in the gradient as you like by adding more array elements.

```
var colors:Array = [0xCCCCCC, 0x333333];
var alphas:Array = [255, 255];
var ratios:Array = [0, 255];
```

The arrays are as follows:

- The `colors` array contains the two colors that you want to use.
- The `alphas` array has the alpha values of the two colors. These can be values between 0 and 255. 0 means that the color will be completely transparent. 255 means that it will be completely opaque.
- The `ratios` array represents how much of each color should be solid. You need to use a number between 0 and 255. Confusingly, this number represents a percentage. It's the percentage of the gradient's width. It represents the point at which you want the color to be solid.

Does the `ratios` array sound like an impossible concept to comprehend? You're not alone! Let's look at a concrete example.

Let's say you want the second color to be solid from the 40% point of the gradient's width. You would need to give it a value of 102 (102 is 40% of 255). 0 represents the leftmost side of gradient, and 255 represents the rightmost side. Your code would look like this:

```
var ratios:Array = [0, 102];
```

Figure 1-21 shows the effect this will have on the example code. The gradient continues up to the 40% mark. After that, the color is solid.

It takes a lot of practice to get used to this system, so experiment with the `GradientFill.as` source file and see if you can predict how the ratio numbers you enter affect the gradient.

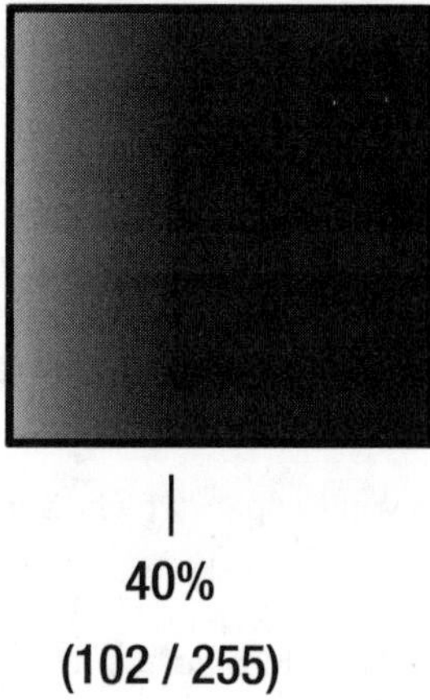

Figure 1-21. Set the gradient:solid color ratio.

The last step is to use the `beginGradientFill` method to apply the gradient.

```
var square:Shape = new Shape();
square.graphics.lineStyle(1)
square.graphics.beginGradientFill
  (
    GradientType.LINEAR, colors, alphas, ratios, matrix
  );
square.graphics.drawRect(0, 0, 50, 50);
square.graphics.endFill();
addChild(square);
```

`beginGradientFill` takes five arguments. The last four are your arrays and the `matrix` object itself. The first is the type of gradient you want to create. You can choose between linear and radial gradients.

```
GradientType.LINEAR
GradientType.RADIAL
```

By combining all these techniques, you have almost infinite flexibility in the kinds of gradients you can create.

Complex shapes

When you're creating complex graphics, it's often a good idea to create a few simple shapes individually and then combine them together into a parent sprite. That way, you need to deal with only one sprite, rather than many shapes.

Drawing the ship

The following code shows how the spaceship graphic was drawn, and the details of how the drawing commands work are shown in Figure 1-22.

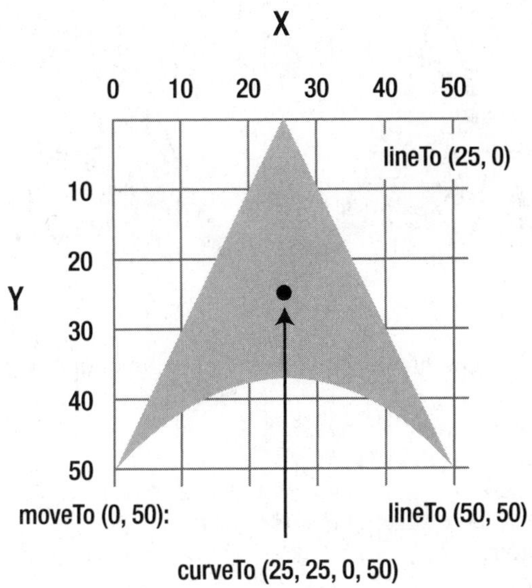

Figure 1-22. Drawing the spaceship

```
var ship:Shape = new Shape();

//1. Leave the lineStyle parameters empty or omit
//including it altogether for an invisible line around the shape
ship.graphics.lineStyle();

//2. Set the optional starting x and y position (the default is 0,0)
ship.graphics.moveTo(0, 50);
```

```
//3. Start the color fill
ship.graphics.beginFill(0x666666);

//4. Draw the connecting lines
ship.graphics.lineTo(25, 0);
ship.graphics.lineTo(50, 50);
ship.graphics.curveTo(25, 25, 0, 50);

//5. End the color fill and display the shape
ship.graphics.endFill();
addChild(ship);
```

Drawing the ship's thruster flame

To make the flame appear under the ship's body, the code that draws the flame should appear before the code that draws the body of the ship (see Figure 1-23).

Figure 1-23. Add the code for the flame first so that it appears under the ship.

```
//Create the gradient box and arrays
var matrix:Matrix = new Matrix();
matrix.createGradientBox(25, 17, (90 * Math.PI / 180), 0, 50);
var colors:Array = [0xFF3300, 0xFFFF00];
var alphas:Array = [100, 0];
var ratios:Array = [0, 255];

//Draw the thruster flame
var flame:Shape = new Shape();
flame.graphics.lineStyle(1, 0x000000, 0);
flame.graphics.beginGradientFill
  (GradientType.LINEAR, colors, alphas, ratios, matrix);
flame.graphics.moveTo(13, 38);
flame.graphics.curveTo(25, 50, (13 * 3), 38);
flame.graphics.lineTo(13, 38);
flame.graphics.endFill();
addChild(flame);
```

Add both shapes to a container sprite

The ship and flame shapes are added to a container sprite. Filters are added, and then the container sprite is centered and rotated 90 degrees (see Figure 1-24). It's rotated by 90 degrees to make it simpler for the code in the ship's model that works out its angle.

```
_angle = _rotationValue * (Math.PI / 180);
```

If the ship isn't rotated by 90 degrees, it won't appear to move in the correct direction, and you'll need to add 90 degrees to its `rotation` to compensate. It's simper just to rotate the graphic into the correct position at its source.

```
//Create a new sprite to contain the shapes
var spaceShip:Sprite = new Sprite();
spaceShip.addChild(flame);
spaceShip.addChild(ship);
addChild(spaceShip);

//Add a bevel and drop shadow filter to the space ship
var shipFilters:Array = new Array();
shipFilters = spaceShip.filters;
shipFilters.push
  (
    new BevelFilter
    (
      2, 135, 0xFFFFFF, 0.50, 0x000000, 0.50, 2, 2
    )
  );
shipFilters.push
  (
  new DropShadowFilter
    (
      2, 135, 0x000000, 0.35, 2, 2
    )
  );
spaceShip.filters = shipFilters;

//Center and rotate it to the right
spaceShip.rotation = 90;
spaceShip.x += 25;
spaceShip.y -= 25;
```

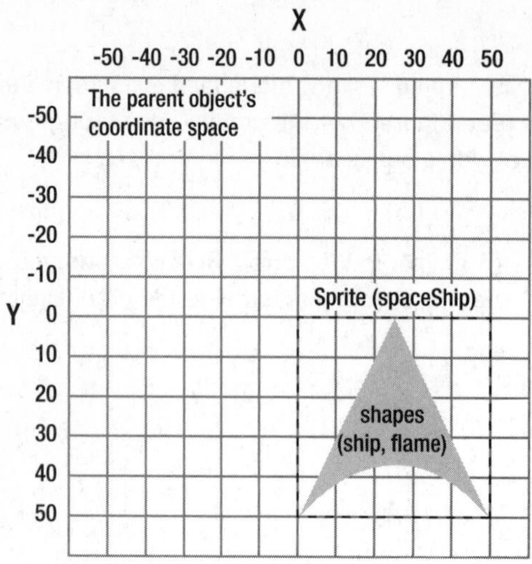

1. Add the shapes to a containing Sprite and add the containing Sprite to the object's display list.

```
var spaceShip:Sprite = new Sprite():
spaceShip.addChild(flame):
spaceShip.addChild(ship):
addChild(spaceShip):
```

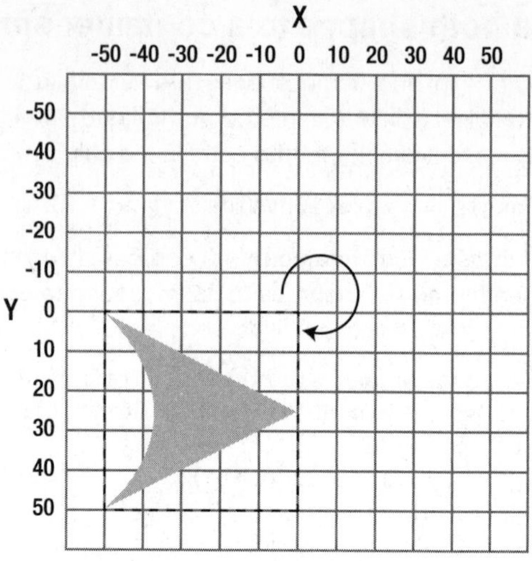

2. Rotate the containing Sprite 90 degrees so that the ship's nose points to the right.

```
spaceShip.rotation = 90:
```

3. Center the containing Sprite inside the object so that its center point is at 0.0.

```
spaceShip.x += 25:
spaceShip.y -= 25:
```

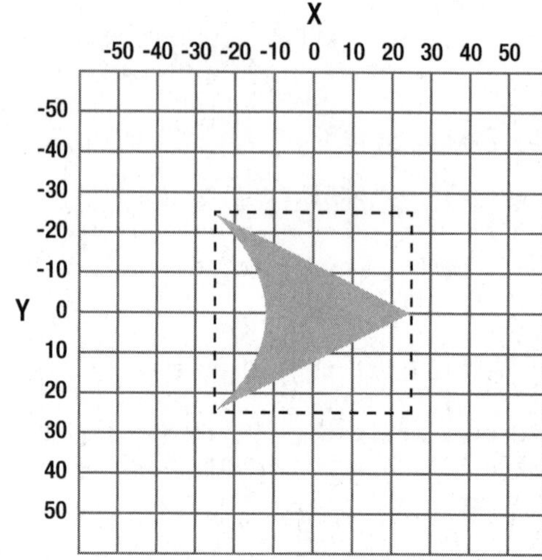

Figure 1-24. Center and rotate the spaceShip sprite.

Using drawPath for really complex shapes

Flash Player 10 includes a new `graphics` method called `drawPath`. You can use it to draw really complex shapes with a lot of points using relatively little code.

Figure 1-25 shows the star shape that the `Star` class draws. How many times do you think you would need to use `lineTo` to draw this shape? It would take 16 `lineTo` commands. Imagine typing all that code in line by line—it would be very tedious and strain to look at.

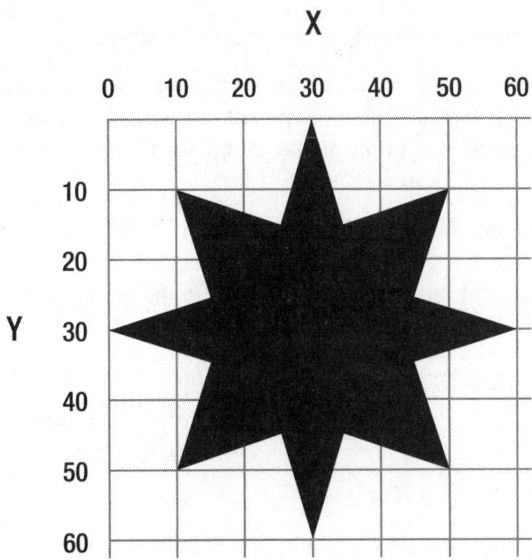

Figure 1-25. Using drawPath to draw a complex shape

The `drawPath` command makes drawing complex shapes like this much easier. Here's the general procedure for using it:

1. Push all the points of your shape into an array.
2. Push all the commands you need to connect them together into another array.
3. Use `drawPath` to draw the shape using the points and commands arrays.

I used the term *array* in these steps, but more correctly I should have said `vector`. In AS3.0, a `vector` is an array whose elements all have the same data type. It's known as a **typed array**. As an example, the following code creates a `Vector` object called `numbers` in which all the elements are `int` types.

```
var numbers:Vector.<int> = new Vector.<int>();
```

This is just an array—the same as the arrays you already know and love. The only difference is that its elements can *only* be integers. That means that you can add elements like this:

```
numbers = [12, 33, 56];
```

But you can't add elements like this:

```
numbers = [12, "Hello!", 3.14];
```

All the elements must be integers, because they were typed using this syntax:

```
<int>
```

This may seem like odd syntax, but it's been borrowed from C++ and Java, which also have Vector classes and type them in the same way. AS3.0, welcome to the club!

The following are the advantages of using a vector over an array:

- Because vector elements are all of the same type, they're much faster to process than arrays. How much faster? This gets mixed reviews. You would need to test this in the context of your game, but it may not be all that significant.
- The compiler can give you an error message if you try to add an element to a vector that's the wrong data type. That's very useful for debugging, because it immediately tells you if your code is trying to do something it shouldn't be doing. Without that extra check, the simple mistake of feeding the wrong data to the wrong array could easily be missed and be very difficult to track down.

> *The `Vector` class has nothing to do with Euclidean vectors, which are the subject of Chapter 2. The `Vector` class is just a typed array.*

So how can we use the `Vector` class and the `drawPath` method to help us draw the star shape? The `DrawingAPI` folder contains a subfolder called `Star` with a working example. Here's the most important section of code:

```
//Create a new Vector object for the drawing coordinates
//This must be typed as Number
var starCoordinates:Vector.<Number> = new Vector.<Number>();

//Push the coordinates into the starCoordinates Vector
starCoordinates.push
  (
    30,0, 35,15, 50,10,
    45,25,60,30, 45,35,
    50,50, 35,45, 30,60,
    25,45, 10,50, 15,35,
    0,30, 15,25, 10,10,
    25,15, 30,0
  );
```

```
//Create a Vector object for the drawing commands
var starCommands:Vector.<int> = new Vector.<int>();

//Push the drawing commands into the starCommands Vector
//1 = moveTo(), 2 = lineTo(), 3 = curveTo()
starCommands.push(1,2,2,2,2,2,2,2,2,2,2,2,2,2,2,2,2,2,2);


//Create the starShape object
var starShape:Shape = new Shape();

//Begin the fill
starShape.graphics.beginFill(0xFFFF00);

//Use the drawPath command to draw the shape using the
//starCommands and starCoordinates Vectors
starShape.graphics.drawPath(starCommands, starCoordinates);

//End the fill
starShape.graphics.endFill();

//Position the star in the center of the sprite
starShape.x -= starShape.width / 2;
starShape.y -= starShape.height / 2;
addChild(starShape);
```

Let's look at how this code works. First, a `Vector` object is created to store all of the x and y coordinates for the shape. These coordinates match those of Figure 1-23.

```
var starCoordinates:Vector.<Number> = new Vector.<Number>();
starCoordinates.push
  (
    30,0, 35,15, 50,10,
    45,25,60,30, 45,35,
    50,50, 35,45, 30,60,
    25,45, 10,50, 15,35,
    0,30, 15,25, 10,10,
    25,15, 30,0
  );
```

Next, it creates another `Vector` object to store the commands used to connect the coordinates. Each number in the vector represents a drawing command:

- 1 for `moveTo()`
- 2 for `lineTo()`
- 3 for `curveTo()`

```
var starCommands:Vector.<int> = new Vector.<int>();
starCommands.push(1,2,2,2,2,2,2,2,2,2,2,2,2,2,2,2,2);
```

Yes, that's 1 `moveTo` command and 16 `lineTo` commands!

Finally, it uses the `drawPath` command to draw the shape. It takes two arguments, the commands vector and the coordinates vector, in that order. These must be vectors; they can't be arrays.

```
starShape.graphics.drawPath(starCommands, starCoordinates);
```

And there you have a very efficient way to draw complex shapes!

Introducing interfaces

Before I close this chapter, I want to introduce the topic of **interfaces**. This is only for reference, however, because none of the code in this book uses interfaces, and I'll never mention them again. So you can skip this section, and you won't have missed a thing. Still interfaces are an important OOP concept, and you'll almost certainly come across them in your programming career. If you need to know what they are and how to use them, here's a quick primer.

What is an interface? It's an AS file, like a class file, that describes the methods that a class can use. If a class then chooses to implement the interface, it must use *exactly* those methods—no more and no less. The class signs a contract that says, "I'm only going to implement the methods in the interface." Why is this important? Because it means that the view can use any model or views that implement the interface, and they will be guaranteed to work.

In the chapter's source files, you'll find a folder called `BasicInterfaceMVC`. It's exactly the same as the example we looked at in this chapter, except that the model and controller implement the two interfaces: `IModel` and `IController`. Let's take a quick look at how it works.

`IModel` is an interface. (By convention, all interface names start with an `I`.) It describes all the methods that any class implementing it must use.

```
package mvc
{
  import flash.events.IEventDispatcher;

  public interface IModel extends IEventDispatcher
  {
    function get direction():String
    function set direction(value:String):void
  }
}
```

This is an interface, not a class, even though it looks very similar to a class. Interfaces need to import any classes they refer to, such as `IEventDispatcher` in this example. Because the model will be dispatching events, it also needs to extend AS3.0's built-in `IEventDispatcher` class.

If the `Model` class wants to use this interface, it needs to say this in its class definition by using the `implements` keyword.

```
public class Model extends EventDispatcher implements IModel
{...
```

Now the model *must use* the methods in the interface—it's signed a contract.

The controller also uses an interface called `IController`.

```
package mvc
{
  import flash.events.KeyboardEvent;

  public interface IController
  {
    function processKeyPress(event:KeyboardEvent):void
  }
}
```

The controller can now implement the `IController` interface.

```
public class Controller implements IController
{...
```

The view can now type both the model to `IModel` and the controller to `IController`.

```
public function View(model:IModel, controller:IController):void
{...
```

Does this seem like a lot of extra code to produce something completely insignificant? Here's why using interfaces is actually very useful:

- The view knows that any object that implements `IModel` or `IController` will work. It means that the model is guaranteed to dispatch the `CHANGE` event that it depends on, and that the methods it calls in the controller actually exist. Without these formal guarantees, the program will generate reams of error message if you accidentally pass the view the wrong type of objects. Or worse, the code could simply fail silently, and you'll never know except for strange bugs that might be extremely difficult to track down.
- It means that you can create other models or controllers that also implement these interfaces, and they'll be guaranteed to work with your existing views. This keeps your code completely modular, and means you can mix and match without the danger of breaking anything.

This is a lot to absorb! My suggestion is that you don't use interfaces while doing your own first experiments with the MVC framework. You have enough on your plate to worry about. Good programming practice suggests that you should *always* use interfaces with MVC, but don't worry, I'll turn a blind eye! I certainly haven't used them in the game examples in this book.

When you feel confident using the MVC framework, come back to this section in the chapter and try to rework your code using interfaces. It may seem like a bit of overkill now, but it's essential for bug-proofing your code in large projects.

Summary

Have you ever started what you thought was a simple game project and realized after a few days of working on it that it was actually monstrously complex? Well, it turns out that "monstrous complexity" is what game designers refer to as "normal complexity." By their very nature, game-design projects are among the most complex things that programmers can attempt.

In this chapter, we've tamed this monster somewhat by implementing the MVC framework and a reliable Verlet integration physics system. Some of the later examples in this chapter had very complex code, but as you can see, their structure makes them predictable, self-managing, easy to read, and easy to extend.

We now have a rock-solid foundation on which to build the rest of the projects in this book. And you can start using the techniques we looked at immediately in your own projects. You might be surprised by how pleasantly bug-free your code becomes when you start implementing the MVC pattern and Verlet integration.

In the next chapter, we're going solve the mystery of collision detection once and for all with a detailed introduction to Euclidean vectors. You'll never need to blindly copy/paste your collision code from a dubious website again!

Chapter 2

Vectors: Ghosts in the Machine

You may not know it, but there's an unseen world of invisible forces at work in your games called **vectors**. They're what make your objects move and detect collisions, and they help you create simulations of real-world physical objects. Vectors are like the atoms and molecules of the game universe—everything is dependent on them, but they're very hard to see with the naked eye.

In this chapter, we're going to peel away the veil of this mysterious realm to examine these smallest but most important components of the video game universe. With the help of a bit of easy math, vectors are the key to decoding the entire geometry of the space of your game environment. Learning how to work with them gives you unlimited control over your games.

How would you feel if you could control gravity, wind, the trajectory of bullets, and the laws of physics and thermodynamics at will? Like a character from the *Matrix*, you will have that kind power in your own game world.

> *Warning! Vectors are not `Vectors`! In this chapter, vectors refer to Euclidean vectors used in geometry, not the `Vector` class. The `Vector` class is an AS3.0 typed array and is completely unrelated to Euclidean vectors. The term also doesn't refer directly to vector graphics, which are used by Flash to draw shapes, although vectors are the underlying mathematical principles on which vector graphics are based.*

What are vectors?

Vectors are lines. They have a start point and an end point. Figure 2-1 shows an example of a vector called v1. The vector starts at point A and ends at point B.

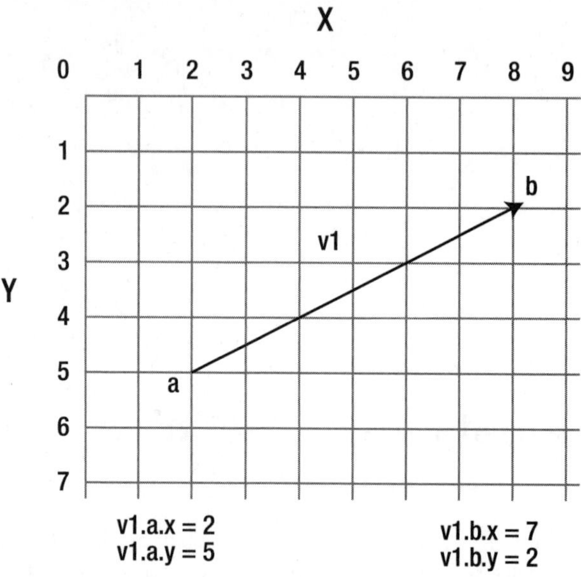

Figure 2-1. A vector called v1 (shorthand for vector 1) with a start point and an end point

Yes, it really is what you think it is: a plain line! Vectors are just lines with a start point and an end point.

What? You were expecting something more complicated than that? Well, I'm sorry to disappoint you! But this is only the beginning of a long chapter, so there's certainly more to the story.

In this chapter, I'm going to use a simple naming convention for describing vectors. Vector names will start with v plus the number of the vector, such as `v1`, `v2`, and `v3`. This will help to keep the code compact and also make it easy for us to use our vectors with arrays.

In the code that we'll be looking at, the start and end points of vectors will be created as `Point` objects. `Point` objects are used to store x and y coordinates. You may have used them in the past if you ever needed to convert a display object's local coordinates to global coordinates. Here's the general code that you would use to create a vector's point A and point B:

```
a:Point = new Point(100, 100);
b:Point = new Point(400, 300);
```

`Point` objects have x and y properties, so you can refer to the specific point coordinates like this:

```
a.x
a.y
```

And you can set the x and y properties like this:

```
a.x = 450;
a.y = 348;
```

Let's say we have a vector called `v1` and want to refer to the x coordinate of point B. We can do so like this:

```
v1.b.x
```

Usually, I would advise you to avoid short, nondescriptive variables names like these, because they're hard to read. But in the case of variables that are going to be used mainly for mathematical calculations, a coded shorthand like this is really useful. Your code will look neat and compact, rather than sprawling off the edge of your code editor, and you'll instantly know what kind of information a variable contains just by glancing at it.

Throughout this chapter, I'll introduce additional abbreviations for common vector properties. The naming conventions are not standardized, and you're free to use any other system you prefer.

Vector characteristics

What can two points that define a line tell us? If the line starts at point A and ends at point B, we can say that the vector is *pointing toward* point B. It has a *direction*.

As you can see in Figure 2-1, the vector tells you where it starts, where it ends, and the direction it's pointing toward. These are the two defining characteristics of vectors:

- Length (often referred to by the more technical term **magnitude**)
- Direction

Does that sound like some sort of information that might be of use in a game? Well, surprise, surprise—you are already using this information. It's called *velocity*!

The x and y components

Whenever a game object moves, it creates a vector. The vector is created by the object's vertical and horizontal velocity, better known as our dear friends, vx and vy, as illustrated in Figure 2-2.

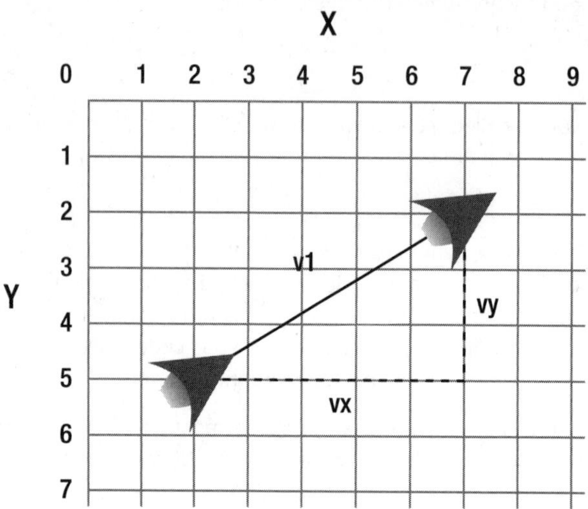

Figure 2-2. When game objects move, their vx and vy properties create a vector.

Any moving object, like our spaceship in the previous chapter, has horizontal velocity (vx) and vertical velocity (vy). When these velocities are combined, the ship moves in some direction. If the spaceship has a vx of 5 and vy of –5, it will appear to move diagonally toward the top right. And when that happens, the ship invisibly creates a vector between its previous position and its new position.

This kind of vector, which is created by an object's movement, is called a **motion vector**. So you've been creating and using vectors all this time without even knowing it!

You have not seen these vectors directly on the stage, but they've been there all along, like other-dimensional puppet masters pulling the strings of your game objects behind the curtains.

vx is known as the vector's **x component**. vy is the vector's **y component**. Figure 2-3 shows how vx and vy fit into the big picture.

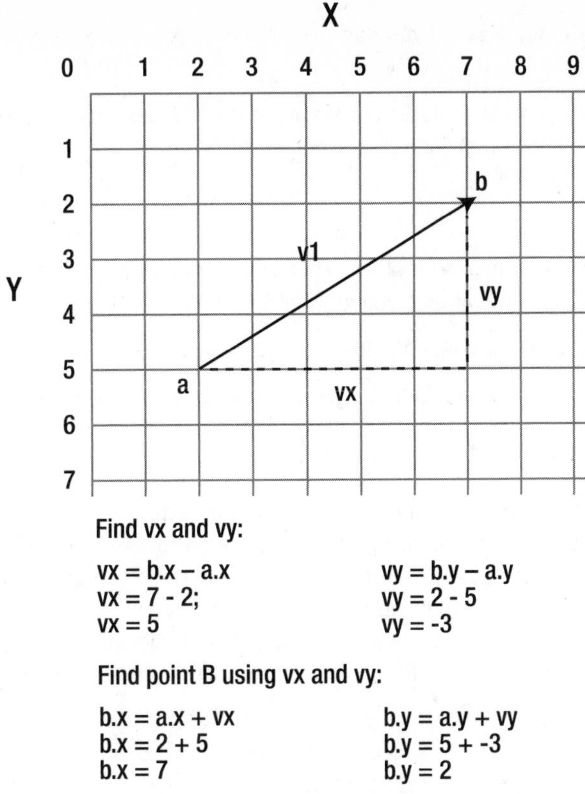

Find vx and vy:

vx = b.x – a.x
vx = 7 - 2;
vx = 5

vy = b.y – a.y
vy = 2 - 5
vy = -3

Find point B using vx and vy:

b.x = a.x + vx
b.x = 2 + 5
b.x = 7

b.y = a.y + vy
b.y = 5 + -3
b.y = 2

Figure 2-3. The vector's x and y components: vx and vy

You can describe any vector using vx and vy values. In fact, vx and vy values *are* vectors. You don't need any more information than that to use vectors effectively.

If you know where the vector starts and where it ends, you can find a vector's vx and vy values using these simple formulas:

```
vx = b.x - a.x;
vy = b.y - a.y;
```

Just subtract the start x and y points from the end x and y points.

If you know only the vector's vx and vy properties and where the vector starts, you can figure out the end point using these formulas:

```
b.x = a.x + vx;
b.y = a.y + vy;
```

Take a look at Figure 2-3 and see if you can work out how the values were found. It's pretty easy if you just take it one small step at a time.

This last set of formulas is particularly important for games, and you've probably used it many times already. Does this look familiar?

```
x += vx;
y += vy;
```

These are identical to the previous formulas. This is just another way of saying, "The new position (point B) is the same as the previous position (point A), plus velocity."

Do you see how easy all these concepts are to grasp? It's just basic math.

A very important thing to remember is that if you have vx and vy properties, you have a vector.

Vector magnitude

All vectors have a length. In geometry, a vector's length is referred to as its **magnitude**. Even though you might find this term confusing at first, we need to use the term magnitude so that it doesn't conflict or create confusion with the AS3.0 `Array length` property. Also, if you begin to get comfortable using the term *magnitude* now, you'll be a small step ahead when you continue learning about vectors outside the pages of this book, especially when you start to do 3D programming. Don't worry—it's not difficult! Just remember that whenever you hear me talk about *magnitude*, I mean the vector's *length*.

It's important to know what a vector's magnitude is so that you can figure out how far away things are or how fast they're moving. If a spaceship's motion vector has a magnitude of 3, then you know what its velocity is. And you can also use that information to anticipate or resolve a collision with another object, as you'll learn in the "Collision and bounce" section later in this chapter.

So how can we find out what a vector's magnitude is? It's the distance between point A and point B. You can easily calculate this with the help of the game designer's reliable old standby, the Pythagorean theorem.

```
m = Math.sqrt(vx * vx + vy * vy);
```

I'm using the variable name `m` to refer to magnitude.

Figure 2-4 illustrates how the vector's magnitude is found.

In a game, a magnitude of 5.8 could tell you how fast a spaceship is moving. Or you could use it to find out how far away the ship is from an enemy.

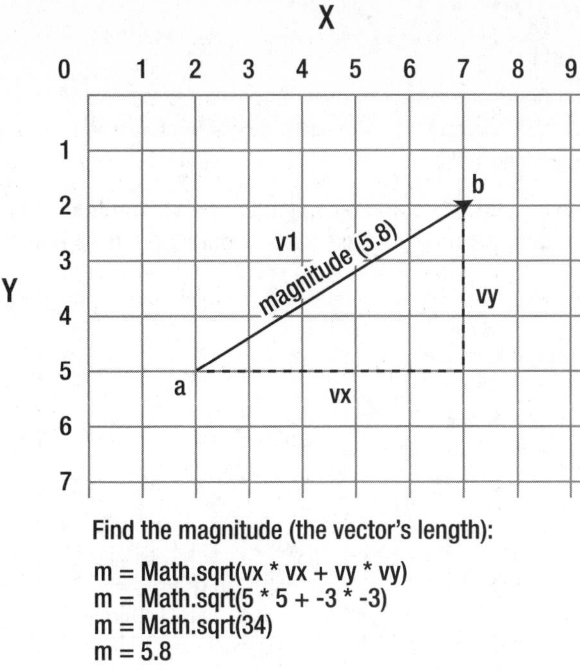

Find the magnitude (the vector's length):

m = Math.sqrt(vx * vx + vy * vy)
m = Math.sqrt(5 * 5 + -3 * -3)
m = Math.sqrt(34)
m = 5.8

Figure 2-4. Use the Pythagorean theorem to find the vector's magnitude. Values have been rounded.

Calculating the angle

It's often useful to know a vector's angle. A bit of simple trigonometry will find it for you.

```
angle = Math.atan2(vy, vx) * 180 / Math.PI;
```

> *With the `Math.atan2` method, the y property is the first argument and the x property is the second. This is unlike every other method in AS3.0, where the x property comes first. So be careful! It's a very common mistake to put the x property first.*

This formula gives you a value in degrees that you can apply to the `rotation` property of any object. (In the pages ahead, you'll see how this trick is used to keep text perfectly aligned to a rotating line.)

There's an interesting flip side to this. How can you find a vector if you have only its angle and magnitude (its length)? A little more trigonometry will help here as well.

```
vx = m * Math.cos(angle);
vy = m * Math.sin(angle);
```

And remember, all you need are the vx and vy properties to calculate any vector. So with these results, you're all set. With vx and vy, you still have a vector, even though it may not have a specific start or end point yet.

These formulas are the keys to being able to switch back and forth from vectors to angles and, as you will see in this chapter, they have endless utility. Figure 2-5 shows how they're used.

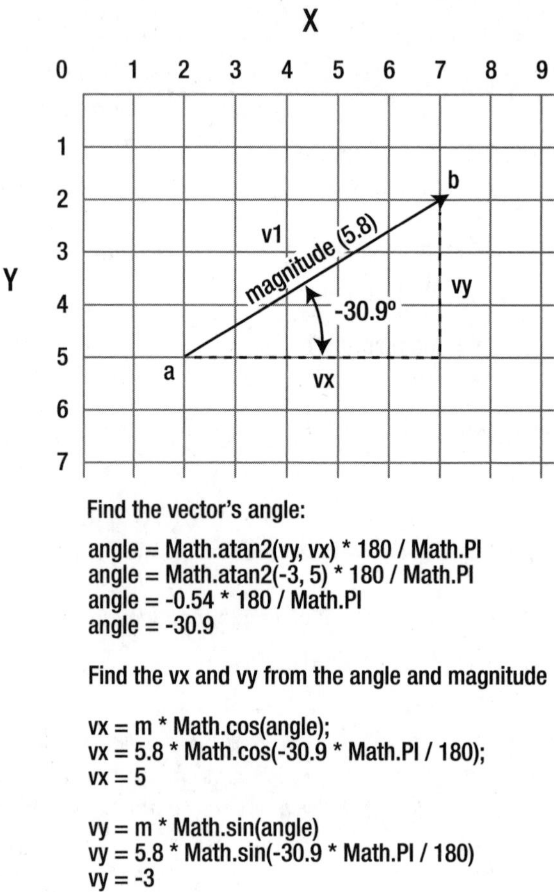
X
0 1 2 3 4 5 6 7 8 9
Y
1
2
3
4
5
6
7
b
v1
magnitude (5.8)
vy
-30.9º
a
vx
Find the vector's angle:
angle = Math.atan2(vy, vx) * 180 / Math.PI
angle = Math.atan2(-3, 5) * 180 / Math.PI
angle = -0.54 * 180 / Math.PI
angle = -30.9
Find the vx and vy from the angle and magnitude
vx = m * Math.cos(angle);
vx = 5.8 * Math.cos(-30.9 * Math.PI / 180);
vx = 5
vy = m * Math.sin(angle)
vy = 5.8 * Math.sin(-30.9 * Math.PI / 180)
vy = -3

Figure 2-5. Finding a vector's angle and finding the vx and vy values

These two formulas are about as much trigonometry as you'll ever need to know while working with vectors. A nice little feature of the vector system is that it produces the same effects as complex trigonometry, but the math involved is much simpler, and the results are concrete and visual. If you've used trigonometry in the past to produce complex motion effects in your games, and only had a vague idea how it was working, you're going to love vectors. They're conceptually much easier to work with.

Vector normals

Vectors hide a deep, dark secret. Clinging to the base of each vector are two invisible and somewhat shadowy additional vectors called **normals**.

One of these normals runs to the left of the vector, and the other runs to its right. They are exactly perpendicular (at 90 degrees) to the main vector. Together, they form a base on which the vector stands. If you think of the vector as a rocket ship pointing up toward the sky, the left and right normals form the ground beneath the rocket. If the rocket tilts to one side, the normals will tilt along with it on the same axis. They always remain perfectly aligned at precisely 90 degrees.

That's actually how the normals got they're name. The normals define the "normal" orientation of the vector. They define the ground that the vector stands on, so you always know which way is "up" in the vector's coordinate system.

Figure 2-6 illustrates how the left and right normals connect with the main vector.

Both the left and right normals are *also* vectors. The left normal is a vector that points to the left, and the right normal points to the right. Whether you want to or not, every time you create a vector, you're actually creating *three* vectors: the main vector and its two normals. The normals have the same magnitude as the main vector. They help to define what's known as the vector's **coordinate space**.

It won't be at all obvious to you yet why this is important or even precisely what it means. In the pages ahead, I'll clarify the role of normals with very detailed and practical examples. What's important to be aware of right now is that the left and right normals exist and can be calculated mathematically. And they also happen to be spectacularly important in helping us figure out the angle of a collision.

The left normal is represented by the variables `lx` and `ly`. They're very easy to calculate.

```
lx = vy;
ly = -vx;
```

As you can see, it's just a 90-degree twist on the main vector's `vx` and `vy` properties.

The right normal is found like this:

```
rx = -vy;
ry = vx;
```

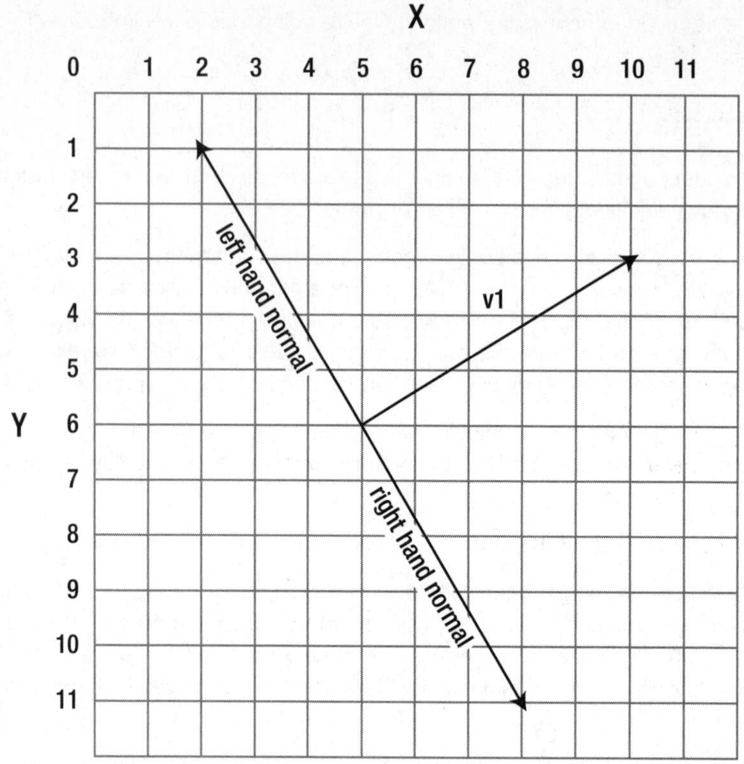

Figure 2-6. The left and right normals are perpendicular to the main vector and help define the vector's coordinate space.

Once you've found the left and right normals' `lx`, `ly`, `rx`, and `ry` values, you can easily figure out the rest of the vector information. Their start point (`a`) will always be the same as the main vector, so you can calculate their end points (`b`) like this:

```
leftNormal.b.x =  v1.a.x + lx;
leftNormal.b.y = v1.a.y + ly;
rightNormal.b.x =  v1.a.x + rx;
rightNormal.b.y = v1.a.y + ry;
```

And now you have two completely new vectors if you need them. You can apply any of the other vector calculations in this chapter to these new vectors.

It's much easier to understand all this visually, so take a look at Figure 2-7 to see how all these values are found. Keep this information close at hand, because you're going to need to use it soon.

> *Remember that abstract calculations always correspond to real coordinates on the stage. If you ever feel confused about what a calculation does, take out a pencil and a sheet of graph paper, and break it down step by step as I've done in the diagrams here.*
>
> *Did I just say "pencil" and "paper"? I did! Try it. You might find you actually enjoy that short break away from your computer.*

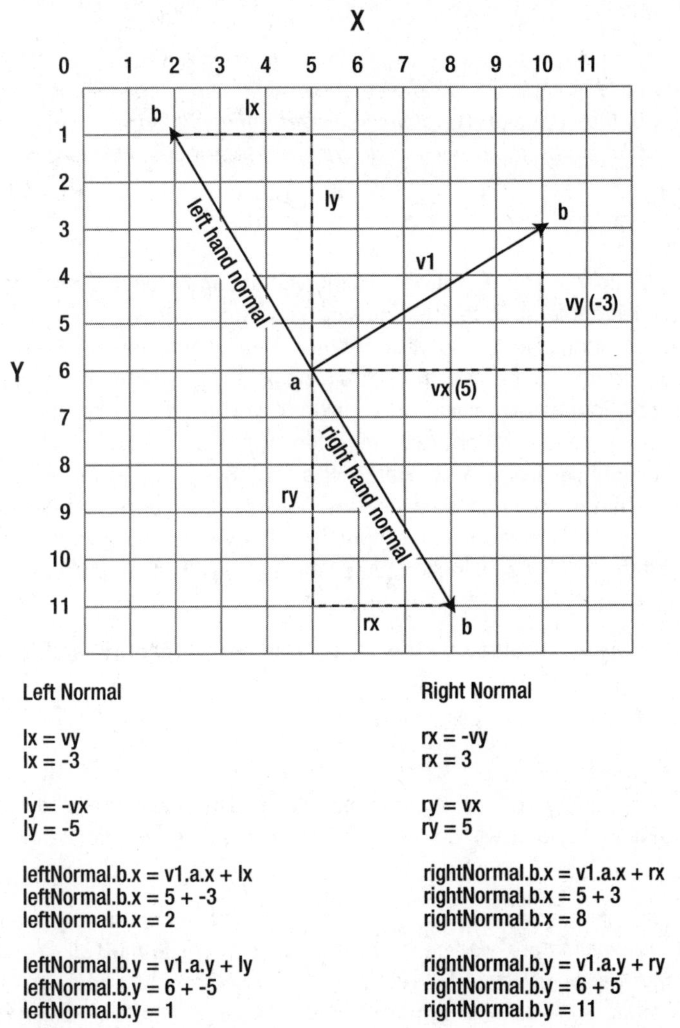
X
0 1 2 3 4 5 6 7 8 9 10 11
Y
1 2 3 4 5 6 7 8 9 10 11
b
lx
ly
b
left hand normal
v1
vy (-3)
a
vx (5)
right hand normal
ry
rx
b
Left Normal
lx = vy
lx = -3
ly = -vx
ly = -5
leftNormal.b.x = v1.a.x + lx
leftNormal.b.x = 5 + -3
leftNormal.b.x = 2
leftNormal.b.y = v1.a.y + ly
leftNormal.b.y = 6 + -5
leftNormal.b.y = 1
Right Normal
rx = -vy
rx = 3
ry = vx
ry = 5
rightNormal.b.x = v1.a.x + rx
rightNormal.b.x = 5 + 3
rightNormal.b.x = 8
rightNormal.b.y = v1.a.y + ry
rightNormal.b.y = 6 + 5
rightNormal.b.y = 11

Figure 2-7. The left and right normals are perpendicular to the main vector and help define the vector's coordinate space.

Normalizing vectors

Sometimes you need to know the direction that a vector is pointing. Where is an object going? And, more important, can you use that information to orient other objects in the same direction?

This is where the technique of **normalizing** a vector becomes important. Normalized vectors have a definite direction, but have their magnitude scaled to 1, which is the smallest size that a vector can be. If you first make the vector as small as possible, you can easily scale it up to any size and keep it perfectly proportioned.

> *Don't confuse normalizing with vector normals. Very confusingly (and it is confusing!), they are two completely separate things. Normals are the vectors perpendicular to the main vector. Normalizing is a technique used to scale a vector.*

Let's consider a pet story to see how a normalized vector can be useful. Your cat loves to chase squirrels, and you see some up in the tree outside your window that she might enjoy tormenting. But how can you communicate this to your cat? Your cat doesn't speak English, but thanks to studiously deciphering the numbers on the kitchen clock to calculate meal times, she has become pretty good at math. Fortunately, sitting on your desk, you have a vector that's 3 feet long and happens to be pointing up toward the tree where the squirrels are playing. The magnitude of the vector is useless to your cat. Three feet? Ha! Child's play! She can leap 20 feet in one bound. But is there some way that you can at least use the vector's direction to tell her the direction she should leap in? Yes! All you need to do is normalize the vector and give the result to your cat. That will give her the squirrels' direction, and she can scale it to 20 feet without losing its direction.

Normalized vectors are represented by the variable names `dx` and `dy`, and they are found like this:

```
dx = vx / m;
dy = vy / m;
```

You just divide the `vx` and `vy` by the vector's magnitude. The result is a really tiny vector with a length of 1. In a Flash game, it will be the size of a single pixel. Figure 2-8 illustrates how this works.

> *Normalized vectors are also called* ***unit vectors*** *because their size is 1, which is the smallest possible whole unit that the vector can be. You can use unit vectors to scale a vector to any size, either larger or smaller. Have you ever wondered what the magic ingredient was in that bottle that Alice drank? It was a unit vector!*

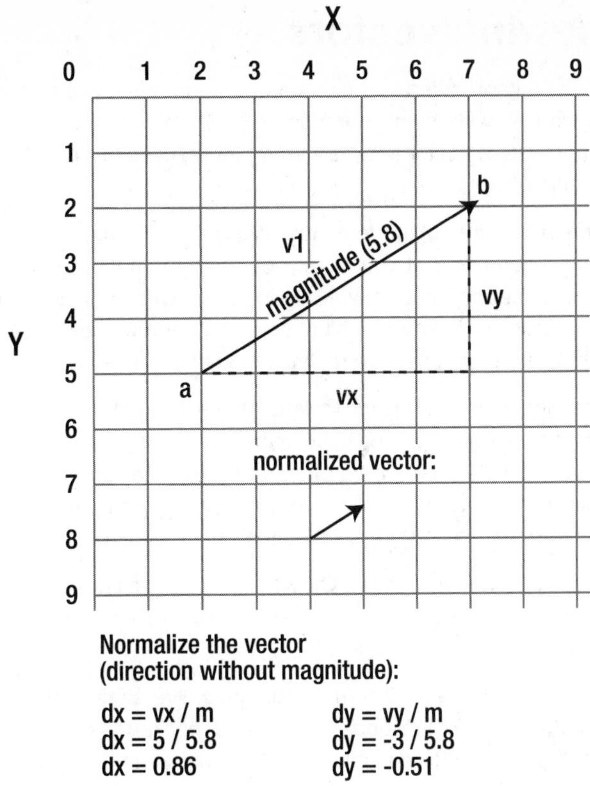

Figure 2-8. Normalize the vector to help you scale it to a different magnitude.

The normalized vector doesn't have any start or end points, so you can think of it as just hanging in space, waiting for someone to tell it what it should do. But most important, the numbers that result are useful for figuring out the vector's direction. If you give the `dx` and `dy` values to your cat, she'll effortlessly find the squirrels in the tree and still be back in time for lunch.

How can your cat do this? We don't know yet! As is, those `dx` and `dy` values seem pretty useless, don't they? But all shall be revealed in the pages ahead. For now, just try to understand what normalized vectors are. We'll be coming back to them again quite soon.

> *What does the d in dx and dy mean? It stands for delta, which in mathematics is often used to show that there has been a change in a value. It's usually used to indicate that a large value has been reduced to a smaller one. By convention, dx and dy are used to represent normalized vx and vy values.*

Using and viewing vectors

Isn't it amazing how much information you can squeeze out of just two little points? Really, at its heart, that's all we're working with: point A and point B. Whenever you have two points anywhere in your game, you can create a vector between them and access this wealth of information about the geometry of your space.

Don't worry about memorizing any of the formulas. In the next few steps, we're going to automate all of these vector calculations so that you never need to look at them again (that is, if you don't want to). However, it is important that you understand what concepts like magnitude and normalize mean. If you're not sure, spend a bit of time going through the previous section until the concepts start to click. There's no reason to rush through any of this.

The vector properties and formulas we've looked at are fundamental to what vectors are all about. In fact, they're so fundamental that you can hardly make a move in a vector universe without needing to invoke a half dozen or so of them at any time. And not only that, but you'll be using exactly the same formulas in exactly the same way, over and over again for a lot of mundane tasks. Does this seem to suggest something?

Yes, you guessed correctly! The miracle of OOP comes to our rescue again! The only sensible or manageable way to deal with vectors is to create a custom class that contains all of these properties and formulas.

Although I encourage you to create your own vector class, I've saved you the trouble by creating one for you. You'll find it here in the book's download package: `com/friendsofed/vector/VectorModel.as`. `VectorModel` includes all of the properties and formulas we've just discussed. It allows you to create a vector object, and automatically figures out its magnitude, left and right normals, normalized `dx` and `dy` values, and angle. All those tedious calculations that you'll no longer need to worry about.

If you hadn't already guessed, the `VectorModel` class is a model in an MVC system. It comes with a corresponding `VectorView` class that visually displays the vector on the stage if you need to see it.

Let's take a look at how to use these classes to build and test the vectors you use in your games.

Creating the vector model

To create a `VectorModel` object, import the class and instantiate it like this:

```
private var _v1:VectorModel = new VectorModel(a.x, a.y, b.x, b.y);
```

The arguments are the x and y positions of the vector's start and end points. These arguments are actually optional, because you can add the start and end points later with the class's `update` method. We'll take a close look at how to do this ahead. But it means you can also create a `VectorModel` object without any arguments, like this:

```
private var _v1:VectorModel = new VectorModel();
```

You can also create a `VectorModel` without start and end points, as long as you know the `vx` and `vy` values.

```
private var _v1:VectorModel = new VectorModel(0,0,0,0, vx, vy);
```

Assign 0 (zero) for the start and end points, and add the `vx` and `vy` values as the last arguments.

The following is the complete `VectorModel` class. It's long, but most of its bulk is due to extra checks that need to be made to find out whether the vector has start and end points or just `vx` and `vy` values.

```
package com.friendsofed.vector
{
  import flash.geom.Point;
  import flash.events.Event;
  import flash.events.EventDispatcher;

  public class VectorModel extends EventDispatcher
  {
    //Start and end points for the main vector
    private var _a:Point = new Point(0, 0);
    private var _b:Point = new Point(0, 0);
    private var _vx:Number = 0;
    private var _vy:Number = 0;

    public function VectorModel
      (
        startX:Number = 0, startY:Number = 0,
        endx:Number = 0, endy:Number = 0,
        newVx:Number = 0,
        newVy:Number = 0
      ):void
    {
      update(startX, startY, endx, endy, newVx, newVy);
    }

    public function update
      (
        startX:Number = 0,
        startY:Number = 0,
        endx:Number = 0,
        endy:Number = 0,
        newVx:Number = 0,
        newVy:Number = 0
      ):void
    {
      if(newVx == 0 && newVy == 0)
      {
        _a.x = startX
```

```
      _a.y = startY;
      _b.x = endx
      _b.y = endy;
      dispatchEvent(new Event(Event.CHANGE));
    }
    else
    {
      _vx = newVx;
      _vy = newVy;
      dispatchEvent(new Event(Event.CHANGE));
    }
  }

  //Start point
  public function get a():Point
  {
    return _a;
  }

  //End point
  public function get b():Point
  {
    return _b;
  }

  //vx
  public function get vx():Number
  {
    if(_vx == 0)
    {
      return _b.x - _a.x;
    }
    else
    {
      return _vx;
    }
  }

  //vy
  public function get vy():Number
  {
    if(_vy == 0)
    {
      return _b.y - _a.y;
    }
```

```
    else
    {
      return _vy;
    }
  }

  //angle (degrees)
  public function get angle():Number
{
    var angle_Radians:Number = Math.atan2(vy, vx);
    var angle_Degrees:Number = angle_Radians * 180 / Math.PI;
    return angle_Degrees;
}

  //magnitude (length)
  public function get m():Number
  {
    if(vx != 0 || vy != 0)
    {
       var magnitude:Number = Math.sqrt(vx * vx + vy * vy);
       return magnitude;
    }
    else
    {
      return 0.001;
    }
  }

  //Left normal VectorModel object
  public function get ln():VectorModel
  {
    var leftNormal:VectorModel = new VectorModel();

    if(_vx == 0
    && _vy == 0)
    {
      leftNormal.update
        (
          a.x, a.y,
          (a.x + this.lx),
          (a.y + this.ly)
        );
    }
    else
    {
      leftNormal.update(0, 0, 0, 0, vx, vy);
    }
```

```
  return leftNormal;
}

//Right normal VectorModel object
public function get rn():VectorModel
{
  var rightNormal:VectorModel = new VectorModel();

  if(_vx == 0
  && _vy == 0)
  {
    rightNormal.update
      (
        a.x, a.y,
        (a.x + this.rx),
        (a.y + this.ry)
      );
  }
  else
  {
    rightNormal.update(0, 0, 0, 0, vx, vy);
  }
  return rightNormal;
}

//Right normal x component
public function get rx():Number
{
  var rx:Number = -vy;
  return rx
}

//Right normal y component
public function get ry():Number
{
  var ry:Number = vx;
  return ry;
}

//Left normal x component
public function get lx():Number
{
  var lx:Number = vy;
  return lx
}
```

```
    //Left normal y component
    public function get ly():Number
    {
      var ly:Number = -vx;
      return ly;
    }

    //Normalized vector
    //The code needs to make sure that
    //the magnitude isn't zero to avoid
    //returning NaN
    public function get dx():Number
    {
      if(m != 0)
      {
        var dx:Number = vx / m
        return dx;
      }
      else
      {
        return 0.001;
      }
    }
    public function get dy():Number
    {
      if(m != 0)
      {
        var dy:Number = vy / m
        return dy;
      }
      else
      {
        return 0.001;
      }
    }
  }
}
```

As you can see, the `VectorModel` class just codifies all the vector properties and calculations that we looked at earlier in this chapter. It also has an `update` method that dispatches a `CHANGE` event. This is important because it means we can use this model to create a custom view of its data.

One important detail is that the `dx` and `dy` getters need to check to make sure that the vector's magnitude isn't zero. Whenever there is a chance—even an extremely improbable chance—that a variable used in a division calculation might evaluate as zero, you should check for this and provide an alternative. Instead of zero, dx and dy return 0.001, which is small enough to have the actual effect of zero in the applications where we'll be using it.

Division by zero will result in the code returning NaN (which stands for Not A Number). This could completely break the code in your game, and you wouldn't know division by zero was the cause unless you were tracing the values.

A feature of the VectorModel class is that it creates two subobjects, ln and rn, which are the left and right normals. Here's how the left-hand vector object is created.

```
public function get ln():VectorModel
{

  var leftNormal:VectorModel = new VectorModel();

  if(_vx == 0
  && _vy == 0)
  {
    leftNormal.update
      (
        a.x, a.y,
        (a.x + this.lx),
        (a.y + this.ly)
      );
  }
  else
  {
    leftNormal.update(0,0,0,0, vx, vy);
  }

  return leftNormal;
}
```

Are you following this?

First, it checks to see whether the vector has start and end points, or whether it just has vx and vy values. It creates the vector with different values in the constructor arguments based on that.

But what's really interesting is how it's creating the vector. It's actually creating a new instance of the very same class that it's a part of!

```
var leftNormal:VectorModel = new VectorModel();
```

This directive is *in the* VectorModel *class itself*. Pretty cool, huh? It may seem sort of crazy, but it's a perfectly legitimate thing to do in AS3.0, and in this case, it's extremely useful. It means that every time you create a VectorModel object, you're actually creating *three* VectorModel objects: one for the main vector and one each for the left and right normals.

If your main vector is called `_v1`, you can access its left and right normal vectors like this:

```
_v1.ln
_v1.rn
```

And because `ln` and `rn` are themselves `VectorModel` objects, they contain all of the same properties as the parent object. For example, to find the end point of the left normal, you could write some code that looks like this:

```
_v1.ln.b
```

To find the right normal's angle, you could use this:

```
_v1.rn.angle
```

Thank you, OOP!

Creating the vector view

Once you've created a `VectorModel`, you can display it with the `VectorView` class. Here's how:

```
private var _v1:VectorModel = new VectorModel();
private var _v1View:VectorView = new VectorView(_v1, "status", 1);
```

The `VectorView` class takes three arguments:

- The `VectorModel` object
- A `String`, which is the type of display you would like. This can be one of the following:
  - `basic` displays a single straight line between the vector's start and end points.
  - `detailed` displays the main vector, its `vx` and `vy`, and the left and right normals.
  - `status` includes a status box that displays all of the vector's data.
- A number, which is the vector's scale. If you don't want to scale the vector, leave it at 1 (which is its default value).

We'll look at examples of how to customize the view using these three arguments in the examples ahead.

Feel free to examine the `VectorView` class, but it's really just a utility to help you view `VectorModel` objects. It's pretty complex, so I won't go into detail about it here. I've commented most of the code if you're curious as to how it works. Except for a few small details, there's nothing new there that you haven't seen before in other contexts.

Let's see what those vectors look like!

OK, I know I've been taking my time getting here, but it's worth the wait. With all the pieces now together, we can plot and display vectors on the stage.

In the chapter's source files, you'll find a folder called `VectorBasics`. Run the SWF, and you'll see something that looks like Figure 2-9. You can fly the spaceship around the screen using the cursor keys, and the program draws a vector between the center of the stage and the ship's x and y position. It also plots the vx and vy, plots the left and right normals, and displays the VectorModel's data in a status box.

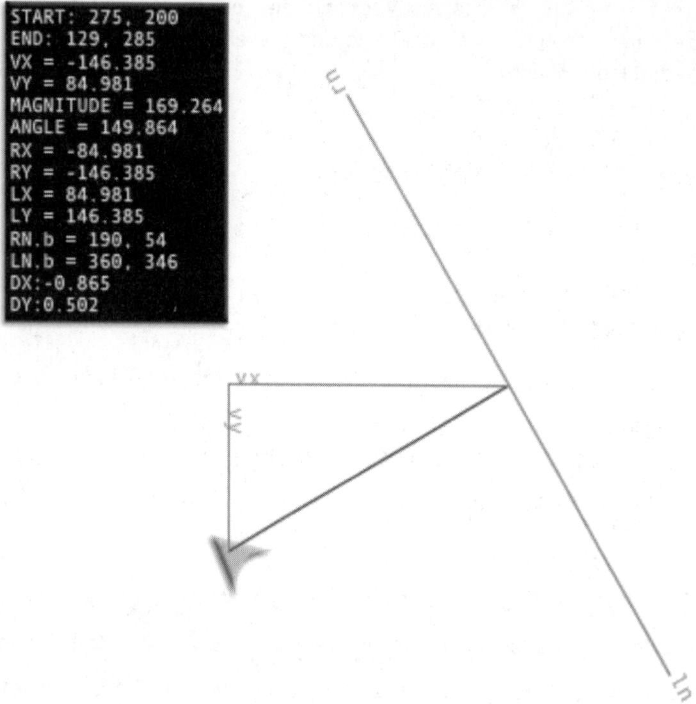

Figure 2-9. Fly the ship around the stage, and watch how the vector and its normals change.

Take a bit of time with this and see if you can connect the dots in your own mind as to how the lines you see on the stage relate to the vector's data. It's all the theory that we've covered so far, but now it's interactive and visual.

Here's the VectorBasics application class that makes all this happen:

```
package
{
  import flash.events.Event;
  import flash.display.Sprite;
  import com.friendsofed.utils.*;
  import com.friendsofed.gameElements.spaceShip.*;
  import com.friendsofed.vector.*;
```

```
[SWF(backgroundColor="0xFFFFFF", frameRate="60",
width="550", height="400")]

public class VectorBasics extends Sprite
{
  //The spaceship
  private var _shipModel:ShipModel
    = new ShipModel();
  private var _shipController:ShipController
    = new ShipController(_shipModel);
  private var _shipView:ShipView
    = new ShipView(_shipModel, _shipController);

  //The vector
  private var _v1:VectorModel = new VectorModel();
  private var _v1View:VectorView = new VectorView(_v1, "status", 1);

  public function VectorBasics()
  {
    //Add the ship view and set the ship model position
    addChild(_shipView);
    _shipModel.setX = 275;
    _shipModel.setY = 200;

    //Add the vector view
    addChild(_v1View);

    addEventListener(Event.ENTER_FRAME, enterFrameHandler);
  }

   private function enterFrameHandler(event:Event):void
  {
    //Update the ship model
    _shipModel.update();
    StageBoundaries.wrap(_shipModel, stage);

    //Update the vector model
    _v1.update(275, 200, _shipModel.xPos, _shipModel.yPos);
  }
 }
}
```

Let's look at some interesting details of this program a bit more closely.

> *Notice that the model and view objects were both declared and instantiated in the class definition.*
>
> ```
> private var _shipModel:ShipModel = new ShipModel();
> ```
>
> *In Chapter 1, this was broken into two steps. First, the variable was declared:*
>
> ```
> private var _shipModel:ShipModel;
> ```
>
> *and then it was instantiated in the class constructor:*
>
> ```
> _shipModel = new ShipModel();
> ```
>
> *Adobe recommends that if you need to initialize a property to a default value, you do this at the same time as you declare it. Except for a few places where this might obscure clarity, the code will follow this convention throughout the rest of the book.*

Updating the vector each frame

The `VectorModel`'s `update` method is called each frame.

```
_v1.update(275, 200, _shipModel.xPos, _shipModel.yPos);
```

The arguments are the x and y positions of the vector's start and end points.

> *In your own projects, you might want to modify this system so that the vector model is automatically updated based on changes to the ship model. This would not be hard to implement, but to keep this code as flexible and clear as possible, I've opted to update it manually each frame. It helps to expose very clearly what is going on behind the scenes.*

When the vector model updates, its `CHANGE` event is fired, and the view redraws the vectors on the stage. How does it do that?

In Chapter 1, we looked at how you can use the drawing API to draw lines and shapes on the stage. If you want those lines and shapes to change every frame, you need to use the `graphics.clear` method. The `graphics.clear` method erases the drawing from the previous frame and redraws the line or shape with the new updated coordinates. To use it, just call it as the first drawing method. This example from the `VectorView` class draws the main vector line:

```
_mainVector.graphics.clear();
_mainVector.graphics.lineStyle(1, 0xFF0000, 1);
_mainVector.graphics.moveTo(_startX, _startY);
_mainVector.graphics.lineTo(_endX, _endY);
```

Without clearing the graphics each frame, the previous line will stay on the stage, and the new line will be drawn over it. Figure 2-10 shows what the `VectorBasics` SWF would look like if it were compiled without the `graphics.clear` method in the preceding code. In many cases, this actually might be a desirable effect.

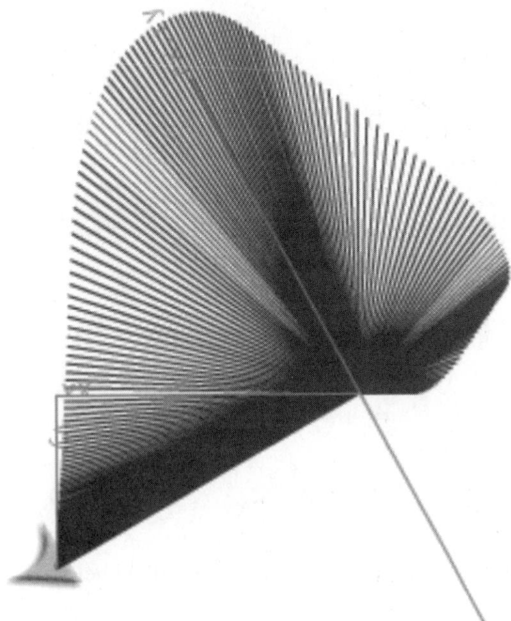

Figure 2-10. This is what happens if you don't use the graphics.clear method before you redraw the lines and shapes each frame.

Rotating text

You might be wondering what specific code makes all the lines rotate. Surprisingly, the answer is nothing at all. The appearance of the lines rotating is simply a result of the vector's data being displayed. A new line is just being drawn between the vectors' start and end points each frame. Nothing has been done to the original `VectorModel` data; it's just being displayed on the stage, as is. Rotation is a by-product. That's the great thing about using a vector system: You can achieve effects that are identical to complex trigonometry, but there's not a `cos`, `sin`, or `atan` in sight!

> *Sometimes you will have sprites or movie clips in your games that aren't using vectors. A nonvector object might need to know how a vector is aligned so that it can update its `rotation` property to match the vector's orientation. In those cases, use the `VectorModel`'s `angle` property to tell the `Sprite` or `MovieClip` object how to align.*

You'll notice that the text used to label the left and right normals (`ln` and `rn`) rotates in precise alignment with them, as illustrated by Figure 2-11. How is this accomplished?

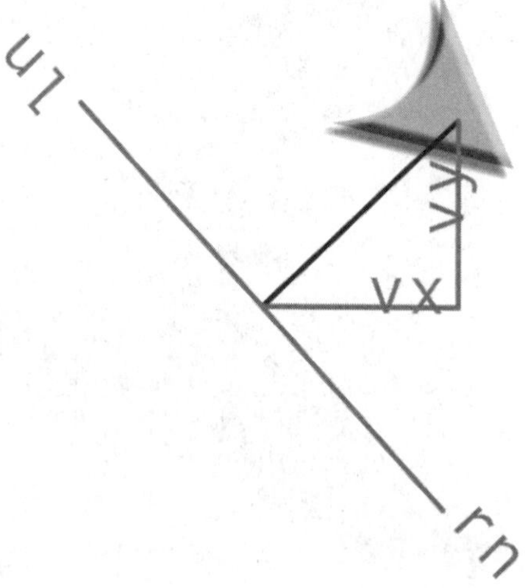

Figure 2-11. The left text rotates in precise alignment with the vectors.

The label text is a custom `RotationText` object, which extends the `Sprite` class. You'll find the `RotationText` class in the `com/friendsofed/utils` folder. Its main job is to wrap text in a `Sprite` container so that it can make use of the `Sprite`'s `rotation` property. To rotate a `RotationText` object, all you need to do is find the vector's angle and assign it to the `rotation` property. For more information about the `RotationText` class, see the "A crash course in embedding assets" section later in this chapter.

Remember that the `VectorModel` has an `angle` property. Also remember that the left and right normals (`ln` and `rn`) are `VectorModel` objects as well, so they have an `angle` property, too. It's therefore the simplest thing in the world to assign this value to the text's `rotation` property:

```
_rn_Label.rotation = _v1.rn.angle;
_ln_Label.rotation = _v1.ln.angle;
```

That's all there is to it! The text rotates in precise alignment with the vectors. You could use exactly the same technique to align the rotation of any `Sprite` or `MovieClip` object.

> *Before you can rotate text, make sure that you're using an embedded font. The "A crash course in embedding assets" section later in this chapter explains how to embed fonts and images directly into your AS class files.*

Rounding numbers to a specific number of decimal places

The final new technique in the `VectorBasics` application class we'll look at is how to round numbers to a specific number of decimal places.

You'll notice that the numbers displayed in the status box have all been rounded to three decimal places. I rounded the numbers in the `VectorView` class so that they would be easier to read. Otherwise, most of them would have 16 trailing decimal places and would be a big blur of information that would be difficult to absorb. Figure 2-12 compares the rounded values to the raw values—which would you prefer to look at?

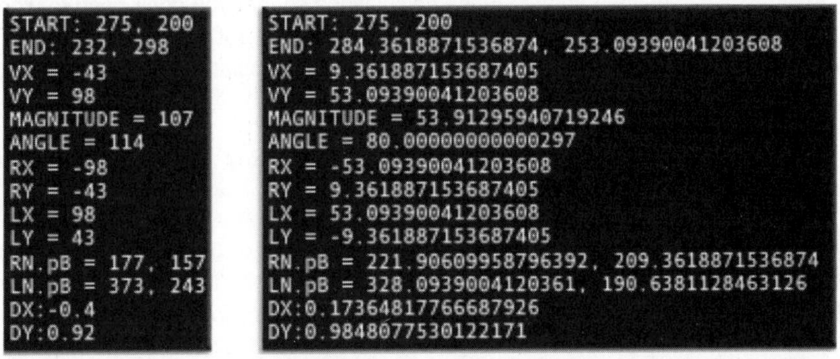

```
START: 275, 200
END: 232, 298
VX = -43
VY = 98
MAGNITUDE = 107
ANGLE = 114
RX = -98
RY = -43
LX = 98
LY = 43
RN.pB = 177, 157
LN.pB = 373, 243
DX:-0.4
DY:0.92
```

```
START: 275, 200
END: 284.3618871536874, 253.09390041203608
VX = 9.361887153687405
VY = 53.09390041203608
MAGNITUDE = 53.91295940719246
ANGLE = 80.00000000000297
RX = -53.09390041203608
RY = 9.361887153687405
LX = 53.09390041203608
LY = -9.361887153687405
RN.pB = 221.90609958796392, 209.3618871536874
LN.pB = 328.0939004120361, 190.6381128463126
DX:0.17364817766687926
DY:0.9848077530122171
```

Figure 2-12. Rounded versus raw data

The numbers were rounded to three decimal places using AS3.0's built-in `Math.round` method, like this:

```
Math.round(_vx * 1000) / 1000;
```

In some debugging situations, you might need the detail of raw data. In those cases, just remove `Math.round` from the `VectorView` class.

To increase the number of decimal places, just add more zeros to 1000. Easy stuff!

There may be some cases where you want a number to be rounded to one decimal place, but still display a trailing zero, such as 4.30 or 56.80. The trailing zero is mathematically meaningless to AS3.0, so the compiler always truncates it. For display purposes, however, you might sometimes need it. You can use the `toFixed` method to achieve this. For example, the following rounds 4.3457894 and displays it as 4.30:

```
var number:Number = 4.3457894;
var roundedNumber:Number = Math.round(number * 10 ) / 10;
trace(roundedNumber.toFixed(2));
```

The number that `toFixed` returns is actually a `String`, so it can be used only for display.

The `VectorBasics` example file is intended to show you how to use the `VectorModel` and `VectorView` classes to help you visualize vectors. Don't let all the extra code confuse you! At it heart lies the very simple calculations we looked at earlier in the chapter. If you understand its basic vector concepts and calculations, that's all you need to know.

The `VectorModel` class helps automate these calculations so that you don't need to worry about them. You're free to concentrate on making creative games. But you don't have to use the `VectorModel` class. If you prefer, you can just use the basic calculations as is, without building a class around them.

Adding and subtracting vectors

You can think of vectors as forces. A vector with a magnitude of 5 is a force that makes your spaceship move 5 pixels each frame. Sometimes in a game, you'll have more than one force acting on an object. Maybe the force of gravity is pulling your spaceship down, and wind is pushing it to the right. You can create vectors for gravity and wind, and then add or subtract those vectors to your ship's motion vector to find the ship's new direction.

Let's take gravity as an example. Imagine that your ship's motion vector has a magnitude of 5, and in your game, you have a gravity vector with a magnitude of 2. If gravity is acting on your spaceship, you want to subtract 2 from 5 to find the ship's new motion vector, which will be 3.

Subtracting the magnitudes of vectors isn't useful in most cases, because the magnitude alone doesn't tell you the vector's direction. Instead, you need to subtract the vector's vx and vy values in two separate calculations. This is incredibly easy to do.

As an example, imagine that you have a spaceship hovering above a flat planet surface. The force of gravity on the y axis is pulling the ship down. If the force of gravity is 2, you can describe its vx and vy properties like this:

```
gravity_Vx = 0;
gravity_Vy = 2;
```

Don't forget that in Flash's backward coordinate system, gravity will have a positive value, so you'll need to *add* it to you ship's motion vector to pull the ship downward.

Remember that if you have a vx and a vy value, you have a vector. It might not have start or end points, but it's still a vector. In this case, the gravity acts only on the y axis, so you don't need a value for vx.

Here's how you can add the force of gravity to the ship's motion vector:

```
shipModel.vy += gravity_Vy;
```

If the ship started with a vy of –5, its new value would now be –3. This would pull the ship down in the next frame. Figures 2-13 and 2-14 illustrate how this vector addition works.

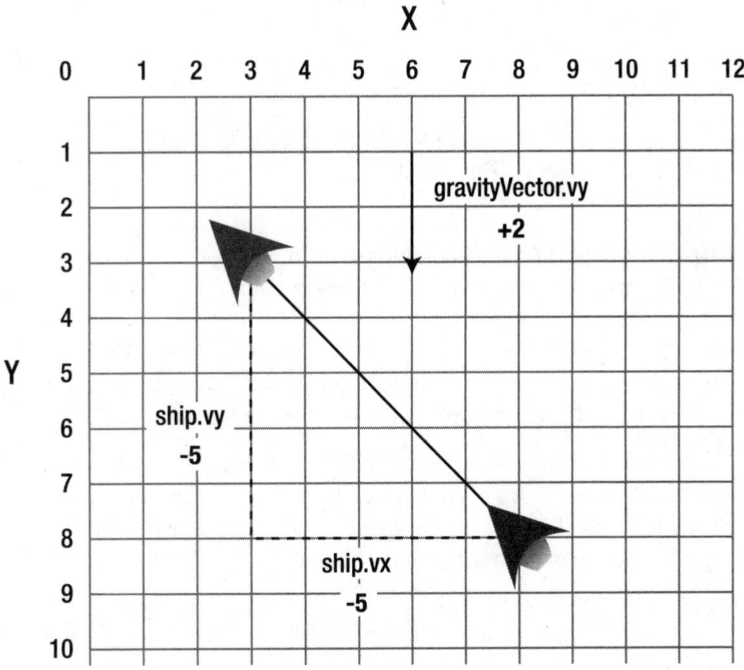

Figure 2-13. What happens when you combine a gravity vector and the ship's motion vector? In this example, the ship's vy value is –5, and the gravity vector is +2.

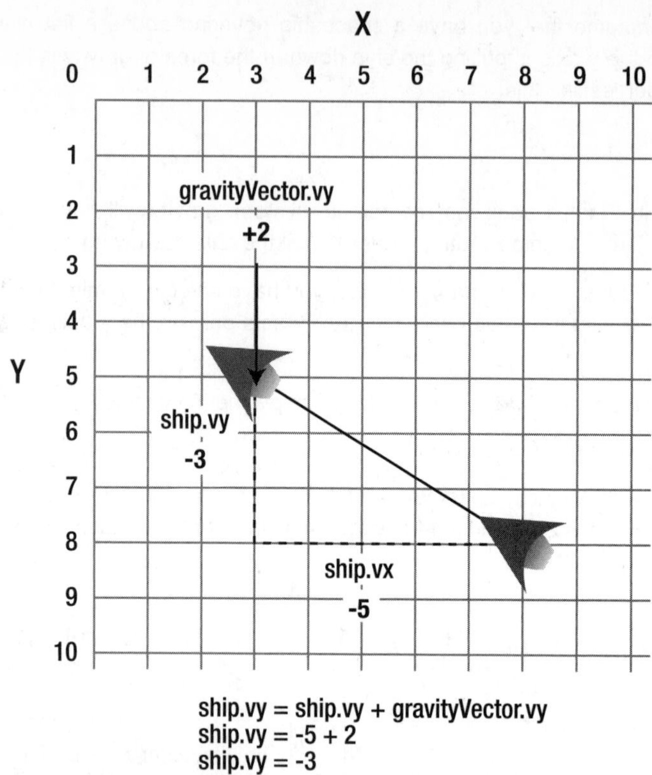

Figure 2-14. When the two vectors are added together, a new vector results, which combines their forces. This pulls the ship down toward the planet surface.

When you add vectors together like this, the result is a new vector. It's a combination of the downward pull of gravity and the upward push of the ship. As you can see, the math is amazingly simple, but it's a very accurate description of what happens in the real world.

You've probably used this same kind of vector addition in many of your own games, but never realized the mechanics behind it. It's a pretty easy concept to grasp, especially if you visualize it like this. Don't forget how this simple example works, because even the most complex combination of forces uses these exact same mechanics.

Next, we'll look at a more complex example.

Scaling vectors

In our simple gravity example, the ship was pulled down on the y axis. This is fine in a platform or pinball game, where "down" is the bottom of the stage. But suppose your spaceship is circling a planet? Which way is down? Take a look at Figure 2-15 and see if you can figure it out.

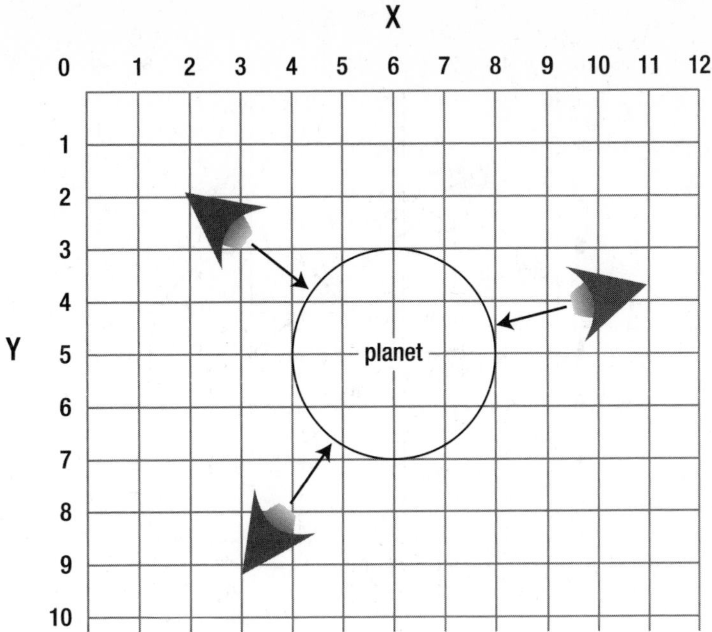

Figure 2-15. To pull a spaceship toward a round planet, gravity must act on both the x and y axes.

Looking at that diagram, two things should come to mind.

- The ship needs to know where the center of the planet is.
- To move the ship toward the planet's center, gravity must act on the both the x and y axes.

Here are the steps to figuring out the force of gravity for a round planet.

1. Create a vector between the ship and the center of the planet. This provides the ever-useful vx and vy values, which are going to help us in the next step.
2. The magnitude of the vector is actually useless to us. We don't need to know the distance between the ship and planet. However, we do need to know the vector's *direction*.
3. Does that ring a bell? It should. Whenever you need a vector's direction but not its magnitude, you normalize the vector. That means reducing it to its smallest possible size. A normalized vector, or unit vector, is represented by the variables dx and dy. To find those values, divide vx and vy by the vector's magnitude.
4. Figure 2-16 shows how to calculate the dx and dy from the ship-to-planet vector.

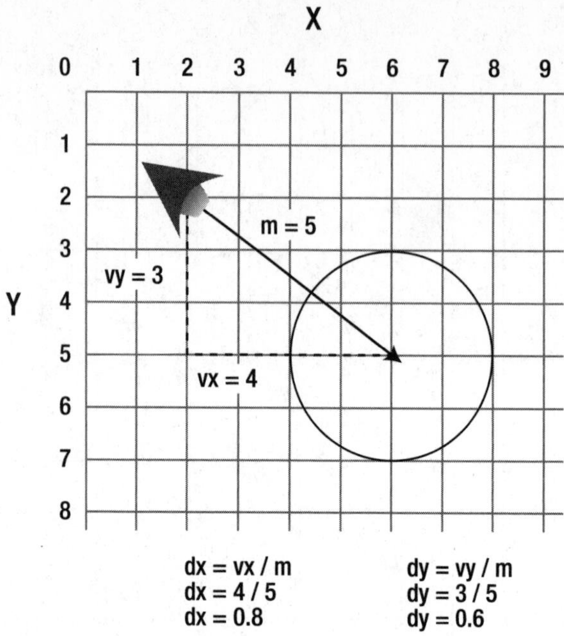

Figure 2-16. Create a vector from the ship and the planet. Find its dx and dy, which tells you the vector's direction.

5. We can use the unit vector to create a new gravity vector. How strong do you want gravity to be? For most games, you'll want it to be about half to a tenth of the value of dx and dy for a realistic effect. In this example, let's scale the gravity vector to 2, so that you can see the effect more clearly.

```
gravity_Vx = dx * 2
gravity_Vy = dy * 2
```

6. Now we have a gravity vector, working in both the x and y axes, that's pointing directly toward the center of the planet. The direction is the same as the original vector, but the magnitude is different.

7. Figure 2-17 shows how the original vector was scaled and the new gravity vector derived.

8. Finally, we can apply the gravity vector to the ship's motion vector.

```
ship.vx += gravity_Vx
ship.vy += gravity_Vy
```

9. The ship will very naturally be drawn toward the center of the planet, no matter which side of the planet it's on. Figure 2-18 shows how the position of the ship is influenced by this new gravity vector. Compare it to Figure 2-15 to see the difference.

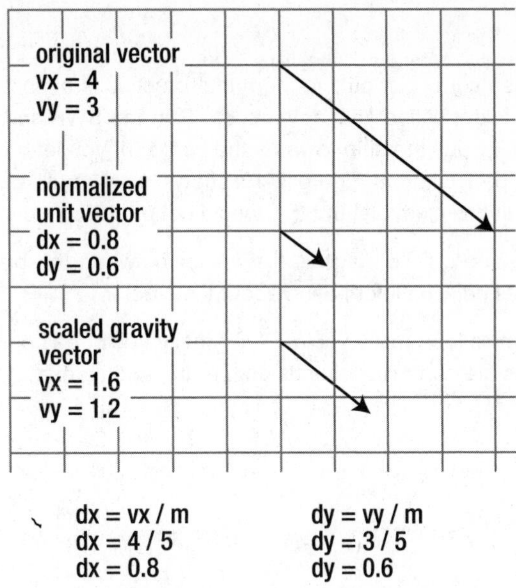

Figure 2-17. If you normalize a vector, you can scale it to any size.

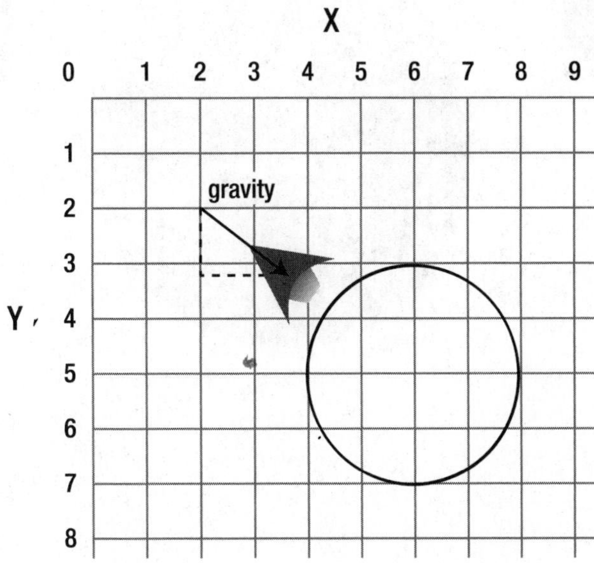

Figure 2-18. Adding gravity to the ship's motion vector pushes it toward the planet.

Gravity in action

If you understand all these concepts, putting them into practice is almost trivial. In the chapter's source files, you'll find a folder called `AddingVectors`. Run the SWF and fly the ship around the planet. Gravity will gradually pull the ship towards the center. If you let it run for a while, the ship will gradually fall into a perfect orbit. Figure 2-19 shows what you'll see. There's no collision detection with the planet in this example, but that would not be difficult to implement.

The vector that you can see on the stage is the vector between the planet and the ship. The status box on the left gives detailed information about that vector.

The status box on the right is the gravity vector. The gravity vector has only `vx` and `vy` properties, so its start and end points are zero. However its `angle`, `dx`, and `dy` exactly match that of the ship-to-planet vector.

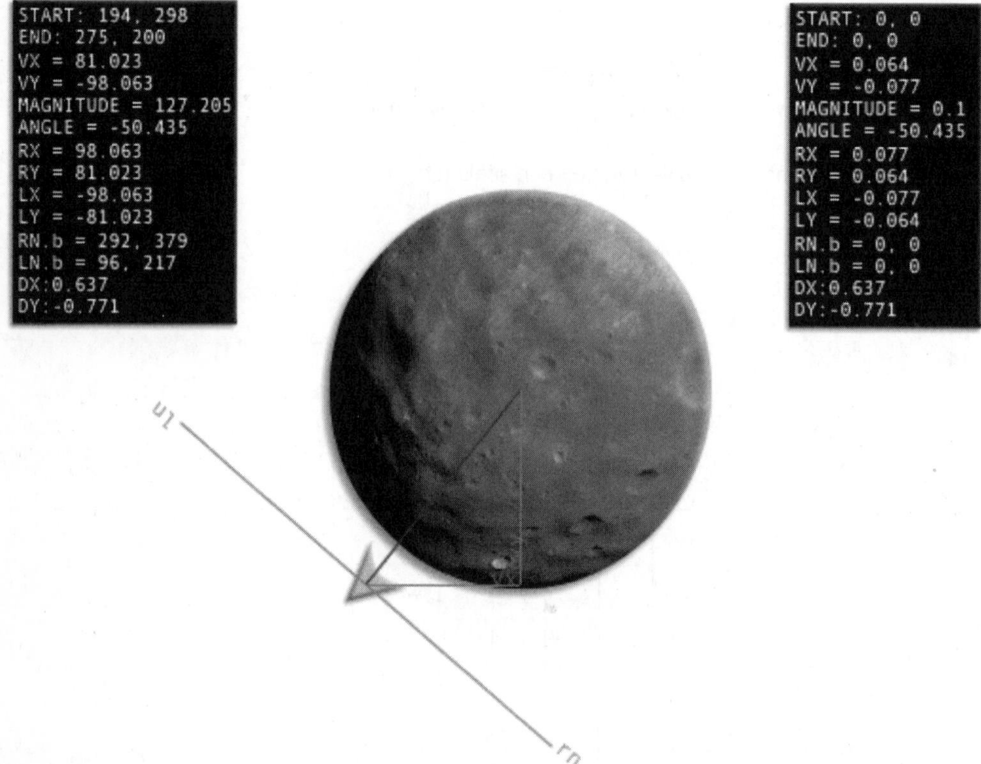

Figure 2-19. The gravity vector is added to the ship's motion vector, which gradually pulls the ship to the center of the planet.

How big is the gravity vector? The status box shows that its `m` (magnitude) property is `0.1`. It has been scaled to one-tenth the size of the normalized vector, which is really, really small. It's so small that it's impossible to plot visibly on the stage. But it's this amount that is nibbling away at the spaceship's velocity each frame and causing it to move toward the center of the planet.

Let's take a look at the code that makes this happen, and I'll explain some of the specifics.

```
package
{
  import flash.events.Event;
  import flash.display.Sprite;
  import com.friendsofed.utils.*;
  import com.friendsofed.gameElements.spaceShip.*;
  import com.friendsofed.vector.*;
  import planet.Planet;

  [SWF(backgroundColor="0xFFFFFF", frameRate="30",
  width="550", height="400")]

  public class AddingVectors extends Sprite
  {
    private var _shipModel:ShipModel
      = new ShipModel();
    private var _shipController:ShipController
      = new ShipController(_shipModel);

    private var _shipView:ShipView
      = new ShipView(_shipModel, _shipController);

    //Ship-to-planet vector
    private var _v1:VectorModel = new VectorModel();
    private var _v1View:VectorView = new VectorView(_v1, "status", 1);

    //Gravity vector
    private var _gravityVector:VectorModel
      = new VectorModel();
    private var _gravityVectorView:VectorView
      = new VectorView(_gravityVector, "status", 1);

    //Planet
    private var _planet:Planet = new Planet(100, 0x999999, 280);

    public function AddingVectors()
    {
      //Add the planet
      addChild(_planet);
      _planet.x = stage.stageWidth / 2;
      _planet.y = stage.stageHeight / 2;
```

```
      //Add the ship
      addChild(_shipView);
      _shipModel.setX = 100;
      _shipModel.setY = 200;

      //Add the vector views
      addChild(_v1View);
      addChild(_gravityVectorView);
      _gravityVectorView.x = 450;

      //Set ship's friction to 1 (no friction) for realistic orbiting effect
      _shipModel.frictionConstant = 1;

      addEventListener(Event.ENTER_FRAME,enterFrameHandler);
    }
    private function enterFrameHandler(event:Event):void
    {
      //Update the ship model
      _shipModel.update();
      StageBoundaries.wrap(_shipModel, stage);

      //Update the ship-to-planet VectorModel
      _v1.update
        (
          _shipModel.xPos,
          _shipModel.yPos,
          _planet.x,
           _planet.y
        );

      //Calculate gravity
      //Use the normalized vector to create a new
      //vector with a new magnitude.
      //This new vector will be the "force of gravity"
      //that we can add to the ship's existing vx and vy vector
      var gravity_Vx:Number = _v1.dx * 0.1;
      var gravity_Vy:Number = _v1.dy * 0.1;

      //Update the gravity vector model
      _gravityVector.update(0,0,0,0, gravity_Vx, gravity_Vy);

      //Trace the gravity vector's magnitude to check its size
      trace(_gravityVector.m);

      //Add the gravity vector to the ship's motion vector
      _shipModel.vx += _gravityVector.vx;
      _shipModel.vy += _gravityVector.vy;
    }
  }
}
```

A glance at this code should tell you that 90% of it is routine. The gravity magic happens in the last few lines.

> *A small technical detail that the code needs to take care of is to remove the effect of friction on the spaceship by setting its `frictionConstant` property to `1`.*
>
> ```
> _shipModel.frictionConstant = 1;
> ```
>
> *This is important so that friction doesn't slow down the ship and obscure the orbiting effect. The `ShipModel` initializes friction to 0.98, which will gradually cause the ship to slow. Setting it to `1` overrides the initial setting and allows the spaceship to orbit without any inertia, as it would in deep space.*
>
> *If you're wondering how the planet was created, flip ahead to the "A crash course in embedding assets" section later in this chapter.*

Here are the steps for making the gravity work:

1. Create a vector between the ship and the planet. This is important, because from it we can derive the direction on which gravity needs to act on the ship.

```
_v1.update
  (
    _shipModel.xPos,
    _shipModel.yPos,
    _planet.x,
    _planet.y
  );
```

2. This vector, `_v1`, is updated in an `ENTER_FRAME` loop, so its start and end points are always changing. It's this vector that is plotted on the stage.

3. Create the gravity `vx` and `vy` using `_v1`'s `dx` and `dy` properties. They're multiplied by 0.1 to create a really small vector. A larger number will increase the force of gravity, and a smaller number will weaken it.

```
var gravity_Vx:Number = _v1.dx * 0.1;
var gravity_Vy:Number = _v1.dy * 0.1;
```

4. Use `gravity_Vx` and `gravity_Vy` to update the `gravityVector` `VectorModel` object.

```
_gravityVector.update(0,0,0,0, gravity_Vx, gravity_Vy);
```

5. This is actually an optional step. Really, all you need are the `gravity_Vx` and `gravity_Vy` values from step 2. I decided to create a gravity `VectorModel` object in this code for two reasons:

   - I want to show you how you can make a `VectorModel` object using only `vx` and `vy` values. You don't need start or end values to make a vector. It also underlines that, yes, gravity is a real-live vector, just like any other vector. It just happens to be too small to see on the stage.
   - It easily allows you to display the vector's data using a `VectorView`.

> *If performance is an issue, you probably shouldn't create a whole `VectorModel` object around these values because it could add unnecessary overhead to your game. You'll need to test this on a case-by-case basis, but you may find that your game runs faster if you manually calculate vector properties as you need them. If so, use the formulas that we looked at earlier in this chapter, and calculate the values only when and if they're used in the game. There's no point weighing down your game with extra code that you don't use. For learning and testing purposes however, creating `VectorModel` objects is pretty useful because they can help you visualize and diagnose tricky design problems, as well as save you from needing to write reams of repetitive code.*

6. Finally, combine the ship's motion vector and the gravity vector.

   ```
   _shipModel.vx += _gravityVector.vx;
   _shipModel.vy += _gravityVector.vy;
   ```

7. These are very small values, but over time, they compound for a very noticeable effect on the stage gravity!

8. As I mentioned before, you could instead use the `gravityVx` and `gravityVy` values directly, like this:

   ```
   _shipModel.vx += gravity_Vx;
   _shipModel.vy += gravity_Vy;
   ```

When I first started learning game design, I would wonder in amazement at examples like this. Certainly the minimum requirement for writing code like this must be an advanced degree in astrophysics and maybe a minor in metaphysics. When I eventually built up the courage to start researching it, I was surprised to discover, "Hey, it's just basic math!" Addition, subtraction, multiplication, and division are all it takes to make the world—or even an entire solar system—go round. Makes you think!

Real gravity

There's one small problem with our spaceship example that you may have noticed. The force of gravity is the same no matter how far away the ship is from the planet. In space, the force of gravity between objects weakens as they move further apart. Also, large objects with a lot of mass will have a greater gravitational attraction than smaller objects. We can implement a more realistic gravitational system with just a bit more tweaking.

First, create some variables that represent the mass of the planet and the spaceship. The values you use will depend on trial and error, but the following values work well in this example:

```
var planetMass:Number = 5;
var shipMass:Number = 1;
```

Next, replace the directives that calculate the gravity `vx` and `vy` with these new directives:

```
var gravity_Vx:Number = _v1.dx * (planetMass * shipMass) / _v1.m;
var gravity_Vy:Number = _v1.dy * (planetMass * shipMass) / _v1.m;
```

Recompile the SWF with this code, and you'll notice that the gravity is weaker when the ship moves farther away from the planet. If you now watch the gravity vector's `m` property, you'll notice that it's no longer just static at 0.1. It becomes smaller when the ship moves farther from the planet and larger when it approaches it.

```
0.123
0.116
0.109
0.103
0.097
0.091
```

If you add a few more planets with different masses and initial velocities, you could use this to create a complex, gravity-based space exploration game with realistic physics. Start building your own universe!

Projecting vectors

Remember the left and right normals? They are those mysterious secondary vectors that form the base of every vector. They always exist, as mathematical entities, whether you want them to be there or not. But what are they good for? Let's take a closer look at some of the properties of normals and how to put them to some useful work in a game.

Here's a fact: the left normal will always be to the left of the main vector, and the right normal will always be to the right.

Oh, you don't believe me? How can that be true if very often the right normal appears on the left side of the stage, and the left normal appears on the right side of the stage, as in Figure 2-20?

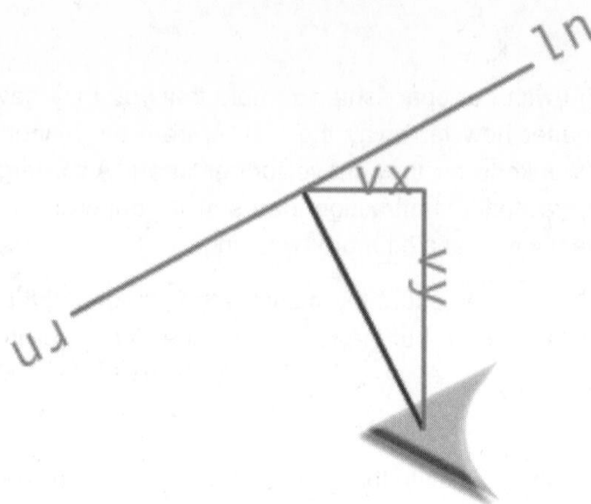

Figure 2-20. The left normal is on the right, and the right normal is on the left. The curious case of the not-so-normal normals!

To understand how this works, imagine that you're standing on the North Pole. Your head is pointing up toward the sky. To your left is your left arm; to your right is your right arm. But hey, the North Pole is freezing cold, so maybe it will be a little warmer on the other side of the planet?

After a long walk, you finally end up on the South Pole, which to your great disappointment is even colder than the North Pole! But still, after all of the adventure getting there, you're happy just to still be in one piece. To make sure, you check: yes, your left arm is still to your left and your right arm is still to your right. Your head is still firmly connected to your body, and it is still pointing up toward the sky.

But how can that be? If you think about it, on the South Pole, your left and right have actually become reversed, and your head is pointing *down*, not up. Figure 2-21 illustrates this conundrum. At least, that's what it would look like to an objective observer watching your antics from the moon.

From your point of view, however, nothing has changed. You have your own coordinate system, which is separate from the coordinate system of the world around you. Up is always up, and left and right are always left and right, no matter on which side of the planet you're standing.

Vectors work in the same way. No matter how they're oriented, the main vector will always be pointing up, and the left and right normals will always be to the left and right of it, at exactly 90 degrees. This is the vector's own coordinate system.

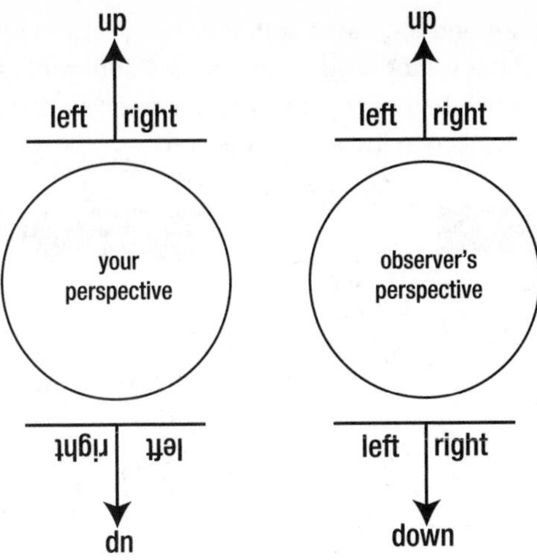

Figure 2-21. Which way is up?

In your games, vectors often will need to share information about their orientation and coordinate system. The classic problem—and the one we're going to solve by the end of this chapter—is an object bouncing off an angled surface. The bouncing object creates a vector when it moves, and the angled surface is another vector. To find the correct angle that the object should bounce away, you need to **project** one vector's coordinate system onto the other. The resulting compromise between coordinate systems will produce a new vector that will become the bouncing object's new velocity.

Again, it's "basic math," as I like to say. But there are a few little bumps along the road that we have to navigate around to get there. The first, is finding out whether two vectors are pointing in the same direction.

Are the vectors pointing in the same direction?

You can mix, match, add, and multiply vectors as much as you like, and all kinds of interesting numbers are produced as a result. One of these numbers is called the **dot product**. You can use it to find out whether two vectors are pointing in the same direction or in opposite directions.

Imagine you have the two vectors `_v1` and `_v2`. You can find their dot product like this:

```
dotProduct = _v1.vx * _v2.dx + _v1.vy * _v2.dy
```

If the dot product is positive, the vectors are pointing in the same direction. This rather quaint but otherwise useless seeming bit of information can actually give a very powerful description of where your game objects are in the relation to each other.

A live example is the best way to see how this works. In the chapter's source files, find the folder called `DotProduct` and run the SWF. You'll see a vector that has been plotted between two circles, which you can drag around the stage with the mouse. Dragging the circles changes the magnitude and orientation of the vector. You'll also see the spaceship's motion vector, extending from the center of the ship, which has been scaled to ten times its original size. A status box tells you whether the vectors are pointing in the same direction.

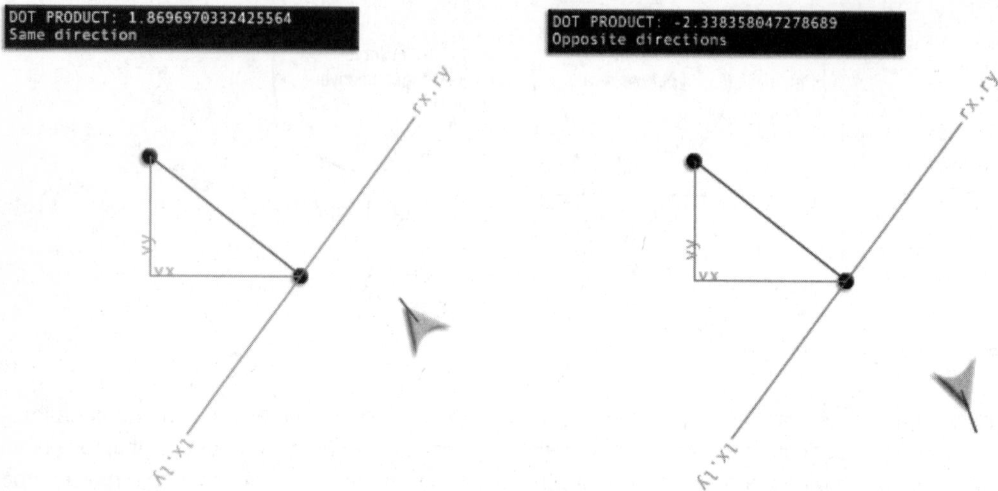

Figure 2-22. The dot product tells you whether vectors are pointing in the same direction.

You'll notice that when the vectors are pointing in the same direction, the dot product is positive. Even if you drag the circles around to change the orientation of the vector, the dot product will always be able to tell you "which way is up." It might seem like a small detail, but the dot product is the key to synchronizing the coordinate systems of two vectors.

Much of the code is similar to the previous examples, and you can see all the specifics in the source file. Here, we'll take a quick look at the new things.

DragHandle objects

The draggable circles are `DragHandle` objects. You'll find the `DragHandle` class in the `com.firendsofed.utils` package. They're useful for testing, and you can create them like this:

```
var dragHandle = new DragHandle();
```

With two `DragHandle` objects on the stage, it's very easy to create a vector between them. Just create a `VectorModel` object for the vector between them, like so:

```
private var _v2:VectorModel = new VectorModel();
```

Then update the `VectorModel` in the `enterFrameHandler`:

```
_v2.update(_handle1.x, _handle1.y, _handle2.x, _handle2.y);
```

Scaling a vector object's view

The spaceship's motion vector was scaled by 10 so that it's easy to see on the stage. That red line extending from the center of the ship points in the direction that the ship is traveling. Scaling very small vectors like this is also something that's useful while you're testing, because it's quite difficult to see a vector that's only a few pixels long. You can scale a vector by providing a number either greater or smaller than 1 as the third argument in the `VectorView` constructor.

```
private var _v1View:VectorView = new VectorView(_v1, "basic", 10);
```

The scaling affects only the `VectorView`. The `VectorModel` contains the original unchanged vector.

The spaceship's motion vector is represented by only `vx` and `vy` properties. It's one of those "hanging in space" vectors, like gravity, that doesn't have start and end points. So that you can actually see it on the stage, you need to give it a definite start point and calculate the end point. You can use the spaceship's x and y position as a start point.

```
_v1.update
  (
    _shipModel.xPos, _shipModel.yPos,
    (_shipModel.xPos + _shipModel.vx),
    (_shipModel.yPos + _shipModel.vy)
  );
```

The vector's end point is calculated by adding the `vx` and `vy` properties to the ship's x position.

The VectorMath class

The `com.friendsofed.vector` package contains a custom class called `VectorMath`. This class has some static methods that can be used for common vector math calculations. The `VectorMath.dotProduct` method finds the dot product of two vectors, like this:

```
var dotProduct:Number = VectorMath.dotProduct(_v1, _v2);
```

You can reverse the `_v1` and `_v2` arguments and, even though the actual number returned will be different, it will still be positive only when the vectors are pointing in the same direction.

The `VectorMath.dotProduct` method looks like this:

```
static public function dotProduct(v1:VectorModel, v2:VectorModel):Number
{
   var dotProduct:Number =  v1.vx *  v2.dx + v1.vy * v2.dy;
   return dotProduct;
}
```

Although you may already see some uses for calculating a dot product in a game, it really comes into its own when used as the basis for projecting a vector onto another vector.

> *The formula I'm using to calculate the dot product in this book is scaled to the magnitude of the first vector (`v1` in this example):*
>
> ```
> dotProduct =  v1.vx *  v2.dx + v1.vy * v2.dy
> ```
>
> *The first vector is multiplied by the second vector's normalized unit vector. This gives you a very useful number that you can use to help resolve collisions (among other things). However, it's not the standard formula for calculating the dot product. Here's the textbook formula:*
>
> ```
> dotProduct =  v1.vx *  v2.vx + v1.vy * v2.vy
> ```
>
> *This version doesn't use `v2`'s `dx` value. Instead, it uses the `vx` value of `v2`. This produces a number that isn't scaled. Again, this formula isn't used in this book.*

Projection in action

Projection is when you overlay a vector onto another vector's coordinate system. It's a slightly tricky concept to grasp when you first start working with it, so let's first look at a simple analogy.

Imagine that you're standing on the sidewalk. It's a sunny day, and the sun is behind you casting your shadow on the concrete. Your shadow is the *projection* of you onto the sidewalk. If you think of yourself as a vector, and the sidewalk as another vector, your shadow is a third vector. It has a lot of your qualities, but conforms to the sidewalk's coordinate system.

That's all a projection is: *the vector's shadow on another vector.* Figure 2-23 shows two examples of `v1` projected onto `v2`. The projection itself becomes a new vector.

A live example is the best way to see projection at work. In the chapter's source files, you'll find a folder called `ProjectingVectors`. Run the SWF and fly the ship around the stage. Now let's explore how it works.

The program uses three vectors:

- `v1` is the vector between the ship and the right drag handle.
- `v2` is the vector between the two drag handles.
- `v3` is a new vector that is a projection of `v1` onto `v2`. This is `v1`'s shadow on `v2`.

To reduce the clutter on the stage, I haven't added a view for `v2`, the vector between the drag handles. Just imagine a line drawn between those points. The view for `v1` is `basic`, displaying only the vector and not its normals. `v3`, the projected vector, is displayed with its `vx`, `vy`, and normals. To help you make sense of what's happening here, take a look at Figure 2-24, which shows all the vectors at work in this example. Keep this diagram at hand when you're referring to the source file or SWF, so you understand which vectors are which.

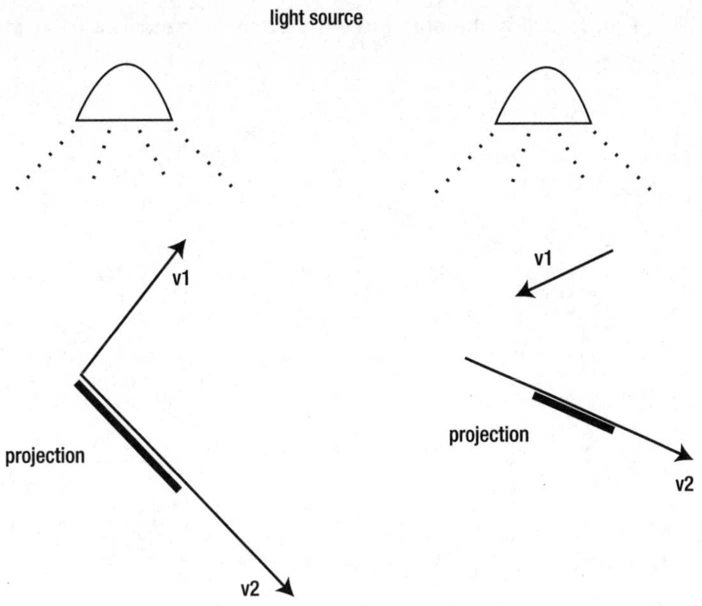

Figure 2-23. Projections are the shadows of vectors on other vectors.

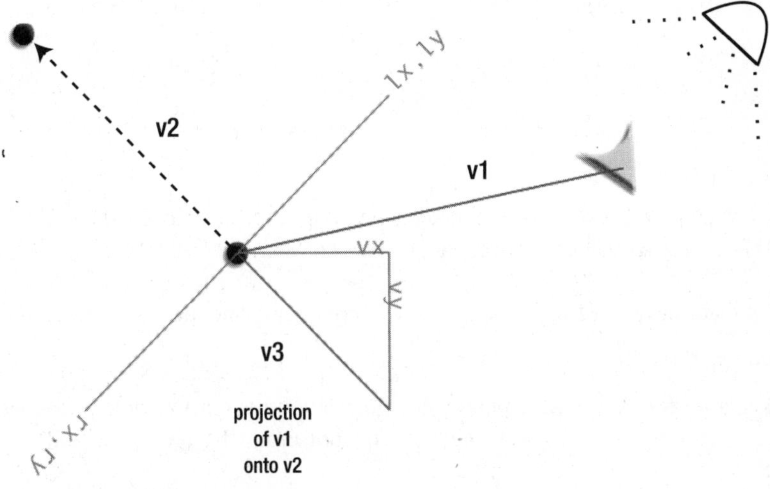

Figure 2-24. v3 is the shadow of v1 projected onto v2.

To get a clear understanding of how this example works, open the SWF and fly the ship around a bit for yourself, as in Figure 2-25. `v3` is the projection of `v1` onto `v2`. Flying the ship around changes `v1`. `v3` tries to match that change, but it's constrained by `v2`'s coordinate system.

Imagine an invisible light following the ship around casting a shadow of v1 onto v2. v3 is that shadow.

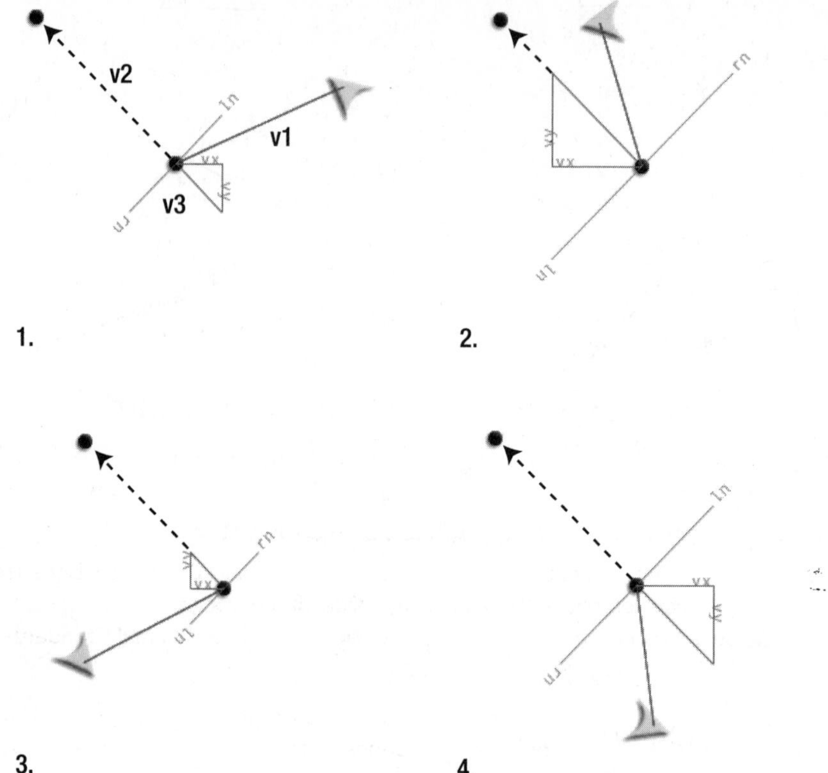

Figure 2-25. The projected vector tries the match both dimensions of the original but is trapped in one dimension. The result is a one-dimensional compromise between the original vector's vx and vy.

The math to project v1 onto v2 in this example is simple. First, find the dot product of v1 and v2:

```
var dotProduct:Number = VectorMath.dotProduct(_v1, _v2);
```

The projection is a new vector. As you know by now, if you have a vx value and a vy value, you have a vector. So the next step is to multiply the dot product by v2's dx and dy to find the projected vector:

```
var projection_Vx:Number = dotProduct * _v2.dx;
var projection_Vy:Number = dotProduct * _v2.dy;
```

And that's it, You have your projected vector!

The example file goes one step further and uses the projection's vx and vy values to create a VectorModel object. This is purely for display purposes, so it's necessary only if you want to see the projected vector on the stage or need some of its additional properties, such as its magnitude or angle.

```
_v3.update
  (
    _handle1.x,
    _handle1.y,
    (_handle1.x + projectedVx),
    (_handle1.y + projectedVy)
  );
```

Again, the math is simple. But the concept is a little tricky to grasp, so don't rush ahead until you feel you have a grip on it. Understanding projection is crucial to being able to make objects bounce off angled surfaces.

Using vector projection for environmental boundaries

Now you know that you can cast a shadow of a vector onto any other vector. A vector's shadow is called a *projection*. The projection is itself a new vector.

Remember that a vector's normals are *also* vectors. That means that you can project a vector onto another vector's left or right normal. Why would you want to do this? Because the dot product that results can tell you exactly on which side of the vector another object is. This is important because it means you can use a vector to create an environmental boundary—that is, a solid surface that things can bounce off. Here's how:

1. Project v1 onto one of v2's normals. Change the ProjectingVectors application class so that v2's left normal becomes the surface onto which v1 is projected (the bold code shows the changes):

   ```
   var dotProduct:Number = VectorMath.dotProduct(_v1, _v2.ln);
   var projectedVx:Number = dotProduct * _v2.ln.dx;
   var projectedVy:Number = dotProduct * _v2.ln.dy;
   ```

2. It doesn't matter whether you project onto the left or right normal.

3. Save, recompile, and run the file to make sure that the left normal is actually being targeted properly. Figure 2-26 shows what you'll see. The new projected vector is aligned along v2's normals.

4. So that the effect is a little easier to see, let's simplify the vector views slightly. Disable the VectorViews for v1 and v3. They'll spoil the show if they're visible.

5. Create a view for v2. Set its second argument to "basic" so that only a simple line is drawn between the two drag handles.

   ```
   private var _v2View:VectorView = new VectorView(_v2, "basic", 1);
   ```

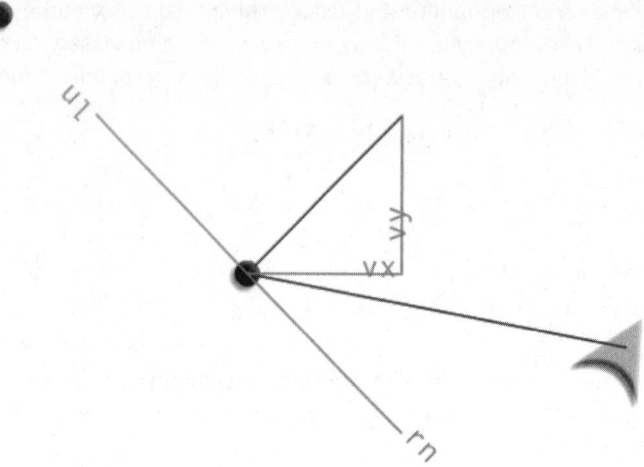

Figure 2-26. Project v1 onto v2's normal.

6. Use `addChild` to add the `_v2View` to the stage.
7. Save, recompile, and run the file.

You'll see a single line drawn between the drag handles. The other vectors aren't visible, but are quietly working their magic behind the scenes.

Fly the ship through the vector and keep your eye on the dot product displayed in the status box. When the ship is on the right side of the vector, the dot product is negative. When it's on the left side, it's positive. The dot product is exactly zero at the point at where the ship crosses the vector. Figure 2-27 illustrates this.

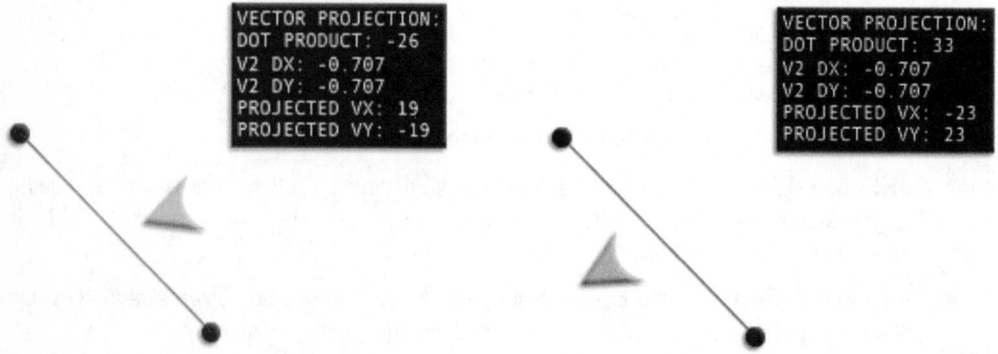

Figure 2-27. A positive dot product means the ship is on the left side of the vector. A negative dot product means its on the right.

You now have a foolproof way of knowing on which side of the line the ship is. `v2` has become a clear environmental boundary.

This bit of information has amazing potential:

- You can use it find out whether an object has crossed a boundary, no matter what the angle of the vector is.
- You can trigger a collision.

Don't worry about completely understanding exactly how this works just yet. We'll take a detailed look at the math behind it and why it's useful in the section on collision a little further ahead.

Crossing the boundary, however, is only the first part of the problem. You also need to know the exact point where the intersection happens. Let's figure that out next.

Intersection

Now that we have a way to figure out if the spaceship has collided with the vector, we need to find out exactly where the collision happened. But let's first consider when it *won't* happen.

When two vectors are parallel, they'll never intersect. And that means that a collision between them will never happen. What do I mean by "parallel vectors"? Those are vectors that are pointing in exactly the same direction or exactly opposite directions. Figure 2-28 shows three examples of parallel vectors. They run alongside each other like the two rails of a train track. You can always tell when two vectors are parallel because their `dx` and `dy` values will be exactly the same.

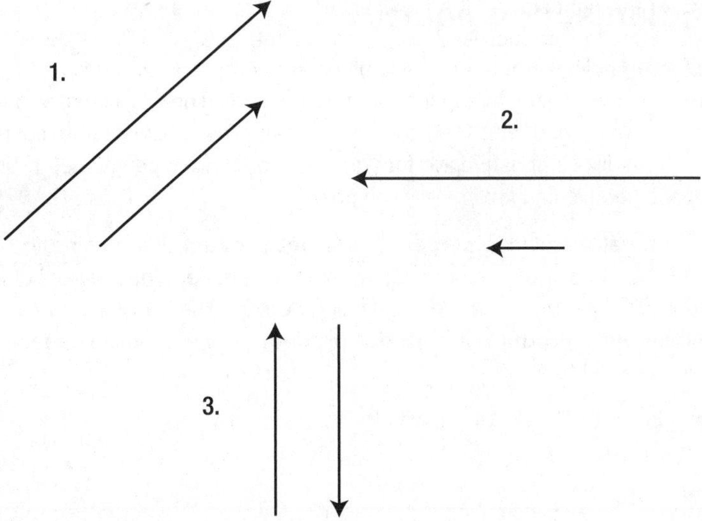

Figure 2-28. These vectors are parallel and will never intersect.

Most vectors aren't parallel and will intersect at some point or another. Sometimes the intersection will happen in the future; other times the intersection has already happened in the past. Figure 2-29 illustrates two pairs or intersecting vectors.

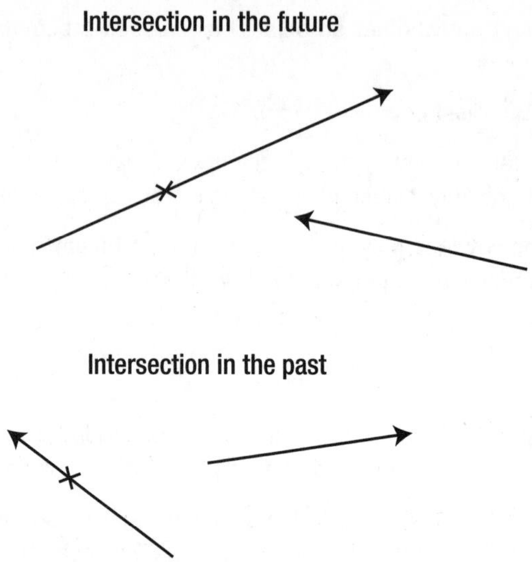

Intersection in the future

Intersection in the past

Figure 2-29. The X marks the intersection point.

Finding the intersection point

Finding the intersection point is not hard. A little bit of math comes to our rescue again. Figure 2-30 illustrates the general idea behind finding the intersection point. The key is that you need to extend a third vector between `v1` and `v2`. The third vector helps us calculate the coordinates of the intersection point. `v3` is like a ghost vector that quietly and invisibly contributes a bit of extra data that your calculations need to find the intersection point.

The math involves a value called a **perpendicular dot product**. It's nothing to be afraid of! In fact, it's exactly the same as finding an ordinary dot product, except that instead of using `v1` in the equation, you use `v1`'s normal: the perpendicular vector. The perpendicular dot product is sometimes called the **perp product** or **perp-dot product**. In the example code, it's represented by a variable named `perpProduct`.

```
perpProduct = v1.ln.vx *  v2.dx + v1.ln.vy * v2.dy;
```

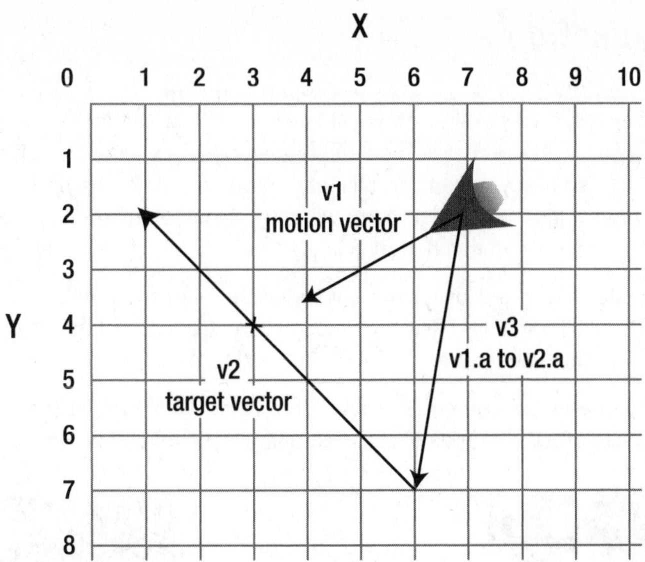

Figure 2-30. The crosshair marks the intersection point.

No big deal, right? We've used this sort of calculation before. You can use either the right or left normal, and the result will be the same.

Here's how to use a perp-dot product to find the intersection point of `v1` on `v2`:

1. Find the perp-dot product of `v3` and `v2`.

   ```
   perpProduct1 = v3.ln.vx *  v2.dx + v3.ln.vy * v2.dy
   ```

2. Find the perp-dot product of `v1` and `v2`.

   ```
   perpProduct2 = v1.ln.vx *  v2.dx + v1.ln.vy * v2.dy
   ```

3. Find the ratio between `perpProduct1` and `perpProduct2`. This is just a matter of dividing the two values together. (`t` is for *tangent*, the point of intersection, and is a common convention for representing this value.)

   ```
   t = perpProduct1 / perpProduct2
   ```

4. With the value of `t` in our pocket, we now have enough information to pinpoint the precise intersection point with real x and y coordinates. We can find this by adding `v1`'s start point to its velocity and multiplying it by `t`.

   ```
   intersectionX = v1.a.x + v1.vx * t
   intersectionY = v1.a.y + v1.vy * t
   ```

5. And there we have the coordinates for the intersection point.

I can just imagine the giddy delight on the faces of the first mathematicians who first figured this out. Mathematicians: 1; Mysteries of the Universe: 0.

Intersection in action

Now let's see how this works in a live example. In the chapter's source files, you'll find a folder called `Intersection`. Run the SWF, and you'll see something that looks like Figure 2-31. The ship's intersection point with the line is marked by a small crosshair. (The ship's motion vector has been scaled by 10 so that you can see it clearly.) You can move the drag handles to change the line's inclination, and the intersection mark will have no problem keeping up. The status box also displays whether the intersection happens in the future or might have happened in the past.

Because the intersection is found using the ship's velocity, not the direction its pointing in, the ship often looks like it's going to miss the intersection. But the intersection point is always predicted with spooky, pinpoint accuracy.

Again, most of the code in the source files is routine. Here, we'll look at the important sections that create the intersection. The names of the vectors are the same as in Figure 2-30.

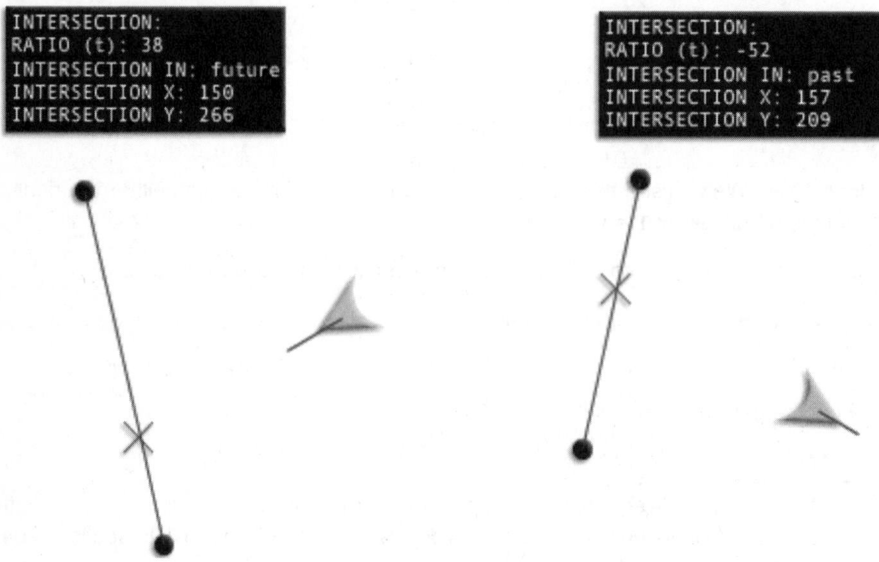

Figure 2-31. The code predicts where the intersection will take place.

First, we need three vectors: `v1` is the ship's motion vector, `v2` is the target vector on which we want to find the intersection, and `v3` is the helper vector between `v1` and `v2` that helps to calculate the correct point.

```
//v1: the ship's motion vector
_v1.update
  (
    _shipModel.xPos,
    _shipModel.yPos,
    (_shipModel.xPos + _shipModel.vx),
    (_shipModel.yPos + _shipModel.vy)
  );

//v2: the vector between the drag handles
_v2.update(_handle1.x, _handle1.y, _handle2.x, _handle2.y);

//v3: the vector between v1 and v2
_v3.update(_shipModel.xPos, _shipModel.yPos, _handle1.x, _handle1.y);
```

Next, we calculate the ratio of the perp-dot product of `v3` and `v2`, and of `v1` and `v2`.

```
var t:Number
  = VectorMath.perpProduct(_v3, _v2)
  / VectorMath.perpProduct(_v1, _v2);
```

The `VectorMath` class has a `perpProduct` method that does this calculation for us.

```
static public function perpProduct(v1:VectorModel, v2:VectorModel):Number
{
  var perpProduct:Number = v1.ln.vx *  v2.dx + v1.ln.vy * v2.dy;
  return perpProduct;
}
```

Next, we combine `v1`'s position and velocity, and multiply it by the ratio (`t`) to find the intersection point.

```
var intersection_X:Number = _v1.a.x + _v1.vx * t;
var intersection_Y:Number = _v1.a.y + _v1.vy * t;
```

Finally, we position the intersection mark.

```
_mark.x = intersection_X;
_mark.y = intersection_Y;
```

(The visible *X* that you see on the stage is created from the `IntersectionMark` class in the `vectors` package. It draws a simple crosshair.)

There's one small problem with this example that I'm sure you've noticed. The intersection mark doesn't know that it should be limited to the magnitude of `v2`. It thinks that `v2` goes on forever. As a result, it finds intersections beyond the limits of `v2`, as you can see in Figure 2-32. This isn't actually incorrect as it has been coded, but we would have a much more usable system if intersections were found only within the vector's point A and B.

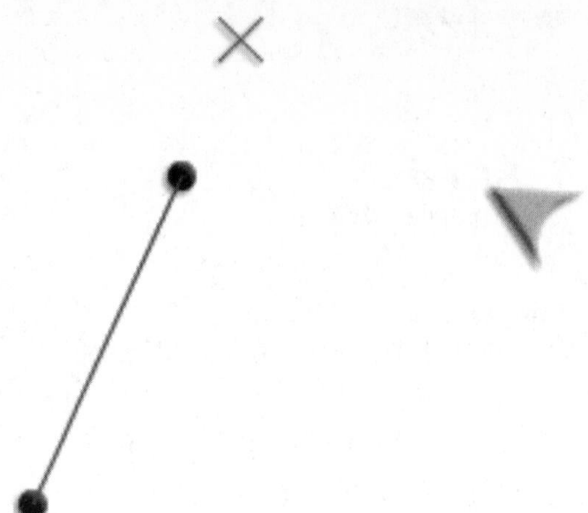

Figure 2-32. Intersections are found outside the limits of the vector.

We need to conjure up a little more vector magic to help us solve this problem.

In the chapter's source files, you'll find a folder called `LimitingIntersection`. Run the SWF, and you'll notice that the intersection point is now mapped only on the length of the vector, and not beyond it. This is very easy to implement. The source code is exactly the same as the previous example, except for these additions:

1. Extend a vector from `v2`'s start point to the intersection point.

```
var v4:VectorModel = new VectorModel
  (_v2.a.x, _v2.a.y, intersection_X, intersection_Y);
```

2. Extend another vector running in the opposite direction from `v2`'s end point to the intersection point.

```
var v5:VectorModel = new VectorModel
  (_v2.b.x, _v2.b.y, intersection_X, intersection_Y);
```

3. If the magnitude of either of these vectors is larger than `v2`'s magnitude, then you know that the intersection point falls beyond `v2`'s bounds.

```
if(v4.m > _v2.m || v5.m > _v2.m)
{
   //The intersection point is outside the magnitude of v2
   intersection_X = 0;
   intersection_Y = 0;
}
```

You can decide what actions to take on this. In this simple example, the intersection point is moved to position 0,0, which keeps it out of trouble. In a more complex game environment, you'll probably have many more variables to consider.

Figure 2-33 illustrates how this works. It's a very simple concept, and once you become more comfortable using vectors, it's the kind of thing you'll easily be able to figure out for yourself.

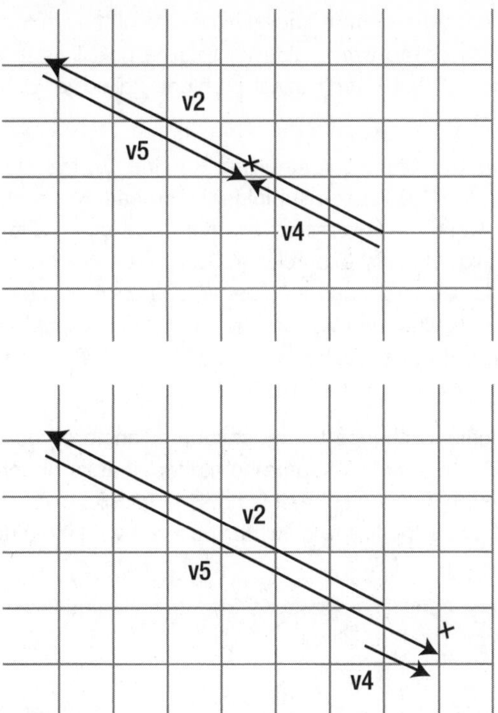

Figure 2-33. If the magnitude of either v4 or v5 is greater than v2, then the intersection point is not within the bounds of v2.

Collision and bounce

You can relax now! We've covered almost everything you need to know about vectors for 2D game design. The theory class is over, and we can now put some of this new information to practical use.

Now we're going to solve the classic problem of **line-versus-point collision**. This is collision between a two-dimensional line segment and a one-dimensional point. **Points** are objects with no height or width, just a position. They're often called **particles**, so that's how I'll be referring to them from now on. Collisions between lines and particles are the most basic form of collision detection that you can do. Once you understand these fundamentals, you'll find shape-versus-shape collision, which we'll look at in the next chapters, much easier to comprehend.

Collision on one side of the line

As you know by now, vectors have two sides: a left side and a right side. A particle can collide with either side. But how does the particle know which side of the vector it's on? And how does it know which is the right side or the wrong side for it to be on? This is important information for line-versus-particle collision. These aren't trivial problems to solve, but we can use some nifty vector tricks to help us.

First, let's looks at collision from one side of the line. Run the `Collision.swf` file in the chapter's source file (You'll find it in the `Collision` subfolder.) You can fly the ship anywhere around the stage, but it's not able to cross the vector from the right side into the left side. The ship's center point is blocked by the line. (In this example, the ship's center point is our one-dimensional particle.) And although you can fly around the line, you can't cross into the space defined by the vector's left normal. If you do, the ship will be placed at its intersection point with the line. This looks like a bug, but it's actually just the expected behavior of this system. We'll be improving this to handle double-sided collision later in the chapter.

You can use the drag handle to change the magnitude or angle of the vector however you like, and you'll see that the effect remains the same no matter what its orientation is. You can fly into the line at any speed, and the ship won't be able cross it. It looks and feels like a solid boundary, but it's really just math! Figure 2-34 illustrates what you'll see when you run the SWF.

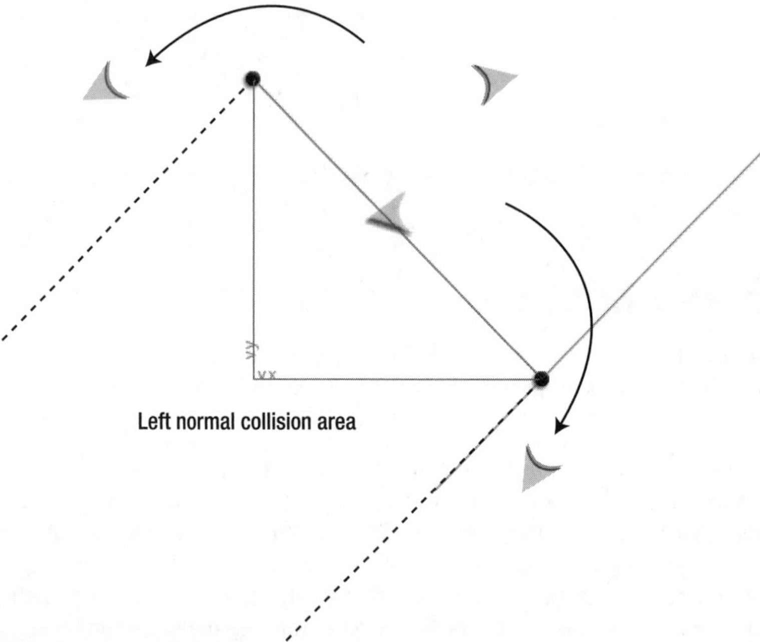

Figure 2-34. You can fly anywhere except in the area defined by the vector's left normal.

There are two important things going on in this example:

- The collision-detection system "knows" the magnitude and orientation of the line to create the collision space. This allows the ship to fly around the line's edges.
- The left side of the line has been created as the collision boundary. The ship is stopped dead in its tracks on the vector if it tries to cross from the right side to the left.

We'll look at these features one at a time. Here's most of the example's `enterFrameHandler`, so you can see the context of the code we'll be examining:

```
private function enterFrameHandler(event:Event):void
{
  //Update the ship model
  _shipModel.update();
  StageBoundaries.wrap(_shipModel, stage);

  //v1: the ship's movement vector
  _v1.update
    (
      _shipModel.xPos, _shipModel.yPos,
      (_shipModel.xPos + _shipModel.vx),
      (_shipModel.yPos + _shipModel.vy)
    );

  //v2: the drag handle vector
  _v2.update(_handle1.x, _handle1.y, _handle2.x, _handle2.y);

  //v3: the vector between v1 and v2
  _v3.update
    (_shipModel.xPos, _shipModel.yPos, _handle1.x, _handle1.y);

  //Dot products
  var dp1:Number = VectorMath.dotProduct(_v3, _v2);
  var dp2:Number = VectorMath.dotProduct(_v3, _v2.ln);

  //Check if ship is within the vector's scope
  if(dp1 > -_v2.m && dp1 < 0)
  {
     //Check if ship's motion vector has crossed the vector from right to left
     if(dp2 <= 0)
     {
          //Find the collision vector
          var collisionForce_Vx:Number = _v1.dx * Math.abs(dp2);
          var collisionForce_Vy:Number = _v1.dy * Math.abs(dp2);
```

```
            //Move ship out of the collision
            _shipModel.setX = _shipModel.xPos - collisionForce_Vx;
                _shipModel.setY = _shipModel.yPos - collisionForce_Vy;
           //Set the velocity to zero
           _shipModel.vx = 0;
           _shipModel.vy = 0;
        }
      }

    //Display the result in a status box
    //...
}
```

> *Important! For this system to work accurately, you need to make sure that changing the ship model's `setX` and `setY` properties leads to a `CHANGE` event being dispatched. If it doesn't, the ship's view won't update immediately, and the collision will appear to be off by one frame. In the `ShipModel` class, `setX` and `setY` modify the public `xPos` and `yPos` properties, and those in turn dispatch a `CHANGE` event that updates the ship's view on the stage.*

Getting the vector magnitude and orientation

The vector creates a collision boundary for the ship. To create that boundary, we need to know the vector's magnitude and orientation. Where is it and how long is it? The ship needs to know where the line starts and ends so that it can fly around it.

`v2` is the vector that you can see on the stage. An invisible vector called `v3` runs between the ship and `v2`'s start point. The dot product of these vectors can tell us whether the ship is within the line's scope.

- If the dot product is greater than zero, the spaceship will be beyond `v2's` scope, at the bottom.
- If the dot product is less than the negative of `v2`'s magnitude, then the ship is beyond `v2`'s scope at the top.

If this sounds confusing, a picture will help. Take a look at Figure 2-35 and compare the value of `dp1` with `v2.m` (the magnitude of the line). If `dp1` is greater than –98 or less than 0, the ship is in a position to possibly collide with the line.

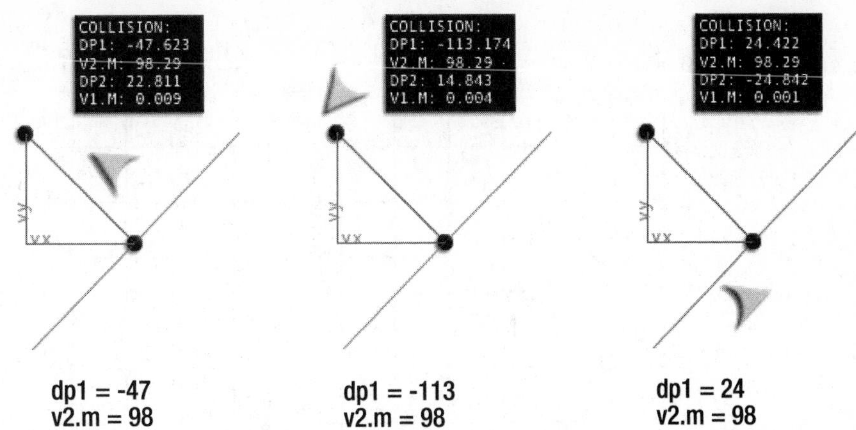

Figure 2-35. dp1 can tell is whether the ship is within the scope of v2.

Here's the code that figures this out and checks whether a collision might be possible:

```
var dp1:Number = VectorMath.dotProduct(_v3, _v2);

if(dp1 > -_v2.m && dp1 < 0)
{… a collision might be possible…
```

If this is false, the ship is free to fly around the top or bottom of the line. This relationship remains the same, even if `v2` changes its magnitude or orientation, so it's an extremely useful bit of information.

Detecting a collision

`dp2` is the dot product of `v3` (the vector between the ship and the start point of `v2`) and `v2`'s normal. Earlier in the chapter, we looked at how we can use this dot product to find out on which side of the line the ship is. Let's review that again here, as it's crucial to understanding how vector-based collision works.

Take a look at Figure 2-36. The spaceship is flying straight toward the line. It's probably going to hit it, so it will be useful to know when it hits and with how much force. In these examples, the collision plane is represented by a vector called `v2`.

To get the information we need, we extend a vector from the spaceship to the collision plane's start point. In these examples, this new vector is called `v3`, and you can see it illustrated in Figure 2-37. This new vector will help us get a bit more extra information about the collision.

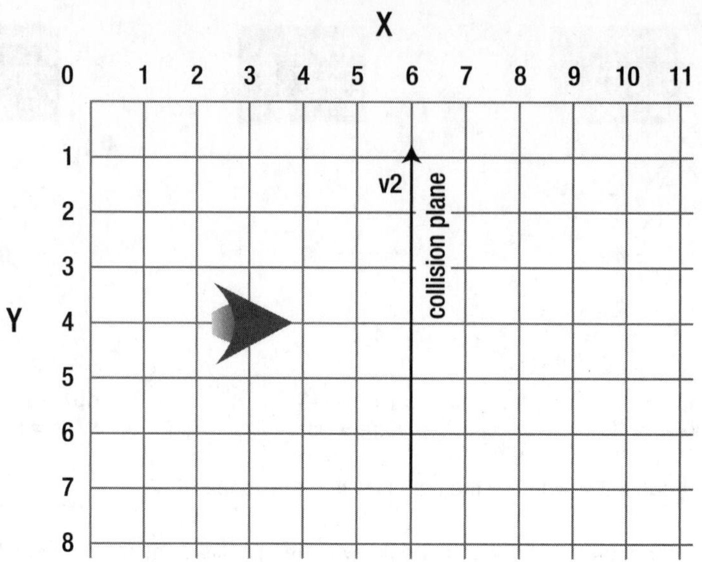

Figure 2-36. A collision between the spaceship and the line is imminent.

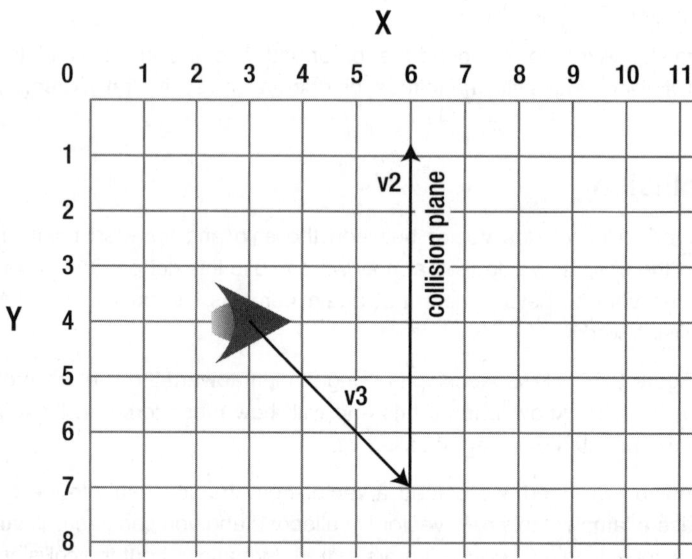

Figure 2-37. Extend a new vector between the spaceship and the collision plane's start point.

There is a magic number that will help us easily solve the collision problem. That number is the dot product between the new vector, v3, and v2's normal. (You can use either the left or right normal, the result will be the same.) Figure 2-38 shows how this dot product is found. In these examples, this dot product is called dp2.

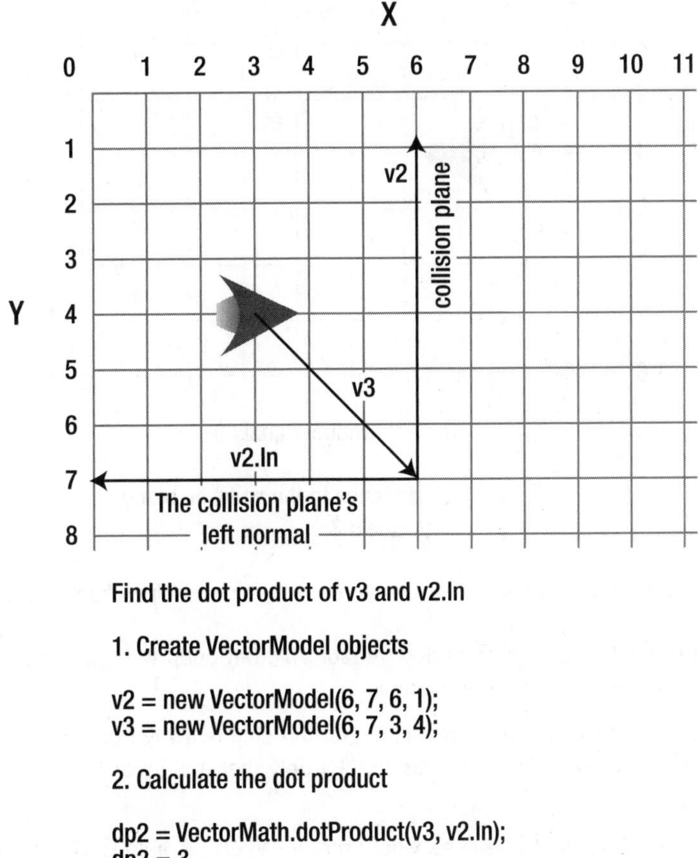
X
0 1 2 3 4 5 6 7 8 9 10 11
Y
1 2 3 4 5 6 7 8
v2
collision plane
v3
v2.ln
The collision plane's
left normal
Find the dot product of v3 and v2.ln
1. Create VectorModel objects
v2 = new VectorModel(6, 7, 6, 1);
v3 = new VectorModel(6, 7, 3, 4);
2. Calculate the dot product
dp2 = VectorMath.dotProduct(v3, v2.ln);
dp2 = 3

Figure 2-38. Find the dot product of v3 and v2 to help calculate the collision.

The dot product in this example has a value of 3. Does that value seem significant in some way? It is. Look carefully, and you'll see that that the spaceship is three cells away from the collision plane. As illustrated in Figure 2-39, the dot product can tell you exactly how far away the ship is from the line.

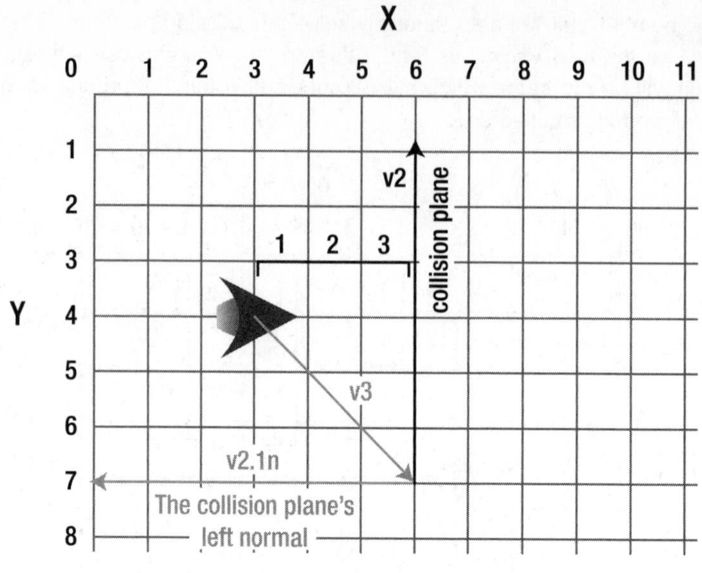

Figure 2-39. The dot product can tell you how far away the spaceship is from the collision plane.

This remarkable coincidence is like a buried treasure hidden deep within the math. It holds true no matter what the angle of the collision plane is.

Because you can use this information to tell how far the ship is away from the line, you can also use it to figure out if there has been a collision. Not only that, but it can tell you with how much force the ship has collided.

Take a look at Figure 2-40, and you'll see what I mean. When the ship is exactly on the line, the dot product is zero. When it has crossed the line by three cells, the dot product is –3.

This means that you know the ship is colliding with the line if the dot product is less than zero. That's the flag that triggers a collision. In the `Collision` example code, it's represented like this:

```
if(dp2 <= 0)
{
  //…We have a collision!
```

Now we have a way to detect a collision. Next, we need to find a way to resolve the collision.

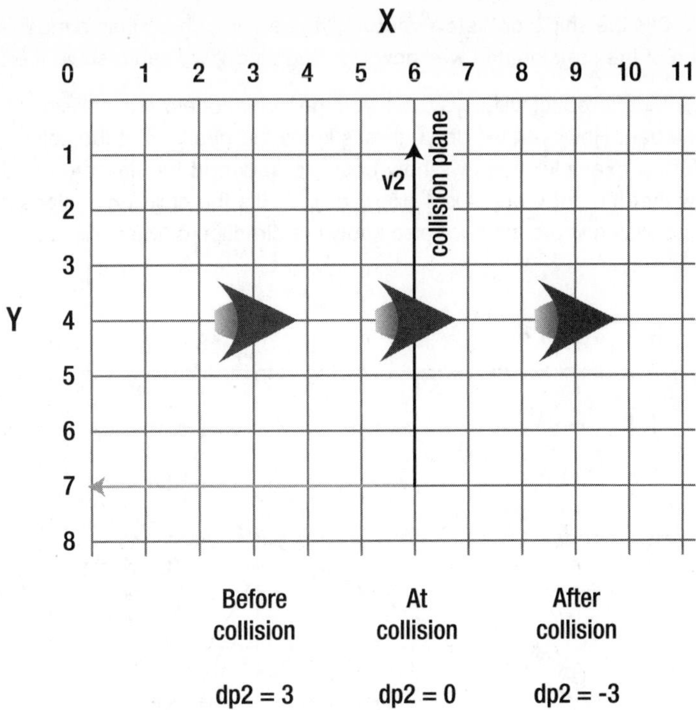

Figure 2-40. Use the dot product to tell you when a collision has occurred and what the collision force is.

Resolving the collision

In Figures 2-35 through 2-39, the spaceship and the collision plane are aligned to the x and y axes. This makes the math really easy to understand and visualize. But in a real-world collision, it's likely that the ship and line will be colliding at weird angles. Fortunately, the math holds up no matter at what angle the collision happens.

When the ship collides with the line, we need to know by how much it has crossed the line. This is important so we can move the ship out of the collision. We need to move it back to the exact point of collision with the line (the point where the dot product is zero). In Figure 2-39, it's easy to see that the ship has overshot the line by three cells. If we move the ship back by 3, it will be positioned exactly at the point of collision.

We can say that –3 is the ship's **collision vector**. The collision vector has a magnitude of 3. If we know the direction of the collision and we know the magnitude, we can resolve the collision.

As you've seen, the dot product will always tell you the magnitude of the collision vector. We have that number in the bag. However, we don't always know the *direction* of the collision. Take a look at Figure 2-41 for an example. It shows how both the ship and the line are colliding at strange angles. We know that the dot product is 4 (rounded). That's the collision vector's magnitude. But we can't create a collision vector until we also know the direction of the collision.

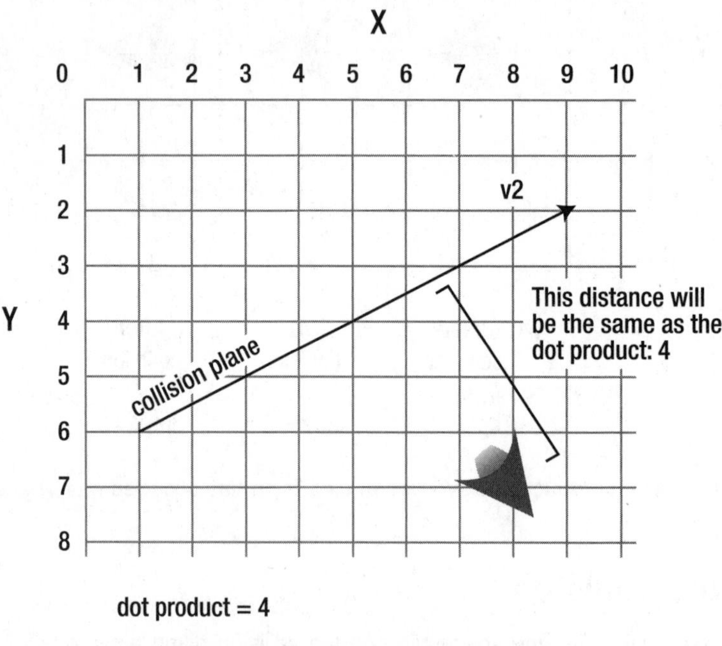
X
0 1 2 3 4 5 6 7 8 9 10
Y
1 2 3 4 5 6 7 8
v2
collision plane
This distance will be the same as the dot product: 4
dot product = 4
The collision vector's magnitude will be 4, but how do we know what its direction is?

Figure 2-41. The ship has collided with the line. The magnitude of the collision will be the same as the value of the dot product. But what's the direction?

How can we figure out from which direction the ship is colliding with the line? Surprise—we already know it! It's the ship's motion vector, `v1`.

Figure 2-42 shows the spaceship's motion vector, `v1`. It's definitely pointing in the right direction. The only problem is that it's too long. Its magnitude is 7 (rounded). What would Goldilocks do?

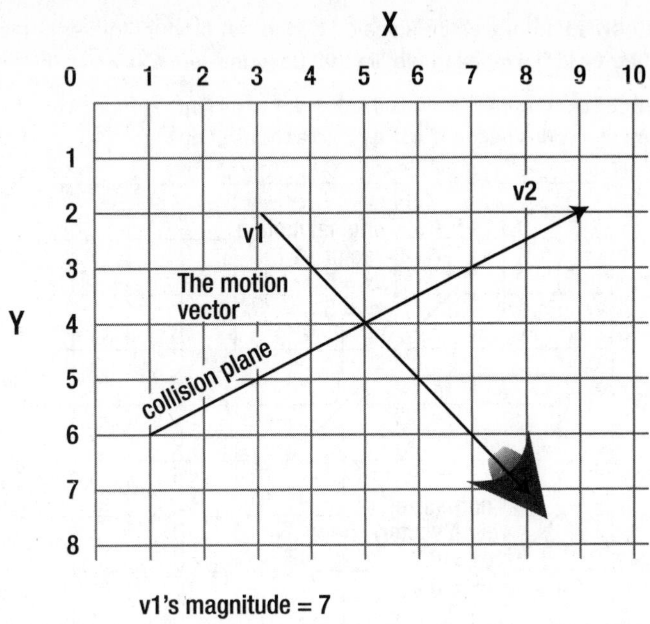

Figure 2-42. The ship's motion vector is pointing in the right direction, but its magnitude is too long.

We need a vector that's pointing in the same direction as `v1` but has the same magnitude as the dot product. Aha! That should ring a bell.

We can use a *unit vector* to help solve this problem. Remember that normalized unit vectors are the smallest size a vector can be. They have the magical property of pointing in a specific direction, but can be scaled to any size. Unit vectors are the "Drink Me!" of Vectorland.

How can we use a unit vector in this case?

1. Normalize the ship's motion vector, `v1`. That will allow us to keep its direction but scale it to any other size.
2. Multiply `v1`'s unit vector by the value of the dot product, 4. The resulting vector is the new collision vector.

Figure 2-43 shows how `v1`'s unit vector is scaled by the dot product to create the collision vector. Here's the code in the `Collision` example file that does this work.

```
var collisionForce_Vx:Number = _v1.dx * Math.abs(dp2);
var collisionForce_Vy:Number = _v1.dy * Math.abs(dp2);
```

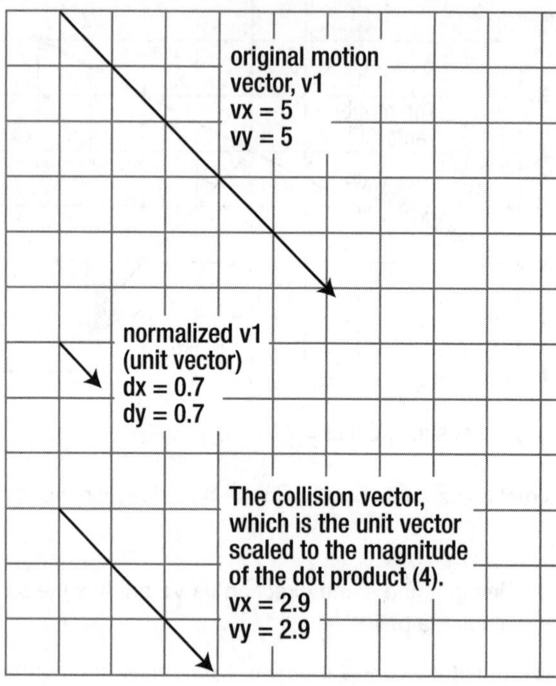

collisionForce_Vx = _v1.dx * Math.abs(dp2)
collisionForce_Vy = _v1.dy * Math.abs(dp2)

Figure 2-43. Scale v1 to the magnitude of the dot product to create the collision vector.

The new collision vector precisely describes the force of the collision. You can see in Figure 2-44 that it fits exactly in the space between the line and ship. (It's been rounded up to 3 because we're working with whole pixel values.) It tells us how far the ship has intersected the line.

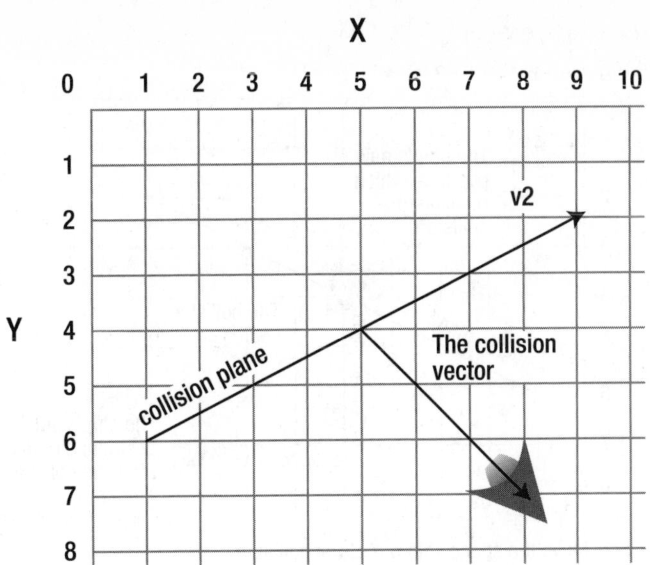

Figure 2-44. The collision vector perfectly decribes how far the ship has crossed the line.

Next, we need to use this information to move the ship back to the collision point. Why? Because the collision plane is supposed to be a solid surface. The spaceship should never seem to cross the line. It should stop right on the collision plane.

All we need to do is take the ship's position and subtract the collision vector. That gives us the collision vector's start point. That point happens to be the exact point of collision between the ship and the line. If we move the ship to that point, we've resolved the collision. Figure 2-45 illustrates how this works.

The code in the `Collision` example file that does the work looks like this:

```
_shipModel.setX = _shipModel.xPos - collisionForce_Vx;
_shipModel.setY = _shipModel.yPos - collisionForce_Vy;
```

It also sets the ship's velocity to `0`, which puts on the brakes.

```
_shipModel.vx = 0;
_shipModel.vy = 0;
```

With the help of normals, normalized unit vectors, and the dot product, we have a simple solution to a complex problem.

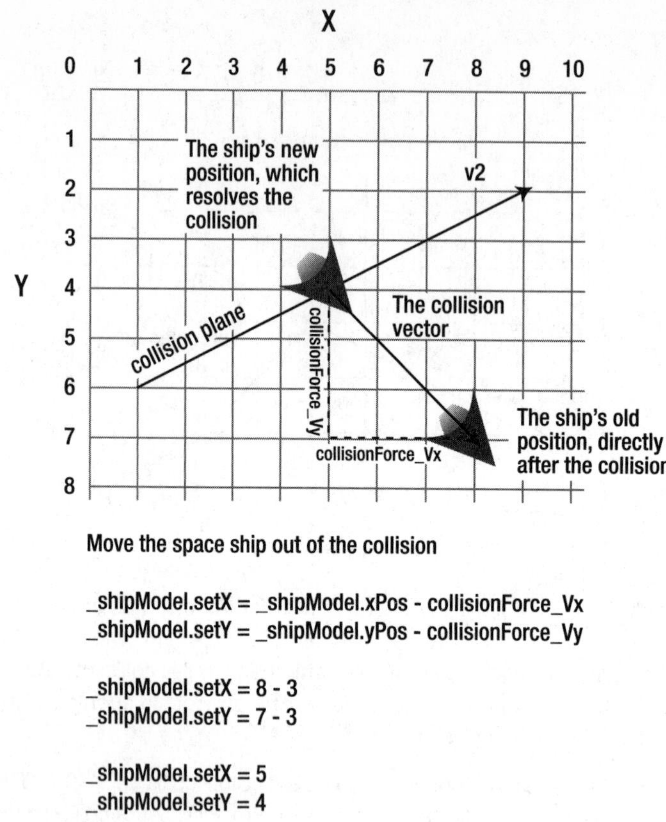

Figure 2-45. Subtract the collision vector from the spaceship's position to find the exact point of collision with the line.

> *Collision detection in video games tends to fall into two main categories:*
>
> - ***Posteriori**: Checking for a collision after the collision has already happened.*
> - ***Priori**: Checking for a collision before it happens*
>
> *This book uses posteriori collision detection. Because all the collision objects are using the MVC system, the code can model the collision and resolve it before the result is displayed on the stage. This allows us to implement stable and accurate collision detection that doesn't suffer from off-by-one-frame errors.*

Bounce

When an object hits an angled line, it needs to ricochet at the correct angle. Here's where the technique of projection saves the day. Let's take a look at the general procedure for making an object bounce.

First, we need to combine the motion vector with the angle of the line with which it's colliding. The first step is to project `v1` onto `v2` and `v2`'s normal. Figure 2-46 illustrates this. (The projected vectors are called `p1` and `p2` in this example.)

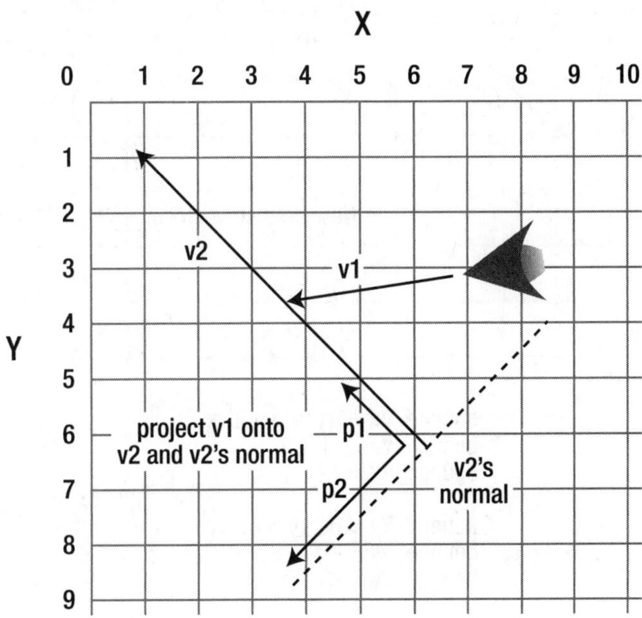

Figure 2-46. Project v1 onto v2 and v2's normal.

The next thing to do is *reverse* the `p2` vector. We want our collision object to bounce, so reversing this projection will create a force directly opposite to the collision force. To reverse a vector, simply multiply its `vx` and `vy` values by -1. Next, add the `vx` and `vy` values of both projected vectors together. This gives you a new bounce vector. Figure 2-47 illustrates this.

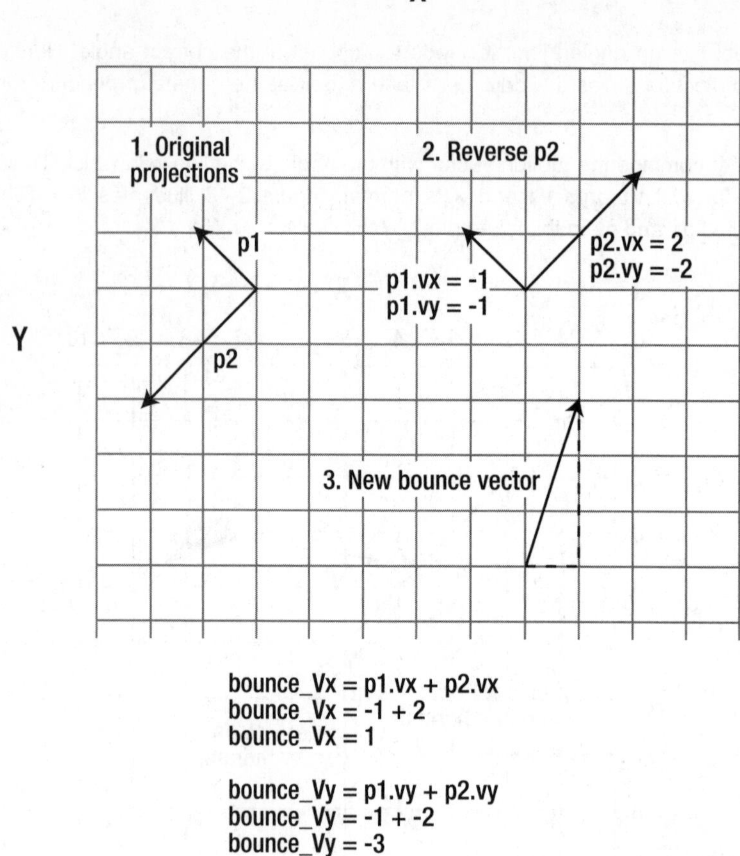
X
Y
1. Original
projections
p1
p2
2. Reverse p2
p1.vx = -1
p1.vy = -1
p2.vx = 2
p2.vy = -2
3. New bounce vector
bounce_Vx = p1.vx + p2.vx
bounce_Vx = -1 + 2
bounce_Vx = 1
bounce_Vy = p1.vy + p2.vy
bounce_Vy = -1 + -2
bounce_Vy = -3

Figure 2-47. Reverse p2, and add the projections together to create a new bounce vector.

The last step is to apply this new bounce vector to the collision object's velocity (`v1`). The object will bounce away at exactly the right angle, no matter what the angle of the line is. Compare the bounce vector in Figure 2-47 with the way that it has been applied in Figure 2-48, and you'll see that it's exactly the same vector.

Let's see how to translate these concepts into AS3.0 code. In the chapter's source files, you'll find a folder called `Bounce`. Run the SWF and you find a working example, as shown in Figure 2-49.

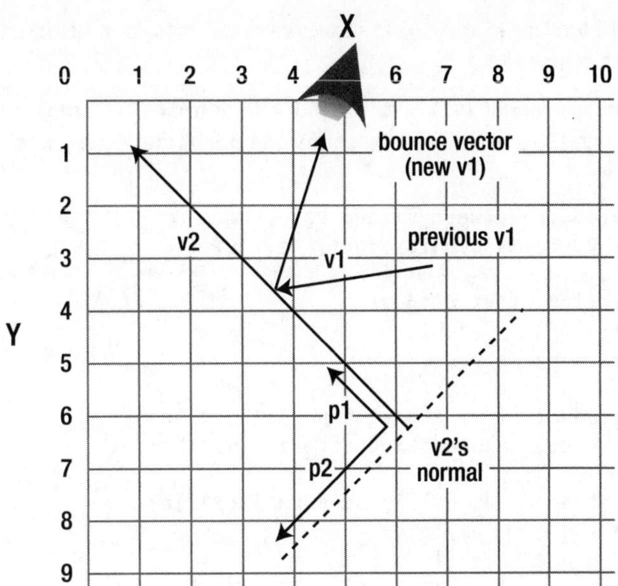

Figure 2-48. Assign the new bounce vector to the object's velocity.

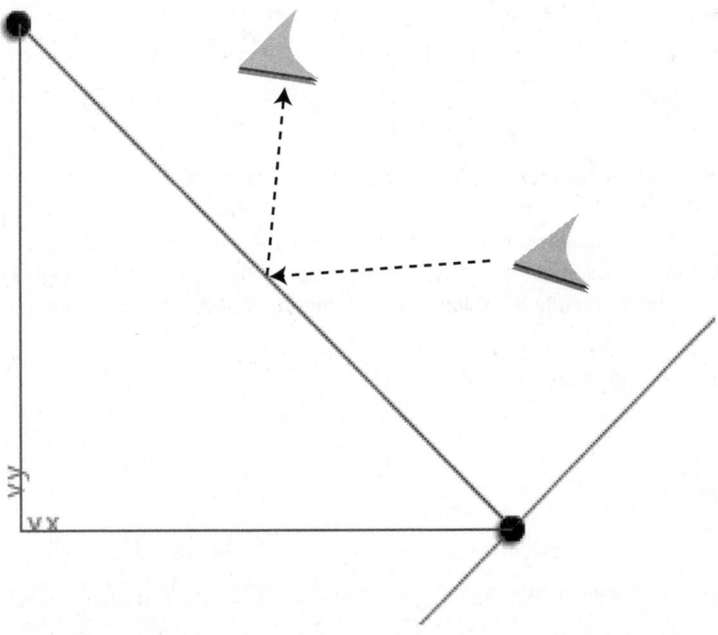

Figure 2-49. Perfect bounce at any angle

The code is almost identical to the Collision example. Let's look at how the new code that makes the spaceship bounce.

Project the ship's motion vector (v1) onto v2 and v2's normal. This creates two new projected vectors. (Again, creating VectorModel objects for them isn't necessary because we need only their vx and vy values.)

```
//Find the dot product between v1 and v2
var dp3:Number = VectorMath.dotProduct(_v1, _v2);

//Find the projection of v1 onto v2
var p1_Vx:Number = dp3 * _v2.dx;
var p1_Vy:Number = dp3 * _v2.dy;

//Find the dot product of v1 and v2's normal (v2.ln)
var dp4:Number = VectorMath.dotProduct(_v1, _v2.ln);

//Find the projection of v1 onto v2's normal (v2.ln)
var p2_Vx:Number = dp4 * _v2.ln.dx;
var p2_Vy:Number = dp4 * _v2.ln.dy;
```

Next, reverse the projection on v2's normal by multiplying it by –1. This will create the bounce effect.

```
p2_Vx *= -1;
p2_Vy *= -1;
```

Then add up the projected vectors' vx and vy values to create a new bounce vector.

```
var bounce_Vx:Number = p1_Vx + p2_Vx;
var bounce_Vy:Number = p1_Vy + p2_Vy;
```

Finally, assign the bounce vector to the spaceship's velocity. Optionally, multiply it by another number to exaggerate or dampen the bounce effect. Multiplying it by 0.8 reduces the bounce force by 20%, which simulates loss of energy when the ship hits the line. Multiplying it by a number greater than 1 will make the bounce force more powerful than the original collision force, which creates a trampoline effect. Multiplying by 0 means that there's no bounce at all.

```
_shipModel.vx = bounceVx * 0.8;
_shipModel.vy = bounceVy * 0.8;
```

Bounce solved!

Momentum

In this book, I've chosen to collide and bounce objects using these steps:

1. When the objects collide, move the objects to the exact point of the collision.
2. Bounce them apart from that collision point.

There is a problem with this: it's not entirely accurate. By repositioning the object at the point of collision, its motion vector can become truncated. Part of its movement from the previous frame might be lost.

Imagine that you're driving along the street and absently run through a red light. You slam on the brakes and skid halfway through the intersection, leaving a long black trail of molten rubber tracing you path. You sheepishly back up, and wait for the light to change.

This is how this the collision code is working. It stops the car exactly at the red light, whether or not the car still has any momentum left. That momentum—the skid marks—is lost. It's not added to the car's new position when the lights change.

I've chosen this style of collision because, for games, it can actually appear more accurate. By positioning colliding objects exactly at the point of collision, it allows the eye to see the point of contact between objects. This is a psychological cue that makes the brain think, "They collided!"

Without this visual cue, the collision can appear less precise or fuzzy, because we never see the objects actually touch each other. Instead, we see them a few pixels apart before they collide, and then a few pixels apart in the next frame when they bounce apart. Even though this might be more accurate, we never see them touch.

This is purely a stylistic decision, so you'll need to decide whether it's appropriate for your games. If you prefer greater accuracy, don't position the colliding object at the collision point. Instead, subtract the collision vector from `p2` and reverse it. You can call the new vector that results the "momentum vector." The distance from the collision point to the momentum vector's point B is the new position you should give your object in the next frame. This way, none of the object's original momentum is lost.

Solid objects

To keep the examples so far as clear as possible, they've involved only one line. But you can add as many lines as you like, and join them together to form solid shapes. Just push all the lines into an array and loop through the array each frame to check for collisions.

The one thing you need to remember is that only one side of the line should face the collision object (the spaceship in our example) at all times. In the last few examples, the ship could fly to the right of the line, but not directly behind it on its left side. There shouldn't be any chance that the object enters the dreaded "left normal collision area" illustrated earlier in Figure 2-34.

With that in mind, you could easily create an irregular terrain for a planet surface or perhaps the interior of a lunar cave, as shown in Figure 2-50. The right side of the lines represents negative space, and the left side represents positive space.

You can also use these techniques to create polygons of any shape. But there's a problem that you need to take into account. Take a look Figure 2-51. Even if your collision object is facing the right side of a line, it will still fall into the collision area from a line on the *opposite side of the polygon*.

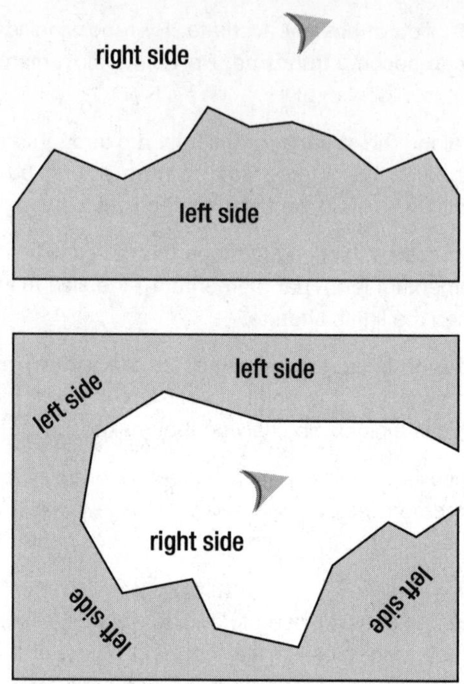

Figure 2-50. Construct environments with the right of the lines facing the collision object.

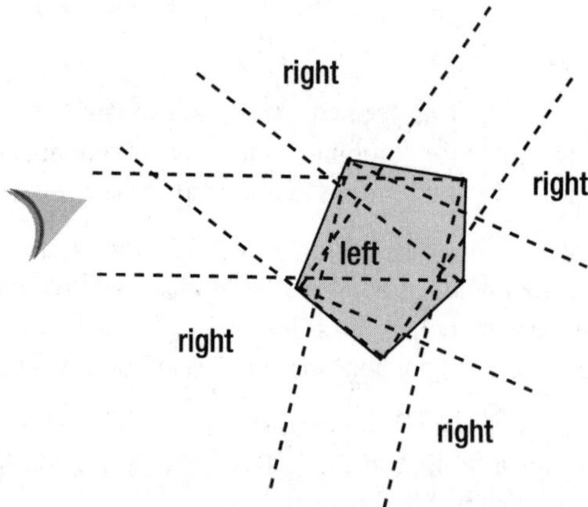

Figure 2-51. The ship may be to the right of the closest line, but it's falling within the left normal collision area from a line on the opposite side of the polygon.

There is a simple solution to this: check only for collisions with lines that intersect with the ship's motion vector. If there's an intersection with more than one line, just check for a collision with the *closest* intersecting line. Figure 2-52 shows an example.

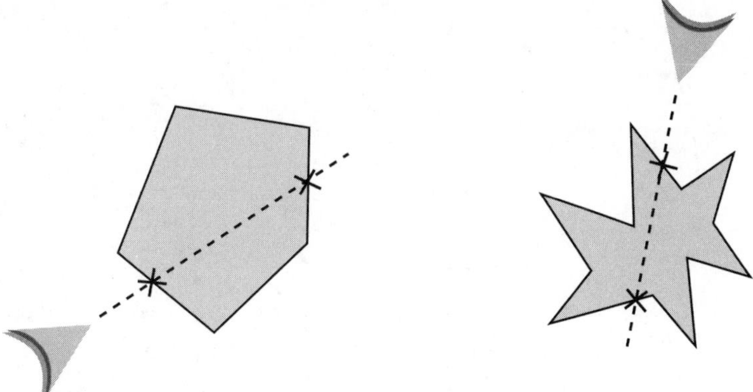

Figure 2-52. Only check for a collision with the closest intersecting line.

Try it! If you're a little uncertain about checking collisions on multiple objects, you'll find more details in Chapter 3.

> *If you're using Verlet integration, you can use vectors to create* ***Verlet sticks*** *and* ***Verlet structures****. These are shapes created by drawing vectors between particles and constraining them to a fixed distance so that they become "solid" and react like solid objects when they collide. They can be used as the basis for building very reliable physics engines. Keith Peters has an excellent introduction to this subject in AdvancED ActionScript 3.0 Animation (friends of ED, 2008), which is a perfect complement to this chapter.*

Collision on both sides of the line

We're now going to use our newfound vector voodoo to create a collision system that works on both sides of the line. To see what it can do, run the `doubleSidedCollision` SWF in the chapter's source files. Fly the ship around both sides of the line, and bounce against it a few times. Figure 2-53 shows what you'll see.

Just what we need! There are actually quite a few different approaches you can take to doing this, but I'm going to show you a method that's both bulletproof and versatile. To make it work, we need to use all of our now formidable number of vector tricks. There's a lot going on in this code, so now might be a good time to review any concepts you're a little fuzzy on.

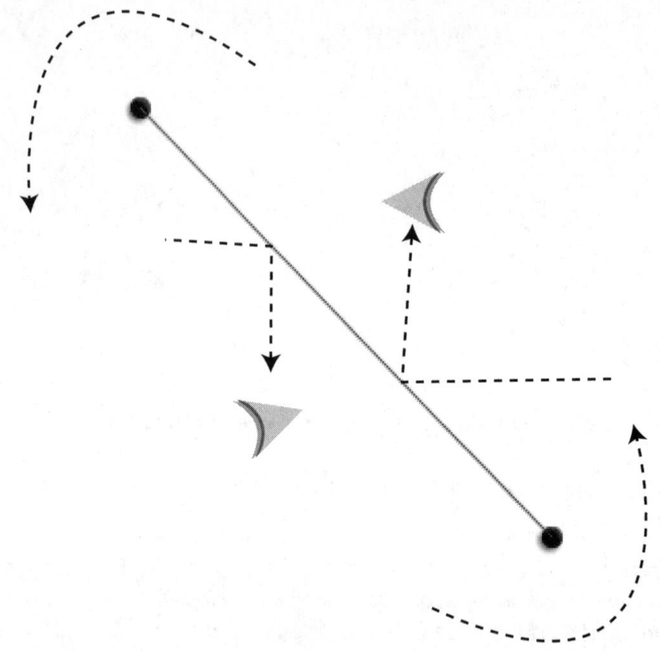

Figure 2-53. Collision and bounce on both sides of the line

Take a look at the `DoubleSidedCollision.as` file, and I'm sure you'll notice a lot of code you recognize. Here's how it works in general terms:

- We need to know which side of the line the spaceship is on. Is it on the right or left side? A new variable called `_lineSide` tracks this.
- The code uses a dot product to find out on which side of the line the ship is. The code uses the dot product to set the `_lineSide` variable to `"left"` or `"right"`.
- The collision boundary is based on the value of the `_lineSide` variable. It's exactly the same technique we used in the previous two examples, but modified to work for collision on both the right and left.
- The `_lineSide` variable is reset when the ship moves around the edges of a line using the same technique used in the previous two examples. The `_lineSide` variable is also reset when the ship wraps around the edges of the stage.

Here's the important code from the enterFrameHandler that does all this work. You'll notice that the code for creating the bounce vector has been offloaded to the VectorMath class. Take a look at the VectorMath.bounce method. It's almost identical to the code in the previous example, except that it returns VectorModel objects to the main program.

```
//The dot product that tells you whether the ship is within
//the scope of the line's magnitude
var dp1:Number = VectorMath.dotProduct(_v3, _v2);
//The dot product that tells you which side of the line
//the ship is on
var dp2:Number = VectorMath.dotProduct(_v3, _v2.ln);

//If the ship is within the scope of the line's magnitude
//then set its line side to left or right
if(dp1 > -_v2.m && dp1 < 0 )
{
  if(_lineSide == "")
  {
    if(dp2 < 0 )
    {
      _lineSide = "left";
    }
    else
    {
      _lineSide = "right";
    }
  }
}
else
{
  //If the ship is not within the line's scope (such as rounding
  //a corner) clear the _lineSide variable.
  _lineSide = "";
}

//Reset the _lineSide variable if the ship has wrapped
//around the edges of the stage
if(_shipModel.yPos > stage.stageHeight
|| _shipModel.yPos < 0
|| _shipModel.xPos < 0
|| _shipModel.xPos > stage.stageWidth)
{
   _lineSide = "";
}
```

```
//Create an environmental boundary based on whether
//the ship has collided from the right or left
if(dp2 > 0 && _lineSide == "left"
|| dp2 < 0 && _lineSide == "right")
{
  //Create the collision vector
  var collisionForce_Vx:Number = _v1.dx * Math.abs(dp2);
  var collisionForce_Vy:Number = _v1.dy * Math.abs(dp2);

  //Move ship out of the collision
  _shipModel.setX = _shipModel.xPos - collisionForce_Vx;
  _shipModel.setY = _shipModel.yPos - collisionForce_Vy;

  //Create a bounce vector
  var bounce:VectorModel = VectorMath.bounce(_v1, _v2);

  //Bounce the ship
  _shipModel.vx = bounce.vx * 0.8;
  _shipModel.vy = bounce.vy * 0.8;
}
```

There are no new techniques here. It just includes some extra logic to figure out on which side of the line the ship is. Let's untangle it and figure out what's happening.

First, we need our usual pair of loyal dot products to help us make sense of our space. They'll be playing the same role as in the previous examples.

```
var dp1:Number = VectorMath.dotProduct(_v3, _v2);
var dp2:Number = VectorMath.dotProduct(_v3, _v2.ln);
```

What side of the line is the spaceship on? We only care if the ship is within the scope of the line's magnitude, because that's when a collision may be likely. If it's not—if the ship is beyond the top or bottom edge of the line—then the `_lineSide` variable should be cleared so that it can be set to something else later. If it is within the line's scope, then use `dp2` to find out whether it's on the left or right side of the line, and set `_lineSide` to that value.

```
//Is the ship within the scope of v2's magnitude?
if(dp1 > -_v2.m && dp1 < 0 )
{
  //If the answer is yes, set _lineSide to the correct value
  if(_lineSide == "")
  {
    if(dp2 < 0 )
    {
      _lineSide = "left";
    }
```

```
    else
    {
      _lineSide = "right";
    }
  }
}
else
{
  //If the ship is not within the line's scope (such as rounding
  //a corner) clear the _lineSide variable.
  _lineSide = "";
}
```

We need to clear the _lineSide variable if the ship wraps around the edges of the stage. If we don't do this, the code might think that the ship is on the wrong side of the line when it reemerges from the opposite side of the stage.

```
if(_shipModel.yPos > stage.stageHeight
|| _shipModel.yPos < 0
|| _shipModel.xPos < 0
|| _shipModel.xPos > stage.stageWidth)
{
   _lineSide = "";
}
```

Now that we know which side of the line the ship is on, we need to check if it crosses the line. For example, if we know that the ship is on the right, and dp2 suddenly becomes less than zero, we know that the ship has just intersected. We have a collision!

```
if(dp2 > 0 && _lineSide == "left"
|| dp2 < 0 && _lineSide == "right")
{…
```

The logic behind the collision code is identical to the previous examples. The only difference is that it has been made more compact by delegating the work of creating the bounce vector to the VectorMath class.

```
//Create the collision vector
var collisionForce_Vx:Number = _v1.dx * Math.abs(dp2);
var collisionForce_Vy:Number = _v1.dy * Math.abs(dp2);

//Move the ship out of the collision
_shipModel.setX = _shipModel.xPos - collisionForce_Vx;
_shipModel.setY = _shipModel.yPos - collisionForce_Vy;

//Create a bounce vector
var bounce:VectorModel = VectorMath.bounce(_v1, _v2);
```

```
//Bounce the ship
_shipModel.vx = bounce.vx * 0.8;
_shipModel.vy = bounce.vy * 0.8;
```

As you can see, it's nothing new—just a bit of simple logic. You can use this technique to create solid objects and complex environments, like a maze, just as you could with the previous examples. Push all the lines into an array and loop through them to check for collisions. However, because this technique depends on a variable to track the side of the line the ship is on, you'll also need a `lineSide` variable for each line. You can store and track these `lineSide` variables in another array.

Bounce, friction, and gravity

For the grand finale, let's round up all the star and bit players of this chapter, and get them to help us solve one of the classic problems of game design: a falling particle hitting, bouncing, and sliding off a line. There are many ways you could do this. I'll show you the way I've done it and explain all the principles involved. My hope is that you'll take this information and run with it to build system that's customized for a game of your own.

You'll find the sample file in the `BouncingParticle` folder. Run the SWF file, and you'll see something that looks like Figure 2-54. A particle falls, hits a line, and bounces. If it gradually comes to a rest on the line, it will slide off. You can move the drag handles to change the orientation of the line.

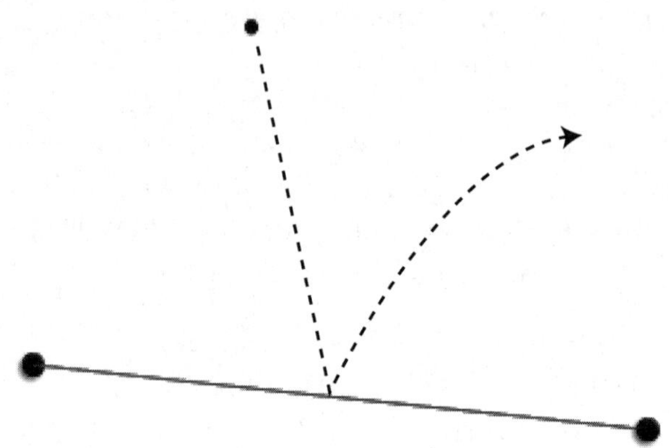

Figure 2-54. A bouncing particle

This example is not coded to handle collision with a moving line. You'll see some weird things happen to the particle if you move the line upwards while the particle is resting on it. The line's drag handles are implemented with `startDrag` and `stopDrag`. When you move objects with the mouse using `startDrag` and `stopDrag`, Flash updates the position of those objects on the stage at a different rate than the movie's frame rate. That means that their change in position won't be synchronized with the code in your `enterFrameHandler`. For a reliable collision system with a moving line, you'll first need to implement a drag-and-drop system that runs within the same `enterFrameHandler` as the rest of the collision code. (Chapter 10 of my book Foundation Game Design with Flash describes such a system in detail.)

Also, if you move the line while the particle hits it or is resting on it, you may want to transfer some of that force to the particle. To do that, you'll need to work out the force and the direction of that force, and add that to the particle's velocity. Does that sound strangely familiar? It should, because it just means you need to figure out the drag handle's motion vector when it moves. I'll let you work out the details, but everything you need to know to do this is in this chapter.

You might not find it surprising that all we're doing in this example is mixing together our ingredients in a slightly different combination. Here's the basic recipe:

1. Add the force of gravity to the particle's velocity.
2. When the particle crosses the line, figure out by how much it has overshot. That becomes your collision force. Add the current gravity to the collision force. Use these values to move the particle out of the collision
3. Calculate bounce as in the previous examples.
4. If you want the particle to slide off an inclined line, you need to calculate friction. This is very easy to do: add the projection of `v1` onto `v2` to the particle's velocity.

Now, let's see how I've cooked this recipe for the `BouncingParticle` example.

First, I created a `particleModel` object. It has a model and view.

```
private var _particleModel:ParticleModel = new ParticleModel();
private var _particleView:ParticleView = new ParticleView(_particleModel);
```

The `ParticleModel` class extends the `AVerletModel` class. All the important code is actually in the `AVerletModel` class. It's essentially the same as the `ShipModel` class we've been using in the previous examples, but simpler and with an added provision for adding gravity to the object's velocity. In Chapter 3, I'll explain exactly how `AVerletModel` works and how to extend it to create new classes. For now, all you need to know is that the code that makes the `particleModel` object move is in the `AVerletModel` class. Its most important part is its `update` method.

```
public function update():void
{
  temporaryX = xPos;
  temporaryY = yPos;

  vx += acceleration_X;
  vy += acceleration_Y;

  vx *= friction;
  vy *= friction;

  xPos += vx + friction_Vx + gravity_Vx;
  yPos += vy + friction_Vy + gravity_Vy;

  previousX = temporaryX;
  previousY = temporaryY;

  //This "update" event is not used in this example,
  //so you can ignore it for now:
  dispatchEvent(new Event("update"));
}
```

Notice that gravity is now a force that can potentially act on the particle's position.

```
xPos += vx + friction_Vx + gravity_Vx;
yPos += vy + friction_Vy + gravity_Vy;
```

It can be applied on both the x and y axes. In this example, it's going to be applied only on the y axis. (The particle's `friction` property is set to `1` by the application, so its own internal friction is not a factor in this example.)

In the `BouncingParticle` application class, the `_particleModel`'s gravity is set to `0.1` when its view is added to the stage.

```
addChild(_particleView);
_particleModel.setX = 150;
_particleModel.setY = 150;
_particleModel.friction = 1;
_particleModel.gravity_Vy = 0.1;
```

The only difference in the `BouncingParticle` code from the previous example is in the `if` statement block that checks for a collision. Here's that entire section:

```
if(dp2 > 0 && _lineSide == "left"
|| dp2 < 0 && _lineSide == "right")
{
   //Create the collision vector
   var collisionForce_Vx:Number = _v1.dx * Math.abs(dp2);
   var collisionForce_Vy:Number = _v1.dy * Math.abs(dp2);
```

```
    //Move the particle out of the collision
    _particleModel.setX
       = _particleModel.xPos
       - collisionForce_Vx;

     _particleModel.setY
       = _particleModel.yPos
       - collisionForce_Vy
       - _particleModel.gravity_Vy;

    //Find the projection vectors
    var p1:VectorModel = VectorMath.project(_v1, _v2);
    var p2:VectorModel = VectorMath.project(_v1, _v2.ln);

    //Calculate the bounce vector
    var bounce_Vx:Number = p2.vx * -1;
    var bounce_Vy:Number = p2.vy * -1;

    //Calculate the friction vector
    var friction_Vx:Number = p1.vx;
    var friction_Vy:Number = p1.vy;

    //Apply bounce and friction to the particle's velocity
    _particleModel.vx = (bounce_Vx * 0.6) + (friction_Vx * 0.98);
    _particleModel.vy = (bounce_Vy * 0.6) + (friction_Vy * 0.98);
}
```

Let's look at how it works.

When a collision is detected, the particle is moved out of the collision by subtracting the force of impact from its velocity. Gravity is an additional force, so we need to subtract that as well.

```
_particleModel.setX
   = _particleModel.xPos
   - collisionForce_Vx;

_particleModel.setY
   = _particleModel.yPos
   - collisionForce_Vy
   - _particleModel.gravity_Vy;
```

Gravity is acting only on the y axis. It's *adding* to the particle's vy to pull it down. By subtracting it from the collision vector, gravity is neutralized. It means that when the particle is resting on the line, it's being pushed down and pushed up by exactly equal forces. This allows the friction effect to work without being crushed by the force of gravity.

Next, we need to find the projection vectors. The `VectorMath.project` method does this work for us, and returns the projection vectors as `VectorModel` objects.

```
var p1:VectorModel = VectorMath.project(_v1, _v2);
var p2:VectorModel = VectorMath.project(_v1, _v2.ln);
```

Here's where it gets interesting. Let's do a quick review and introduce some new terms.

We have two projection vectors, and each projection represents a component of the particle's velocity. The motion vector is split down the middle into two separate parts:

- `p1` is the projection of `v1` onto `v2`. This represents the particle's `vx` projected onto the line. It's known as the **parallel component**. The parallel component handles the friction on the surface of the line. This makes sense if you think of it as the "across" axis of the vector's plane.
- `p2` is the projection of `v1` onto `v2`'s normal. This represents the particle's `vy` projected onto the line. It's known as the **perpendicular component**. The perpendicular component handles bounce. This makes sense because it's the "up and down" axis of the vector's plane.

Figure 2-55 illustrates these components.

The short story is that `p2` handles bounce, and `p1` handles surface friction. And if you understand that, the rest is almost laughably easy. No, really, it is! You'll see that it's true in the next calculations.

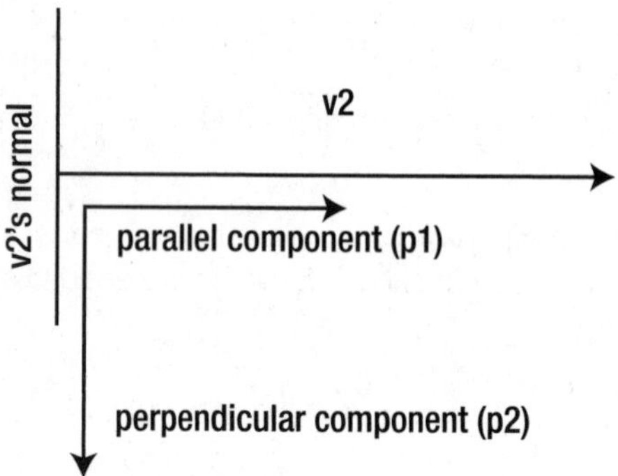

Figure 2-55. The parallel and perpendicular components

We calculate bounce by reversing `p2` and adding it to the particle's velocity.

```
var bounce_Vx:Number = p2.vx * -1;
var bounce_Vy:Number = p2.vy * -1;

_particleModel.vx = (bounce_Vx * 0.6) + (friction_Vx * 0.98);
_particleModel.vy = (bounce_Vy * 0.6) + (friction_Vy * 0.98);
```

This is exactly the same as the way we calculated bounce in the previous example; the context is just slightly different.

Friction *is* p1. It doesn't need to be reversed or have any calculations done to it. However, if you want the particle to gradually slow down, multiplying it by a number less than 1 (such as 0.98) will do the trick.

```
var friction_Vx:Number = p1.vx;
var friction_Vy:Number = p1.vy;

_particleModel.vx = (bounce_Vx * 0.6) + (friction_Vx * 0.98);
_particleModel.vy = (bounce_Vy * 0.6) + (friction_Vy * 0.98);
```

Experiment with different bounce and friction multipliers until you find a combination you like.

Line-versus-particle collision solved!

A crash course in embedding assets

Before you can use assets like images, fonts, and sounds in your game, you need to embed them. If you're using the Flash Professional IDE, you can embed them directly into your SWF using the IDE. Check Flash's documentation on how to do this if you don't already know how. Here, I'm going to show you how to embed assets using pure AS3.0 code, which is often more convenient and possibly easier to manage, especially if you're writing a lot of code.

Embedding fonts

Use the `Embed` metatag to embed the font and assign it to a class. This must be done in the class definition, where you declare all your instance variables. Here's the basic format:

```
public class AnyClass extends Sprite
{

[Embed(systemFont="Andale Mono", fontName="embeddedFont",
fontWeight="normal",
advancedAntiAliasing="true", mimeType="application/x-font")]

  //… declare class instance variables
```

This embeds the Andale Mono font, which is a font installed on my system. You can use the name of any font that you have installed.

Its `fontName` parameter is `"embeddedFont"`. If I want to use this font anywhere else in the class, I need to refer to it by this name. The other parameters should be self-evident.

You'll notice that there's a `Class` variable just below the `Embed` tag called `EmbeddedFontClass`.

```
private var EmbeddedFontClass:Class;
```

The font is actually *stored in this class*. Yes, I know what you're thinking: There's no assignment operator to show this, and it doesn't look like it could possibly be standard AS3.0 syntax. No, it's not a messy hack. It actually *is* the proper way to assign an embedded asset to its own class. You can give the variable any name you like, but it must be declared directly after the `Embed` tag.

If you've embedded assets using the Flash Professional IDE in the past, these steps are the same as importing an asset to the Library, exporting it for ActionScript, and giving it a class name in the Symbol Properties window.

After you've embedded the font, you can use it in your class if you follow these steps:

1. Import the `flash.text` package.

   ```
   import flash.text.*;
   ```

2. Create a `TextFormat` object. `TextFormat` objects contain all the formatting options for your text.
3. Create a `TextField` object and use the `TextFormat` object to format the text it contains.
4. Optionally, add the `TextField` class to a `Sprite` object. That means you can use a sprite as a container for text. This allows you to use the sprite's properties to do things like add filters or rotate the text. You can rotate *only* text that uses embedded fonts. (If the font isn't embedded, the text field will be blank.)

You can see a working example of how to use an embedded font in the `RotationText` class (`com.friendsofed.utils`). Here's a modified version code of the code in that class:

```
//1. Create a text format object
var format:TextFormat = new TextFormat();
format.size = 12;
format.color = 0x000000;

//The name of the font should match
//the "name" parameter in the Embed tag
format.font = "embeddedFont";

//2. Create a TextField object
var textField:TestField = new TextField();
textField.embedFonts = true;
textField.autoSize = TextFieldAutoSize.LEFT;
textField.text = "The text you want to display in the text field";
textField.setTextFormat(format);
textField.antiAliasType = flash.text.AntiAliasType.ADVANCED;

//3. Create a Sprite object and add the _textContainer to it
var textContainer:Sprite = new Sprite();
addChild(textContainer);
textContainer.addChild(textField);
```

You'll find more information and some useful links to help you debug problems with embedded fonts in the comments in the `RotationText` class.

Embedding images

You can embed images in two ways:

- **At runtime**: Images are external to the SWF and are loaded when they're needed. This keeps the size of the SWF small, and is a good idea if you have a large number of images that won't be needed immediately when the game loads. However, there's always a chance that images may not load if network traffic is interrupted.
- **At compile time**: Images are embedded directly into the SWF. This is the recommended way to embed images (and other assets) for games because it means that your game won't break if images fail to load for some reason. It means that your SWF will be larger, but that's usually a fair trade to make for increased reliability.

The examples in this book use compile-time embedding. Let's take a look at how the image of Mars's moon Phobos is embedded in the `AddingVectors` example that we looked at earlier in the section about gravity. Figure 2-56 shows its folder structure.

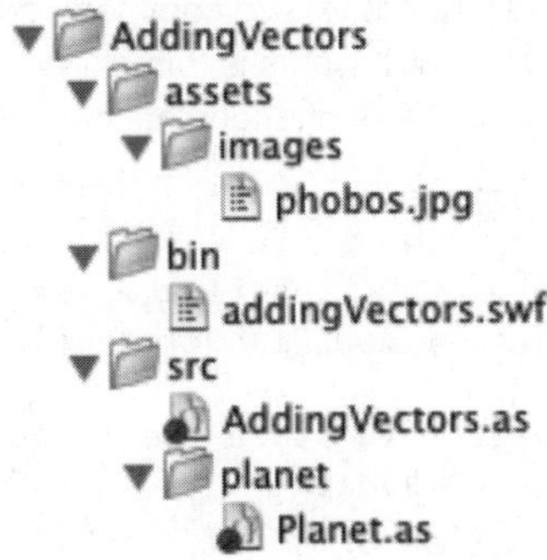

Figure 2-56. The structure of the AddingVectors project

The `Planet` class embeds the image using the `Embed` metatag. Its `source` parameter is the path to the `phobos.jpg` file.

```
[Embed(source="../../assets/images/phobos.jpg")]
private var PlanetImage:Class;
```

The image is assigned to its own class, `PlanetImage`. You can instantiate it like this:

```
var planetImage:DisplayObject = new PlanetImage();
```

That's really all you need to do to embed and display an image in a class. However, if you want a little more control over how the image is displayed, you'll probably take it a few steps further.

To scale the image and use it as a background fill for a shape, you need to import the `BitmapData` and `Matrix` classes.

```
import flash.display.BitmapData;
import flash.geom.Matrix;
```

Both of these classes are little mini-universes of complexity in their own right, and we'll look at both of them more closely in later chapters. For now, you need to know that the `BitmapData` class helps display the image. The `Matrix` class scales, centers, and rotates it.

The `drawPlanet` method uses these classes to plot the image. It works by scaling the image to the value of `_radius`. The radius of the planet is provided by the `Planet` class's constructor arguments in the `AddingVectors` application class.

```
private var _planet:Planet = new Planet(100, 0x999999, 280);
```

The radius is 100. Its rotation is 280.

The image is then used as a bitmap fill for a circle shape (which is also the same size as the radius). The circle shape with the bitmap fill of the image of Phobos is what finally becomes the planet.

The following is the entire `drawPlanet` method. I've commented each line with a brief description of what it does. The best way to learn how it works is to make some small changes, recompile the `AddingVectors` class, and observe how your changes affect the display of the planet.

```
private function drawPlanet():void
{
  //1. Create a new instance of the PlanetImage class
  var planetImage:DisplayObject = new PlanetImage();

  //2. Create a BitmapData object to store the image
  var image:BitmapData = new BitmapData
   (planetImage.width, planetImage.height, false);

  //3. Draw the image, and create a new Matrix as a parameter
  image.draw(planetImage, new Matrix());

  //3a. Optionally, create a Matrix to scale (or optionally rotate) the image
  var matrix:Matrix = new Matrix();

  //3b. Find the correct scale for the image based
  on the size of the planet (its radius)
  var scale:Number = ((_radius * 2) / planetImage.width);

  //3c. Adjust the scale by 20% so that the image margins
  //are slightly cropped
  var adjustedScale:Number = scale * 1.2;

  //3d. Apply the scale amount to the matrix
  matrix.scale(adjustedScale, adjustedScale);
```

```
  //3e. Center the bitmap so that its mid point is 0,0
  matrix.translate(-_radius, -_radius);

  //3f. Rotate the bitmap 280 degrees (the value of _rotation)
  matrix.rotate(_rotation * Math.PI / 180);

  //4. Draw the planet shape
  var planetShape:Shape = new Shape();

  //Use a beginBitmapFill function to draw the bitmap onto the shape
  //The "true" parameter refers to whether the bitmap should be tiled
  //or just drawn once
  planetShape.graphics.beginBitmapFill(image, matrix, true);
  planetShape.graphics.drawCircle(0, 0, _radius);
  planetShape.graphics.endFill();
  addChild(planetShape);

  //5. Add a bevel and drop shadow filter to the planet
  var planetFilters:Array = new Array();
  planetFilters = planetShape.filters;
  planetFilters.push
   (
     new BevelFilter
       (
         4, 135, 0xFFFFFF, 0.50,
         0x000000, 0.50, 4, 4
       )
    );
  planetFilters.push(new DropShadowFilter(4, 135, 0x000000, 0.35, 4, 4));
  planetShape.filters = planetFilters;
}
```

As you can see, it's a lot of code, but you do have very fine control over how the image is displayed.

Important vector formulas

Here's a cheat sheet of all the important formulas used in this chapter.

Create vectors

To create a vector, you need two points: a point called A and a point called B. Both points have x and y values.

```
vx = b.x - a.x;
vy = b.y - a.y ;
```

When you have vx and vy values, you have a vector.

Vector magnitude

The magnitude (m) of a vector tells you how long the vector is. It's the distance between point A and point B.

```
m = Math.sqrt(vx * vx + vy * vy);
```

This is formula is the Pythagorean theorem.

Vectors and angles

Find a vector's angle (in degrees):

```
angle = Math.atan2(vy, vx) * 180 / Math.PI;
```

If you know only a vector's angle and magnitude, you can find its vx and vy values like this:

```
vx = m * Math.cos(angle);
vy = m * Math.sin(angle);
```

Left and right normals

Normals are vectors that are exactly perpendicular (at 90 degrees) to the main vector. Find the left normal (lx) like this:

```
lx = vy;
ly = -vx;
```

Find the right normal (rx) like this:

```
rx = -vy;
ry = vx;
```

The left and right normals start at the base of the main vector and extend outward. That means that their start points (point A) will always be the same as the main vector's start point. You can find their point B coordinates like this:

```
leftNormal.b.x =  v1.a.x + lx;
leftNormal.b.y = v1.a.y + ly;

rightNormal.b.x =  v1.a.x + rx;
rightNormal.b.y = v1.a.y + ry;
```

Normalized vectors (unit vectors)

Unit vectors are the smallest size that a vector can be, while still retaining the vector's direction. Normalized unit vectors are represented by the variable names dx and dy. Find them like this:

```
dx = vx / m;
dy = vy / m;
```

Scaling vectors

If you have a unit vector, you can scale it to any size. Multiply the dx and dy values by any amount.

```
scaledVector_Vx = dx * multiplier;
scaledVector_Vy = dy * multiplier;
```

Gravity

To create a gravity effect between a spaceship and a round planet, follow this procedure:

1. Create a vector between the ship and the planet with values that are updated each frame.

   ```
   shipToPlanet_Vx = planet.x - spaceShip.x;
   shipToPlanet_Vy = planet.y - spaceShip.y;
   ```

2. Find its unit vector.

   ```
   m = Math.sqrt
      (
        shipToPlanet_Vx * shipToPlanet_Vx
        + shipToPlanet_Vy * shipToPlanet_Vy
      );

   shipToPlanet_Dx = shipToPlanet_Vx / m;
   shipToPlanet_Dy = shipToPlanet_Vy / m;
   ```

3. Create a gravity vector by scaling the ship-to-planet vector with a small number, like 0.1.

   ```
   gravity_Vx = shipToPlanet_Dx * 0.1;
   gravity_Vy = shipToPlanet_Dy * 0.1;
   ```

4. Assign the gravity vector to the ship's vx and vy velocity values.

   ```
   spaceShip.vx += gravity_Vx;
   spaceShip.vy += gravity_Vy;
   ```

5. For gravity that weakens as the objects move farther apart, add mass to the equation.

   ```
   planetMass = 5;
   shipMass = 1;

   gravity_Vx = shipToPlanet_Dx * (planetMass * shipMass) / m;
   gravity_Vy = shipToPlanet_Dy * (planetMass * shipMass) / m;
   ```

Dot product

The dot product tells you whether vectors are pointing in the same direction.

```
dp = v1.vx * v2.dx + v1.vy * v2.dy;
```

If the dot product is positive, the vectors point in the same direction. If it's negative, they point in opposite directions.

Projection

A vector's projection is the shadow of the vector on another vector. The projection is itself a new vector. First, find the dot product of the vector you want to project (v1) and the vector that will be the surface for the projection (v2).

```
dp = v1.vx * v2.dx + v1.vy * v2.dy;
```

Next, multiply the dot product by the surface vector's (v2's) dx and dy values.

```
projection_Vx = dotProduct *  v2.dx;
projection_Vy = dotProduct *  v2.dy;
```

The result is the new projection vector. It's the shadow of v1 on v2.

Define an environmental boundary

Here's the procedure for using a vector to define an environmental boundary:

6. Create a vector to use as an environmental boundary. This will be vector v2.
7. Create a vector between a game object (like the center of a space ship) and v2's point A. This will be vector v3.
8. Find the dot product of v3 and v2's left normal (v2.ln).

```
dp = v3.vx * v2.ln.dx + v3.vy * v2.ln.dy;
```

If the dot product is less than zero, you know that the game object has crossed with the environmental boundary (v2).

Resolve a collision with a vector

Find the dot product between v3 and v2.ln, as shown in the previous section. The game object needs a motion vector called v1. Multiply the absolute value of the dot product by v1's unit vector. This produces a collision vector.

```
collisionForce_Vx = v1.dx * Math.abs(dp);
collisionForce_Vy = v1.dy * Math.abs(dp);
```

Subtract the collision vector from the game object's x and y position.

```
gameObject.x = gameObject.x - collisionForce_Vx;
gameObject.y = gameObject.y - collisionForce_Vy;
```

This gives you the exact position where the game object collides with the environmental boundary, v2.

Bounce

To bounce a motion vector (v1) off a surface (v2), follow this procedure:

1. Find the dot product of v1 and v2.

   ```
   dp1 = v1.vx * v2.dx + v1.vy * v2.dy;
   ```

2. Project v1 onto v2.

   ```
   p1_Vx = dp1 * v2.dx;
   p1_Vy = dp1 * v2.dy;
   ```

3. Find the dot product of v1 and v2's normal (v2.ln).

   ```
   dp2 = v1.vx * v2.ln.dx + v1.vy * v2.ln.dy;
   ```

4. Project v1 onto v2.ln.

   ```
   p2_Vx = dp2 * v2.ln.dx;
   p2_Vy = dp2 * v2.ln.dy;
   ```

5. Reverse the projection on v2's normal.

   ```
   p2_Vx *= -1;
   p2_Vy *= -1;
   ```

6. Add up the projections to create a new bounce vector.

   ```
   bounce_Vx = p1_Vx + p2_Vx;
   bounce_Vy = p1_Vy + p2_Vy;
   ```

7. Assign the bounce vector to a game object's velocity. This should be the same object whose motion vector (v1) was used in the preceding steps. Use a multiplier, like 0.8, to dampen or exaggerate the bounce.

   ```
   gameObject.vx = bounce_Vx * 0.8;
   gameObject.vy = bounce_Vy * 0.8;
   ```

Friction

Follow the same steps as for bounce. `p1_Vx` and `p1_Vy` are the friction values. You can use them as is or optionally multiply them with another number, like 0.98, to gradually slow down an object.

```
friction_Vx = p1_Vx * 0.98 ;
friction_Vy = p1_Vy * 0.98;
```

Assign friction to the game object's velocity.

```
gameObject.vx = friction_Vx;
gameObject.vy = friction_Vy;
```

Summary

In this chapter, we covered one of the great black arts of game design. It's the key to understanding advanced collision detection. If you understand vectors, you have total control over the geometry of your game space. Combined with the technical efficiencies of the MVC framework and Verlet integration, it gives you a killer system to form the basis of a solid physics-based game engine.

Of course, this is just a start. I haven't gone into detail about how to use these techniques for collision detection with solid objects. But I'm sure you can see that it's not that difficult. Join a few vectors together, create a loop to check for collisions with the closest intersecting vector, and you can build polygons of any shape. However, in Chapter 4, we'll be looking at a better way to handle collision between polygons.

In the next chapter, we're going to explore collision detection between circles. We'll look at a few more classic collision-detection problems such as billiard-ball physics and how to check for collisions with multiple objects.

Until then, why not design a simple game using all the techniques from this chapter? A remake of the classic game Gravitar or Omega Race might be fun.

Have fun designing your game, and I'll meet you in Chapter 3 when you're ready!

Chapter 3

Collisions Between Circles

This is the first of two chapters that will take you on a grand tour of collision-detection strategies for 2D games. By the end of the next chapter, you'll have all your bases covered for games ranging from action and platform games to basic physics-simulation games.

This chapter covers collision detection between circles. Circles are a good place to start because they have the same dimensions all the way around. If you understand collision detection between circles, understanding collision detection between polygons becomes much easier.

This chapter covers the following topics:

- Using abstract classes to help you build games with extensible and reusable code
- Handling collisions between moving and stationary circles
- Handling collisions between a circle and a line
- Dealing with collisions when both circles are moving
- Handling collisions between multiple circles on the stage at the same time
- Implementing gravity and bounce
- Dealing with collisions between really fast moving circles

This chapter also features a flexible working prototype of a billiards style game. By the end of the chapter, you'll have the skills you need to turn it into a full-featured game.

Abstract classes

As I'm sure you've already realized, making games can become a rather complex business. Before we look at collision detection and reaction between circles, we need to develop a strategy for efficiently managing the already quite complex code we've written so that we can seamlessly reuse it in different contexts. Here, I'll show you how to use abstract classes and concrete classes with the MVC design pattern. We'll then use those new classes to make circles for the examples in this chapter.

Understanding abstract and concrete classes

One of the best things about OOP is that it gives you the ability to create a library of reusable code. That means that if you've written a chunk of complex code that works really well, you need to write that code only once, and never again. You can use that code in your programs with the complementary techniques of **inheritance** and **composition**.

Composition is when you instantiate a class and then use that class to help you instantiate another class. The MVC design pattern is based on composition. Here's some code from the previous chapter that's a typical example of composition at work:

```
private var _particleModel:ParticleModel = new ParticleModel();
private var _particleView:ParticleView = new ParticleView(_particleModel);
```

The `_particleModel` is fed into the `ParticleView`'s arguments so that the `ParticleView` class can use it in its own code.

Composition's big advantage over inheritance is that you can feed any class into any other class, and as long as it's the right type of class, it will work. This way, you can write very general code that keeps your classes completely independent. This helps to isolate bugs from infecting other classes, and means that you can mix and match classes on a whim to try new things without breaking the code you've already written. It helps to achieve the OOP goal of **encapsulation**. Yay, composition!

The other game in town is inheritance. Inheritance is when a new class *extends* a preexisting class so that the new class acquires all of the old class's properties and methods. Whenever you create a new class using the keyword `extends`, you're using inheritance.

```
public class BouncingParticle extends Sprite
```

`BouncingParticle` is a class that needs to be displayed on the stage. It would be painstaking and tedious to tell `BouncingParticle` in code how to display itself on the stage. It would be much better if we could just say, "Hey, `BouncingParticle`! I'm really busy. I can't be bothered to tell you how to display yourself on the stage. But `Sprite` already knows how to do this. Please just borrow its code." So `BouncingParticle` extends `Sprite` and inherits all of `Sprite`'s properties and methods. It means that you can use all of the `Sprite` class's properties, like `alpha` and `visible` in your new class without needing to code them yourself.

But what is the `Sprite` class, exactly? Have you ever seen its actual code? Neither have I! It's actually embedded into Flash Player and written in C++, so even if you could see it, your AS3.0 skills wouldn't help you much in understanding how it works.

That's actually a good thing. The fact is that we *are* really busy making games, so the less time we spend fiddling with the minutia of code, the more time we have to make really good games. If we can apply the same "make-and-forget" approach to our own programming, we can create games quickly and efficiently with libraries of preexisting code that we never really need to look at again after we've created them. Yay, inheritance!

Abstract classes can help us with this. An abstract class is a class that is packed with useful methods and properties but never instantiated itself. Instead, another class will extend the abstract class. The new class that extends it is then instantiated.

You make an abstract class like this:

```
public class AbstractClass
{
  //Properties and methods that you want all classes derived
  //from this class to inherit
}
```

Yes, it's just a plain-old class—nothing special! Only two main features of an abstract class make it different from any other class:

- **General methods and properties**: Its methods and properties are very general, so that they can be used by as wide a number of other classes as possible. For example, it's very likely that many objects in your game might need a `color` property. This could apply to enemy objects, environment objects, or player objects. All of them could extend a general abstract class that includes a `color` property. It's a property that applies to all your objects.
- **Not instantiated**: You make a promise to yourself not to instantiate an abstract class. It's used only to make other classes. Other programming languages like Java allow you to specifically declare a class as `Abstract`, and the compiler will prevent you from instantiating it if you try. AS3.0 doesn't have this feature, but that's no big deal; just tell yourself not to instantiate it.

By convention, AS3.0 programmers add an uppercase `A` to abstract class names to signal that the class is abstract and shouldn't be instantiated:

```
public class AThisClassIsAbstract
{
}
```

The classes that you make from abstract classes are called **concrete classes**. You create them by extending the abstract class.

```
public class ConcreteClass extends AbstractClass
{
  //Additional, specific properties and methods
}
```

A concrete class inherits all the properties and methods of the abstract class that it extends. Because a concrete class is "subclassed" from another class, it's also, perhaps not surprisingly, called a **subclass**.

Concrete classes are different from abstract classes in two important ways:

- **Specific methods and properties**: Their methods and properties are *specific*. That means that if you have an enemy object class, it might contain a method called `targetPlayer`. That's a method that only enemy objects would find useful. However, the enemy object class will also be able to access any of the general properties, like `color`, that it shares with other classes that extended the same abstract class that it has.
- **Instantiated**: Concrete classes are instantiated. That means that you actually make objects from them using the `new` operator.

So, you can do this:

```
var concreteObject:ConcreteClass = new ConcreteClass();
```

But you should never do this:

```
var abstractClass:AbstractClass = new AbstractClass();
```

Again, abstract classes should never be instantiated. They should be written for the sole purpose of being extended by other classes. They're puppet masters, never seen on the stage, but quietly pulling the strings in the dark behind the curtains.

You can think of an abstract class as a concrete class's "parent." The kids go out to play, and the parent class keeps a dutiful eye on them from the kitchen window. To avoid confusion with AS3.0's use of the keyword `parent` for display objects, abstract classes are referred to as a **superclass**. AS3.0 has a keyword called `super`, which lets you access the abstract class from the concrete class, and you'll see how this is used in the examples ahead.

Actually, I should qualify this example slightly. It's acceptable, and often preferable, to type the concrete class as the abstract class, like this:

```
var concreteObject:AbstractClass = new ConcreteClass();
```

`concreteObject` has an `AbstractClass` type, but it's still being instantiated as a `ConcreteClass`.

Why would you want to do this? Because it allows you keep your code really general. It means that if you have another class that also extends the abstract class, you can instantiate it like this:

```
var anotherClass:AbstractClass = new AnotherClass();
```

Because both classes are typed as the `AbstractClass`, you can use either of them in a method that accepts `AbstractClass` objects in its parameters.

```
public function someMethod(gameObject:AbstractClass):void
{...
```

That means both `concreteObject` and `anotherClass` can be passed to this method, and, because they both extend `AbstractClass`, it will work. It means you need only one method for two or more different classes of objects. It also means that because they share the same type (their parent `AbstractClass`), you can switch classes on a whim, like this:

```
anotherClass = new NewClass();
```

This has great potential for games, where you might want to switch the behavior of an object, like an enemy, in the middle of a game. This technique allows you to do this. Programmers call this *programming to the interface, not the implementation*. I just call it really cool!

The relationship between abstract and concrete classes is based on inheritance. Despite being extremely convenient, inheritance comes with a couple of risks:

- **Bloat**: Your concrete classes risk inheriting code from the abstract class that they won't need.
- **Dependency**: If you make a change to the abstract class, all the concrete classes that extend it will inherit that change. That might be just fine, but there's a risk that you could make a change that conflicts with code in the concrete classes. This could break your program. In a small project with just a few classes, you'll be able to track this down and fix it reasonably easily. In a big project with hundreds or possibly thousands of classes, it could be fatal.

> *As a safety check, you may prefer to use an interface. An interface is like an abstract class, but locks you into implementing a limited set of methods that can't be changed after you've established them. This is good, because it prevents your creativity from messing up your work. If you want to implement a new method, you'll need to create a new interface for it, and have your concrete class extend that new interface. This prevents you from changing code that's working fine. Interfaces only specify the methods that classes must use. They don't allow you to create default behaviors, and that's one big advantage that abstract classes have, and why they're still worth the risk. For a brief introduction to interfaces, see Chapter 1. For more details, refer to Adobe's online AS3.0 documentation,* ActionScript 3.0 Language and Components Reference, *and the book* Object-Oriented ActionScript 3.0 *by Todd Yard, Peter Elst, and Sas Jacobs (friends of ED, 2007).*

These potential dangers are why programmers tend to favor using composition over inheritance. However, you can mitigate much of this by using inheritance wisely. AS3.0's `Sprite` class, for example, is built on *six layers of inheritance*:

```
Sprite ➤ DisplayObjectContainer ➤ InteractiveObject ➤
DisplayObject ➤ EventDispatcher ➤ Object
```

So, obviously Adobe's engineers weren't afraid of this dependency when designing AS3.0.

You'll find many cases in your own work where inheritance is safe to use and the best solution to a problem. One of these cases is creating and using abstract classes.

Creating and implementing abstract classes

Now we're ready for some practical examples of how to create and implement abstract classes. We'll start with one for the Verlet motion code we've been using in the previous chapters.

Creating an abstract Verlet motion class

I spent a lot of time creating and testing the Verlet motion code that we've been using in the previous two chapters. Do I really want to rewrite all that code every time I have an object that uses Verlet integration? Of course not. I would rather just write the code once, and then tell other classes to use it if they need it. This is the perfect opportunity to use an abstract class.

In the chapter's source files, you'll find a folder called `Circle`. Run the SWF, and you'll see that it's a simple program that allows you to move a circle around the stage by using the arrow keys or clicking the stage with the mouse (see Figure 3-1).

Figure 3-1. Click anywhere on the stage or use the arrow keys to move the circle.

The circle is created using the `CircleModel` class and is displayed using the `CircleView` class. All the classes we'll be using in this chapter are in the `com/friendsofed/gameElements/primitives` folder. The `primitives` folder contains classes that form the very basis of game design elements, and you can use them to build many different kinds of objects for your games.

The `CircleModel` class extends another class called `AVerletModel`. `AVerletModel` contains all the essential methods and properties, like the venerable `update` method, that game objects need to use if they want to move around the stage using Verlet integration. It's an abstract class. If any other class wants to move around the stage, all it needs to do is extend `AVerletModel`.

Let's take a detailed look at `AVerletModel` and how `CircleModel` extends it. `AVerletModel` forms the basis of any motion system you may want to build yourself, so it's an important reference for you to have at hand between the covers of this book.

```
package com.friendsofed.gameElements.primitives
{
  import flash.events.Event;
  import flash.events.EventDispatcher;

  //ABSTRACT CLASS - Do not instantiate
  public class AVerletModel extends EventDispatcher
  {
    //Properties that don't require validation
    public var previousX:Number = 0;
    public var previousY:Number = 0;
    public var temporaryX:Number = 0;
    public var temporaryY:Number = 0;
    public var rotationSpeed:Number = 0;
    public var acceleration_X:Number = 0;
    public var acceleration_Y:Number = 0;
    public var acceleration:Number = 0;
    public var frictionConstant:Number = 0.96; //Global friction
    public var friction:Number = frictionConstant;
    public var friction_Vx:Number = 0;
    public var friction_Vy:Number = 0;
    public var width:uint = 1;
    public var height:uint = 1;
    public var gravity_Vx:Number = 0;
    public var gravity_Vy:Number = 0;
    public var color:uint = 0x999999;

    //Properties that require validation
    //by getters and setters
    private var _xPos:Number = 0;
    private var _yPos:Number = 0;
    private var _angle:Number = 0;
    private var _visible:Boolean = true;
    private var _rotationValue:Number = 0;

    public function AVerletModel():void
    {
    }

    public function update():void
    {
      temporaryX = xPos;
      temporaryY = yPos;

      vx += acceleration_X;
      vy += acceleration_Y;
```

```
  vx *= friction;
  vy *= friction;

  //Optional: speed trap
  /*
  if((Math.abs(vx) < 0.05) && (Math.abs(vy) < 0.05))
  {
    _acceleration_X = 0;
    _acceleration_Y = 0;
  }
  */

  xPos += vx + friction_Vx + gravity_Vx;
  yPos += vy + friction_Vy + gravity_Vy;

  previousX = temporaryX;
  previousY = temporaryY;

  //Listen for optional "update" events if you need to
  //synchronize any code with this object's frame updates
  dispatchEvent(new Event("update"));
}

//angle
public function get angle():Number
{
  return _angle;
}
public function set angle(value:Number):void
{
  _angle = value;
  dispatchEvent(new Event(Event.CHANGE));
}

//vx
public function get vx():Number
{
  return _xPos - previousX;
}
public function set vx(value:Number):void
{
  previousX = _xPos - value;
}
```

```
//vy
public function get vy():Number
{
  return _yPos - previousY;
}
public function set vy(value:Number):void
{
  previousY = _yPos - value;
}

//xPos
public function get xPos():Number
{
  return _xPos;
}
public function set xPos(value:Number):void
{
  _xPos = value;
  dispatchEvent(new Event(Event.CHANGE));
}

//yPos
public function get yPos():Number
{
  return _yPos;
}
public function set yPos(value:Number):void
{
  _yPos = value;
  dispatchEvent(new Event(Event.CHANGE));
}

//setX
public function set setX(value:Number):void
{
  previousX = value - vx;
  xPos = value;
}

//setY
public function set setY(value:Number):void
{
  previousY = value - vy;
  yPos = value;
}
```

```
    //visible
    public function get visible():Boolean
    {
      return _visible;
    }
    public function set visible(value:Boolean):void
    {
      _visible = value;
      dispatchEvent(new Event(Event.CHANGE));
    }

    //rotationValue
    public function get rotationValue():Number
    {
      return _rotationValue;
    }
    public function set rotationValue(value:Number):void
    {
      _rotationValue = value;
      if(_rotationValue > 360)
      {
        _rotationValue = 0;
      }
    }
  }
}
```

> *Note that the `frictionConstant` property was not created as a true constant because it could change during the game.*

You can see that this is a typical model class. It's a data storage object, with a specific method called `update` that helps process that data. You can tell it's an abstract class because of the uppercase `A` in the class name and the comment to remind you to not instantiate it.

```
//ABSTRACT CLASS - Do not instantiate
public class AVerletModel extends EventDispatcher
{...
```

One thing that's different from the model classes that we looked at in the previous two chapters is that the `update` method fires an `"update"` event.

```
dispatchEvent(new Event("update"));
```

This is important because sometimes your games will need to know exactly when a model is being updated, without needing to be informed of other `CHANGE` events. You'll see some examples of how this event is used in the chapters ahead.

We can use this abstract class to make a concrete class. The CircleModel class is such a class. It extends AVerletModel and adds its own new property, radius. Here's the CircleModel class.

```
package com.friendsofed.gameElements.primitives
{
  import flash.events.Event;
  import flash.events.EventDispatcher;

  public class CircleModel extends AVerletModel
  {
    private var _radius:Number = 0;

    public function CircleModel
      (radius:uint = 30, color:uint = 0x999999):void
    {
      this.radius = radius;
      this.color = color;
    }

    //radius
    public function get radius():uint
    {
      return _radius;
    }
    public function set radius(value:uint):void
    {
      _radius = value;
      this.width = radius * 2;
      this.height = radius * 2;
    }
  }
}
```

A quick glance at this code shows the main advantages of using an abstract class: It's brief and manageable! You won't need to exert any extra brain-strain sifting through AVerletModel. Because CircleModel extends AVerletModel, it inherits all of its properties.

You can see this clearly in the radius setter. CircleModel doesn't contain its own height or width properties. this.height and this.width refer to the height and width properties invisibly inherited from AVerletModel. (The use of the keyword this is optional.)

CircleModel is a concrete class. And, like any good concrete class, it adds a new property, radius, which is specific to circles.

We have the circle's model. The next step is to create its view.

Creating an abstract view class

As I'm sure you're already noticed, there are many repetitive methods required to display an object on the stage. It makes a lot of sense to create a general abstract view class that *all* display objects can use. This will save us the tedium of typing those laborious ADDED_TO_STAGE and REMOVED_FROM_STAGE events over and over again. Better just to set them up once and forget about them. Let's do it!

The primitives folder contains an AVerletView class that does just this.

```
package com.friendsofed.gameElements.primitives
{
  import flash.display.*;
  import flash.events.Event;

  //ABSTRACT CLASS - Do not instantiate
  public class AVerletView extends Sprite
  {
    private var _shape:Shape;

    //Variable that refers to the model.
    //Note that it's "protected"
    //so that it can be accessed by other classes
    //in this same package, but not outside it
    protected var model:Object;

    public function AVerletView(verletModel:AVerletModel):void
    {
      model = verletModel;
      model.addEventListener(Event.CHANGE, changeHandler);
      addEventListener(Event.ADDED_TO_STAGE, addedToStagHandler);
    }

    private function addedToStagHandler(event:Event):void
    {
      //Draw the object
      draw();

      //Position the object
      this.x = model.xPos;
      this.y = model.yPos;

      //Add listeners
      addEventListener
        (Event.REMOVED_FROM_STAGE, removedFromStageHandler);
    }
```

```
    private function removedFromStageHandler(event:Event):void
    {
      removeEventListener
        (Event.ADDED_TO_STAGE, addedToStagHandler);
      removeEventListener
        (Event.REMOVED_FROM_STAGE, removedFromStageHandler);
    }

    //The draw method is also protected
    protected function draw():void
    {
    }

    protected function changeHandler(event:Event):void
    {
      this.x = model.xPos;
      this.y = model.yPos;

      //If any of your objects use rotation, add this line:
      this.rotation = model.angle;

      //If any of your objects depend on visibility, use this:
      this.visible = model.visible;
    }
  }
}
```

The `model` property is declared as `protected`.

```
protected var model:Object;
```

`protected` properties can be accessed by the class in which they've been declared and in any subclasses that extend this class. The `CircleView` class extends `AVerletView`, so it will need to access the `model` property.

You'll also notice that `model` is typed as `Object`. I've done this just to improve the readability of the code a little. Strictly speaking, it should be typed as `AVerletModel`, like this:

```
protected var model:AVerletModel;
```

However, if it's typed as `AVerletModel`, you will need to explicitly cast the children of `AVerletModel` when you want to use their specific properties in other classes. I know that sounds confusing! Let's look at a practical example.

The `CircleModel` class extends `AVerletModel`. But `CircleModel` also adds a property called `radius`. If you want to use the `model` object's `radius` property in a class that extends `AVerletView`, you will need to use code that looks like this: `CircleModel(model).radius`. This is **casting**. It forces the `model` object to be interpreted as a `CircleModel` and not as its parent, `AVerletModel`. By typing `model` as `Object`, you don't need to cast it. You just refer to the `model`'s `radius` property directly, like this: `model.radius`.

> *Typing `model` as `Object` works because `Object` is a **dynamic class**. Dynamic classes aren't picky about any properties that you attempt to access on objects. This is convenient, but could lead to problems if you try to access properties that don't exist. I'll leave it for you to decide how important this might be in your own code. I'll discuss dynamic classes in much greater detail in later chapters.*

The `draw` method is also `protected`. And, strangely, it doesn't include any directives.

```
protected function draw():void
{
}
```

Again, it's `protected` so that the `CircleView` class can use it. It's been left blank so that the `CircleView` class can override the `draw` method and add its own directives. The `AVerletView` class does the job of calling the `draw` method when it's created but leaves the specific details of what to actually draw for `CircleView` to fill in. The `CircleView` class will draw a circle, but another class that extends `AVerletView` could draw another shape.

This is typical of how abstract classes should be coded. They should be as general as possible, but if there's a method that all concrete classes will use, it should be included, even if that method doesn't contain any directives. `AVerletView` also takes over the mundane tasks of positioning the object on the stage and implementing the `changeHandler` that listens for changes in the model. These are tasks that are common to all Verlet view objects.

Creating a concrete CircleView class

With the abstract class ready to go, we can now extend it to make specific objects, like circles, particles, and rectangles. The concrete `CircleView` class does just that.

```
package com.friendsofed.gameElements.primitives
{
  import flash.display.Shape;
  import flash.filters.*;

  public class CircleView extends AVerletView
  {
    public function CircleView(circleModel:CircleModel):void
    {
      super(circleModel);
    }
    override protected function draw():void
    {
      var shape:Shape = new Shape();
      shape.graphics.lineStyle(1);
      shape.graphics.beginFill(model.color);
```

```
            shape.graphics.drawCircle(0, 0, model.radius);
            shape.graphics.endFill();
            addChild(shape);
        }
    }
}
```

It's delightfully succinct, because most of the work is done by the superclass, `AVerletView`.

The `CircleView` class takes one parameter: a `CircleModel` object. It needs to send that parameter back to `AVerletView` to be processed. The `super` method does this work.

```
super(circleModel);
```

`super` is used to send information from a subclass to a parent superclass. In this case, `circleModel` will be fed directly into `AVerletView`'s constructor parameters.

You can use `super` whenever a subclass needs to communicate with its superclass. It comes in two forms. `super()` is used to specifically call the superclass's constructor method. You can pass any arguments to the superclass that you need to, as long as they match the number of parameters and the class type. You can use this only once in the class, in the constructor method, and never again. If you don't add `super()` yourself, the compiler will do it for you automatically. This means that the superclass's constructor method will *always* be called, whether you want it to be or not. But don't worry—that's a good thing! It's part of why inheritance is so convenient.

The other form is `super.`*`methodName`*`()`, which you can use to target a specific method in the superclass. You may have a case where a subclass wants to use a superclass's default method, but add a few directives of its own. You can do this using the `super` keyword. Imagine that the superclass has a method called `display`. It has a default directive that traces some text.

```
protected function display():void
{
  trace("Hello from the superclass!");
}
```

The subclass has its own `display` method, but it wants to also use the existing directive from the superclass. Here's how it can do that:

```
override protected function display():void
{
  super.display();
  trace("Hello from the subclass!");
}
```

This will trace like this:

```
Hello from the superclass!
Hello from the subclass!
```

The superclass's directives will run first, followed by the subclass's directives.

Do you recall that the `draw` method in `AVerletView` was `protected`? `CircleView` can use that method and insert its own directives using the `override` keyword.

```
override protected function draw():void
{…
```

`override` tells the complier, "Ignore the superclass's `draw` method and use the directives in my `draw` method instead."

Keyboard and mouse control

The `Circle` application class does the job of composing all of the elements and displaying the `CircleView` object, `_c1`, on the stage. It's a typical MVC system.

```
private var _c1:CircleModel = new CircleModel(30);
private var _UIController:UIController = new UIController(_c1);
private var _c1_View:CircleView = new CircleView(_c1);
private var _UIView:UIView = new UIView(_c1, _UIController, stage);
```

But there's one big difference between this implementation of the MVC and those we looked at in previous chapters: *The circle has two views*.

As I mentioned in Chapter 1, the keyboard and mouse input are a kind of view. Because of this, it often makes sense to split the visual view and the input view into two separate classes. This keeps them modular so you can easily change your input system if necessary.

The input view in this application is called `UIView`. It accepts input from the mouse and keyboard, and sends it to the controller for processing. Again, so that you have a reference at hand to create a similar class of your own, here's the complete `UIView` class:

```
package com.friendsofed.gameElements.primitives
{
  import flash.display.Sprite;

  //Keyboard Events
  import flash.events.Event;
  import flash.events.KeyboardEvent;
  import flash.ui.Keyboard;

  //Mouse Event
  import flash.events.MouseEvent;

  public class UIView extends Sprite
  {
    private var _model:Object;
    private var _controller:Object;
    private var _stage:Object;
```

```
    public function UIView
      (
        model:AVerletModel,
        controller:UIController,
        stage:Object
      ):void
    {
      this._model = model;
      this._controller = controller;
      this._stage = stage;

      _stage.addEventListener
        (KeyboardEvent.KEY_DOWN,keyDownHandler);
      _stage.addEventListener
        (KeyboardEvent.KEY_UP,keyUpHandler);
      _stage.addEventListener
        (MouseEvent.MOUSE_DOWN, mouseDownHandler);
      _stage.addEventListener
        (MouseEvent.MOUSE_UP, mouseUpHandler);
    }
    private function keyDownHandler(event:KeyboardEvent):void
    {
      _controller.processKeyDown(event);
    }
    private function keyUpHandler(event:KeyboardEvent):void
    {
      _controller.processKeyUp(event);
    }
    private function mouseDownHandler(event:MouseEvent):void
    {
      _controller.processMouseDown(event, _stage);
    }
    private function mouseUpHandler(event:MouseEvent):void
    {
      _controller.processMouseUp(event);
    }
  }
```

If you needed to, you could further separate keyboard and mouse input views into their own classes.

The `UIController` class has the job of processing all this input. Its methods are declared as `internal` because it needs to share them only with classes that are part of its same package.

```
package com.friendsofed.gameElements.primitives
{
  import flash.events.KeyboardEvent;
  import flash.ui.Keyboard;
  import flash.events.MouseEvent;
```

```
public class UIController
{
  private const EASING:Number = 0.1;
  private var _model:Object;
  private var _stage:Object;

  public function UIController(model:AVerletModel):void
  {
    _model = model;
  }

  internal function processKeyDown(event:KeyboardEvent):void
  {
    _model.friction = 1;
    if(event.keyCode == Keyboard.LEFT)
    {
      _model.acceleration_X = -0.1;
    }
    if(event.keyCode == Keyboard.RIGHT)
    {
      _model.acceleration_X = 0.1;
    }
    if(event.keyCode == Keyboard.UP)
    {
      _model.acceleration_Y = -0.1;
    }
    if(event.keyCode == Keyboard.DOWN)
    {
      _model.acceleration_Y = 0.1;
    }
  }

  internal function processKeyUp(event:KeyboardEvent):void
  {
    if(event.keyCode == Keyboard.LEFT
    ||(event.keyCode == Keyboard.RIGHT))
    {
      _model.acceleration_X = 0;
    }
    if(event.keyCode == Keyboard.UP
    ||(event.keyCode == Keyboard.DOWN))
    {
      _model.acceleration_Y = 0;
    }
    _model.friction = _model.frictionConstant;
  }
```

```
    internal function processMouseDown
      (event:MouseEvent, stage:Object):void
    {
      _model.friction = 1;

      //Calculate the distance from the object to the mouse
      var vx:Number = stage.mouseX - _model.xPos;
      var vy:Number = stage.mouseY - _model.yPos;

      //Optimized easing (does away with Math.sqrt)
      var m:Number = vx * vx + vy * vy;
      var range:uint = 1;

      //Move the object if it is more than 1 pixel away from the mouse
      if (m >= range * range)
      {
        _model.vx += (stage.mouseX - _model.xPos) * EASING / 2;
        _model.vy += (stage.mouseY - _model.yPos) * EASING / 2;
      }
    }
    internal function processMouseUp(event:MouseEvent):void
    {
      _model.friction = _model.frictionConstant;
    }
  }
}
```

The mouse movement works using a standard easing formula. Usually, `Math.sqrt` is used to calculate the distance from the object to the mouse, like this:

```
var m:Number = Math.sqrt(vx * vx + vy * vy);
if (m >= 1)
{...
```

If the distance from the mouse to the object is greater than 1 pixel, then ease the object to the new position.

This works just fine, but `Math.sqrt` happens to be one of the most processor-intensive math functions you can use. If there's any way to avoid it, you should, because you'll gain a noticeable performance boost.

`UIController` uses an optimized formula for calculating distance. It adds an extra variable into the mix, but does away with `Math.sqrt`.

```
var m:Number = vx * vx + vy * vy;
var limit:uint = 1;
if (m >= limit * limit)
{...
```

How does this do away with Math.sqrt? Let's put in some real numbers and see how they turn out. Here's what the unoptimized version of the formula looks like with 50 as the vx and vy values:

```
var m:Number = Math.sqrt(50 * 50 + 50 * 50);
m = 70
```

The distance from the mouse to the center of the object is 70.

We need another number to tell us the range in which to activate easing. To make this example clearer, let's say the range is 20.

```
if (70 >= 20)
{
  //… ease the object
```

Now here's the optimized version:

```
var m:Number = 50 * 50 + 50 * 50;
m = 5000
```

The distance of 5000 is, of course, nowhere near 70. However, this is compensated for because the code multiplies the value of range by itself.

```
if (5000 >= range * range)
{…
```

If range is 20, the if statement will look like this:

```
if (5000 >= 400)
{…
```

Now you may be thinking that the ratio between 5000 and 400 is completely different than the ratio between 70 and 20. You would be right.

```
5000 / 400 = 12.5
70 / 20 = 3.5
```

However, 3.5 squared is 12.25. And what's the square root of 5000? You guessed it, 70!

```
3.5 * 3.5 = 12.25
Math.sqrt(5000) = 70
```

Yes, I know, it's a bit of a brain-twister, but it works!

In the UIController class, the value of range is 1.

```
var m:Number = vx * vx + vy * vy;
var range:uint = 1;
if (m >= range * range)
{…
```

One multiplied by one also equals one, so unless your `range` was another number, you can actually skip the additional multiplication step in the conditional statement and just use 1.

If you are using another number, such as 20, you could precalculate the value—20 times 20 equals 400.

```
if (m >= 400)
{…
```

This is a very small optimization, but if you are performing this calculation on hundreds of objects each frame, you will notice a performance improvement.

Enough theory for now! Let's go back to doing what game designers love to do most: figuring out cool new ways to smash objects together! We'll start with a couple of circles.

Collision-handling basics

At the end of the previous chapter, we took a detailed look at how to handle collisions between a particle and a line. A particle is essentially just a one-dimensional object, without height or width. However, most objects in your games will have height and width.

Circles are a good place to start because the height and width of a circle are equal. A circle's **radius** is the distance between the center of the circle and its edge. The radius is both the circle's height *and* width. Because the dimensions of a circle are even all the way around, collision detection involving circles is simpler by about half than dealing with collisions between bulky polygons like rectangles and triangles.

Circle collisions fall into two categories:

- Collisions between moving circles and stationary circles
- Collisions between moving circles

The solutions to these two types of collision problems are related, but the second problem is a little more complex. So let's first take a look at the easiest problem to solve: collision between a moving circle and one that isn't moving.

Collisions between moving and stationary circles

Run the SWF file called `CircleVsCircle` in the chapter's source files. You'll see two circles on the stage. With the mouse or keyboard, bump one circle into the other. You'll see that there's a precise collision, and the circle bounces away at the correct angle, as shown in Figure 3-2.

You may be surprised at how trivial the code that does this is actually is. We've done most of the hard work of calculating distance and bounce vectors in the previous chapter, so we can just recycle that code here. Also, all of our motion code is tucked away in other classes (The `AVerletModel` class), so we don't need to bother with any of that either. The application class must deal with only the specific problem of collision detection and reaction, and that makes for easy coding.

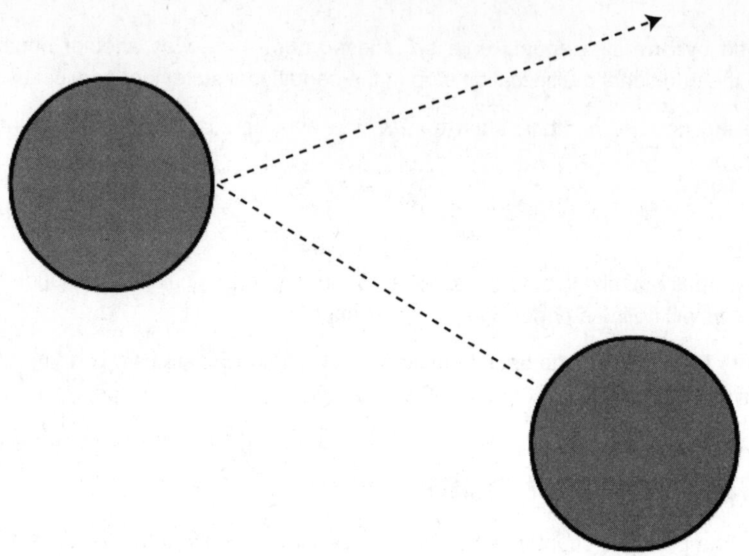

Figure 3-2. The player's circle hits the stationary circle and bounces away at the correct angle.

Here's the entire CircleVsCircle application class:

```
package
{
  import flash.events.Event;
  import flash.display.Sprite;
  import com.friendsofed.utils.*;
  import com.friendsofed.gameElements.primitives.*;
  import com.friendsofed.vector.*;

  [SWF(width="550", height="400",
  backgroundColor="#FFFFFF", frameRate="60")]

  public class CircleVsCircle extends Sprite
  {
    //Circle 1 (player's circle)
    private var _c1:CircleModel
      = new CircleModel(30);
    private var _UIController:UIController
      = new UIController(_c1);
    private var _c1_View:CircleView
      = new CircleView(_c1);
    private var _UIView:UIView
      = new UIView(_c1, _UIController, stage);
```

```
//Circle 2
private var _c2:CircleModel = new CircleModel(30);
private var _c2_View:CircleView = new CircleView(_c2);

//Status box
private var _statusBox:StatusBox = new StatusBox;

public function CircleVsCircle():void
{
  //Circle 1
  addChild(_c1_View);
  _c1.setX = 300;
  _c1.setY = 200;0

  //Circle 2
  addChild(_c2_View);
  _c2.setX = 200;
  _c2.setY = 200;

  //Add the status box
  addChild(_statusBox);

  addEventListener(Event.ENTER_FRAME, enterFrameHandler);
}

private function enterFrameHandler(event:Event):void
{
  //Update c1 (player's circle)
  _c1.update();
  StageBoundaries.wrap(_c1, stage);

  //Update c2
  _c2.update();
  StageBoundaries.wrap(_c2, stage);

  //Vector between the circles
  var v0:VectorModel
    = new VectorModel(_c1.xPos, _c1.yPos, _c2.xPos, _c2.yPos);

  //Calculate the radii of both circles combined
  var totalRadii:Number = _c1.radius + _c2.radius;

  if(v0.m < totalRadii)
  {
    //A collision is happening.
    //Find the amount of overlap between circles
    var overlap:Number = totalRadii - v0.m;

    _c1.setX = _c1.xPos - (overlap * v0.dx);
    _c1.setY = _c1.yPos - (overlap * v0.dy);
```

```
        //_c1's motion vector
        var v1:VectorModel
          = new VectorModel
          (
             _c1.xPos,
             _c1.yPos,
             _c1.xPos + _c1.vx,
             _c1.yPos + _c1.vy
          );

        //Create c1's bounce vector
        var bounce_C1:VectorModel = VectorMath.bounce(v1, v0.ln);

        //Bounce _c1
        _c1.vx = bounce_C1.vx;
        _c1.vy = bounce_C1.vy;
      }
      else
      {
        //No collision
      }

      //Update status box
      _statusBox.text = "CIRCLE VS CIRCLE:";
    }
  }
}
```

In this example, first we plot a vector called v0 between the centers of both circles.

```
var v0:VectorModel = new VectorModel(_c1.xPos, _c1.yPos, _c2.xPos, _c2.yPos);
```

We need to know the combined radii (the half widths) of the circles. (To keep this code as clear as possible, I've created this as a local variable in the enterFrameHandler, but you should almost certainly precalculate this value if you don't expect the radii of the circles to change during the course of the game.)

```
var totalRadii:Number = _c1.radius + _c2.radius;
```

When the magnitude of the v0 vector is less than the combined radii (half widths) of the circles, then a collision has occurred, as shown in Figure 3-3.

```
if(v0.m < totalRadii)
{
  //A collision is happening
```

Next, we figure out the amount of overlap between the circles, as shown in Figure 3-4.

```
var overlap:Number = totalRadii - v0.m;
```

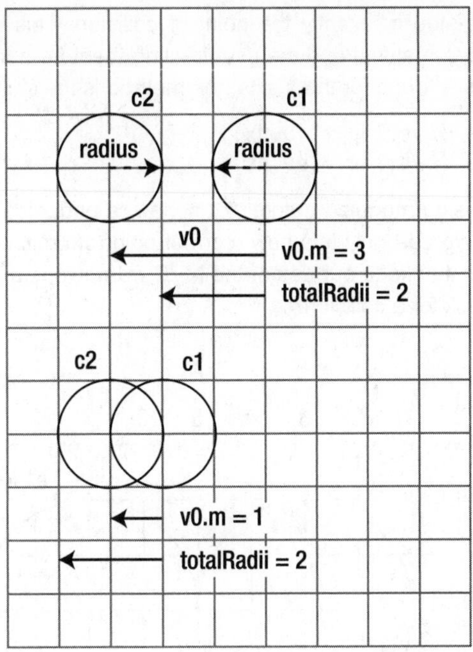

Figure 3-3. A collision occurs when the magnitude of the vector between the circles is less than their combined radii.

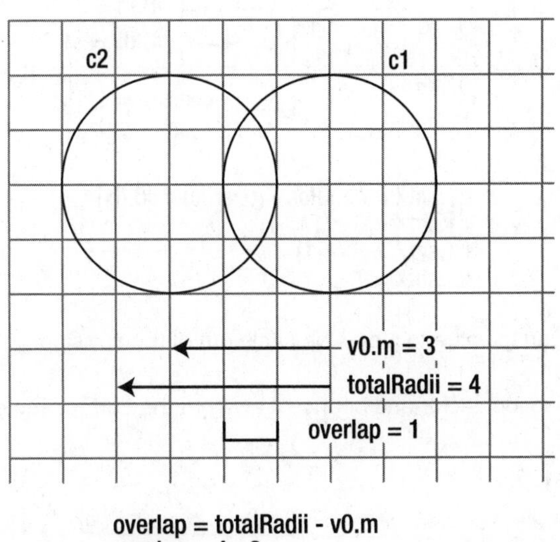

Figure 3-4. Find the amount of overlap.

Then we make the circle stop at exactly the point of collision. This is done by multiplying the overlap with v0's dx and dy values, and then subtracting them from the circle's current position. Figure 3-5 shows how this is found for the x axis (the method is the same for the y axis).

```
_c1.setX = _c1.xPos - (overlap * v0.dx);
_c1.setY = _c1.yPos - (overlap * v0.dy);
```

Because the collision is being modeled before _c1's view is updated, we never see any overlap when the circles collide. We see only this new, correct point of contact between them. This very clean collision detection is thanks to our use of the MVC framework, and because we're updating the models before we check for a collision.

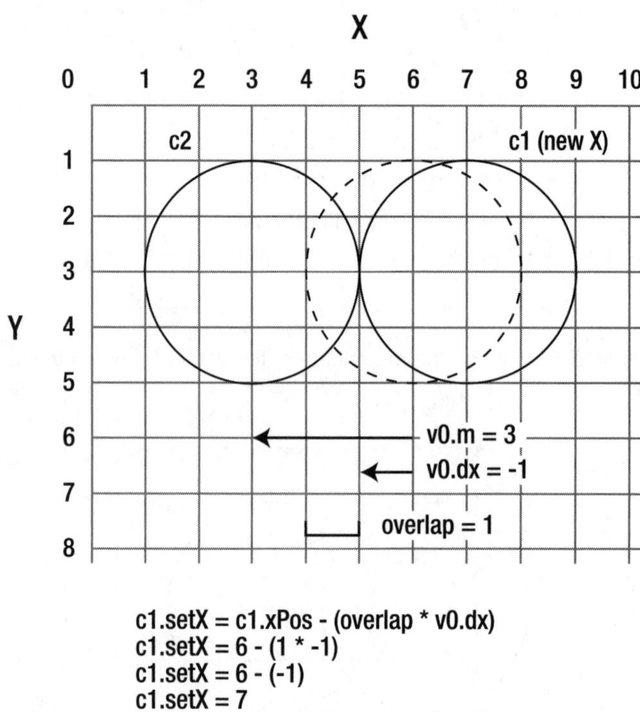

Figure 3-5. Use the overlap value to move the circle out of the collision.

Finally, we find _c1's motion vector and bounce it away at the correct angle.

```
var v1:VectorModel
  = new VectorModel
  (
    _c1.xPos,
    _c1.yPos,
    _c1.xPos + _c1.vx,
    _c1.yPos + _c1.vy
);
```

```
var bounce_C1:VectorModel = VectorMath.bounce(v1, v0.ln);

_c1.vx = bounce_C1.vx;
_c1.vy = bounce_C1.vy;
```

The code uses a clever trick to bounce the circle away at the correct angle. Imagine that the circle is hitting a wall created by v0's normal. (Take a quick look back at Chapter 2 if you need a refresher on vector normals.) All we need to do is bounce _c1's motion vector against this imaginary wall. It's the same solution to the problem of bouncing the particle against the line in the previous chapter. The only difference is that we can't "see" the line that the circle is bouncing against. It just exists mathematically. Figure 3-6 shows what this imaginary wall created by v0's normal would look like if it were visible.

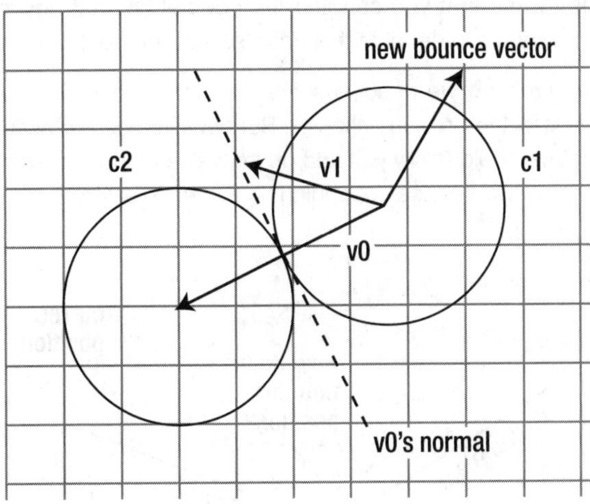

Figure 3-6. The new bounce vector is found by bouncing the circle's motion vector (v1) against the invisible wall created by the normal of the vector between the two circles (v0).

You can use this trick any time you need to bounce an object at any angle. Just create a vector, at whatever inclination you need, and bounce the object's motion vector against it. The vector doesn't even need coordinates on the stage—any vx and vy values will do the trick. It works like a charm!

Collision between a circle and a line

We finished Chapter 2 with a look at how to detect a collision between a particle and a line. Your games will probably more likely require you to find out what to do when a solid object, like a circle, hits a line.

Although we've already done most of the heavy lifting in the previous chapter, collision detection between circles and lines comes with its own special problems:

- How do you find the closest point of contact between the circle and the line?
- What happens when the circle hits the corners of the line?
- How should the circle react when it hits a corner?

We're going to solve each of these problems one at a time in a way that builds on the code we've already written and paves the way for solving other interesting problems ahead.

Finding the point of contact

There are actually many ways that you can find the point of contact between a circle and a line. We're going to look at two ways in detail in this chapter and the next.

Figure 3-7 illustrates the problem we need to solve. The center point of the circle is really just the particle that we were using in the previous chapter. But now we need to account for the radius of the circle. You may think that we could easily just add on the value of the circle's radius to find the contact point, but we can't. That point will change depending on the angle at which the circle hits the line.

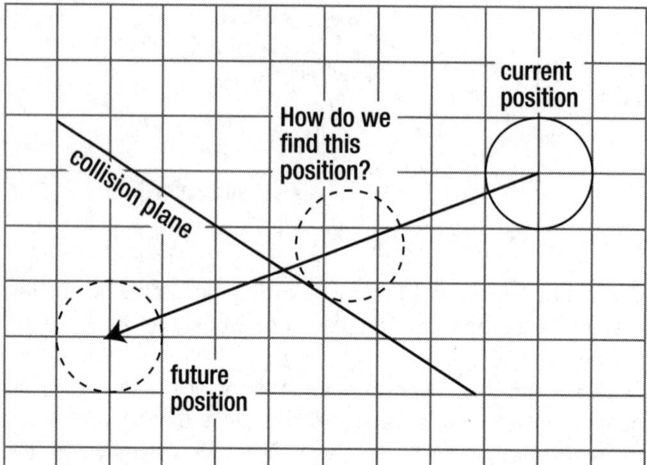

Figure 3-7. How do you find the point of contact between the circle and the line?

But there's something interesting that you might notice if you stare at Figure 3-7 long enough. Draw a vector from the center of the circle to its closest point of contact on the collision plane. It will look like the single spoke of a bicycle wheel. That vector happens to be exactly parallel to the collision plane's normal, as illustrated in Figure 3-8.

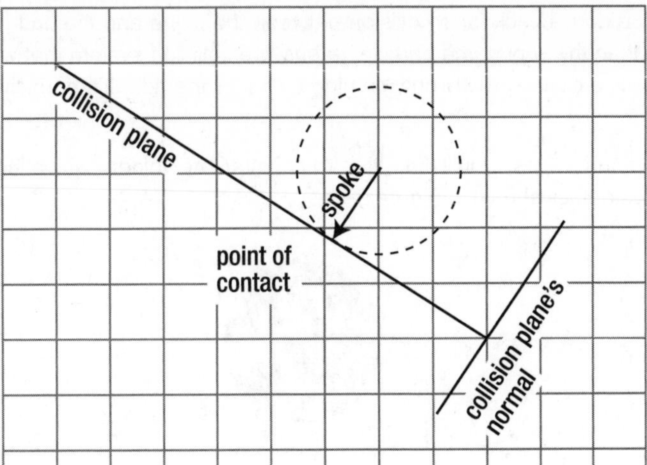

Figure 3-8. The vector from the center of the circle to its edge is parallel to the collision plane's normal.

And (drum roll please!) that means the point of collision is at the very end of that spoke. If you know what the collision plane's normal is, and you know the distance from the end of the spoke to the collision plane, you can work out the point of contact. This turns out to be true no matter what angles are involved.

As you can see from Figure 3-8, if we can create this spoke vector, we'll always know where the point of collision between the circle and the plane will be. But how can we create it?

There are two things we know about this spoke vector:

- Its magnitude is exactly the same as the circle's radius.
- Its angle is exactly the same as the collision plane's normal.

This means we can take the collision plane's normal and scale it to the magnitude of the circle's radius. Here's the simple formula to do this:

```
spoke_Vx = circlesRadius * collisionPlane.ln.dx;
spoke_Vy = circlesRadius * collisionPlane.ln.dy;
```

This is the standard formula for scaling vectors that we looked at in Chapter 2. It gives you a vector that's the same magnitude as the circle's radius, but points in the direction of the collision plane's normal. It's like a spoke of a bicycle wheel, but one that *always* points toward the ground, like a plumb line.

Now all we need to do is check for a collision between the plane and the end point of this spoke. It's nothing more than the very same particle-versus-line collision system that we examined at the end of Chapter 2. The circle is really only coming along for the ride. It's bouncing like a child on a pogo stick.

In the chapter's source files, you'll find the `CircleVsLine` folder, which contains a working example of this system, as shown in Figure 3-9.

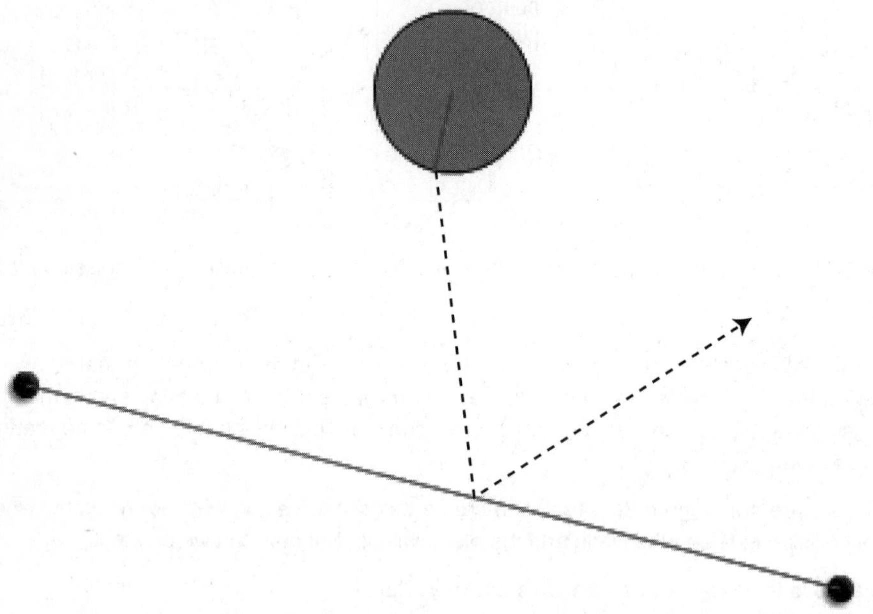

Figure 3-9. Calculate the collision from the end point of the spoke.

Run the SWF and change the inclination of the collision plane. You'll notice that the circle's spoke always changes its angle to match the angle of the collision plane's normal, so the collision point is always correct.

You'll be happy to know that we need to make only minor changes to our particle-versus-line collision code to implement this system. Except for this new code, the rest of the code is identical to the code in the previous example in Chapter 2.

First, we need to create the spoke vector that runs from the center of the circle to its edge. In the `CircleVsLine` application class, this vector is called `v0`. The spoke needs to know which side of the line the circle is on so that it points in the correct direction. If the circle is on the left side of the line, the spoke aligns according to the collision plane's left normal. If it's on the right side, it uses the right normal.

```
if(_lineSide == "" || _lineSide == "left")
{
  _v0.update
    (
      _circleModel.xPos,
      _circleModel.yPos,
      _circleModel.xPos + _v2.rn.dx * _circleModel.radius,
      _circleModel.yPos + _v2.rn.dy * _circleModel.radius
    );
}
else
{
  _v0.update
    (
      _circleModel.xPos,
      _circleModel.yPos,
      _circleModel.xPos + _v2.ln.dx * _circleModel.radius,
      _circleModel.yPos + _v2.ln.dy * _circleModel.radius
    );
}
```

Now instead of calculating the circle's velocity (`_v1`) from its center, calculate it *from the end of the spoke* (`v0`'s point B).

```
_v1.update
(
  _v0.b.x,
  _v0.b.y,
  _v0.b.x + _circleModel.vx,
  _v0.b.y + _circleModel.vy
);
```

And that's all there is to it!

However, there is one big flaw in this system that I'm sure you've noticed if you ran the SWF. The circle doesn't know when it has hit one of the corners of the line. If it hits a corner, it will either fall through or flip sides on the line if the angle is shallow enough, as shown in Figure 3-10.

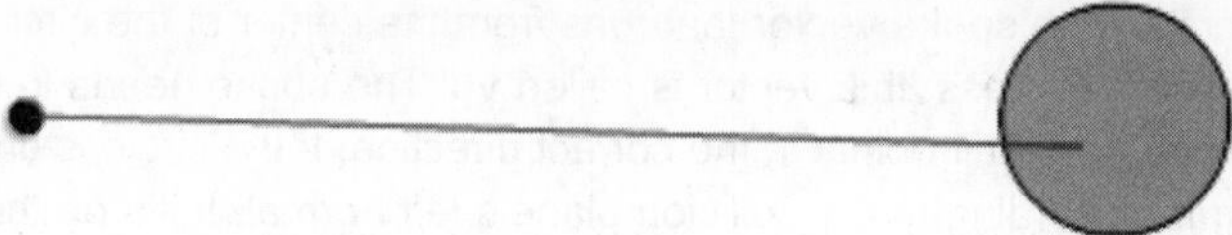

Figure 3-10. The circle can't detect the corners of the line.

As it turns out, collision with "the corners of the line" needs to be handled using a different type of collision detection altogether.

You can think of the single point that defines the very edge of the line as a particle. That means that our line is actually made up of three distinct pieces:

- A particle that represents point A (the start of the line)
- A vector between point A and point B (the end of the line)
- A particle that represents point B

So far, we've addressed how to resolve the collision with the vector between the points. To handle the other two parts, we need to solve another kind of collision-detection problem: collisions between a circle and a particle.

But hey, we've already done that! A particle is really just a circle with a radius of 1, as illustrated in Figure 3-11. We can use exactly the same technique that we used to solve our circle-versus-circle collision problem.

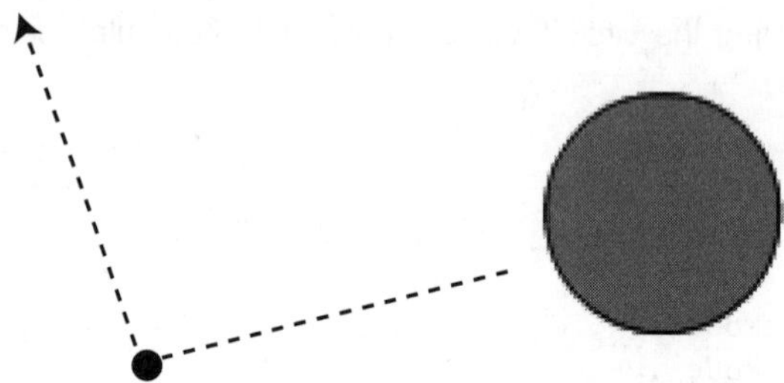

Figure 3-11. A particle is just a circle with a radius of 1.

The circle hits the one-dimensional particle and bounces off in the right direction.

Finding the edge of the line

We've solved the first two problems of circle-versus-line collisions, and have only one left to tackle: How does the circle know whether it should check for a collision with the line or with one of the corners?

The solution to this problem depends on knowing whether the circle is within the region of space defined by the left and right sides of the line or just outside it. If the circle is within the region, then we need to solve a circle-versus-line collision problem. If it's outside the region, it becomes a circle-versus-particle collision problem. Figure 3-12 illustrates this.

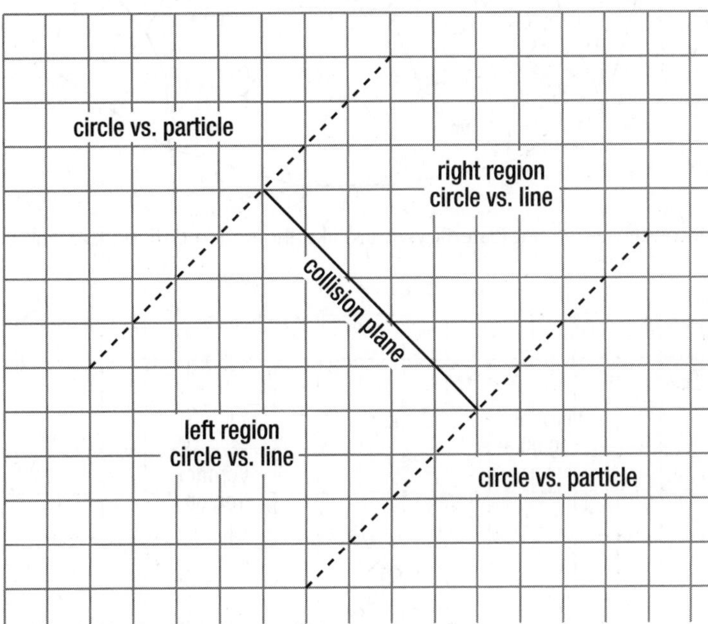

Figure 3-12. Change the type of collision system depending on which region the circle resides.

The kind of "region of space" that we're interested in is called a **Voronoi region** (named after Russian mathematician G. F. Voronoi). You may run across this term if you do much reading outside the pages of this book. A simple way to understand Voronoi regions is as honeycombs or a cluster of soap bubbles. The space inside each honeycomb or bubble is a Voronoi region, as illustrated in Figure 3-13.

For the purposes of this book, however, we can simplify this concept. You can think of a Voronoi region as the space defined by a vector and its normal. Take a look at Figure 3-14, and you'll see that it's a pretty easy concept to grasp, Figure 3-14 shows that you can use the collision plane and its normals to divide the space up into four Voronoi regions. These regions are easily defined by the vector math concepts we covered in Chapter 2.

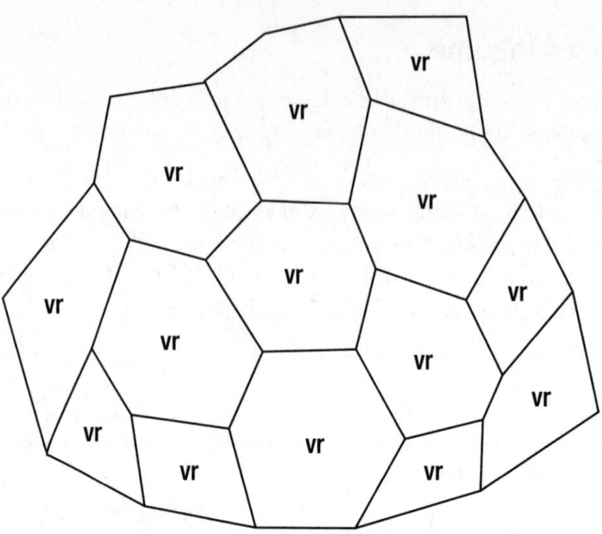

Figure 3-13. Voronoi regions, indicated by vr, are like the space defined by soap bubbles or honeycombs.

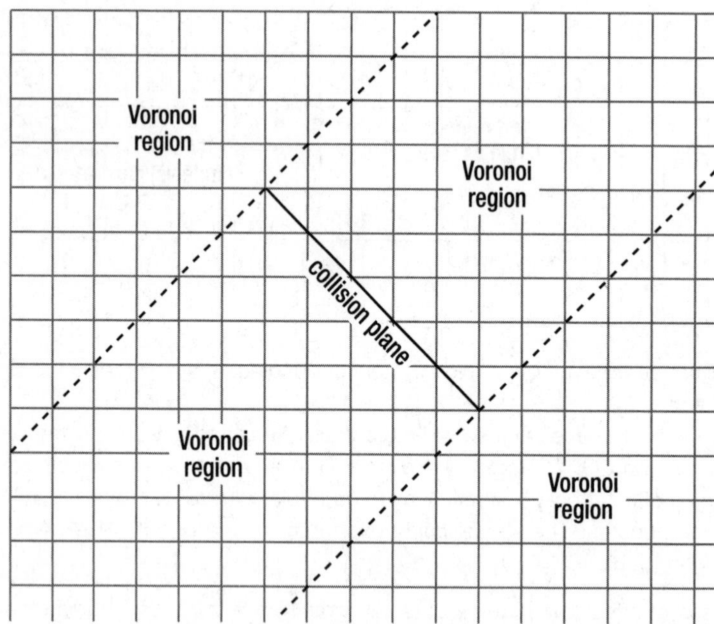

Figure 3-14. The collision plane and its normal can be used to define four Voronoi regions.

Voronoi regions are especially helpful in efficiently detecting collisions between circles and polygons, like rectangles and triangles. They allow you to apply a different collision strategy depending on the region where the object resides. We'll be taking a closer look at how to calculate them in Chapter 4.

For now, it's enough that our line-versus-particle code from the previous chapter already does the job of finding out which region the circle occupies. Let's do a quick review of those concepts.

First, the code knows whether the object is on the left side or right side of the line. In the example code that we've been using, `v2` is a vector that represents the collision plane. Another vector called `v3` runs from the end of the spoke (`v0`) to the start of the collision plane, as shown in Figure 3-15.

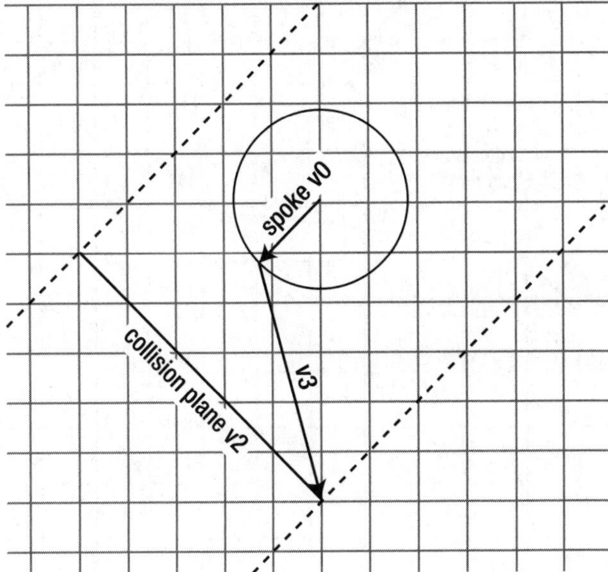

Figure 3-15. A vector called v3 runs between the end of the spoke and the start of the collision plane. The dot product between v3 and v2.ln tells you on which side of the collision plane the end of the spoke is located.

If the dot product between `v3` and `v2`'s left normal (`v2.ln`) is greater than zero, then the end of the spoke is on the left side of the collision plane. If the dot product is less than zero, then the end of the spoke is on the right side. Figure 3-16 illustrates how this works. This is the same basic collision code that we covered in Chapter 2.

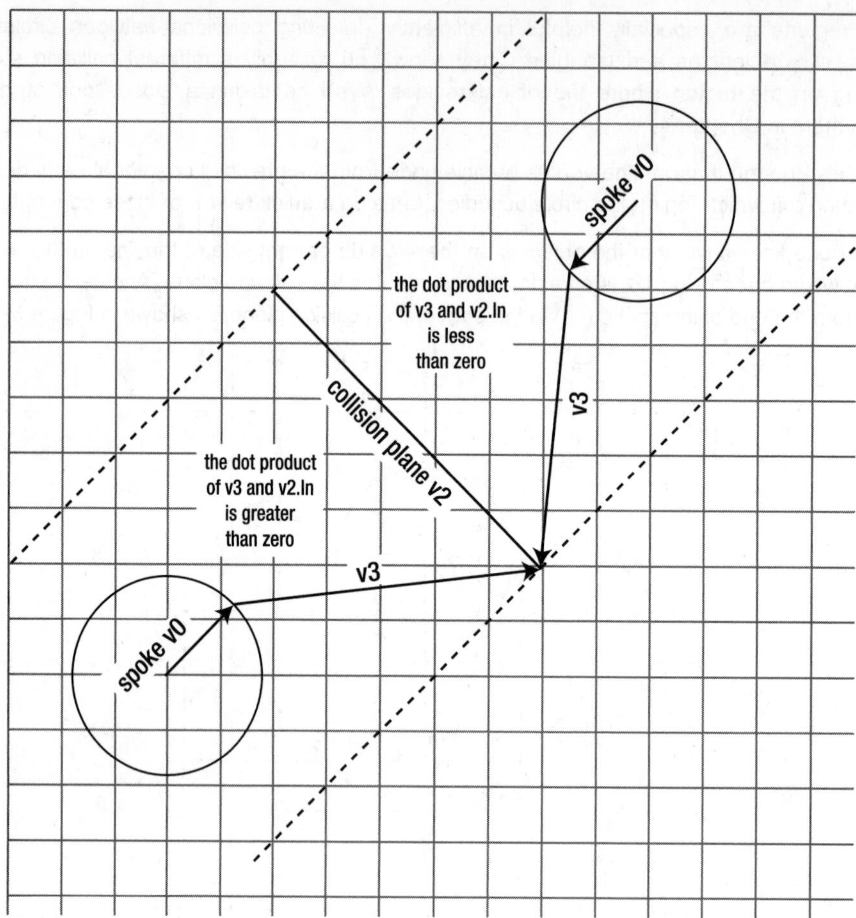

Figure 3-16. Use the dot product between v3 and v2.ln to find out on which side of the collision plane the circle is located.

The code also knows whether the object is beyond the start and end point of the collision plane. This is also worth a quick review.

The code calculates another dot product, between `v3` and `v2`. If this dot product is greater than zero, then the end of the spoke is beyond the collision plane's start point. If this dot product is greater than `v2`'s negative magnitude (`-v2.m`), then it's beyond the collision plane's end point. Figure 3-17 illustrates these concepts.

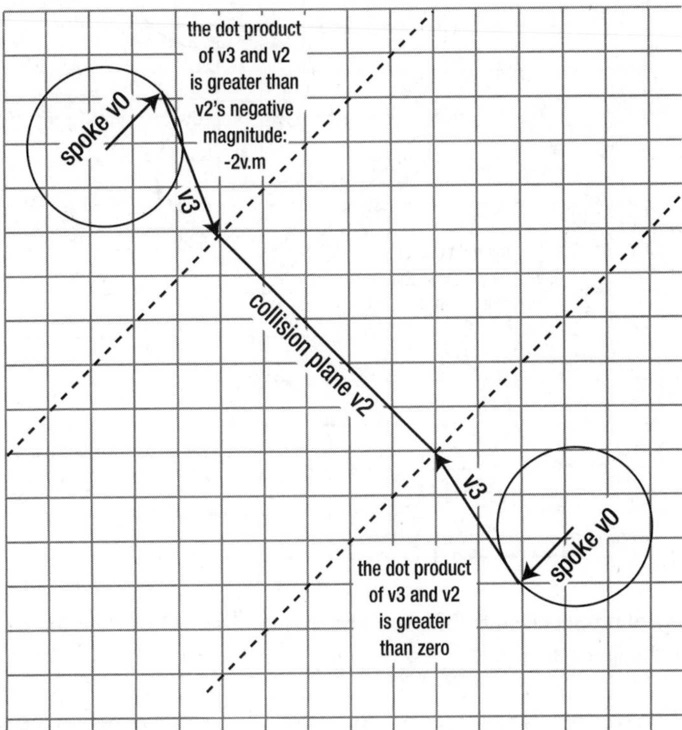

Figure 3-17. Use the dot product between v3 and v2 to find out whether the circle is beyond the collision plane's start and end points.

The flip side of this is that you can tell whether the circle is within the collision plane's start and end points This will be true if the dot product is greater than `-v2.m` and less than zero, as illustrated in Figure 3-18. The code that checks for this in the examples looks like this:

```
dp1 > -_v2.m && dp1 < 0
```

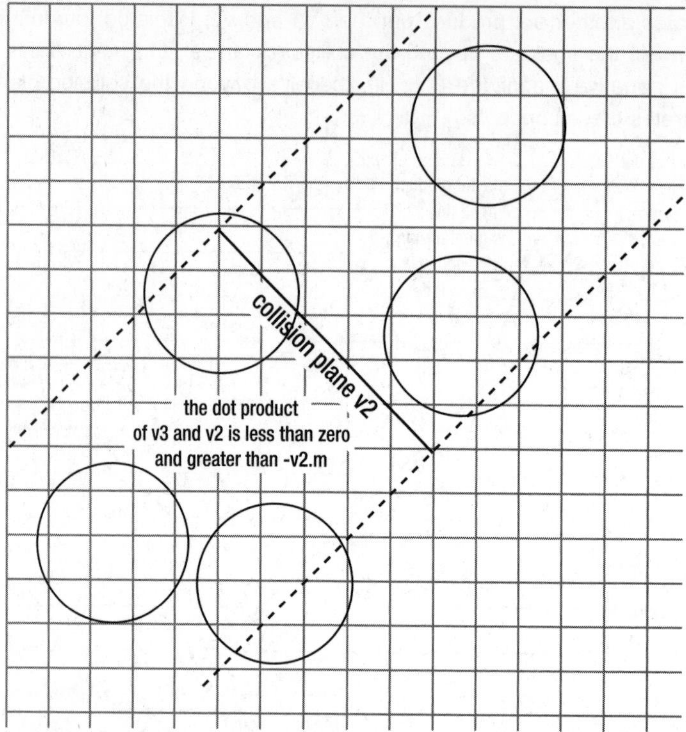

Figure 3-18. If the dot product is less that zero and greater than -v2.m, then the circle will be somewhere within the line's scope.

All this means is that we can use this math to figure out which Voronoi region the circle occupies, and we can switch the collision strategy accordingly.

- If the circle is between the collision plane's start and end points, we know to check for a collision between the circle and the line. We can use a particle-versus-line strategy.
- If it's outside that space, we know to check for a collision between the circle and one of the line's end points. It then becomes a circle-versus-particle collision problem.

In the source files, you'll find the `CircleVsCorner` folder. Run the SWF file, and you'll see that this system is used to accurately bounce the circle off the corners of the line, as shown in Figure 3-19.

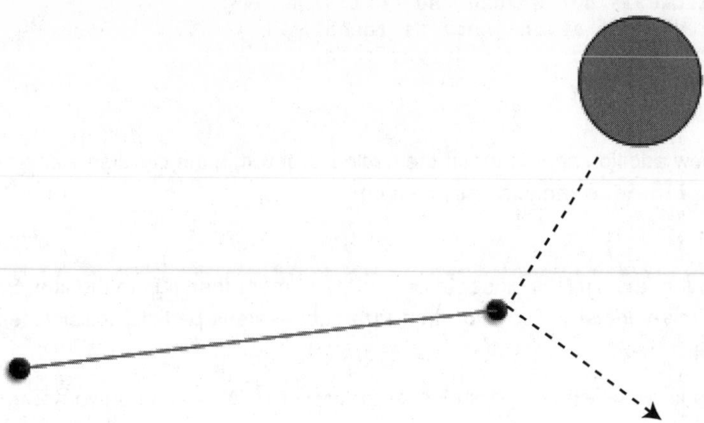

Figure 3-19. Bounce the circle off the corner of the line.

Here's the bit of code from the `enterFrameHandler` that finds the dot products and decides which side of the line, if any, the circle is on.

```
//The dot product that tells you whether the circle is within
//the scope of the collision plane's magnitude (its Voronoi region)
var dp1:Number = VectorMath.dotProduct(_v3, _v2);

//The dot product that tells you which side of the collision plane
//the circle is on
var dp2:Number = VectorMath.dotProduct(_v3, _v2.ln);

//If the circle is within the region of space defined
//by the collision plane and its normals
//then set its line side to left or right
if(dp1 > -_v2.m && dp1 < 0 )
{
  if(_lineSide == "")
  {
    if(dp2 < 0 )
    {
      _lineSide = "left";
    }
    else
    {
      _lineSide = "right";
    }
  }
}
else
{
```

```
    //If the circle is not within the collision
    //plane's region of space (such as rounding
    //a corner) clear the _lineSide variable.
    _lineSide = "";
}
```

The important new addition here is that if the circle is not within the collision plane's start and end points, then the `_lineSide` variable has no value.

```
_lineSide = "";
```

This must mean that the circle is closer to one of the corners than it is to the line. So, we need to switch from a circle-versus-line collision test to a circle-versus-particle collision test with one of the corner points.

We also need to know which corner is closest to the circle. We can use two new vectors to help us find this:

- `_v4` is a vector between the center of the circle and the start point of the line.
- `_v5` is a vector that runs between the center of the circle and the end point of the line.

Figure 3-20 illustrates these two new vectors.

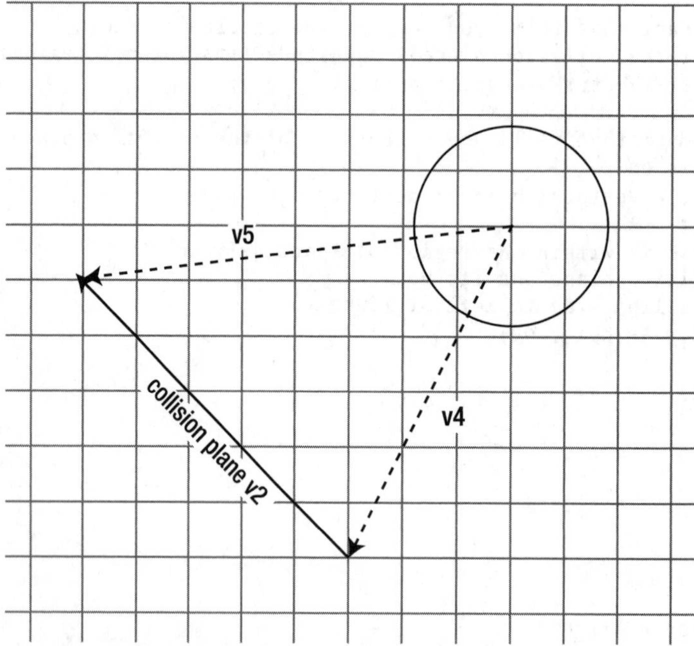

Figure 3-20. Vectors between the center of the circle and the collision plane's start and end points help detect a collision with the plane's corners.

The vector with the smallest magnitude indicates the corner that the circle is nearest. Here's the code from the `CircleVsCorner` application class that figures out which corner to check for a collision:

```
if(_lineSide == "")
{
  //Check for a collision with the corners
  if(_v4.m < _circleModel.radius
      || _v5.m < _circleModel.radius)
  {
    //Bounce the circle on the closest corner
    if(_v4.m < _v5.m)
    {
      //The circle is closest to the start of the line
      cornerBounce(_circleModel, _v4);
    }
    else
    {
      //The circle is closest to the end of the line
      cornerBounce(_circleModel, _v5);
    }
  }
}
```

The `cornerBounce` method bounces the circle, using the same basic bounce code we used in earlier examples.

```
public function cornerBounce
  (circleModel:CircleModel, distanceVector:VectorModel):void
{
  //Find the amount of overlap
  var overlap:Number = circleModel.radius - distanceVector.m;

  //Move the circle out of the collision
  circleModel.setX
    = circleModel.xPos
    - (overlap * distanceVector.dx);
  circleModel.setY
    = circleModel.yPos
    - (overlap * distanceVector.dy);

  //Calculate the circle's motion vector
  var motion:VectorModel
    = new VectorModel
    (
      circleModel.xPos,
      circleModel.yPos,
      circleModel.xPos + circleModel.vx,
      circleModel.yPos + circleModel.vy
    );
```

```
    //Create the circle's bounce vector
    var bounce:VectorModel
      = VectorMath.bounce(motion, distanceVector.ln);

  //Bounce the circle
  circleModel.vx = bounce.vx;
  circleModel.vy = bounce.vy;
}
```

You'll find the full code in the `CircleVsCorner.as` file in the chapter's source files.

Collision between moving circles

In many games, like billiards or marbles, you'll need both circles to react to a collision. When the circles collide, each circle transfers its motion force to the other circle.

When the collision occurs, you need to separate the circles and then figure out their new bounce velocities. These are the same concepts we looked at in earlier examples. However, when both circles are in motion, there are some important differences:

- **Separation**: If one circle is moving and the other isn't, it's easy to separate them in a collision. We did this in the first example in this chapter by simply positioning the moving circle at the boundary of the stationary circle. But when both circles are moving, where is that boundary? You need to find a compromise position: separate each by a proportional amount. Luckily, a very simple formula can help us do that.
- **Bounce**: When moving circles collide, their new bounce vectors are not only determined by the angle of collision, but also by the force with which the other circle is hitting it. The circles need to transfer their motion vectors to each other.

Again, there are no big surprises here, and you already have the tools you need for the solution.

In the chapter's source files, run the `movingCircles.swf` file. You'll see a small circle and much larger one. Both are pulled to the bottom of the stage by gravity. Bounce the small circle into the larger circle, and you can see that they both bounce against each other and around the stage very realistically. You can try to balance one circle on top of the other, and trap the smaller one in a corner, as shown in Figure 3-21. It's actually a lot of fun to play with. It may look like it takes extremely complex algorithms and formulas to create something like this, but it's all done with a few sparse lines of pretty familiar code and some simple logic.

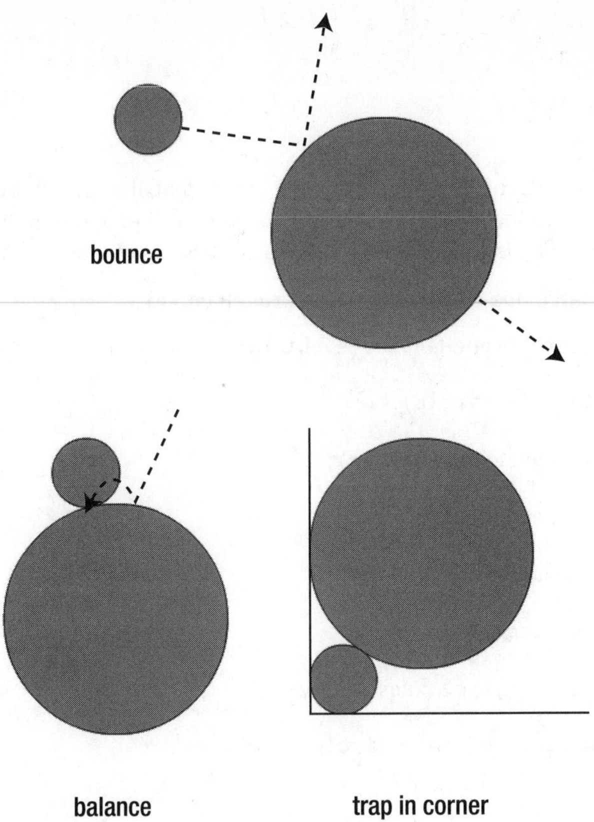

Figure 3-21. Realistic collision reaction and bounce between circles

You can give these circles any radius value, with or without gravity, and you'll get similarly realistic effects.

Let's take a tour of the most import parts of the `MovingCircles` application class.

Gravity is added by setting the circles' `gravity_Vy` properties to `0.1` when they're added to the stage by the circle models' class constructors.

```
//Circle 1
addChild(_c1_View);
_c1.setX = 300;
_c1.setY = 200;
_c1.gravity_Vy = 0.1;
```

```
//Circle 2
addChild(_c2_View);
_c2.setX = 200;
_c2.setY = 200;
_c2.gravity_Vy = 0.1;
```

gravity_Vy is a property of the AVerletModel class that the CircleModel class inherits. Optionally, you could give the circles a friction value of 1 to exaggerate the effects of bounce and gravity. (Default friction is 0.96, which gives the circles a bit of drag.)

The most important part of the class is the enterFrameHandler:

```
private function enterFrameHandler(event:Event):void
{
  //Update c1 (player's circle)
  _c1.update();
  StageBoundaries.bounce(_c1, stage);

  //Update c2 (the second circle)
  _c2.update();
  StageBoundaries.bounce(_c2, stage);

  //Vector between circles
  var v0:VectorModel = new VectorModel
    (_c1.xPos, _c1.yPos, _c2.xPos,_c2.yPos);

  //Calculate the radii of both circles combined
  var totalRadii:Number = _c1.radius + _c2.radius;

  if(v0.m < totalRadii)
  {
    //A collision is occurring.
    //Find the amount of overlap
    var overlap:Number = totalRadii - v0.m;

    //Create an overlap vector
    var collision_Vx:Number = Math.abs(v0.dx * overlap * 0.5);
    var collision_Vy:Number = Math.abs(v0.dy * overlap * 0.5);

    //Variables that track whether _c1 is above, below,
    //to the left or to the right of _c2
    var xSide:int;
    var ySide:int;
```

```
//xSide is 1 when _c1 is to the right of _c2,
//and -1 when it's to the left of _c2.
//ySide is 1 when _c1 is below _c2,
//and -1 when it's above _c2
_c1.xPos > _c2.xPos ? xSide = 1 : xSide = -1;
_c1.yPos > _c2.yPos ? ySide = 1 : ySide = -1;

//Reposition _c1 out of the collision.
//Use xSide and ySide to make the overlap vector either
//negative or positive, depending on the side of the collision
_c1.setX = _c1.xPos + (collision_Vx * xSide);
_c1.setY = _c1.yPos + (collision_Vy * ySide);

//Reposition _c2
_c2.setX = _c2.xPos + (collision_Vx * -xSide);
_c2.setY = _c2.yPos + (collision_Vy * -ySide);

//We've moved the circles out of the collision. Now we
//need to bounce them away at the correct angle

//_c1's motion vector
var v1:VectorModel
  = new VectorModel
  (
    _c1.xPos,
    _c1.yPos,
    _c1.xPos + _c1.vx,
    _c1.yPos + _c1.vy
  );

 //_c2's motion vector
 var v2:VectorModel
    = new VectorModel
    (
      _c2.xPos,
      _c2.yPos,
      _c2.xPos + _c2.vx,
      _c2.yPos + _c2.vy
    );

 //Project v1 onto v0 and v0.ln
 var p1a:VectorModel = VectorMath.project(v1, v0);
 var p1b:VectorModel = VectorMath.project(v1, v0.ln);

 //Project v2 onto v0 and v0.ln
 var p2a:VectorModel = VectorMath.project(v2, v0);
 var p2b:VectorModel = VectorMath.project(v2, v0.ln);
```

```
    //Mix and match the results of p1 and p2 to
    //find the correct bounce vectors

    //Bounce c1
    //using p1b and p2a
    _c1.vx = p1b.vx + p2a.vx;
    _c1.vy = p1b.vy + p2a.vy;

    //Bounce c2
    //using p1a and p2b
    _c2.vx = p1a.vx + p2b.vx;
    _c2.vy = p1a.vy + p2b.vy;
}
```

A collision is detected when the magnitude of the vector between the circles is less than their combined radii. This is exactly the same way a collision was detected in our first example.

But because both circles are moving, we have a new problem. When only one circle was moving, it was easy to know which circle to reposition after the collision: the moving one. Now that both circles could be moving, which circle do we reposition, and by how much?

To figure that out, we need to do the following:

1. Find out the amount by which the circles overlap when they collide.

   ```
   var overlap:Number = totalRadii - v0.m;
   ```

   This is the same code that we used to find the overlap in the example with the stationary circle.

2. Create a **collision vector**. This will give us the vx and vy values we need to separate the circles. This vector must be divided in half so that we can share it between the two circles. One half will go to circle 1, and the other half will go to circle 2.

   ```
   var collision_Vx:Number = Math.abs(v0.dx * overlap * 0.5);
   var collision_Vy:Number = Math.abs(v0.dy * overlap * 0.5);
   ```

   The vector is found by scaling v0's magnitude to the amount of overlap. By multiplying the overlap by v0's dx and dy, we have a new vector inclined at the same angle as v0 but with the same magnitude as the overlap. Figure 3-22 shows how this vector is found.

   The vx and vy values need to be absolute (without a plus or minus sign). We need these values to be neutral because we want the flexibility to decide whether to add or subtract this vector to each circle's position (you'll see how in the next step).

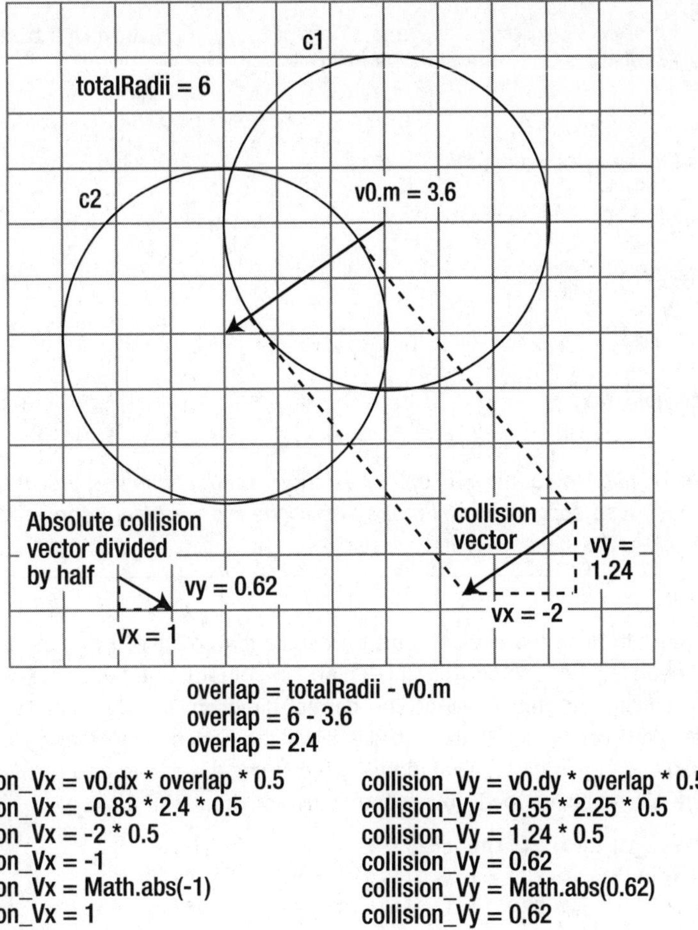
c1
totalRadii = 6
c2
v0.m = 3.6
Absolute collision vector divided by half
vy = 0.62
vx = 1
collision vector
vy = 1.24
vx = -2
overlap = totalRadii - v0.m
overlap = 6 - 3.6
overlap = 2.4
collision_Vx = v0.dx * overlap * 0.5
collision_Vx = -0.83 * 2.4 * 0.5
collision_Vx = -2 * 0.5
collision_Vx = -1
collision_Vx = Math.abs(-1)
collision_Vx = 1
collision_Vy = v0.dy * overlap * 0.5
collision_Vy = 0.55 * 2.25 * 0.5
collision_Vy = 1.24 * 0.5
collision_Vy = 0.62
collision_Vy = Math.abs(0.62)
collision_Vy = 0.62

Figure 3-22. Find the collision vector, divide it by half, and make it absolute.

3. Is the first circle above, below, to the right of, or to the left of the second circle? We need to know this information so that we can correctly add or subtract the overlap vector to each circle's position. The easiest way to track this is by creating variables that are assigned `1` or `-1`, depending on where the circles are in relation to each other. Why we need to do this will become clear in the next step.

```
var xSide:int;
var ySide:int;

_c1.xPos > _c2.xPos ? xSide = 1 : xSide = -1;
_c1.yPos > _c2.yPos ? ySide = 1 : ySide = -1;
```

> *This bit of code illustrates the use of the* ***ternary operation****. It's a shorthand style of writing* `if / else` *statements. This line of code...*
>
> ```
> _c1.xPos > _c2.xPos ? xSide = 1 : xSide = -1;
> ```
>
> *... is the same as writing this:*
>
> ```
> if(_c1.xPos > _c2.xPos)
> {
>   xSide = 1;
> }
> else
> {
>   xSide = -1;
> }
> ```
>
> *For short, simple conditional tests, the ternary operation is very helpful. It takes up much less space and will make your code more readable once your eyes get used to the syntax. Try it!*

4. We need to push the circles apart to resolve the collision. For example, on the x axis, we'll need to push one circle to the left and the other to the right. The collision vector that we calculated in step 2 will be the correct direction for one of the circles, but not the other. However, we know that the directions the circles need to move in will be the polar opposites of each other. That means we can use the `xSide` and `ySide` variables (which will be `1` or `-1`) to correctly invert one of the vectors.

```
//Move _c1 out of the collision
_c1.setX = _c1.xPos + (collision_Vx * xSide);
_c1.setY = _c1.yPos + (collision_Vy * ySide);

//Move _c2 out of the collision
_c2.setX = _c2.xPos + (collision_Vx * -xSide);
_c2.setY = _c2.yPos + (collision_Vy * -ySide);
```

The orientation of the circles will always be changing, so we can never know which circle's overlap vector to invert. Luckily, the `xSide` and `ySide` variables take care of keeping track of that for us automatically. Figure 3-23 shows how the circles' new positions are found.

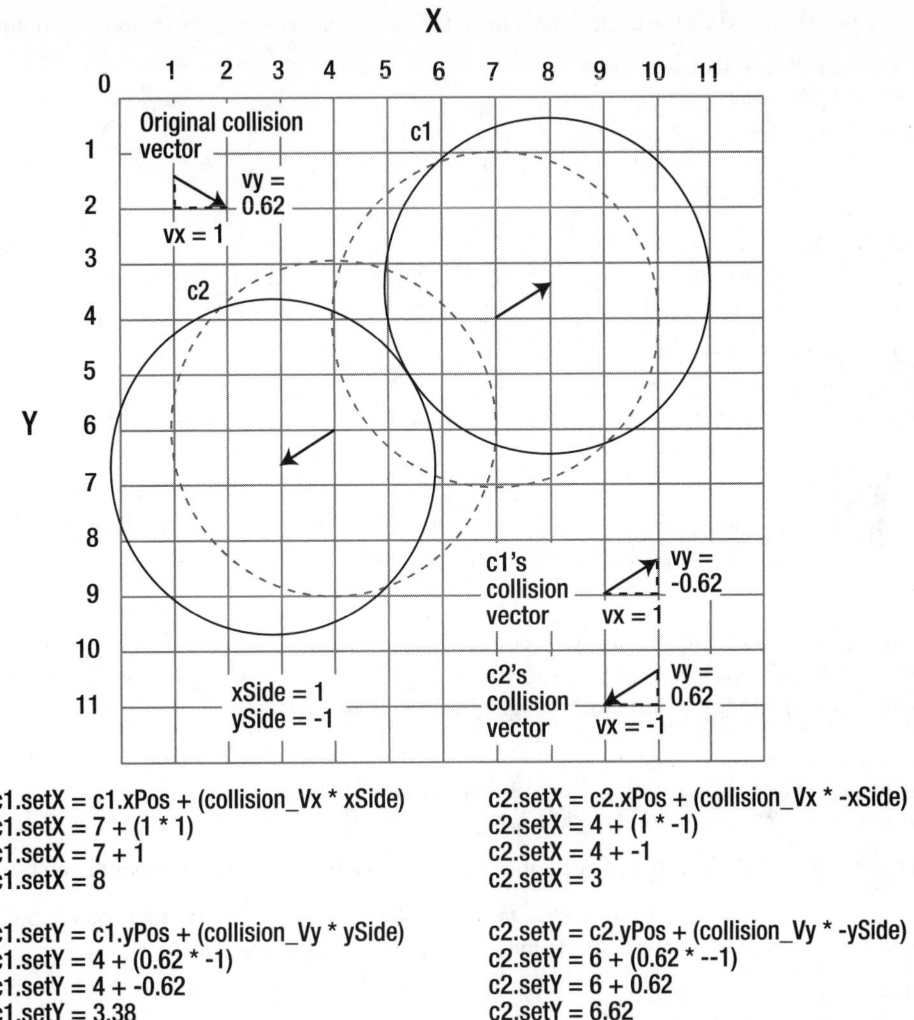
X
0 1 2 3 4 5 6 7 8 9 10 11
Y
1 2 3 4 5 6 7 8 9 10 11
Original collision vector
vy = 0.62
vx = 1
c1
c2
c1's collision vector
vy = -0.62
vx = 1
c2's collision vector
vy = 0.62
vx = -1
xSide = 1
ySide = -1
c1.setX = c1.xPos + (collision_Vx * xSide)
c1.setX = 7 + (1 * 1)
c1.setX = 7 + 1
c1.setX = 8
c1.setY = c1.yPos + (collision_Vy * ySide)
c1.setY = 4 + (0.62 * -1)
c1.setY = 4 + -0.62
c1.setY = 3.38
c2.setX = c2.xPos + (collision_Vx * -xSide)
c2.setX = 4 + (1 * -1)
c2.setX = 4 + -1
c2.setX = 3
c2.setY = c2.yPos + (collision_Vy * -ySide)
c2.setY = 6 + (0.62 * --1)
c2.setY = 6 + 0.62
c2.setY = 6.62

Figure 3-23. Use the collision vector to move the circles out of the collision.

Now that we've moved the circles out of the collision, we need to calculate their bounce vectors. When the circles collide, they transfer their motion vectors to each other.

First, we need to calculate the circles' motion vectors and project them onto v0 and v0's normal.

```
//_c1's motion vector
var v1:VectorModel
  = new VectorModel
  (
    _c1.xPos,
    _c1.yPos,
    _c1.xPos + _c1.vx,
    _c1.yPos + _c1.vy
  );

//_c2's motion vector
var v2:VectorModel
  = new VectorModel
  (
    _c2.xPos,
    _c2.yPos,
    _c2.xPos + _c2.vx,
         _c2.yPos + _c2.vy
  );

//Project v1 onto v0 and v0.ln
var p1a:VectorModel = VectorMath.project(v1, v0);
var p1b:VectorModel = VectorMath.project(v1, v0.ln);

//Project v2 onto v0 and v0.ln
var p2a:VectorModel = VectorMath.project(v2, v0);
var p2b:VectorModel = VectorMath.project(v2, v0.ln);
```

This is the first step in calculating any bounce vector, so it should be pretty familiar to you by now.

Now here's the freaky part. Both circles must transfer their velocities to each other, but also bounce away at the correct angle. To do this, *mix and match the projections.*

```
//Bounce c1
//using p1b and p2a
_c1.vx = p1b.vx + p2a.vx;
_c1.vy = p1b.vy + p2a.vy;

//Bounce c2
//using p1a and p2b
_c2.vx = p1a.vx + p2b.vx;
_c2.vy = p1a.vy + p2b.vy;
```

Each circle's velocity is a combination of its projections plus the other circle's projections. Dr. Frankenstein would be proud! It's a difficult thing to visualize, but as you can see, the code is quite straightforward and symmetrical. This gives you a perfectly natural collision reaction that you can use in any game where two circles collide.

> *It might make sense to make the large circle heavier than the smaller one, so that its bounce is in proportion to its size. You can do this by giving it some mass. Just divide the bounce vector by any number larger than 1, and the bounce effect will be dampened accordingly*
>
> ```
> var mass:uint = 5;
> _c2.vx = (p1a.vx + p2b.vx) / mass;
> _c2.vy = (p1a.vy + p2b.vy) / mass;
> ```
>
> *Dividing the bounce vector by 5 will make the large circle appear much heavier when the small circle bumps into it. You might want to consider making mass a property of the `CircleModel` class, or working out a formula for mass based on the circles' radii.*

Multiple-object collision

Two circles are good, but ten are better! To check for a collision with more than one object on the stage, use this strategy:

- Push all of your objects into an array.
- Loop through the array once each frame and check each object for a collision with another object.

If that sounds pretty simple, it is! The one hiccup is that you need to be careful that your loop doesn't check for a collision with two pairs of objects twice. If it does, you'll spend precious CPU cycles doing unnecessary checking, and that will ultimately slow down your game.

There's a standard algorithm for detecting multiple object collision that solves this problem. It's a **nested `for` loop** (a loop within a loop) that makes sure that no two objects are compared twice.

Imagine you have an array called `objects` that contains all of your game objects, and a method called `checkCollision` that performs the collision check. The multiple-object collision check algorithm will look like this:

```
for (var i:int = 0; i < objects.length; i++)
{
  var object_1:GameObject = objects[i];

  for (var j:int = i + 1; j < objects.length; j++)
  {
     var object_2:GameObject = objects[j];
     checkCollision(object_1, object_2);
  }
}
```

The key to making this work is that the inner loop starts its loop counter at a number that is *one greater than the outer loop*.

```
var j:int = i + 1;
```

This prevents any two objects from being checked more than once.

Let's combine this technique with the moving circle collision system we used in the previous example. In the chapter's source files, you'll find a folder called `MultipleObjectCollision`. Run the SWF, and you'll see a basic prototype of a billiards-style game, as shown in Figure 3-24. It's not much more than a fusion of our circle-versus-circle collision system and the multiple object collision algorithm.

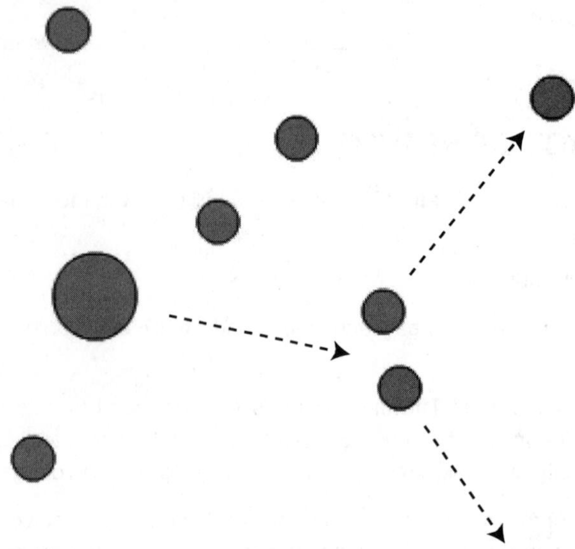

Figure 3-24. Check for collisions with many circles to create a simple billiards-style simulation.

The circles are plotted at random positions on the stage. If any of them overlap when the game starts, the collision system pushes them apart.

For this to work, all the objects need to be pushed into arrays. Because we're using an MVC system, each object actually has two parts: its model and its view. Each needs to be pushed into its own array.

```
private var _models:Array = new Array();
private var _views:Array = new Array();
```

We also need a variable that tells the program how many circles to create.

```
private var _numberOfCircles:Number = 10;
```

The MultipleObjectCollision constructor method does the work of creating the models and views and pushing them into their arrays.

```
public function MultipleObjectCollision():void
{
 for(var i:int = 0; i < _numberOfCircles; i++)
 {
   //Create the circle model and give it a random position
   var radius:uint = 10;
   var circleModel:CircleModel = new CircleModel(radius);
   circleModel.setX
     = Math.round(Math.random() * stage.stageWidth);
   circleModel.setY
     = Math.round(Math.random() * stage.stageHeight);

   //Optional gravity:
   //circleModel.gravity_Vy = 0.1;

   //Push the Model into the _models array
   _models.push(circleModel);

   //Create the circle view
   //add it to the views array and add it to the stage
   var circleView:CircleView = new CircleView(circleModel);
   _views.push(circleView);
   addChild(circleView);
 }

 //Add the player's circle
 _models.push(player);
 player.setX = 275;
 player.setY = 200;
 _views.push(playerView);
 addChild(playerView);

 addEventListener(Event.ENTER_FRAME, enterFrameHandler);
}
```

The big circle on the stage is the player's circle, which is represented by the player object in this code. It's added to the stage outside the loop, but added to the same _models and _views arrays.

> *In this example, adding the circle views to a _views array is optional, because the code doesn't reference them after they've been added to the stage. However, if you want to expand this demo into a full-featured game, you'll need to be able to reference the circles in the _views array in order to remove them from the stage. The sample Block Game in Chapter 4 has a working example of how to do this.*

The player object is created in the class definition using exactly the same code we've using throughout this chapter.

```
private var player:CircleModel = new CircleModel(20);
private var _UIController:UIController = new UIController(player);
private var playerView:CircleView = new CircleView(player);
private var _UIView:UIView = new UIView(player, _UIController, stage);
```

The enterFrameHandler implements the loop that checks for collisions. It also updates the models and checks for stage boundary collisions in a separate loop.

```
private function enterFrameHandler(event:Event):void
{
  //First update the models and check for stage boundary collisions
  for (var i:int = 0; i < _models.length; i++)
  {
    _models[i].update();
    StageBoundaries.bounce(_models[i], stage);
  }

  //Loop through all the circles and check for collisions
  for (var j:int = 0; j < _models.length; j++)
  {
    //The first model
    //to use in the collision check
    var c1:CircleModel = _models[j];

    for (var k:int = j + 1; k < _models.length; k++)
    {
      //The second model
      //to use in the collision check
      var c2:CircleModel = _models[k];

       //Check for a collision
       checkCollision(c1, c2);
    }
  }
}
```

The loop that updates the models needs to run first so that none of the circles visibly overlap when they collide. This allows the collision to be modeled first, before it's displayed on the stage. Only the result of the collision will be displayed on the stage, you'll never see them overlap.

The checkCollision method does the work of finding whether the two objects are actually colliding. Its code is identical to the collision code in the previous example.

With just a little more work, you can develop this example into a full-featured billiards game. Add some pockets, graphics for the table, and a scoring system. You could also create a visible vector as a cue to help you align your aim correctly.

This system is very robust. You'll never find that the circles "stick together" or overlap when they collide, even in very crowded, chaotic situations. This is thanks to accurate separation calculations and the fact that using the MVC framework allows us to model the collisions before we display the results on the stage.

As a stress test, give the circles a random radius, create more of them, and add some gravity. Figure 3-25 shows what happens: They fall to the bottom of the stage and politely jostle around a bit until they find a comfortable formation, which is different every time. It has a compelling beauty, and it's easy to forget that this behavior is being produced by nothing more than a few simple algorithms.

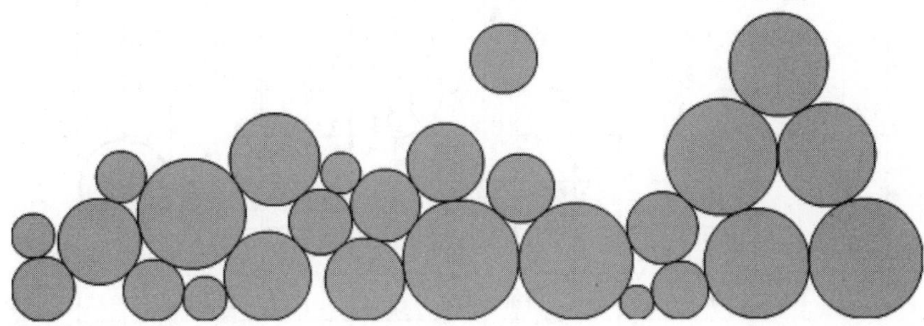

Figure 3-25. Pebbles at the bottom of a riverbed? Organic complexity that is the result of objects obeying the logic of the program in unexpected ways.

Fast-moving circles

This engine that we've built over the past few pages will hold you well for most of the games you'll build using circle collisions. But there's one scenario where it won't work. If the circles are very small and traveling very quickly, there's a chance that they could "skip over" each other, and the collision will never be detected. Any games involving very fast-moving projectiles will face this problem.

You don't think that this will be a problem in your game? Truth be told, I've never found occasion to use it in any of my game projects, so this may be the case for you as well. Hey, no worries—Chapter 4 is waiting for you! You won't miss anything essential by skipping this last section of the chapter.

For the rest of you, let's take a look at a solution that you can keep in your back pocket in case you need to use it. It could be a lifesaver at some point.

Let's flash back to the highways of France and catch up on our friend Loup Verlet, who we met in Chapter 1. There he is at the side of road, taking snapshots of our lime-green Citroen every 10 minutes. If we bump into something really big, like a mountain, he'll be there with his camera snapping away. In the scale of your games, most of the things that your objects will be colliding with will be the size of mountains, so our collision system has no problem detecting them.

But there's a fatal flaw. Our system uses the radii of the circles to determine whether a collision has occurred. It assumes that the each circle's velocity will never be greater than the combined radii of both circles. If it is greater, then the vector between the circles (v0) will never be smaller than that combined radii, and a collision won't be detected. Figure 3-26 illustrates this problem.

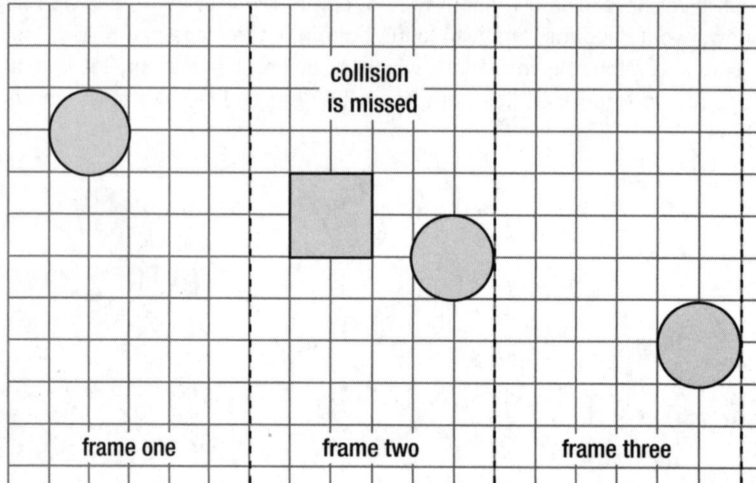

Figure 3-26. A collision won't be detected if a moving object's velocity is greater than the width of the object with which it's colliding.

That means that if we're traveling 100 kilometers an hour and Verlet is taking snapshots every 10 minutes, the mountain we bump into will need to be pretty big. Its base must be wider than 10 kilometers for Verlet to catch the collision with his camera.

But what if it's much smaller? What if the object is not a mountain, but a coffee shop at the side of the road? We could quickly pull over, grab a cinnamon brioche at the drive-through, and, except for a few suspicious crumbs, Verlet would be none the wiser when we wave to him through our sunroof at the overpass a few kilometers down the road. Heh, heh … guilty pleasures!

Not to be outdone, Verlet hatches a plan. He knows that we *always* stop at coffee shops. And so even though he can't see them, he has a map that lists all of the coffee shops along the highway. He knows that if our route passes a coffee shop, we'll stop. Collision detected!

Here's how we can solve this problem using AS3.0 code:

1. Find out whether the objects have trajectories that are likely to intersect.
2. If they do, check their velocities to find out whether they're going to intersect in the next frame.
3. If the velocities intersect, then we have a collision. Use their current positions and velocities to find the exact places they'll be when they collide, and then move them to that collision point.

In the chapter's source files, you'll find the `FastMovingCircles` folder. Run the SWF file, and you'll see two tiny circles on the stage, one of which you can move with the keyboard or by clicking with the mouse. A thin, black line extends from the circle to the mouse. Use this line to aim your circle so that it's in a trajectory that intersects with the other circle. Smash the circles together, and watch them collide and bounce apart. Even at extremely high velocities, the collision works perfectly. Figure 3-27 shows what you'll see and what happens.

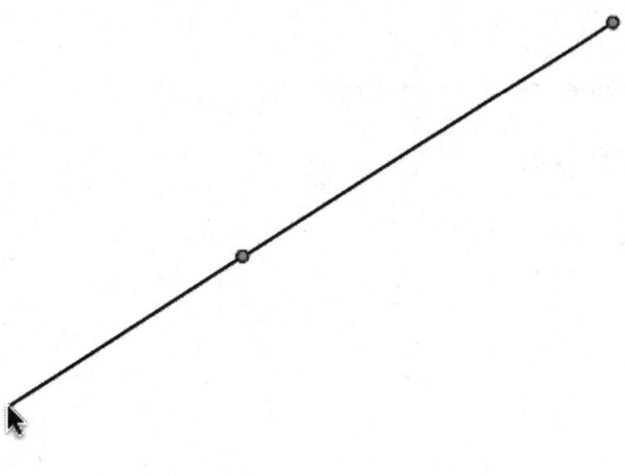

A. Line up the target

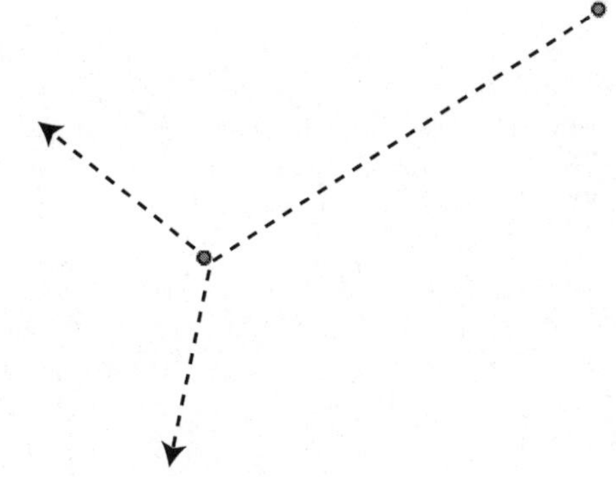

B. Watch the collision

Figure 3-27. Collision at high velocities

The code is densely packed, although you'll see that it's full of the usual suspects. I've listed `enterFrameHandler` here, with comments to help you see how it all fits together.

```
private function enterFrameHandler(event:Event):void
{
  //Update c1 (player's circle)
  _c1.update();
  StageBoundaries.bounce(_c1, stage);

  //Update c2
  _c2.update();
  StageBoundaries.bounce(_c2, stage);

  //Vector between circles
  var v0:VectorModel
    = new VectorModel
    (
      _c1.xPos,
      _c1.yPos,
      _c2.xPos,
      _c2.yPos
    );

  //c1's motion vector
  var v1:VectorModel
    = new VectorModel
    (
      _c1.xPos,
      _c1.yPos,
      _c1.xPos + _c1.vx,
      _c1.yPos + _c1.vy
    );

  //c2's motion vector
  var v2:VectorModel
    = new VectorModel
    (
      _c2.xPos,
      _c2.yPos,
      _c2.xPos + _c2.vx,
      _c2.yPos + _c2.vy
    );
```

```
//Two motion vectors are difficult to deal with.
//Simplify this problem
//by creating a new vector, v3
var v3:VectorModel
  = new VectorModel
  (
    0,0,0,0,
    _c1.vx - _c2.vx,
    _c1.vy - _c2.vy
  );

 //Project v0 onto v3.
 //This gives you the closest
 //point of c1 to c2
 var p1:VectorModel = VectorMath.project(v0, v3);

  //Plot a vector from p1.b to the center of c2
  var v4:VectorModel
    = new VectorModel
    (
      _c1.xPos + p1.vx,
      _c1.yPos + p1.vy,
      _c2.xPos,
      _c2.yPos
    );

  //Calculate the radii of both circles combined
  var totalRadii:Number = _c1.radius + _c2.radius;

  //Find the difference between the total radii
  //and the magnitude of v4
  var difference:Number = totalRadii - v4.m;

  if(difference > 0)
  {
    //Possible collision! c1 is in a trajectory that may
    //intersect with c2. Let's find out if it does.

    var overlap:Number
      = Math.sqrt(totalRadii * totalRadii - v4.m * v4.m);

    //Find the possible new position for c1
    var new_X:Number =  v4.a.x - overlap * v3.dx;
    var new_Y:Number =  v4.a.y - overlap * v3.dy;

    //Create a vector between v1.a and the new x and y points
    var v5:VectorModel
      = new VectorModel(_c1.xPos, _c1.yPos,  new_X, new_Y);
```

```
    //Find the dot product between v0 and v1
    var dp:Number = VectorMath.dotProduct2(v5, v1);

    if(v5.m < v3.m
    && dp > 0)
    {
      //The motion vectors will intersect in the next frame
      //so the circles will definitely collide
      var ratio:Number = v5.m / v3.m;

      //Move the circles to the collision point
      _c1.setX = _c1.xPos + ratio * _c1.vx;
      _c1.setY = _c1.yPos + ratio * _c1.vy;

      _c2.setX = _c2.xPos + ratio * _c2.vx;
      _c2.setY = _c2.yPos + ratio * _c2.vy;

      //Bounce them apart
      //Project v1 onto v0 and v0.ln
      var p1a:VectorModel = VectorMath.project(v1, v0);
      var p1b:VectorModel = VectorMath.project(v1, v0.ln);

      //Project v2 onto v0 and v0.ln
      var p2a:VectorModel = VectorMath.project(v2, v0);
      var p2b:VectorModel = VectorMath.project(v2, v0.ln);

      //Mix and match the results of p1 and p2 to
      //find the correct bounce vectors

      //Bounce c1
      //p1b and p2a
      _c1.vx = p1b.vx + p2a.vx;
      _c1.vy = p1b.vy + p2a.vy;

      //Bounce c2
      //p1a and p2b
      _c2.vx = p1a.vx + p2b.vx;
      _c2.vy = p1a.vy + p2b.vy;
    }
  }
}
```

Although it solves the problem, there are two flaws in this system:

- Because velocity is calculated only when the circles start to move, the collision detection starts in the second frame of movement. This means that a collision could be missed if the objects are very close together before they start moving.
- Because it's dependent on velocity calculations, the collision detection starts to fall apart at low speeds.

I recommend that you use this solution only in games where these drawbacks won't be a problem. For example, in a game where the player is using artillery fire to deflect the enemy's artillery fire, it will work just fine. If these problems will be a limitation, I suggest that you fuse this solution with earlier solutions, and modify how you treat your collision detection depending on the circles' velocities.

Summary

Some of the earliest games known to humankind, and still some of the most popular in the present day, involve getting some sort of ball from one side of the playing field to the other. It holds some sort of innate fascination for us all. It was no coincidence that the game to start the video game revolution in the 1970s was Pong. You now know everything you need to get started to create and re-create old and new types of ball games. The bit of work that it takes to understand these concepts can have a big payback in the wide variety of games you can make.

But we're not done yet. Bouncing circles are a good start, but it would be even better if they had an environment to bounce around in. In the next chapter, we're going look at how you can make such an environment using rectangles and triangles of all sizes. These could be used for a physics-based pinball-style game or an environment for an action platform game. We'll also bring many of the concepts together from first the few chapters to build a breakout-style game prototype.

Until then, how about finishing off that billiards game? Drop me a line when you do—I'd love to play it!

Chapter 4

Collisions Between Polygons

Polygons are shapes with at last three straight lines or angles. Squares, rectangles, and triangles are all polygons—those delightful little shapes we spent our primary school years snipping from colored paper. Collision detection between polygons is more complex than collision detection between circles because you must account for not only width (the circle's radius), but also for height and often an angled plane, like the slope of a triangle. But if you can manage collision detection between different kinds of polygons, as well as between polygons and circles, you'll be able to handle most collision-detection problems that your games with throw at you.

In this chapter, we're going to look at these topics:

- Collisions between rectangles
- Collisions between rectangles and circles
- Collisions between rectangles, circles, and triangles

We'll then take a detailed look at two important case studies that use all the techniques we've covered in this book so far, along with a few new ones. We'll begin with an introduction to the technique that lets us do efficient polygon collision detection.

This chapter assumes that you're fluent in the vector math concepts covered in Chapters 2 and 3. If you think you're a little hazy on any vector math topics, review those earlier chapters, and work through the concepts and code in your own projects. There's no need to rush into this chapter until you're fully confident you understand the previous material.

The separating axis theorem

At the end of Chapter 2, I explained how you can make polygons by joining a series of lines. Checking for a collision with the polygon then just becomes a question of checking for collisions with all of the lines. So if you're testing for a collision between a particle and a hexagon, for example, your code checks whether the particle is intersecting with any of the hexagon's six lines that make up its sides. This works, and for many scenarios, it may be all you need. But its one big drawback is that it checks for collisions that have no likelihood of ever occurring.

Imagine that you have 100 hexagons on the stage, and one particle that could collide with any of them. You know that your particle is only ever going to collide with one side of one hexagon. If you check each side of every hexagon on the stage, you'll be doing 599 more collision checks than necessary. This eats a huge hole in your game's performance budget. It's as if you spent $1 on a slice of pizza, but unwittingly dropped $599 on the floor of the pizza parlor while digging through your pockets for your change. Multiply that by 30 or 60 times per second, and you have a real problem! This is what programmers refer to with the technical term **expensive**, and I'm sure you will agree with them.

Doing collision detection wisely means doing collision tests only between objects that are likely to collide. If you're checking for collisions between a particle and those 100 hexagons, you should consider that of those 100 hexagons, the particle is only ever going to collide with hexagons that it can reach within one frame of movement. That means just those hexagons that are within range of its velocity vector—perhaps only three or four of them. If you can find those few hexagons, you've immediately saved 96% of your performance budget! This applies not only to polygons, like squares and hexagons, but also to circles and particles.

Checking for collisions with objects that are in the immediate vicinity of each other is called **broad-phase collision detection**. The simplest way of doing a broad-phase collision check is to overlay a grid onto the stage and compare only those objects that are in directly adjacent cells in the grid. It requires quite a bit of computing overhead to manage a broad-phase collision system, so the performance benefit is usually apparent only if you're testing for collisions between more than a few hundred objects each frame.

Once you've found the most likely hexagon to collide with, you need to determine which side of the hexagon the particle is hitting. Checking all six sides arbitrarily is very inefficient, so you need to narrow down the search to the most likely sides. This step in the process, where you test for collisions between individual objects, is called **narrow-phase collision detection**.

The broad-phase step of this process is covered in Chapter 8. In this chapter, we'll work with one of the most widely used and efficient techniques for doing narrow-phase collision detection with polygons: the separating axis theorem (SAT).

Understanding SAT

The SAT is an observation about how polygons intersect. It's widely regarded as the most efficient way to check whether polygons are colliding. It's also pretty easy to understand:

- If there is an axis on which any two objects *don't* overlap, then there's no collision between the objects. In the case of two rectangles, this means that if the rectangles overlap on the x axis but not the y axis, then they're not colliding. The axis on which they don't intersect is the *separating axis* that gives the theorem its name.
- If the objects overlap on all their axes (both x and y), then a collision has occurred.
- The axis with the smallest amount of overlap is the axis on which the collision is occurring.

> *The SAT was first formulated by legendary computer scientist and software engineer Stefan Gottschalk. It caught the eye of the Flash game design world in an online tutorial by Metanet, makers of the highly respected Flash and PlayStation game N.*

In any game, the chance that two objects are *not* colliding is far more likely than that they *are* colliding. The SAT capitalizes on this fact. It's very efficient because you can find out immediately whether two objects are overlapping just by testing one axis. If there's no overlap on that one axis, you have your answer: there's no collision. It's a quick escape, and you've just saved yourself some processing power. You don't need to bother testing any of the other axes.

In the case of rectangles, this means you can reduce collision checks by up to half. In the case of a complex polygon, like a hexagon, it means needing to do up to three times fewer collision checks.

However, if you find that two objects are overlapping on one axis, it doesn't mean that the objects are actually colliding. It means that they could be, but you don't know yet. So, you next need to check another axis to be sure. In the case of rectangles, if you find an overlap on both the x and y axes, then the rectangles are definitely overlapping and you have a collision. If you find any axis without an overlap, then there's no collision, and you can stop further checking.

Anyway, that's the theory. If this all sounds a bit too abstract, let's take a step back and look at a practical example.

Using SAT

The simplest polygon collision detection you do is between two squares or two rectangles. Imagine that you need to check for a collision between two squares on the stage. In pseudo code, a basic SAT algorithm for squares looks like this:

```
if(the squares overlap on the x axis)
{
  //There might be a collision! Let's check:
  if(the squares overlap on the y axis)
  {
```

```
    //The squares overlap on both axes, so there's definitely a collision
    //The collision is occurring on the axis with the smallest amount of
    overlap
  }
  else
  {
    //There's no overlap on the y axis, so there's no collision
  }
}
else
{
  //There's no overlap on the x axis, so there's no collision
}
```

What do I mean by "if the squares overlap on the x or y axis"?

Take a look at Figure 4-1, which depicts two squares on the stage. They're obviously not intersecting, which we can plainly see with our eyes. But we need to find a way to describe this in programming code so that our games can also see it.

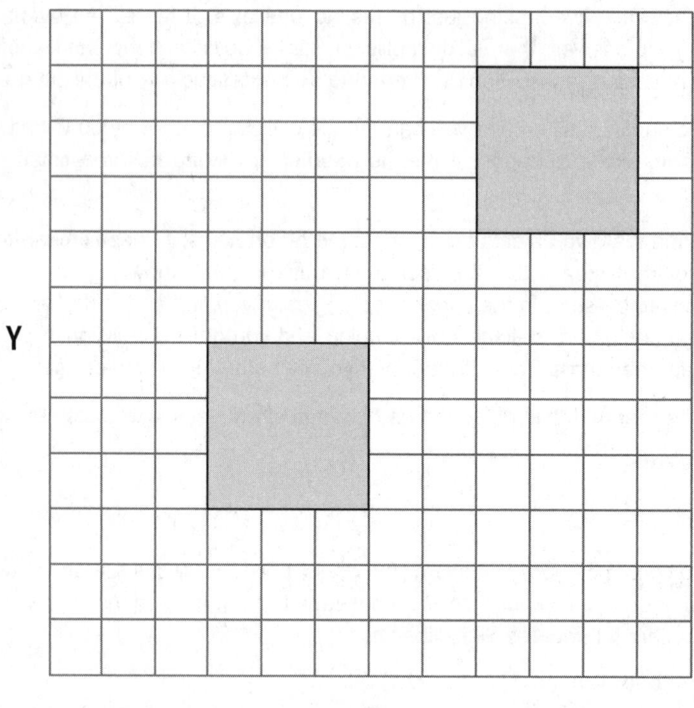

Figure 4-1. Two squares that are not intersecting. How can we describe this in code?

You can see from Figure 4-1 that those two squares exist on a stage with an x axis and a y axis. Conveniently enough, the sides of the squares are also aligned to the stage's x and y axes:

- Their top and bottom sides are parallel to the x axis.
- Their left and right sides are parallel to the y axis.

> *In technical collision detection literature, squares or rectangles whose sides are aligned to the x and y axes are called* ***axis-aligned bounding boxes****, or* ***AABBs****. In other words, the stage is rectangular and the squares are rectangular. Nothing is rotated. This is the simplest collision scenario you can have. Game designers will often wrap odd-shaped, nonrectangular objects in AABBs because using them for collision detection is extremely fast.*

To check whether the squares are intersecting, we don't need to check all four sides of each square against all four sides of the other square. We just need to check whether the sides of the squares are intersecting on the two axes. To do this, we need to use projection. We must project each square onto the x and y axes. You'll recall from Chapter 2 that the projection of a shape is the shadow that it casts if you were standing behind it shining a light. In this case, each square needs to cast two shadows: one shadow onto the x axis and another onto the y axis. Figure 4-2 illustrates this.

How can we use these projections to find out whether the squares are intersecting?

The SAT says that if the projections of the shapes don't overlap on any axes, then the shapes don't overlap. Bingo! That pretty much sums up Figure 4-2. You can clearly see that the projections don't overlap at all.

How will our SAT pseudo code handle this "no collision" condition? First, it will check for any overlaps on the x axis. It finds none, so it knows that there is no collision. It can skip a whole block of code and jump straight to the end. The code in bold indicates the code that's being triggered.

```
if(the squares overlap on the x axis) //They don't
{
  //There might be a collision! Let's check:
  if(the squares overlap on the y axis)
  {
    //The squares overlap in both axes, so
    //there's definitely a collision. The collision is occurring on
    //the axis with the smallest amount of overlap
  }
    else
    {
    //There's no overlap on the y axis, so there's no collision
    }
}
```

```
else
{
  //There's no overlap on the x axis, so there's no collision
}
```

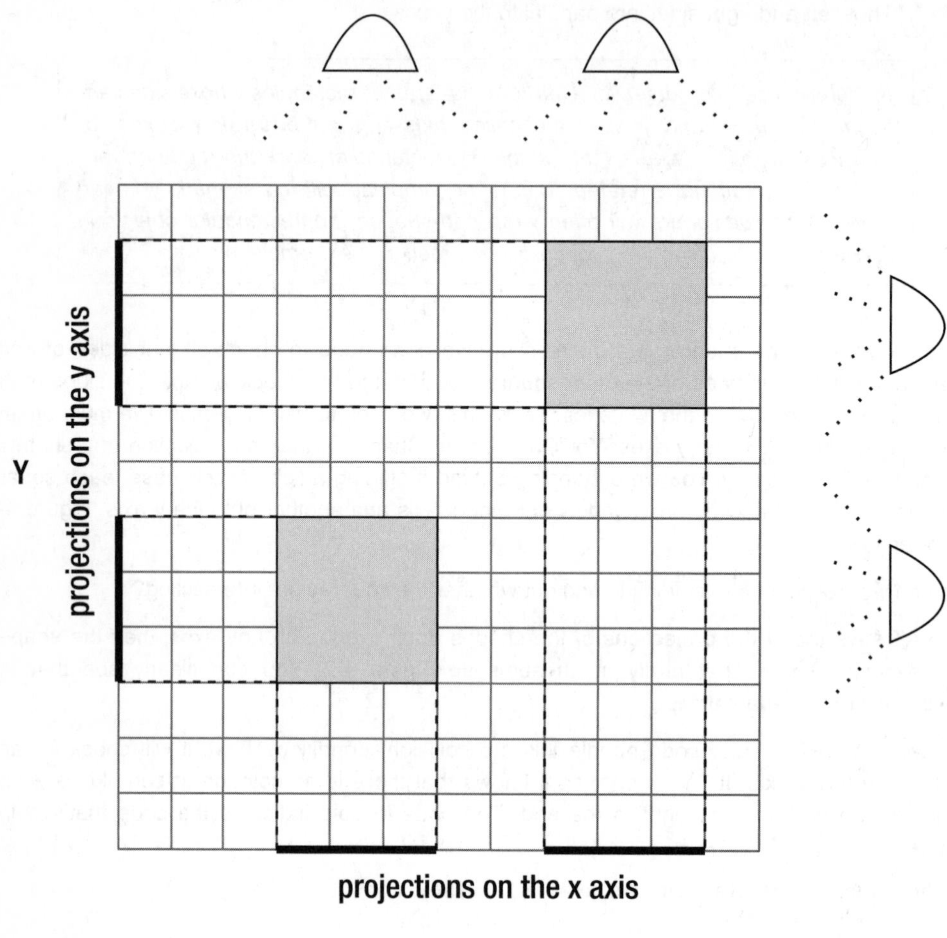

Figure 4-2. Project the squares onto the x and y axes.

This is why using the SAT is so efficient: it doesn't do any extra checking.

So what happens if the squares overlap on the x axis? Let's find out.

In Figure 4-3, you can see that the top square has moved to the left. The projections of both squares are now overlapping on the x axis.

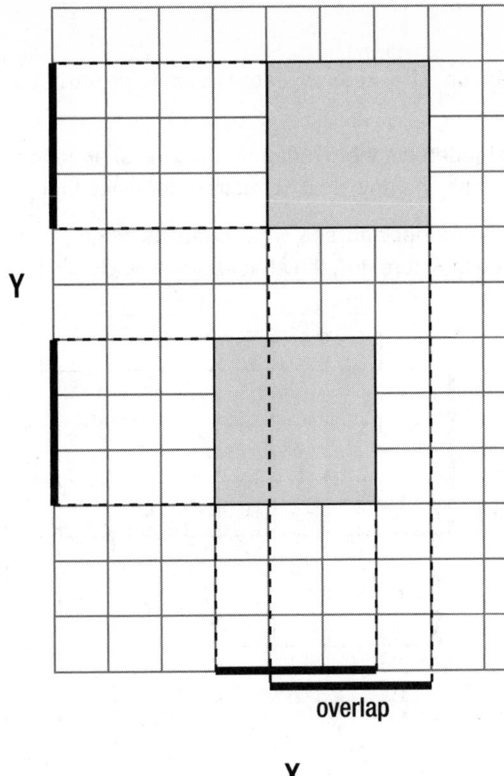

Figure 4-3. The projections overlap on the x axis.

Of course, you can see that even though they overlap on the x axis, the squares still don't intersect. Let's see if our SAT pseudo code agrees with us.

```
if(the squares overlap on the x axis) //They do
{
  //There might be a collision! Let's check:
  if(the squares overlap on the y axis) //They don't
  {
    //The squares overlap in both axes, so
    //there's definitely a collision. The collision is occurring on
    //the axis with the smallest amount of overlap
  }
    else
    {
    //There's no overlap on the y axis, so there's no collision
    }
}
```

```
else
{
  //There's no overlap on the x axis, so there's no collision
}
```

Yes, it does agree with us! It detects the overlap on the x axis, and then goes on to check for an overlap on the y axis. It doesn't find any, so it correctly determines that there's no collision.

Now let's push the example further and see what happens when the squares overlap on the y axis as well. As you can see in Figure 4-4, the shapes are now clearly intersecting.

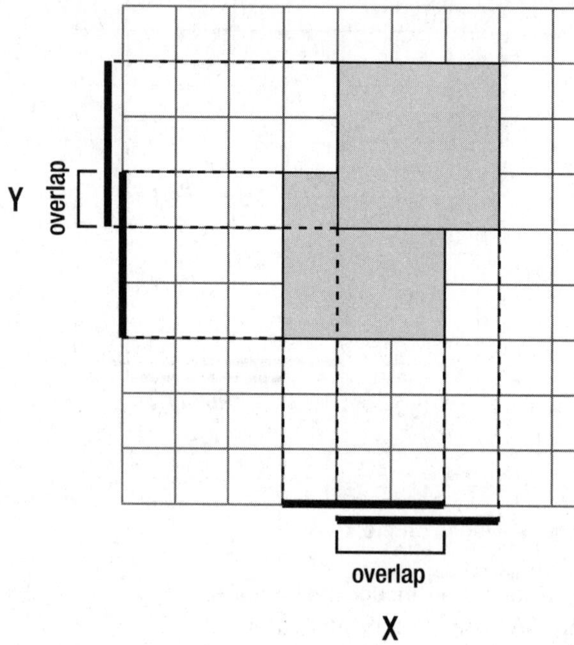

Figure 4-4. The squares overlap on both axes, so we have a collision. The collision occurs on the y axis, which has the smallest amount of overlap.

What will the SAT have to say about this?

```
if(the squares overlap on the x axis) //They do
{
  //There might be a collision! Let's check:
  if(the squares overlap on the y axis) //They do
  {
    //The squares overlap in both axes, so
    //there's definitely a collision. The collision is occurring on
    //the axis with the smallest amount of overlap
  }
```

```
    else
    {
    //There's no overlap on the y axis, so there's no collision
    }
}
else
{
  //There's no overlap on the x axis, so there's no collision
}
```

Not only does it detect the collision, but it also knows that the collision is happening on the y axis, which is the axis with the smallest amount of overlap.

This, in a nutshell, is the SAT.

An SAT limitation

Before continuing, you need to be aware of a fundamental problem of the SAT system that could give you unexpected results if your game objects move too far in one frame. If objects are moving very quickly, the axis with the smallest amount of overlap might not be the one on which the collision is occurring.

For example, look at Figure 4-4 and imagine that the upper square is moving at a high velocity, from the right side of the stage to the left, and that it has collided with the lower square from the right. Imagine that it was moving so fast that it managed to penetrate more than halfway into the lower square. Our eyes would tell us that the collision is happening on the x axis, which is correct. But the SAT would notice that the overlap is less on the y axis, and tell us that the collision happened from above. If we used this information to resolve the collision in a game, the upper square would appear to be unnaturally pushed up above the lower square.

This is an unavoidable aspect of the SAT algorithm, so you'll need to decide whether this is something you can live with. The speed and efficiency of the SAT is usually enough compensation, but if your game demands greater precision, here are some work-arounds to help you live with it:

- Limit you game engine so that it's never possible for the velocities of any objects to be greater than the half width of the smallest object.
- Even if the axis information is not what you want, you can still use the SAT to tell you whether a collision is occurring. Just don't use its overlap values to resolve the collision. Instead, resolve the collision in another way:
  - Use the line-versus-point collision techniques from Chapter 2 to resolve the collision.
  - If you know the direction of the collision, and you know where the collision boundary is, use that boundary to resolve the collision. In Chapters 8 and 9, we'll look at some efficient ways of resolving collisions that you can use if you set up your game world with fixed collision boundaries.

SAT detects collisions very efficiently, and that alone is a good enough reason to use it. But you'll need to decide whether the information it tells you about the direction of the collision is useful or correct in the context of your game.

Finding the amount of overlap

So far, so good, but there are a few more details we need to figure out before we have a complete working system. We're going to look at how to project the shapes onto each axis in detail in the pages ahead, as this varies in complexity depending on the kinds of polygons you're using. Here, I'll show you how to determine whether the projections are overlapping, and how to calculate the amount of overlap.

We need a vector that runs between the centers of both squares. This is the distance vector. The distance vector also needs to be projected onto each axis, as shown in Figure 4-5.

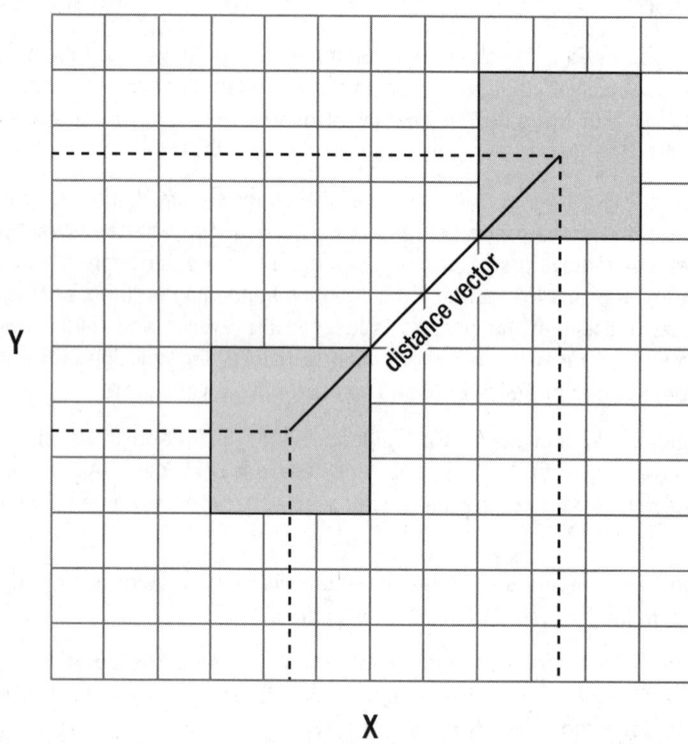

Figure 4-5. Plot a distance vector between the shapes and project it onto the x and y axes.

Use the distance vector's projections like a measuring stick to measure the distance between the centers of the projections of the squares on each axis, as illustrated in Figure 4-6.

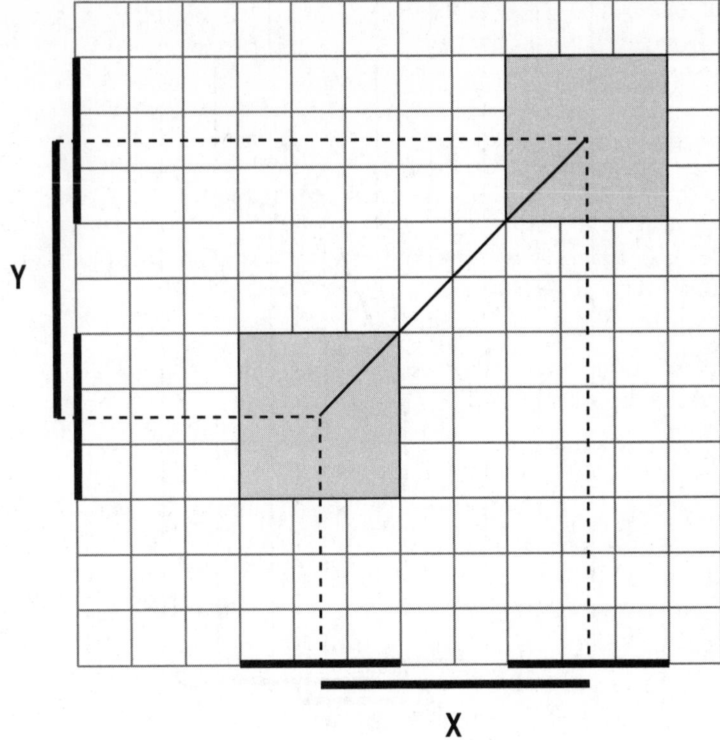

Figure 4-6. Measure the distance between the projections of the shapes to find out whether they overlap.

Follow these steps to find out whether there's any overlap:

1. Add the projections of the shapes together, and divide that number in half. In Figure 4-5, the total of the projections of the squares on the x axis is 6. Half of 6 is 3.
2. If the magnitude of the projected distance vector is less than the value in step 1 (in other words, if it's less than 3), then the shapes overlap on that axis.
3. The amount of overlap between the shapes is the difference between the value from step 1 and the projected distance vector's magnitude.

It's much easier to see in pictures than it is to read, so take a good look at Figure 4-7. (The convention I'm using in this book is that variable names that start with `p` refer to projection vectors.)

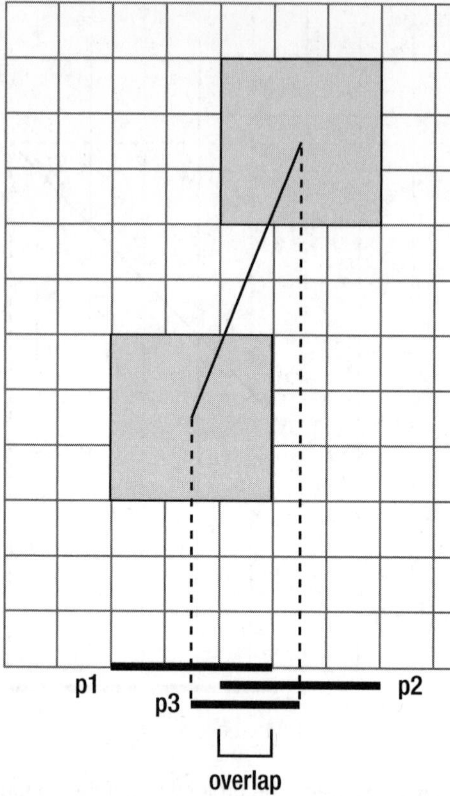

$$overlap = (p1 + p2) / 2 - p3$$
$$overlap = (3 + 3) / 2 - 2$$
$$overlap = 3 - 2$$
$$overlap = 1$$

Figure 4-7. Measure the distance between the projections of the shapes to find out whether they overlap.

Finding the collision side

Now that we know on which axis the collision is happening, we need to find out on which side of the square it's taking place. This is easy to figure out by checking whether the distance vector's vx and vy are greater or less than zero.

- If the collision is happening on the x axis, is it happening on the right or left side of the square? Find the distance vector's vx. If it's greater than zero, then the collision is happening on the right. If it's less than zero, the collision happens on the left.
- If the collision is happening on the y axis, is it happening on the top or bottom side of the square? Find the distance vector's vy. If it's greater than zero, the collision is happening on the top. If it's less than zero, the collision happens on the bottom.

Figure 4-8 shows how to find the collision side. It may look a bit confusing at first so take a moment for the logic to sink in.

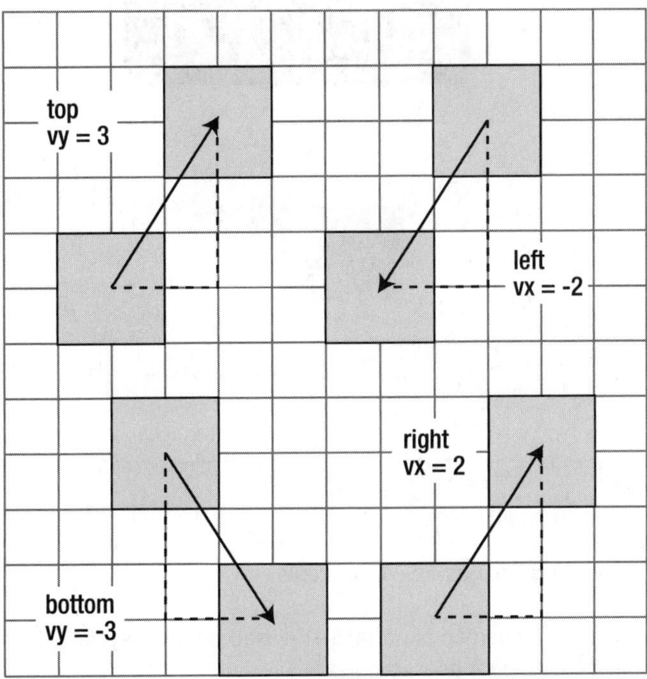

Y Axis

```
if (vy > 0)
{
  side = top
}
else
{
  side = bottom
}
```

X Axis

```
if (vx > 0)
{
  side = right
}
else
{
  side = left
}
```

Figure 4-8. Find the collision side.

You can find a working example of this entire system in the chapter's source files in the `SeparatingAxis` folder. The example looks like Figure 4-9 when you run it. Strangely, I'm going to recommend that you *not* look the source code yet. The source code has been written to exactly match the concepts we've covered so far, so the `SeparatingAxis` SWF is really just an interactive illustration of these concepts. But if you're just working with rectangles, there are shortcuts you can take that can greatly simplify your code. In the next section, we'll address the specifics of using the SAT with rectangles.

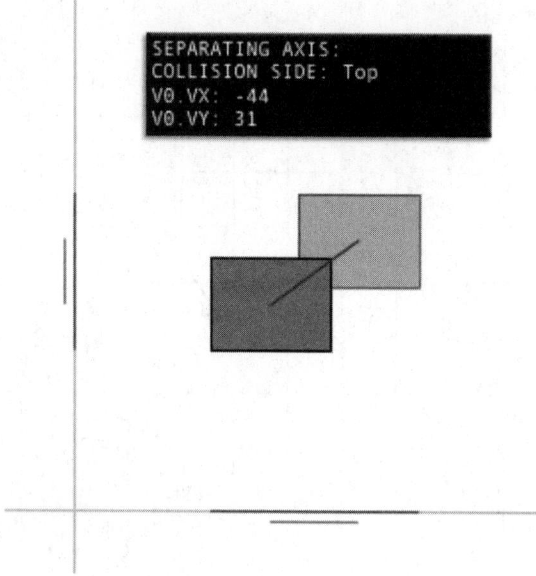

Figure 4-9. A working example of basic SAT concepts.

I've shown you the general fundamentals of a SAT-based collision system. It's the basic theory, and applies to all shapes, no matter how complex.

As you've seen, collisions between squares and rectangles with the SAT are very easy to understand. If you start using the SAT with complex irregular shapes and find yourself getting confused, just come back to these pages to remind yourself of the process and review the examples. If you understand the SAT with squares, you can apply those same principles to all polygons. Just take it slowly, and apply each principle step by step.

Rectangle collisions

Collision detection with squares or rectangles that are aligned to the stage's x and y axes is the simplest implementation of the SAT. In fact, it's even simpler than my description of it in the previous section. There are three important reasons why:

- If a rectangle is aligned to the stage's x and y axes, you don't need to do any projection. A rectangle's projection on the x axis is the same as its width, and its projection on the y axis is the same as its height, as illustrated in Figure 4-10. That means you just need to use the height and width values.

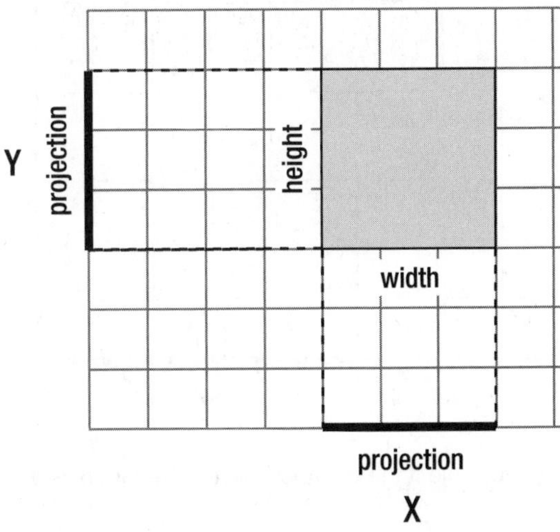

Figure 4-10. Because the rectangle is aligned to the stage's x and y axes, it's height and width equal its projections.

- The distance vector's vx and vy are the same as its projections on the x and y axes, as shown in Figure 4-11.
- You can greatly simplify your calculations if you use half-width and half-height values. This is true not only for rectangles, but also for all polygons, no matter their orientation. (If you need to project a polygon's side onto an axis, divide the projection in half.) You'll see how in the examples ahead.

The short story is that because of all these shortcuts, applying the SAT with rectangles requires only some very basic vector math. It's something every game designer should know, and I'll walk you through each step of the way.

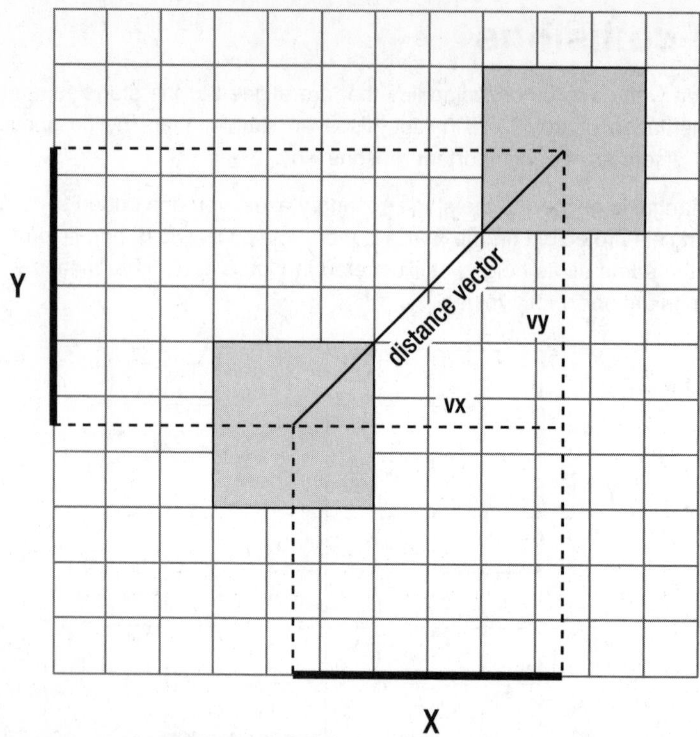

Figure 4-11. You don't need to project the distance vector, because its vx and vy are the same as its projections.

Rectangle collision handling in action

Run the SWF file `RectangleVsRectangle` in the chapter's source files. Use the mouse or arrow keys and move the left rectangle into the right one. It hits it and bounces away at the correct angle. Graphs show you the rectangles' total half widths and half heights, and how they compare to the distance vector's `vx` and `vy`.

In Figure 4-12, you can see that the distance vector's `vy` is less than the total half widths. This indicates that the rectangles are overlapping on the y axis. When they overlap on both axes, a collision is detected.

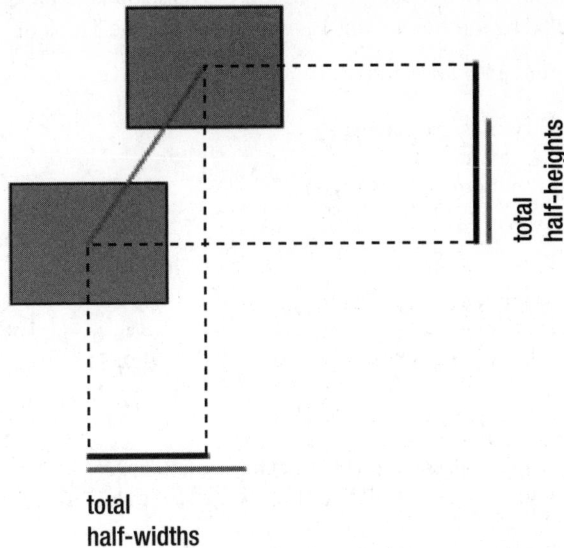

Figure 4-12. The rectangle reacts to the collision with correct bounce and friction.

From the SWF and Figure 4-12, it should be quite how clear how the collision is found.

This example also uses bounce and friction. When you run the SWF, the bounce effect is evident, but what may not be that obvious is the surface friction. The player's rectangle can slide against the surface of the stationary rectangle, and the exact slipperiness of that surface is the direct result of the friction calculation. You'll be glad to know that bounce and friction are calculated in *exactly the same way* that we calculated them in the previous two chapters, so there's nothing new to learn. The implementation is just slightly different, as I'll explain in the pages ahead.

Take a look at the source file, and you'll see that the rectangles are made using `RectangleModel` and `RectangleView` objects. These are the same as the `CircleModel` and `CircleView` objects we used in the previous chapter, except that they create rectangles. `RectangleModel` and `RectangleView` also extend the abstract `AVerletModel` and `AVerletView` classes, so the underlying code is the same as we've been using for circles.

The most important section of the code is the `enterFrameHandler`, and I'll list it here so that you can see how it works in context. These are the names of the important objects that are used:

- `_r1` is the `RectangleModel` that serves as the player's rectangle. This is the rectangle you can move with the mouse and keyboard.
- `_r2` is the stationary rectangle.
- `_v0` is the distance vector between the rectangles.

Follow the comments through the code to see how the collision is detected and resolved. Bounce and friction are handled by the `bounceOnPlane` method, and we'll look at how that works next.

```
private function enterFrameHandler(event:Event):void
{
  //Update _r1 (player's rectangle)
  _r1.update();
  StageBoundaries.bounce(_r1, stage);

  //Update _r2
  _r2.update();
  StageBoundaries.bounce(_r2, stage);
  //Vector between rectangles
  _v0.update(_r1.xPos, _r1.yPos, _r2.xPos, _r2.yPos);

  //Check whether the projection on the
  //x axis (in this case the v0's vx)
  //is less than the combined half widths
  if(Math.abs(_v0.vx) < _r1.width * 0.5 + _r2.width * 0.5)
  {
    //A collision might be occurring! Check the other
    //projection on the y axis (v0's vy)
    if(Math.abs(_v0.vy) < _r1.height * 0.5 + _r2.height * 0.5)
    {
      //A collision has occurred! This is good!

      //Find out the size of the overlap on both the x and y axes
      var overlap_X:Number
        = _r1.width * 0.5
        + _r2.width * 0.5
        - Math.abs(_v0.vx);

      var overlap_Y:Number
        = _r1.height * 0.5
        + _r2.height * 0.5
        - Math.abs(_v0.vy);

      //The collision has occurred on the axis with the
      //*smallest* amount of overlap. Let's figure out which
      //axis that is

      if(overlap_X >=  overlap_Y)
      {
        //The collision is happening on the x axis
        //But on which side? _v0's vy can tell us
        if(_v0.vy > 0)
        {
          _collisionSide = "Top";
```

```
      //Move the rectangle out of the collision
      _r1.setY = _r1.yPos - overlap_Y;
    }
    else
    {
      _collisionSide = "Bottom";

      //Move the rectangle out of the collision
      _r1.setY = _r1.yPos + overlap_Y;
    }


    //The rectangle needs a vector to bounce against.
    //Plot the x axis at r1's position
    var xAxis:VectorModel
      = new VectorModel
      (
        _r1.xPos - _r2.width * 0.5,
        _r1.yPos,
        _r1.xPos + _r2.height * 0.5,
        _r1.yPos
      );

    //Bounce the rectangle using the bounceOnPlane method
    bounceOnPlane(_r1, xAxis, 0.1, 0.98);
  }
  else
  {
    //The collision is happening on the y axis
    //But on which side? _v0's vx can tell us
    if(_v0.vx > 0)
    {
      _collisionSide = "Left";

      //Move the rectangle out of the collision
      _r1.setX = _r1.xPos - overlap_X;
    }
    else
    {
      _collisionSide = "Right";

      //Move the rectangle out of the collision
      _r1.setX = _r1.xPos + overlap_X;
    }
```

```
        //The rectangle needs a vector to bounce against
        //Plot the y axis at r1's position
        var yAxis:VectorModel
          = new VectorModel
          (
            _r1.xPos,
            _r1.yPos - _r2.height * 0.5,
            _r1.xPos,
            _r1.yPos + _r2.height * 0.5
          );

        //Bounce the rectangle using the bounceOnPlane method
        bounceOnPlane(_r1, yAxis, 0.1, 0.98);
      }
    }
    else
    {
      _collisionSide = "No collision";
    }
  }
  else
  {
    _collisionSide = "No collision";
  }
  //...Display graphs and update the status box...
}
```

Bounce and friction

When the squares collide, they need a surface to collide against so that the code can calculate bounce and friction. This "surface" is just a vector that describes the axis on which the collision happens. This vector doesn't actually need to be visible on the stage, and can be calculated just when it's needed.

When the squares collide on the y axis, a vector is created that describes that axis:

```
var yAxis:VectorModel
  = new VectorModel
  (
    _r1.xPos,
    _r1.yPos - _r2.height * 0.5,
    _r1.xPos,
    _r1.yPos + _r2.height * 0.5
  );
```

It's not visible on the stage, but Figure 4-13 shows what it would look like if you could actually see it.

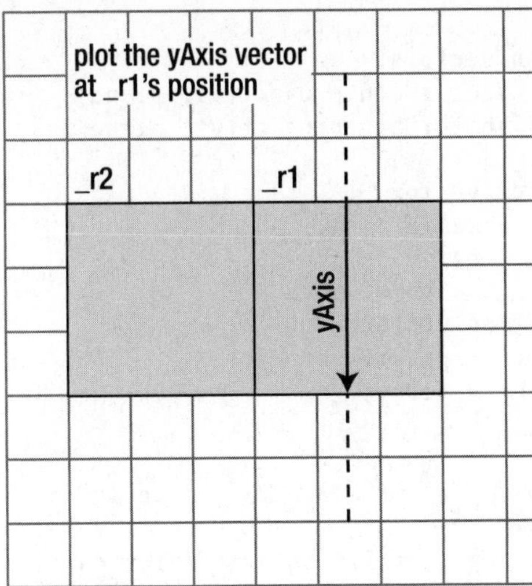

Figure 4-13. Create an imaginary vector that descibes the axis that the collision is happening on. It's needed to calculate bounce and friction.

This is the same kind of "imaginary surface" that we created in Chapter 3 to bounce two circles together. It's just used to give the bounce and friction calculations some accurate numbers.

We can now take this vector and send it to the `bounceOnPlane` method, along with the name of the rectangle and the bounce and friction values.

```
bounceOnPlane(_r1, yAxis, 0.1, 0.98);
```

The `bounceOnPlane` method is a general method that can accept any objects that extend the `AVerletModel` class. This includes `RectangleModel` objects.

```
public function bounceOnPlane
  (
    verletModel:AVerletModel,
    plane:VectorModel,
    bounce:Number,
    friction:Number
  ):void
{
  //The model's movement vector
  var v1:VectorModel
    = new VectorModel
    (
      verletModel.xPos,
      verletModel.yPos,
      verletModel.xPos + verletModel.vx,
      verletModel.yPos + verletModel.vy
    );
```

```
    //Find the projection vectors
    var p1:VectorModel = VectorMath.project(v1, plane);
    var p2:VectorModel = VectorMath.project(v1, plane.ln);

    //Calculate the bounce vector
    var bounce_Vx:Number = p2.vx * -1;
    var bounce_Vy:Number = p2.vy * -1;

    //Calculate the friction vector
    var friction_Vx:Number = p1.vx;
    var friction_Vy:Number = p1.vy;

    verletModel.vx
      = (bounce_Vx * bounce) + (friction_Vx * friction);
    verletModel.vy
      = (bounce_Vy * bounce) + (friction_Vy * friction);
}
```

`v1` is the rectangle's movement vector, and, as you can see, it's calculated when only it's needed. (The `bounceOnPlane` method is also available in the `VectorMath` class in the `com.friendsofed.vector` package.)

This is the same formula that we've been using to calculate bounce and friction in Chapters 2 and 3, so make sure you review those sections for more details on how this works.

Triangle collisions

Finding the separating axis for rectangles is easy because you have only two axes to worry about. And because those axes are aligned to the stage axes, you don't need to do any projection. Things get a bit more complicated when you start using polygons that have angles that aren't at 90 degrees

Triangles are a good next step, because in addition to x and y axes, they have an additional axis: the **hypotenuse**, which is the triangle's slope, as shown in Figure 4-14. (In this chapter, all the examples involve right-angled triangles, which are formed by a 90-degree angle.)

Our job is to figure out a way to find out if another polygon is intersecting the hypotenuse. The SAT can help us, but the solution won't be obvious right away.

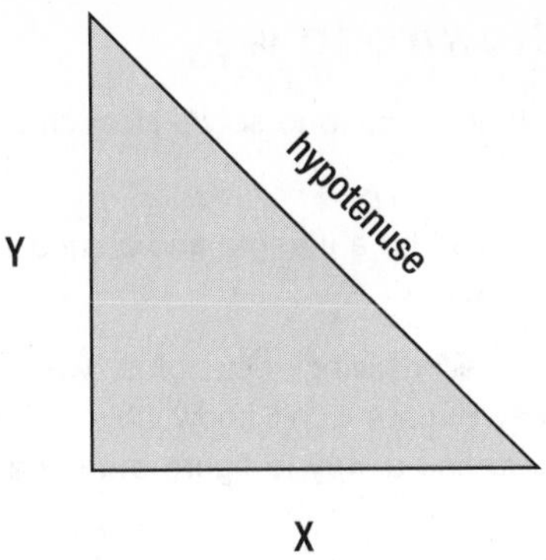

Figure 4-14. Right angles have three axes: x, y, and the hypotenuse.

I'm going to issue an unusual warning about the next few sections. You will need to be very comfortable with the SAT and projecting vectors to fully appreciate the code and examples. If you find it a bit overwhelming, don't panic! Take a few steps back and make sure that you fully understand the SAT with rectangles and can write your own rectangle-versus-rectangle collision code. That's very important, and forms a core game-design technique. Only continue when you feel comfortable with the code and the concepts for rectangle collisions.

You'll be pleased to know that SAT collisions with triangles and other nonrectangular polygons are not essential game-design techniques. You can have a flourishing game-design career without ever needing to develop the collision code from scratch yourself. APIs like the open source Box2D contain libraries of code that do all of this math for you, and probably much more efficiently than you could if you were writing the code yourself from scratch. If you are reading this section and thinking, "This is just too technical!" don't worry. Box2D and other physics libraries will handle it for you.

However, even if you don't implement any of this code yourself, I do think it's a good idea to get some general familiarity with the concepts and problems you'll need to think about. You never know when it might be useful. It's also an important step to writing your own game physics engine, which some of you may want to do. But if it's just too much for now, jump ahead to the Block Game case study at the end of the chapter. You won't miss any crucial information by skipping the next few sections.

SAT with triangles—the wrong way

Let's take a look at the problem that we need to solve. How can we find out whether the triangle and square are intersecting?

Figure 4-15 shows all the axes formed by a triangle and a square: the x axis, the y axis, and the hypotenuse, which is a new, third axis.

As you've seen from the examples involving rectangles, we now know how to check for an intersection on the x and y axes. But we don't know how to check for an intersection on the hypotenuse. Somehow we need to find a way to figure out if the square is intersecting this new third axis.

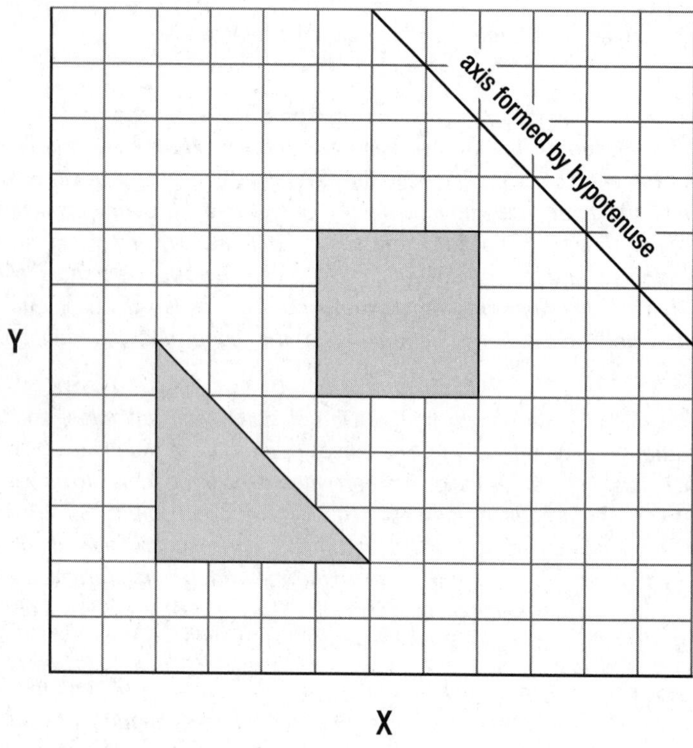

Figure 4-15. The axes formed by a triangle and a square.

To solve this problem with the SAT, we need to first project each shape onto each axis. This is the first, most basic step in any SAT system. Figure 4-16 shows what this will look like.

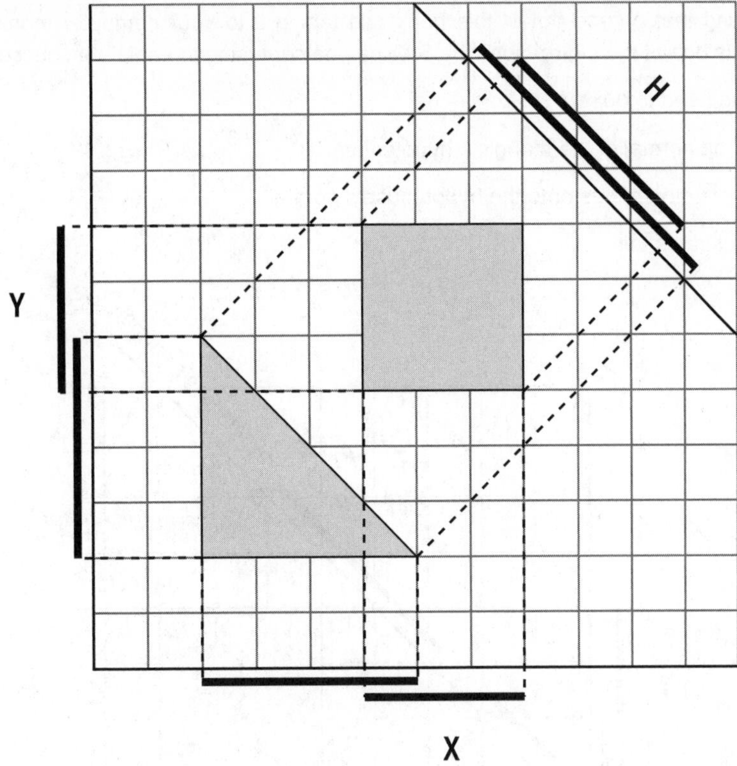

Figure 4-16. The wrong way to look for an intersection with the triangle's hypotenuse

You can see that each shape is casting a shadow of itself on each axis. Each of these shadows is a projection vector that you can calculate using the techniques described in Chapters 2 and 3.

But take a close look at Figure 4-16—isn't something wrong there?

This is what we know so far about the SAT: if the projections of the shapes overlap on all axes, then the shapes overlap. In Figure 4-16, all the projections of both the shapes *do overlap*. According to the SAT, shouldn't that mean that the shapes are intersecting? However, you can clearly see that the shapes themselves are not intersecting. What's going on here?

SAT with triangles—the right way

This exposes a deep truth to the SAT, and one which is often confusing for game developers just coming to grips with using it for the first time.

Don't project the shapes on to the axis; project them onto the ***axis's*** **normal**.

It's worth cutting that phrase out of this book and taping it to your computer monitor, because forgetting this is one of the big reasons the SAT can be confusing to implement successfully.

Here's what we need to do:

1. Find the normal of the triangle's hypotenuse.
2. Project both shapes onto the hypotenuse's normal.

Figure 4-17 illustrates this.

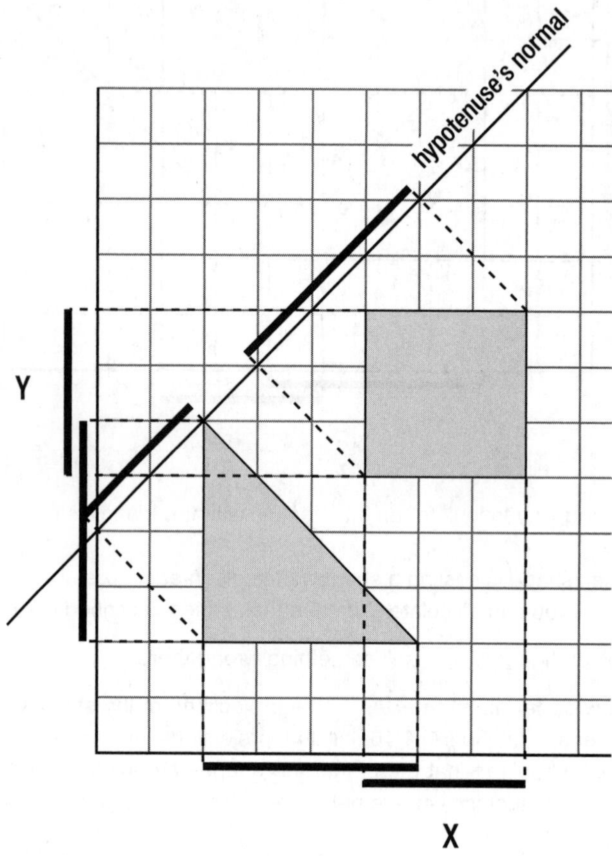

Figure 4-17. The right way: project the shapes onto the hypotenuse's normal.

The distance between the square and the triangle will be the same as the distance between their projections on the hypotenuse's normal, as shown in Figure 4-18.

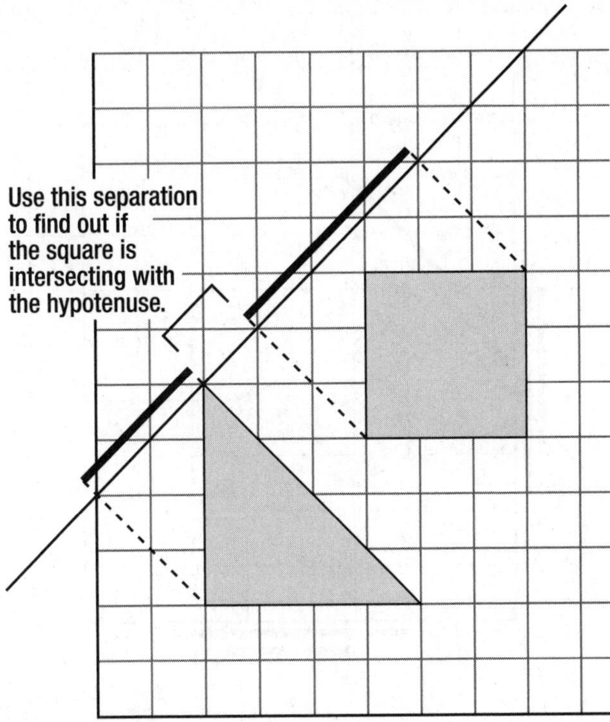
Use this separation
to find out if
the square is
intersecting with
the hypotenuse.

Figure 4-18. The right way: project the shapes onto the hypotenuse's normal.

You can see in Figure 4-19 that when the shapes are overlapping, they overlap on all three axes.

All we need to do next is measure the amount of overlap, and we'll know how much to separate the shapes after they collide. Thanks to the SAT, we also know that the square is overlapping on the hypotenuse because it's the axis on which the overlap is the smallest. Very cool!

But this brings up a big question: When we were using the SAT with rectangles, we didn't need to project onto the normals of the x and y axes. Why not?

Because, very simply, *the x axis is the normal of the y axis*, and vice versa. Remember that a normal is just a vector that's at 90 degrees to the main vector. So actually we *were* projecting on the axis normals, but we didn't need to think of them in that way. This is another very beneficial shortcut to using rectangles. But whenever you have a polygon, like a triangle, that has an axis that isn't at 90 degrees, you must remember to project the shapes onto that axis's normal.

We've got the theory down, now our next job is translate it into usable code.

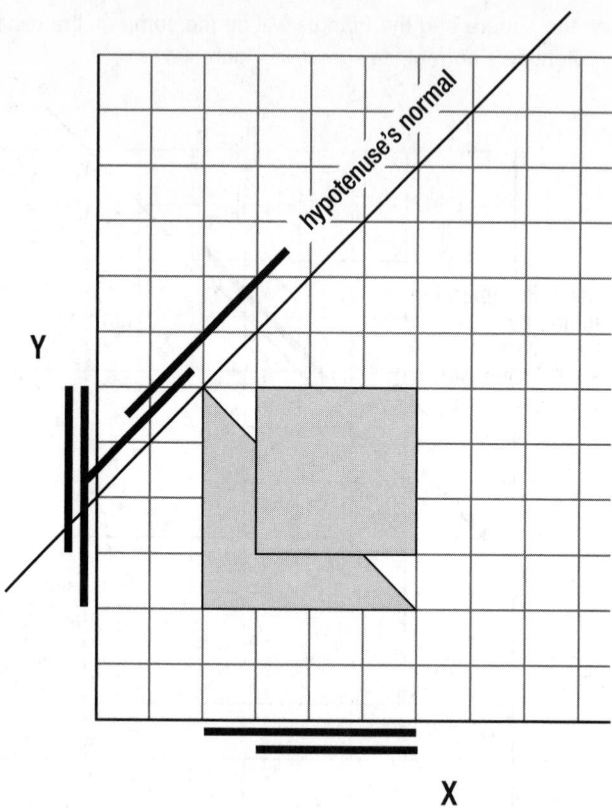

Figure 4-19. If the projections of the shapes overlap on all axes, then the shapes themselves overlap.

Triangle collision handling in action

You can find a working example of this system in the `RectangleVsTriangle` folder. Run the SWF, and you'll see that the collision detection between the rectangle and triangle works just as you would expect, as shown in Figure 4-20. A red line represents the projection of the square onto the hypotenuse. (It's actually half of the square's projection. Why only half the projection is used is explained soon.) Bounce and friction are created with the same `bounceOnPlane` method that we used in the previous example.

Rather than deluge you with source code, I'll take you step by step through the code that makes this work. In the diagrams that follow, I've given all the vectors and shapes the same names as in the source code. I'll highlight the important bits from the source code that match the diagrams, so you can use this as a map to understanding how the code works. Or better yet, use it a basis for writing your own code. Writing your own code is always the best way to learn.

Figure 4-20. Collision between a rectangle and a triangle

Make the shapes

The first step is to make the shapes. `_r1` is the `RectangleModel`. `t1` is the `TriangleModel`. You'll find the `TriangleModel` and `TriangleView` classes in the `com.friendsofed.gameElements.primitives` package. They follow the same format as the classes we used for circle and rectangle objects. The one difference is that you assign the triangle's `inclination`. This is a string that can be `"right"` or `"left"` depending on which way you want the triangle's hypotenuse to face.

This code produces a triangle that faces toward the left:

```
private var _t1:TriangleModel = new TriangleModel(60, 80, "left");
```

Its default value is `"right"`.

Plot the hypotenuse as a vector

Step 2 is to plot the hypotenuse as a vector. The triangle's hypotenuse is a `VectorModel` object, just like any other `VectorModel` object that we've used so far. We need to determine where it starts and ends so that we can figure out how to project the shapes onto its normal , as shown in Figure 4-21.

```
private var _hypotenuse:VectorModel = new VectorModel();

_hypotenuse.update
  (
    _t1.xPos - _t1.width * 0.5,
    _t1.yPos - _t1.height * 0.5,
    _t1.xPos - _t1.width * 0.5 +  _t1.width,
    _t1.yPos - _t1.height * 0.5 + _t1.height
  );
```

I've calculated it like this in the source code so that the process is as clear as possible. However, `TriangleModel` objects also allow you to access the `hypotenuse` as a built-in property. The `hypotenuse` is worked out for you automatically when you create a `TriangleModel` object, and you can access it like this:

```
_t1.hypotenuse
```

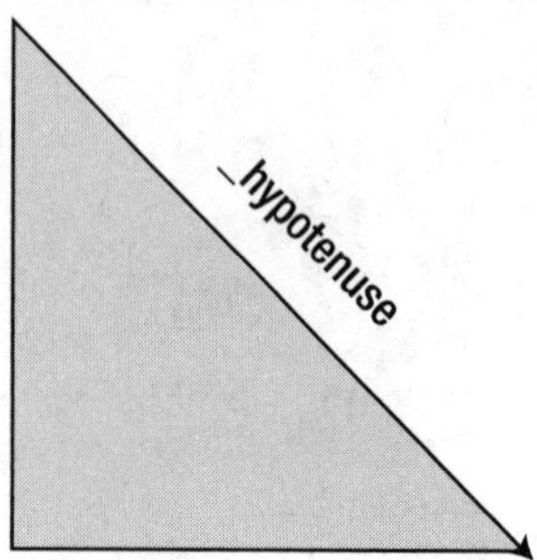

Figure 4-21. Plot the hypotenuse as a vector.

Create a distance vector between the centers of the objects

Step 3 is to create a distance vector between the center of the rectangle and the center of the triangle. Figure 4-22 illustrates this step.

```
private var _v0:VectorModel = new VectorModel();
_v0.update(_r1.xPos, _r1.yPos, _t1.xPos, _t1.yPos);
```

The triangle's "center" is measured from its top-left corner by adding half its height and half its width.

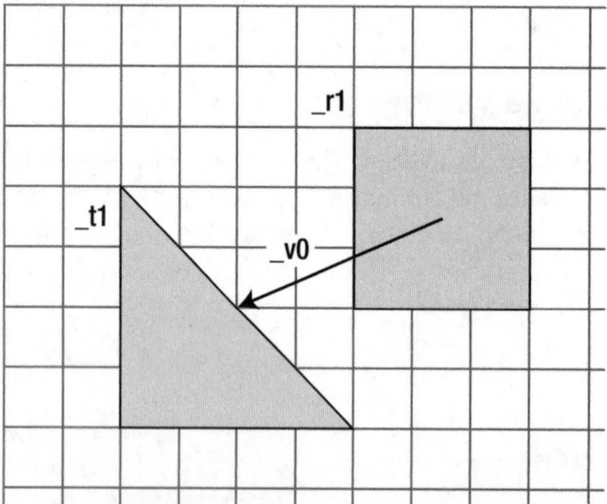

Figure 4-22. A distance vector between the rectangle and the triangle

Project the distance vector onto the hypotenuse's normal

Step 4 is to project the distance vector onto the hypotenuse's normal. Position the projection so that it starts at point A of the hypotenuse's left normal and extends as far as the projection's vx and vy. Figure 4-23 illustrates this step.

```
var v0_P:VectorModel = VectorMath.project(_v0, _hypotenuse.ln)
_v0_P.update
  (
    _hypotenuse.ln.a.x,
    _hypotenuse.ln.a.y,
    _hypotenuse.ln.a.x - v0_P.vx,
    _hypotenuse.ln.a.y - v0_P.vy
   );
```

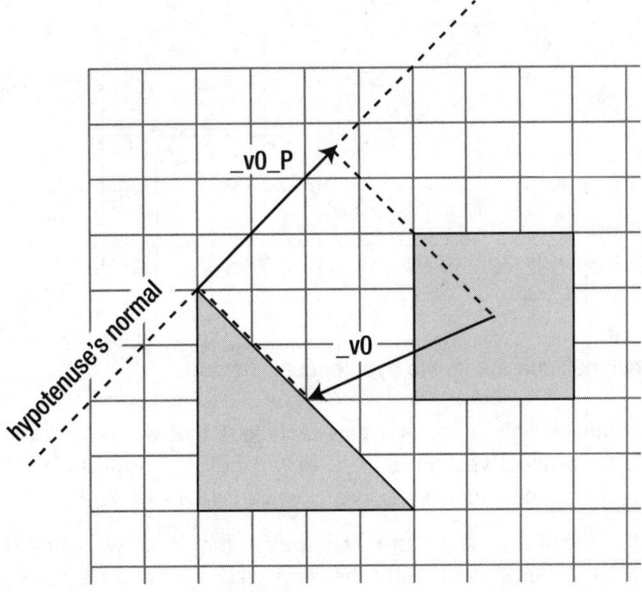

Figure 4-23. Project the distance vector onto the hypotenuse's normal.

Any time you see an uppercase P in the code, it refers to the projected version of the vector.

Project the square onto the hypotenuse's normal

Step 5 is to project the square onto the hypotenuse's normal. Imagine that that there's a light behind the square that's casting a shadow on the normal, as shown in Figure 4-24.

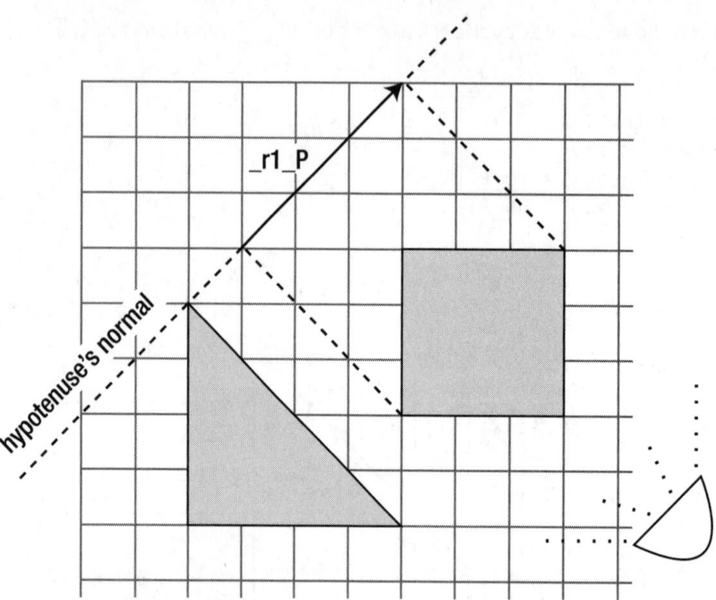

Figure 4-24. Project the square onto the hypotenuse's normal.

Projecting an entire shape onto a line is a new technique that we haven't looked at yet. You've seen how to project individual vectors onto other vectors, but now we need to project a two-dimensional shape onto a one-dimensional line. How can we do that?

If that shape is a rectangle, there are two ways: the long way and the shortcut. The `RectangleVsTriangle` source code uses the long way, because it's more flexible and you'll need to learn how to do it if you project polygons that are more complex than rectangles. But let's look at the shortcut first, because it's easy to do and you'll find many good opportunities to use it in your game projects.

Extend a vector from the bottom-left corner of the square to the top-right corner. You can then project that new vector onto the hypotenuse, as shown in Figure 4-25. If you're using squares or rectangles, this will save you a few extra calculations.

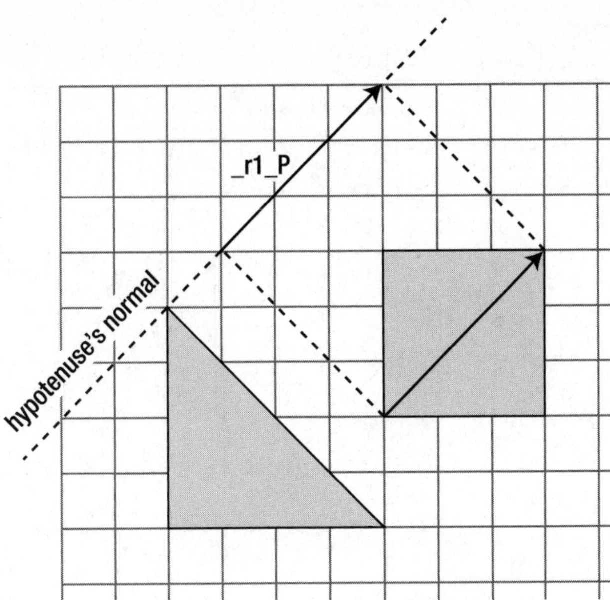

Figure 4-25. The shortcut: create a diagonal vector through the square and project it onto the hypotenuse's normal.

The long way is more flexible because it will work with shapes whose sides don't form right angles:

- Plot each side of the shape as a vector.
- Individually project each side onto the hypotenuse.

Figure 4-26 illustrates this approach.

Remember that the whole point of doing all this is to figure out how big the gap is between the hypotenuse and the projection of the square. We're not quite there yet, but we have all the pieces of the puzzle and are just about ready to solve it.

It turns out that we can vastly simplify this problem if, instead of projecting the square's width and height, we project its *half width and half height*, as shown in Figure 4-27. This reduces the number of calculations we need to do by almost four times. This is because if we combine half of the square's width and height projections, and then subtract the projection of the distance vector, the result will tell us exactly how much space is in the gap between the square and the hypotenuse.

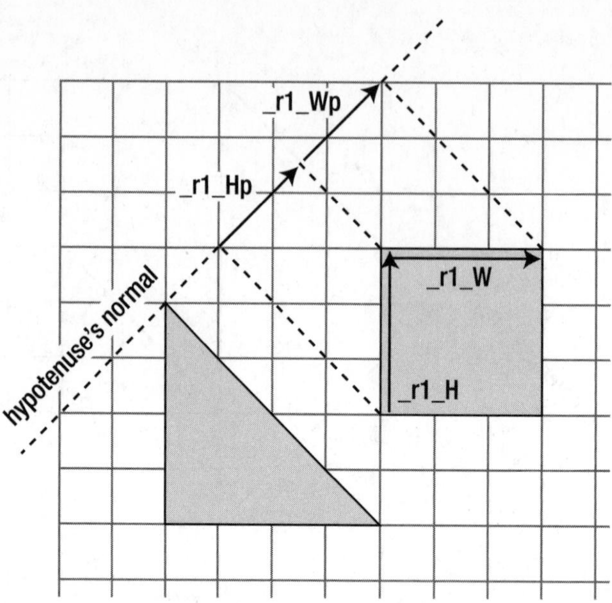

Figure 4-26. Project two sides of the square onto the hypotenuse's normal.

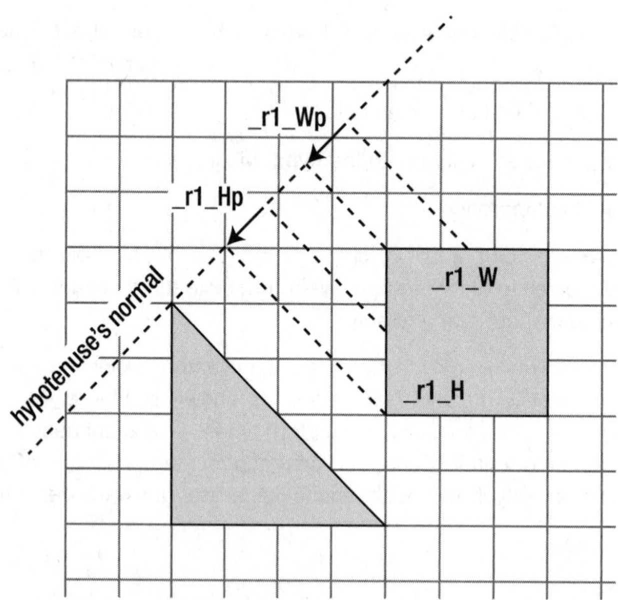

Figure 4-27. Simplify the calculations by projecting the half widths and half heights.

Next, add those projections together to create a new vector, as shown in Figure 4-28. You can see this new vector as the red moving line in the `RectangleVsTriangle` SWF.

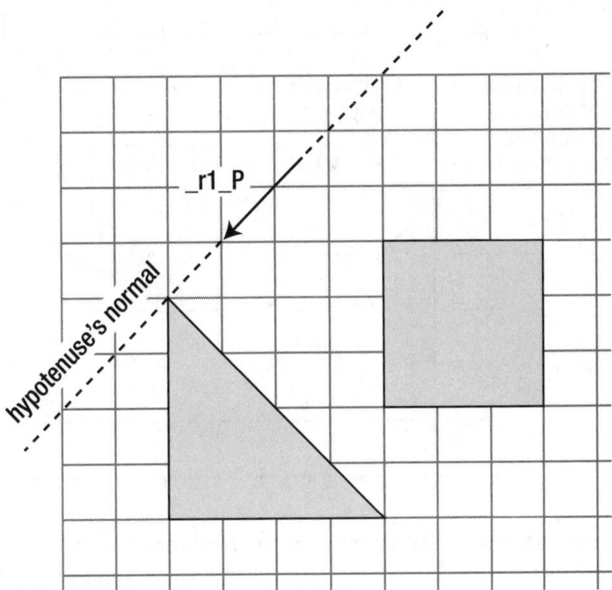

Figure 4-28. Add the projections together.

Finally, if you subtract this new vector from the projection of the distance vector, you can find the gap, as shown in Figure 4-29. It doesn't matter which direction this vector points toward.

Here's the code that finds and projects the square's half height and half width onto the hypotenuse's normal:

```
var r1_W:VectorModel = new VectorModel(0,0,0,0, _r1.width / 2, 0);
var r1_Wp:VectorModel = VectorMath.project(r1_W, _hypotenuse.ln);
var r1_H:VectorModel = new VectorModel(0,0,0,0, 0, _r1.height / 2);
var r1_Hp:VectorModel = VectorMath.project(r1_H, _hypotenuse.ln);

_r1_P.update
  (
    _hypotenuse.ln.a.x + _v0_P.vx,
    _hypotenuse.ln.a.y + _v0_P.vy,
    _hypotenuse.ln.a.x + _v0_P.vx - (r1_Wp.vx - r1_Hp.vx),
    _hypotenuse.ln.a.y + _v0_P.vy - (r1_Wp.vy - r1_Hp.vy)
  );
```

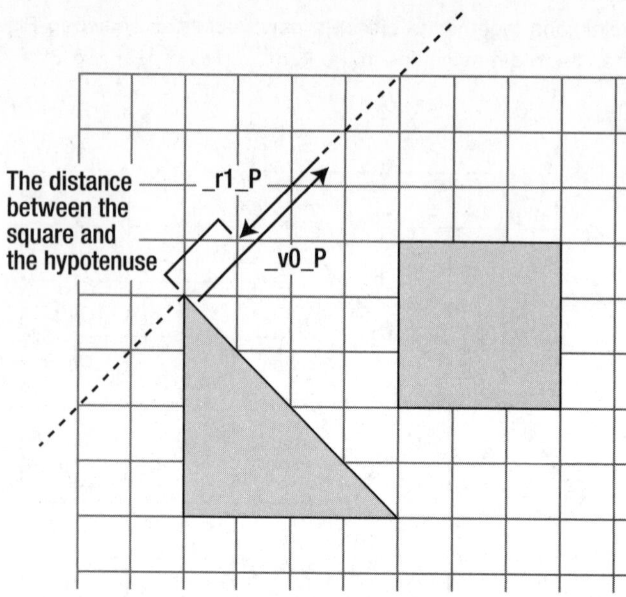

Figure 4-29. The distance between the square and the hypotenuse is equal to the projection of the distance vector minus the projection of the shape's half width and half height.

> *After I wrote this code, I stared at it for a moment and thought, "Wow, what a big mess of code!" It looks pretty intricate, and it is. But, if you step through it slowly, you'll see that it just uses basic math to describe what you can see visually in Figure 4-29. While I was writing this, I wasn't actually thinking about the code at all. My head was just full of little diagrams of vectors, and the code that resulted seemed to just happen incidentally.*
>
> *You'll find it easy to write your own code like this if you forget about the numbers for a while and just think about the pictures. It all amounts to nothing more than projecting, adding, and subtracting vectors—and you've been doing that for at least 100 pages already!*
>
> *You'll also find that it's much easier to write code like this yourself from scratch than it is to look at someone else's code (like mine) and work backward to try to understand it. As I've been encouraging you to do all along, use these concepts and write your own code. That's by far the best way to learn and internalize all these concepts. Maybe even the only way.*

Create a gap vector between the square and hypotenuse

Step 6 is to create a vector to represent the gap between the square and the hypotenuse, as shown in Figure 4-30. If you create a vector to represent it, you'll have a few more numbers you can play with. In the source code, this vector is called `hDistance` because it represents the distance between the square and the hypotenuse.

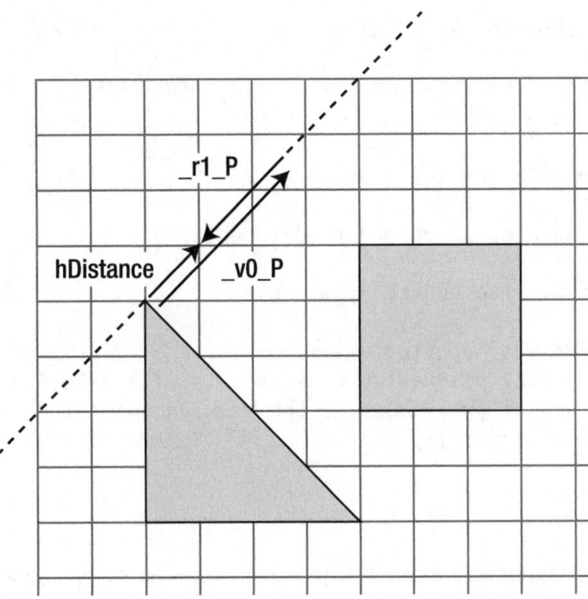

Figure 4-30. Create a vector to represent the distance between the square and the hypotenuse.

```
var hDistance:VectorModel
  = new VectorModel
  (
    _hypotenuse.ln.a.x,
    _hypotenuse.ln.a.y,
    _hypotenuse.ln.a.x - _v0_P.vx - _r1_P.vx,
    _hypotenuse.ln.a.y - _v0_P.vy - _r1_P.vy
  );
```

Find the dot product

Step 7 is to find the dot product between the `hDistance` and the hypotenuse's left normal. This is the last number that we need. It will help us to check whether the two shapes are overlapping.

```
var dp:Number = VectorMath.dotProduct(hDistance, _hypotenuse.ln);
```

Check if the shapes are overlapping

Step 8 is to Check each axis to find out if the shapes are overlapping. We have three axes to check. We know from the SAT algorithm that if there's an overlap on all three axes, then the shapes themselves are overlapping.

This is what the logic for this looks like in pseudo code:

```
if(there's an overlap on the x axis)
{
  //There might be a collision, but we don't yet know.
  //Let's check the y axis:

  if(there's an overlap on the y axis)
  {
    //We're getting closer, but we need to check one more axis to be sure

    if(there's an overlap on the hypotenuse)
    {
      //A collision has occurred!
      //Find the amount of overlap on each axis. The axis with
      //smallest amount of overlap is the axis on which the
      //collision is occurring.
    }
  }
}
```

The process for checking for an overlap on the x and y axes is exactly the same as checking for an overlap on those axes using rectangles.

The third axis that we need to check for is the hypotenuse. We can find out whether there's an overlap on this axis by using the dot product we calculated in the previous step. If the dot product is greater than zero, then an overlap is occurring. The amount of overlap equals the value of the dot product, so that's easy to find.

Here's what all this looks like in the source code:

```
//Check whether the projections are overlapping on the x axis
if(Math.abs(_v0.vx) < _r1.width * 0.5 + _t1.width * 0.5)
{
  //A collision might be occurring! Check the other
  //projection on the y axis (v0's vy)
```

```
if(Math.abs(_v0.vy) < _r1.height * 0.5 + _t1.height * 0.5)
{
  //Check the projection on the hypotenuse's normal

  if(dp > 0)
  {
    //A collision has occurred! This is good!
    //Find out the size of the overlap on the x, y and hypotenuse axes
    var overlap_X:Number
      = _r1.width * 0.5
      + _t1.width * 0.5
      - Math.abs(_v0.vx);

    var overlap_Y:Number
      = _r1.height * 0.5
      + _t1.height * 0.5
      - Math.abs(_v0.vy);

    var overlap_H:Number = Math.abs(dp);
```

Move the square out of the collision

Finally, we need to move the square out of the collision. Compare the size of the overlap on each axis. The collision will be happening on the axis with the smallest overlap. If that turns out to be the hypotenuse, we can move the square out of the collision and bounce it like this:

```
if(overlap_H < overlap_Y
&& overlap_H < overlap_X)
{
  //The collision is happening on the hypotenuse
  //Use the hDistance's vx and vy to correctly
  //reposition the rectangle
  _r1.setY = _r1.yPos + hDistance.vy;
  _r1.setX = _r1.xPos + hDistance.vx;

  //Bounce and friction
  VectorMath.bounceOnPlane(_r1, _hypotenuse, 0.1, 0.98);
}
```

This is slightly modified from the source code, so be sure to check the `RectangleVsTriangle` application class to see it in its proper context.

Triangle collision wrap-up

Congratulations! You've just survived a foray into deepest, darkest, and most dangerous corner of the SAT jungle. It doesn't get more complicated than this, so if you've suffered no greater harm than a few ruffled feathers, rest assured that it all gets a lot easier from here on out.

This also happens to be the most complex application of vector math in the entire book, and probably the most complex math you'll ever find yourself doing in your entire game design career. But as I hope you've seen, the overall complexity is easy to manage if you break it down into small steps. Each of the steps in this process involves the basic vector concepts we've been using since Chapter 2.

And, yes, in case you had any doubt, you now have all the skills you need to use the SAT with polygons of any degree of complexity.

But if it was all a bit of a blur, that's OK, too. This is not an essential core game-design technique. It will get you started on the path to building your own physics engine if that's something you want to do, but that's a much more specialized area. Generalist game designers tend to use third-party APIs like Box2D to handle the really complex geometry and physics. As long as you're comfortable handling collisions between rectangles and circles, and understand the basics of vectors, as well as how to implement bounce and friction, that's all you need to know to follow the rest of the content in this book. The fact is that collisions between game objects are almost always handled by rectangular or circular bounding boxes.

And after this example, our next one is going be like a holiday in the Caribbean!

Oriented bounding box collisions

Earlier, we looked at rectangles that have their x and y axes oriented to the stage axes. The technical name for these is axis-aligned bounding boxes (AABBs). They're the most common shape used to enclose game objects for doing collision detection.

That's all well and good. But what if the rectangles aren't aligned to the stage's axes? What if they're rotated at odd angles, as in Figure 4-31?

Figure 4-31. Oriented bounding boxes are rectangles that aren't aligned to the stage axes.

These are called **oriented bounding boxes** (**OBBs**). They're widely used in games, most obviously as collision shapes for overhead driving games. Just imagine that each of the rectangles has four wheels and a fancy paint job, and I'm sure you'll see what I mean.

There are two important things that you need to know about OBBs if you want to use them for collision detection:

- You can use all the SAT principles that we've looked at so far to find the collision.
- Because rectangles form 90-degree angles, you don't need to project the shapes onto the axis normals. This makes testing for collisions with OBBs much easier than with other angled polygons like triangles, where the angles aren't at 90 degrees.

Let's see how we can apply our knowledge of the SAT to this problem.

1. **Find the axes**. How many axes are there? Each rectangle has four sides, but two of those sides are aligned to the same axis. That means that there are only four axes between the two rectangles that we need to worry about, as shown in Figure 4-32. As you can see, each axis matches the rectangles' top or bottom and left or right sides.

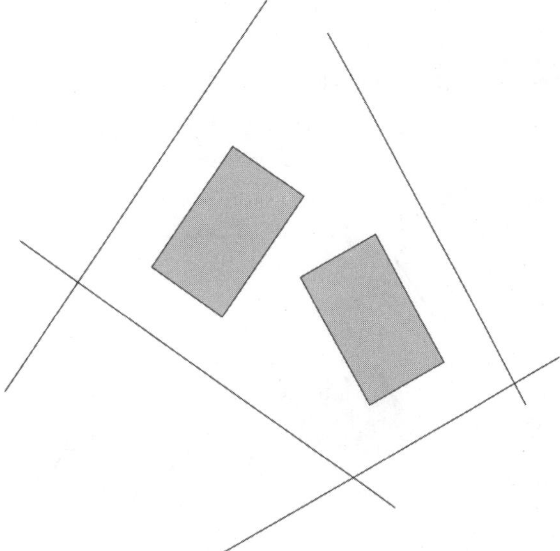

Figure 4-32. Two rectangles have a maximum of four axes.

2. **Project each shape onto each axis**. Two rectangles projected onto four axes means that you need to do a total of eight projections. This can make for a rather chaotic-looking diagram, so I've broken this step into three diagrams. Figure 4-33 shows the projections of the left rectangle onto the axes. Figure 4-34 shows all the projections of the right rectangle onto the axes. If we put all these projections together, we end up with Figure 4-35.

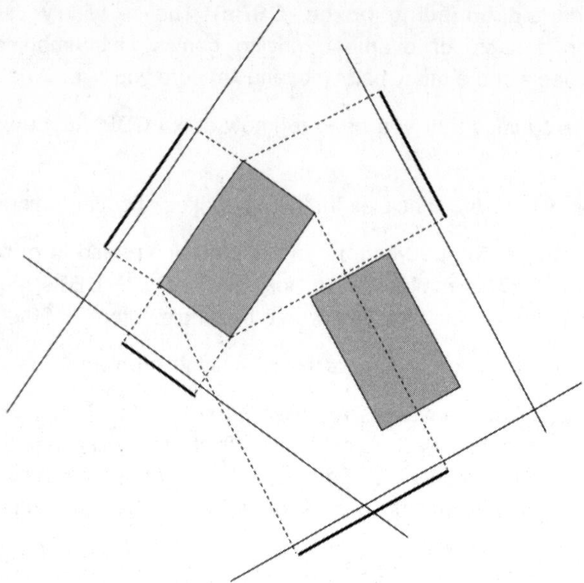

Figure 4-33. Project the left rectangle onto all four axes.

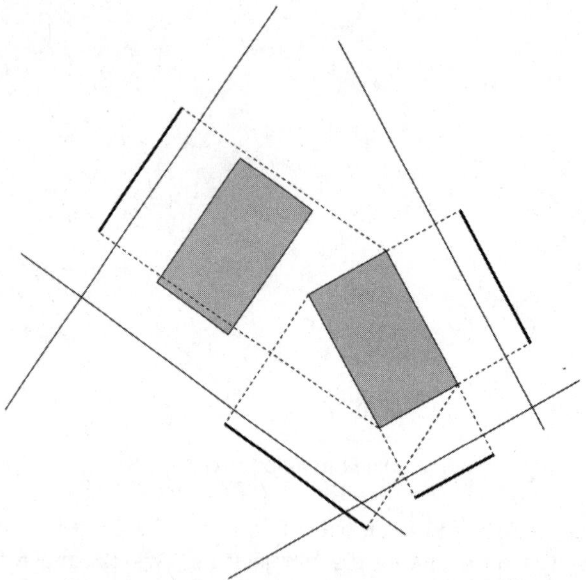

Figure 4-34. Project the right rectangle onto all four axes.

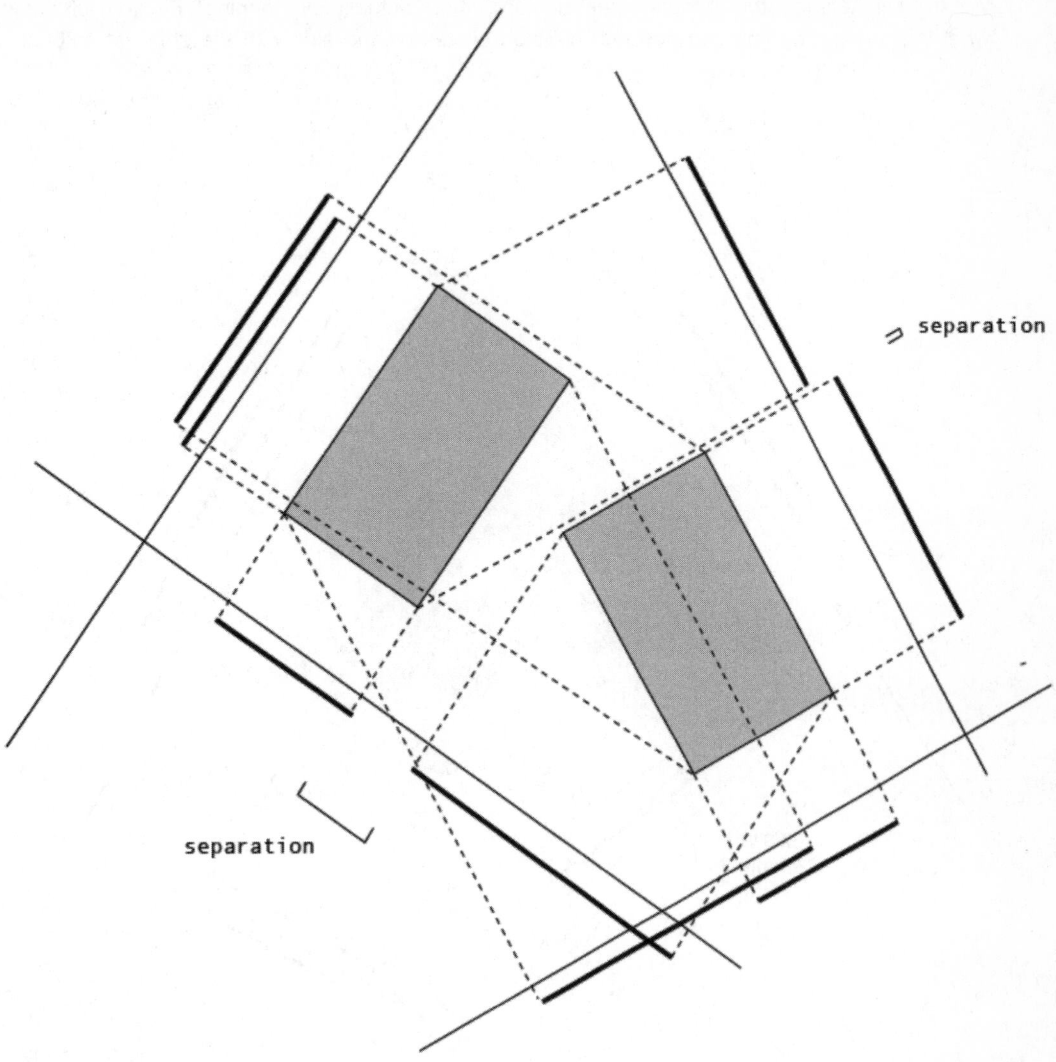

Figure 4-35. With all projections visible, you can see the separating axes. This proves that the shapes don't overlap.

In addition to giving Mondrian a run for his money, this diagram is interesting for another reason. You can clearly see that there are two separating axes. According to the SAT, all axes need to overlap if the shapes themselves are overlapping, so this is proof that the shapes don't overlap.

Will this still hold together if the shapes themselves are actually overlapping? Figure 4-36 shows what this looks like. You can see that collision occurs on the axis with the smallest amount of overlap.

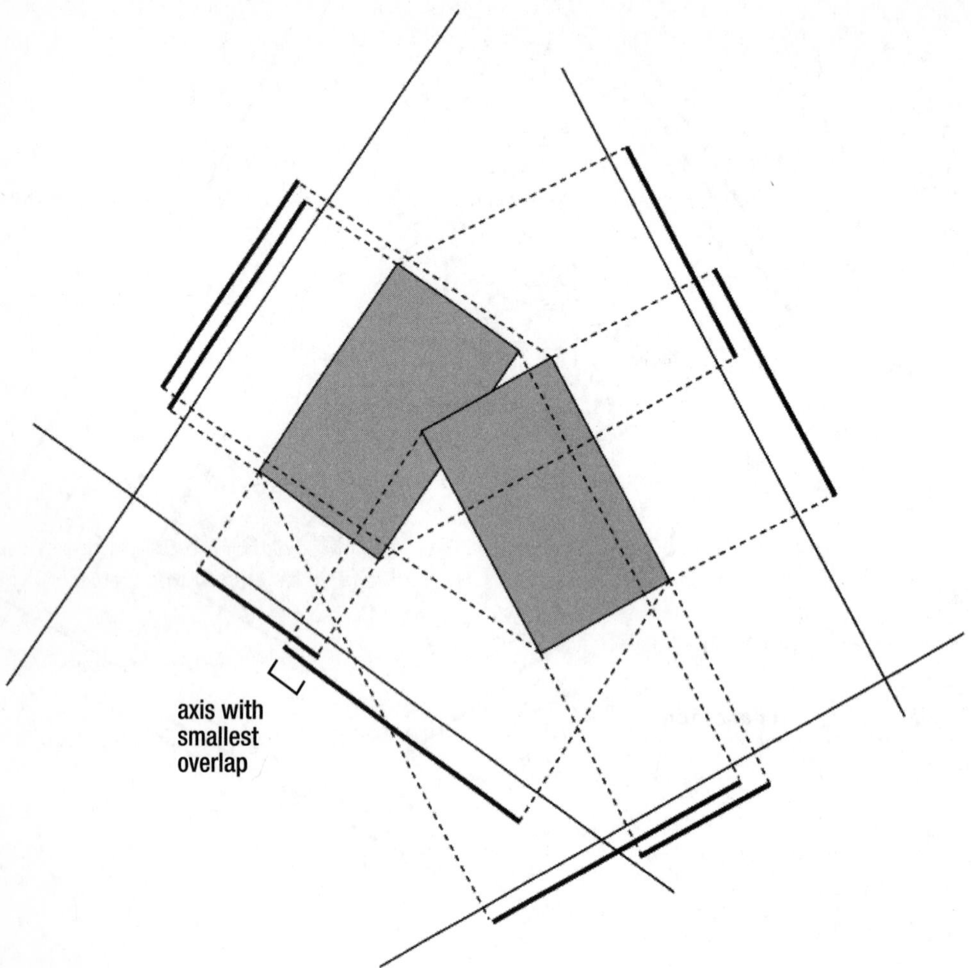

Figure 4-36. When the shapes overlap, the collision is occurring on the axis with the smallest amount of overlap.

Here's how to resolve the collision:

1. Create a collision vector. Multiply the collision axis's `dx` and `dy` values by the amount of overlap.
2. Move the colliding rectangle out of the collision using the collision vector's `vx` and `vy`. If both rectangles are moving, split the difference using the same approach we looked at in Chapter 3 for dealing with two moving circles.
3. Use the axis and axis's normal to calculate the bounce and friction.

These are the standard steps that we've been using to resolve collisions, so they should be pretty familiar to you by now. All these calculations will be much easier to do if you project the rectangles' half widths and half heights.

When I said that this example was going to be like a Caribbean holiday, I actually meant that it was going to be a Caribbean holiday for me! Why? Because I'm going to assign you the actual work of translating these concepts into code. But as I said, it's just the usual routine of projection and separation, which should be old hat to you by now. There are many ways that you could write this code, but the best way is always your own way.

And always remember this: *if you understand the pictures, you can write the code*!

However…

If you're doing an overhead car-driving game, the SAT might be overkill. The SAT is good for a super-precise physics simulation, but there are simpler ways to do the collision detection that could be just as effective. Here are some options:

- Surround each car by an invisible bounding circle. The collision then becomes a simple circle-versus-circle problem that we looked at in Chapter 3.
- For more precision, use two circles for each car: one for the front of the car and another for the back.
- Just check for collisions with the corner points. Each car has four corners, so check each point against the other car's side. You can use the same techniques we used in Chapter 2. This would give you as much precision as the SAT approach and might be at least as efficient.

Simple solutions are often the best.

Polygon and circle collisions

You know about circles. You know about squares. You know about triangles. But what if you want to mix circles and squares and triangles together, as in Figure 4-37?

This is the kind of collision horror scenario that can turn the blood cold of even the most battle-hardened Flash game designer. But it's not as difficult as you might think. It's just a matter of applying a bit of logic to the skills you already have. Let's see how.

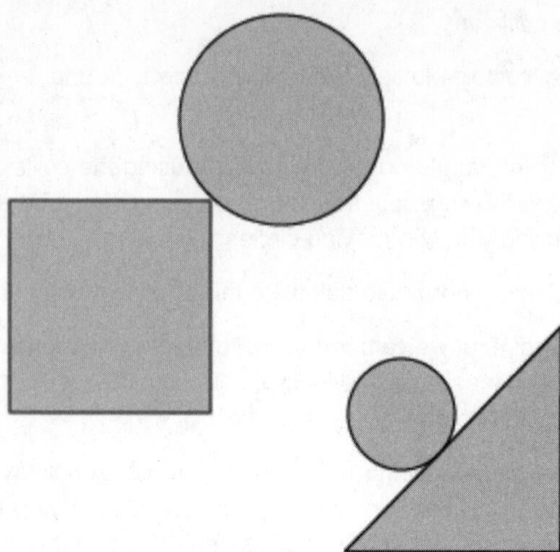

Figure 4-37. Mixing and matching polygons and circles

Circle and square collisions

The problem we need to solve is how to deal with the corners. In fact, it's the same problem we needed solve when working out how to deal with the corners in collisions between circles and lines in Chapter 3. It means that to solve a collision between a circle and a square, you need to break it into two parts:

- When the circle is closer to the sides of the square than it is to the corners, it becomes a rectangle-versus-rectangle collision problem.
- When the circle is closer to any of the corners than it is to the sides, it becomes a circle-versus-particle collision problem. The x and y coordinates of the square's corners are the particles.

To know when to use which collision strategy is just a matter of logic, and this is not at all hard to work out. You just need to find out which region of space (Voronoi region) the circle occupies, and apply the correct collision strategy for that region. Figure 4-38 illustrates where these regions are and which strategy to use for each.

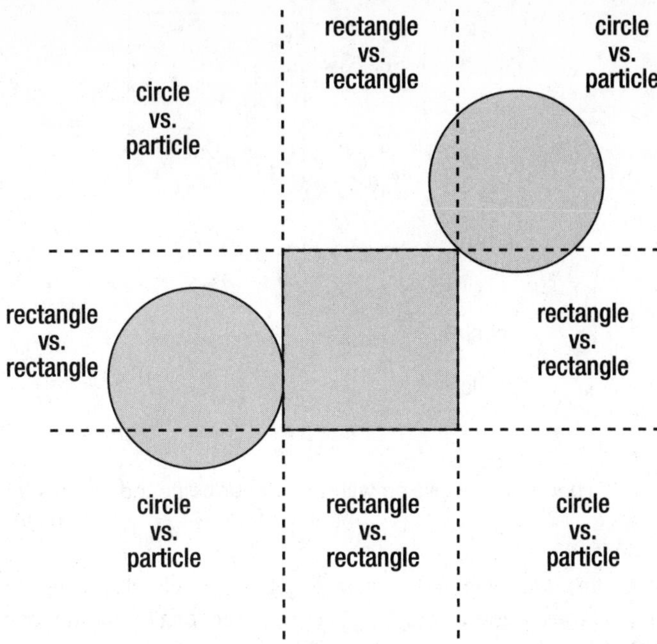

Figure 4-38. Choose the collision strategy based on which region the circle occupies.

You can figure out which region the circle is in by comparing its center position to the square's position, plus its half height and half width.

When the circle is in a rectangle-versus-rectangle region, it literally *becomes* a square for collision purposes, as shown in Figure 4-39. It might look like a circle on the stage, but the collision code sees it as a square.

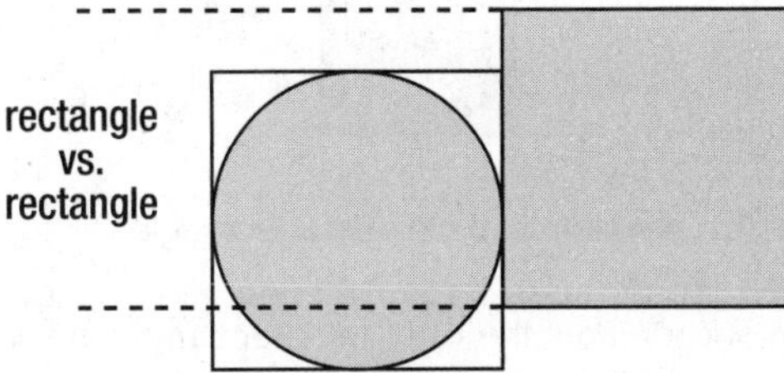

Figure 4-39. The collision code treats the circle like a square when it's in a rectangle-versus-rectangle region.

When the circle is in a circle-versus-particle region, it completely ignores the square shape and just checks for a collision with the square's closest corner point, as shown in Figure 4-40. This is the same circle-versus-particle collision strategy we looked at in Chapter 3.

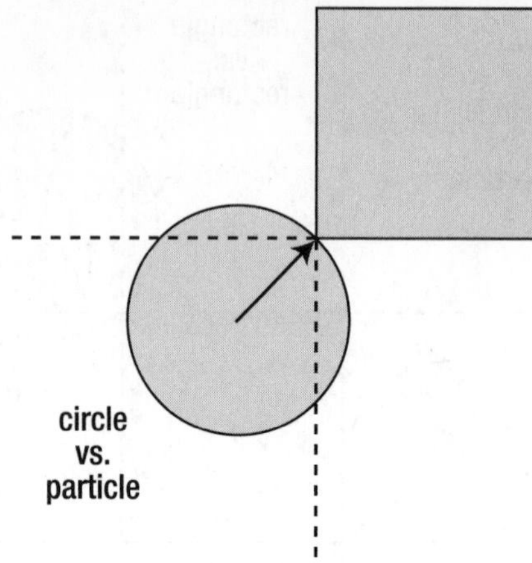

Figure 4-40. The circle checks for a collision with the corner point and ignores the square completely.

Once you understand this, the logic behind selecting the correct collision strategy almost writes itself. But to help you get started, look at `CircleVsRectangle` in the source files, which implements this system, as shown in Figure 4-41. That's right, my holiday is over!

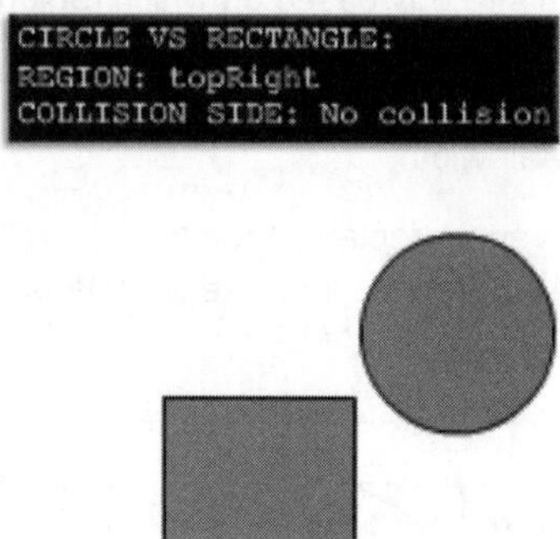

Figure 4-41. Collision detection between a circle and a rectangle

The following is the section of code from the `CircleVsRectangle` application class that finds the region in which the circle resides. (`_r1` is the rectangle, and `_c1` is the circle.) It compares the circle's position to the rectangle's position and size, and figures out which of the eight regions it currently occupies.

```
//Is the circle above the rectangle's top edge?
if(_c1.yPos < _r1.yPos - _r1.height * 0.5)
{
  //If it is, we need to check whether it's in the
  //top left, top center or top right
```

```
  if(_c1.xPos < _r1.xPos - _r1.width * 0.5)
  {
    region = "topLeft";
  }
  else if (_c1.xPos > _r1.xPos + _r1.width * 0.5)
  {
    region = "topRight";
  }
  else
  {
    region = "topMiddle";
  }
}
//The circle isn't above the top edge, so it might be
//below the bottom edge
else if (_c1.yPos > _r1.yPos + _r1.height * 0.5)
{
  //If it is, we need to check whether it's in the
  //bottom left, bottom center or bottom right
  if(_c1.xPos < _r1.xPos - _r1.width * 0.5)
  {
    region = "bottomLeft";
  }
  else if (_c1.xPos > _r1.xPos + _r1.width * 0.5)
  {
    region = "bottomRight";
  }
  else
  {
    region = "bottomMiddle";
  }
}
//The circle isn't above the top edge or below the bottom
//edge, so it must be on the left or right side
else
{
  if(_c1.xPos < _r1.xPos - _r1.width * 0.5)
  {
    region = "leftMiddle";
  }
  else
  {
    region = "rightMiddle";
  }
}
```

Next, the code uses the `region` value to figure out which collision strategy to use. It chooses either a circle-versus-point strategy or a rectangle-versus-rectangle strategy, depending in which region the circle resides. The following is the code from the enterFrameHandler that does this. This is all code that you've seen from earlier examples.

```
//If the circle is in the topMiddle,
//bottomMiddle, leftMiddle or rightMiddle
//perform a standard rectangle vs. rectangle collision check

if(region == "topMiddle"
|| region == "bottomMiddle"
|| region == "leftMiddle"
|| region == "rightMiddle")
{
  //Check whether the projection on
  //the x axis (in this case the v0's vx)
  //is less than the combined half widths
  if(Math.abs(_v0.vx) < _c1.width * 0.5 + _r1.width * 0.5)
  {
    //A collision might be occurring. Check the other
    //projection on the y axis (v0's vy)

    if(Math.abs(_v0.vy) < _c1.height * 0.5 + _r1.height * 0.5)
    {
      //A collision has occurred

      //Find out the size of the overlap on both the x and y axes
      var overlap_X:Number
        = _c1.width * 0.5
        + _r1.width * 0.5
        - Math.abs(_v0.vx);

      var overlap_Y:Number
        = _c1.height * 0.5
        + _r1.height * 0.5
        - Math.abs(_v0.vy);

      //The collision has occurred on the axis with the
      //*smallest* amount of overlap. Let's figure out which
      //axis that is

      if(overlap_X >=  overlap_Y)
      {
        //The collision is happening on the x axis
        //But on which side? v0's vy can tell us
        if(_v0.vy > 0)
        {
          _collisionSide = "Top";
          _c1.setY = _c1.yPos - overlap_Y;
        }
```

```
      else
      {
        _collisionSide = "Bottom";
        _c1.setY = _c1.yPos + overlap_Y;
      }
      //Plot the x axis at r1's position
      var xAxis:VectorModel
        = new VectorModel
        (
          _c1.xPos - _r1.width * 0.5,
          _c1.yPos,
          _c1.xPos + _r1.height * 0.5,
          _c1.yPos
        );

      VectorMath.bounceOnPlane(_c1, xAxis, 0.1, 0.98);
    }
    else
    {

      //The collision is happening on the y axis
      //But on which side? v0's vx can tell us
      if(_v0.vx > 0)
      {
        _collisionSide = "Left";
        _c1.setX = _c1.xPos - overlap_X;
      }
      else
      {
        _collisionSide = "Right";
        _c1.setX = _c1.xPos + overlap_X;
      }

      //Plot the y axis at r1's position
      var yAxis:VectorModel
        = new VectorModel
        (
          _c1.xPos,
          _c1.yPos - _r1.height * 0.5,
          _c1.xPos,
          _c1.yPos + _r1.height * 0.5
        );

      VectorMath.bounceOnPlane(_c1, yAxis, 0.1, 0.98);
    }
  }
```

```
    else
    {
      _collisionSide = "No collision";
    }
  }
  else
  {
    _collisionSide = "No collision";
  }
}

//The circle isn't in danger of intersecting
//with any of the rectangle's planes,
//so it has to be closer to one of the four corners
//The checkCornerCollision method does the
//work of the collision detection
//It takes four arguments:
//1. The CircleModel object
//2. The x position of the corner
//3. The y position of the corner
//4. The bounce multiplier which
//determines the amount of "bounciness"

if(region == "topLeft")
{
  checkCornerCollision
    (
      _c1,
      _r1.xPos - _r1.width * 0.5,
      _r1.yPos - _r1.height * 0.5,
      0.6
    );
}
else if(region == "topRight")
{
  checkCornerCollision
    (
      _c1,
      _r1.xPos + _r1.width * 0.5,
      _r1.yPos - _r1.height * 0.5,
      0.6
    );
}
else if(region == "bottomLeft")
{
  checkCornerCollision
    (
      _c1,
      _r1.xPos - _r1.width * 0.5,
```

```
      _r1.yPos + _r1.height * 0.5,
      0.6
    );
}
else if(region == "bottomRight")
{
  checkCornerCollision
    (
      _c1,
      _r1.xPos + _r1.width * 0.5,
      _r1.yPos + _r1.height * 0.5,
      0.6
    );
}
```

The `checkCornerCollision` method bounces the circle off the square's corners.

```
public function checkCornerCollision
  (
    circle:CircleModel,
    corner_X:Number,
    corner_Y:Number,
    bounceAmount:Number
  ):void
{
  //Vector between circle and particle (the square's corner)
  var v0:VectorModel
    = new VectorModel
    (
      circle.xPos,
      circle.yPos,
      corner_X,
      corner_Y
    );

  if(v0.m < circle.radius)
  {

    //Find the amount of overlap
    var overlap:Number = circle.radius - v0.m;

    circle.setX = circle.xPos - (overlap * v0.dx);
    circle.setY = circle.yPos - (overlap * v0.dy);
    //circle's motion vector
    var v1:VectorModel
      = new VectorModel
      (
        circle.xPos,
        circle.yPos,
```

```
        circle.xPos + circle.vx,
        circle.yPos + circle.vy
      );

    //Create the circle's bounce vector
    var bounce:VectorModel = VectorMath.bounce(v1, v0.ln);

    //Bounce the circle
    circle.vx = bounce.vx * bounceAmount;
    circle.vy = bounce.vy * bounceAmount;
  }
}
```

This code is almost identical to the circle-versus-particle code we looked in Chapter 3.

Circle and triangle collisions

To check for a collision between a circle and a triangle's hypotenuse, we apply a circle-versus-line collision strategy. This is the same collision strategy we covered at the beginning of Chapter 3. The hypotenuse also determines how the regions are divided, as shown in Figure 4-42.

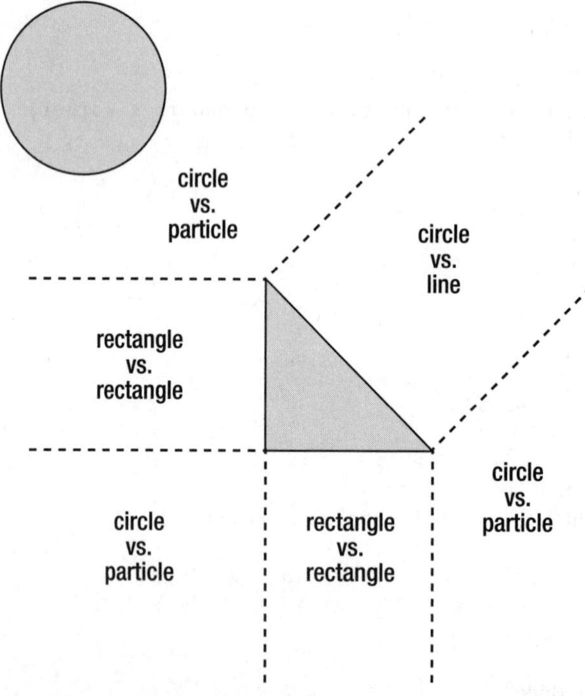

Figure 4-42. Use a circle-versus-line collision strategy to check for a collision between the circle and the triangle's hypotenuse.

To find out whether the circle is within the hypotenuse region, we just need to reach into our bag of tricks and roll this one onto the table:

- Extend a vector between the center of the circle and the start point of the hypotenuse.
- If the dot product between this vector and the hypotenuse is less than zero and greater than the negative value of the hypotenuse's magnitude, you know that it's within this region.

Figure 4-43 shows what you need to find.

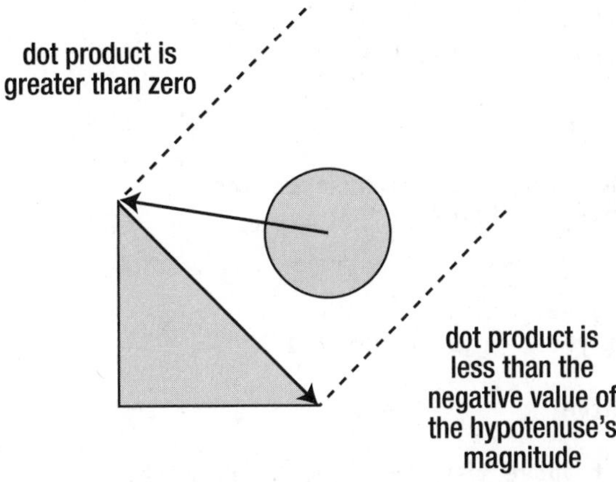

Figure 4-43. The dot product of the two vectors will tell you whether the circle is within the hypotenuse's region.

Check back to Chapter 3 for a quick review of how this works, just in case you've forgotten.

You'll find a working example in the `CircleVsTriangle` folder, as shown in Figure 4-44.

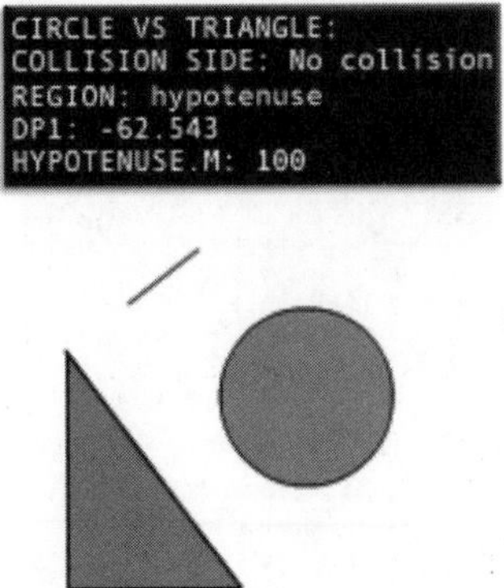

Figure 4-44. Circle-versus-triangle collision.

Again, we just need to use logic to figure out in which region the circle resides. However, there are a few little minefields to sidestep that won't be obvious at first, and I'll point these out as we walk through the example.

Let's take a look at the code in the source that finds the regions. There are a few different ways you could code this, and although this one isn't the most efficient, it's the most understandable.

```
//Which region is the circle in?
//First check the hypotenuse
if(dp1 < 0
&& dp1 > -_hypotenuse.m
&& _c1.xPos > _t1.xPos - _t1.width / 2
&& _c1.yPos < _t1.yPos + _t1.height / 2)
{
  region = "hypotenuse";
}
//If the circle isn't in the hypotenuse region,
//check the other possibilities
else
{
  //Check the top corner
  if(_c1.yPos < _t1.yPos - _t1.height / 2)
  {
    region = "topCorner";
  }
  //The circle isn't above the top edge, so it might be
  //below the bottom edge
  else if (_c1.yPos > _t1.yPos + _t1.height / 2)
  {
    //If it is, we need to check whether it's in the
    //bottom left, bottom center or bottom right
    if(_c1.xPos < _t1.xPos - _t1.width / 2)
    {
      region = "bottomLeftCorner";
    }
    else if(_c1.xPos > _t1.xPos + _t1.width / 2)
    {
      region = "bottomRightCorner";
    }
    else
    {
      region = "bottomMiddle";
    }
  }
```

```
    //The circle isn't above the top edge or below the bottom
    //edge, so it must be on the left or right side
    else
    {
      if(_c1.xPos < _t1.xPos - _t1.width / 2)
      {
        region = "leftMiddle";
      }
      //If all the previous tests fail, then
      //the circle must be within the wedge of space between the
      //bottom-right corner and the the hypotenuse's region
      else
      {
        region = "bottomRightCorner";
      }
    }
}
```

First, we check whether the circle is in the hypotenuse region, as shown in Figure 4-45.

```
if(dp1 < 0
&& dp1 > -_hypotenuse.m
&& _c1.xPos > _t1.xPos - _t1.width / 2
&& _c1.yPos < _t1.yPos + _t1.height / 2)
{
  region = "hypotenuse";
}
```

In addition to checking the value of the dot product, we also must make sure that the circle is above the bottom of the triangle and to the right of its left edge. This is important because the dot product condition could be true if the circle is on the opposite side of the hypotenuse. These extra checks make sure that it's on the correct side of the triangle.

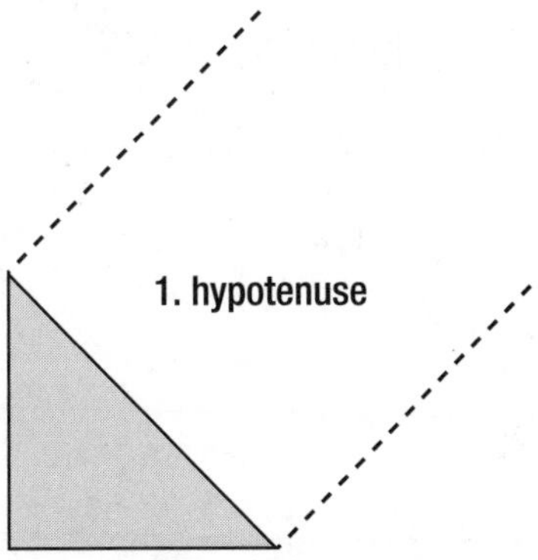

Figure 4-45. Check the hypotenuse region.

Next, check the top corner, as shown in Figure 4-46. Because we checked the hypotenuse first, we know that the circle can't possibly be in the hypotenuse region. This makes the conditional statement for this odd-shaped region very simple.

```
else
{
  if(_c1.yPos < _t1.yPos - _t1.height / 2)
  {
    region = "topCorner";
  }
```

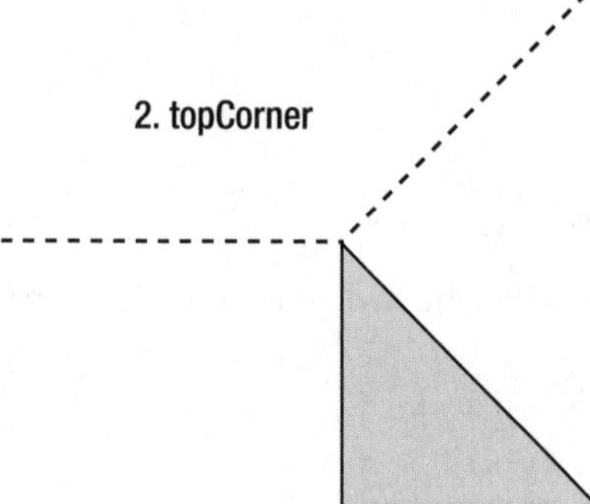

Figure 4-46. Check the top corner.

We've eliminated the top regions of the circle, so we can now check the bottom and sides. The next bit of code checks whether the circle is below the triangle. There are actually three regions below the triangle, so we need to check for each of them, as shown in Figure 4-47.

```
else if (_c1.yPos > _t1.yPos + _t1.height / 2)
{

  if(_c1.xPos < _t1.xPos - _t1.width / 2)
  {
    region = "bottomLeftCorner";
  }
  else if(_c1.xPos > _t1.xPos + _t1.width / 2)
  {
    region = "bottomRightCorner";
  }
  else
  {
    region = "bottomMiddle";
  }
}
```

There's one little anomaly that's not accounted for here, but the next step will fix this oversight.

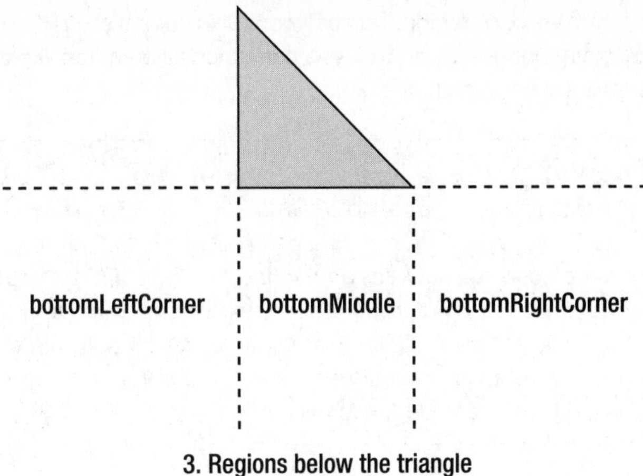

Figure 4-47. Check the regions below the triangle.

Lastly, we need to check the right and left sides. Most of the right side belongs to the hypotenuse region, except for a wedge of space just below it. This wedge belongs to the `bottomRightCorner`, as shown in Figure 4-48.

```
else
{
  if(_c1.xPos < _t1.xPos - _t1.width / 2)
  {
    region = "leftMiddle";
  }
  else
  {
    region = "bottomRightCorner";
  }
}
```

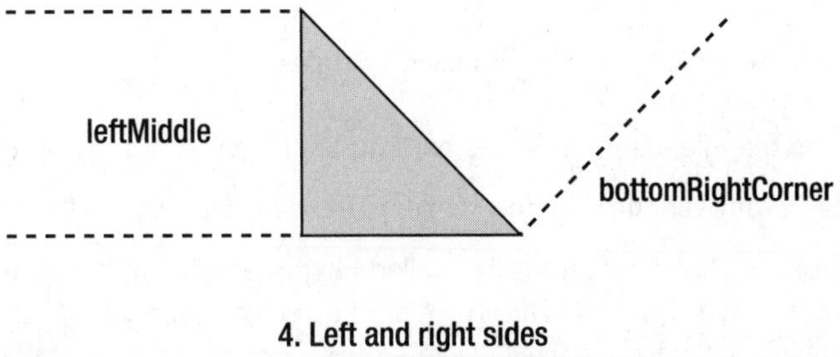

4. Left and right sides

Figure 4-48. The right side also includes the part of the bottomRightCorner region.

When you're working out Voronoi regions for polygons like this, it's often a good idea to draw them with a pencil on graph paper first, so that you can catch little snafus like this before you start coding. Paper and pencil—a wonderful medium!

> *When you deal with the circle-versus-hypotenuse collision, you can use the same circle-versus-line technique we used in Chapter 3. It will work just fine. However, the `CircleVsTriangle` source code handles it differently. It uses the technique that we used to check for an overlap between the rectangle and the hypotenuse. But instead of projecting the rectangle's half width and half height, it projects the circle's radius. Neither method is necessarily better than the other, but it's important to know that there's often more than one way to solve a problem. Check the source code for details.*

Left-facing triangles

In the chapter's source files you'll find a folder called `CircleVsTriangleLeft`. The application class allows you to create triangles that are facing either to the right or to the left, as shown in Figure 4-49.

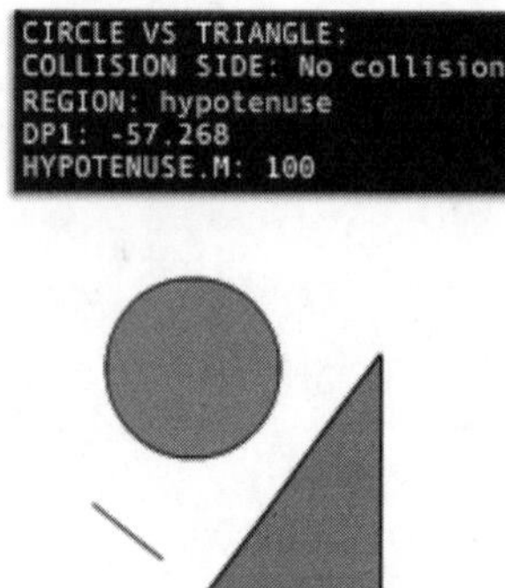

Figure 4-49. Reverse the logic to create left-facing triangles.

To create a left-facing triangle, use `"left"` as an argument in the `TriangleModel`'s constructor.

```
private var _t1:TriangleModel = new TriangleModel(60, 80, "left");
```

`TriangleModel` objects have a property called `hypotenuse` that returns the triangle's hypotenuse as a `VectorModel` object. The `hypotenuse` vector is calculated differently depending on whether the triangle's inclination is `"left"` or `"right"`.

The logic used to find the Voronoi regions for left-facing triangles is exactly the same as for right-facing triangles, but some of the values are reversed. You'll find all the details in the source itself—there aren't any surprises.

Case studies

Now it's time to see how everything you've learned works in actual games. We'll look at two case studies that demonstrate the techniques we've covered so far, as well as some new ones. These case studies supply several important items you can use for your own games:

- A complex physics-based game environment for platform and action games
- A prototype for a breakout-style game
- A flexible template for building games that can be scaled to accommodate games of almost any size or complexity

Case study 1: Polygon environment

We've spent this chapter making the building blocks of game environments. And what do you do with building blocks? Build things! So, like an industrious three-year-old, I emptied my bag of blocks on the kitchen floor and came up with `PolygonEnvironment`, which you'll find in the chapter's source files. Figure 4-50 shows the environment.

Use the mouse or arrow keys to explore the environment. The circle can bounce, roll, slide, and find corners to rest in, as shown in Figure 4-51.

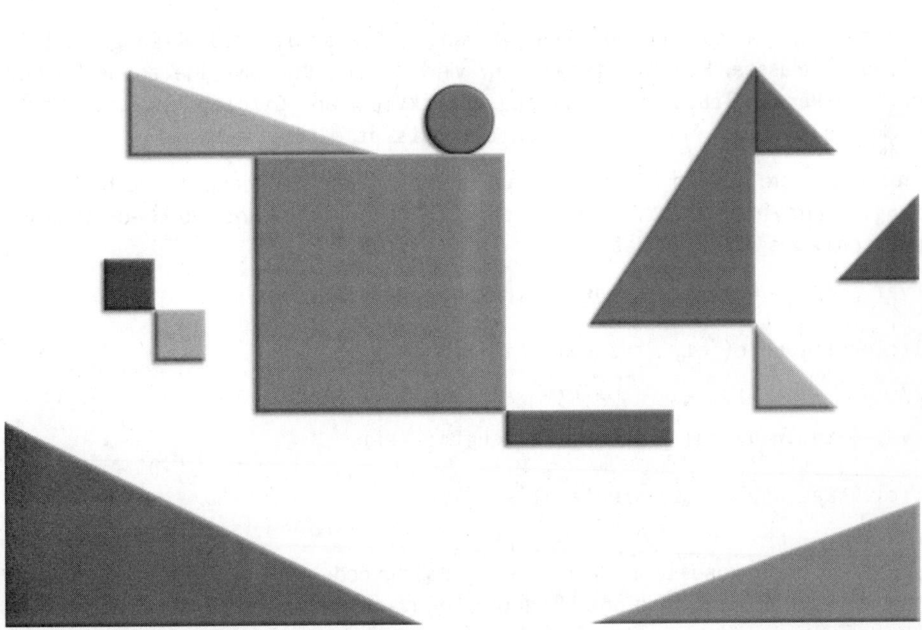

Figure 4-50. An interactive polygon environment with physics and gravity

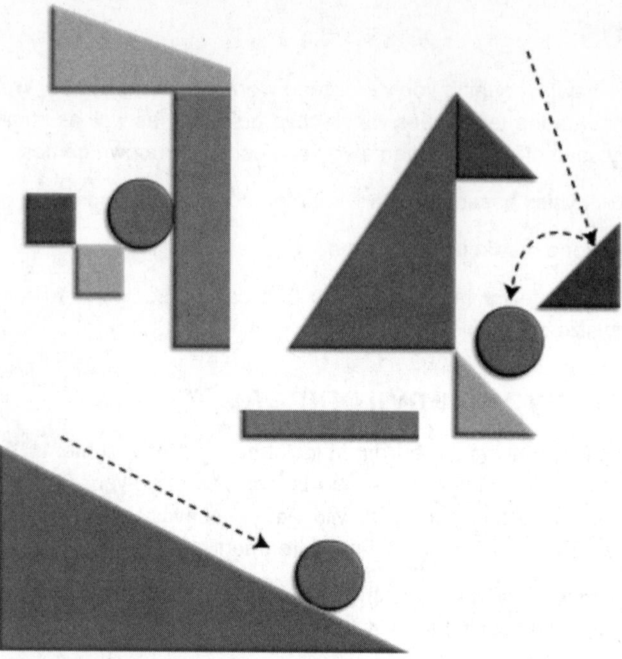

Figure 4-51. Bounce, slide, and hide in a corner.

The shapes that you can see on the stage use the `RectangleModel`, `TriangleModel`, and `CircleModel` classes. But I've created new view classes that give the shapes a beveled appearance: `RectangleBlockView`, `TriangleBlockView`, and `CircleBlockView`. (You'll find these classes in the `com.friendsofed.gameElements.primitives` package.)

The rectangles are pushed into a `_rectangles` array, and the triangles are pushed into a `_triangles` array. The `enterFrameHandler` loops through each array to check each type of shape for collisions with the circles.

```
for(var i:int = 0; i < _triangles.length; i++)
{
  circleVsTriangle(_c1, _triangles[i]);
}

for(var j:int = 0; j < _rectangles.length; j++)
{
  circleVsRectangle(_c1, _rectangles[j]);
}
```

`PolygonEnvironment` uses all the techniques and all the code we've covered in this chapter. I've intentionally kept all the code in one big application class so that you can easily see how it fits together.

Handling slopes

There's a new feature in `PolygonEnvironment`. When the circle rolls up and down the sloping triangles, it behaves like a real ball. It rolls slowly uphill and accelerates quickly downhill. And if it rolls uphill, it will gradually slow down, stop, and roll back down the hill again. This is exactly the effect that gravity has on balls rolling on real hills in the real world.

I haven't made any changes in how gravity affects the circle to achieve this effect. The star of the show this time is friction. I've made an addition to the code so that slopes have less friction when the circle is traveling downhill, and more friction when the circle is traveling uphill.

To figure out whether the circle is traveling uphill or downhill, you need to check its velocity. If its velocity is greater than zero, then you know its traveling downhill, and you need to reduce friction. (The `friction` value is calculated just before the `bounceOnPlane` method.)

```
var friction:Number;
c1.vy > 0 ? friction = 1.05 : friction = 0.98;
VectorMath.bounceOnPlane(c1, t1.hypotenuse, 0.6, friction);
```

If the circle is traveling downhill, `friction` will be greater than 1. The effect of this is cumulative, so that the circle gradually picks up speed as it rolls downhill, as shown in Figure 4-52. You'll find this bit of code in the `circleVsTriangle` method that checks for collisions between the circle and the triangles.

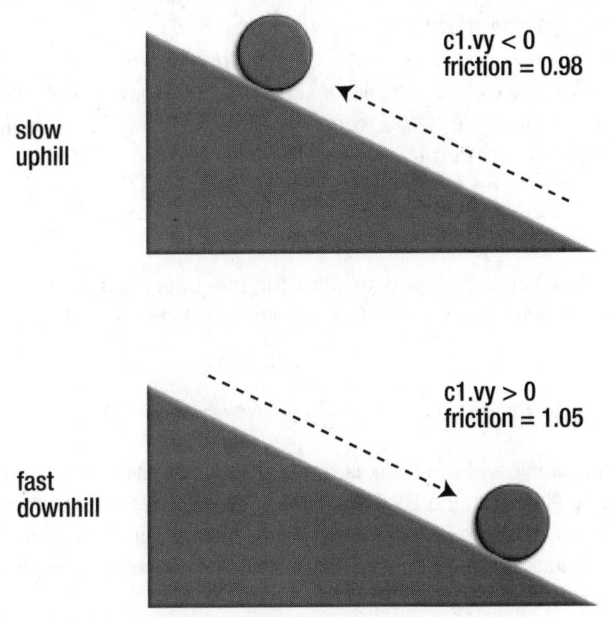

Figure 4-52. Use the circle's velocity to vary the slope's friction.

Building game worlds

With proper game graphics to replace these example shapes, you're well on your way to building game environments that are as complex as any you might need, for a huge variety of games. If you can start to see shapes as containers or bounding boxes for game objects, you'll realize how valuable this chapter has been.

The code used in `PolygonEnvironment` is predictable, but there's also a lot of it—more than 600 lines the last time I checked. If you add some enemies, AI, menus, and a scoring system, you'll soon end up with an application class that's thousands of lines long, and that would be completely unmanageable.

The solution is to break down these responsibilities into separate classes. That's easy enough to say, but how do you do it? If you take the wrong approach, you can end up with folders and subfolders full of classes, and start to forget halfway through the project which classes do what or how they communicate with one another. Classes alone are not answer.

Good planning could solve some of this, but if you're designing a new type of game for the very first time, you often won't know what to anticipate. Game designers like to work on the cutting edge, and the inspired thrill of trying something new in the middle of a project is what drives innovation and keeps games fresh.

> *There is a technical term for "trying lots of new stuff until something works." Game designers call this **iteration**. Iteration, as a design style, means trying something new, observing its effect, and then using what you've learned to try again. That's almost always how game designers work. So, the next time your boss asks you to describe your work methodology, you can reply with confidence, "I employ the **iterative process**." It will sound much better than saying, "I make it up as I go along."*

So, yes, you can plan, but you also need to plan for the unexpected. And expect that the unexpected will become the plan! There's certainly no single solution to this, but the next section suggests a good one.

Case study 2: Block Game

Our first complete game prototype of the book is the imaginatively titled `BlockGame`, which you'll find in the chapter's source files. Run the SWF, and you'll see that it's a familiar paddle-and-brick game in the style of Breakout, as shown in Figure 4-53. Use the mouse to move the paddle and break the bricks. When 30 bricks have been hit, a "Game Over" message is displayed.

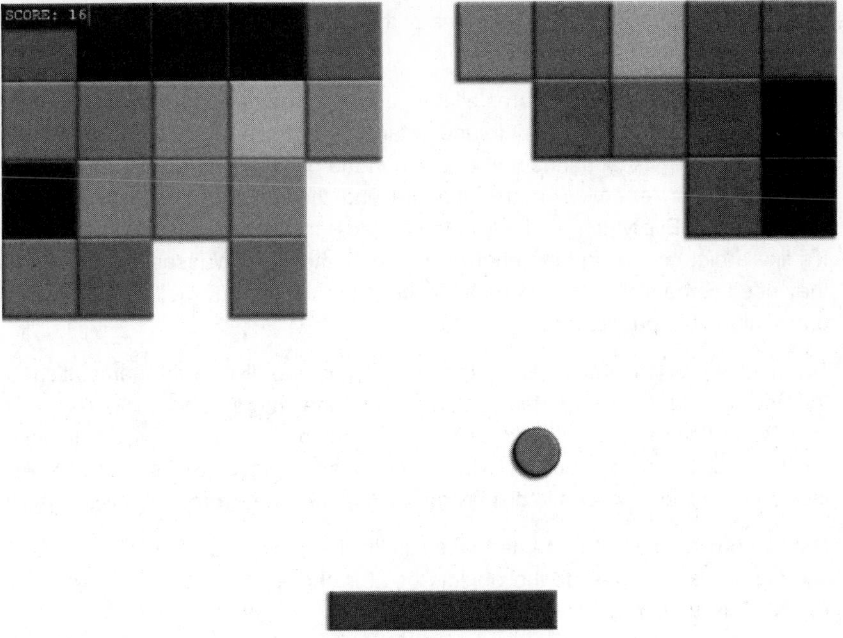

Figure 4-53. A classic brick-and-paddle game

This is a bare-bones skeleton of a game, which I've kept as simple as possible so that you can clearly see how all the pieces fit together. It's important for two reasons:

- It employs the circle-versus-square collision system that we looked in this chapter, which is a core game-design technique. It shows that it's just as effective when both the circle and square are in motion.
- It's structured like a complete game. You can use this structure to build games of great complexity and flexibility once you understand it.

Let's pull this example apart and see how all the pieces fit together.

MVC saves the day again!

The game is built around an all-encompassing MVC structure. You understand how the MVC concept works with individual game objects, like spaceships. What you need to do now is expand that concept so that it envelops an entire game. (If you need a refresher on how MVC works, be sure the review the relevant sections in Chapter 1.)

The basic concept isn't hard to grasp, but some of the details aren't obvious right away. Here are the main components:

- **Game model**: A class that stores all the data of the game. This includes numerical data, such as the score. That's easy to understand, but what's a little trickier to grasp is that it also has all the visual things you can see in the game. This includes the game objects (like the player, enemies, and platforms) and the `sprites`, which contain the entire game screen. Everything that exists in the game must be contained in the game model. It's like a big, centralized storehouse where all the other classes know they can look if they need something. This will be a bit confusing at first, but we'll look at how this works practically in the pages ahead.
- **Game view**: A class that uses the game model data to display the game. It's responsible for adding and removing game elements to the stage. This includes game levels, menus, and score displays. It doesn't handle any game logic; however, it includes logic for the user interface, such as what to do when a player clicks a button. And it also includes any logic it needs to display game data, like the score or to switch levels.
- **Game controller**. All the game logic: initialization, level setup, collision detection, and scoring. It also creates all the objects used in the game and adds them to the game model. This is the most complex class.
- **Application class**: This is the game's common point of entry. Use the application class to compose the MVC system and add the game view to the stage. The application class has privileged access to the `stage` object, so we need to feed it a reference to the `stage` to the view and controller classes.

Figure 4-54 shows how this all fits together.

Take a look at the `BlockGame` folder, and you'll find four files, each of which corresponds with the preceding main components:

- `BlockGame.as` (the application class)
- `GameModel.as`
- `GameView.as`
- `GameController.as`

We'll take a look at each of these in turn and see how they work together to build the game.

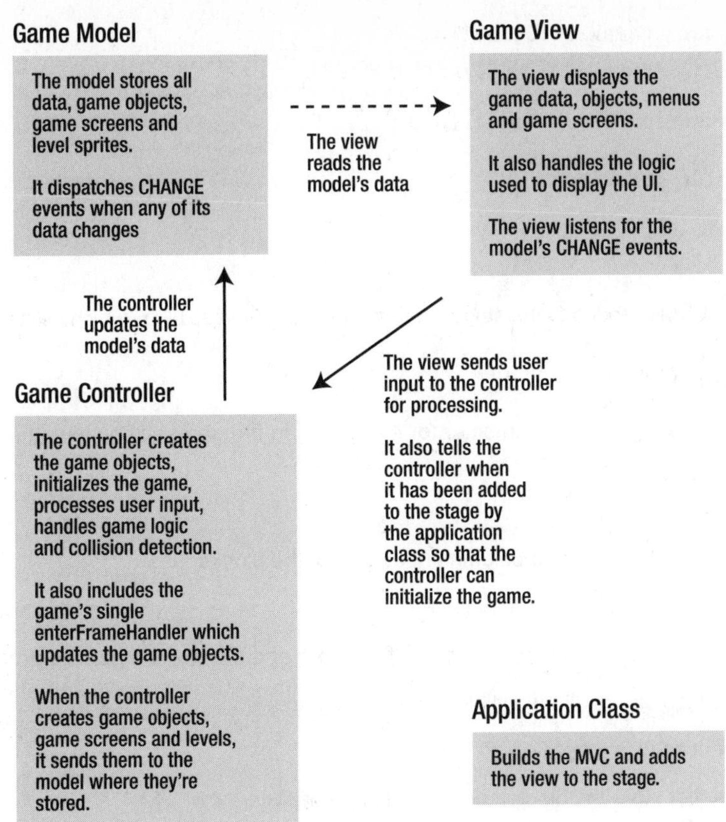
Game Model
The model stores all data, game objects, game screens and level sprites.
It dispatches CHANGE events when any of its data changes
The view reads the model's data
Game View
The view displays the game data, objects, menus and game screens.
It also handles the logic used to display the UI.
The view listens for the model's CHANGE events.
The controller updates the model's data
The view sends user input to the controller for processing.
It also tells the controller when it has been added to the stage by the application class so that the controller can initialize the game.
Game Controller
The controller creates the game objects, initializes the game, processes user input, handles game logic and collision detection.
It also includes the game's single enterFrameHandler which updates the game objects.
When the controller creates game objects, game screens and levels, it sends them to the model where they're stored.
Application Class
Builds the MVC and adds the view to the stage.

Figure 4-54. Use the MVC framework to organize your game.

The application class

The application class is the hook that gets the game up and running. It composes the MVC framework and adds the view to the stage. Here's the entire BlockGame application class:

```
package
{
  import flash.events.Event;
  import flash.display.Sprite;

  [SWF(width="550", height="400", backgroundColor="#FFFFFF", frameRate="60")]

  public class BlockGame extends Sprite
  {
    private var _gameModel:GameModel
      = new GameModel();
    private var _gameController:GameController
      = new GameController(_gameModel, stage);
```

```
    private var _gameView:GameView
      = new GameView(_gameModel, _gameController, stage);

    public function BlockGame():void
    {
      addChild(_gameView);
    }
  }
}
```

When the _gameView is added to the stage, it alerts the _gameController, which initializes the game.

The GameModel

The GameModel is a big storage container for everything in the game. It contains the values for all the game's data:

- The score
- The number of rows and columns used to plot the blocks
- The width and height of each block

The GameController uses this data to create the game and monitor the game's progress.

The GameModel also stores all the visible objects in the game:

- References to the paddle and ball
- Arrays that store the block models and block views

What's important to keep in mind is that the GameModel *doesn't create any of these objects*. The GameController creates them when the game is initialized. However, the GameModel needs to have storage containers ready for them, when the models are first created.

The GameModel does create one object, however. And it's a somewhat unusual object: a screen sprite. This represents the visible stage. The GameController will add the paddle, ball, and block views to this sprite when it initializes the game. The GameView adds this sprite to the stage when the game starts. It's the game screen that you can see when you play the game.

Keep your eye on this screen object! It's the key to understanding how our whole MVC system works. You'll see how this screen sprite is used by the GameController and GameView soon.

It's important to understand that the screen sprite is part of the GameModel's data. This highlights an important point: *everything in the game is data*. Data isn't just numbers and strings. It's also all visible objects and their container sprites on the stage. And in bigger games, this includes complete levels and menus.

The strategy behind this is to pack everything in the game into the GameModel so that it can be found by any object that needs it. The GameModel doesn't make any decisions about what to do with this data or how to display it, but makes it accessible in one central location to any other class or object that needs it.

Here's the entire GameModel class:

```
package
{
  import flash.events.Event;
  import flash.events.EventDispatcher;
  import flash.display.Sprite;
  import com.friendsofed.gameElements.primitives.*;

  public class GameModel extends EventDispatcher
  {
    //The number of rows and columns
    public const ROWS:uint = 4;
    public const COLUMNS:uint = 11;

    //The GameModel needs references to the game objects
    //The paddle and the ball
    public var paddle:RectangleModel;
    public var ball:CircleModel;

    //The blocks
    public var blockWidth:uint = 50;
    public var blockHeight:uint = 50;
    public var blockModels:Array = [];
    public var blockViews:Array = [];

    //The game screen, which is visible on the stage.
    //The GameController will add objects to this Sprite
    //and the GameView will add it to the stage.
    public var screen:Sprite = new Sprite();

    //Game variables
    private var _score:uint = 0;
    public var maxScore:uint = 30;

    public function GameModel():void
    {
    }

    //score
    public function get score():uint
    {
      return _score;
    }
```

```
    public function set score(value:uint):void
    {
      _score = value;
      dispatchEvent(new Event(Event.CHANGE));
    }
  }
}
```

Can you see that the screen sprite is being initialized in the GameModel?

The GameView

The GameView does these jobs:

- Adds the GameModel's screen sprite to the stage
- Creates a status box that displays the score
- Listens for changes to the GameModel's score and displays it in the status box
- Figures out if the score is greater or less than the GameModel's maxScore
- If the score is greater than the GameModel's maxScore, removes the screen sprite and displays a "Game Over" message in the status box

The GameView doesn't actually build the level; that's the job of the GameController. It just handles the bigger picture of adding and removing the screen sprite on the stage and displaying the score and "Game Over" message.

Here's the entire GameView class:

```
package
{
  import flash.events.Event;
  import flash.display.Sprite;
  import flash.ui.Mouse;
  import com.friendsofed.gameElements.primitives.*;
  import com.friendsofed.utils.*;

  public class GameView extends Sprite
  {
    private var _gameModel:GameModel;
    private var _gameController:GameController;
    private var _stage:Object;

    //Status box to display the score
    private var _statusBox:StatusBox = new StatusBox;
```

```
public function GameView
      (
        model:GameModel,
        controller:GameController,
        stage:Object
      ):void
    {
      _gameModel = model;
      _gameModel.addEventListener(Event.CHANGE, changeHandler);
      _gameController = controller;
      this._stage = stage;
      addEventListener(Event.ADDED_TO_STAGE, addedToStageHandler);
    }

    private function addedToStageHandler(event:Event):void
    {
      //Display the screen Sprite
      addChild(_gameModel.screen);

      //Add the status box
      addChild(_statusBox);
      _statusBox.text = "SCORE:";

      //Hide the mouse
      Mouse.hide();

      //Add listeners
      addEventListener(Event.REMOVED_FROM_STAGE, removedFromStageHandler);
    }

    private function removedFromStageHandler(event:Event):void
    {
      removeEventListener
        (Event.ADDED_TO_STAGE, addedToStageHandler);
      removeEventListener
        (Event.REMOVED_FROM_STAGE, removedFromStageHandler);
    }
    private function changeHandler(event:Event):void
    {
      if(_gameModel.score < _gameModel.maxScore)
      {
        _statusBox.text = "SCORE: " + _gameModel.score;
      }
      else
      {
        removeChild(_gameModel.screen);
        _statusBox.text = "GAME OVER";
        _statusBox.text += "\n" + "SCORE: " + _gameModel.score;
```

```
            _statusBox.x = _stage.stageWidth / 2 - _statusBox.width / 2;
            _statusBox.y = _stage.stageHeight / 2 - _statusBox.height;
            Mouse.show();
          }
        }
      }
    }
```

The GameController

The GameController has a lot of work to do:

- Create all the objects and add them to the GameModel's screen sprite
- Construct the level, and initialize the colors and positions of all the game objects
- Run the game's single enterFrameHandler that updates the paddle and ball, and check for collisions
- Contain all the collision methods
- Update the score, which it sends to the GameModel

The GameController class is listed here, but to save a bit of space, I've omitted the collision code. It's identical to the code that we covered earlier in the chapter, so refer to the source for the specifics if you need them. Some of what's happening will be a bit confusing at first glance, so we'll take a look at some of the details after the code listing.

```
package
{
  import flash.events.Event;
  import flash.events.KeyboardEvent;
  import flash.ui.Keyboard;
  import flash.events.MouseEvent;
  import flash.display.DisplayObject;
  import com.friendsofed.utils.*;
  import com.friendsofed.gameElements.primitives.*;
  import com.friendsofed.vector.*;

  public class GameController
  {
    private var _gameModel:GameModel;
    private var _stage:Object;

    //The paddle
    private var _paddleModel:RectangleModel;
    private var _MousePaddleController:MousePaddleController;
    private var _MousePaddleView:MousePaddleView;
    private var _paddleView:RectangleBlockView;
```

```
//The ball
private var _ballModel:CircleModel;
private var _ballView:CircleBlockView;

public function GameController(model:GameModel, stage:Object):void
{
  _gameModel = model;
  _stage = stage;
  _stage.addEventListener(Event.ENTER_FRAME, enterFrameHandler);
  createLevel();
}
public function createLevel():void
{
  //Create the paddle
  _paddleModel = new RectangleModel(150, 25);
  _MousePaddleController = new MousePaddleController(_paddleModel);
  _MousePaddleView = new MousePaddleView
    (_paddleModel, _MousePaddleController, _stage);
  _paddleView = new RectangleBlockView(_paddleModel);

  //Add the _paddleModel to the GameModel and the _paddleView
  //to the GameModel's screen Sprite
  _gameModel.paddle = _paddleModel;
  _gameModel.screen.addChild(_paddleView);

  //Position the paddle at the bottom of the stage and give it a color
  _gameModel.paddle.setX = _stage.stageWidth / 2;
  _gameModel.paddle.setY
    = _stage.stageHeight - _gameModel.paddle.height / 2;
  _gameModel.paddle.color = 0x4E4E4E;

  //Create the ball
  _ballModel = new CircleModel(15);
  _ballView = new CircleBlockView(_ballModel);

  //Add the _ballModel to the GameModel and the _ballView
  //to the GameModel's screen Sprite
  _gameModel.ball = _ballModel;
  _gameModel.screen.addChild(_ballView);

  //Position the ball, give it an initial velocity
  //and set its friction and color
  _gameModel.ball.setX = 275;
  _gameModel.ball.setY = 250;
  _gameModel.ball.vy = 5;
  _gameModel.ball.vx = 3;
  _gameModel.ball.friction = 1;
  _gameModel.ball.color = 0xC27D96;
```

```
    //Create the blocks and position them in rows and columns
    //Array to store block colors
    var blockColors:Array
      = [0xBDCEA8, 0x90AE9A, 0x769690, 0x6C8388, 0x061737F];

    var currentBlock:uint = 0;
    for(var columns:int = 0; columns < _gameModel.COLUMNS; columns++)
    {
      for(var rows:int = 0; rows < _gameModel.ROWS; rows++)
      {
        //Create the block models
        var blockModel:RectangleModel
          = new RectangleModel
            (
              _gameModel.blockWidth,
              _gameModel.blockHeight
            );

        //Position the blockModels in a grid
        blockModel.setX
          = columns * _gameModel.blockWidth
          + _gameModel.blockWidth / 2;
        blockModel.setY
          = rows * _gameModel.blockHeight
          + _gameModel.blockHeight / 2;

        //Assign a random color
        var color:uint = Math.round(Math.random() * blockColors.length);
        blockModel.color = blockColors[color];

        //Push the block model into the GameModel's blocks array
        _gameModel.blockModels.push(blockModel);

        //Create the block views and add it to
        //the GameModel's screen sprite
        var blockView:RectangleBlockView
          = new RectangleBlockView(blockModel);
        _gameModel.blockViews.push(blockView);
        _gameModel.screen.addChild(blockView);

        //Increment the currentBlock counter to plot the next element
        currentBlock++;
      }
    }
  }
```

```
private function enterFrameHandler(event:Event):void
  {
    //Update the paddle and ball Models
    _gameModel.paddle.update();
    StageBoundaries.stop(_gameModel.paddle, _stage);

    _gameModel.ball.update();
    StageBoundaries.bounce(_gameModel.ball, _stage);

    //Check for a collision between the ball and the paddle
    circleVsRectangle(_gameModel.ball, _gameModel.paddle);

    //Check for a collision between the ball and the blocks
    //by looping through all the elements in the blockModels
    //array and calling the circleVsRectangle collision method
    for(var i:int = 0; i < _gameModel.blockModels.length; i++)
    {
      circleVsRectangle
        (_gameModel.ball, _gameModel.blockModels[i]);

      //Remove the block if it has been hit. If it has,
      //its "visible" property will have been set to "false"
      //by the circleVsRectangle method above
      if(_gameModel.blockModels[i].visible == false)
      {
        _gameModel.screen.removeChild(_gameModel.blockViews[i]);
        _gameModel.blockViews.splice(i, 1);
        _gameModel.blockModels.splice(i, 1);

        //Update the score
        _gameModel.score++;
        }
    }
}

    //The main collision method:
    public function circleVsRectangle(c1:CircleModel, r1:RectangleModel):void
    {
      //… Standard circle vs. rectangle code from the earlier in the chapter.
      //Check the source code for details.

      //If a collision is found on the sides of the
      //rectangle and the rectangle isn't
      //the player's paddle, then the rectangle's
      //"visible" property is set to "false".
      //This flags it to be removed from the blockModels
      //and blockViews arrays in the enterFrameHandler
```

```
      if(r1 != _gameModel.paddle)
      {
        r1.visible = false;
      }

      //If a collision isn't found on the sides of the rectangle,
      //this method calls checkCornerCollision to check whether
      //the ball has hit any of the corners
    }

    //Check for a collision with the rectangle's four corners
    private function checkCornerCollision
      (
        circle:CircleModel,
        corner_X:Number,
        corner_Y:Number,
        bounceAmount:Number
      ):void
    {
      //…Bounce the ball if it hits a corner, set the
      //rectangle's visible property to "false" so that it's
      //flagged for removal by the enterFrameHandler

      if(r1 != _gameModel.paddle)
      {
        r1.visible = false;
      }
    }
  }
}
```

The GameController is the brains of the game. It takes on many of the roles that had been the responsibility of the application classes in our previous example files.

The first thing it does is to create the objects. The paddle object is its own self-contained MVC system.

```
_paddleModel = new RectangleModel(150, 25);
_MousePaddleController = new MousePaddleController(_paddleModel);
_MousePaddleView = new MousePaddleView
  (_paddleModel, _MousePaddleController, _stage);
_paddleView = new RectangleBlockView(_paddleModel);
```

The MousePaddleController very simply fixes the paddle's x position to the mouse position. (You'll find it in the com.friendsofed.gameElements. primitives package.)

The next bit is interesting: the paddle model is passed to the GameModel's paddle property.

```
_gameModel.paddle = _paddleModel;
```

From now on, whenever the GameController needs to access the paddle, it does so through the GameModel. This is centralized so that other objects, like the GameView, can access it. The efficiency of this won't be immediately obvious in a small example, but in a complex game, it means that multiple views can access the same data from a common location in the GameModel.

Next, the paddle view is added to the GameModel's screen sprite.

```
_gameModel.screen.addChild(_paddleView);
```

All the views of the game objects will be added to the GameModel's screen sprite. The GameView can then access and display them. Figure 4-55 illustrates how this all fits together.

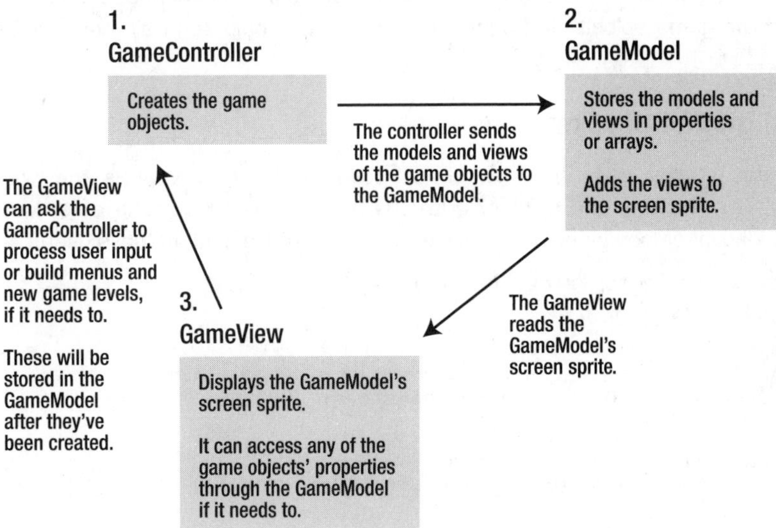

Figure 4-55. The GameController creates the game objects and stores them in the GameModel. The GameView reads them from the GameModel.

The GameController also gives the game objects their initial positions and colors.

```
_gameModel.paddle.setX = _stage.stageWidth * 0.5;
_gameModel.paddle.setY = _stage.stageHeight - _gameModel.paddle.height * 0.5;
_gameModel.paddle.color = 0x4E4E4E;
```

But hold on a moment! This is visual information relating to the display. In an MVC system, isn't that the job of the view? Shouldn't positions and colors be assigned in the GameView?

Let's review what we know about MVC:

- Only the controller should change values in the model.
- The view should only read the model's data.
- If the view needs any values changed, it should pass that request to the controller first.

Our GameController code is sticking to this formula. The x, y, and color information are all properties of objects that exist in the GameModel. That means that only the GameController should be allowed to change it. It's visual data, yes, but it's *data.* All data—visual or otherwise—should be centralized in the GameModel, and only the GameController can change it.

However, that doesn't prevent the GameView from creating its own objects and accessing them directly. In this simple example, the GameView creates a StatusBox object to display the score. The GameModel doesn't' need to know anything about the StatusBox, because the StatusBox has nothing to do with the data of the game. It's purely for display purposes. The GameView can create and modify any other objects it needs, like borders, buttons, or menus to showcase that data. The only thing it can't do is directly change properties in the GameModel. It can't change the properties of the game objects. If it thinks it needs to, it should send all those requests to the GameController.

Plotting the grid of blocks

The last detail of this code that we should take a closer look at is the way that the GameController plots the grid of blocks. It uses a nested for loop. The outer loop plots the columns, and the inner loop plots the rows. Here's the general algorithm that's used:

```
//A counter variable to track the current block
var currentBlock:uint = 0;

//Columns
for(var columns:int = 0; columns < _gameModel.COLUMNS; columns++)
{
  //Rows
  for(var rows:int = 0; rows < _gameModel.ROWS; rows++)
  {
    //Create the block
    var block = new Block();

    //Set the x and y position
    //(assuming the block's x and y point is its center)
    block.x = columns * block.width + block.width * 0.5;
    block.y = rows * block.height + block.height * 0.5;

    //Push the block into an array
    blockArray.push(block);

    //Increment the currentBlock counter to plot the next element
    currentBlock++;
  }
}
```

This is skeletal code so that you can better understand the underlying system for plotting a grid of rectangles. The actual code in the GameController class (listed earlier) also does the additional work of assigning colors and adding the block views to the GameModel's screen sprite. It also adds the blocks' views and models to arrays so that they can easily be removed after a collision.

This algorithm for plotting a grid is another fundamental game-design technique. You're going to see it many more times in this book in various contexts.

Multilevel games

It takes a bit of practice and a bit of discipline to code like this. The payoff is that you have an abstract model of your game running behind the scenes that any object can access. And because the data is largely decoupled from the other objects, it can be displayed or processed in an endless variety of ways without disrupting the rest of the structure.

It also doesn't make any assumption about what the content of the game is, so it's a blank slate. It will work just as well as a general structure whether you're designing a video game or an interactive information kiosk for a museum.

Using an MVC system for organizing your game is also very flexible because you can add as many new components to this system as you need to without breaking the components that are already working together. This is great for creatively designing your game while you code it. An example of this is building a multilevel game, with many game screens and different styles of play. In this simple game, there's only one level and then the game ends. But how could we expand this to create more game levels? Very simply: create a model, view, and controller *for each level*.

For level one, you might have three classes: `LevelOneModel`, `LevelOneView`, and `LevelOneController`. They would be functionally almost identical to the three classes we've just looked at. However, in a multilevel game, you would also use a `GameModel`, `GameView`, and `GameController`. Their tasks would be to manage the overall running of the game.

The `GameModel` would track the global data, like the score, that's needs to run the game, and set the overall conditions for winning and losing. Optionally, you might also find it useful to store individual levels as data in the game. This is the same concept as storing the `screen` sprite as data, except on a wider scope. Game levels are a kind of data, so it might make sense for `GameModel` to store them. This is especially true if data needs to be shared between levels. The `GameModel` can then act as a single resource for this data.

The `GameView` would switch levels and handle the game's menus and user interface. (Specific menus for each level are handled by the level's view.) It would listen for changes in the model to figure out when it should switch levels. It then would ask the `GameController` to create a new level.

The `GameController` would create the levels. Levels are complete, self-contained MVC systems in their own right. They would consist of three classes, such as `LevelOneModel`, `LevelOneView`, and `LevelOneController`. The details of level creation are handled by the `LevelController`.

Something to consider is that the `LevelOneModel` might also need to access to the `GameModel`'s, data. If so, you could create the `LevelOneModel` like this:

```
private var _levelOneModel:LevelOneModel = new LevelOneModel (_gameModel);
```

It's also quite likely that the LevelOneController would need access to the GameModel, to alert it to update the global score, among other things. In that case, you could create the LevelOneController like this:

```
private var _levelOneController:LevelOneController
  = new LevelOneController(_levelOneModel, _gameModel, stage);
```

It's quite acceptable for a model in an MVC system to have more than one controller.

In addition to this, you'll almost certainly need two more items:

- A gameElements package that contains the MVC components for your game objects. This could include the player character, enemies, backgrounds, and platforms.
- A Collision class. It's very likely that your collision code will be common to all game levels, so it makes sense to centralize it.

There are a few different ways that you could handle these specifics, but this will be enough to get you started. Figure 4-56 shows the basic file structure you might end up with a three-level game.

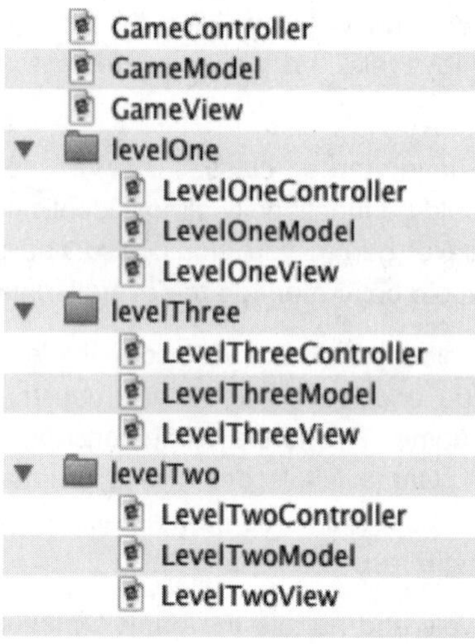

Figure 4-56. Structure for a multilevel game.

Chapter 7 takes a more detailed look at game structure using this system and how to manage a complex game. It also explains how to manage different game states.

Remember that this *is merely a suggested way of organizing your code*. It works, and works well, but there's no one-size-fits-all solution that will cover all game design problems. Look carefully at each game project before you start to determine whether this solution will work for you. Also, don't feel you need to understand all of this just by reading through this chapter. This is one situation where the best way to learn is to jump in and start coding a game. You'll soon find out whether this is the right system for you to use for what you're trying to accomplish.

To get you started, I've created a basic template file in the chapter's source files called `GameTemplate`. It's a blank template based on the `BlockGame` example. It includes a `GameModel`, `GameView`, `GameController`, and document class. There's enough there for you start filling in the details of your own game. And let me know when you're done—I'd love to play it!

In Chapter 8, we're going to take a detailed look at an alternative system to manage multiple levels using a tile-based game engine.

Summary

The core physics and geometry that we've covered so far in this book should be basic knowledge for any serious game designer. Learn it, understand it, practice it, and let it become the currency of your game-design universe. The concepts and math are as useful for making games using AS3.0, as it is for making games with Java, C++, Objective C, or some future programming language yet to be invented. You now have the skills to control the entire geometry of your space and the motion of all your game objects. You are able to handle almost any collision-detection problem that might come up. (Yes, I said "almost," because there's one more collision scenario that you still need know about, which we'll look at in the next chapter.)

The concepts that we've covered are so fundamental to game design, in any programming language or medium, that if you want to try your hand at more complex physics, you have this book as a reference to move on to the next level. All the math and concepts that we've covered have built a solid foundation for you to continue developing your skills.

In the next chapter, we're going to start putting these skills to some practical use and learn about how to use bitmaps for pixel-perfect collision and making destructible environments.

Chapter 5

Pixel-Perfect Collision and Destructible Environments

Circles, squares, and triangles are great, but for some games, they just won't cut it. Sometimes you need to make a game with bumpy, jagged shapes—for example, for an uneven rocky landscape. And sometimes it's fun to make a game where players can interactively destroy the game world, down to the smallest pixel. Actually, that sounds like a lot of fun!

The techniques we've looked at so far won't help with pixel-perfect collision—at least, not easily. To create environments that are malleable on the smallest pixel level, we need to tackle one more great collision-detection system every Flash game designer should know: **bitmap collision**.

We're going to cover many interesting topics in this chapter. You'll learn how to do the following:

- Convert sprites and movie clips to bitmaps.
- Figure out if two bitmap objects are colliding.
- Separate colliding bitmaps to create a solid collision boundary.
- Build concave and convex bitmap environments for game objects.
- Create a mini-map for a huge, scrolling environment.
- Interactively cut holes into bitmaps to destroy parts of the environment.

And if we're going to create environments that can be destroyed, we need something to destroy them with. We're going to a build a pair of objects with wide application for games: a lander spacecraft that is typical of many side-scrolling sci-fi action games and a rotating gun turret that fires bullets (a video-game staple!)

Of course, bitmap collision involves bitmaps, so we need to start with what bitmaps are and why we need to use them.

Vector vs. bitmap graphics

The two main ways that computers create images are by using **vector graphics** and **bitmap graphics**.

All the graphics that we've used in this book so far have used vector drawing techniques. Vector graphics are made by plotting points and drawing connecting lines or curves between those points. When I first started using Flash, it was billed as a vector graphics animation tool, and although it's far more than that in its current form, it's still great for making vector art.

> *Vector graphics are not the same as the mathematical Euclidean vectors that we've been using in the previous chapters. Vector graphics are actually made using Euclidean vectors, but this is something that is largely hidden by the software that makes the graphics.*

If you ever did a connect-the-dots puzzle as a child, you already know how vector graphics work. The computer knows where point A is and where point B is, and it knows that it must draw a line between them. Those connecting lines are the vectors. Vectors can make any shape, like stars or spaceships, just by joining a lot of points together. If you have complex shapes, like butterflies, the points are very close together and the lines between them are very short. Curves are handled with a mathematical formula, usually for a Bezier curve.

Vector graphics are handy because the only information stored about them is the minimum math required to plot the shape's points. This means that vector graphic file sizes tend to be very small. They contain just a few x and y coordinates, with perhaps the formula for a Bezier curve or two.

Because they just exist as mathematical formulae, vector graphics can be scaled to any size without losing detail. If you have a small vector image of a butterfly the size of your palm, you can scale it to the size of an apartment building without losing detail or increasing the file size. Just multiply all the points equally by a big number. The numbers that make up the butterfly's points will be increased proportionately, but no new information will be added to the file. You'll end up with a huge butterfly, but the file size will be no bigger than the original.

Small file size and seamless scaling are the two big advantages of vector graphics. But they have some drawbacks as well:

- **Slow to render**: Vector graphics are, at their heart, little mathematical formulae. Math is handled by your computer's CPU, and if the CPU is busy calculating points, it has less processing power to run other parts of your game. If you have a lot of vector graphics moving around the stage, there could be hundreds of thousands of points the CPU must calculate each frame, and that eats up a big part of your performance budget.
- **Lack surface detail**: Vector graphics just contain information about the points that make up the corners of the shape. They don't store any information about the inside area of the shape. For example, a vector graphic file of a triangle just contains the x and y coordinates of the triangle's three corners. This means that you can't change the color of individual pixels in the inner area of the triangle, because there's no way to access that information.

These weak areas of vector graphics are where bitmap graphics show their strength.

Bitmaps are rectangular grids made up of rows and columns of single pixels. (They're a "map" of "bits.") Each pixel in the grid contains a color, and by putting the right colors next to each other in the right cells in the grid, bitmaps create shapes. If vector graphics are connect-the-dots, then bitmap graphics are paint-by-numbers. Figure 5-1 shows how vectors and bitmaps represent the same shape differently.

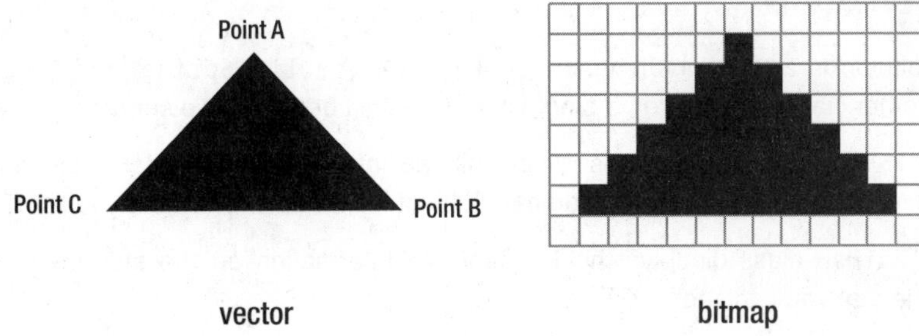

Figure 5-1. A vector graphic represents the triangle as points. A bitmap graphic represents it as a grid of pixels.

Each pixel in a bitmap graphic can be accessed and changed, and this means that you have fine control over the color of even the smallest pixel. All digital photographs are bitmaps because this surface detail is essential for photographs.

Because bitmaps don't need to calculate points, they don't have any mathematical overhead that drains CPU power from your game. But bitmaps have their own drawbacks:

- **Lack information**: Bitmaps are clueless: All they know is the height and width of their grid, and the color information for each pixel in the grid. They don't know anything about the kind of image or shape those pixels represent.

- **Don't scale well**: Because they don't understand their content, they can't be scaled. You can certainly try, but if you do, things get ugly, fast. The bitmap will mindlessly balloon the size of each pixel so that you end up with a terribly blocky, pixelated image. This might be cool for retro-style games, but not for almost everything else.
- **Use a lot of memory**: The vector triangle in Figure 5-1 will have a very small file size because the only information that's stored is its three corner points, the fill color, and a calculation—four pieces of data and a simple formula that explains how to connect the points together. On the other hand, the bitmap triangle must store the color information of every single pixel in the grid. It's an 8-by-13 grid, totaling 104 bits of data to store. That makes it about 26 times bigger than the vector graphic. The bitmap is essentially spending on memory what it saves on CPU power.

But the fact that you can access individual pixels of a bitmap makes up for all these shortcomings. It means you can do accurate collision detection between irregularly shaped objects. It also means you can control single pixels or groups of pixels inside shapes. Using bitmaps opens up realms of possibilities for our games that would be nearly impossible with vector graphics alone.

Using bitmaps

In AS3.0, a bitmap is a `DisplayObject`, just like the `MovieClip`, `Sprite`, and `Shape` classes. Unlike those other classes, however, a single bitmap is split between two separate classes:

- The `BitmapData` class stores all the bitmap information. It contains the grid and the color of each pixel in the grid. You can think of it as a data file or array full of numbers.
- The `Bitmap` class displays the `BitmapData` information on the stage. It's the bitmap image that you can see.

To create and use a single bitmap, you work with both of these classes together.

The reason for splitting bitmaps into two classes is the same reason we've been splitting our game objects into model and view classes. If you can separate the data from the display of that data, you have much more control and flexibility. `BitmapData` is the model class, and `Bitmap` is the view class. You'll see how useful this separation is when it comes to building a mini-map for a big scrolling environment later in this chapter.

To use bitmaps in your games, you have three options:

- Import a bitmap image, such as a digital photograph. For example, in Chapter 2, we imported and displayed the image of Mars's moon, Phobos, in the gravity demonstration.
- Create a new bitmap from scratch using pure AS3.0 code.
- Create a bitmap object from an already existing `Shape`, `Sprite`, or `MovieClip` object.

After you have your bitmaps in your games, the next step is dealing with collisions between them.

Bitmap collisions

In this chapter's source files, you'll find a folder called `BitmapCollision`. Run the SWF, and you'll see two stars on the stage. You can move one of the stars around the stage with the mouse. If any part of the stars touch, they register a collision in the status box, as shown in Figure 5-2. The collision detection is perfect, no matter which sides or parts of the shapes are touching.

Figure 5-2. Pixel-perfect collision detection using bitmaps

Can you imagine the brain-melting math involved if you attempted this kind of collision detection using the SAT, as in the previous chapter? I get queasy just thinking about. The amazing thing is that this collision detection is done using just one method:

```
bitmapData.hitTest
```

There's no math at all!

Let's see how this works.

Checking for a collision

To use bitmapData.hitTest, both collision objects must be bitmaps. The BitmapCollision application class has a method called makeStar that draws the stars using the drawing API techniques we covered in Chapter 1. It creates them first as vector graphics using the Shape class. It then uses those shapes to create Bitmap and BitmapData objects. Those objects are then returned to the main part of the program and used in the collision.

I know that's a bit difficult to absorb all at once, so let's go through the code. First, create the star objects.

```
//Star 1 (player's star)
private var _s1:Object = makeStar();

//Star 2
private var _s2:Object = makeStar();
```

The stars, _s1 and _s2, are typed as Object. Creating the stars as Object types means that a single star can contain both the Bitmap and BitmapData objects. This shortcut simplifies the code a bit.

The makeStar method draws each star, and returns it as Bitmap and BitmapData. The star shape is first drawn as a vector object, and then turned into a bitmap. Here's the abridged version of the method:

```
private function makeStar():Object
{
  //Create the starShape vector graphic
  var starShape:Shape = new Shape();

  //… draw the star using the standard drawing API

  //Create the BitmapData to store the star graphic
  var starBitmapData:BitmapData = new BitmapData(200, 200, true, 0);

  //Draw the vector star shape into the BitmapData
  starBitmapData.draw(starShape);

  //Use the BitmapData to create the Bitmap image of
  //the star that will be visible on the stage
  var starBitmap:Bitmap = new Bitmap(starBitmapData);

  //Create the star object to return to the caller.
  //The star object contains both the BitmapData and the Bitmap
  var star:Object = new Object;
  star.bitmapData = starBitmapData;
  star.bitmap = starBitmap;
  star.shape = starShape;

  return star;
}
```

The star is first drawn as a vector graphic using the same drawing API methods that we've used to draw all the graphic elements in the book so far. But we need to convert the star into a bitmap so we can use pixel-perfect bitmap collision.

First, we create a `BitmapData` object to store the bitmap information. This creates an empty grid of pixels that is the same height and width as the original star vector graphic.

```
var starBitmapData:BitmapData = new BitmapData(200, 200, true, 0);
```

The first two parameters are the height and width of the grid: 200 by 200. The third parameter, `true`, means that the bitmap will have areas of alpha transparency. This is very important, because it allows us to use transparent areas to define the edges of the shape. This will be crucial for our pixel-perfect collision system to work properly.

The last parameter is `0`. That's the **fill color**. Zero here means that any areas of the bitmap that don't have a defined color should be made transparent. Again, this is very important for our collision system to work. However, you could use any fill color you like. If you used `0x000000`, for example, the fill color would be black. The result in this example would be that the gray star would be enclosed in a black square. This could be useful in some cases, as you'll when we build a mini-map for a scrolling environment later in this chapter.

Now that we have a blank `BitmapData` object, we need to copy the star shape into it. The `draw` method does this.

```
starBitmapData.draw(starShape);
```

This is like taking a snapshot or photocopy of the star. `BitmapData`'s `draw` method looks at the `starShape` and figures out the pixel positions and colors on the grid it needs to switch on to create a pixel map of the star.

> *The `draw` method has many other parameters that you can set to fine-tune how the shape is drawn into the bitmap, and you'll find details in Adobe's online AS3 documentation,* ActionScript 3.0 Language and Components Reference. *In the examples later in this chapter, we'll look at some of these in much greater detail, but for now, this basic format will serve you well.*

Next, we use `BitmapData` to create the `Bitmap` display object.

```
var starBitmap:Bitmap = new Bitmap(starBitmapData);
```

The `starBitmap` is the actual, visual bitmap image that will be displayed on the stage. It looks exactly like the original vector shape, but it has been converted into pure pixels.

Now that we've made the `BitmapData` and `Bitmap` objects, we need to get them back to the rest of the program. The simplest way to do this is to wrap them up into a single `Object`, and return that `Object` to the method's caller.

```
var star:Object = new Object;
star.bitmapData = starBitmapData;
star.bitmap = starBitmap;
star.shape = starShape;

return star;
```

We now have our star bitmaps, so we can use them to do bitmap collision. This is done inside an ENTER_FRAME loop.

```
private function enterFrameHandler(event:Event):void
{
  //Make the star follow the mouse
  _s1.bitmap.x = stage.mouseX - 100;
  _s1.bitmap.y = stage.mouseY - 100;

  if(_s1.bitmapData.hitTest
     (
       new Point(_s1.bitmap.x, _s1.bitmap.y),
       255,
       _s2.bitmap,
       new Point(_s2.bitmap.x, _s2.bitmap.y),
       255
     )
   )
  {
    _collision = "true";
  }
  else
  {
    _collision = "false";
  }

  //Update the status box
  _statusBox.text = "BITMAP COLLISION:";
  _statusBox.text += "\n" + "COLLISION: " + _collision;
}
```

When bitmaps are created, their registration point is the top-left corner of the grid, as shown in Figure 5-3. This is important to remember. That means that we need to find the center of the bitmap by working down and across from that top-left corner. This bit of code determines the bitmap's center point:

```
bitmapCenter_X = bitmap.x + bitmap.width * 0.5;
bitmapCenter_Y = bitmap.y + bitmap.height * 0.5;
```

This is unlike all of the other game objects we've created in the book so far, which have been positioned directly in the center of their containing sprites. I did this so that the calculations are a little more intuitive to work out. Nothing is stopping you from centering a bitmap so that its center point has an x/y position of 0, but it doesn't make bitmaps happy. Some versions of Flash Player produce glitchy bitmap displays if the x and y position values of bitmaps contain negative numbers. It also makes some other bitmap calculations more confusing than they need to be. For these reasons, I'm going to keep the registration point at the top-left corner for all the bitmaps in the next few chapters. Keep this in mind when you look at any code that involves the width, height, or center points of bitmaps. That's why, in the code from `BitmapCollision`, the star bitmap is centered to the mouse's position like this:

```
_s1.bitmap.x = stage.mouseX - 100;
_s1.bitmap.y = stage.mouseY - 100;
```

The star's size is 200 by 200 pixels. To center it over the mouse, its top-left corner must be 100 pixels above and to the left of the mouse's position.

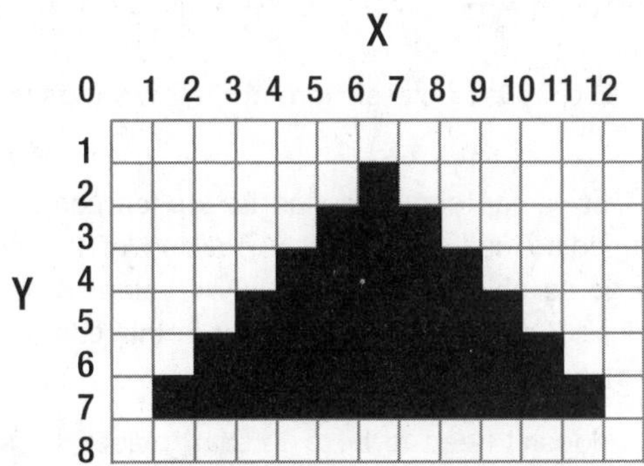

Figure 5-3. Bitmap registration points are at the top-left corner.

There's a magic formula for bitmap collision with the `BitmapData.hitTest` method. This is it:

```
bitmapData_A.hitTest
  (
    new Point(bitmapA.x, bitmapA.y),
    alphaValueA,
    bitmapB,
    new Point(bitmapB.x, bitmapB.y),
    alphaValueB
  )
```

I know, it's a rat's nest to look at! Figure 5-4 is diagram that decodes what's going on for you. When you get a bit of practice using it, you'll see that it's not as bad as it looks at first. You'll be using this same standard format over and over again. The formula contains a lot of information, but it's all really helpful. (The line breaks are just to help make the code a bit more readable, so, if you want to, you can keep everything on one really long line.)

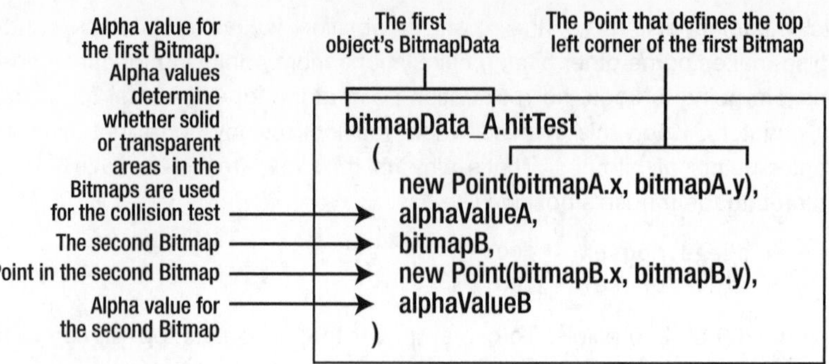

Figure 5-4. BitmapData's hitTest method

`hitTest` is a method of the `BitmapData` class. Here are a few things you need to know about its parameters:

- The point for the first bitmap should define its top-left corner. However, *it can be any point*. You don't need to use the x and y position of the bitmap. In these first few example files, the game objects' `xPos` and `yPos` values from their model classes are used, which is typical. But in the examples later in this chapter, you'll see how useful it can be to use different values.
- The second object doesn't need to be a `Bitmap` object. It can also be a `Point` or a `Rectangle` object. If you want pixel-perfect collision, then it should be a `Bitmap` object. But if you don't need as much accuracy, `Point` and `Rectangle` objects are faster to process. You'll see how this works when we look at destroying things, near the end of the chapter. If the second object isn't a `Bitmap` object, you don't need to include the second `Point` object.
- The alpha values determine the "solid" parts of the bitmap. If the value is 255, completely opaque (solid) parts of the bitmap are used for the collision test. A value of 0 means that completely transparent areas are used for testing. You can use any value between 0 and 255 to define points of semitransparency to be used for the collision test.

Don't worry if you feel like that's a lot of information right now. For most games, it's unlikely that you'll need to modify any of the parameters from what we've used in this example. Copy and paste with glee!

The problems with bitmap collision

Pixel-perfect collision without any math? Is it too good to be true?

Sadly, yes! As helpful as bitmap collision can be, it comes at a very high price:

- It's dreadfully slow.
- Collision? What's a collision?

Bitmaps have no information about the shapes they're testing. They figure out which parts of the bitmap they need to test by methodically comparing every pixel from bitmap A against every other pixel in bitmap B. They just throw them all against a wall and see which of them stick. For example, if you're testing two 100-by-100 bitmaps, each bitmap has 10,000 pixels that must be checked against 10,000 pixels in the other bitmap. Thankfully, this is done by super-optimized C++ code running in Flash Player, and it takes many shortcuts. But it's still hugely taxing. If you have any more than a small handful of objects using bitmap collision in your game, the frame rate will drop dramatically.

> *Programmers refer to the technique of trying every possible combination to solve a problem by the very colorful term* ***brute force****. Usually you want to avoid brute-force checking because it's so extremely inefficient. But sometimes it's the only way. And other times, brute force can actually be faster, if it the alternative solution involves doing a lot of very complex, CPU-intensive calculations.*

Also, our poor clueless bitmaps have absolutely no information to give us about the collision that happens. Because there's no mathematical information about the shapes, there's no way to find out by how much the shapes have intersected, the side of the shape where the collision happened, or the angle of the collision.

These are serious problems. The performance hit alone means that bitmap collision detection should only ever be a last resort in your games. Still, it's undeniably useful for complex shapes, and it's essential in some situations. So let's see how we can make it work.

Finding the collision boundary

All collision-detection systems must have a clear collision boundary. You need to know where and by how much the objects have intersected so that you can separate them and send them on their merry way. If your shapes are defined by vectors, you have detailed information that you can use to do this. Chapters 2, 3, and 4 were proof of that.

As you've learned, bitmaps don't have any information about their content except pixel positions and colors. Without any mathematical information about the colliding shapes, how can we possibly do the kind of separation and collision reaction that we've been doing with vectors over the past few chapters? Easy—we use vectors!

In the chapter files, you'll find a folder called `BlockMovement`. Run the SWF, and you'll see something that looks very much like the previous example. But in this version, the stars don't overlap when they collide. They remain cleanly separated the entire time, no matter where you move the mouse, as shown in Figure 5-5.

Here's the `ENTER_FRAME` loop from the `BlockMovement` application class that does this:

Figure 5-5. Use a bit of simple vector math to keep the shapes perfectly separated when they collide.

```
private function enterFrameHandler(event:Event):void
{
   _s1.bitmap.x = stage.mouseX - 100;
   _s1.bitmap.y = stage.mouseY - 100;

   //Distance vector between the stars
   var v0:VectorModel
     = new VectorModel
       (
         _s1.bitmap.x,
         _s1.bitmap.y,
         _s2.bitmap.x,
         _s2.bitmap.y
       );

  //Use a while loop to figure out if the stars are touching
  while
    (
      _s1.bitmapData.hitTest
        (
          new Point(_s1.bitmap.x, _s1.bitmap.y),
          255,
          _s2.bitmap,
          new Point(_s2.bitmap.x, _s2.bitmap.y),
          255
        )
      )
  {
    //Separate _s1 by 1 unit vector until
    //it is no longer touching _s2
    _s1.bitmap.x -= v0.dx;
    _s1.bitmap.y -= v0.dy;
  }
}
```

That's all there is to it! Let's see how it works:

The first thing the code does is to create a distance vector between the two stars.

```
var v0:VectorModel
     = new VectorModel
       (
        _s1.bitmap.x,
        _s1.bitmap.y,
        _s2.bitmap.x,
        _s2.bitmap.y
       );
```

Next, it does a `hitTest` collision check inside a `while loop`.

```
while
  (
    _s1.bitmapData.hitTest
      (
        new Point(_s1.bitmap.x, _s1.bitmap.y),
        255,
        _s2.bitmap,
        new Point(_s2.bitmap.x, _s2.bitmap.y),
        255
      )
    )
{...
```

If you haven't used a `while` loop before, don't worry, it's very easy to use. The loop runs for as long as the condition in the parentheses is `true`:

```
while(this condition is true)
{
  ...run this code
}
```

In this case, the condition is `true` if the two bitmaps are touching. That means you can understand the logic of the `while` loop like this:

```
while(the two bitmaps are touching)
{
  ...push the stars apart
}
```

The actual code looks more confusing than this because the unavoidably wordy `hitTest` method is *inside* the `while` loop's conditional statement. But take a careful look at it, and you'll see that its structure is no more complex than the pseudo code. I've used some custom formatting to make it a little more readable.

The code that runs inside the `while` loop is very simple.

```
_s1.bitmap.x -= v0.dx;
_s1.bitmap.y -= v0.dy;
```

All it does is push the stars out of the collision by a tiny bit. When the shapes no longer touch, the `while` loop quits.

How much is "a tiny bit"? It's the value of the distance vector's `dx` and `dy` values. In case you've forgotten, the `dx` and `dy` values are unit vectors. They're the smallest units that a vector can be.

The `while` loop does this so quickly that even if it needs to run 200 loops before it separates the shapes, you'll never notice. This all happens in one frame, and quicker than the blink of an eye. Only the end result is displayed on the stage, so you never see the separation at work. This is another example of brute force, but a `while` loop does this sort of thing very efficiently. It has a minimal impact on performance if used wisely and sparingly. Yay, `while` loop!

Figure 5-6 is a slow-motion view of the loop so that you can clearly see what it's doing over the duration of one frame.

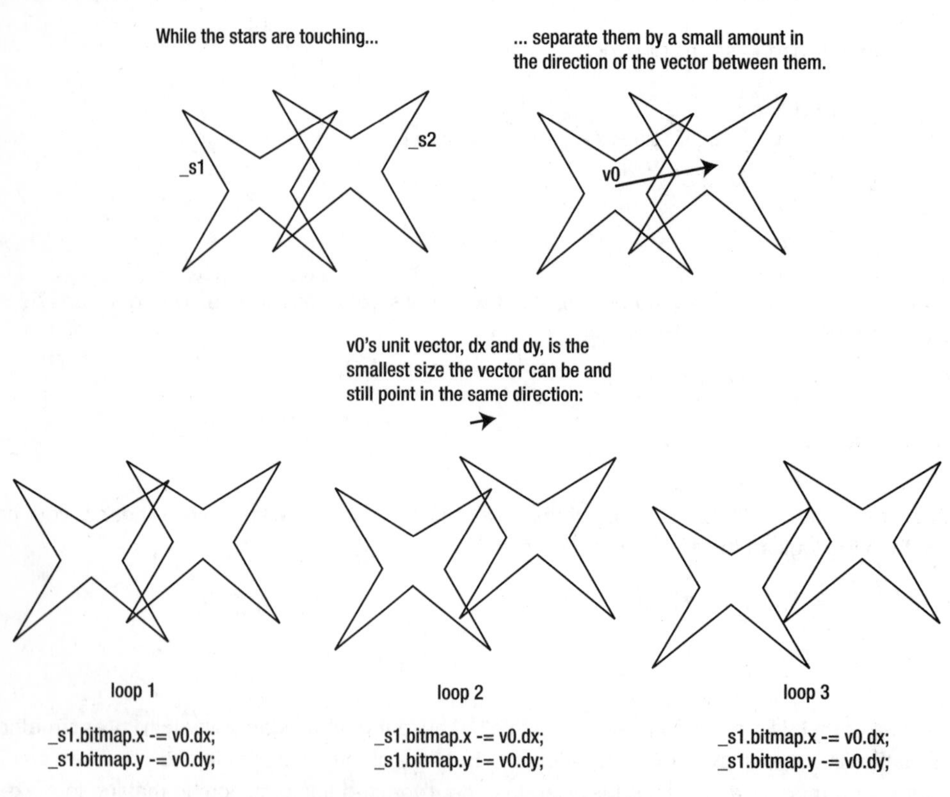

Figure 5-6. Use a bit of simple vector math to keep the shapes perfectly separated when they collide.

Now aren't you glad that you spent all that time learning about vectors? Vectors are central to almost every advanced game-design technique, and they have plenty more tricks up their sleeves.

Now for the warning: `while` loops are dangerous! If you use a `while` loop, you must make sure that the condition it checks for eventually becomes `true`. If it doesn't, the loop will run forever, and Flash Player will hang. In fact, if you play around with the `blockMovement` SWF long enough, you can probably make it hang, and you may need to force Flash Player to quit. "Bhwahahaha!" laughs the evil Flash game designer!

Don't look so shocked; there's an easy solution! We can modify the code slightly so that we can guarantee that the `while` loop eventually quits. An extra `if` statement and loop counter variable will help us out. Here's the solution:

```
//Distance vector between the stars
var v0:VectorModel
  = new VectorModel
  (
    _s1.bitmap.x,
    _s1.bitmap.y,
    _s2.bitmap.x,
    _s2.bitmap.y
  );
//Use a while loop to figure out if the stars are touching,
//but limit the number of times the loop runs by
//using a counter variable and incrementing it by "1" each loop

var loopCounter:int = 0;
while (loopCounter++ != 200)
{
  //An if statement inside the while loop
  //checks for a collision
  if
    (
      _s1.bitmapData.hitTest
        (
          new Point(_s1.bitmap.x, _s1.bitmap.y),
          255,
          _s2.bitmap,
          new Point(_s2.bitmap.x, _s2.bitmap.y),
          255
        )
    )
  {
    //Separate _s1 by 1 unit vector until
    //it is no longer touching _s2
    _s1.bitmap.x -= v0.dx;
    _s1.bitmap.y -= v0.dy;
  }
}
```

You'll find a working example of this code in the `SafeBlockMovement` folder. In this version of the code, the loop will run for a maximum of 200 times.

```
while (loopCounter++ != 200)
{…
```

The `loopCounter` variable is incremented directly in the conditional statement itself. Yes, I know that's a bit sneaky, but it works great! The `while` loop is now guaranteed to quit after 200 loops, whether or not the `hitTest` method returns `true`. This is a fail-safe way to make sure that there's no danger of an infinite loop.

The work of checking for a collision is done by the `while` loop's nested `if` statement. If it finds a collision, it will move the shape out of the collision by a maximum of 200 increments.

For this to work in a game, you need to make sure the loop will run enough times to separate the shapes. That means that the value of `loopCounter` shouldn't be less than the maximum velocity at which you expect your objects to be traveling. For example, if a game spaceship is traveling at 15 pixels per second and hits an asteroid, your loop will need to run up to 15 times to make sure that it resolves the collision on that frame. If it doesn't, it will finish resolving it on the next frame, and you'll see the spaceship blip through the asteroid slightly.

When I tested this example, I found that I had to run the loop up to 200 times each frame because the shapes are very large and I was moving the mouse quickly. For most games, however, between 10 and 20 loops should be just fine. If your velocities have limits, this solution will work flawlessly. Although you want your loops to run as few times as possible, `while` loops are very efficient and will be the least of your performance worries.

You now have all the basics of bitmap collision detection down, and you'll be happy to know it doesn't get any more difficult than this. Yes, I know, I've said that before, but this time I mean it! The next step is to find out how to apply these techniques in practical ways to games.

Bitmap collision-detection strategies

There are three basic bitmap collision-detection strategies that will serve you well for all types of games:

- **Convex shapes**: When your shapes are roundish or squarish with a solid center, like the star shapes in the previous example.
- **Surfaces**: When the collision is from only one side, like a wall at the side of the stage or the ground at the bottom of the stage.
- **Concave shapes**: When the shapes have a hollow center, like a cave.

Over the next pages, we'll tour all these strategies in real-live game contexts.

Convex shapes

In the chapter's source files, find the `Asteroid` folder and run the SWF. You'll see a small Lunar Lander-style spacecraft that you can fly around the stage with the arrow keys. The lander, as its name implies, can land anywhere on the asteroid. I've made the vector between the lander and asteroid visible so that you can more easily understand the relationship between them.

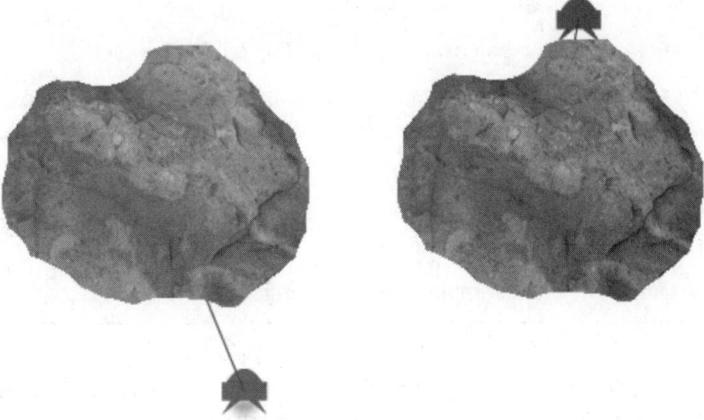

Figure 5-7. Fly around the asteroid and land anywhere on it.

> *In all the examples in this chapter and the next, I haven't used any filters on the display objects. I've omitted them so that the bitmap edges are more clearly defined. This makes testing and debugging easier because you can clearly see how accurate the collision is. Feel free to add filters like drop shadows and bevel effects on bitmaps in your own games if they don't negatively affect performance.*

The collision detection and reaction work in the same way as the previous example with the two stars. When the shapes collide, the lander is separated incrementally from the asteroid in the direction of the vector using a `while` loop. That's not new.

What is new is that the lander is being pulled to the bottom of the stage by gravity, and it also uses variable velocity—it has `vx` and `vy` values. For the collision reaction to be accurate, we need to compensate for the values of these new variables.

But first, let's look at how the asteroid and lander bitmaps were created.

Creating bitmaps from sprites

If you're curious about how the lander works, take a peek in the `com.friendsofed.gameElements.lunarLander` package. It's just a variation of the player control systems you've seen before, so there's won't be any surprises.

Like the other game objects, it's rendered as a `Sprite` object. To use bitmap collision, we must turn it into a `Bitmap` object.

> *If your game involves bitmap collision, and your objects don't need any of the features of `Sprite` or `MovieClip` objects, always create them natively as bitmaps in their view classes. Converting from a sprite to a bitmap is just an extra, unnecessary step that you should avoid.*
>
> *I've broken this rule in many examples in this book for two reasons:*
>
> - *To show you how to turn sprites into bitmaps. Sometimes it's extremely useful to be able to do this, and the performance hit may be negligible.*
> - *To make sure that the `Bitmap` and `BitmapData` classes are completely exposed in the application classes, which is very useful to see while you're still learning.*
>
> *But don't follow my bad example in your own games!*

The lander has a model and view class, just like the other game objects in previous chapters. To turn it into a bitmap, send its model and view to the `createBitmap` method.

```
var landerBitmap:Object = createBitmap(_lander, _lander_View);
```

The `createBitmap` method will return an `Object` that contains the `BitmapData` and `Bitmap` objects. You can access those objects like this:

```
landerBitmap.bitmap
landerBitmap.bitmapData
```

The `createBitmap` method is near the end of the `Asteroid` application class.

```
private function createBitmap
  (model:AVerletModel, view:AVerletView):Object
{
  //Create the BitmapData and Bitmap objects based
  //on the lander's model and view
  var bitmapData:BitmapData
    = new BitmapData(model.width, model.height, true, 0);
  bitmapData.draw(view);
  var bitmap:Bitmap = new Bitmap(bitmapData);

  //Create the object to return to the caller
  var bitmapObject:Object = new Object;
  bitmapObject.bitmapData = bitmapData;
  bitmapObject.bitmap = bitmap;

  return bitmapObject;
}
```

This method does what the heart of the `makeStar` method did in the previous example. Can you see how neatly the model matches the `BitmapData` and the view matches the `Bitmap`?

> *Because `Bitmap` objects have their registration points at the top corner, we need to adjust the screen wrapping code to compensate for this with a special `StageBoundaries.wrapBitmap` method.*
>
> ```
> StageBoundaries.wrapBitmap(_lander, stage);
> ```
>
> *The `com.friendsofed.utils` package also contains special bitmap methods for stopping and bouncing objects at the stage edges. You can use them like this:*
>
> ```
> StageBoundaries.stopBitmap(_lander, stage);
> StageBoundaries.bounceBitmap(_lander, stage);
> ```

The bitmap of the lander is created every frame and is just used for the collision check. It's not added to the stage. The image of the lander that you see on the stage is the vector shape created by the lander's view class. This demonstrates how you can display vector graphics on the stage and just use matching bitmaps for behind-the-scenes collision detection.

Creating the asteroid bitmap

The asteroid is a PNG image with alpha transparency. The alpha transparency is important because it's the contrast between the transparent and opaque parts of the image that defines the asteroid's shape.

I dropped the PNG image into the project's `images` folder:

`Asteroid ➤ assets ➤ images ➤ asteroid.png`

PNG images *are* bitmap images. But we can't just use them as is. We need to import them into our program and then copy them into a `BitmapData` class. This makes them readable by AS3.0.

The following steps outline how to import the asteroid PNG image into the program. I've abridged a lot of the code to avoid repeating material that you should know all too well by now. Make sure to check the complete code in the source files to see it all in its proper context.

1. The image is embedded in the class definition using the `Embed` metatag. A class called `AsteroidImage` is used to contain the image. Remember that in an odd quirk in AS3.0 syntax, the class that contains the image must come directly after the `Embed` tag.

```
public class Asteroid extends Sprite
{

  //…
```

```
//Variables required to display the asteroid bitmap
private var _asteroidBitmap:Bitmap;
private var _asteroidBitmapData:BitmapData;

//Embed the image of the asteroid using a relative path to the PNG image
//Create a class to store the image
[Embed(source="../assets/images/asteroid.png")]
private var AsteroidImage:Class;
```

2. In the `Asteroid` constructor, a new instance of the `AsteroidImage` class is created.

```
public function Asteroid():void
{
  //...
  var asteroidImage:DisplayObject = new AsteroidImage();
```

`asteroidImage` must be typed as a `DisplayObject` This is a bit confusing because it's obviously an instance of `AsteroidImage`. The problem is that the `AsteroidImage` class won't be available to the compiler when it tries to compile the SWF. If you try to type it as `AsteroidImage`, you'll get the error "Type was not found or was not a compile-time constant: AsteroidImage." This just means that the compiler doesn't know what the `AsteroidImage` class is, and it doesn't know where to look for it. Because the `AsteroidImage` class is created in the class definition, it's hidden to the compiler. This is a little technical nuisance, but easily handled. Just use the more general `DisplayObject`, and all will be well.

3. Use the `asteroidImage` instance to create the asteroid's `BitmapData` and draw the PNG image into it.

```
_asteroidBitmapData = new BitmapData(asteroidImage.width,
asteroidImage.height, true, 0);
_asteroidBitmapData.draw(asteroidImage);
```

This code should be starting to look quite familiar to you by now.

4. Finally, create the `Bitmap` object, add it to the stage, and position it.

```
_asteroidBitmap = new Bitmap(_asteroidBitmapData);
addChild(_asteroidBitmap);
_asteroidBitmap.x = 200;
_asteroidBitmap.y = 100;
```

Via two completely different routes, we now have two bitmaps that we can use for collision detection. This is where the fun starts!

Collision with the asteroid

The collision system is essentially the same as the collision between the two stars in the earlier example. There's a vector between the lander and the asteroid, which is used to separate the shapes when they collide. Here's the code from the `enterFrameHandler` that does this:

```
//The distance vector between the lander and the asteroid
_v0.update
  (
    _lander.xPos + _lander.width * 0.5,
    _lander.yPos + _lander.height * 0.5,
    _asteroidBitmap.x + _asteroidBitmap.width * 0.5,
    _asteroidBitmap.y + _asteroidBitmap.height * 0.5
  );

//Check for a collision
var loopCounter:int = 0;
while (loopCounter++ != 10)
{
  if(landerBitmap.bitmapData.hitTest
      (
        new Point(_lander.xPos, _lander.yPos),
        255,
        _asteroidBitmap,
        new Point(_asteroidBitmap.x, _asteroidBitmap.y),
        255
      )
    )
  {
    //Switch off gravity
    _lander.gravity_Vy = 0;

   //Move the lander out of the collision in the direction
   //of the distance vector
   _lander.setX = _lander.xPos - _v0.dx;
   _lander.setY = _lander.yPos - _v0.dy;
   _lander.vx = 0;
   _lander.vy = 0;
 }
 else
 {
   break;
 }
}
```

For a precise-looking collision, the code switches off the lander's gravity and set its velocity to 0. If this isn't done, the lander will appear to wobble slightly when it's resting on the asteroid. This is because the forces that are pushing and pulling it are not quite equal.

If we switch gravity off when the lander is on the asteroid, we need to switch it back on again when it leaves. But there's a problem: when the lander is "resting on the asteroid," it's actually not touching the asteroid any more. It's just slightly above it.

Remember that the `while` loop pushes the lander and asteroid apart. The loop quits when they're no longer touching each other. That means that you can't run the same collision test to find out if the lander is actually on the asteroid, because it will always return `false`. The loop has done its job and separated the objects perfectly. The lander and asteroid will be directly adjacent to each other, but they won't overlap by even 1 pixel. The problem is that because they're completely separated, we have no way to detect when the lander is resting on the asteroid.

To solve this, we need to run a second collision check that tests to see if there is any ground directly below the lander. It checks to see if 1 pixel below the lander is in contact with the asteroid. If it is, then we know the lander is still "on the asteroid." If there's no ground directly below it, then we know the lander isn't in contact with the ground, and we can switch gravity back on again.

This will be easier for you understand if you can visualize it before you look at the code. Figure 5-8 illustrates the logic of what we want to accomplish.

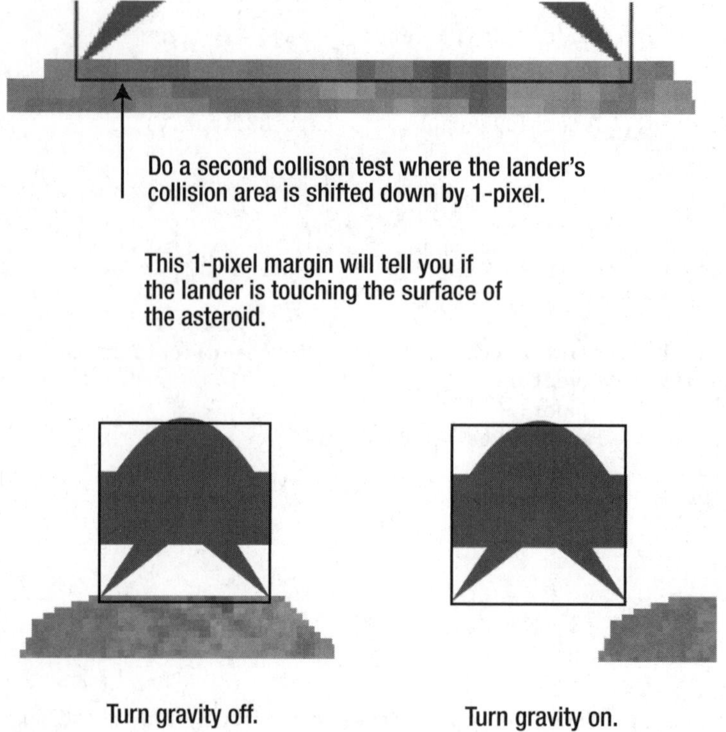

Figure 5-8. Check whether the lander is on the surface of the asteroid.

The code for this second collision test is saying, "If an area 1 pixel below the lander isn't touching the asteroid, turn gravity on."

Here's what it looks like:

```
if(!landerBitmap.bitmapData.hitTest
    (
      new Point(_lander.xPos, _lander.yPos + 1),
      255,
      _asteroidBitmap,
      new Point(_asteroidBitmap.x, _asteroidBitmap.y),
      255
    )
  )
{
  _lander.gravity_Vy = 0.1;
}
```

Note that it checks whether a collision is *not* happening.

```
if(!...
```

The `+ 1` is highlighted in the code so that you can clearly see where it shifts the collision area down by a pixel.

```
new Point(_lander.xPos, _lander.yPos + 1),
```

In environments where game objects rest on steep surfaces, you will need a bit more clearance. You'll be able tell this if the object appears to wobble slightly when it should be resting. If that's the case, use `+2`, `+3`, `+4`—keep increasing that number until the wobble disappears.

Inside out

There's one amazing side effect to this technique. The asteroid is a convex object, but you can use the same technique to check for collisions with concave objects. A "cave" is a perfect example of a concave object. Take a look at Figure 5-9 for an example of what I mean.

You can see in Figure 5-9 that there's a vector between the center of the cave and the lander. In the asteroid example, that same vector was used to push the asteroid and lander apart. However, inside the cave, the lander can fly around, and it's stopped when it bumps into the ground or walls, just as you would expect. This effect exactly inverts what was happening with the asteroid.

The collision technique is exactly the same. The small difference is that, instead of *pushing* the objects apart, it's *pulling* the objects apart. The direction of the vector has been reversed. The only change that needs to be made to the code to accomplish this is to change the minus sign to a plus sign, in these two lines of code:

```
_lander.setX = _lander.xPos + _v0.dx;
_lander.setY = _lander.yPos + _v0.dy;
```

Isn't that effortless?

This will work as long as the concave environment is enclosed on four sides. It won't work if you want the lander to fly around the cave entrance to the outer wall. I'll explain why and provide a solution to such a situation in the "Concave shapes" section ahead.

You'll find a full working example of this in the `Crater` folder in the chapter's source files.

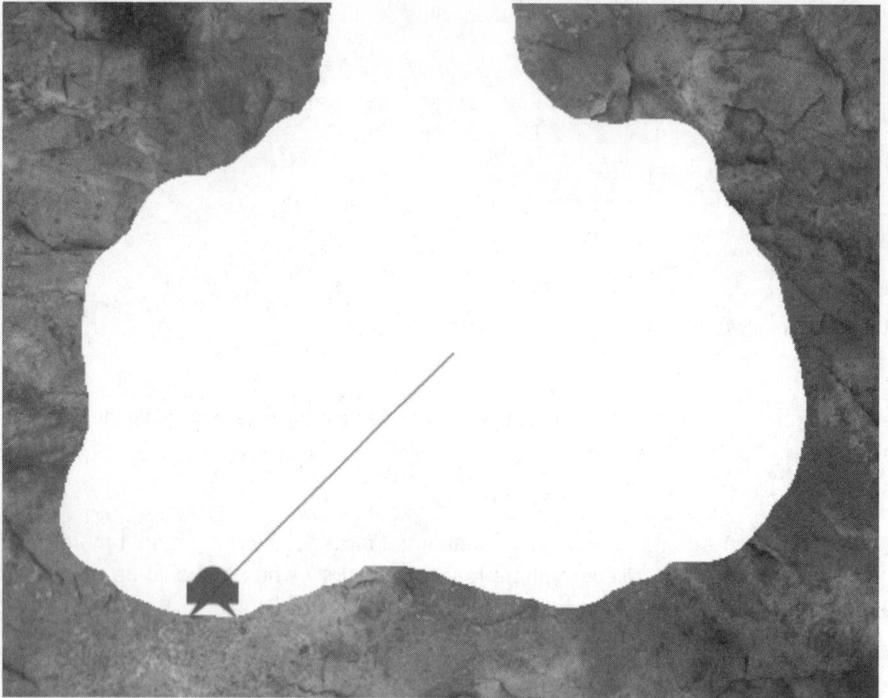

Figure 5-9. Reverse the direction of the collision separation to create an enclosed concave environment.

Surfaces

A very common requirement for game objects is to move about and interact with an uneven ground surface, like one with hills or rocks. This is very easy to implement using bitmap collision. In fact, the code is much simpler than the previous code.

We've been doing a lot of traveling through the empty reaches of deep space over the past few chapters. What can I say? It's a big universe out there! But now our space travelers have spotted a nearby planet and are going to take the lander down for a closer look.

Run the `PlanetSurface` SWF, and you'll see a scene that looks like Figure 5-10. When you land the lander on the surface, you can use the left and right arrow keys to drive it up and down the hills. It moves smoothly and evenly over the hilly surface in a very natural way. If you approach a hill with enough speed, you can even stylishly coast over its lip and "get some air," like a skateboarder going over a ramp.

Figure 5-10. Land on the planet surface and drive up and down the hills.

The technique used to separate the lander from the planet surface is almost identical to the techniques we used in the previous example. But it's simpler, because the collision can only ever happen on the y axis. That means we don't need to plot a distance vector. When the objects collide, we just push the lander directly up on the y axis until it's free of the collision.

Here's the section in the `enterFrameHandler` that handles the collision. I've highlighted the line of code that pushes the lander up and out of the collision.

```
var loopCounter:int = 0;
while (loopCounter++ != 10)
{
  if(landerBitmap.bitmapData.hitTest
      (
        new Point(_lander.xPos, _lander.yPos),
        255,
        _planetSurfaceBitmap,
        new Point
          (_planetSurfaceBitmap.x, _planetSurfaceBitmap.y),
        255
      )
    )
  {
    //Switch off gravity
    _lander.gravity_Vy = 0;
```

```
    //Move the lander out of the collision on the y axis
    _lander.setY = _lander.yPos - 1;
    _lander.vy = 0;
  }
  else
  {
    break;
  }
}
```

Again, we need to switch gravity back on again if the lander isn't touching the ground.

```
if(!landerBitmap.bitmapData.hitTest
    (
      new Point(_lander.xPos, _lander.yPos + 1),
      255,
      _planetSurfaceBitmap,
      new Point(_planetSurfaceBitmap.x, _planetSurfaceBitmap.y),
      255
    )
  )
{
  _lander.gravity_Vy = 0.1;
}
```

This bit of code is identical to the previous example.

> *If you want the lander to struggle up the sides of hills, as if battling the tug of gravity, just multiply its vy by a fractional number when it's moving up. This is the same technique we looked at for handling slopes in the polygon environment case study near the end of Chapter 4.*

Concave shapes

With convex and surface strategies, you can build very complex game environments. You can use the convex strategy to build the inner walls of a maze, and the surface strategy to build its outer walls. These techniques are extremely robust. They should be the first techniques you employ to build complex environments using bitmap collision.

But there's one situation where these strategies can't help you. Imagine that the lander is flying around the asteroid and discovers that it's hollow inside. The lander enters the hollow area and flies into the very heart of the asteroid.

This is a problem for us. The convex collision strategy depends on a vector between the center of the asteroid to the center of the lander. The vector is always pushing the lander away from the asteroid's center. If the lander touches the inner surface of the asteroid's cave, it will be pushed through the cave wall to the outside of the asteroid. Figure 5-11 illustrates what will happen.

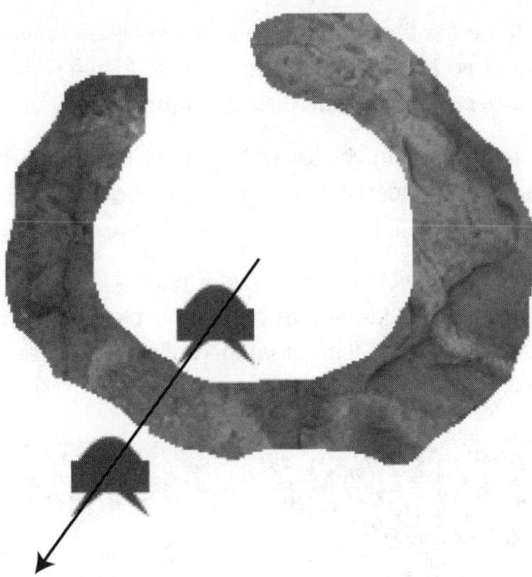

Figure 5-11. Concave shapes pose a problem. The distance vector will push the lander away from the center, through the asteroid's wall.

Obviously, this means we can't use the distance vector to separate the objects. We need another way to do it.

What are our options? Here are two contenders which, although promising, tripped over their ski poles in the qualifying round:

- Figure out whether the lander is inside or outside the asteroid, and reverse the direction of the separation accordingly. This might work, but how can we determine where the outside starts and in the inside ends? It's a complex problem, and I haven't found a simple solution to it. Let me know if you think of one! Also, it might work with roundish or squarish shapes, but not complex maze structures with many inner compartments.
- Use the lander's motion vector. For example, if the lander is moving forward and bumps into the asteroid's wall, we can push it back in a direction opposite to its velocity. This actually works quite well, but it breaks down if the lander gets pushed diagonally into a corner formed by two adjoining pixels. It doesn't know which way to go. It either gets stuck or flits off the screen in a blip. This isn't a robust enough solution.

And the winner is …

Bitmaps are made up of pixels. Pixels are just little squares. Squares have only four sides. That means that when two bitmaps collide, they're only ever touching on one of four sides. If you zoomed in really closely, you would see the flat square side of the first bitmap's pixels touching the flat square side of the other bitmap's pixels.

This simplifies things a lot. It means that we can think of a collision between bitmaps as a collision between squares. That should be an easy problem to solve. All we need to do is find out which of the four sides the collision is occurring on, and push the lander away in the opposite direction.

We can't solve this problem with math, because we don't have any mathematical information about the bitmaps. And anyway, who really wants to do more math? The solution is actually straightforward, and you know part of it already.

The chapter's source files contain a working example. Find the `Cave` folder and run the SWF. The lander has found an entrance to a hidden cave below the planet's surface. It can fly anywhere inside it. Bump into any surface, and you'll see that the collision is clean and precise, as shown in Figure 5-12.

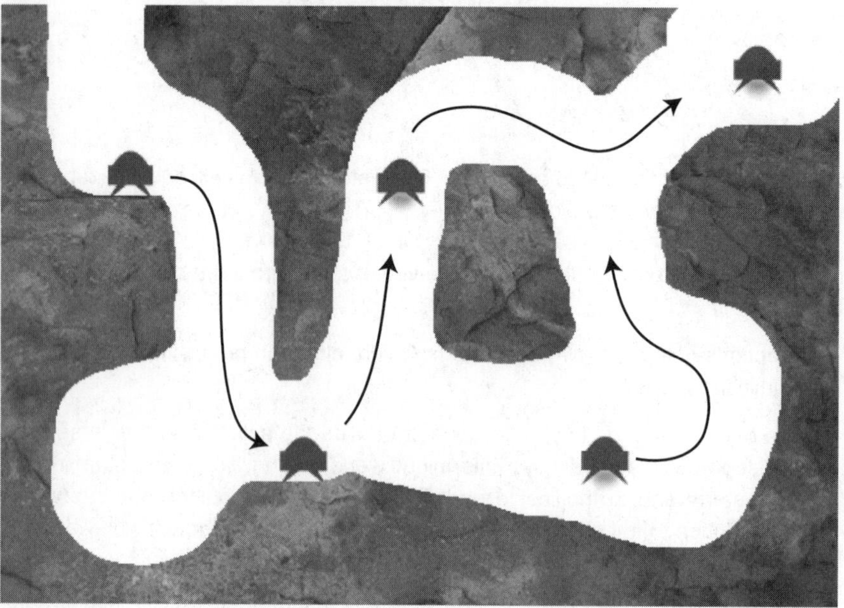

Figure 5-12. Fly anywhere inside the cave and bump into any surface.

To make this work, the code does five collision checks. It first checks to see if a collision is occurring—any collision. If it finds a collision, it does four more checks to find out whether the top, bottom, left, or right side of the lander is touching the cave wall. It then pushes the lander in the opposite direction of the collision side.

The code does this by creating what I call **collision boxes** to do the checking. Imagine that the lander is surrounded by four boxes, and each box is checking for a collision with the cave walls, as shown in Figure 5-13. The box that finds a collision is the box that determines on which side the collision is happening. Each box extends outward from the lander by 10 pixels. They're like a beetle's feelers or antennae that can sense a collision with a wall.

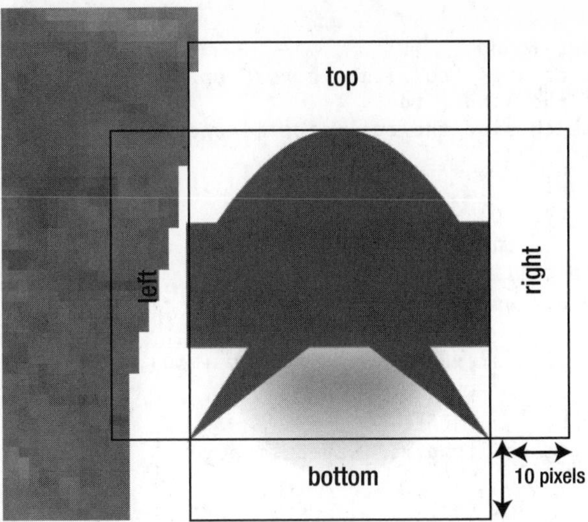

Figure 5-13. Create four collision boxes around the lander to check for collisions with the cave walls.

These collision checks run inside a `while` loop. The following is the entire `enterFrameHandler` from the `Cave` application class that does this collision checking.

```
private function enterFrameHandler(event:Event):void
{
  //Update the lander
  _lander.update();
  StageBoundaries.wrapBitmap(_lander, stage);

  //Create the lander bitmap object
  var landerBitmap:Object = createBitmap(_lander, _lander_View);

  //Check for a collision between the lander and the cave
  var loopCounter:int = 0;
  while (loopCounter++ != 10)
  {
    if(landerBitmap.bitmapData.hitTest
        (
          new Point(_lander.xPos, _lander.yPos),
          255,
          _caveBitmap,
          new Point(_caveBitmap.x, _caveBitmap.y),
          255
        )
      )
```

```
{
  //A collision was found.
  //Next the code creates "collision boxes" on all
  //four sides of the lander to
  //find out on which side the collision is occurring

  //Switch off gravity
  _lander.gravity_Vy = 0;

  //1. Check for a collision on the bottom
  if(landerBitmap.bitmapData.hitTest
      (
        new Point(_lander.xPos, _lander.yPos + 10),
        255,
        _caveBitmap,
        new Point(_caveBitmap.x, _caveBitmap.y),
        255
      )
    )
  {
    //Move the lander out of the collision
    _lander.setY = _lander.yPos - 1;
    _lander.vy = 0;
    _collisionSide = "bottom";
  }

  //2. Check for a collision on the top
  else if
    (landerBitmap.bitmapData.hitTest
      (
        new Point(_lander.xPos, _lander.yPos - 10),
        255,
        _caveBitmap,
        new Point(_caveBitmap.x, _caveBitmap.y),
        255
      )
    )
  {
    //Move the lander out of the collision
    _lander.setY = _lander.yPos + 1;
    _lander.vy = 0;
    _collisionSide = "top";
  }

  //3. Check for a collision on the right
  if(landerBitmap.bitmapData.hitTest
      (
        new Point(_lander.xPos + 10, _lander.yPos),
        255,
```

```
          _caveBitmap,
          new Point(_caveBitmap.x, _caveBitmap.y),
          255
        )
      )
    {
      //Move the lander out of the collision
      _lander.setX = _lander.xPos - 1;
      _lander.vx = 0;
      _collisionSide = "right";
    }

    //4. Check for a collision on the left
    else if
      (landerBitmap.bitmapData.hitTest
        (
          new Point(_lander.xPos - 10, _lander.yPos),
          255,
          _caveBitmap,
          new Point(_caveBitmap.x, _caveBitmap.y),
          255
        )
      )
    {
      //Collision on left
      _lander.setX = _lander.xPos + 1;
      _lander.vx = 0;
      _collisionSide = "left";
    }
  }
  else
  {
    break;
  }
}
//Switch gravity back on if there is no ground below the lander.
//Adding "+1" to the lander's y position in the collision
//test is the key to making this work
if(!landerBitmap.bitmapData.hitTest
  (
    new Point(_lander.xPos, _lander.yPos + 1),
    255,
    _caveBitmap,
    new Point(_caveBitmap.x, _caveBitmap.y),
    255
  )
)
```

```
    {
      _lander.gravity_Vy = 0.1;
    }

    //Update status box
    _statusBox.text = "CAVE:";
    _statusBox.text += "\n" + "GRAVITY: " + _lander.gravity_Vy;
    _statusBox.text += "\n" + "COLLISION SIDE: " + _collisionSide;
}
```

(The `collisionSide` variable is just used to update the status box, and isn't part of the collision system.)

This collision system works well, but it's not quite as robust as using distance vectors. If the spaces that the lander needs to fly through are too narrow, the code will get confused about the direction of the collision, and the lander will flit through the wall in the wrong direction. However, you can easily manage this with careful level design and a lot of testing. Don't make the spaces too small, and it will work just fine.

Why did I choose to extend the collision boxes by 10 pixels? This is pretty arbitrary. You might find you have to use a larger or smaller number in your games. The smaller you make the number, the narrower the spaces can be that the lander flies though, but the more prone to error the collision detection will be. You want to find the smallest possible number that still provides accurate collision detection. A value of 10 is a good starting point, but only trial and error in your own games will tell you what numbers you need to use.

Despite these quirks, this system works reliably enough. And it is so easy to implement that I've used it as the primary collision system for all the remaining examples in this chapter and the next. The collision detection is as precise and accurate as you could ever want it to be.

The other great thing about this system is that it's quick and easy to create game levels. All you need to do is draw them! Your level design can be as complex as you like, but you'll only ever need to do a collision test with one bitmap.

> *The image of the cave in the `Cave` example was easy to make. Early one January morning, I was taking a walk along the frozen shores of Lake Ontario, when I spotted an interesting piece of Precambrian shale jutting up through the ice. I took a picture of it with a small pocket camera. When I got home, I loaded the image in Photoshop. It took me less than 5 minutes with my all-time-favorite tool, the Eraser, to create the cave you see in Figure 5-12. I just erased the bits or rock I didn't want and, voila, the cave was born!*
>
> *I then resized the image so that it matched the stage dimensions (550 by 400) and saved it as a 32-bit PNG file. 32-bit PNG files contain alpha transparency information, which is used to define the shapes in the bitmap collision system that we're using.*
>
> *This is an extremely fun way to create game levels and quickly try out new ideas.*

A really huge cave

Small caves are cool, but big caves are cooler! How big can we make the cave? This was something I had to find out. My favorite games as a child always involved exploring big environments. I loved classic cave-flyer games like Thrust, Gravitar, and Scramble, along with epic scrolling, role-playing games like the original Zelda and Final Fantasy. But I never took the slightest notice of my score. What kept me playing was just the thrill of finding out what was around the next corner.

So for the next example, I decided to use the full-size 6-megapixel photograph of the slab of Precambrian shale I used for the first `Cave` example. I wanted to create a really huge, scrolling underground cave for the lander to explore. And I thought, while I'm at it, why not create a GPS-style mini-map to help me find my way through this colossal environment? You can find the result in the `BigCave` folder. It looks like Figure 5-14.

Figure 5-14. Can you find your way out of this scrolling underground cave?

Fly the lander though the cave and try to find the exit sign. The cave scrolls as the lander moves, and a yellow dot traces its progress on a map at the top-left corner. Yes, I used the entire 6-megapixel photograph to make this cave, and yes, I had a lot of fun using the Eraser tool in Photoshop! Figure 5-15 illustrates the lander's journey through the cave.

Figure 5-15. Trace your journey on the map as you fly through the cave to the exit.

Before you start to panic, let me reassure you that it's not complex or difficult to make this. In fact, the point of this example is to demonstrate that you don't need complex code to produce a complex-looking result. The collision techniques are identical to the previous example; I copy/pasted most of the code from that project into this one. The scrolling system is the same one I described in *Foundation Game Design with Flash*. The only really new thing is the mini-map, but that's created with only a few short lines of code, most of which you've already seen before. The result appears complex, but the components it's built from are routine. You'll see how easy this is in the explanations ahead.

> *What about that big, red exit sign that the lander can bump into, fly around, and land on? It looks like it might be scarily complicated to make something like that, but it's just part of the big cave bitmap. I added the text to the photograph using Photoshop. As far as the code is concerned, that text is just part of the single bitmap shape, like the cave walls and passages. It's just more pixels—no big deal! This is a great side effect of this system: you can create radically different game levels just by editing the background image in Photoshop.*

Scrolling

If you've read *Foundation Game Design with Flash*, you'll recognize this scrolling system. Four values define the inner boundary area of the stage.

```
private var _rightInnerBoundary:Number
  = (stage.stageWidth * 0.5) + (stage.stageWidth * 0.25);
private var _leftInnerBoundary:Number
  = (stage.stageWidth * 0.5) - (stage.stageWidth * 0.25);
private var _topInnerBoundary:Number
  = (stage.stageHeight * 0.5) - (stage.stageHeight * 0.25);
  private var _bottomInnerBoundary:Number
  = (stage.stageHeight * 0.5) + (stage.stageHeight * 0.25);
```

> *`*0.5` is the same as `/2`, and `*0.25` is the same as `/4`. Flash Player processes multiplication about twice as quickly as division, so this is good optimization trick.*

When the lander reaches the stage boundary, it stops moving, and the cave bitmap moves opposite to the lander's velocity.

```
if (_lander.xPos < _leftInnerBoundary)
{
  _lander.setX = _leftInnerBoundary;
  _rightInnerBoundary = (stage.stageWidth * 0.5) + (stage.stageWidth * 0.25);
  _caveBitmap.x -= _lander.vx;
}
else if (_lander.xPos + _lander.width > _rightInnerBoundary)
{
  _lander.setX = _rightInnerBoundary - _lander.width;
  _leftInnerBoundary = (stage.stageWidth * 0.5) - (stage.stageWidth * 0.25);
  _caveBitmap.x -= _lander.vx;
}
if (_lander.yPos < _topInnerBoundary)
{
  _lander.setY = _topInnerBoundary;
  _bottomInnerBoundary
    = (stage.stageHeight * 0.5) + (stage.stageHeight * 0.25);
  _caveBitmap.y -= _lander.vy;
}
else if (_lander.yPos + _lander.height > _bottomInnerBoundary)
{
  _lander.setY = _bottomInnerBoundary - _lander.height;
  _topInnerBoundary = (stage.stageHeight * 0.5) - (stage.stageHeight * 0.25);
  _caveBitmap.y -= _lander.vy;
}
```

There's also an additional check that stops the cave bitmap background from moving if it reaches the edge of the cave. This bit of code also extends the inner boundary so that the lander can fly straight to the stage edges when the cave stops moving.

```
if (_caveBitmap.x + _caveBitmap.width < stage.stageWidth)
{
  _caveBitmap.x = stage.stageWidth - _caveBitmap.width;
  _rightInnerBoundary = stage.stageWidth;
}
else if (_caveBitmap.x > 0)
{
  _caveBitmap.x = 0;
  _leftInnerBoundary = 0;
}
if (_caveBitmap.y > 0)
{
  _caveBitmap.y = 0;
  _topInnerBoundary = 0;
}
else if (_caveBitmap.y + _caveBitmap.height < stage.stageHeight)
{
  _caveBitmap.y = stage.stageHeight - _caveBitmap.height;
  _bottomInnerBoundary = stage.stageHeight;
}
```

It's a very effective illusion and allows for environments of any size.

> *Chapter 8 demonstrates how to implement an alternative scrolling system using the `scrollRect` method.*

The mini-map

At the beginning of this chapter, I mentioned that a bitmap is made up of two parts. The `BitmapData` object is the raw information that describes the size of the grid and the pixel color of every cell in that grid. The `Bitmap` object displays that data. I said that the reason for this is to separate the data from the display. It means that we can use the data from one bitmap to create a completely new bitmap using the same data.

This feature pays off fabulously in helping to create the GPS mini-map. The map is just a tiny version of the huge 6-megapixel cave bitmap. All we need to do is take the cave's `BitmapData` and scale it to the desired size.

We first need two variables for the map's `BitmapData` and `Bitmap` objects:

```
private var _mapBitmapData:BitmapData;
private var _mapBitmap:Bitmap;
```

The class constructor then creates these objects by taking the cave's BitmapData and scaling it down to a small size. Here's the code that does that:

```
//1. Determine the scale factor
var scaleFactor:Number = 0.04;

//2. Determine the map's size based on
//the _caveBitmap's full height and width
var mapWidth:Number = _caveBitmapData.width * scaleFactor;
var mapHeight:Number = _caveBitmapData.height * scaleFactor;

//3. Create the map's BitmapData based on the scaled height and width
var _mapBitmapData:BitmapData = new BitmapData
  (mapWidth, mapHeight, false, 0x000000);

//4. Create a Matrix to scale the cave's BitmapData to the new size
var scaleMatrix:Matrix = new Matrix();
scaleMatrix.scale(scaleFactor, scaleFactor);

//5. Use the scaled Matrix along with the _caveBitmapData to
//draw the scaled image of the cave into the _mapBitmapData
_mapBitmapData.draw(_caveBitmapData, scaleMatrix);

//6. Create the map's Bitmap using the new scaled _mapBitmapData
_mapBitmap = new Bitmap(_mapBitmapData);
```

I know that you don't like the look of that Matrix object, but you'll soon see that it's not nearly as intimidating as it seems. Let's go through the code.

We first have to figure out how big we want the mini-map to be—25 times smaller is a good size.

```
var scaleFactor:Number = 0.04;
```

This value can now be applied to other values to keep the scaling consistent.

How big is "25 times smaller" in actual pixels? Let's work that out:

```
var mapWidth:Number = _caveBitmapData.width * scaleFactor;
var mapHeight:Number = _caveBitmapData.height * scaleFactor;
```

The original cave bitmap dimensions are 2816 by 2112 pixels. The map's dimensions are worked out to be 112 by 84 pixels.

We next need to make the map's BitmapData. This line of code should be quite familiar to you, as it's how we've been creating BitmapData objects throughout this chapter. But there are two different values in the arguments, which I've highlighted here.

```
var _mapBitmapData:BitmapData = new BitmapData
  (mapWidth, mapHeight, false, 0x000000);
```

Those two values are very important:

- `false` means that there will be no areas of transparency in the bitmap.
- `0x000000` means that the bitmap's fill color will be black. Any areas of the bitmap that don't have assigned colors will be filled with black.

This gives the mini-map a nice solid, black background, which you can see in Figure 5-15. This is very different from the other bitmaps in this chapter, which were all created with transparent fill areas. It's important to remember that you can create bitmaps with any fill color you like.

Up till now, we've just been using transparent fills because they've been necessary for collision checking. An object's shape was defined by the transparent pixels that surrounded it.

Figure 5-16. The map uses a black background fill color.

If the map is 25 times smaller than the original bitmap, it will use 25 times fewer pixels. That means that we need to throw out most of the cave bitmap's pixels, but still end up with an image that looks like the original.

If you think about it, this is a pretty sophisticated problem. We're compressing each group of 25 pixels into 1 pixel. That single pixel must represent the approximate combined color values of the whole group of 25.

To do this, we need to put the cave's bitmap data through a mathematical filter. The filter must churn through all of the original data and squeeze it so that it's very small but contains correct approximations of the original pixel colors.

Luckily, AS3.0 does this for us. In fact, it has a whole class dedicated to doing mathematical filtering: the Matrix class.

> *If reading the explanation of the Matrix class in the AS3.0 documentation makes your head swim and eyes blur over after the second sentence, don't worry! All you really need to know about the Matrix class is this:*
>
> *It's used to mathematically describe the position, rotation, scaling, and skewing of display objects—in other words, their shape, size, and position.*
>
> *The details of how it does these things can become complex, but they're also very specific to each task. That means you don't need to understand everything about the Matrix class right away. Just learn a little about how it works in the context that you're using it. With enough practical examples, which you'll find in this chapter and those ahead, it will start to click.*

The Matrix class has a method called scale that can help us squeeze the bitmap down to size. To use it, we need to make a Matrix object.

```
var scaleMatrix:Matrix = new Matrix();
scaleMatrix.scale(scaleFactor, scaleFactor);
```

The scale method takes two arguments: the scale factors on the x and y axes (the value of scaleFactor is 0.04, which we defined earlier). Those are the amounts by which we want to scale the object.

Now that the Matrix is loaded and ready to go, we can use it to draw the mini-map's BitmapData:

```
_mapBitmapData.draw(_caveBitmapData, scaleMatrix);
```

The BitmapData's draw method accepts a Matrix as a second argument precisely to do the job we're now asking it to do. This line of code takes the cave's bitmap and scales it down using the Matrix's scale factors. It works out how many pixels to use and finds the approximate pixel colors.

The last job is to create the map's Bitmap using the scaled _mapBitmapData.

```
_mapBitmap = new Bitmap(_mapBitmapData);
```

(The BigCave application class also gives the map a drop shadow and bevel filter to help it stand out from the background.)

It's this final _mapBitmap which is the visible mini-map that is added to the stage.

```
addChild(_mapBitmap);
```

There's a fabulous bonus to the map sharing the same data as the cave. If you decide to change the design of the cave in Photoshop and resave the PNG file, the mini-map will automatically read the cave's new BitmapData and update itself accordingly. You don't need to change a single line of code or even think about it. This is one of the great advantages of separating the data from the display.

The map marker

A small, yellow square marks the place on the map that matches the lander's real location in the cave. It's just a rectangle created by the drawing API. The position for the marker is found by scaling the lander's x and y positions by the same amount that the cave's bitmap is scaled. The marker's position is plotted from the top-left corner of the map.

```
_mapMarker.x = _mapBitmap.x + ((-_caveBitmap.x + _lander.xPos) * 0.04);
_mapMarker.y = _mapBitmap.y + ((-_caveBitmap.y + _lander.yPos) * 0.04);
```

The only extra detail here is that we need to subtract the cave bitmap's position to compensate for its scrolling.

Adding objects to scrolling environments

Games are usually pretty crowded, frenetic places full of enemies, treasures, and traps that can help or hinder your goal. Yes, life can be pretty hard in a video-game universe. Up until now, our little lander has had it pretty easy, wouldn't you say? Oh, if it only knew what's to come!

Let's take a look at how you can add objects to big, scrolling environments. In the chapter's source files, find the CaveObjects folder and run the SWF. The lander can fly around the same cave, but now the cave is populated by four mysterious green orbs. The position of the orbs is shown on the map, and they scroll along with the background, as shown in Figure 5-17.

All the objects in a scrolling environment must move at the same rate and in the same direction as the background. There are two ways that you can handle this:

- Put every object that needs to scroll into a single Sprite or MovieClip object. That way, you need to scroll only that one container object. All the other subobjects will automatically scroll with it. The disadvantage is that whenever you want to check for a collision with any of the game objects and the player, you need to convert the objects' x and y coordinates from local to global.
- Scroll all the objects individually, in the same way that you scroll the background. This keeps everything in the same coordinate space, but means the scrolling won't happen automatically. You'll need to code the scrolling individually for each object or group of objects.

I don't know about you, but my brain always starts to hurt whenever I have to convert points from local to global coordinates. Also, I find it much easier to write and debug the collision code if all the objects share the same coordinate space. It just feels more natural to me. So, I've opted for the second option for the scrolling examples in this book. This is purely a personal choice. if you're more comfortable with a single scrolling background, by all means, use it. The amount of code involved in both systems is the same, and there doesn't appear to by any performance difference.

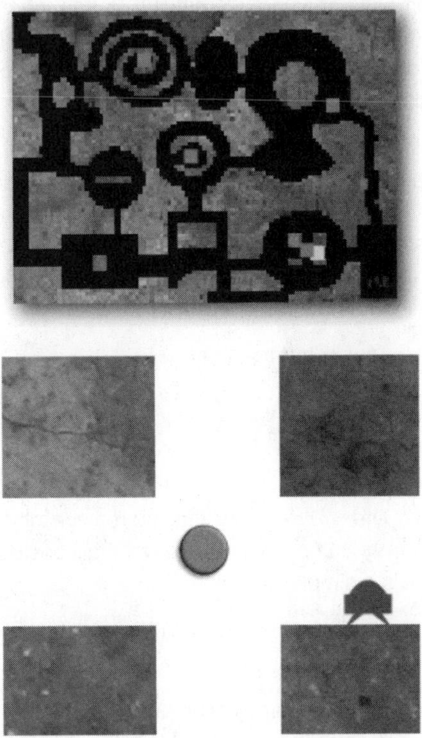

Figure 5-17. The locations of the orbs are shown by green dots on the map.

To position the green orbs in the cave, I went back to the original photograph of Precambrian shale that I was editing in Photoshop. I found the x and y coordinates of each of the four positions on the photograph where I wanted an orb to be and made a note of them. That's a total of eight numbers to keep track of, which is not much (four orbs, each with an x and y value). But it's very common for games to store and track hundreds of numbers for groups of objects like this. So rather than taking the lazy route of creating each orb and individually assigning positions to them, I'm going to show you how treat them as a single group. They all share the same properties and behave the same way, so it makes sense to work with them together as a single unit. Let's see how we can do this efficiently.

Using two-dimensional arrays

The first step is to make a little database of the orb positions. When you think of storing data, arrays immediately come to mind. We could store all the positions of the orbs in an array like this:

```
private var _orbPositions:Array = [969,378, 1298,1045, 2109,1696, 2301,700];
```

Each pair of numbers represents the x and y positions of one of the orbs.

This will work, but I'm sure you can immediately see a few problems here. One is that it's difficult to read. Even with a bit of creative spacing, it's difficult to see where one pair of numbers ends and the other begins. This might not be problem with 8 numbers, but can you imagine what it would look like with 200? It could be very difficult to isolate and debug a problem if you made a mistake entering any of the data.

Another problem is that looping becomes complicated. The great value to storing data in arrays is that you can loop though the data and perform repetitive tasks on hundred of objects with just a few lines of code. Our problem in this case is that the data is not uniform. The first number of each pair is an x position value, and the second is a y position value. That means to get or set these values on one object, the loop would need to count in twos, like this: 0, 2, 4, 6, and so on. That's fine. We could create a loop that counts in twos like this:

```
for(var i:int = 0; i < array.length; i += 2)
{
  _orbs[i].x = _orbPositions[i];
  _orbs[i].y = _orbPositions[i + 1];
}
```

But do you see the problem? The `_orbs` array that stores the objects will also skip though its values in twos. It means that only half of them will have their positions set. We could use some math get around this, but there's a simpler way.

It makes more logical sense to group each x and y value as its own single unit. Let's see how to take that approach.

First, put each pair of numbers into its own array. The array will contain only two values. That means that if you have four objects, each object's position will be stored in a single array. You'll end up with four arrays, with each array containing two numbers. The code might look something like this:

```
var position1:Array = [969, 378];
var position2:Array = [1298,1045];
var position3:Array = [2109,1696];
var position4:Array = [2301,700];
```

Next, put those four position arrays *into another array*.

```
var positions:Array = [position1, position2, position3, position4];
```

Yes, it's just like a big fish eating a lot of smaller fish.

Now you can loop though all the array objects as you normally would. When you want to change the position of the object, you can access the subarrays.

```
for(var i:int = 0; i < array.length; i += 2)
{
  _orbs[i].x = _ positions[i][0];
  _orbs[i].y = _ positions [i][1];
}
```

To access the position values, you first need to locate the array in which they're stored, and then the specific x and y values. This is what the syntax looks like:

```
_positions[containingArray][subArray];
```

or, if you prefer:

```
_positions[bigFish][smallFish];
```

In the context of a loop, it looks like this:

```
_positions[i][0];
_positions[i][1];
```

On the first loop, the preceding code will be read like this:

```
_positions[position1][969];
_positions[position1][378];
```

On the second loop, it will look like this:

```
_positions[position2][1298];
_positions[position2][1045];
```

Neat, huh? This is called a **two-dimensional array**. It's an array that contains other arrays.

There's a short form for creating two-dimensional arrays. You can create both the containing array and the subarrays in one step, like this:

```
private var _orbPositions:Array
  =[[969,378],[1298,1045],[2109,1696],[2301,700]];
```

But it's much easier to read if you format it like this:

```
private var _orbPositions:Array
  =
  [
    [969,378],
    [1298,1045],
    [2109,1696],
    [2301,700]
  ];
```

Can you see why it's called a two-dimensional array? When you format it in this way, you can clearly see that the data creates a grid. It has height and width, just like a two-dimensional shape.

This is conceptually an extremely important thing to understand. If you can "see" the shape of this data grid, it makes certain calculations in your games much easier for you to understand. You'll see how useful this is in Chapters 8 and 9, where two-dimensional arrays actually become the visual representation of the game level. But even in this example, a quick glance at that array reveals where the pairs of x and y values are. You could also think of them as two columns. This makes it very easy to edit and debug the data.

Two-dimensional arrays offer a great solution to our problem. Figure 5-18 helps you to visualize how they work.

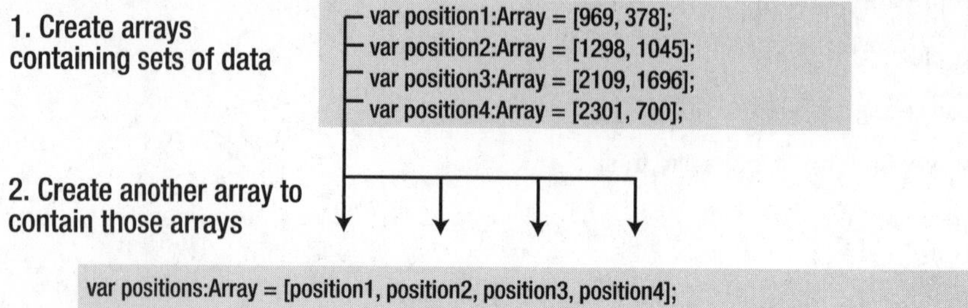
1. Create arrays containing sets of data
var position1:Array = [969, 378];
var position2:Array = [1298, 1045];
var position3:Array = [2109, 1696];
var position4:Array = [2301, 700];
2. Create another array to contain those arrays
var positions:Array = [position1, position2, position3, position4];

3. Loop through the containing array to access the the sub-arrays

```
for(var i:int = 0; i < positions.length; i++)
{
  _orbs[i].x = positions[i][0];
  _orbs[i].y = positions[i][1];
}
```

4. The values for each loop

```
_orbs[0].x = 969;
_orbs[0].y = 378;
```

```
_orbs[1].x = 1298;
_orbs[1].y = 1045;
```

```
_orbs[2].x = 2109;
_orbs[2].y = 1696;
```

```
_orbs[3].x = 2301;
_orbs[3].y = 700;
```

Use this short-form syntax to create two-dimensional arrays quickly

```
var positions:Array
 =
[
  [969,378],
  [1298,1045],
  [2109,1696],
  [2301,700]
];
```

Figure 5-18. Creating and using two-dimensional arrays

Creating and adding the objects

Getting back to the example file, the positions of the orbs are now in a two-dimensional array called _orbPositions. The example file also uses another array, simply called _orbs, to store the orb shapes. The next job is to create the orbs and add them to the stage in the correct positions on the map.

The orbs are positioned with a for loop. We can assume that we need one orb for each of the four map positions. That means we can use the _orbPosition array's length property to determine how many orbs to make. This is really handy, because if we ever add more positions to the _orbPosition array, new orbs will be automatically created and added to the stage without us needing to change any other code.

```
for(var i:int = 0; i < _orbPositions.length; i++)
{
   //Create the orb Shape
   var orb:Shape = new Shape();

   //…draw the shape and add filters

  //Add the shape to the _orbs array
  _orbs.push(orb);

  //Add the orb to the stage
  addChild(orb);

  //Set the initial orb positions using the values from
  //the two-dimensional array
  orb.x = _caveBitmap.x + _orbPositions[i][0];
  orb.y = _caveBitmap.y + _orbPositions[i][1];
}
```

For each orb, we also need a corresponding marker to show its position on the mini-map. These map markers are just little square shapes made with the drawing API. An array called _mapMarkers stores them. We can again use the _orbPosition array's length property to figure out how many of them to make.

This is the loop that creates the map markers, pushes them into the _mapMarkers array, adds them to the stage, and positions them on the map:

```
for(var j:int = 0; j < _orbPositions.length; j++)
{
  //Create the marker shape
  var mapMarker:Shape = new Shape();
  //… draw the shape
```

```
  //Push the shape into the _orbMarkers array
  _orbMarkers.push(mapMarker);

  //Add the marker to the stage
  addChild(mapMarker);

  //Position the marker on the map
  mapMarker.x = _mapBitmap.x + ((-_caveBitmap.x + _orbs[j].x) * 0.04);
  mapMarker.y = _mapBitmap.y + ((-_caveBitmap.y + _orbs[j].y) * 0.04);
}
```

The orbs and map markers are now on the stage in the correct positions. The next job is to scroll the orbs so that they stay synchronized with the background.

Scrolling the objects

The four orbs all have fixed positions. Their positions don't change after they've been added to the stage. This makes it quite easy to scroll them.

In the `enterFrameHandler`, a loop uses the orbs' positions from the two-dimensional array and plots them from the top-left corner of the `_caveBitmap` background.

```
for(var i:int = 0; i < _orbs.length; i++)
{
  _orbs[i].x = _caveBitmap.x + _orbPositions[i][0];
  _orbs[i].y = _caveBitmap.y + _orbPositions[i][1];
}
```

This ensures that whenever the `_caveBitmap` moves, the orbs will remain fixed at the same relative position. They will correctly move in and out of the stage depending on the position of the bitmap.

For this example, this code works just fine. But what if you had a game where, after you assigned the orbs their initial position, they started moving around the cave by themselves? Maybe you've programmed them with some AI to try and hunt down the player. You would have no way of knowing where they were supposed to be relative to the background's top-left corner.

The solution is to calculate a **scroll velocity**. Figure out the velocity at which the background is moving, and add that velocity to the objects' positions. This allows the objects to move around within a scrolling environment.

Calculating a scroll velocity is the same as calculating velocity for any other object.

1. Store the scrolling background's x and y positions in temporary variables before it scrolls.
2. Scroll the background.
3. Subtract the temporary position from the new position to find the velocity.

Here's the code in the enterFrameHandler that does this (the code that scrolls the background has been abridged, but it's exactly the same as the previous example):

```
//Capture the current background x and y positions before
//they're changed by scrolling
var temporaryX:Number = _caveBitmap.x;
var temporaryY:Number = _caveBitmap.y;

//…scroll the background

//Calculate the scroll velocity
var scroll_Vx:Number = _caveBitmap.x - temporaryX;
var scroll_Vy:Number = _caveBitmap.y - temporaryY;
```

The game can now use the scroll velocity to scroll the orbs:

```
for(var i:int = 0; i < _orbs.length; i++)
{
   _orbs[i].x += scroll_Vx;
   _orbs[i].y += scroll_Vy;
}
```

The beauty of this is that you don't need to know where any of the orbs should be. They work that out for themselves based on their current positions and the scroll velocity.

This technique is indispensable if your scrolling objects move, and you'll see it widely used in the case study in Chapter 7.

Building a rotating gun turret

Our lander is having quite a jolly old time floating about in space caverns, but this is a video-game universe. Sooner or later, something bad is going to happen! We need to give our little lander something to defend itself with.

The perfect weapon, and video-game staple, is the multitalented **rotating gun turret**. If we attach one to the lander, it will be able shoot down any enemies that cross its path. You'll find an example in the Bullets folder. Run the SWF file, and you'll see that the lander has acquired a cannon. Use the mouse to rotate it and fire bullets, as shown in Figure 5-19.

The turret is a completely separate MVC system from the lander. It's a separate object and just follows the lander's position. Turrets are such useful things in games that I felt it would give me more flexibility to keep it as a separate game component.

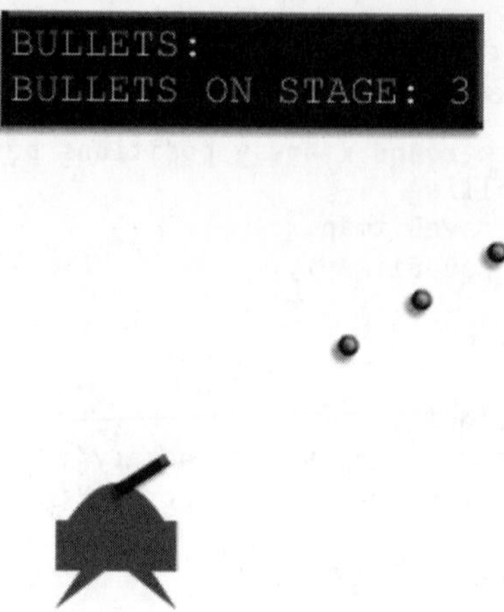

Figure 5-19. Aim and fire bullets with the mouse.

You'll find the turret's model, view, and controller in the `com.friendsofed.gameElements.turret` package. Its MVC components follow the same format as the lander's. The `Bullets` application class creates it like this:

```
private var _turret:TurretModel
  = new TurretModel(15, 3, 0x000000, -20, -160);
private var _turretUIController:TurretUIController
  = new TurretUIController(_turret);
private var _turret_View:TurretView
  = new TurretView(_turret);
private var _turretUIView:TurretUIView
  = new TurretUIView(_turret, _turretUIController, stage);
```

In a big game, it would probably makes sense to create the turret as a sub-MVC system *inside* the lander MVC. I've created it in the application class just to more clearly expose the nuts and bolts of how it works.

Drawing and rotating the cannon

The `TurretView` class draws a rectangle that represents the barrel of the cannon. Its middle center is at 0, and the rectangle is drawn toward the left, as shown in Figure 5-20.

```
_turretShape.graphics.drawRect
  (0,model.height / 2, -model.width, -model.height);
```

This aligns the shape accurately so that it rotates correctly according to the formula we'll use.

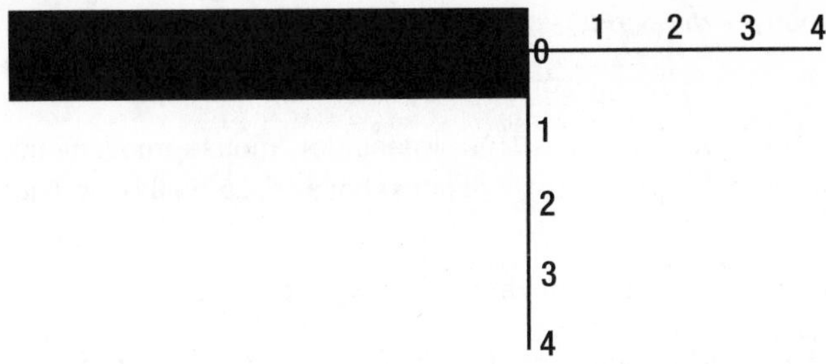

Figure 5-20. Set the barrel of the cannon so that it's aligned to the left of the shape's middle center point.

This puts it at a starting rotation position of 0 degrees. You can think of this position as lying flat on the ground.

You'll notice in the SWF that the cannon can't make a full 360-degree rotation around the lander. The rotation is constrained within a certain range. This creates the effect of the lander's hull blocking the cannon's movement, as shown in Figure 5-21.

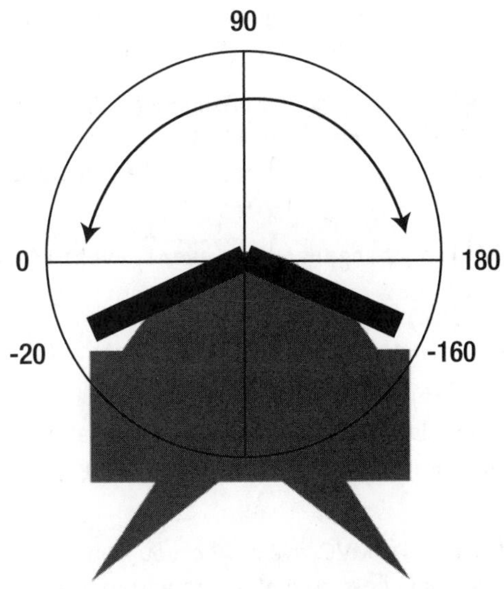

Figure 5-21. Constrain the cannon's rotation within a specific range.

The cannon can move freely between –20 to –160 degrees, but not outside that range.

The `TurretModel` has `constrainLeft` and `contrainRight` properties, which can be initialized in its constructor. They are the last two arguments in the constructor method:

```
private var _turret:TurretModel = new TurretModel
```

```
(15, 3, 0x000000, -20, -160);
```

The first three arguments set the cannon's width, height, and color.

To move the cannon, the `TurretUIView` listens for mouse movements and sends that information to the `TurretUIController`'s `processMouseMove` method to figure out what should happen.

```
internal function processMouseMove(stage:Object):void
{
  //Figure out the angle based on the mouse's stage position
  var angle:Number = Math.atan2
    (_model.yPos - stage.mouseY, _model.xPos - stage.mouseX);

  //Constrain angle to the top arc of the lander
  if(angle * 180 / Math.PI > _model.constrainLeft
  || angle * 180 / Math.PI < _model.constrainRight)
  {
    _model.angle = angle;
  }
}
```

This is the same formula for calculating an angle of rotation using `Math.atan2` described in *Foundation Game Design with Flash*.

The `TurretModel` has an `angle` property that it has inherited from its parent, the `AVerletModel` superclass. When the `angle` changes, `AVerletModel` dispatches a `CHANGE` event. The `TurretView` listens for that event, and its `changeHandler` updates the rotation of the turret shape.

```
override protected function changeHandler(event:Event):void
{
  super.changeHandler(event);
  _turretShape.rotation = model.angle  * 180 / Math.PI;
}
```

This is the same way that view classes update an object's visual position on the stage based on changing `xPos` and `yPos` values in the model. Instead of changing its x and y position, it's just changing its angle.

Figure 5-22 is a map of the turret's MVC system so you can see how it all fits together. I've removed all but the most essential code, so make sure you refer to the original source files for a complete working example. This diagram is just to help you understand the relationship between the classes.

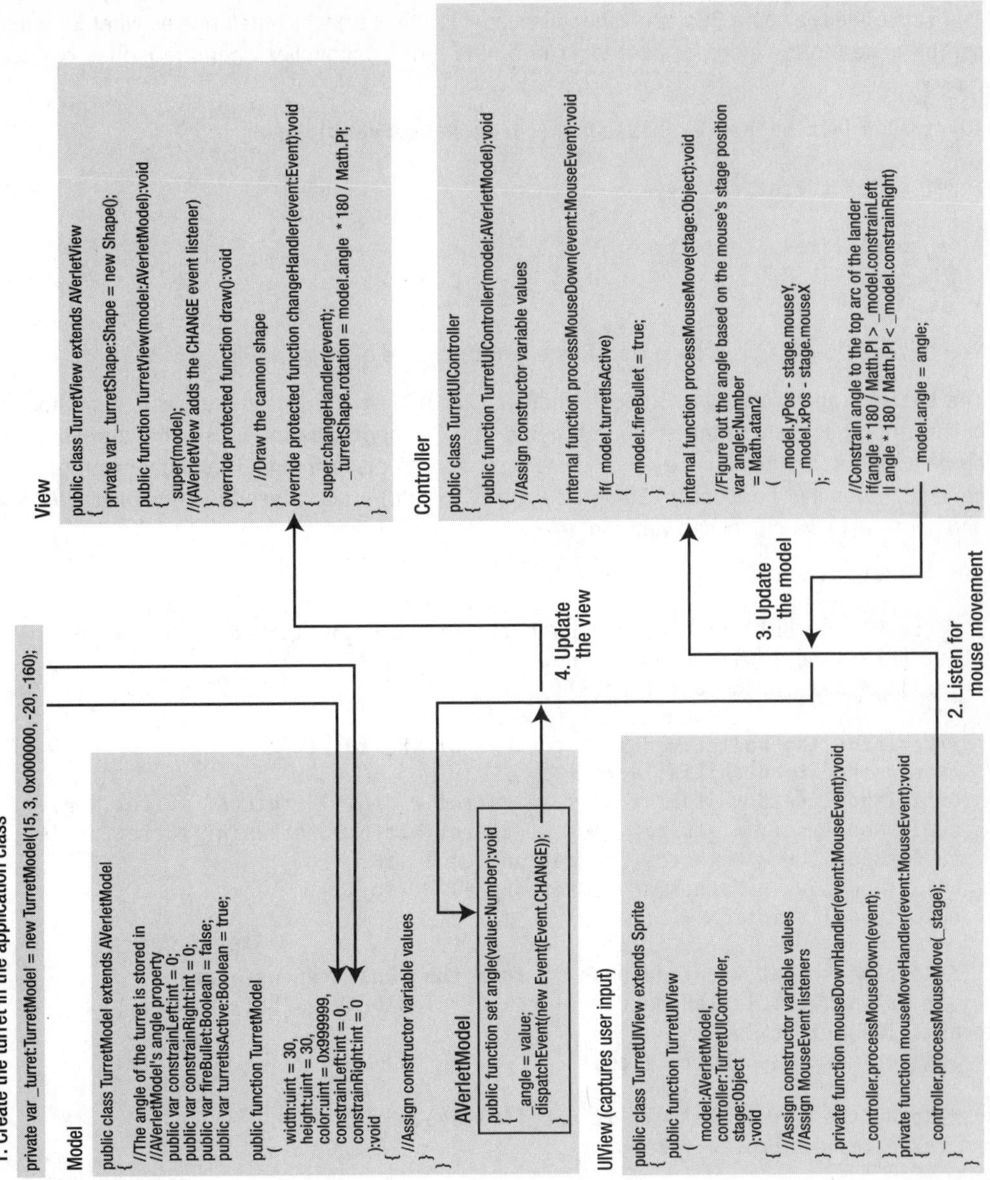

Figure 5-22. The turret's MVC system

Firing bullets

The turret doesn't actually fire any bullets. It just *gives permission* to the application class to add them to the stage.

The TurretModel has a Boolean variable called fireBullet, which determines whether bullets can be added to the stage. It's set to true by the turret's controller when the mouse button is clicked.

```
internal function processMouseDown(event:MouseEvent):void
{
  if(_model.turretIsActive)
  {
    _model.fireBullet = true;
  }
}
```

You can see how this bit of code fits into the grand scheme of things in Figure 5-22.

The Bullets application class checks whether fireBullet is true. In that case, it creates the bullets and adds them to the stage at the end of the cannon's barrel. It uses the turret's angle property and some trigonometry to find the right spot to place them. (This trigonometry is also covered in detail in *Foundation Game Design with Flash*.) It also gives them their initial velocity and adds the bullet model and views to arrays.

```
if(_turret.fireBullet == true)
{
  //Create the bullet model and push it into the _bulletModels array
  var bulletModel:CircleModel = new CircleModel(2);
  _bulletModels.push(bulletModel);

  //Position the bullet model at the end of the turret
  //and give it an initial velocity
  bulletModel.setX = _turret.xPos - _turret.width * Math.cos(_turret.angle);
  bulletModel.setY = _turret.yPos - _turret.width * Math.sin(_turret.angle);
  bulletModel.vx = Math.cos(_turret.angle) * -10;
  bulletModel.vy = Math.sin(_turret.angle) * -10;
  bulletModel.friction = 1;

  //Add the bullet view and push it into the _bulletViews array
  var bulletView:CircleBlockView = new CircleBlockView(bulletModel);
  addChild(bulletView);
  _bulletViews.push(bulletView);

  //Reset the turret so that it can fire again
  _turret.fireBullet = false;
}
```

The last thing it does is set the turret's fireBullet property to false. This prevents a bullet from firing again until the next mouse click.

Moving and removing bullets

The bullet models and views are now conveniently in arrays. That means we can deal with all of them just by looping through the number of bullets that have been created. The application class has the next few tasks to perform:

- Call the bullets' `update` methods so that they move across the stage.
- Remove the bullet views if they cross the stage boundaries. This involves removing them from the stage and splicing them from both the model and view arrays.

A single `for` loop takes care of both these steps.

```
for(var i:int = 0; i < _bulletModels.length; i++)
{
  //Update the bullet model
  _bulletModels[i].update();

  //Remove the bullet if it crosses the stage boundary
  if(_bulletModels[i].yPos < 0
  || _bulletModels[i].yPos > stage.stageHeight
  || _bulletModels[i].xPos < 0
  || _bulletModels[i].xPos > stage.stageWidth)
  {
    _bulletModels.splice(i, 1);
    removeChild(_bulletViews[i]);
    _bulletViews.splice(i, 1);
    i--;
  }
}
```

I find that it's much easier to manage adding and removing objects when these tasks are done in the application or game controller class.

Make sure you take a good look at the `Bullets` application class so that you can see all this code in its proper context.

Destroying things!

What's the point of discovering new and mysterious worlds in distant corners of the galaxy if we can't destroy them? Our little lander has a new toy to play with, so we're going to let it loose and make this chapter live up to its promise!

Run the `BitmapErase` SWF for a taste of the trouble to come. The lander can fly around the cave and blast holes in the rock, as shown in Figure 5-23. The lander can use these holes as new routes to fly through and perch on new ledges that the holes make, as shown in Figure 5-24.

Figure 5-23. Blast holes in the rock.

Figure 5-24. The new environment can change the game in unexpected ways. Hide from enemies or plan attacks.

Being able to interactively change the game world at the pixel level has tremendous potential in games. It means that players can use the environment to strategically solve puzzles, hide from enemies, or plan attacks. It also means that the game is different each time it's played. **Terrain deformation** is big topic in game design, and many action-strategy games, like Worms, make it a central part of their game engines. If you design and plan your games carefully, terrain deformation can help you create a game with unexpected outcomes that are exciting to play and replay.

Although the effect is impressive and extremely useful, terrain deformation with AS3.0 can be accomplished with only a few lines of code. Actually, it all boils down to one line.

It will be easier for you to understand the code if you know what we're asking it to do. Think of the stage as a big grid. Each pixel position on the stage represents a cell on the grid. Remember that bitmaps are also just big grids full of pixel information. In that way, they're exactly like the grid that makes up x and y stage positions. The only difference is that they also contain pixel color information.

When one of the bullets hits the bitmap, the code plots a circle onto the cave bitmap in the same place as the bullet's stage position. The circle is then erased from the cave bitmap. That leaves a gaping hole in the cave the same size as the circle. Because those pixels have been erased, they're no longer involved in the bitmap collision check, and the lander can fly through the hole.

Bitmap collision using points

Collision detection between the bullets and the cave bitmap uses the same `Bitmapdata.hitTest` method as in previous examples. However, there's one big difference. The bullets are really small, so we don't need to bother checking whether their entire area is hitting the cave, just their center points.

The `Bitmapdata.hitTest` method has an option for checking bitmaps against single points. All you do is specify the second object in the collision as a `Point` object.

Here's the code in the `BitmapErase` application class that checks for a collision between the bullets and the cave (I've highlighted the important new code):

```
if(_caveBitmapData.hitTest
    (
      new Point(_caveBitmap.x, _caveBitmap.y),
      255,
      new Point(_bulletModels[i].xPos, _bulletModels[i].yPos)
    )
  )
{ …
```

The second object is just a point. It can be any `Point` object. In this case, the bullet's x and y position is converted into a `Point` object.

Bitmap collision detection is extremely processor-intensive, so whenever you have a chance to substitute a `Point` for a `Bitmap` object, do it! It will give your game a noticeable performance boost.

You can also specify `Rectangle` objects as the second object in the collision. Here's an example:

```
if(_caveBitmapData.hitTest
    (
      new Point(_caveBitmap.x, _caveBitmap.y),
      255,
      new Rectangle(x, y, width, height)
    )
  )
{ ...
```

(The x and y positions refer to the top-left corner of the rectangle.)

This essentially checks for a collision between the bitmap and an object's bounding box. Rectangular bounding boxes are widely used for collision checking in games because of their speed and simplicity, and you can harness those benefits here. As with `Point` objects, using `Rectangle` objects means that your game doesn't need to process more pixel information, and that's a big performance saving. If you don't need absolute pixel-perfect collision detection, make sure you use `Point` and `Rectangle` objects every chance you get.

Erasing the bitmap

Just as in the previous example, the bullets are stored in two arrays: `_bulletModels` and `_bulletViews`.

> *Now that you know about two-dimensional arrays, you could store both the model and views in the same array, following the same format we used for storing positions in the object scrolling example. This will make your code a bit more compact, but also possibly a little less readable, so I'll leave it up to you to decide whether or not to try it.*

A `for` loop cycles through each bullet, updates it, and checks for collisions. When it finds a collision between the bullet and cave, it carves a hole in the cave bitmap. Here's all the code that does this, and I'll explain in detail how the hole is created in the section that follows.

```
for(var i:int = 0; i < _bulletModels.length; i++)
{
  //Update the bullet model
  _bulletModels[i].update();

  //Check for a collision between the cave bitmap and the
  //bullet's x and y position
  if(_caveBitmapData.hitTest
```

```
      (
        new Point(_caveBitmap.x, _caveBitmap.y),
        255,
        new Point(_bulletModels[i].xPos, _bulletModels[i].yPos)
      )
    )
  {
    //Assign a radius for the circle
    var radius:int = 40;

    //Create a circle shape using the above radius value
    var circle:Shape = makeCircle(radius);

    //Create a Matrix object. The Matrix's
    //"translate" method is used to
    //position the circle shape in the
    //right place on the cave bitmap
    var matrix:Matrix = new Matrix();
    matrix.translate(_bulletModels[i].xPos, _bulletModels[i].yPos);

    //Redraw the cave bitmap using the
    //circle shape and the matrix.
    //The BlendMode.ERASE argument tells the cave's BitmapData
    //to erase the circle shape at the
    //position specified by the matrix
    _caveBitmapData.draw(circle, matrix, null, BlendMode.ERASE);

    //Remove the bullet
    _bulletModels.splice(i, 1);
    removeChild(_bulletViews[i]);
    _bulletViews.splice(i, 1);
    i--;
  }
}
```

Only five lines of code do the job of creating the hole in the bitmap. The first thing the code needs to do is create a circle shape.

```
var radius:int = 40;
var circle:Shape = makeCircle(radius);
```

This is handled by the `makeCircle` method that you'll find near the end of the application class.

```
private function makeCircle(radius:int = 30):Shape
{
  //Create the shape
  var shape:Shape = new Shape();
  shape.graphics.lineStyle(0);
  shape.graphics.beginFill(0xFFFFFF);
```

```
  shape.graphics.drawCircle(0, 0, radius);
  shape.graphics.endFill();

  return shape
}
```

Its job is just to return a circle Shape object.

Realize that you can use *any* shape you like. I've just used circles for the sake of clarity, but in a game, you might use different shapes and vary them depending on the kind of destruction you want. (You'll see an example of this in the next section.) Also, you are not restricted to Shape objects. You can use sprites, movie clips, or other bitmaps—any display object will work. With enough time and attention to detail, you could create very realistic and intricate destruction effects.

> *You don't want the imaginative destruction of players to cause bugs in the game, so you'll need to do a lot of testing and set limits where necessary.*

The next step is to create a Matrix object that stores the position of the bullet where it hits the cave. The Matrix class has a translate method that stores x and y position values.

```
var matrix:Matrix = new Matrix();
matrix.translate(_bulletModels[i].xPos, _bulletModels[i].yPos);
```

Again, don't let that Matrix class put you off! We need to use it so that we can communicate the position of the bullet to the bitmap. The bitmap can't read the bullet's position directly. The position must be wrapped inside a Matrix class object.

Finally, we need to redraw the cave's BitmapData with this new information.

```
_caveBitmapData.draw(circle, matrix, null, BlendMode.ERASE);
```

This is another way of saying, "Redraw the cave's bitmap, but erase a circle shape at whatever position the matrix says you should."

The null in the arguments just says that there's no ColorTransform object involved in the mix. A ColorTransform object allows you to adjust the colors of the bitmap.

And that's it! As I said, the effect is really just created by one line of code. But what a line of code it is! With a bit of imagination, you have a whole new universe of possibilities and directions that you can take your games.

Jagged rocks

I mentioned that you can use any shapes to create your destructible environment, not just circles. You'll find a working example of this in the JaggedBitmapErase folder. In this example, the lander is able to blast jagged rock shapes into the cave wall and fly through the new spaces, as shown in Figure 5-25.

Figure 5-25. Cut holes in the environment bitmap using different shapes, and randomize them for an organic effect.

The code is identical to the previous example, except that the shape is created by this new `makeBrokenRock` method:

```
private function makeBrokenRock(scaleFactor:int = 8):Shape
{
  //Create a new Vector object for the drawing coordinates
  var coordinates:Vector.<Number> = new Vector.<Number>();

  //Create the broken rock shape
  //in a 1:1 grid
  coordinates.push
    (
      0,0, 4,2, 7,0, 10,2,
      8,6, 10,10, 6,9, 4,10,
      3,9, 0,10, 2,7, 0,5,
      1,3, 0,0
    );

  //Scale to the correct size, and center the shape
  for(var i:int = 0; i < coordinates.length; i++)
  {
    //Scale the shape to the scaleFactor value
    coordinates[i] *= scaleFactor;

    //Center the shape at 0,0
    coordinates[i] -= (scaleFactor * 10) * 0.5;
  }

  //Create a Vector object for the drawing commands
  var commands:Vector.<int> = new Vector.<int>();
```

```
  //1 = moveTo(), 2 = lineTo(), 3 = curveTo()
  commands.push(1,2,2,2,2,2,2,2,2,2,2,2,2,2);

  //Create the shape
  var shape:Shape = new Shape();
  shape.graphics.lineStyle(0);
  shape.graphics.beginFill(0xFFFFFF);
  shape.graphics.drawPath(commands, coordinates);
  shape.graphics.endFill();

  return shape
}
```

The coordinates for the shape are in a 10-by-10 grid.

```
coordinates.push
    (
    0,0, 4,2, 7,0, 10,2,
    8,6, 10,10, 6,9, 4,10,
    3,9, 0,10, 2,7, 0,5,
    1,3, 0,0
    );
```

Figure 5-26 illustrates this.

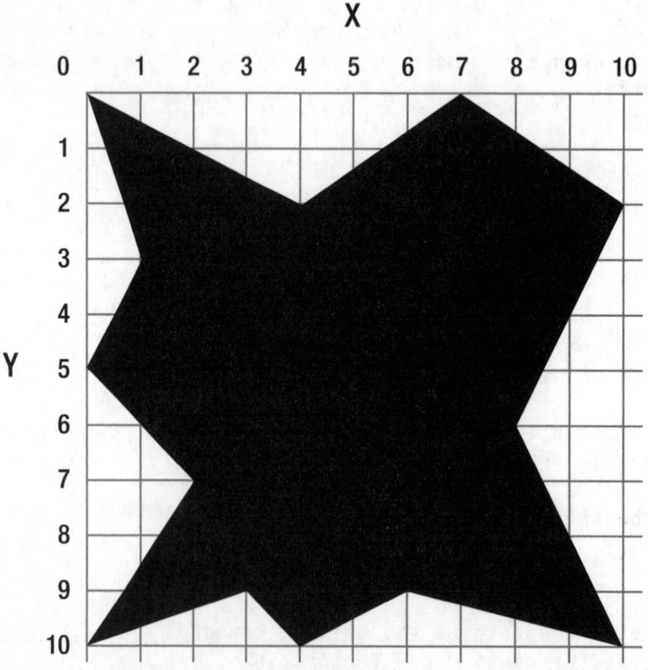

Figure 5-26. The shape of broken rock is plotted on a 10-by-10 grid.

I created this shape in a 10-by-10 grid because it's a convenient size to plot the points and makes it easy to scale. The only problem is that if we used the shape as is, it would produce a 10-by-10-pixel bitmap. That's too small. The code needs to scale it up to a much larger size so that the shape will cut a sizable chunk out of the cave wall.

The `makeBrokenRock` method has a `scaleFactor` variable that's initialized with a value of `8`. If we multiply all the values in the grid by 8, we'll end up with an 80-by-80-pixel shape, which is a much better size for the game. The `for` loop multiplies all the values in the grid by 8:

```
coordinates[i] *= scaleFactor;
```

But that's not the end of the story. We also want the shape to be centered. So the next line in the loop subtracts `40` from all the values.

```
coordinates[i] -= (scaleFactor * 10) * 0.5;
```

This pushes the shape 40 pixels to the left and 40 pixels up. It means that the center of the shape will be exactly at point 0—perfectly centered.

> *Yes, I could have created this shape in a centered 80-by-80 grid to begin with. But it's important to demonstrate how you can scale and center a shape like this. It means you can create shapes of many different sizes just by changing the `scaleFactor` value.*

You could create a more realistic effect by having the method randomly choose one of three or four different shapes each time the method is called, and vary the sizes slightly. This would make the effect organic and unpredictable.

Summary

Within the first few weeks of getting in to Flash game design, I had filled up every Flash message board on the Internet (the two that existed then!) with question after question about how to do pixel-perfect collision between irregular shapes. That was back in what now seems like the medieval period of Flash 4, when I was still learning ActionScript, and almost everyone else on the message boards was about as puzzled about this as I was. There were some great theories proposed, but no workable solutions. Why oh why, we lamented, did Flash not provide an easy way to check for collisions between irregular shapes?

When I finally had a chance to revisit the problem, Flash 8 had arrived, and with it most of the tools to do the kind of bitmap collision covered in this chapter. But surprisingly, it was rarely used. In the interim, not only had Flash game developers found plenty of creative work-arounds, but many of those work-arounds proved to work better for most collision problems than using bitmaps. Game developers had figured out that bounding boxes or AABB collision were perfectly adequate most of the time and, as a bonus, really fast. And if you needed circles or weird shapes, use math. Mathematical solutions, as you've seen in Chapters 2, 3, and 4, are not only fast, but give you a lot of information about the collision that you can use for things like bounce and friction.

That's still pretty much all true. All things being equal, doing bitmap collision testing is slow. Game designers will do whatever they can to squeeze any extra CPU juice out of their system, and if that means not using pixel-perfect collisions, so be it.

But pixel-perfect collision is amazing! And, as you've seen from this chapter, it allows you to achieve some effects that would be very complicated to do otherwise. For creating destructible environments or bumpy surfaces, bitmap collision testing is essential.

How slow is it? You certainly would not want to do hundreds of bitmap collision tests each frame, because Flash Player would grind to a halt. But if you use bitmap collision wisely for a limited number of objects, it's plenty fast enough for most games. Just assume that it's going to be slow, use it conservatively, do a lot of testing, and you'll be fine. In Chapter 8, I'm going to introduce broad-phase collision testing, which will help you to optimize this even further. You really shouldn't have any excuse not to use pixel-perfect collision in your games. It's great!

But enough talk; this is a book about video games, so let's blow some things up!

Chapter 6

Explosions, Blitting, and Optimization

Hey, it's break time! I'm going to give you 5 minutes to play a quick game of Luxor, Zookeeper, or Bejeweled. But just 5 minutes … promise?

After playing any of those games, can you focus on this sentence, or are you still shaken from a nonstop barrage of flashing, exploding, shimmering, and bouncing things that fill every square millimeter of the screen? What separates great commercial games like Luxor and Bejeweled from games you'll make while you're learning is the attention they pay to surface detail. Everything shimmers, flashes, explodes, and sparkles with unceasing bubbly giddiness at every opportunity. It makes those games incredibly tactile, so that you feel you can touch them. It's an illusion, of course, but a brilliant one, which increases the fun factor immeasurably.

A lot of those effects can be created in a very simple way. At a point of contact between two objects, add a third object. The third object is an animated sprite that displays the effect and then quickly fades away. In this chapter, I'm going to show you how to do just that, by creating explosions and particle effects.

Although the explosion effects we're going to look at are specific to this chapter's examples, you can adapt them to any kind of visual effect you like: a starburst, a puff of smoke, a flash of light, or even animated text that displays your score for picking up an item. The basic technique of adding and removing the visual effect from the stage will be the same. Using surface effects like this—even just a few of them—will add an extra layer of polish to your games that starts to push them toward professional standards.

We'll approach this in very gradual step-by-step way, starting with something simple and finishing the chapter with a complex example. Along the way, we'll cover these important topics:

- Using timer events for animation
- Adding dynamic properties
- Breaking a bitmap into particles and using those particles as bits of an explosion
- Using `Rectangle` and `Point` objects to take a snapshot of a section of a bitmap
- Creating a tile sheet
- Making starburst explosions
- Creating smoke trails using Perlin noise
- Calculating frame rates
- Using `copyPixels` and bit-block transfer (blitting) for really fast particle effects
- Creating lookup tables to improve performance
- Using an explosion controller to help manage complex particle effects

So let's start blowing things up!

A simple particle explosion

You'll find the first explosion effect we'll be making in the `ParticleExplosion` folder. The screenshot in Figure 6-1 doesn't do the effect justice, so make sure you run the SWF to get a feeling for it.

Figure 6-1. Blast the rock and watch the fireworks.

When the bullets hit the rock, 100 little rotating squares of varying color and transparency fly away in different directions, like a fireworks explosion, as shown in Figure 6-2. Gravity pulls the fragments downward, and they all quickly fade away.

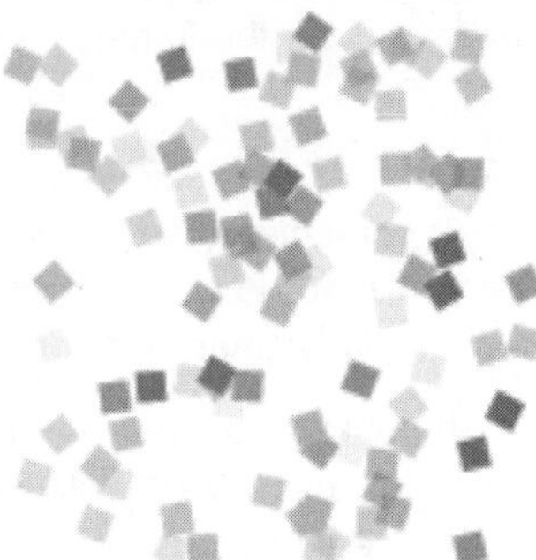

Figure 6-2. The explosions are made up of little rotating squares of different colors.

The explosion is a single, self-contained sprite that's superimposed over the background. The sprite creates 100 little squares internally; gives them random velocity, rotation, and fade rates; and makes them move. It's all done by the `Explosion` class, which you'll find in the `com.friendsofed.gameElements.effects` package.

There's one very important new technique that the `Explosion` class uses. Instead of updating the positions of the particles each frame, it updates their positions using a timer.

Using timer events for animation

A particle explosion creates a lot of moving objects on the stage. Whenever many things start moving around quickly in your games, you need to start thinking about optimization. Explosion effects using a few hundred particles will start to put a strain on the CPU, and your game will slow down, stutter, and crawl. Even in this simple example, if you fire off five or ten bullets at time, you'll probably notice a drop in the frame rate.

One widely used optimization technique is to run less important animations at frame rates that are slower than the rest of the game. Players really notice only the frame rates of objects that they're directly interacting with: the player's character, enemies, and bullets. Those need to run at the highest possible frame rates for the players to feel immersed in the game. But players don't notice the frame rates of background objects or little extras, like explosions. If you can update those nonessential animations at low frame rate, you have much more juice left over for the main action. This can give your game a big performance saving. This is also a very simple solution to put into place. All it amounts to is this:

Update the object positions with a `TIMER` *instead of an* `ENTER_FRAME` *event.*

There are no other changes you'll need to make to the code and, except for one important difference, the animation effect on the stage will be identical.

The difference is that if you use a timer event, the objects will still continue to be animated at a constant rate, even if the game's frame rate drops. Timer events run independently from the SWF's frame rate, so they're not affected by a drop in the frame rate. If the frame rate does drop, the objects will calculate their new positions as if the game were running at full speed. The result on stage is that objects will essentially skip over the frames they've missed and jump to their new positions.

This isn't usually a desirable effect for the main objects in the game, like the player's character, because players will suddenly see their character jump to a new position. And even though that position will be the correct one, the fact that the player didn't see its gradual, frame-by-frame transition to that point makes the player feel disconnected from the control of the game.

But for nonessential animations, this approach is perfect. Because they continue to run at a constant rate, timer-based animations can also give the illusion that the game is running at a higher frame rate than it is, even if the frame rate drops. And, while you're building and testing the game, you can modify the rate at which objects animate to find the perfect balance between animation speed and performance.

To help you understand how to use timer events, here's a simple class template containing all the essential elements. (You'll find this template in the chapter's source files.)

```
package
{
  import flash.events.Event;
  import flash.events.TimerEvent;
  import flash.utils.Timer;

  public class TimerAnimationTemplate extends Sprite
  {
    //Instantiate the timer based on the desired rate at which
    //you want to update the animation.
    //"16" is about 60 fps. 32 is about 30 fps. Divide 1000 (milliseconds)
    //by the target frame rate to find the correct value
    private var _animationTimer:Timer = new Timer(16);

    public function TimerAnimationTemplate():void
    {
      _animationTimer.addEventListener
        (TimerEvent.TIMER, animationEventHandler);
      _animationTimer.start();

      //Removed from stage listener
      addEventListener
        (Event.REMOVED_FROM_STAGE, removedFromStageHandler);
  }
```

```
    private function animationEventHandler(event:TimerEvent):void
    {
      //Add your animation code here.
      //This behaves the same as an ENTER_FRAME loop
    }

    private function removedFromStageHandler(event:Event):void
    {
       _animationTimer.removeEventListener
          (TimerEvent.TIMER, animationEventHandler);
       removeEventListener
          (Event.REMOVED_FROM_STAGE, removedFromStageHandler);
    }
  }
   }
```

In this template, the timer is set to fire every 16 milliseconds. That's about 60 frames per second. Divide 1000 by your target frame rate to figure out what value to use. Remember that changing the update rate will also affect the velocities of your objects. That means that if you use a lower rate, you'll need to increase your objects' velocities to compensate.

It's very important to remove the `animationEventHandler` when the object is removed from the stage, because it *will* continue to run in the background and slow down your whole game. (You won't need an `ADDED_TO_STAGE` event unless the class is dependent on the `stage` object.)

Animating with a timer event is a simple optimization, but it's important not to underestimate how valuable it can be. By far, the biggest drag on the CPU is displaying things on the stage, so any savings you make in this area has a huge performance payoff.

Creating the Explosion class

You'll be happy to know that, apart from using a timer event to handle the animation, there's nothing that the `Explosion` class does that you have not already seen. And you could certainly have figured it out for yourself. But, like learning any new thing, a different context can sometimes make something look a little more confusing than it actually is.

The following is the complete `Explosion` class from the `com.friendsofed.gameElements.effects` package. I've commented every important line. Read through it carefully.

```
package com.friendsofed.gameElements.effects
{
  import flash.events.Event;
  import flash.display.*;
  import flash.filters.*;
  import flash.events.TimerEvent;
  import flash.utils.Timer;
```

```
public class Explosion extends Sprite
{
  private var _speedLimit:int = 5;
  private var _fadeRate:Number = 0.01;
  private var _numberOfParticles:int = 100;
  private var _gravity:Number = 0.1;
  private var _colors:Array = [0xFF6600, 0xFF9900, 0xFFCC00];
  private var _animationTimer:Timer = new Timer(16);
  private var _particles:Array = [];

  public function Explosion
    (
      numberOfParticles:int = 100,
      fadeRate:Number = 0.01
    ):void
  {
     this._numberOfParticles = numberOfParticles;
     this._fadeRate = fadeRate;

     //Create all the particles
     for (var i:uint = 0; i< _numberOfParticles; i++)
     {
        //Draw the particle.
        //In this example, particles are MovieClip objects
        //so that properties like vx, vy, and
        //fadeRate can be added dynamically.
        //This is just for convenience
        var particle:MovieClip = new MovieClip();

        //Create a random color based on the _colors Array.
        //Casting the random number as uint has the same effect
        //as Math.floor, but it's faster
        var randomColor:uint = uint(Math.random() * _colors.length);
        particle.graphics.beginFill(_colors[randomColor]);

        //Draw the particle
        particle.graphics.drawRect(-2, -2, 4, 4);
        particle.graphics.endFill();

        //Add the particle to this Explosion object
        addChild(particle);

        //Give the particle a random rotation
        particle.rotation = Math.floor(Math.random() * 360) - 180;

        //Give it a random initial alpha
        particle.alpha = Math.random() + 0.5;
```

```
      //Give it a random velocity
      particle.vx = (Math.random() * _speedLimit) - _speedLimit * 0.5;
      particle.vy = (Math.random() * _speedLimit) - _speedLimit * 0.5;

      //Give the particle a custom rate at which it will fade out
      particle.fadeRate = Math.random() * _fadeRate + 0.02;

     //Push the particle into the particles array
     _particles.push(particle)
  }

  _animationTimer.addEventListener
    (TimerEvent.TIMER, animationEventHandler);
  _animationTimer.start();

  //Removed from stage listener
  addEventListener
    (Event.REMOVED_FROM_STAGE, removedFromStageHandler);
}

private function animationEventHandler(event:TimerEvent):void
{
  for (var i:uint = 0; i < _particles.length; i++)
  {
    //Set the alpha, update the position, and add gravity
    _particles[i].alpha -= _particles[i].fadeRate;
    _particles[i].x += _particles[i].vx;
    _particles[i].vy += _gravity;
    _particles[i].y += _particles[i].vy;

    //Remove the particle if its alpha is less than zero
    if(_particles[i].alpha <= 0)
   {
      removeChild(_particles[i]);
      _particles.splice(i, 1);
      i--;
      //If there are no more particles left,
      //dispatch an event to inform the parent that the
      //explosion is finished so that it can be removed
      if(_particles.length == 0)
      {
        dispatchEvent(new Event("explosionFinished"));
      }
    }
  }
}
```

```
    private function removedFromStageHandler(event:Event):void
    {
      _animationTimer.removeEventListener
        (TimerEvent.TIMER, animationEventHandler);
      removeEventListener
        (Event.REMOVED_FROM_STAGE, removedFromStageHandler);
    }
  }
}
```

There are two important features of this class:

- It uses **dynamic properties** to create particle objects.
- It dispatches an event to inform other classes that the explosion effect is finished.

Let's look at each of these features in detail.

Dynamic properties

Each explosion that you can see on the stage is a self-contained `Explosion` object. It's essentially just a single `Sprite`. An instance of the `Explosion` class is added to the stage when a bullet hits the cave wall. The explosion particles that you can see flying away from the center of the explosion are *all contained inside* that single explosion `Sprite`.

The particles are created by the `Explosion` class as `MovieClip` objects.

```
var particle:MovieClip = new MovieClip();
```

The `MovieClip` class is *dynamic*. That means you can add new properties to `MovieClip` objects whenever you need them, like this:

```
particle.vx = (Math.random() * _speedLimit) - _speedLimit * 0.5;
particle.vy = (Math.random() * _speedLimit) - _speedLimit * 0.5;
particle.fadeRate = Math.random() * _fadeRate + 0.02;
```

`vx`, `vy`, and `fadeRate` aren't properties of the `MovieClip` class. I created them on the spur of the moment in this code because I needed them. Dynamic properties don't need to be defined in a class ahead of time. You can make them up as you go along.

Dynamic classes are very convenient. Using them, you can keep all the code for the explosion in one class without needing to create a separate `Particle` class that defines the custom properties you need. If you don't need the precision or detail of a full MVC system, dynamic properties are a quick-and-easy solution that save you from having to write a lot of unnecessary supporting code.

The `Object` class is also dynamic, and you'll see how we put it to similar use in the examples ahead.

> *You can make any of your own custom classes dynamic by adding the `dynamic` keyword to the class constructor, like this:*
>
> ```
> dynamic public function ClassName()
> {...
> ```
>
> *This means that you can add any new properties to instances of this class. Those new properties don't need to be defined inside the class itself.*

Adding and removing explosions

The `ParticleExplosion` application class creates an instance of `Explosion` every time a bullet hits the cave wall. Each time it creates an `explosion` instance, it does three things:

- Stores a reference to the `explosion` instance in an `_explosions` array.
- Adds the `explosion` instance to the stage.
- Adds an event listener to the `explosion` instance. The event listener is used to find out when the explosion is finished, so that it can be removed from the stage and removed from the `_explosions` array.

Here's an abridged version of the `for` loop in the application class that adds the explosion. (The rest of the code in the application class is identical to the code from the examples in Chapter 5.)

```
for(var i:int = 0; i < _bulletModels.length; i++)
{
  //...Update the bullet

  //Check for a collision between the cave and the bullet
  if(_caveBitmapData.hitTest
      (
        new Point(_caveBitmap.x, _caveBitmap.y),
        255,
        new Point(_bulletModels[i].xPos, _bulletModels[i].yPos)
      )
    )
  {
    //...Cut a hole in the cave bitmap

    //Create the explosion
    var explosion:Explosion = new Explosion();
    explosion.x = _bulletModels[i].xPos;
    explosion.y = _bulletModels[i].yPos;

    //1. Add the explosion to the stage
    addChild(explosion);
```

```
    //2. Push the explosion instance into the _explosions array
    _explosions.push(explosion);

    //3. Add a listener to the explosion to find
    //out when it finishes
    explosion.addEventListener
      ("explosionFinished", removeExplosion);

    //Remove the bullet
  }
}
```

It's now the job of the Explosion class to make the explosion effect. It creates all the particles, animates them, and removes them from the display list when their alpha reaches zero.

When the Explosion class creates a particle, it adds it to the _particles array.

```
for (var i:uint = 0; i< _numberOfParticles; i++)
{
  //Create the particle
  var particle:MovieClip = new MovieClip();

  //… create the particle's properties

  //Push the particle into the _particles array
  _particles.push(particle);
}
```

It removes the particle from that array when the particle is completely invisible. If there are no particles left in the array, it sends an "explosionFinished" event.

```
if(_particles[i].alpha <= 0)
{
  removeChild(_particles[i]);
  _particles.splice(i, 1);
  i--;

  if(_particles.length == 0)
  {
      dispatchEvent(new Event("explosionFinished"));
  }
}
```

This is the event that the ParticleExplosion application class is listening for. As soon as it hears the event, it runs the code in its removeExplosion method.

```
public function removeExplosion(event:Event):void
{
  removeChild(Explosion(event.target));
  _explosions.splice(_explosions.indexOf(event.target), 1);
}
```

This code removes the explosion from the stage and splices it from the `_explosions` array. It uses the very fast `indexOf` method.

This is the first time we've used `indexOf` to remove objects from an array. Using `indexOf` means you don't need to loop through every element of the array to find what you're looking for. The `indexOf` method does this for you automatically using very optimized code that runs behind the scenes in Flash Player. It's faster than using a `for` loop to do the same job, and the code is much more compact.

`indexOf` is an `Array` and `Vector` class method. It tells you the array index number of the object you're seeking. Let's look at how it works in this context.

`event.target` is the `Explosion` object that fired the event. The `removeExplosion` method first removes it from the stage.

```
removeChild(Explosion(event.target));
```

Notice that `event.target` must be cast as `Explosion`. This is just a bit of hand-holding we need to do to reassure the compiler that, "Yes, don't worry, it's an `Explosion` object. I know what I'm doing here. You don't have to give me any errors or warnings." The compiler usually needs this reassurance with `Event` objects.

The next job is to remove the explosion from the `_explosions` array. Usually, you would loop through all the array elements looking for a match, and then splice the array when you've found the index number of the object. I'm sure you'll recognize this code:

```
for(var i:int = 0; i < _explosions.length; i++)
{
  if(event.target == _explosions[i])
  {
    removeChild(_explosions[i]);
    _explosions.splice(i, 1);
    i--;
    break;
  }
}
```

This will work, and is how we removed the bullets in the previous chapter. But we don't need to do all this. We can just use `indexOf` to find the index number of the object automatically, and then splice the array in one line of code:

```
_explosions.splice(_explosions.indexOf(event.target), 1);
```

`_explosions.indexOf(event.target)` has the same array index value as the value of `i` in the `for` loop. The only difference is that the loop is being run for us internally by Flash Player. It's running highly optimized, compiled machine code, which is much faster than any interpreted code we could write in AS3.0.

> *`indexOf` will be faster only if you need to search for an object in an array. If you're already looping through array elements one by one to do things such as animate them or check for collisions, you won't see any speed benefit by using it.*

This is a very basic particle explosion effect, but I've left the door open for you to fiddle, tinker, and experiment with it until you find something that works for your game. Start with this basic format and run with it.

Of course, the particles in the explosions don't need to be little colored squares. They could be circles, stars, or even tiny photographs of sparks or flames. Each particle could also be another little animated particle explosion itself. The only limits to what you can create are your imagination and performance budget. Give Luxor and Bejeweled a run for their money!

A more realistic explosion

That particle explosion was cool, but what could make it cooler?

How about if we could create the explosion using pixels from the real thing being exploded? What if we could actually obliterate the rock into hundreds of pieces, like shattering a sheet of glass on the ground? That sounds a lot cooler to me! And it's completely possible with AS3.0.

It works like this:

- Take a snapshot of the area in the bitmap that you want to explode.
- Cut the snapshot into tiny squares, and use those squares as particles in the explosion. Send them flying away in different directions. The particles will exactly match the pixels in the bitmap that you're destroying.

First, I'll show you how to take snapshots of things on the stage, and then I'll show you how to cut them up and turn them into particles.

> *The basic technique covered in this section is not only important for creating particle explosions, but for any game where you slice a bitmap into smaller sections. It would be great for creating a mix-and-match puzzle game using photographs, for example.*

Taking a snapshot

In the chapter's source files, find the `BitmapSnapshot` folder and run the SWF. When the bullet hits the cave wall, the program takes an 80-by-80-pixel snapshot of the cave bitmap at the point where the bullet hit. It then displays the snapshots in a row at the top of the stage. Each snapshot represents the section of the cave bitmap that was destroyed by the explosion. Figure 6-3 illustrates what's happening.

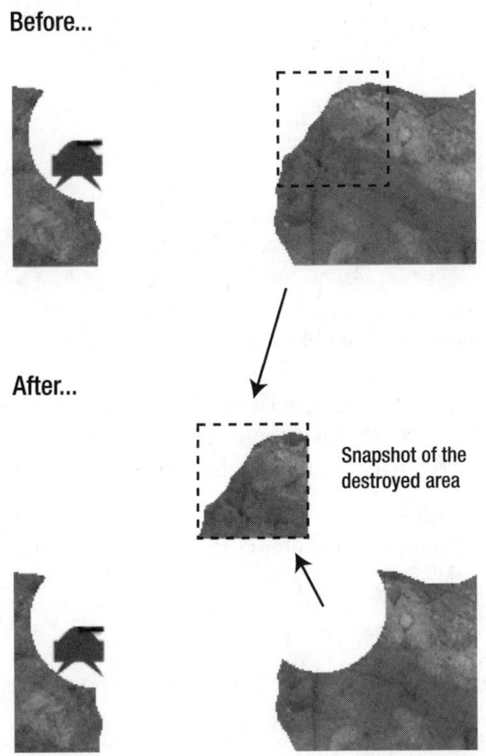

Figure 6-3. A snapshot of the area the bullet hits

The result is a quirky *memento mori* of the destroyed environment, as shown in Figure 6-4.

Figure 6-4. The snapshots record all the bits of the environment that have been destroyed.

If seeing something like this gives you a delirious thrill, then you're definitely reading the right book! The potential uses for this technique are legion—far greater than this simple example implies. It can be put to all sorts of novel and entertaining uses in games.

Here's the code from the bullet collision test in the `BitmapSnapshot` application class that performs this magic. The comments numbered 1 to 5 are the important lines of code. I'll explain them in detail ahead.

```
if(_caveBitmapData.hitTest
    (
      new Point(_caveBitmap.x, _caveBitmap.y),
      255,
      new Point(_bulletModels[i].xPos, _bulletModels[i].yPos)
    )
  )
{
  //Add the circle
  var radius:int = 40;
  var circle:Shape = makeCircle(radius);

  //Take a snapshot of the area being hit
```

```
  //1. Create a blank BitmapData object to store the snapshot
  //It should be the same size as the circle that's cutting the
  //hole into the cave bitmap
  var snapshotBitmapData:BitmapData = new BitmapData(80, 80, true, 0);

  //2. Create a rectangle object that's also the same size as the circle.
  //This is the viewfinder that finds the right spot on the bitmap to copy
  var rectangle:Rectangle
    = new Rectangle
    (
      _bulletModels[i].xPos - 40,
      _bulletModels[i].yPos - 40,
      80, 80
    );

  //3. Create a Point object, which is needed to define the top-left corner
  //of the new snapshot bitmap.
  //Leave this at 0,0 unless you need to offset it
  var point:Point = new Point(0, 0);

  //4. Copy the pixels from the _caveBitmapData into the new
snapshotBitmapData.
  //The Rectangle and Point objects specify which part to copy
  snapshotBitmapData.copyPixels(_caveBitmapData, rectangle, point);

  //5. Create a new Bitmap based on the snapshotBitmapData
  var snapshot:Bitmap = new Bitmap(snapshotBitmapData);

  //Add the snapshot to the stage and position it
  addChild(snapshot);
  snapshot.x = _snapshot_X;
  snapshot.y = 20;
  _snapshot_X += 90;

  //Reset the snapshot x position if it moves too far to the left
  if(_snapshot_X > stage.stageWidth - 90)
  {
    _snapshot_X = 10;
  }

       //… cut a hole in the cave bitmap using code from the previous chapter
}
```

First, we need a blank BitmapData object to create the snapshot. It should be the same size as the circle. That means that if the circle has a radius of 40, then a square, 80-by-80 bitmap will be a perfect fit.

```
var snapshotBitmapData:BitmapData = new BitmapData(80, 80, true, 0);
```

This is a blank canvas to receive the snapshot.

The next step is to figure out which part of the cave we want to copy. The code uses a `Rectangle` object for this. You can think of the rectangle as a camera's viewfinder on the cave bitmap. The center of the rectangle is the bullet's x and y position.

```
var rectangle:Rectangle
  = new Rectangle
  (
    _bulletModels[i].xPos - 40,
    _bulletModels[i].yPos - 40,
    80,
    80
  );
```

This is hard to visualize, so Figure 6-5 will help you see what it's doing. The code creates an 80-by-80 rectangle whose top-left corner is 40 pixels above and to the left of the bullet. Its dimensions match the blank `snapshotBitmapData` that we created in the previous step.

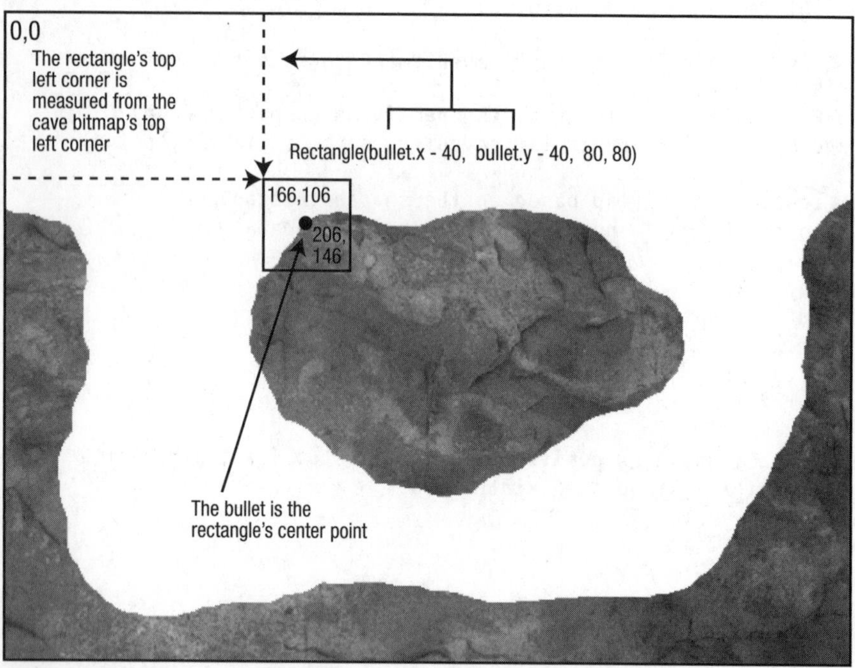

Figure 6-5. The Rectangle object acts like a camera's viewfinder to help capture the section of the bitmap we want to copy.

This works well in this example because the cave bitmap happens to exactly match the dimensions of the stage. If you wanted to use a bitmap that was bigger or smaller than the stage, you would need to offset the bullet's position with the difference between the bitmap's and stage's dimensions. (The Escape! case study in Chapter 7 has a working example of just such a situation.) For another type of game, you could use any x or y position, such as the position of the mouse, to help you plot this rectangle.

Next, we need to create a `Point` object that will define the top-left corner for the new snapshot bitmap. You can leave this at 0,0, unless you want to offset the image in the snapshot for some reason.

```
var point:Point = new Point(0, 0);
```

We're now finally ready to create the snapshot. This is done using the `BitmapData`'s `copyPixels` method. `copyPixels` copies the section from the cave bitmap onto the snapshot.

Using `copyPixels` is like baking a cake. You take `Rectangle` and `Point` objects that you've just created and mix them together with the `BitmapData` object that you want to copy. The result is copied into the snapshot.

```
snapshotBitmapData.copyPixels(_caveBitmapData, rectangle, point);
```

Hot out of the oven with this new `BitmapData`, we can make the final `Bitmap`:

```
var snapshot:Bitmap = new Bitmap(snapshotBitmapData);
```

That's the actual bitmap image of the destroyed area of the environment that you can see on the stage.

And the rest is history! Isn't AS3.0 amazing? Just a few lines of code can produce a complex and spectacular result.

Note that to be perfectly accurate, the snapshot should be circular, so that it precisely matches the round hole cut into the bitmap. You can do this by creating a circle shape and using the snapshot's `BitmapData` as the circle's bitmap fill color. Replace this line of code:

```
var snapshot:Bitmap = new Bitmap(snapshotBitmapData);
```

with these lines:

```
var snapshot:Shape = new Shape();
snapshot.graphics.beginBitmapFill(snapshotBitmapData, null, true);
snapshot.graphics.drawCircle(radius, radius, radius);
snapshot.graphics.endFill();
```

This uses `beginBitmapFill`, which is the same technique used in Chapter 2 to create the image of Phobos. It's essentially a bitmap mask effect. You can see the result in Figure 6-6. It's just like taking a bite out of a cookie. You can use any shape that you like, no matter how complex.

Figure 6-6. Use beginBitmapFill to create snapshots that exactly match the shape used to cut a hole in the cave bitmap.

Slicing and dicing

Now that you have bitmaps that match the destroyed cave, you can do anything with them. Add some collision detection and velocity, and they can become new objects in your game world. Use them with a gravity gun as weapons against enemies, or use them to build a defense against attacks. Or maybe they could be collected as fuel for the mother ship, or used as pieces in a puzzle to help solve the planet's ancient mystery. Build a game around them if you're feeling creative.

But for now, we're just going to blow them up! To see what I mean, run the SWF in the `BitmapParticleExplosion` folder and try destroying parts of the cave, as shown in Figure 6-7.

It's actually a real kick, and I'm a bit embarrassed to admit that I've spent far more time destroying rocks while testing this example than I can account for professionally. Breaking things is fun!

Figure 6-7. Obliterate the rock using the actual pixels from the cave bitmap.

In this example, the bits of rock are all similar in color, and the photographs in this book are black and white, so the effect may seem a little muted. But imagine a space action game where you're blasting away at colorful baddies at light speed. They would explode in a cascade of color that exactly matches pixels they're made of. It's true, pixel-perfect destruction.

I'll first explain how this works, and then show you the specifics of the code. If you're thinking, "Yeah, that's nice, but I don't think I'll really need to use this in any of my games," I still encourage you to read through this section, even just as an intellectual exercise. It introduces some extremely important new concepts and techniques that form a cornerstone for many of the examples to come.

In the previous section, we took a snapshot of a square area of the cave bitmap. Now we need to cut that snapshot into a lot of little squares. That means we need to take a lot of tiny, square snapshots of each section of the big snapshot. We can then use each tiny snapshot to represent a single particle.

It works like this:

1. Decide on how big you want to make each particle (each piece of the rock you're exploding). It may be 4 pixels, 10 pixels, or whatever—it's up to you.
2. Create a grid that matches the dimensions of the snapshot. Each cell in the grid should be the size of one particle.
3. Loop through the grid, and take mini-snapshots of every cell. If the grid has 100 cells, you'll take 100 little snapshots.

4. Wrap each of those mini-snapshots in its own `MovieClip` container. You can then animate those movie clips using the same techniques as the previous example.

Figure 6-8 illustrates what we want to accomplish.

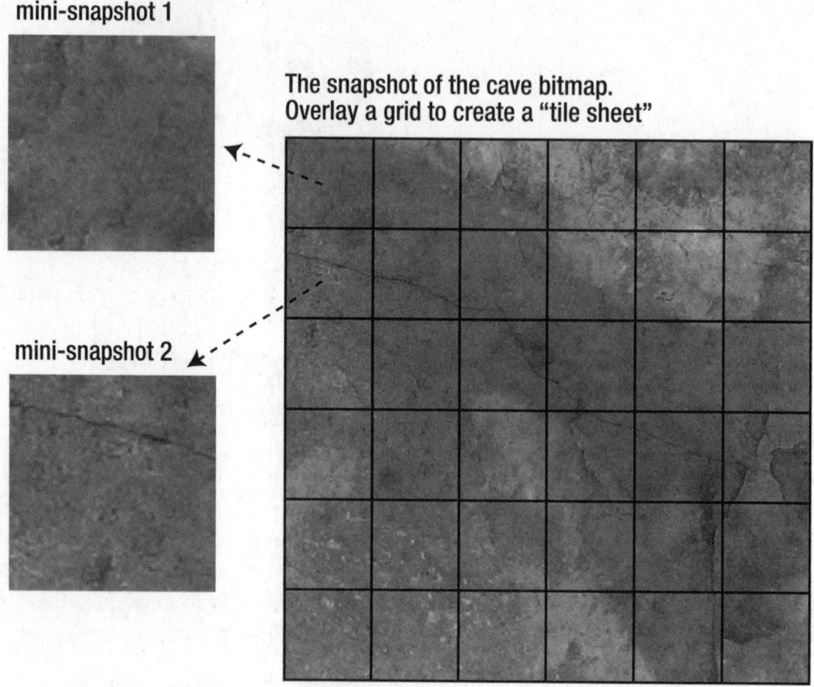
mini-snapshot 1
The snapshot of the cave bitmap.
Overlay a grid to create a "tile sheet"
mini-snapshot 2
... create mini-snaphots for every cell in the grid.
Each mini-snapshot becomes an independent particle
which can be animated.

Figure 6-8. Use a grid to take mini-snapshots of every section of the bitmap.

Tiles, tile sheets, and grids

Take a close look at the image of the grid in Figure 6-8. What does it remind you of? Perhaps the tile work in your shower or the expensive tiled floor in the lobby of a bank? That's why the term for a bitmap with a grid overlaid on it is a **tile sheet**. Each cell in a tile sheet is called a **tile**.

So how do you "overlay a grid onto a bitmap"?

You actually already know how to make a grid. Think back to the enigmatic Block Game from Chapter 4. A nested `for` loop helped us plot the blocks on the stage in a grid pattern. Here's a simplified version:

```
for(var column:int = 0; column < numberOfColumns; column++)
{
  for(var row:int = 0; row < numberOfRows; row++)
  {
    //Position of block
   block.x = column * gridCellSize;
   block.y = row * gridCellSize;
  }
}
```

It simply loops through each column, and then loops through each row of that column, to find the new grid position. The grid position is a combination of the current row and column, multiplied by the size of an individual grid cell.

This bit of code is a video-game staple. You'll need to become comfortable looking at it because we're going to be using it a lot from here on out. Whenever you see it, you should think, "Aha! It's a grid!" We can use this same bit of code to help solve our current problem.

Let's pretend that the size of each tile is 10 pixels.

```
tileSize = 10;
```

We then need to divide the width or height of the snapshot by the `tileSize` to give us the number of cells in each row or column

```
gridSize = snapshot.width / tileSize;
```

If the snapshot is 80 pixels wide, this will give us 8. That means there will be eight rows and eight columns in the grid. This is all we need for a square grid where the height and width are the same. You need to make sure that the tile size will divide evenly into the grid size.

Now that we have that information, we can use it to loop through every cell, calculate its x and y coordinates, and take a mini-snapshot of that section of the bitmap. Because the dimensions of the grid exactly match the dimensions of the snapshot, the cells align perfectly to the corresponding positions on the snapshot.

```
for(var column:int = 0; column < gridSize; column++)
{
  for(var row:int = 0; row < gridSize; row++)
  {
    //1. Find the x and y coordinates of this tile.
    //2. Use those coordinates to take a mini-snapshot of the tile
    //3. Wrap the mini-snapshot in a MovieClip container so that it can be
animated
  }
}
```

That's not so hard, is it?

Making the bitmap explosion

If you understand how to take snapshots using copyPixels, and you understand how to loop through cells in a grid, you've got it! The actual code that creates the bitmap explosion effect doesn't do anything more than this. It may seem complicated at first glance, but don't be fooled! Again, it's just the new context that may make it a little disorienting.

The BitmapExplosion class in the com.friendsofed.gameElements.effects package does all this work. Take a look at the entire class, and then read the detailed explanation that follows.

```
package com.friendsofed.gameElements.effects
{
  import flash.events.Event;
  import flash.display.*;
  import flash.filters.*;
  import flash.geom.Point;
  import flash.geom.Rectangle;
  import flash.events.TimerEvent;
  import flash.utils.Timer;
  import com.friendsofed.vector.*;

  public class BitmapExplosion extends Sprite
  {
    private var _speedLimit:int = 5;
    private var _fadeRate:Number = 0.01;
    private var _numberOfParticles:int = 100;
    private var _gravity:Number = 0.2;
    private var _colors:Array = [0xFF6600, 0xFF9900, 0xFFCC00];
    private var _animationTimer:Timer = new Timer(16);
    private var _particles:Array = [];

    public function BitmapExplosion
    (
      bitmapData:BitmapData,
      tileSize:int = 10,
      numberOfParticles:int = 100,
      fadeRate:Number = 0.01
    ):void
  {
    var gridSize:uint = uint(bitmapData.width / tileSize);

    //Slice the bitmap into small squares called "tiles"
    for(var column:int = 0; column < gridSize; column++)
    {
      for(var row:int = 0; row < gridSize; row++)
      {
        //Create a tile
        var tileBitmapData:BitmapData
          = new BitmapData(tileSize, tileSize, true, 0);
```

```
//Create a rectangle object that's also the
//same size as the tile.
//This is the viewfinder that finds the
//right spot on the bitmap to copy
var sourceRectangle:Rectangle
  = new Rectangle
  (
    column * tileSize,
    row * tileSize,
    tileSize,
    tileSize
  );

//A Point object, which is needed to define the
//upper-left corner of the bitmap.
//Leave this at 0,0 unless you need to offset it
var point:Point = new Point(0, 0);

//Copy the pixels from the original image's
//BitmapData into the new tileBitmapData.
//The Rectangle and Point objects specify which part to copy
tileBitmapData.copyPixels
   (bitmapData, sourceRectangle, point);

 //Create a new Bitmap based on the tileBitmapData
 //and add it to the stage
 var tile:Bitmap = new Bitmap(tileBitmapData);

 //Create a particle MovieClip
 var particle:MovieClip = new MovieClip();
 addChild(particle);

 //Wrap the tile Bitmap in the particle MovieClip.
 //This allows it to be easily faded and rotated
 particle.addChild(tile);

 //Position in the correct place on the stage
 particle.x = column * tileSize - (bitmapData.width * 0.5);
 particle.y = row * tileSize - (bitmapData.width * 0.5);

 //Give the particle a random rotation
 particle.rotation = Math.floor(Math.random() * 360) - 180;

 //Give it a random velocity
 particle.vx
   = (Math.random() * _speedLimit) - _speedLimit * 0.5;
```

```
        particle.vy
         = (Math.random() * _speedLimit) - _speedLimit * 0.5;

         //Give the particle a custom rate at which it will fade out
         particle.fadeRate = Math.random() * _fadeRate + 0.02;

         //Push the particle into the _particles array
         _particles.push(particle);
       }
     }

     _animationTimer.addEventListener
       (TimerEvent.TIMER, animationEventHandler);
     _animationTimer.start();

     addEventListener
       (Event.REMOVED_FROM_STAGE, removedFromStageHandler);
   }

   private function animationEventHandler(event:TimerEvent):void
   {
     //Make the particles move and gradually fade them out
     for (var i:uint = 0; i < _particles.length; i++)
       {
       //Set the alpha, update the position, and add gravity
       _particles[i].alpha -= _particles[i].fadeRate;
       _particles[i].x += _particles[i].vx;
       _particles[i].vy += _gravity;
       _particles[i].y += _particles[i].vy;

       //Remove the particle if its alpha is less than zero
       if(_particles[i].alpha <= 0)
       {
         removeChild(_particles[i]);
         _particles.splice(i, 1);
         i--;
         if(_particles.length == 0)
         {
           dispatchEvent(new Event("explosionFinished"));
         }
       }
     }
   }
```

```
    private function removedFromStageHandler(event:Event):void
    {
      _animationTimer.removeEventListener
        (TimerEvent.TIMER, animationEventHandler);
      removeEventListener
        (Event.REMOVED_FROM_STAGE, removedFromStageHandler);
    }
  }
}
```

The `BitmapExlposion`'s constructor does the job of looping through each cell in the grid and turning the mini-snapshot tiles into `MovieClip` particles.

Its first task is to take a snapshot of the tile at the correct position in the tile sheet. A blank `BitmapData` object is created to store the mini-snapshot tile.

```
var tileBitmapData:BitmapData = new BitmapData(tileSize, tileSize, true, 0);
```

If the `tileSize` is 4 pixels, it creates a blank 4-by-4 square.

A `Rectangle` object is created that will find the correct place on the tile sheet to take the mini-snapshot. The rectangle will also be 4 by 4 pixels. Its top-left corner is found by multiplying the row or column by the size of the tile.

```
var sourceRectangle:Rectangle
    = new Rectangle
    (
      column * tileSize,
      row * tileSize,
      tileSize,
      tileSize
  );
```

This might be a little too abstract to grasp at first, so let's take a closer look.

Let's say that the loop has run a few times, and it is currently at column 5 and row 3. If `tileSize` is 4, the x and y positions of the rectangle will be read like this:

```
sourceRectangle.x = 4 * 4;
sourceRectangle.y = 3 * 4;
```

That equals this:

```
sourceRectangle.x = 16;
sourceRectangle.y = 12;
```

These numbers happen to exactly match the correct tile's pixel location on the tile sheet. Remember that this rectangle is like the camera's viewfinder. It finds the spot on the bitmap to copy. Figure 6-9 shows how these coordinates find exactly the right tile. The rectangle's top-left corner determines the correct position.

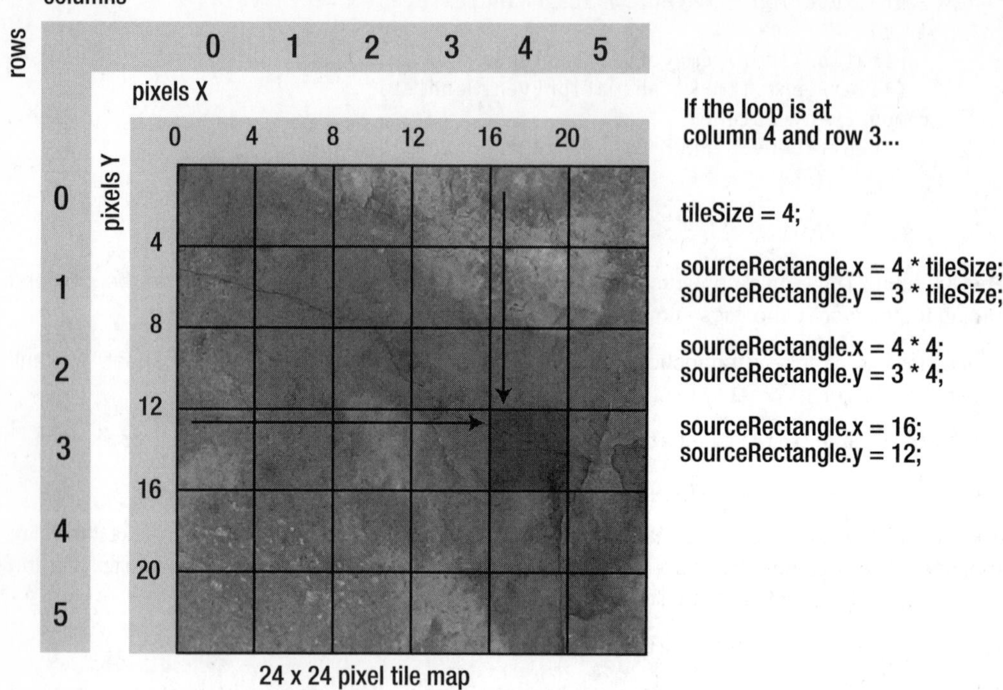

Figure 6-9. If you know the tile size, you can calculate the correct x and y positions of the tile using the grid's column and row.

Now we need to create a `Point` object to determine the rectangle's offset.

```
var point:Point = new Point(0, 0);
```

There's no need for any offset in this case, so we can leave the point's coordinates at 0,0.

Finally, we can use `copyPixels` to copy the section of the snapshot into the tile's `BitmapData`, and create the tile bitmap:

```
tileBitmapData.copyPixels(bitmapData, sourceRectangle, point);
var tile:Bitmap = new Bitmap(tileBitmapData);
```

We now have a tile we can work with to create a particle.

The second phase of this code wraps the tile bitmap in a `MovieClip`. The only reason for doing this is so that we can add custom properties, like velocity and the fade rate. The `Bitmap` class is not dynamic, so it's not possible to add custom properties to `Bitmap` objects as you need them. A `Sprite` object isn't dynamic either.

We create a `MovieClip` instance called `particle` and add it to the display list.

```
var particle:MovieClip = new MovieClip();
addChild(particle);
```

Then we add the tile bitmap to the `particle` movie clip's display list.

```
particle.addChild(tile);
```

This next bit of code is very important. It takes the square particle and adds it to a position on the stage that exactly matches its original position on the tile sheet. This will be the starting positions of all the particles in the center of the `BitmapExplosion`.

```
particle.x = column * tileSize - (bitmapData.width * 0.5);
particle.y = row * tileSize - (bitmapData.width * 0.5);
```

When the loop finishes placing all the particles, the result is an image that looks identical to the original tile sheet, but with one huge difference. Instead of it just being one image, it's actually composed of a lot of little squares, each of which can be individually targeted and controlled. It's like taking all the pieces of a puzzle and laying them down in exactly the right location.

> *If any tiles in the snapshot are transparent, they will be also be turned into particles. There's nothing necessarily wrong with this, but it could be a bit wasteful if your snapshots contain many areas of transparency. You could consider optimizing this system by not including any tiles that are entirely transparent. To find the color value of any given pixel, you can use the `BitmapData` class's `getPixel32` method. See the getPixel32 entry in Adobe's online* ActionScript 3.0 Language and Components Reference *for more information about how to do this.*

To explode the particles, we need to give them all the individual velocities. These velocities are assigned randomly, along with random fade rates and rotations.

```
//Initial rotation
particle.rotation = Math.floor(Math.random() * 360) - 180;

//Random velocity
particle.vx = (Math.random() * _speedLimit) - _speedLimit * 0.5;
particle.vy = (Math.random() * _speedLimit) - _speedLimit * 0.5;

//Random fade rate
particle.fadeRate = Math.random() * _fadeRate + 0.02;
```

Finally, push the particle into an array so that we can animate it along with all the other particles in a single loop.

```
particles.push(particle);
```

Now that the particles have been created and assigned their initial values, we can animate them. The BitmapExplosion does this using a timer event, just as our first example did. In fact, the code is identical to our first example.

```
private function animationEventHandler(event:TimerEvent):void
{
  //Make the particles move and gradually fade them out
  for (var i:uint = 0; i < particles.length; i++)
  {
    //Set the alpha, update the position, and add gravity
    particles[i].alpha -= particles[i].fadeRate;
    particles[i].x += particles[i].vx;
    particles[i].vy += _gravity;
    particles[i].y += particles[i].vy;

    //Remove the particle if its alpha is less than zero
    if(_particles[i].alpha <= 0)
    {
      removeChild(_particles[i]);
      _particles.splice(i, 1);
      i--;

      //If there are no more particles in the array,
      //dispatch an event to inform the parent that the
      //explosion has finished
      if(_particles.length == 0)
      {
        dispatchEvent(new Event("explosionFinished"));
      }
    }
  }
}
```

The code loops through all the particles and updates their positions based on their velocities and their alpha based on their fade rates. If the alpha of any particle reaches zero, it's removed from the display list and the particles array. When the array is empty, the method dispatches an "explosionFinished" event to inform any other classes that might be listening.

To create this explosion on the stage, the BitmapParticleExplosion application class uses this code:

```
var explosion:BitmapExplosion
  = new BitmapExplosion(snapshotBitmapData, 4);

explosion.x = _bulletModels[i].xPos;
explosion.y = _bulletModels[i].yPos;
```

```
addChild(explosion);
_explosions.push(explosion);
explosion.addEventListener("explosionFinished", removeExplosion);
```

The `BitmapExplosion` constructor takes two parameters: the `BitmapData` of the image you want to explode and the size of each individual particle.

```
var explosion:BitmapExplosion
  = new BitmapExplosion(snapshotBitmapData, 4);
```

This information is used by the `BitmapExplosion` class to plot the grid and tile sheet.

As with our first example, the application class removes the explosion when the explosion fires an `"explosionFinished"` event.

```
public function removeExplosion(event:Event):void
{
  removeChild(BitmapExplosion(event.target));
  _explosions.splice(_explosions.indexOf(event.target), 1);
}
```

In this case, `event.target` must be cast as `BitmapExplosion`, because it's a `BitmapExplosion` object.

As you can see from the example SWF, this works really well. But there's one small problem and one big problem that we need to solve before we can say we really have a grip on particle explosions.

- **The small problem**: The particle velocities are random. In a real explosion, they should all fly away from the center.
- **The big problem**: It's dreadfully slow. Fire off a few bullets, and you'll soon notice a severe drop in frame rate when you have a few hundred particles flying around the stage. This is because of the overhead associated with moving `MovieClip` (or `Sprite`) objects around the stage.

Both of these problems are solvable, and their solutions will reveal some indispensable new techniques. This has been a step in the learning process, but let's refine our approach a bit more so that we have a usable particle system that will work well for games.

Starburst explosions

If you run the BitmapParticleExplosion SWF again and watch the explosion effect carefully, you'll notice it doesn't explode from the center like a real explosion. Instead, each particle flies away in a different direction. The particles flutter around at random. It's the same effect that you would get if you picked up a stack of papers and threw them out of a window, as you did on your last day of school. This makes sense, because the velocities of the particles are completely random. Figure 6-10 illustrates this effect.

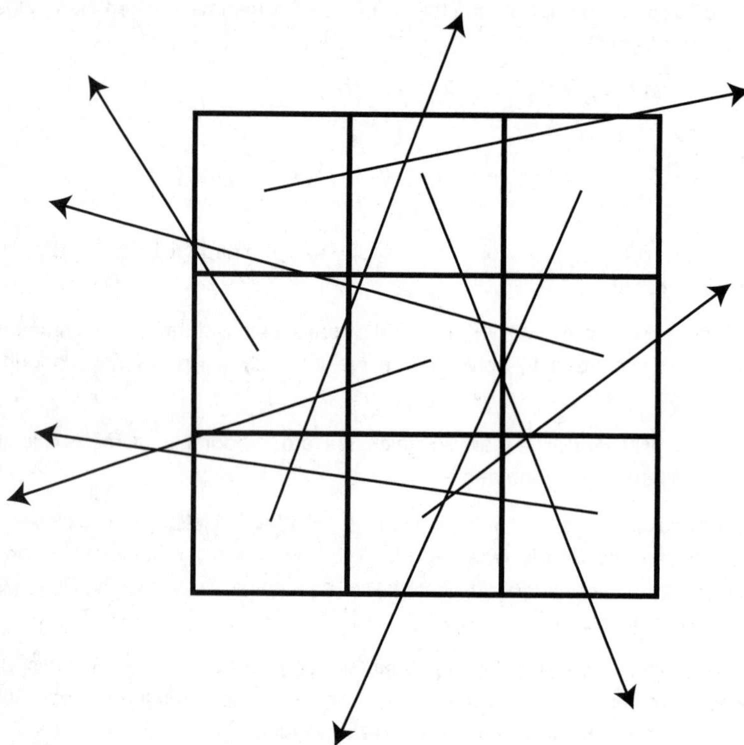

Figure 6-10. Random directions create an interesting effect, but not a natural-looking explosion.

In a real explosion, the directions of the particles aren't random. Particles are forcibly pushed away from the explosion's center, as shown in Figure 6-11. This is the kind of effect you really wanted to achieve on your last day of school, but various bothersome laws prevented you from accomplishing.

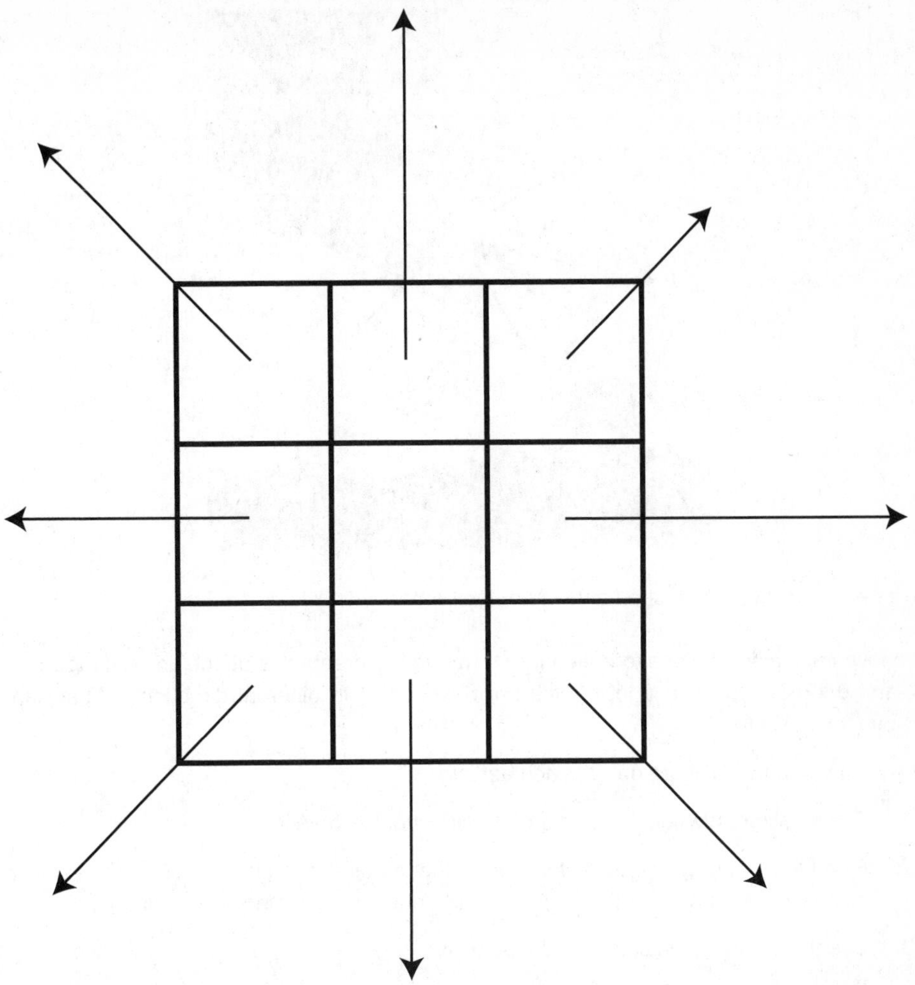

Figure 6-11. Real explosions burst from the center of the object.

Some of these particles may travel faster or slower than other particles, but they all have a definite direction. They move away from the center of the grid.

You'll find a working example of this in the `BitmapStarburstExplosion` folder, Figure 6-12 shows the effect.

Figure 6-12. Particles are pushed away from the center.

Only a few small modifications to the code are needed to create this effect. Look at Figures 6-10, 6-11, and 6-12. Do you see a lot of little arrows pointing in different directions? That can only mean one thing: vectors!

Here's what you need to figure out for each particle:

1. Plot a vector between the center of the tile sheet and an individual tile.
2. Find the dx and dy of that vector. This is that magical and oh-so-useful unit vector, which gives us the direction of the original vector, but can be scaled to any magnitude.
3. Use the `dx` and `dy` to calculate the velocity.

Figure 6-13 illustrates what this looks like. All we need to do is translate this logic into code.

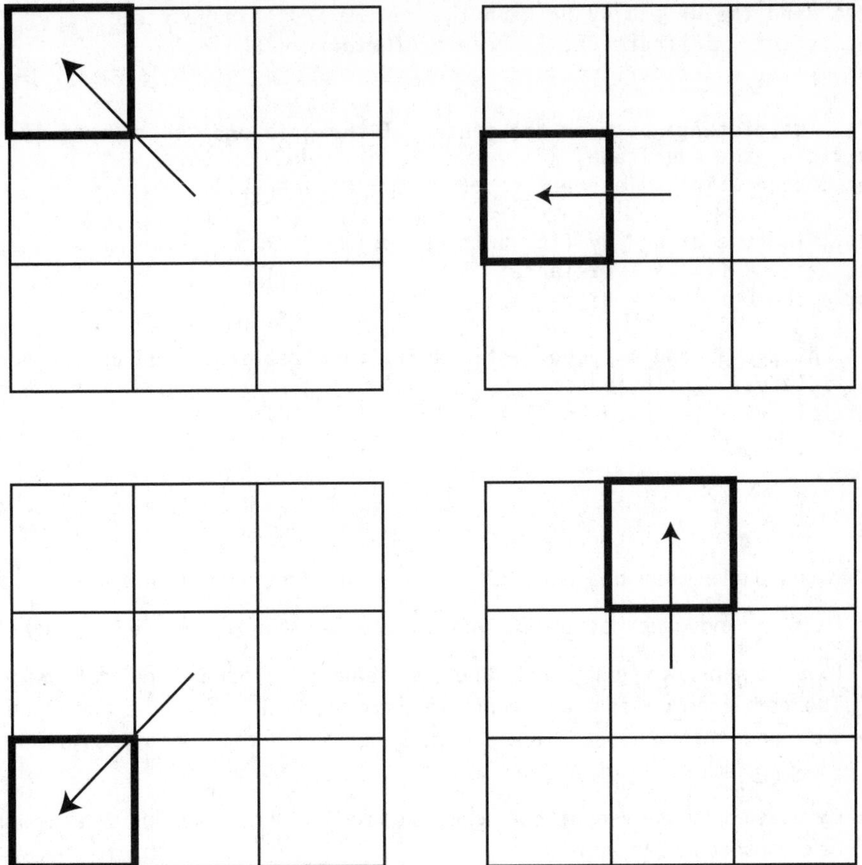

Figure 6-13. Loop through each particle and plot a vector between it and the center of the tile sheet.

The `StarburstExplosion` class in the `com.friendsofed.gameElements.effects` package contains the code. This class is identical to the `BitmapExplosion` class, except for these lines of code:

```
for(var column:int = 0; column < gridSize; column++)
{
  for(var row:int = 0; row < gridSize; row++)
  {
    //...

    //1. Find the center of the grid
    var centerOfGrid:uint = gridSize * 0.5;
```

```
        //2. Find the vx and vy between the center and this particle
        var vx:int = int(particle.x - centerOfGrid);
        var vy:int = int(particle.y - centerOfGrid);

        //3. The distance between the center of the grid and the current ↵
        particle (the magnitude)
        var distance:int = int(Math.sqrt(vx * vx + vy * vy));

        //4. Find the dx and dy (the unit vector)
        var dx:Number = vx / distance;
        var dy:Number = vy / distance;

        //5. Assign a random speed, but a definite direction based on the vector
        particle.vx = (Math.random() * _speedLimit) * dx;
        particle.vy = (Math.random() * _speedLimit) * dy;

        //...
    }
}
```

I could have used a VectorModel to simplify this, but I didn't for three reasons:

- I want to expose the math behind creating vectors, just in case you've forgotten!
- I want to remind you that you don't need to create a VectorModel object to use vectors. The math is really simple, and by not creating a whole class around a vector, you gain a slight performance boost. This is especially significant for CPU-heavy tasks like making a lot of particles.
- By sidestepping the VectorModel class, I could force the vx, vy, and distance values to be processed as int types.

  ```
  var vx:int = int(particle.x - centerOfGrid);
  ```

  This saves the CPU from needing to process decimal places. It's a very tiny savings, but it all adds up if you're working with hundreds of particles. (The dx and dy values must be typed as Number, because they are, by their very nature, fractional values.)

There's another technical problem with this bit of code: an awful lot of math going on. Remember that this explosion is created in one frame, and in that time, all these particles must be created and assigned velocities. Math.sqrt is also miserably slow, so whenever you use it, red flags should come up. Its performance impact will be noticeable.

A good solution is to *precalculate* all of this math when you initialize the game. An array of precalculated values is called a **lookup table**. It's one of the most important optimization techniques you can ever use. You'll get the details in the "Lookup tables" section later in this chapter.

Fast particle explosions

A major problem with all the particle effects we've looked at so far is that they're slow. As soon as you have more than a few hundred particles flying around the stage, the frame rate takes a dramatic nosedive. These examples have been an essential step in the learning process, but for almost any practical or professional game project, they're not usable. Yes, I mean they're useless!

The particles we have worked with are composed of `Sprite` or `MovieClip` objects. These objects are very convenient to work with for several reasons:

- They're simple to create and manage.
- They can be easily rotated, faded, and scaled.
- It's easy to change the stacking order (which objects appear in front of or behind other objects).

But that convenience comes with a big processing overhead. If there's any way we can display things on the stage without sprites or movie clips, we can win back bucket-loads of CPU power.

It turns out, there is a way.

Introducing bit-block transfer

What's bit-block transfer? It sounds like the final stage of some devious human/machine cybernetics experiment, or perhaps even more distressingly, a particularly uninspired children's educational board game.

Well, my dears, we've arrived at the obligatory section of the book where I'm going to ask you to brew yourself a pot of cinnamon-clove rooibos tea, do a few sun salutations, and then settle down under a shady tree in a secluded forest glen, with nothing but the fluttering of butterfly wings and the whir of your laptop's fan to disturb you. I need you to have your senses at their sharpest as I introduce a topic that is not only essential for creating usable particle-explosion effects, but also a cornerstone game-design technique. Yes, it's **bit-block transfer**!

All the examples in this chapter have made use of a funky little method called `copyPixels`. It's used to copy pixels from one bitmap to another. La-di-da! But this seemingly mundane task holds a deep, dark secret that if you use it to your advantage, can completely revolutionize what your Flash games are capable of doing.

Adobe's AS3.0 documentation, as useful as it is, is not known for its gripping narrative style. And there's certainly no trace of the personality of whoever wrote it—except for one, telling moment. If you look up the entry for `copyPixels`, you'll find this:

> *[copyPixels] provides a fast routine to perform pixel manipulation between images ...*

Whoever the anonymous author was, he or she invoked Herculean restraint in writing that sentence. The only trace of what the author is attempting to imply is the word *fast*, which I'm sure was added with immense pride by Adobe's engineering team. Because, in reality, that sentence should read like this:

> *[copyPixels] provides a staggeringly, Earth-shatteringly, hair-raisingly fast routine to perform pixel manipulation between images that will blow your mind, man!*

How fast is it? Depending on how you cut the cake, you can use it to move things around the stage about three to five times faster than with `Sprite` or `MovieClip` objects. Five times more processing power at your disposal means five times more things moving around the stage, or five times more power to do other important processing in your game.

> *A series of comprehensive tests by Jeff and Steve Fulton, authors of* The Essential Guide to Flash Games *(friends of ED, 2010), showed that in certain circumstances, using* `copyPixels` *can actually be up to 20 times faster. Performance is notoriously dependent on context, so you'll need to run some tests in your own projects to find out exactly what kind of performance saving you can get from bit-block transfer.*

Not only that, but using `copyPixels` to move objects around the stage uses less code than moving around sprites or movie clips, and it's delightfully elegant to implement. This leads to only one conclusion:

Always use `copyPixels` *to move objects whenever you can.*

Use `Sprite` or `MovieClip` objects if you need the extra icing sugar they provide—often you won't.

How then can you harness the speed of `copyPixels`? This is where the technique of bit-block transfer comes in. It's an ancient and venerable video-game animation technique that has been around since the days of Pong. It's used to copy pixels from one bitmap into a new place in a second bitmap. Bit-block transfer isn't a phrase that rolls easily off the tongue, so it's more affectionately known as **blit** or **blitting.**

For a basic blit, you start with a bitmap image that contains all the objects you want to use in your game. Yes, that's right: *all the objects in one big bitmap*. Arrange them in a grid formation. These can be characters, elements of the environment, rendered text, or whatever you like. In a nutshell, the image should contain all of your game graphics.

The single bitmap that they're contained in is called a **tile sheet**. The bitmap file can be a PNG, JPEG, or GIF. The graphics are organized in a grid layout, and should be contained in grid rectangles or squares of the same size. You can use any bitmap image-editing software you like, such as Photoshop, Fireworks, or GIMP.

The tile sheet can be any size you like, but bitmaps render more quickly if you uses sizes that are multiples of 2, 8, 16, 32, 64, 128, and so on. Those are numbers that make computers happy, because computers do calculations with powers of 2 very efficiently.

Figure 6-14 is an example of a tile sheet containing some game characters and objects. The tile sheet is 128 by 128 pixels. Each grid in the tile sheet is 32 by 32 pixels. The objects that fill each individual tile can be any shape or dimension, but their height or width shouldn't exceed the size of the tile they occupy.

Figure 6-14. A 128-by-128 square tile sheet. Each object occupies a 32-by-32 tile.

The next step is to create a blank bitmap that's exactly the same size as the stage. Let's call it the **stage bitmap**.

Copy tiles from the tile sheet onto new places on the stage bitmap. If you do this in an `ENTER_FRAME` loop, and change their positions slightly each frame, the objects will move.

You can think of it this way: the objects from the tile sheet are being projected onto a new bitmap at new places. On every frame, they're projected onto a slightly different place than the previous frame. Figure 6-15 illustrates this.

The original tile sheet isn't altered in any way. It's simply a source that is read by `copyPixels` each frame. You can think of the tile sheet as just an array of pictures. If you want to change your game objects, just swap in a new tile sheet with different graphics.

The effect is identical to moving sprites or movie clips; it's just vastly easier for the CPU to process.

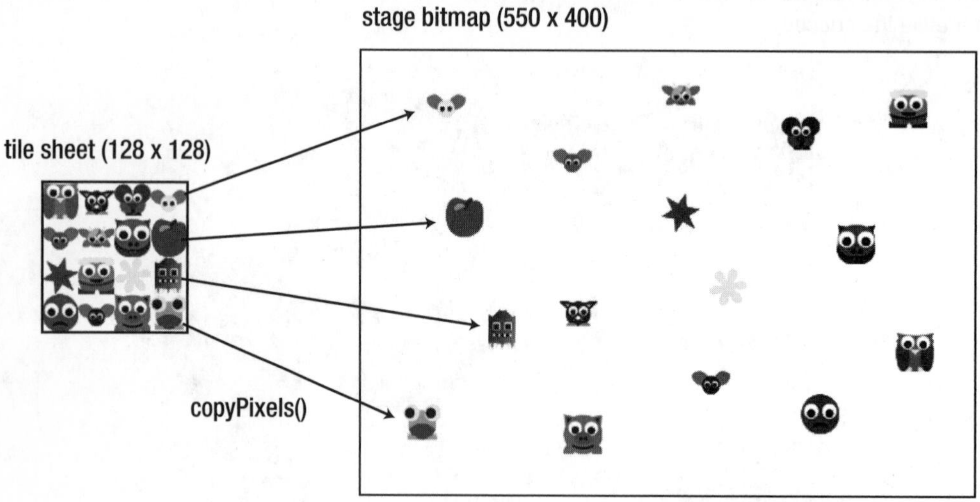

Figure 6-15. copyPixels reads the tiles in the tile sheet and copies them to new positions on the stage bitmap.

Those are the only new techniques you need to learn. Everything else you know about velocity, physics, and controlling objects remains exactly the same. The only difference is how those objects are displayed on the stage. Because we've been separating data from display in all our code since Chapter 1, swapping one display scheme for another is a no-brainer.

And the other good news? All this is done with just a few lines of code, most of which will be very familiar. Let's see how!

Basic blitting

In the chapter's source files, you'll find a folder called `BitBlockTransfer`, which demonstrates a simple example. Run the SWF, and you'll see 16 numbered squares on the stage (from 0 to 15). They move around and bounce off the stage edges, as shown in Figure 6-16.

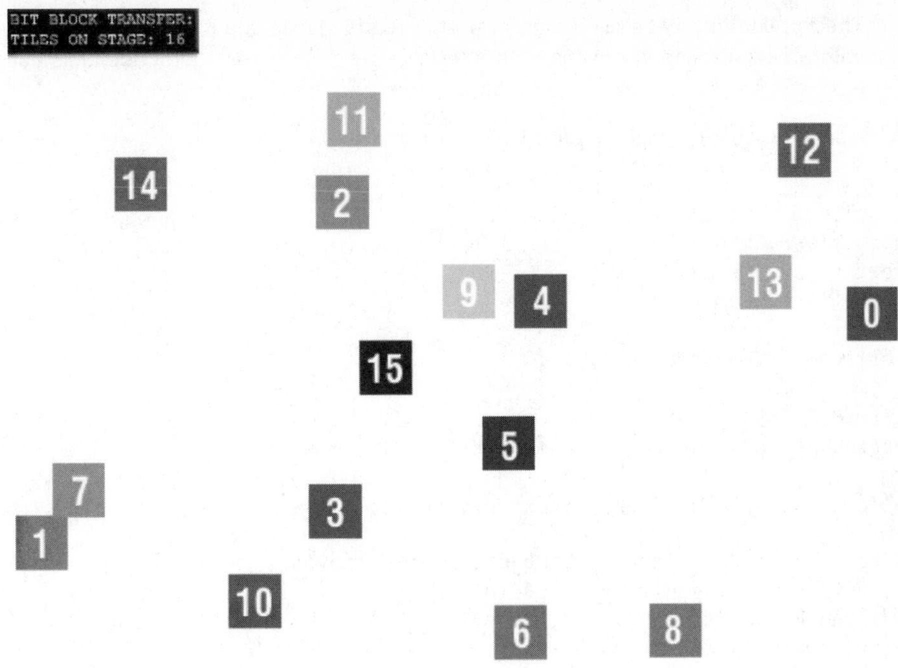

Figure 6-16. Move graphics around the stage without the help of Sprite or MovieClip objects.

This is nothing spectacular, except for one aspect: not a single `Sprite` or `MovieClip` object is doing any of the work. How is it possible?

There are two components to this example:

- **A tile sheet**: A PNG file in the `assets/images` folder called `tileSheet.png`. It's a 128-by-128 bitmap image of those 16 numbered squares, as shown in Figure 6-17.

Figure 6-17. The tilesheet is just a 128-by-128 PNG bitmap of numbered squares.

- **The application class**: BitBlockTransfer reads the tile sheet and copies each tile onto a new position in a bitmap that's the same size as the stage. It does this each frame.

Here's the entire BitBlockTransfer application class:

```
package
{
  import flash.events.Event;
  import flash.display.*;
  import flash.geom.Point;
  import flash.geom.Rectangle;
  import com.friendsofed.utils.*;

  [SWF(width="550", height="400",
  backgroundColor="#FFFFFF", frameRate="60")]

  public class BitBlockTransfer extends Sprite
 {
    //Create a blank BitmapData object as the canvas
    private var _stageBitmapData:BitmapData
      = new BitmapData(550, 400, true, 0);
    private var _stageBitmap:Bitmap
      = new Bitmap(_stageBitmapData);

    //The size of each tile square in the tile sheet
    private var _tileSize:uint = 32;
    private var _gridSize:uint = 4;

    //Speed limit
    private var _speedLimit:int = 3;

    //Variables required to display the tile sheet bitmap
    private var _tileBitmap:Bitmap;
    private var _tileSheetImage:DisplayObject;
    private var _tileBitmapData:BitmapData;

    //An array to store the tiles
    private var _tiles:Array = new Array();

    //Status box
    private var _statusBox:StatusBox = new StatusBox;

    //Embed the image of the tile sheet
    [Embed(source="../assets/images/tileSheet.png")]
    private var TileSheet:Class;
```

```
    public function BitBlockTransfer():void
    {
      //Create a new instance of the TileSheet class
      _tileSheetImage = new TileSheet();

      //Create a BitmapData object to store the tile sheet
      _tileBitmapData
        = new BitmapData(_tileSheetImage.width, _tileSheetImage.height, true,
0);
      _tileBitmapData.draw(_tileSheetImage);

      //Add the stage bitmap.
      //This bitmap will be updated automatically when
      //the _stageBitmapData is changed.
      //Everything visible on the stage is displayed on this bitmap
      addChild(_stageBitmap);

      //Add the status box
      addChild(_statusBox);

      //Initialize the tiles
      initializeTiles();

      addEventListener(Event.ENTER_FRAME, enterFrameHandler);
    }

    //Create tile models and map them to the
    //correct positions on the tile sheet
    private function initializeTiles():void
    {
      //Loop through each tile in the tile sheet
      for(var column:int = 0; column < _gridSize; column++)
      {
        for(var row:int = 0; row < _gridSize; row++)
        {
          //Create a tile object to store the tile's original
          //position and give it an initial velocity.
          //This becomes the tile's "model"
          var tileModel:Object = new Object();

          //Record the tile's position on the _tileSheet image
          //so that the correct section of the _tileSheet can be found
          //when the tile is copied onto the stage bitmap
          tileModel.tileSheet_X = column * _tileSize;
          tileModel.tileSheet_Y = row * _tileSize;

          //Set the tile's start x and y position on the stage
          tileModel.x = tileModel.tileSheet_X;
          tileModel.y = tileModel.tileSheet_Y;
```

```
                //Give the tile a random velocity
                tileModel.vx = (Math.random() * _speedLimit) - _speedLimit / 2;
                tileModel.vy = (Math.random() * _speedLimit) - _speedLimit / 2;

                //Push the tile into the tiles array
                _tiles.push(tileModel);
            }
        }
    }

    private function enterFrameHandler(event:Event):void
    {
        //Clear the bitmap from the previous frame so that it's
        //blank when you add the new particle positions
        _stageBitmapData.fillRect(_stageBitmapData.rect, 0);

        //Move the tiles by working out their new positions based
        //on the velocity's and positions of the tileModels
        for(var j:int = 0; j < _tiles.length; j++)
        {
            //1. Update the models
            //Update the position and velocity of the tileModels
            _tiles[j].x += _tiles[j].vx;
            _tiles[j].y += _tiles[j].vy;

            //Check stage boundaries
            //Check left and right
            if(_tiles[j].x + _tileSize > _stageBitmapData.width
            || _tiles[j].x < 0)
            {
                _tiles[j].vx = -_tiles[j].vx;
            }
            //Check top and bottom
            if(_tiles[j].y + _tileSize > _stageBitmapData.height
            || _tiles[j].y < 0)
            {
                _tiles[j].vy = -_tiles[j].vy;
            }

            //2. Create the views: display the tiles on the stage bitmap

            //Find the tileModel's corresponding tile in the tileMap's
            //BitmapData and plot it to a new position in the containing stage
            bitmap.
            //This is the tile's "view"
```

```
        //Create a Rectangle object that's aligned to the correct spot on the
        //tile sheet. It's top-left position matches the top-left position on
        //the tile sheet based on the tile we need. These positions are
        //stored in the tile model objects
        var sourceRectangle:Rectangle
          = new Rectangle
          (
              _tiles[j].tileSheet_X,
              _tiles[j].tileSheet_Y,
              _tileSize,
              _tileSize
          );

        //Create a Point object that defines the new position of the
        //tile on on the stage bitmap.
        //This is tile's stage position
        var destinationPoint:Point
          = new Point(_tiles[j].x, _tiles[j].y);

        //Copy the tile from the original tile sheet and project it onto the
        //correct new place on the stage bitmap.
        //If your original tile bitmap uses any areas of transparency, make
sure↵
 to add the last
        //"true" parameter. This is mergeAlpha. It lets transparent areas
show through
        _stageBitmapData.copyPixels
          (
            _tileBitmapData,
            sourceRectangle,
            destinationPoint,
            null,
            null,
            true
          );
      }

      //Update the status box
      _statusBox.text = "BIT BLOCK TRANSFER:";
      _statusBox.text += "\n" + "TILES ON STAGE: " + _tiles.length;
    }
  }
}
```

Let's take a close look at how this all works.

The class embeds the tileSheet.png file and turns it into a BitmapData object.

```
[Embed(source="../assets/images/tileSheet.png")]
private var TileSheet:Class;

public function BitBlockTransfer():void
{
  //Create a BitmapData of the tile sheet
  _tileSheetImage = new TileSheet();
  _tileBitmapData = new BitmapData(_tileSheetImage.width,
_tileSheetImage.height,↩
 true, 0);
  _tileBitmapData.draw(_tileSheetImage);
```

It doesn't display the tile sheet on the stage. The tile sheet just exists as BitmapData so that its pixel information can be read. It's a storage container for your game object images.

The application class also creates a stage bitmap. This bitmap is blank and fills the whole stage. The tiles from the _tileBitmapData will be copied onto it. With blitting, the game objects are not added to the stage. They're projected onto a big bitmap that's the same size as the stage. That's what the _stageBitmap is.

```
private var _stageBitmapData:BitmapData = new BitmapData(550, 400, true, 0);
private var _stageBitmap:Bitmap = new Bitmap(_stageBitmapData);
//…
public function BitBlockTransfer():void
{
  //…
 addChild(_stageBitmap);
```

However, the stage bitmap itself is added to the stage. It's the blank screen on which the tiles will be projected.

Remember that BitmapData and Bitmap have a model-view relationship. Whenever the BitmapData changes, the Bitmap automatically updates itself to match the changes. This means that to change the way the stage Bitmap looks, we just need to change its BitmapData. You'll see how in the steps ahead.

The initializeTiles method creates models of the tiles. These models store important information about each tile:

- Its location on the tile sheet. This is important because copyPixels will use this information to locate the correct tile to display on the stage bitmap.
- The tile's initial x and y positions on the stage. This will be the same as its position on the tile sheet when the class is initialized, but will change when enterFrameHandler runs.
- It's velocity (which is random in this example).

This is all done inside a nested for loop. As in earlier examples, the loop finds the tile's correct position because it knows the size of the tile sheet and the size of each individual tile. The loop simulates the dimensions of the tile sheet to find the information it needs.

```
private function initializeTiles():void
{
  //Loop through each tile in the tile sheet
  for(var column:int = 0; column < _gridSize; column++)
 {
    for(var row:int = 0; row < _gridSize; row++)
   {
      //Create a tile model
      var tileModel:Object = new Object();

      //Record the tile's position on the _tileSheet image
      //so that the correct section of the _tileSheet can be found
      //when the tile is copied onto the stage bitmap
      tileModel.tileSheet_X = column * _tileSize;
      tileModel.tileSheet_Y = row * _tileSize;

      //Set the tile's start x and y position on the stage
      tileModel.x = tileModel.tileSheet_X;
      tileModel.y = tileModel.tileSheet_Y;

      //Give the tile a random velocity
      tileModel.vx = (Math.random() * _speedLimit) - _speedLimit / 2;
      tileModel.vy = (Math.random() * _speedLimit) - _speedLimit / 2;

      //Push the tile into the tiles array
      _tiles.push(tileModel);
    }
  }
}
```

It's important to remember that these tile models are just bits of data. They don't contain any visual information about the tiles. But because their tileSheet_X and tileSheet_Y values match the correct tile's position on the tile sheet, you can use them to refer to the tile you want. This is the same kind of data abstraction that we've used in other MVC systems throughout this book. It has the same advantage here.

When the enterFrameHandler runs, the first thing it does is clear the stage bitmap:

```
private function enterFrameHandler(event:Event):void
{
  //Clear the stage bitmap
  _stageBitmapData.fillRect(_stageBitmapData.rect, 0);
```

It fills the stage bitmap with a big, blank rectangle, which matches the stage's dimensions. This is important because it erases the display from the previous frame. Without this step, all the objects would leave traces of their previous positions on the stage, as shown in Figure 6-18. (This effect might actually be useful at some point, for a drawing application, for example, so keep it in mind.)

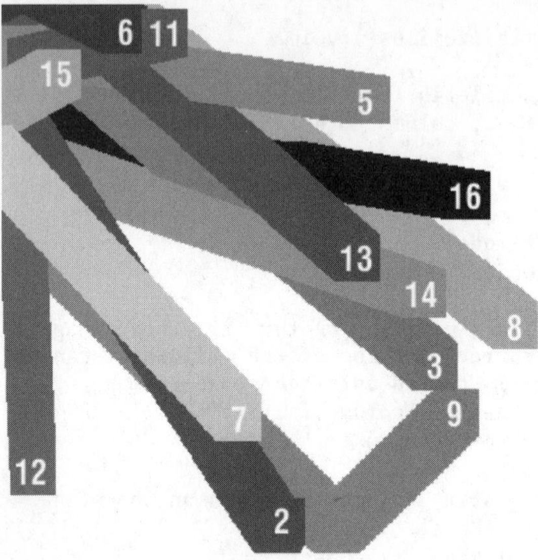

Figure 6-18. Objects wil leave traces of their previous positions if you forget to clear the stage bitmap each frame.

The `enterFrameHandler` loops through all the tile models in the `_tiles` array. It does two important things:

- **Updates the models**: It moves the tile models based on their velocities. It also checks stage boundaries.
- **Updates the view**: It checks each model and finds its corresponding tile in the tile sheet. It copies those pixels from the tile sheet and displays them on the stage bitmap at the same position as the model.

As you can see from the following code, the procedures for moving the objects around the stage and checking stage boundaries are identical to how you work with `Sprite` and `MovieClip` objects.

```
for(var j:int = 0; j < _tiles.length; j++)
{
  //Update the models
  //Update the position and velocity of the tileModels
  _tiles[j].x += _tiles[j].vx;
  _tiles[j].y += _tiles[j].vy;
```

```
  //Check stage boundaries
  //Check left and right
  if(_tiles[j].x + _tileSize > _stageBitmapData.width
  || _tiles[j].x < 0)
  {
    _tiles[j].vx = -_tiles[j].vx;
  }
  //Check top and bottom
  if(_tiles[j].y + _tileSize > _stageBitmapData.height
  || _tiles[j].y < 0)
 {
    _tiles[j].vy = -_tiles[j].vy;
  }
  //...
}
```

The only indication that we're working in a slightly different universe is that the `width` and `height` of the `_stageBitmapData` are checked, rather than the `width` and `height` of the stage.

The really interesting part of all this is how the tiles are displayed on the stage. It's done with just three directives.

```
for(var j:int = 0; j < _tiles.length; j++)
{
  //...
  //1. Create the views: display the tiles on the stage bitmap.
  //Create a Rectangle object that's aligned to the correct spot on the tile
  //sheet.
  var sourceRectangle:Rectangle
    = new Rectangle
    (
      _tiles[j].tileSheet_X,
      _tiles[j].tileSheet_Y,
      _tileSize,
      _tileSize
    );

  //2. Create a Point object that defines the new position on the stage
  //bitmap
  var destinationPoint:Point
    = new Point(_tiles[j].x, _tiles[j].y);

  //3. Copy the tile from the original tile sheet and project it onto the
  //correct new place on the stage bitmap
  _stageBitmapData.copyPixels
    (
      _tileBitmapData,
      sourceRectangle,
```

```
      destinationPoint,
      null,
      null,
      true
    );
}
```

These three directives are what blitting is all about. Let's look at how they work.

First, we create a `Rectangle` object. The top-left corner of this rectangle should match the top-left corner of the corresponding tile in the tile sheet.

```
var sourceRectangle:Rectangle
  = new Rectangle
  (
    _tiles[j].tileSheet_X,
    _tiles[j].tileSheet_Y,
    _tileSize,
    _tileSize
  );
```

This can be a little abstract to visualize, so let's look at it more concretely.

Imagine that the loop has run ten times (starting from zero). The code will read like this:

```
var sourceRectangle:Rectangle
  = new Rectangle
  (
    _tiles[9].tileSheet_X,
    _tiles[9].tileSheet_Y,
    32,
    32
  );
```

It creates a 32-by-32 square rectangle. The top-left corner of that rectangle is offset by the values `_tileSheet_X` and `_tileSheet_Y`. But what are those values?

If it's the tenth tile, they'll have these values:

```
_tiles[9]._tileSheet_X = 64
_tiles[9]._tileSheet_Y = 32
```

That exactly matches the coordinates of the tenth tile on the tile sheet. Figure 6-19 shows how this is found.

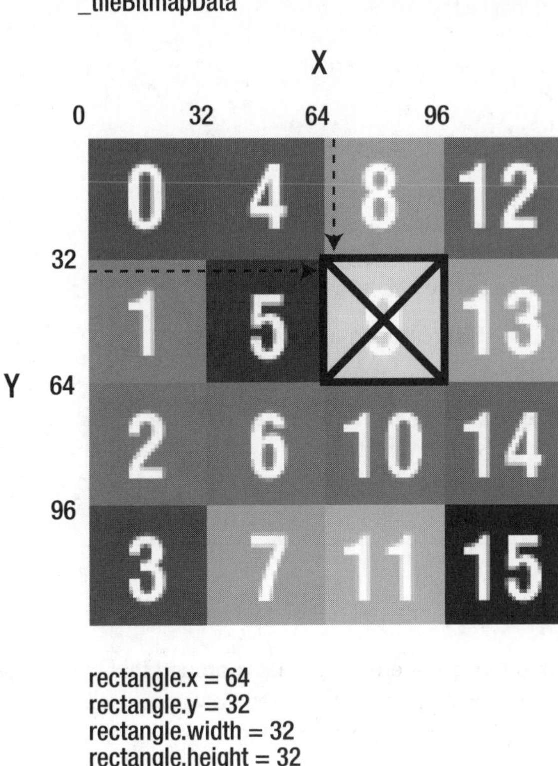

Figure 6-19. Use the values from the tile model to create a Rectangle object with the same dimensions and position as the corresponding tile on the the tile sheet. This is like taking a snapshot of the tile.

You can think of this rectangle object as a camera's viewfinder that examines the tile sheet and takes a snapshot of the correct tile.

Now that we've found the correct tile, we need to find where on the stage to copy it. This is done by creating a `Point` object. The Point's x and y coordinates match the position on the stage bitmap where you want to place the tile.

```
var destinationPoint:Point
  = new Point(_tiles[j].x, _tiles[j].y);
```

These coordinates refer to the tile's top-left corner. Those x and y positions were worked out in the earlier section of code by calculating the tile model's velocity.

Finally, use `copyPixels` to copy the tile to the stage bitmap.

```
_stageBitmapData.copyPixels
  (
    _tileBitmapData,
    sourceRectangle,
    destinationPoint,
    null,
    null,
    true
  );
```

This is exactly the same use of `copyPixels` as in the other examples in this chapter.

And there you have it! Super-fast blitting in a nutshell.

> *There's one little detail that you need to keep in mind if your tile sheet contains transparency. Make sure that `copyPixel`'s sixth parameter is `true`. This is the `mergeAlpha` parameter, which makes sure that the transparency of the PNG file is preserved.*

How fast is fast?

When your games start to move hundreds of objects around that stage, you're going to notice a drop in the frame rate. And you're also going to need a way to measure that frame rate to figure out how changes you make to your code are affecting it.

Calculating the frame rate and memory usage

A **frame rate tracker** is a simple calculation that compares the time that has elapsed between the current frame and the previous frame. If you divide 1000 milliseconds by that difference, you'll find out at how many frames per second the game is running.

A few lines of code like this in an `ENTER_FRAME` loop will do the job nicely:

```
_time = getTimer();
_fps = 1000 / (_time - _previousTime);
_previousTime = getTimer();
```

The frame rate can sometimes fluctuate unpredictably over one or two frames, so you'll generally end up with an easier-to-understand number if you calculate the average frame rate over a fixed time. You can do this by pushing the value of each frame into an array, and then calculating the average of all the values in that array over a second or two.

While we're at it, let's create a **memory usage tracker** to find out how much memory your game is using. This can be useful if you suspect your code has an unexpected memory leak somewhere.

Flash Player has a `System.totalMemory` property that tells you amount of memory being used in bytes. Megabytes are a bit easier to read, so here's how you can access `System.totalMemory` and convert its data to megabytes:

1. Import the `System` class.

```
import flash.system.System;
```

2. Convert the memory used by Flash Player from bytes to megabytes.

```
var mb:Number = System.totalMemory / 1024 / 1024;
```

(There are 1024 bytes in one kilobyte, and 1024 kilobytes in one megabyte.)

3. Round to two decimal places.

```
var memory:Number = Math.round(mb * 100) / 100;
```

> *`System.totalMemory` tells you the memory of all the instances of Flash Player currently running on your system. That means that if you have web browser windows open with Flash ads or applications running anywhere on your computer, those will be included in the total as well. For an accurate reading, make sure that the only Flash Player instance running is your game.*

You'll notice that if you track the memory, it will gradually go up. This doesn't mean you have a memory leak, because the Flash Player's garbage collector allows quite a bit of information to accumulate before trashing it. It errs on the side that more information is better to have at hand so it can be accessed quickly, and that means increased memory usage. That's a good thing!

So if just watching memory usage won't tell you whether you have a memory leak, what will? Unexpected spikes and dips in this data can suggest a memory leak, but only if you notice corresponding unexpected changes in performance in your game. If your game runs fine, then there's no need to worry about a memory leak. If you think you might have one, use this data to chart a graph and see if you can pinpoint when or how it occurs.

Here are the most common causes for memory leaks in AS3.0:

- Pushing data and objects into arrays and not clearing or limiting data that isn't needed. This is especially true if you're creating objects dynamically, especially in loops.
- Not removing event listeners when you remove the objects that send them.

But there's no need to be paranoid about memory leaks. Most day-to-day code that you write won't ever cause them. Unlike with most other programming languages, memory leaks are a rare occurrence in AS3.0. The Flash Player's automatic garbage collection does a great job of making sure they don't happen.

In the com.friendsofed.utils package, you'll find the PerformanceProfiler class, which tracks the frame rate and memory usage for you. It returns the average frame rate of the past 60 frames. Here's the class:

```
package com.friendsofed.utils
{
  import flash.utils.getTimer;
  import flash.system.System;

  public class PerformanceProfiler
  {
    private var _time:uint;
        private var _previousTime:uint;
    private var _fps:uint;
    private var _times:Array = [];

    public function PerformanceProfiler():void
    {
    }

    public function get fps():uint
    {
      //Calculate the frame rate
      _time = getTimer();
      _fps = 1000 / (_time - _previousTime);
      _previousTime = getTimer();
      _times.push(_fps);

      var average:uint = 0;
      for(var i:int = 0; i < _times.length; i++)
      {
        average += _times[i];

        //Make sure that the array doesn't grow
        //to more than 60 elements
        if(_times.length > 60)
        {
          //Remove the first element from the array
          //if there are more than 60 elements
          _times.shift();
        }
      }
      var averageFps:uint = uint(average / _times.length);

      return averageFps;
    }
```

```
    public function get memory():Number
    {
      //Convert the bytes into megabytes
      var mb:Number = System.totalMemory / 1024 / 1024;

      //Round to two decimal places
      var memory:Number = Math.round(mb * 100) / 100;

      return memory;
    }
  }
}
```

> *Use the Array class's `shift` method to remove the first element in an array.*

To use this class to check the frame rate in a game, first instantiate it in the same way you instantiate any other object:

```
private var _performance:PerformanceProfiler
  = new PerformanceProfiler();
```

Then call its methods inside an `ENTER_FRAME` loop:

```
currentFrameRate = _performance.fps;
memoryUsage = _performance.memory;
```

It's essential to track the frame rate so that you can test how changes to your game affect performance. When you're pushing Flash Player to its limits, many of the decisions about what you can or can't include in your game will be made for you by this simple calculation.

MovieClip vs. copyPixels

Let's track the frame rate to see if `copyPixels` can earn its keep.

In the chapter's source files, you'll find two folders: `LotsOfTiles` and `LotsOfMovieClips`. The SWFs for both these examples are identical. You'll see 160 game objects bouncing around the stage, with the status box displaying the frames per second, as shown in Figure 6-20.

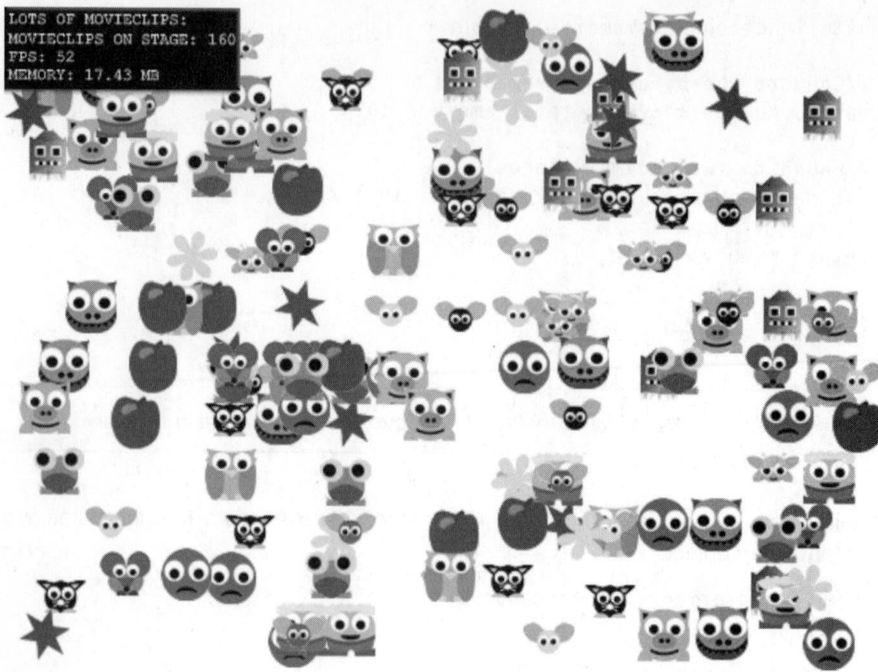

Figure 6-20. Compare the speed of copyPixels and MovieClip objects with two files that produce the same effect in different ways.

Both files loop through an identical 128-by-128 pixel tile sheet to display 16 tiles on the stage a variable number of times. In both examples, you can add more objects to the stage by increasing this variable:

```
private var _timesToRepeat:uint = 10;
```

I've initialized this to `10` in both files, which starts with 160 objects.

The major difference between `LotsOfTiles` and `LotsOfMovieClips` is that `LotsOfTiles` uses `copyPixels` and blitting to display the tiles. `LotsOfMovieClips` reads the tile sheet but wraps each tile in a `MovieClip` object. That `MovieClip` object is then moved around the stage. This is exactly the same technique we followed to create the `BitmapExplosion` example earlier in this chapter.

The important thing to note is the frame rate. With only a few dozen objects on the stage, the difference in the frame rate between them is negligible. At 160, the movie clips run at about half the rate as the blit objects. If you increase that number, things nosedive precipitously. At 1600 objects, `copyPixels` beats out `MovieClip` by about five to one, as shown in Figure 6-21.

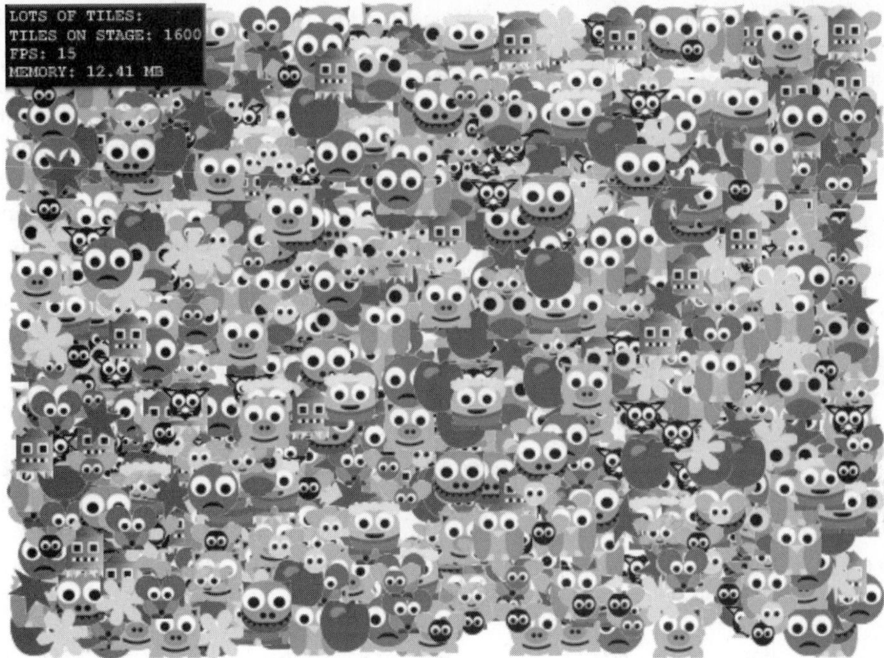

Figure 6-21. It's like 1967 all over again!

These numbers will vary from system to system and the context in which you're using them, but `copyPixels` is a decisive winner every time.

To blit or not to blit?

The bottom line is that blitting is a fast and efficient way to move things around the stage. Even if you're not moving a lot of objects around the stage, you can use your performance savings for other aspects of the game, like AI or calculating vectors. But should you always blit instead of using sprites or movie clips? No, not always.

Sprites and movie clips have many built-in features, like scaling and rotation, that make them very easy to manage. In a smallish game, those advantages might outweigh the performance savings of blitting, especially if you have only a few objects on the stage. And as you can see, even 160 `MovieClip` objects can be animated on the stage smoothly with plenty of juice to spare.

If you blit, you must manually manage rotation, scaling, and fading. That means there's no `rotation` property you can use to rotate an object, there are no `scaleX` and `scaleY` properties to resize it, and no there's no `alpha` property to set its transparency.

To rotate, fade, or scale an image with blitting, you need to *prerender the effect in the tile sheet.* What do I mean by that?

For rotation, you need to have a series of images in the tile sheet that show the object at incremental stages of rotation. You must to draw each stage of the rotation yourself. Figure 6-22 illustrates an example of a tile sheet with tiles that could be used to rotate a game character. You then need to write code that loops through those tiles in the correct order to display the rotation animation on the stage. You essentially need to build your own mini-animation engine from scratch. It's not difficult to write code to do this (you'll see how in the next chapter). And because `Sprite` and `MovieClip` rotation is very CPU-intensive, this approach actually provides another big performance savings. But truthfully, in a small game, it would be overkill. It's a lot more work to manage, and there may not be any noticeable payoff.

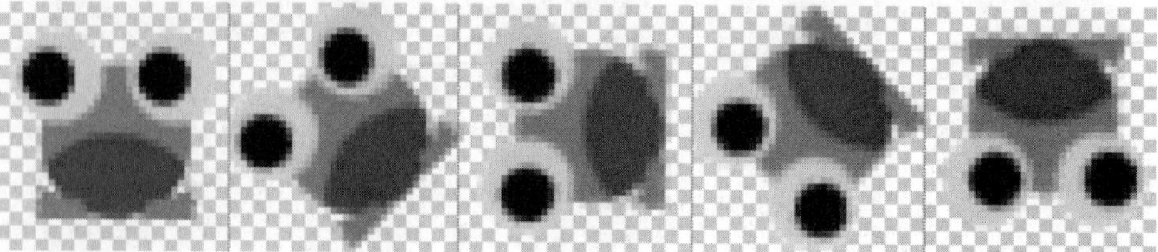

Figure 6-22. To rotate an object with blitting, you prerender the rotation animation in the tile sheet and then write code to display those tiles as an animated sequence.

The same approach applies to fading an image. Prerender the effect in the tile sheet and display those tiles in sequence when you need them, as shown in Figure 6-23. Scaling is the same. You need to use a tile sheet with a series of images that show the object gradually getting smaller and smaller, or bigger and bigger. Every stage must be drawn manually. How about fading, scaling, and rotating at the same time? You need to draw a series of individual tiles that show each gradual change in the transformation, with whatever combination of effects you want.

Figure 6-23. To fade an object, you need a sequence of images of the object at various stages of transparency.

In other words, achieving such image effects is like doing labor-intensive, hand-drawn, frame-by-frame animation. You'll need to plan for this well in advance, and expect that a game with a lot of animation could require tile sheets made up of hundreds or even thousands of tiles. Each tile would represent a single frame of an animated transformation sequence.

Rather than prerendering all of this, you *could* write your own custom graphics classes that work all of it out with code. This would be extremely complex to write, and would probably eat up all the performance savings gained by blitting in the first place. And, what's worse, you would just be reinventing the wheel. That's exactly what the Sprite and MovieClip classes do for you automatically in the first place!

What about collision detection? You can forget about using hitTestObject and hitTestPoint, as those are built-in properties of the Sprite and MovieClip classes. You'll need to roll you own collision code, as we've done in the first few chapters of this book. In Chapters 8 and 9, I'll show you how to handle collision detection in a blit display environment.

The other area where Sprite and MovieClip objects have a clear advantage is **depth sorting**: figuring out which object should appear stacked above or below other objects. When sprites and movie clips are added to the stage with addChild, the **display list** determines their stacking order. You can move a display object to the top of the stack like this:

```
setChildIndex(displayObjectInstance, numChildren - 1);
```

When you blit, you don't add anything to the stage or the display list. So you need to create your own system for managing the stacking order. You determine the stacking order by making sure the objects you want to appear on top are the last to be copied by copyPixels. If all your tiles are in an array called tiles, the last element of that array will appear above the others. If you're using a tile sheet with 16 tiles, the sixteenth tile will be on top.

You might need some control over the stacking order after you create the tile sheet. If so, the solution is to create a new depths array that just determines the stacking order of objects. It will have the same number of elements as the tiles array, but just contain numbers that determine their stacking order on the stage. You can use this depths array to control which tiles are drawn before others. Let's say you have a tile sheet with four tiles. You'll need a matching depths array with four elements:

```
tiles = [tile1, tile2, tile3, tile4];
depths = [3, 2, 0, 1];
```

This determines that tile3 would be at top of the stack at position 0. To actually make tile3 appear at the top, copyPixels must to draw it last. This means you need to sort the tiles array according to the depths array. Then create a new array with the tiles organized according to their stacking order. It's a lot of work. Is it worth it? It might be!

As you can see, it's not always clear-cut whether blitting is going to be a better option than using Sprite or MovieClip objects. It's always going to be faster, but it can be more complex to manage in some ways. You'll need to be the judge of which route you want to take, depending on the particular project.

Where blitting has a clear advantage is moving a lot of things around the stage quickly, and so it's perfect for fast particle explosions.

Blit explosions

Our blitting discussion was a bit of a detour, but an important one. You're now well prepared to use your newfound knowledge to create a fast particle explosion.

You'll find it in the appropriately named `FastParticleExplosion` folder. Run the SWF, and you'll see that the effect is similar to `BitmapStarburstExplosion`, except that there's very little drop in the frame rate, no matter how many particles are on the stage, as shown in Figure 6-24. The only real difference is that a blit system has been used to move the particles rather than wrapping them in `MovieClip` objects.

Figure 6-24. Use blitting to have many more particles on the stage.

The application class makes an explosion by creating a `BlitExplosion` instance and sending it the `snapshotBitmapData` in its constructor argument.

```
var explosion:BlitExplosion = new BlitExplosion
  (
    snapshotBitmapData, 4
  );
```

`snapshotBitmapData` is the snapshot of the section of rock that we want to break into pieces. It plays the same role as the tile sheets in our previous examples on blitting.

The `BlitExplosion` class creates a 500-by-500-pixel blank bitmap. It's the canvas for the explosion. It breaks the `snapshotBitmapData` into tiles and moves them around the canvas.

Here's the entire `BlitExplosion` class so that you can see all the code in its proper context.

```
package com.friendsofed.gameElements.effects
{
  import flash.events.Event;
  import flash.display.*;
  import flash.geom.Point;
  import flash.geom.Rectangle;
  import flash.events.TimerEvent;
  import flash.utils.Timer;
  import com.friendsofed.vector.*;

  public class BlitExplosion extends Bitmap
  {
    private var _speedLimit:int = 5;
    private var _fadeRate:Number = 0.01;
    private var _numberOfParticles:int = 100;
    private var _gravity:Number = 0.2;
    private var _animationTimer:Timer = new Timer(16);
    private var _fadeCounter:int = 50;
    private var _gridSize:uint;
    private var _tileSize:uint;
    private var _sourceBitmapData:BitmapData;

    //Create a blank BitmapData object as the canvas for this bitmap.
    //This is the same as the "stage bitmap" from the
    //previous examples, except that it's only contained within this
    //object. It needs to be big enough to
    //contain all the particles during the explosion
    private var _explosionBitmapData:BitmapData = new BitmapData
      (
        500, 500, true, 0
      );

    //The array that stores the particle tiles
    private var _tiles:Array = [];

    public function BlitExplosion
      (
        bitmapData:BitmapData,
        tileSize:int = 10,
        fadeRate:Number = 0.01
      ):void
   {
      _sourceBitmapData = bitmapData;
      _tileSize = tileSize;
      _gridSize = uint(_sourceBitmapData.width / _tileSize);
```

```
//Add the blank BitmapData to this Bitmap object
this.bitmapData = _explosionBitmapData;

//Slice the _sourceBitmapData into small tiles
for(var column:int = 0; column < _gridSize; column++)
{
  for(var row:int = 0; row < _gridSize; row++)
  {
    //Create a tile object to store the tile's original
    //position and give it initial velocity.
    //This become's the tile's "model"
    var tileModel:Object = new Object();

    //Record the tile's position on the snapshot image
    //so that the correct section of the snapshot can be found
    //when the tile is copied onto the explosions bitmap
    tileModel.tileMap_X = column * _tileSize;
    tileModel.tileMap_Y = row * _tileSize;

    //Center in the correct place inside this explosion object
    tileModel.x
      = column * tileSize - (_sourceBitmapData.width / 2);
    tileModel.y
      = row * tileSize - (_sourceBitmapData.width / 2);

    //Starburst explosion
    //1. Find the center of the grid
    var centerOfGrid:uint = _gridSize * 0.5;

    //2. Find the vx and vy between the center and this particle
    var vx:int = int(tileModel.x - centerOfGrid);
    var vy:int = int(tileModel.y - centerOfGrid);

    //3. The distance between the center of
    //the grid and the current particle
    var distance:int = int(Math.sqrt(vx * vx + vy * vy));

    //4. Find the dx and dy
    var dx:Number = vx / distance;
    var dy:Number = vy / distance;

    //5. Assign a random speed, but a
    //definite direction based on the vector
    tileModel.vx = (Math.random() * _speedLimit) * dx;
    tileModel.vy = (Math.random() * _speedLimit) * dy;

    //Push the tile into the tiles array
    _tiles.push(tileModel);
  }
}
```

```
      _animationTimer.addEventListener
        (TimerEvent.TIMER, animationEventHandler);
      _animationTimer.start();

    addEventListener
      (Event.REMOVED_FROM_STAGE, removedFromStageHandler);
  }

  private function animationEventHandler(event:TimerEvent):void
  {
    //Clear the bitmap from the previous frame so that it's
    //blank when you add the new particle positions
    _explosionBitmapData.fillRect(_explosionBitmapData.rect, 0);

    for(var i:int = 0; i < _tiles.length; i++)
    {
      //1. Update the model.
      //Find the new positions of the particles
      _tiles[i].x += _tiles[i].vx;
      _tiles[i].vy += _gravity;
      _tiles[i].y += _tiles[i].vy;

      //2. Create the particle view and display it on the stage

      //Find the tileModel's corresponding tile in the snapshot's
      //BitmapData and plot it to a new position in this containing
      //bitmap. Create a Rectangle object that's aligned to the
      //correct spot on the snapshot
      var sourceRectangle:Rectangle = new Rectangle
        (
          _tiles[i].tileMap_X,
          _tiles[i].tileMap_Y,
          _tileSize,
          _tileSize
        );

      //Create a Point object that defines the new position of the
      //tile on on the stage bitmap
      var destinationPoint:Point = new Point
        (
          _tiles[i].x + (_explosionBitmapData.width * 0.5),
          _tiles[i].y + (_explosionBitmapData.height * 0.5)
        );

      //Copy the pixels from the original image's BitmapData into
      //the new tileBitmapData. The Rectangle and Point objects
      //specify which part to copy
      _explosionBitmapData.copyPixels
```

```
        (
          _sourceBitmapData,
          sourceRectangle,
          destinationPoint
        );
      }

      //Fade the explosion out if the animation has
      //run for more than 100 frames
      _fadeCounter--;
      if(_fadeCounter < 0)
      {
        this.alpha -= 0.10;
        if(this.alpha <= 0)
        {
          dispatchEvent(new Event("explosionFinished"));
        }
      }
    }

    private function removedFromStageHandler(event:Event):void
    {
      _animationTimer.removeEventListener
        (TimerEvent.TIMER, animationEventHandler);

      removeEventListener
        (Event.REMOVED_FROM_STAGE, removedFromStageHandler);
    }
  }
}
```

As you can see, this is just a mixture of the earlier `BitmapExplosion` with the new blitting techniques.

The entire explosion fades out after it has run for 100 frames. The `_fadeCounter` is initialized to `100` and is decreased by one each frame. When it reaches zero, the explosion's `alpha` is decreased in steps of `0.10`. When the alpha reaches zero, an `"explosionFinished"` event is fired.

```
_fadeCounter--;
if(_fadeCounter < 0)
{
  this.alpha -= 0.10;
  if(this.alpha <= 0)
  {
    dispatchEvent(new Event("explosionFinished"));
  }
}
```

This code will be a good starting point for you to create your own custom particle explosions and effects using blitting.

Lookup tables

There are two big bottlenecks in particle explosions that slow things down:

- Displaying the particles on the stage
- Calculating vectors and velocities

We've largely solved the first problem with blitting. We can solve the second one by using **lookup tables**.

Lookup tables are just arrays containing values. The values are precalculated and copied into the arrays while the game is being initialized. This means that the game will take slightly longer to initialize, but won't suffer any slowdowns due to the CPU trying to do complex math while it's running. Lookup tables save the game from needing to suddenly start doing a lot of calculations while trying to clip along at 60 frames per second. Instead of performing calculations, all it needs to do is read the values that are precalculated in the array.

> *Before the dawn of mechanical computing, lookup tables were actually big, heavy, leather-bound books full of nothing but precalculated values. They were used in fields such as surveying and mapmaking, which required frequent reference to complex but predictable trigonometry calculations. Rather than doing the slow and tedious math by hand, you could just "look up" the answer in the book. Incidentally, the person whose job it was to do this was called a "computer"!*

You'll find a simple example of a lookup table in the `FastColorExplosion` folder. Run the SWF, and you'll see a version of the basic three-color explosion from the beginning of the chapter, as shown in Figure 6-25. This one looks similar, but runs much faster. The particles are displayed using blitting, and their velocities and colors are precalculated in lookup tables.

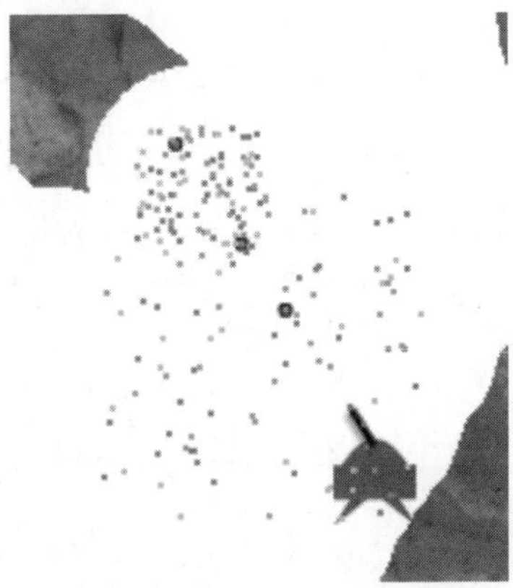

Figure 6-25. Fast multicolored explosions using blitting and lookup tables

The following is an abridged version of the FastColorExplosion application class that shows how the values are precalculated and then used to create the explosion effect. I've included only the code that creates and builds the lookup tables. The values are stored in Vector objects, because their numerical data can be read faster than Array objects.

```
public class FastColorExplosion extends Sprite
{
  //1. Determine the number of particles
  //and their size, maximum speed and colors
  private var _numberOfParticles:uint = 100;
  private var _particleSize:uint = 2;
  private var _speedLimit:int = 5;

  //2. Create Vectors (typed arrays) for the particle velocities
  private var _particle_Vx:Vector.<Number> = new Vector.<Number>;
  private var _particle_Vy:Vector.<Number> = new Vector.<Number>;

  //3. Create a Vector to store the colors
  private var _colors:Vector.<uint> = new Vector.<uint>;
  private var _randomColors:Vector.<uint> = new Vector.<uint>;

  //...

  public function FastColorExplosion():void
  {
    //4. Add colors to the _colors Vector
    _colors.push(0xFF6600, 0xFF9900, 0xFFCC00);

    //5. Create random velocities and colors for all the particles
    //and store them in the Vectors
    for (var i:uint = 0; i< _numberOfParticles; i++)
    {
      //A. Give them a random velocity
      _particle_Vx[i]
        = (Math.random() * _speedLimit) - _speedLimit * 0.5;
      _particle_Vy[i]
        = (Math.random() * _speedLimit) - _speedLimit * 0.5;

      //B. Populate the _colors Vector with random colors
      var randomColor:uint = uint(Math.random() * _colors.length);
      _randomColors.push(_colors[randomColor]);
    }
    //...
  }
}
```

This code creates three vectors: one for the vx values, one for the vy values, and a third for the color values. What does the data in these vectors look like? Each of the three vectors contains 100 numbers. If you trace _particle_Vx, the first ten numbers look like this:

```
0.6410878617316484,
-0.29987990390509367,
-1.9093330716714263,
2.3980771633796394,
0.029475553892552853,
1.3315631006844342,
-2.0507941488176584,
-2.0083568221889436,
2.305694443639368,
-0.6968122068792582,
...
```

This is what a lookup table looks like. It's just a big list of precalculated values.

The next step is to use this information to create the explosions. The vectors and other data are sent to the `ColorExplosion` class, which is the class that creates the explosion. It then adds the new explosion to the stage.

```
var explosion:ColorExplosion
  = new ColorExplosion
  (
    _numberOfParticles,
    _particleSize,
    _particle_Vx,
    _particle_Vy,
    _randomColors
  );

explosion.x =
  _bulletModels[i].xPos - explosion.width * 0.5;
explosion.y =
  _bulletModels[i].yPos - explosion.height * 0.5;

addChild(explosion);
_explosions.push(explosion);
```

The `ColorExplosion` class uses the color and velocity values when it creates the particle objects, and then displays them using blitting. It no longer needs to do any math to figure out the velocities and colors. This removes a big processing bottleneck in the system. You can find the `ColorExplosion` class in the `com.friendsofed.gameElements.effects` package. Take a good a look at how it reads the precalculated values to create the particles. I've highlighted all the most important lines of code.

```
package com.friendsofed.gameElements.effects
{
  import flash.events.Event;
  import flash.display.*;
  import flash.geom.Point;
  import flash.geom.Rectangle;
```

```
import flash.events.TimerEvent;
import flash.utils.Timer;
import com.friendsofed.vector.*;

public class ColorExplosion extends Bitmap
{
  private var _fadeCounter:int = 50;
  private var _numberOfParticles:int = 100;
  private var _gravity:Number = 0.1;
  private var _size:Number;
  private var _animationTimer:Timer = new Timer(16);

  //The array that stores the particles
  private var _particles:Array = [];

  //Create a blank BitmapData object as the canvas for this bitmap
  private var _explosionBitmapData:BitmapData
    = new BitmapData(500, 500, true, 0);

  public function ColorExplosion
  (
    numberOfParticles:uint,
    particleSize:uint,
    particle_Vx:Vector.<Number>,
    particle_Vy:Vector.<Number>,
    randomColors:Vector.<uint>
  ):void
{
  this._numberOfParticles = numberOfParticles;
  this._size = particleSize;

  //Add the blank BitmapData to this Bitmap object
  this.bitmapData = _explosionBitmapData;

  //Create all the particles
  for (var i:uint = 0; i< _numberOfParticles; i++)
  {
    //Create the particle object
    var particle:Object = new Object();

    //Create the particle's BitmapData based on the
    //colors from the precalculated Vector
    particle.bitmapData
      = new BitmapData(_size, _size, false, randomColors[i]);

    //Give it an initial position
    particle.x = 0;
    particle.y = 0;
```

```
    //Assign velocity by reading the velocity Vectors
    particle.vx = particle_Vx[i];
    particle.vy = particle_Vy[i];

    //Push the particle into the particles array
    _particles.push(particle);
  }

  _animationTimer.addEventListener
    (TimerEvent.TIMER, animationEventHandler);
 _animationTimer.start();

 addEventListener
    (Event.REMOVED_FROM_STAGE, removedFromStageHandler);
}

private function animationEventHandler(event:TimerEvent):void
{
  //Clear the bitmap from the previous frame so that it's
  //blank when you add the new particle positions
  _explosionBitmapData.fillRect(_explosionBitmapData.rect, 0);

 for(var i:int = 0; i < _particles.length; i++)
{
      //Update the model
      _particles[i].x +=  _particles[i].vx;
      _particles[i].vy += _gravity;
      _particles[i].y +=  _particles[i].vy;

      //Display the particle in the correct
      //position on this bitmap
      var sourceRectangle:Rectangle
        = new Rectangle(0,0, _size, _size);

      var destinationPoint:Point
        = new Point
        (
          _particles[i].x + (_explosionBitmapData.width * 0.5),
          _particles[i].y + (_explosionBitmapData.height * 0.5)
        );

      _explosionBitmapData.copyPixels
        (
          _particles[i].bitmapData,
          sourceRectangle,
          destinationPoint
        );
    }
```

```
      //Fade the explosion out if the animation has
      //run for more than 100 frames
      _fadeCounter--;
      if(_fadeCounter < 0)
      {
        this.alpha -= 0.10;
        if(this.alpha <= 0)
        {
          dispatchEvent(new Event("explosionFinished"));
        }
      }
    }

    private function removedFromStageHandler(event:Event):void
    {
      _animationTimer.removeEventListener
        (TimerEvent.TIMER, animationEventHandler);

      removeEventListener
        (Event.REMOVED_FROM_STAGE, removedFromStageHandler);
    }
  }
}
```

The class is not doing any math to calculate the color and velocity values. It's just reading the precalculated values from the vectors that were sent to it in its constructor.

Using lookup tables is a small but necessary optimization that you'll almost certainly want to employ when you start moving many hundreds of objects around the stage.

An Explosion Controller

With more than one or two particle effects in your game, your code will start to become very complex very quickly. The solution is to offload all the complexity to a dedicated explosion controller class with these specific responsibilities:

- Create the lookup tables.
- Create instances of explosion objects and add them to the stage.
- Remove explosions from the stage when they're finished.

You'll find an example of just such a system at work in the `ManagingExplosions` folder. When you run the SWF, you'll see that the explosions in this example are a combination of all the techniques we've covered in this chapter so far, as shown in Figure 6-26.

As you can see, I got a bit carried away! I combined both the colored particle and bitmap tile explosions into one effect. The colored particles explode four times faster than the rock tiles and are unaffected by gravity. This makes it look as if the exploding bullets on the rock surface cause the rock to break away. Yes, it's a bit over the top, but it's a good test to see how far we can push these techniques. Creating that explosion involved managing a lot of data. If I had left it all up to the application class, it would consist of about a quarter of the code. But it's just an effect, so I am much happier with it safely tucked away into another class, so I don't need to look at that code after it has been written.

Figure 6-26. A complex explosion effect combining multiple techniques

The application class creates an `ExplosionController` object. This is just a sprite that is added to the stage, and displays the explosions using blitting. You can think of it as a transparent layer that sits above the other objects on the stage and has the job of displaying explosions. The `ExplosionController` also creates the lookup tables, contains most of the values needed to create explosions, and removes them from the display list when the explosions are finished. Figure 6-27 illustrates how the `ExplosionController` fits into the grand scheme of things.

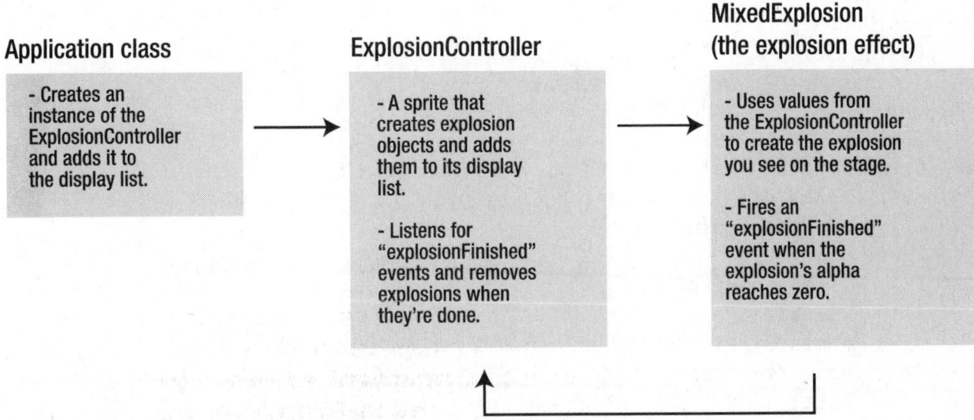

Figure 6-27. Using an ExplosionController

The application class creates an ExplosionController instance and adds it to the display list.

```
private var _snapShotSize:uint = 80;
private var _explosionController:ExplosionController
  = new ExplosionController(_snapShotSize);
//…
addChild(_explosionController);
```

The only value the application class needs to share with the ExplosionController is the _snapShotSize. That's the size of the rectangle we're going to cut out of the cave wall. The ExplosionController is a Sprite object, so it sits invisibly in the top-left corner of the stage.

When the application class needs an explosion, it calls the ExplosionController's createExplosion method.

```
_explosionController.createExplosion
  (
    _bulletModels[i].xPos,
    _bulletModels[i].yPos,
    snapshotBitmapData
  );
```

It sends the bullet's position and the snapshot's BitmapData to the ExplosionController.

The ExplosionController initializes all the values needed to create the explosion, such as the lookup tables and particle velocities. All that data is initialized when the object is created, so it's ready to go when the class is called upon to create an explosion.

The createExplosion method uses the values in the ExplosionController class to make the explosion. It creates an instance of the MixedExplosion class and adds it to the display list.

```
public function createExplosion
  (
    xPos:Number,
    yPos:Number,
        snapshotBitmapData:BitmapData
   ):void
{
   //Create the explosion
      var explosion:MixedExplosion
        = new MixedExplosion
        (
            snapshotBitmapData,
          _tileSize,
          _numberOfParticles,
          _particleSize,
          _particle_Vx,
          _particle_Vy,
          _randomColors,
```

```
        _tile_Vx,
        _tile_Vy,
        _gridSize,
        _snapShotSize
            );

    //Position the explosion so that it matches the
    //x and y position of the bullet on the stage
    explosion.x = xPos - explosion.width * 0.5;
    explosion.y = yPos - explosion.height * 0.5;

    //Add an event listener to the explosion so that
    //it can be removed when its alpha reaches zero
    explosion.addEventListener
      ("explosionFinished", removeExplosion);

    //Add the explosion to the display list
    addChild(explosion);

    //Push the explosion into the _explosions array
    _explosions.push(explosion);
  }
```

Be sure to take a look at the complete `ExplosionController` class in the source files to see how it calculates all those values when it's initialized.

When the `MixedExplosion`'s `alpha` reaches zero, it fires an `"explosionFinished"` event.

```
//Fade the explosion out if the animation has
//run for more than 100 frames
_fadeCounter--;
if(_fadeCounter < 0)
{
  this.alpha -= 0.10;
  if(this.alpha <= 0)
  {
    //Dispatch an event to inform the parent that the
    //explosion is finished so that it can be removed
    dispatchEvent(new Event("explosionFinished"));
  }
}
```

The `ExplosionController` listens for this event and removes the explosion from the display list and its `_explosions` array.

```
public function removeExplosion(event:Event):void
{
  removeChild(MixedExplosion(event.target));
  _explosions.splice(_explosions.indexOf(event.target), 1);
}
```

This will be enough to get you started building your own `ExplosionController`. In Chapter 7, you'll see how you can use specialized controller classes in an MVC system to help manage other aspects of a complex game project.

Smoke trails

The last effect we'll look at in this chapter is smoke trails. It's quite a performance-intensive effect, and that gives us an opportunity to look at few new optimization techniques.

Run the `SmokeTrails` SWF in the chapter's source files to see this effect in action, as shown in Figure 6-28.

Figure 6-28. Give the bullets smoke trails.

How easy is it? Just use a picture of some smoke and add it to the stage at the bullet's position. Rotate it, scale it, fade it, then repeat. When its `alpha` is zero, remove it from the stage. With a lot of these on the stage, it looks like a trail of smoke streaming from the bullet.

Unfortunately, rotating, scaling, and fading alpha are among the most CPU-intensive tasks you can ask Flash Player perform. I'll show you how to cut down on any unnecessary animation and also how to use AS3.0's Perlin noise feature to create a reasonably realistic-looking smoke image without needing to embed another photograph.

The Perlin noise effect

The smoke is an instance of the `Smoke` class from the package `com.friendsofed.gameElements.effects`. It basically just does two important things:

- Creates a smoke pattern
- Animates the pattern by rotating, scaling, and fading it

Here's the entire Smoke class:

```
package com.friendsofed.gameElements.effects
{
  import flash.events.Event;
  import flash.display.*;
  import flash.events.TimerEvent;
  import flash.utils.Timer;

  public class Smoke extends Sprite
  {
    private var _circle:Sprite = new Sprite();
    private var _animationTimer:Timer = new Timer(96);

    public function Smoke():void
    {
      //Create the smoke using a Perlin noise effect:

      //1. Create a random "seed" number to start the pattern
      var seed:Number = Math.floor(Math.random() * 100);

      //2. Determine what color channels you want to use
      var channels:uint
        = BitmapDataChannel.BLUE|BitmapDataChannel.ALPHA;

      //3. Create a blank BitmapData to contain the noise
      var smoke:BitmapData = new BitmapData(5, 5, true, 0);

      //4. Use the perlinNoise method to create the noise
      //based on the random seed number and color channels
      smoke.perlinNoise
        (200, 200, 6, seed, true, false, channels, true, null);

      //5. Create a circle and fill it with the perlinNoise pattern
      _circle.graphics.beginBitmapFill(smoke);
      _circle.graphics.drawCircle(0, 0, 5);
      _circle.graphics.endFill();
      addChild(_circle);
```

```
  _animationTimer.addEventListener
    (TimerEvent.TIMER, animationEventHandler);
  _animationTimer.start();

  addEventListener
    (Event.REMOVED_FROM_STAGE, removedFromStageHandler);
}

private function animationEventHandler(event:TimerEvent):void
{
  _circle.rotation += 3;
  _circle.scaleX += 0.24;
  _circle.scaleY += 0.24;
  _circle.alpha -= 0.08;

  //Dispatch an event so that the parent can remove it
  if(_circle.alpha <= 0)
  {
    dispatchEvent(new Event("smokeFinished"));
  }
}

private function removedFromStageHandler(event:Event):void
{
  _animationTimer.removeEventListener
    (TimerEvent.TIMER, animationEventHandler);
  removeEventListener
    (Event.REMOVED_FROM_STAGE, removedFromStageHandler);
}
}
}
```

The perlinNoise method is a fun effect that's used for making random blotches of pixels in an organic way, as shown in Figure 6-29. It can work well for things like smoke, water, and clouds. I've also seen it used for generating random maps of continents and islands in games, as well as random 3D terrain, like mountain ranges.

> *The algorithms that produce a Perlin noise effect were first developed by Ken Perlin. His work won him an Oscar for Technical Achievement for its use in the 1982 movie, Tron.*

Figure 6-29. A typical Perlin noise pattern

This is the directive that creates the smoke pattern from the `Smoke` class:

```
smoke.perlinNoise(200, 200, 6, seed, true, false, channels, true, null);
```

There are a lot of parameters! But you really need to fully understand only these three:

- **Parameter 4,** `seed`: A *seed* is a number in an algorithm that triggers pattern. In this case, it's the catalyst for the random pattern of pixel blotches you see on the stage. You'll get a different random pattern by keeping all the other parameters the same and changing just this number. In the `Smoke` class, the seed is generated randomly, so each puff of smoke is slightly different. The seed can be *any* number; it doesn't need to be limited to a certain range or size.

  ```
  var seed:Number = Math.floor(Math.random() * 100);
  ```

  Any random number will do; only by experimenting can you see the effect it will have. And the seed number doesn't need to be random. It you keep it fixed at a specific number, you'll always generate the same pattern.

- **Parameter 7,** `channels`: This determines which colors are used. The `Smoke` class uses the `BLUE` and `ALPHA` channels.

  ```
  var channels:uint = BitmapDataChannel.BLUE | BitmapDataChannel.ALPHA;
  ```

  The `ALPHA` channel allows some parts of pattern to be transparent. The four channels to choose from are `RED`, `GREEN`, `BLUE`, and `ALPHA`. Delineate the channels with the **bitwise or operator**, which is the vertical pipe symbol (`|`) you can see between them.

- **Parameter 8,** grayScale: This can be true or false. Smoke is usually a shade of gray, so I've set this as true in the Smoke class.

  ```
  smoke.perlinNoise(200, 200, 6, seed, true, false, channels, true,
  null);
  ```

Those are the most important parameters, but here's what the others do:

- **Parameters 1 and 2**, baseX **and** baseY: These set the size of the pattern.
- **Parameter 3**, octaves: This specifies how many times to repeat the noise pattern. More repetitions create a more detailed effect.
- **Parameter 5**, stitch. This creates a pattern in which the top, bottom, left, and right sides match. You can use this to make a continuous tiled background from one pattern.
- **Parameter 6**, fractal: If this is true, it will produce smoother looking gradients.

But to really understand how all these parameters work, you need to play with them yourself in a live example. To help you get started with Perlin noise effects, I've provided the PerlinNoise.as file in the chapter's source files. It's a simple program that displays a Perlin noise pattern on the stage. Take a look at the perlinNoise entry in the Adobe's *ActionScript 3.0 Language and Components Reference*, and experiment by changing the values of the parameters. Don't worry too much about understanding exactly what those parameters are supposed to do. Just try new values, and when you see something you like, make a note of it. You can't really go wrong. You'll be creating all kinds of interesting patterns in no time, and many of them will be useful for effects in games.

Smoke trail optimization

These smoke trails are such a performance hog that you will need to radically optimize them before they can become usable. I've done this in three ways.

The first important optimization involves the Smoke class's timer event. Instead of updating the smoke's animation at 60 frames per second, I've set it to 10. The Smoke class's _animationTimer is set to fire every 96 milliseconds. That works out to just about one-tenth of a second.

```
private var _animationTimer:Timer = new Timer(96);
```

This seems like a minor thing, but we've just increased our performance budget by sixfold. That's a huge savings. And I promise you that no one will notice that the smoke is animating at just 10 frames per second.

The second important optimization is that smoke is added to the stage only every second frame. The SmokeTrails application class has two variables that keep track of when to add smoke:

```
private var _frameInterval:int = 2;
private var _frameCounter:int = 0;
```

`_frameInterval` determines how often to add smoke. At `2`, it will add smoke every second frame. `_frameCounter` counts the number of frames since the last time smoke was added.

The application class adds the smoke in the same loop that moves the bullets.

```
if(_frameCounter == _frameInterval)
{
  if(_smokeTrails.length < 50)
  {
    var smoke:Smoke = new Smoke();
    smoke.x = _bulletModels[i].xPos;
    smoke.y = _bulletModels[i].yPos;
    addChild(smoke);
    _smokeTrails.push(smoke);
    smoke.addEventListener
        ("smokeFinished", removeSmoke);
  }
}
```

It then increments the `_frameCounter` and resets it if it's greater than the interval.

```
_frameCounter++;
if(_frameCounter > _frameInterval)
    {
  _frameCounter = 0;
}
```

If you want to add smoke to the stage even less frequently, change the `_frameInterval` value to `3` or `4`. Experiment with different values to find one that works well for your game.

The final optimization is that the code adds more smoke only if there aren't more than 50 smoke instances already on the stage.

```
if(_smokeTrails.length < 50)
{…
```

> *Do the smoke trails really need to rotate, scale, or fade? Perhaps they do, but always aim for the minimum possible that you can get away with. Extra effects are always just that: extra. Never be afraid to cut something out or simplify it if makes you game more playable. Remember—fun first! No one will find your game fun if it crawls along at 5 frames per second, no matter how great the effects are.*

These are all minor, easy-to-implement performance optimizations, but they could play a make-or-break difference in the playability of your games.

Summary

Particle effects are a big topic, and an area that many developers specialize in. This chapter has just scratched the surface of the subject. A quick web search will turn up many good examples and source code for different kinds of particle effects that you can adapt for you own projects.

You should now be well prepared to make good use of all those resources, and have more than enough information to create your own original effects. You can usually achieve big changes to an effect by making small changes to the code, so do a lot of experimenting. Build yourself a library of effects to use with your games.

In the next chapter, we'll look at how to use particle explosions in the context of a real game. We're also going to tie together quite a few threads that have been evolving over the last few chapters and use them to create a sophisticated game incorporating sound, music, buttons, and AI.

Chapter 7

Make It Fun! Sound, Music, and AI

Much of this book is about the nuts and bolts of technology—how to make games. And I hope you're having as much fun learning these techniques as I am writing about them. But it's important to remember that the games we make are not about you or me. Games are for players, and players play games because they're fun.

All the technology in the world can't make a game fun. And, what is fun, anyway? In the middle of a big project, it's easy to lose sight of what makes games enjoyable to play.

In this chapter, I'm going to show you how to add several essential game design pieces that help make games fun.

- Sound effects and music
- Interaction by clicking buttons
- Simple but versatile AI routines, including how to figure out if enemies can "see" the player
- Different game screens to bookend your games

Of course, adding these types of elements makes your games more complex. How can you manage this complexity without losing control of the game project?

In this chapter's case study, we'll look at how to structure a very complex sci-fi action game prototype that puts all of these new techniques to work. You'll be able to use it as a model for building your own complex games.

Sounds like fun to me!

Put fun first

Before we get to the code, let's take a look at the bigger picture. Here are some tips to help you make your game fun:

- **Make it responsive**: For every action, have a reaction. If a player collects objects or bumps into something, make a burst of color and play a sound. Our real world is like this. Accelerate too fast, and your tires squeal. Bump your head, and you see stars. Why should games be any different?

  Giving players multisensory tactile information about the game world adds a sense of immersion—players feel that they're inhabiting and interacting with a parallel universe inside the game. That wondrous sense of escape into an alternate reality is part of what makes games so enjoyable to play.

  Responsive feedback from the game, like flashes of color or bursts of sound, will instruct players about how to play the game while they're playing it. Get this right, and you won't need rules or instructions. Pick up and play, all the way!

- **Yes, simpler really is more fun**: Fun doesn't need to be complex or difficult. Watch a kitten playing with a ball of string. Watch most human beings for most of human history play with a ball and a flat surface. Find an amusing interactive toy to play with, like a circle bouncing off a square, and build a game around it.

  This applies to your user interface, too. Use logical keys for game actions, and use the mouse or touch as input wherever you can. The less time players spend figuring out how to play your game, the more time they will have to enjoy playing it.

  Players decide within the first few seconds whether or not they like your game. There's a lot of competition out there, so pull them in right away and keep them playing.

- **Have a goal**: Players like challenges. They like to have a clear goal and then fail to achieve it. Let them play again to see if they can learn from their mistakes. For some strange reason, this makes humans happy! Having a goal is what turns a toy into a game.

  Your goal can be anything you dream up. Find the exit, save the princess, get a high score, find the right pattern, make an interesting object, or just try to survive to the end of the game. But whatever it is, make sure that everything in your game reminds players what that goal is and nudges them toward achieving it.

  That means that if the players do something wrong, tell them! Sound an alarm, create an explosion, or shake them about. If they do something right, make happy sounds, shower them with bright flower petals, or give them some flashing bonus points. Your game world can direct the player into succeeding with the right combination of positive and negative feedback.

- **Give them little victories**: As a child, I was mortified by a story my dad told me. He was watching my sister and I play Super Mario World. "Ah yes, just like rats!" he said.

  "What?" I asked in a hyper-focused, mid-level, bleary-eyed stammer.

  "If rats press a lever, and they get food," he explained, "the rats will keep pressing that lever endlessly, even if they get fed only once in every 100 attempts."

  He was right. I had played that level countless times, but I kept falling off a ledge somewhere in the middle. What kept me going was that I was able to succeed at collecting little coins and stars, and stomping on easy enemies along the way. The fact that I kept falling off that ledge at a critical point didn't matter. I knew I could win, even if I wasn't winning right now. The buzz of my little victories kept me going.

  My dad, a psychologist, was referring to a well-known phenomenon described by B.F. Skinner called **intermittent reinforcement**. It's the crack cocaine of human survival. But unlike crack cocaine, it's free and legal. Use it in your games whenever you can! Reward players for completing small, easy tasks, and they'll approach the more difficult tasks with compulsive abandon. If they know they can succeed eventually, they'll keep pressing that lever over and over again.

- **Involve the player in creating and modifying the game world**: Games with the greatest replay value are those that allow players to contribute something to the game world. Players' actions can interactively change the shape of the game level, or modify the goal. Players can be given a choice of multiple strategies to reach the goal, each with differing outcomes. Let players make something, uniquely on their own, that they can use in the game.

- **Wind them up and let them loose**: Program the enemy AI with simple rules so that they interact with the game world in a specific way. If the game world changes in unexpected ways, the AI should be able to adapt to those changes in equally unexpected ways. This makes the AI seem like intelligent living creatures and adds to the sense of immersion.

Far from being afterthoughts, these tips should be the very first things on your mind when you start designing a game. Tear these pages from this book, and tape them to your bedroom ceiling so that they are the first and last things you see each day (besides your teddy bear, of course!). If you remember to put fun first, the rest of your task becomes so much easier.

Sound effects and music

The more senses you can involve in your game, the more immersive and fun it will become. Sound and music are essential for games, and AS3.0 has some great built-in classes and methods for adding and controlling sounds.

In this section, we're going to a look at the following topics:

- Embedding and playing sound effects
- Creating buttons and how to use them to control sounds
- Playing, stopping, looping, and adjusting the volume and pan of music

As you'll see, with just a bit of code and a little understanding of the concepts AS3.0 uses to play sounds, you'll find it quick and easy to add sound and music to your games. This chapter covers all the sound and music techniques you need to know.

Adding sound effects

Run the SoundEffects SWF in the chapter's source files. You'll find two buttons on the stage, as shown in Figure 7-1. If you click them, a sound will play.

Figure 7-1. Click the buttons to play a sound.

The structure and logic of the code behind this is not difficult to grasp:

- The sounds are embedded into the class from the assets\sounds folder. These are just ordinary MP3 files containing the sound you want to use.
- A CLICK listener is added to a button.
- The listener plays the sound when the button is clicked.

Here's the entire SoundEffects class that does all of this:

```
package
{
  import flash.events.Event;
  import flash.display.*;
  import flash.events.MouseEvent;
  import flash.ui.Mouse;
  import com.friendsofed.utils.*;
```

```
//Classes needed to play sounds
import flash.media.Sound;
import flash.media.SoundChannel;

[SWF(width="130", height="100",
backgroundColor="#FFFFFF", frameRate="60")]

public class SoundEffects extends Sprite
{
  //Embed and create the sounds:

  //Laser gun
  [Embed(source="../assets/sounds/laserGun.mp3")]
  private var LaserGun:Class;
  private var _laserGun:Sound = new LaserGun();
  private var _laserGunChannel:SoundChannel
    = SoundChannel();

  //Explosion
  [Embed(source="../assets/sounds/bigExplosion.mp3")]
  private var Explosion:Class;
  private var _explosion:Sound = new Explosion();
  private var _explosionChannel:SoundChannel
    = new SoundChannel();

  //Status box
  private var _statusBox:StatusBox = new StatusBox;

  public function SoundEffects():void
  {
    //1. LASER
    var laserButton:EasyButton
      = new EasyButton("Laser gun", 12, 100, 25);
    addChild(laserButton);

    //Position the button on the stage
    laserButton.x = 20;
    laserButton.y = 30;

    //Add the button event listener
    laserButton.addEventListener
      (MouseEvent.CLICK, laserHandler);

    //2. EXPLOSION
    var explosionButton:EasyButton
      = new EasyButton("Explosion", 12, 100, 25);
    addChild(explosionButton);
```

```
        //Position the button on the stage
        explosionButton.x = 20;
        explosionButton.y = laserButton.y + 30;

        //Add the button event listener
        explosionButton.addEventListener
          (MouseEvent.CLICK, explosionHandler);

        //Add the status box
        addChild(_statusBox);
        _statusBox.text = "SOUND EFFECTS:";
      }

      private function explosionHandler(event:Event):void
      {
        //Play the button sound
        _explosionChannel = _explosion.play();
      }

      private function laserHandler(event:Event):void
      {
        //Play the button sound
        _laserGunChannel = _laserGun.play();
      }
  }
}
```

First, this class imports two essential classes required for playing sounds: the `Sound` and `SoundChannel` classes.

```
import flash.media.Sound;
import flash.media.SoundChannel;
```

You need to use both these classes together to play sounds.

- `Sound` contains the actual sound that you want to play.
- `SoundChannel` helps you play the sound.

You can think of the `Sound` class as a CD, and a `SoundChannel` as the CD player that actually loads and plays it, as illustrated in Figure 7-2.

Figure 7-2. The Sound and SoundChannel classes work together to play sound effects and music.

To create a new sound to use in a game, you need to embed it, create its `Sound` object, and then create its `SoundChannel` object:

```
//Embed the sound
[Embed(source="../assets/sounds/laserGun.mp3")]
private var LaserGun:Class;

//Create the Sound object from the embedded sound
private var _laserGun:Sound = new LaserGun();

//Create a SoundChannel object that will play the sound
private var _laserGunChannel:SoundChannel = new SoundChannel();
```

The `SoundChannel` can then play the `Sound` whenever it's called on to do so. In this case, it happens with a button click:

```
private function laserHandler(event:Event):void
{
  //Play the button sound
  _laserGunChannel = _laserGun.play();
}
```

And that's really all there is to it. The only thing to keep in mind is this strangely unintuitive syntax:

```
_laserGunChannel = _laserGun.play();
```

`_laserGun.play()` is assigned to the `_laserGunChannel` object. Strangely, the `play` method is on the `Sound`, not the `SoundChannel`. But apart from that little quirk, this is a very routine line of code. It's the equivalent to putting a CD into a CD player and pressing the play button.

Playing music

Playing music is the same as playing any other sound effects. But music is usually longer than the second or two that a simple sound effect might be. If you have a 2-minute music clip, you'll probably need some way of controlling when it starts and stops. You may also need to pause, resume, or loop it. Those are all features of any software music player, and luckily for us, AS3.0 has built-in methods and classes that automate most of these tasks.

You'll find an example of a very basic music player in the MusicPlayer folder. Start playing the music, and you'll hear some ethereal space-game music that loads from an MP3 file. Click some of the other buttons to see what happens. You can rewind, fast-forward, pause, restart, adjust the volume up and down, and pan the music to the left and right. The **POSITION** indicator in the status box tells you for how long, in milliseconds, the music has been playing, as shown in Figure 7-3.

Figure 7-3. A no-frills AS3.0 MP3 player

If you think it might be reasonably complex to build something like this, you're in for a surprise. Just import the sound classes, set up a few common-sense variables, apply some straightforward logic, and you're good to go. The MusicPlayer class is quite long, but follows the same format as the SoundEffects class, so I won't reprint it in its entirety here. But let's take a tour of the main features that make the music player work.

First, the MusicPlayer class imports the SoundTransform class.

```
import flash.media.SoundTransform;
```

The SoundTransform class is used to adjust the volume and the panning of the sound to the left and right speaker. You'll see how it's used in the explanations ahead.

Next, embed the sound, and set up all the objects and variables that you'll need to control it. Here they are:

```
[Embed(source="../assets/sounds/music.mp3")]
private var Music:Class;
private var _music:Sound = new Music();
private var _musicChannel:SoundChannel = new SoundChannel();
private var _playHeadPosition:int = _musicChannel.position;
private var _musicIsPlaying:Boolean = false;
private var _volume:Number = 1;
private var _pan:Number = 0;
```

For controlling music, these are all the standard variables you'll need.

The `MusicPlayer` class then creates buttons and adds listeners to them. All the functionality of the music player happens in the button event handlers. Let's take a closer look at those event handlers.

Playing and pausing

Playing sounds and pausing sounds are very closely related actions. Playing music is the same as playing a sound effect: just assign the `music.play` method to the music's `SoundChannel`.

```
private function playHandler(event:Event):void
{
   if (!_musicIsPlaying
   && _musicChannel != null)
   {
      _musicChannel = _music.play(_playHeadPosition);
      _musicIsPlaying = true;
   }
 }
```

However, you'll notice a few small differences from the code we were using to play sound effects.

First, we don't want to make the music play if it's already playing. The `_musicIsPlaying` Boolean variable can help us check for that.

```
if (!_musicIsPlaying
&& _musicChannel != null)
{…
```

Without that check, another instance of the music sound will start playing every time you click the play button.

`_musicIsPlaying` is set to `true` when the music starts to play, and to `false` when the pause button is clicked.

If there's any chance that the `SoundChannel` object might not be assigned any value, you need to check for that, too:

```
if (!_musicIsPlaying
&& _musicChannel != null)
{
```

There's a greater chance of the SoundChannel object being null in a music player application where sound is likely to be added and removed from the channel. If you don't do this extra check, and _musicChannel does have a null value, you'll get a runtime error.

We also need to know whether we are starting the music from the beginning or if it has already been played and paused. If it has been paused, we need to know at which point to start playing it. A variable called _playHeadPosition tracks the current position of the music. If you provide this value as an argument to the sound's play method, the music will play from that point onward.

```
_musicChannel = _music.play(_playHeadPosition);
```

The SoundChannel class has a property called position. If the SoundChannel is like a CD player, its position property is like the little glowing minutes and seconds on the CD player that tell you how long the track has been playing. Whenever a sound plays, the position property tracks how long it has been playing. You can see the position property output in the status box. It's displayed like this:

```
_statusBox.text
  += "\n" + "POSITION: " + uint(_musicChannel.position);
```

The position property is *read-only*. That means you can use it to find out the current position of the music, but you can't change that position to make that music play from another spot.

To get around that limitation, this program uses a variable called _playHeadPosition. It helps to control where the music should start and stop playing.

When the program is initialized, _playHeadPosition is set to the value of the SoundChannel's read-only position property.

```
private var _playHeadPosition:int = _musicChannel.position;
```

Because the music hasn't started playing yet, the position value will be zero. And that means that _playHeadPosition will also be zero. Zero is always a good place to start!

As soon as the music starts playing, the position value will start to increase, which you can clearly see in the status box. If you click the pause button, the position value is assigned to the _playHeadPosition, and the SoundChannel pauses the sound. (Technically, it "stops" the sound, but it stops it at its current position. It doesn't reset the music to the start point, and so behaves more like CD player's pause button.)

```
private function pauseHandler(event:Event):void
{
  if(_musicChannel != null)
  {
    _playHeadPosition = _musicChannel.position;
    _musicChannel.stop();
    _musicIsPlaying = false;
  }
}
```

This means that `_playHeadPosition` now has a record of the current `position` value. And what's more, you can change its value.

To resume playing directly at the position that the music was stopped, just feed the current value of `_playHeadPosition` to the `play` method. The music will start playing from that point onward.

```
_musicChannel = _music.play(_playHeadPosition);
```

We now have an efficient system that allows the music to resume playing from where it was stopped.

Couldn't we just have used the `_musicChannel.position` property directly to resume playing the sound?

```
_musicChannel = _music.play(_musicChannel.position);
```

Yes, for just pausing and resuming a sound, that would work just fine. The only problem is that there's far more going on in this music player application than just starting or pausing, as you'll see in the next example.

Restarting music

The real usefulness of the `_playHeadPosition` variable pays off when you make the music play from a position other than the current position.

The restart button sets the `_playHeadPosition` variable to `0`, stops the music, and then starts playing it again from that point. Position zero is the start of the music.

```
private function restartHandler(event:Event):void
{
  if(_musicIsPlaying
  && _musicChannel != null)
  {
      _playHeadPosition = 0;
      _musicChannel.stop();
      _musicChannel = _music.play(_playHeadPosition);
    }
  }
}
```

Remember that there's no way to change the value of `_musicChannel.position`, because it's read-only. But now that we've forced the music to play from position zero, `_musicChannel.position` blindly follows along and acquires the new value automatically.

Fast-forwarding and rewinding

We can use this same bit of trickery to fast-forward and rewind the music. The rewind and fast-forward handlers add and subtract 1000 milliseconds (1 second) to the current position, and then tell the music to resume playing from that new point.

```
private function rewindHandler(event:Event):void
{
  if(_musicChannel != null
  && _musicIsPlaying
  && _musicChannel.position - 1000 > 0)
  {
    _playHeadPosition = _musicChannel.position - 1000;
    _musicChannel.stop();
    _musicChannel = _music.play(_playHeadPosition);
  }
}

private function fastForwardHandler(event:Event):void
{
  if(_musicChannel != null
  && _musicIsPlaying
  && _musicChannel.position + 1000 < _music.length)
  {
    _playHeadPosition = _musicChannel.position + 1000;
    _musicChannel.stop();
    _musicChannel = _music.play(_playHeadPosition);
  }
}
```

The other check these two handlers need to make is to ensure that the new rewind and fast-forward values are actually valid for the length of the music. That means that they shouldn't be able to rewind to a position that's *less than zero*.

```
if(_musicChannel != null
&& _musicIsPlaying
&& _musicChannel.position - 1000 > 0)
{...
```

And similarly, you shouldn't be able to fast-forward to a position that's greater than the actual length of the music.

```
if(_musicChannel != null
&& _musicIsPlaying
&& _musicChannel.position + 1000 < _music.length)
{...
```

The `Sound` class has a property called `length` that tells you the total length of the sound in milliseconds.

As you can see, this is a very simple system, but it works well.

Changing the volume and speaker panning

Sound volume and speaker panning are handled together by a separate `SoundTransform` object. First, you need to create a `SoundTransform` object.

```
var transform:SoundTransform
  = new SoundTransform(_volume, _pan);
```

The two arguments in the SoundTransform's constructor are the volume and panning:

- **Volume**: How loud or quiet the sound is. This can be any number, but it's usually set between 0 and 1. A 0 means that the sound is completely inaudible, 0.5 is mid-volume, 1 is normal volume, and 2 is twice normal volume.
- **Pan**: Determines whether the sound is played through the left or right speaker, or at equal volume through both speakers. This can be any number ranging from -1 to 1. At 0, the sound will come through both speakers equally. At -1, it will be heard only through the left speaker. At 1, it will be heard only through the right speaker.

Next, apply the SoundTransform object to the SoundChannel's soundTransform property.

```
_musicChannel.soundTransform = transform;
```

The new volume and speaker panning values will then take effect.

Yes, this can be a bit confusing. The SoundChannel class has a soundTransform property. It has the same name as the SoundTransform class, except for the different capitalization. These are two different things! To change a sound's volume or panning, you need to create an instance of the SoundTransform class and apply it to the SoundChannel's soundTransform property. Confusing as this might appear, just stick to the format in these examples, and you won't go wrong.

With that basic format in place, let's look at the event handlers that make these changes in the MusicPlayer program, beginning with volume adjustments.

The _volume variable in the MusicPlayer program is initialized to 1.

```
private var _volume:Number = 1;
```

Clicking the **Volume Up** button increases the _volume's value by 0.2. It creates a new SoundTransform object with the new volume value, and applies that new volume to the _musicChannel's soundTransform property.

```
private function volumeUpHandler(event:Event):void
{
  if(_musicChannel != null)
  {
     _volume += 0.2;
     var transform:SoundTransform
       = new SoundTransform(_volume, _pan);
    _musicChannel.soundTransform = transform;
  }
}
```

In this example, you can see that _pan has also been included as an argument in the SoundTransform constructor. This is optional. I've done it here because the pan value might have already been changed. If it's not reassigned again to the _musicChannel, along with the volume, the pan will default back to 0, and its previously changed value will be lost.

Turning down the volume follows the same logic. The only difference is that its lowest value is limited to 0. You could, in theory, give it a value less than zero, but there would be no audible difference—you can't hear less than complete silence, can you?

```
private function volumeDownHandler(event:Event):void
{
if(_musicChannel != null
&& _volume > 0)
  {
    _volume -= 0.2;
    if(_volume < 0)
    {
      _volume = 0;
    }
    var transform:SoundTransform
      = new SoundTransform(_volume, _pan);
    _musicChannel.soundTransform = transform;
  }
}
```

Panning follows the same format as changing the volume. The only difference is that the pan values need to be limited to between -1 and 1. That's the range used for panning.

```
private function panLeftHandler(event:Event):void
{
  if(_musicChannel != null
  && _pan > -1)
  {
     _pan -= 0.2;
     if(_pan < -1)
     {
       _pan = -1;
     }
     var transform:SoundTransform
       = new SoundTransform(_volume, _pan);
    _musicChannel.soundTransform = transform;
  }
}

private function panRightHandler(event:Event):void
{
  if(_musicChannel != null
  && _pan < 1)
  {
     _pan += 0.2;
     if(_pan > 1)
```

```
      {
        _pan = 1;
      }
      var transform:SoundTransform
        = new SoundTransform(_volume, _pan);
    _musicChannel.soundTransform = transform;
  }
}
```

Panning has useful applications for games, because you could make sounds play through the speaker that matches the side of the screen where an object is located. This gives a great sense of spatial immersion. You'll see an example of this effect at work in the pages ahead.

Looping music

There are two different ways you can loop sounds and music: with a `play` method argument or with a `SOUND_COMPLETE` event handler.

The `Sound` class's `play` method has a second optional argument, which determines the number of times you want the sound to loop.

```
_musicChannel = _music.play(_playHeadPosition, timesToLoop);
```

If you want the sound to start at position zero (the beginning of the track) and loop ten times, you could use code that looks like this:

```
_musicChannel = _music.play(0, 10);
```

If you want it to loop indefinitely, you can assign the loop argument the value `int.MAX_VALUE`.

```
_musicChannel = _music.play(0, int.MAX_VALUE);
```

`int.MAX_VALUE` is the highest possible value that an integer can be: 2,147,483,647. That means the sound won't loop forever, but it will loop long enough for the player to finish the game, and possibly even continue to loop a few decades well beyond that. That should be long enough!

For simple looping, this technique will work fine. On occasions where you need a bit more flexibility and control, you can create a loop using a `SOUND_COMPLETE` event. First, add a `SOUND_COMPLETE` event handler to the `SoundChannel` object when you play the music.

```
_musicChannel = _music.play(0);
_musicChannel.addEventListener(Event.SOUND_COMPLETE, loopMusicHandler);
```

Next, create a `loopMusicHandler` that plays the music again, and then adds another new `SOUND_COMPLETE` listener.

```
public function loopMusic(event:Event):void
{
  if (_musicChannel != null)
  {
    //Play the music
    _musicChannel = _music.play(0);
```

```
        //Add a new listener
        _musicChannel.addEventListener
          (Event.SOUND_COMPLETE, loopMusicHandler);
      }
   }
```

You also need to remove the listener anywhere in your program whenever the music stops.

```
_musicChannel.stop();
_musicChannel.removeEventListener
  (Event.SOUND_COMPLETE, loopMusicHandler);
```

> *If you loop continuous sounds that don't have a discernible start or end, you might hear a moment of silence before the sound plays again. This is because some MP3 formats store the ID3 tag information (the name of the song, name of the artist, and so on) at the beginning or end of the file. That's the silence you hear. If this proves to be a problem, make sure that you export the MP3 file from your audio software without the ID3 information. Most sound editors have this as an option. If you don't have access to the original uncompressed sound file, use an audio editor to trim the few milliseconds of silence from the beginning or end of the file.*

Using sound and music in a game

In the UsingSounds folder, you'll find an example of how to use these techniques to add sounds and music to a game. Run the SWF, and you'll find that the bullet-firing and explosion effects now have accompanying sounds, and music plays in the background.

Speaker panning matches the position of the effects on the stage. If the explosion happens on the right side of the stage, it can be heard in the right speaker. The bullet-firing sound is also in the speaker that matches its stage position, as shown in Figure 7-4. The amount of right and left speaker panning is proportionate to where the effects are in relation to the left and right side of the stage.

Figure 7-4. Sound panning matches the position of the effect on the stage.

The bullet-firing sound is played whenever the player fires a bullet, and the explosion sound is played when the bullet hits the cave wall.

Panning values range from –1 (the left speaker) to +1 (the right speaker). To create the panning effect, the code needs to convert the x position of the effects on the stage to a value within the –1 to +1 range. This is slightly awkward, but easy to do if you start with a value that represents the half the stage's width.

```
private var _halfStage:uint = uint(stage.stageWidth * 0.5);
```

A simple `if/else` statement can then use that value to figure out whether the pan value should be between –1 and 0 (the left speaker) or 0 and +1 (the right speaker) based on the bullet's position on the stage.

```
if(_bulletModels[i].xPos < _halfStage)
{
  //Left speaker
  _explosionPan = (_bulletModels[i].xPos - _halfStage) / _halfStage;
}
else
{
  //Right speaker
  _explosionPan = (_bulletModels[i].xPos / _halfStage) - 1;
}
```

The `_explosionPan` value can then be used to create the `SoundTransform` object.

```
var explosionTransform:SoundTransform
  = new SoundTransform(_volume, _explosionPan);
```

This new `explosionTransform` object is then used as the third argument in the `SoundChannel`'s `play` method

```
_explosionChannel = _explosion.play(0, 1, explosionTransform);
```

The bullet-firing sound is created in an identical way.

> *The techniques we've covered so far are all the basics you'll need to know for sound and music in games. For building a full-featured music player, you'll obviously need a bit more refinement control. You can start by reviewing all of the properties and methods in the `Sound`, `SoundChannel`, and `SoundTransform` classes in Adobe's online ActionScript 3.0 Language and Components Reference. There are a lot of them! Most usefully, the `Sound` class's `id3` property can be used to find quite a bit of information about the music that's playing.*

Finding sound effects and music

Where can you find music and sound effects for games? Here are some places to start:

- **Record your own sounds**: Record real sounds and add effects to them with audio software. I made the sounds of the lander's thruster in the case study later in this chapter by recording myself saying "Shhhhhhh" into a microphone. I looped it, added phase and delay effects with GarageBand, and ended up with a pretty convincing spaceship sound. You'll be surprised at how many useful game sounds you'll find in your everyday environment once you start listening.

> *Most of the iconic sound effects in the original Star Wars series were created by sound designer Ben Burtt, who recorded real environmental sounds. The famous Star Wars laser gun sound was the sound of a hammer hitting a high-tension wire that was holding up an antenna tower. The sound of the Imperial Walkers in the Empire Strikes Back was created by combining the sound of a machinist's punch press and the sound of a bicycle chain being dropping on concrete. The sound of Luke Skywalker's famous landspeeder was nothing more than a busy Los Angeles highway recorded through a vacuum cleaner tube. Interesting sounds are everywhere!*

- **Buy music and sounds**: Purchase royalty-free sounds and music from a sound library. *Royalty-free* means that you need to pay for the sounds only once. You don't need to pay for them every time you use them in a game.
- **Use software to create music and sounds**: There is software that can help you to create interesting sounds and melodies, even if you can't play an instrument. Take a look at GarageBand on Mac OS X and Magix Music Maker on Windows. For creating old-skool 8-bit video game sounds, the free software sfxr (Windows) and cfxr (Mac OS X) will do the trick. That's what I used to create the laser gun and explosion sounds in these examples. It's great for creating sounds quickly while you're building and testing a game.

All the music in this book was created using WolframTones (`http://tones.wolfram.com`). It's free online software that generates an entire musical score mathematically using **cellular automata**. Cellular automata are essentially grids of ones and zeros created by algorithms that mimic organic patterns found in nature. No two patterns generated by the algorithms are ever the same. It's like the musical version of Perlin noise, which we looked at in Chapter 6.

The quality of most of the music generated by WolframTones would be defined by most normal human artistic standards as "patently horrible," but occasionally, you'll discover something quite nice. The fact that the music is essentially completely random means you never know what you're going to get. The music is generated as a MIDI file, which you can import into audio software to tweak, mix, edit, and add your own instrumentation.

In the case study later in this chapter, you'll see how the sounds and music used in these examples are put to work in a real game project.

Buttons

The sound effects and music from the previous examples were generated by clicking buttons. In a game, most of the sounds will be triggered when something happens, like an explosion. But buttons are useful for many other game elements, like menus and start screens. Let's look at the basics of building buttons that you can use in your games.

Creating simple buttons

AS3.0 has a built-in class called `SimpleButton`, which helps you make buttons quickly. The `SimpleButton` class has built-in properties that determine how the button looks in its various states. Here are the most important of them:

- `downState`: What the button looks like when it's pressed down.
- `overState`: What the button looks like when the mouse is hovering over it.
- `upState`: The button's normal state, when the mouse isn't interacting with it.
- `hitTestState`: A display object that determines the area of the button that is sensitive to the mouse.

These four properties can contain any display object. To change how any of the button states look, just assign a different `Sprite`, `MovieClip`, or `Bitmap` object to any of these properties. I'll show you how to do this in the example ahead.

The `SimpleButton` class also has a few more properties that you may find useful:

- `useHandCursor`: A Boolean value that determines whether the Flash player should display a hand icon when the mouse is over the button.
- `enabled`: A Boolean value that determines whether a button is currently active. If you want to disable a button, set its `enabled` property to `false`.
- `SoundTransform`: Sets a sound's volume and panning. We used it in previous examples in this chapter.
- `TrackAsMenu`: A Boolean variable that determines whether `SimpleButton` or `MovieClip` objects can receive mouse release events

Be sure to check Adobe's online *ActionScript 3.0 Language and Components Reference* for more information about how to use these properties.

Making custom buttons

To make a custom button, create a new class that extends SimpleButton. You can then use all the class's properties to help you create the button.

I've done just that in my own custom class called EasyButton. I used this EasyButton class to create the buttons in the SoundEffects example. You can find the EasyButton class in the com.friendsofed.utils package. You can use it as a model for creating your own custom buttons. Here's the entire EasyButton class:

```
package com.friendsofed.utils
{
  import flash.display.*;
  import flash.filters.*;
  import flash.text.*;

  public class EasyButton extends SimpleButton
  {
    //Button properties
    private var _upColor:uint = 0x333333;
    private var _overColor:uint = 0x666666;
    private var _downColor:uint = 0x333333;
    private var _width:uint = 80;
    private var _height:uint = 80;
    private var _text:String;

    //Text properties
    [Embed(systemFont="Andale Mono", fontName="embeddedFont",
    fontWeight="normal", advancedAntiAliasing="true",
    mimeType="application/x-font")]
    private var EmbeddedFontClass:Class;
    private var _fontSize:uint;
    private var _fontColor:uint;

    public function EasyButton
      (
        textContent:String = "",
        fontSize:uint = 12,
        width:int = 50,
        height:int = 50,
        fontColor:uint = 0xFFFFFF
      ):void
    {
      this._text = textContent;
      this._width = width;
      this._height = height;
      this._fontSize = fontSize;
      this._fontColor = fontColor;
```

```
    //Button properties.
    //These are all built-in properties of the SimpleButton class.
    //They call the displayState method which determines
    //how these button states look.
    downState = displayState(_downColor);
    overState = displayState(_overColor);
    upState = displayState(_upColor);
    hitTestState = overState;
    useHandCursor = true;
  }

  //The displayState method creates a Sprite for each
  //button state. The only difference between button states in this example
  //is the background colors used to differentiate them
  private function displayState(backgroundColor:uint):Sprite
  {
    var sprite:Sprite = new Sprite()
    sprite.graphics.beginFill(backgroundColor);
    sprite.graphics.drawRect(0, 0, _width, _height);
    sprite.graphics.endFill();

    var filters:Array = [];
    filters = sprite.filters;
    filters.push
      (
        new BevelFilter
        (
          2, 135, 0xFFFFFF, 0.50,
          0x000000, 0.50, 2, 2
        )
      );
    filters.push
      (
        new DropShadowFilter
        (
          2, 135, 0x000000, 0.35, 2, 2
        )
      );
    sprite.filters = filters;

    //Create a text format object
    var format:TextFormat = new TextFormat();
    format.size = _fontSize;
    format.color = _fontColor;
    format.font = "embeddedFont"

    //Create a TextField object
    var textField:TextField = new TextField();
    textField.embedFonts = true;
```

```
        textField.autoSize = TextFieldAutoSize.LEFT;
        textField.text = _text;
        textField.setTextFormat(format);
        textField.antiAliasType = flash.text.AntiAliasType.ADVANCED;

        //Add the text to the sprite
        sprite.addChild(textField);
        textField.x = 5;
        textField.y = 3;

        return sprite;
      }
  }
}
```

It could be easy to miss how the button states are created in all that code, so let's take a closer look.

When the button is initialized, three variables determine what the colors of each button state will be:

```
private var _upColor:uint = 0x333333;
private var _overColor:uint = 0x666666;
private var _downColor:uint = 0x333333;
```

These are the colors that differentiate each button state.

Next, the four button states are assigned.

```
downState = displayState(_downColor);
overState = displayState(_overColor);
upState = displayState(_upColor);
hitTestState = overState;
useHandCursor = true;
```

They each call the `displayState` method, but they send a different color as an argument. The `displayState` method returns a `Sprite`. That's what determines how each state looks. The display states all hold a reference to the `Sprite` that's returned to them.

The `displayState` method has the job of creating a `Sprite` for each state based on the unique color assigned to that state. It also adds the button text.

```
private function displayState(backgroundColor:uint):Sprite
{
  //Draws a rectangle using the supplied background color.
  //Adds the text.
  //Returns a Sprite back to the caller
}
```

This is a quick way of giving each button state a unique look.

In this simple example, the only difference I've made to each button state is the background color. This is fine for building a quick prototype, but for a finished professional game, you could create a much more complex button class that changes many more visual details and possibly the text as well. Feel free to rip my `EasyButton` class apart and use it as the basis for your own custom buttons.

> *When you're working on an exciting new game project, there's nothing that can kill the enthusiasm quicker than the tedium of building a user interface. It always helps if you have a few easy-to-use classes for creating text and buttons in your back pocket, so you can quickly add them to a game while you're building and testing a prototype.*
>
> *The `com.friendsofed.utils` package contains a custom class called `EasyText`. It lets you quickly add text to the stage without needing to create all the accompanying text objects or embedding any fonts. Create an `EasyText` object like this:*
>
> ```
> var anyText:EasyText
>   = new EasyText("Hello World!", 32);
> addChild(anyText);
> ```
>
> *This will display "Hello World" on the stage. It's a sprite, so you can position it using x and y properties. The second argument in the constructor, `32`, is the font size.*
>
> *A great resource for simple but effective UI elements is Keith Peters' Minimal Comps (`http://www.minimalcomps.com`). They are easy to use and superb for building quick prototypes with a low overhead.*

Enemy AI: Line of sight

It seems like all those noises and explosions have attracted some unwelcome attention! Just as the lander was leaving the rocky planet's outer atmosphere, it was spotted by an enemy UFO. Can the lander outfly it? Run the `LineOfSight` SWF and try. It's a fun game of cat and mouse.

If the lander is hiding behind the asteroid, the UFO can't see it. But as soon as there's a direct line of sight without obstruction between the lander and UFO, the UFO's red light switches on and it attacks.

This works because a vector has been plotted between the lander and UFO. When the vector is unobstructed by the asteroid, the UFO can "see" the lander. Figures 7-5 and 7-6 illustrate the effect you'll notice when you run the SWF.

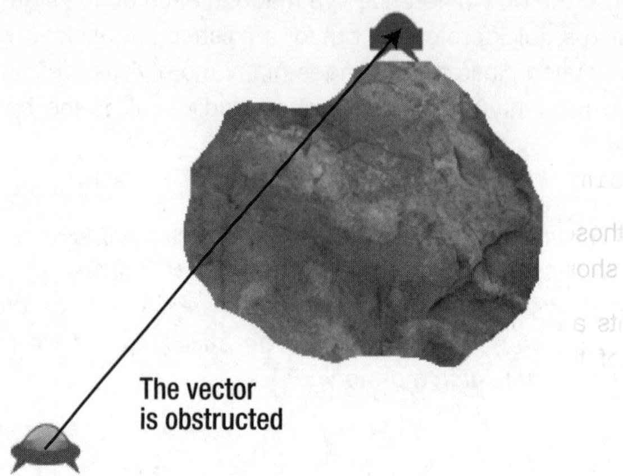

Figure 7-5. When the lander is hiding behind the asteroid, the UFO can't see it. The vector between the objects is obstructed. The UFO waits patiently for the lander to reemerge.

Figure 7-6. The UFO attacks when an unobstructed vector can be drawn between the lander and UFO.

Line of sight is one of the most useful video-game AI techniques. The concept is quite simple:

- Plot a vector from the enemy to the player's object.
- Test points at fixed spaces along the vector to see if they are touching the asteroid or the lander, as shown in Figure 7-7. You can use `hitTest` (for bitmaps) or `hitTestPoint` (for sprites or movie clips) to check for these collisions.
- If any of those points *don't* touch the asteroid, you know the enemy can see the player, as shown in Figure 7-8.
- If the points are spaced too widely along the vector, you could miss small objects. Because of this, the space between each point should not be greater than the smallest object you hope to detect, as shown in Figure 7-9.

Checking the collisions of points along the vector is done inside a `while` loop.

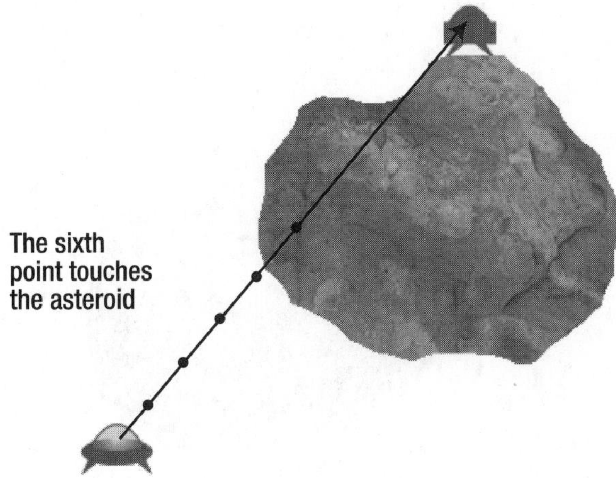
The sixth
point touches
the asteroid

Figure 7-7. Test points along the vector and check to see what they touch. It's almost like an insect's feeler.

The last
point touches
the lander

Figure 7-8. If none of the points touch the asteroid, then the UFO can see the lander and start to attack.

Figure 7-9. The distance between each point should be no greater than the size of the smallest object. The space between each point along the vector is a segment.

Our job now is to translate this logic into code. Because we know all about vectors and `while` loops, it becomes a very simple problem to solve.

I'll first list the entire code in context from the `enterFrameHandler`, and then explain how it works.

> *The UFO is an instance of the `UfoModel` and `UfoView` classes that you'll find in the `com.friendsofed.gameElements.ufo` package. The view draws the UFO, and the model contains a `_playerIsVisible` property that is set to `true` when the lander can be seen. I want to completely expose the vector math in this example, so I haven't used the `VectorModel` class to create vector objects.*

```
//1. Find the center points of the lander and UFO
//These points are measured from the top-left corners of the objects
var lander_X:int = int(_lander.xPos + _lander.width * 0.5);
var lander_Y:int = int(_lander.yPos + _lander.height * 0.5);
var ufo_X:int = int(_ufo.xPos + _ufo.width * 0.5);
var ufo_Y:int = int(_ufo.yPos + _ufo.height * 0.5);

//2. Create the distance vector between the UFO and lander
var vx:Number = lander_X - ufo_X;
var vy:Number = lander_Y - ufo_Y;

//3. Find the vector's magnitude
var magnitude:Number = Math.sqrt(vx * vx + vy * vy);

//4. Find the unit vector
var dx:Number = vx / magnitude;
var dy:Number = vy / magnitude;

//5. Create a segment that is the size of the space
//between each point.
//The segment should be no bigger than the smallest object
//in the game that enemy needs to find. The lander's width
//will do for this example
var segment:int = _lander.width;

//6. Figure out the maximum number of times
//you'll need to run the loop
var numberOfPoints:uint = uint(magnitude / segment);

//7. Create vectors of increasing length from the UFO in
//the direction of the lander.
//If the end point of the vector hits the asteroid
//then you know that the lander isn't visible.
var counter:int = 0;
```

```
while (counter++ != numberOfPoints)
{
  //Scale the vector to the size of the lander's width,
  //multiplied by the current counter value
  var vectorLength:int = segment * counter;

  //Create a Point object at the end of the vector
  var point:Point
    = new Point
    (
      ufo_X + dx * vectorLength,
      ufo_Y + dy * vectorLength
    );

  //Check whether that Point is touching the asteroid
  if(_asteroidBitmapData.hitTest
      (
        new Point(_asteroidBitmap.x, _asteroidBitmap.y),
        255,
        point
      )
    )
  {
    //If the Point does touch the asteroid, then the
    //lander can't be visible and we can break the loop
    _ufo.playerIsVisible = false;
    break;
  }
  else
  {
    //If it's not touching the asteroid, then
    //the player could be visible. If this remains
    //true by the end of the loop, then the UFO
    //can clearly see the player
    _ufo.playerIsVisible = true;
  }
}

//Ease the UFO towards the lander if
//it has line of sight
if(_ufo.playerIsVisible
&& magnitude > 1)
{
   _ufo.vx += dx * 0.1;
   _ufo.vy += dy * 0.1;
}
```

The vector between the objects needs to be plotted from their centers in order for it to be accurate. The code first creates four variables that work out the center x and y positions of the lander and UFO from their top-left corners, as illustrated in Figure 7-10.

```
var lander_X:int = int(_lander.xPos + _lander.width * 0.5);
var lander_Y:int = int(_lander.yPos + _lander.height * 0.5);
var ufo_X:int = int(_ufo.xPos + _ufo.width * 0.5);
var ufo_Y:int = int(_ufo.yPos + _ufo.height * 0.5);
```

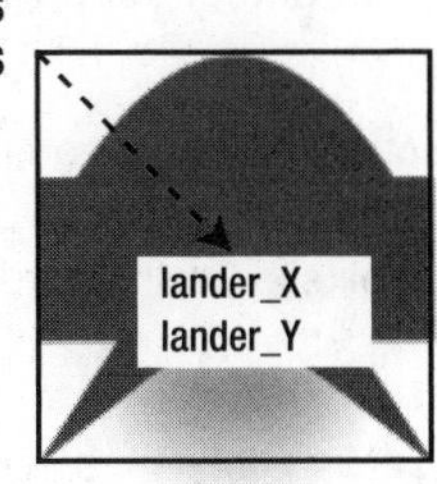

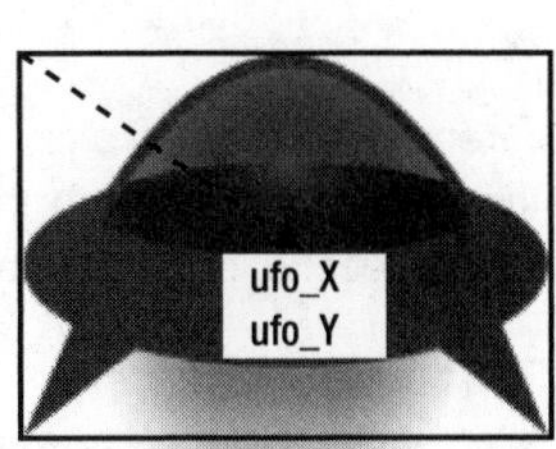

Figure 7-10. Find the center points of the objects.

Next, the code creates a distance vector between the lander and UFO's center x and y positions, calculates its magnitude, and figures out the unit vector (the `dx` and `dy`).

```
var vx:Number = lander_X - ufo_X;
var vy:Number = lander_Y - ufo_Y;
var magnitude:Number = Math.sqrt(vx * vx + vy * vy);
var dx:Number = vx / magnitude;
var dy:Number = vy / magnitude;
```

These are all the standard vector calculations that we covered in Chapter 2.

We need to figure out how much space should be between each point along the vector. I've called these spaces between the points **segments**. Each segment should be no longer than the smallest thing that the UFO needs to find. In this case, the segment will be the width of the lander. You can see these segments in Figure 7-8.

```
var segment:int = _lander.width;
```

We then figure out how many points we'll need along the vector.

```
var numberOfPoints:uint = uint(magnitude / segment);
```

If the vector is 100 pixels long, and each segment is 10 pixels, we'll have 10 points that we'll need to check.

Next, we create a while loop that will run for as many times as we have points

```
var counter:int = 0;
while (counter++ != numberOfPoints)
{…
```

Every repetition of the loop will check for a collision between one of the points along the vector and the asteroid.

Each time the loop repeats, it creates a point along the vector in the direction of the lander. In the first loop, the distance of this point from the UFO will be one times the width of the lander, or about 30 pixels. On the second loop, it will be twice that: 60 pixels. On the third loop, it will be 90.

```
while (counter++ != numberOfPoints)
{
  //Scale the vector to the size of one segment,
  //multiplied by the current counter value
  var vectorLength:int = segment * counter;

  //Create a Point object at the end of the vector
  var point:Point
    = new Point
    (
      ufo_X + dx * vectorLength,
      ufo_Y + dy * vectorLength
    );
  //…
}
```

These points work their way along the entire length of the vector.

This works because we're using the original vector's dx and dy values to scale the vector by the amount of vectorLength. Figure 7-11 illustrates the process.

When we plot a new point on the vector, we then need to run a simple collision test against the point and the asteroid. If the point hits the asteroid, then we know the lander won't be visible, and we can quit the loop.

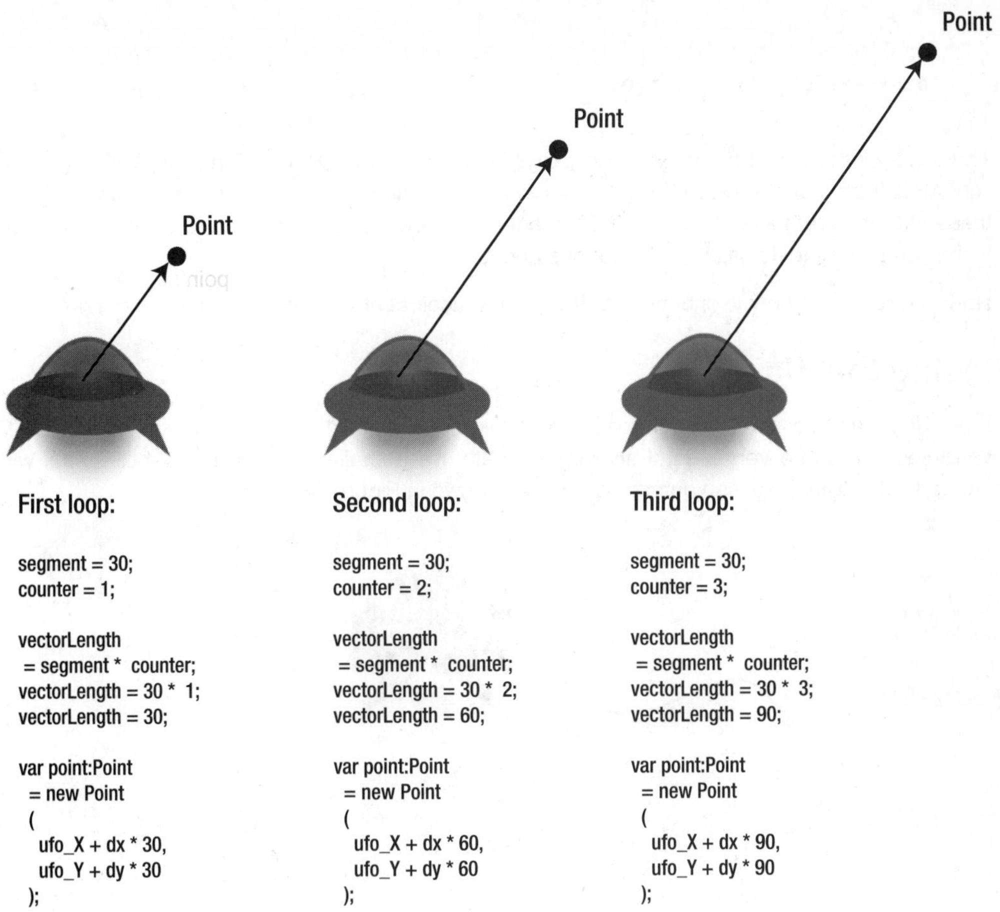
Point
Point
Point
First loop:
segment = 30;
counter = 1;
vectorLength
= segment * counter;
vectorLength = 30 * 1;
vectorLength = 30;
var point:Point
= new Point
(
ufo_X + dx * 30,
ufo_Y + dy * 30
);
Second loop:
segment = 30;
counter = 2;
vectorLength
= segment * counter;
vectorLength = 30 * 2;
vectorLength = 60;
var point:Point
= new Point
(
ufo_X + dx * 60,
ufo_Y + dy * 60
);
Third loop:
segment = 30;
counter = 3;
vectorLength
= segment * counter;
vectorLength = 30 * 3;
vectorLength = 90;
var point:Point
= new Point
(
ufo_X + dx * 90,
ufo_Y + dy * 90
);

Figure 7-11. The while loop uses the dx and dy values of the vector between the objects to place points at ever-increasing positions along the vector.

```
if(_asteroidBitmapData.hitTest
    (
      new Point(_asteroidBitmap.x, _asteroidBitmap.y),
      255,
      point
    )
  )
{
  _ufo.playerIsVisible = false;
  break;
}
```

```
else
{
  _ufo.playerIsVisible = true;
}
```

The _ufo model has a property called playerIsVisible. When it's true, the UFO's glowing light turns from green to red. The UFO also switches on its thruster when it's flying upward. Both these features are handled by the UFO's model and view classes, so be sure to check them out in the source for the details if you're curious about how they work.

Now that you know how to find the line of sight, let's look at how to use that information.

Chasing the player

If the UFO can see the lander, it goes into attack mode and flies toward it. If you run the SWF, you'll see it flies in a very natural and organic path. It's a challenge to evade the UFO, but with enough fancy flying, you can outmaneuver it, as shown in Figure 7-12.

Figure 7-12. The UFO chases the lander by changing its position each frame based on the distance vector between them.

The end result looks complex and eerily lifelike, but it's all done using an extremely simple easing calculation.

```
if(_ufo.playerIsVisible
&& magnitude > 1)
{
  _ufo.vx += dx * 0.1;
  _ufo.vy += dy * 0.1;
}
```

It's calculating the shortest path between the UFO and the lander based on the distance vector, and pushing the UFO's velocity in the correct direction. But the final effect is complex because the distance vector is changing each frame, and friction and acceleration are also at play.

This is a simple and effective chase engine, and for most games, it will probably be all you need. However, you could always throw more variables into the mix to keep the game unpredictable. Here are a few ideas:

- Have the enemy attack only if the player is within a certain radius of it. You'll see an example of this in the case study coming up next.
- Add some randomness to the distance vector between the objects so that the enemy's path is less precise.
- Vary the enemy's speed of attack, and possibly work out a system for determining when the enemy gets tired. Perhaps it could become confused if the player does a bit of fancy flying.

There are many possibilities, but effective enemy AI always comes down to simple logic and a lot of experimentation. In Chapter 9, we'll return to the subject of line of sight and pathfinding, and discover how to navigate complex maze environments.

Case study: Escape!

We've covered a lot of exciting techniques so far. In fact, you now have everything you need at your fingertips to build some very complex games. To give you an idea of what's possible, I've created a sample game prototype called Escape! You'll find it in the `Escape` folder in the chapter's source files.

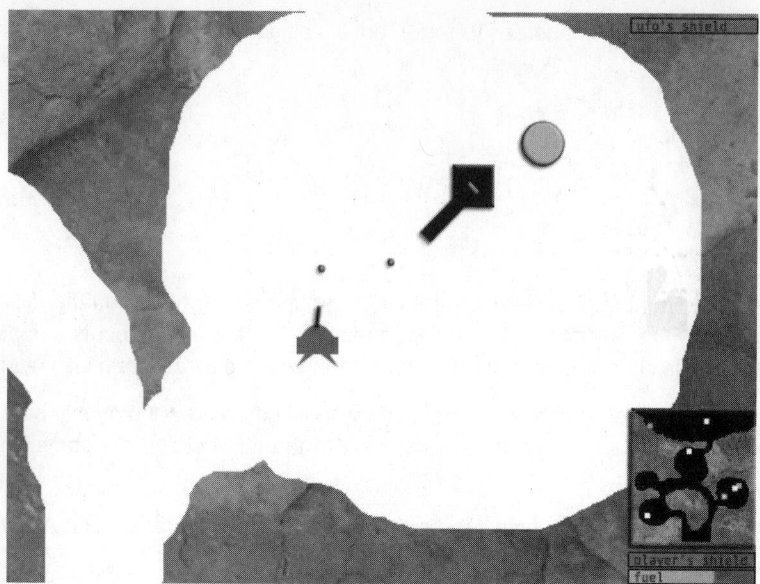

Figure 7-13. Escape! A game prototype combining all the techniques we've covered so far

It's a classic cave-flyer style game, as shown in Figure 7-13, and concludes the plot that we've been gradually developing. Our poor lander has been captured by the UFO and imprisoned deep under the planet's surface. To make matters worse, the lander's cannon has been taken away, leaving it without any defenses. How will it escape? Play the game and see if you can find the cannon, escape from the cave, and destroy the UFO mother ship on the planet's surface before you run out of fuel or shield power. Figure 7-14 illustrates how to play through the game.

Escape! uses all the techniques that we've covered in the book so far:

- Scrolling
- Mini-map
- Bitmap collision detection
- Destructible environment
- Sound effects and music
- Particle explosions
- Game management: collecting objects, managing weapons, fuel and shields

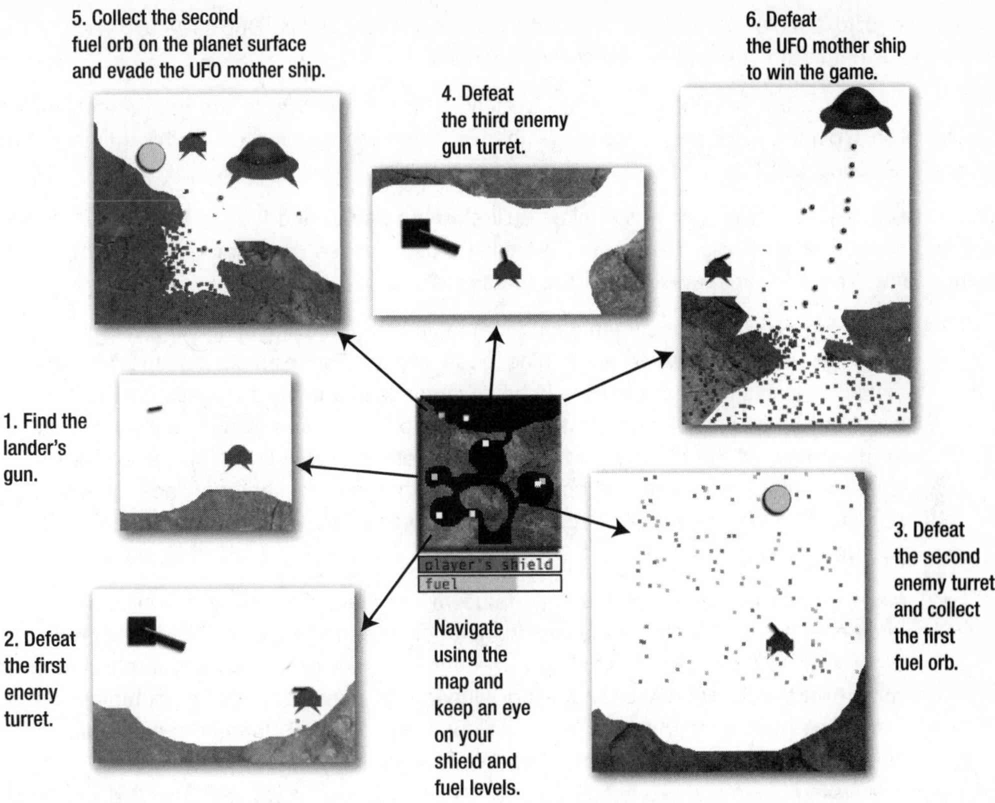

Figure 7-14. Escape from the underground cave by collecting fuel orbs, destroying enemies, and finding your way to the planet surface.

It also introduces two new techniques:

- Multiple game screens
- AI systems for the rotating enemy gun turrets and the UFO mother ship

Escape! is a prototype model for a sci-fi arcade game. You could easily apply the techniques and concepts to build a fantasy role-playing action game, too.

This game has the most complex game structure in the book. We'll start by examining this structure.

Structure: your best friend and worst enemy

I've purposely made Escape! very complex to help illustrate how you can manage complexity in a game project. As I mentioned earlier in the book, "monstrous complexity" is what game designers refer to as "normal complexity." We need to confront it head on. Escape! uses a structure that can be extended to handle any degree of added complexity and detail. But as you'll see, all the components of this structure will be comfortingly familiar.

The entire game is built around a big MVC system, which is identical to the game template we looked at in Chapter 4. However, because there's much more going on in this game, many tasks—like sound, scrolling, and collision—have been delegated to subclasses.

When designing a complex game like this, you'll always need to find the right balance between keeping code together in big classes and breaking those classes down into smaller, abstracted components. There are advantages and disadvantages to both tactics:

- **A few big classes**: If you keep code together in long, rambling classes, you'll always know where to look when something goes wrong. For example, for most of the examples in this book, I've tried to keep all the code in one big application class. This is because if you haven't written the code yourself, it can sometimes be very difficult to grasp how all the different classes work together. However, if you have a really complex game, you could end up with classes that are thousands of lines long, and scrolling through them could become an insufferable chore. You'll soon forget what you were looking for and why.
- **Many small classes**: If you break code down into many little classes, you'll need to remember exactly how those classes work together and share data. If you don't have a good idea of this and don't stick to a consistent set of naming and architecture conventions right from the beginning, debugging could become a nightmare. If something goes wrong, you'll need to follow a trail of scant clues from one class to the next, and hope that you've remembered how you put everything together.

I've taken a pretty conservative, middle-of-the-road approach to structuring Escape!. The discipline of using MVC as a skeletal framework is helpful in reminding me which classes do what. If I have a doubt, I just ask myself, "Hmmm… is displaying the map on the stage the job of the model, view, or controller? It's the job of the view!" Because I understand the well-defined responsibilities of each class, it's easy to find what I need.

But at a certain point, this starts to break down. For example, the job of the controller is to handle all the game logic. That makes sense, but game logic happens to be extremely complex in this game (and in most games). It involves not just tracking shield and fuel levels, but all these jobs as well:

- Playing sounds
- Detecting collisions
- Managing the scrolling of all the objects on the stage

These jobs are very well defined. It makes sense to have dedicated classes that do these things. But how can we make a lot of new classes while still maintaining the structure of the MVC? The answer is to create helper classes for the main MVC classes.

Creating a simple helper class

A **helper class** is a specialized class that helps the main class do its job. You've already seen a number of helper classes in this book: the performance manager class and explosion manager classes from Chapter 6 are examples.

Here's an example of how you could create a helper class to play game sounds. The `GameController` can create an instance of a `SoundController` helper class that does all the work of playing sounds. Whenever it needs to play a sound, it asks this class to do the job of playing it. The `GameController` class might look like this:

```
package
{
  public class GameController
  {
    public function GameController(gameModel:GameModel):void
    {
      //Create the Sound Controller object
      private var _sound:SoundController = new SoundController(gameModel);

      stage.addEventListener(Event.ENTER_FRAME, enterFrameHandler);
    }

    private function enterFrameHandler(event:Event):void
    {
      if(there's a collision)
      {
        //Use the SoundController object to play the sound
        _sound.smallExplosion();
      }
    }
  }
}
```

The `Controller` class creates an instance of the `SoundController`, and sends it a reference of the `GameModel`. The `SoundController` class might look like this:

```
package
{
  import flash.media.Sound;
  import flash.media.SoundChannel;

  public class SoundController
  {
    //Explosion sound
    [Embed(source="../assets/sounds/smallExplosion.mp3")]
    private var SmallExplosion:Class;
    private var _smallExplosion:Sound = new SmallExplosion();
    private var _smallExplosionChannel:SoundChannel;
      = new SoundChannel();
```

```
    public function SoundController(gameModel:GameModel):void
    {
      //Use the gameModel to access any game data if needed
    }
    public function smallExplosion():void
    {
      _smallExplosionChannel = _smallExplosion.play();
    }
  }
}
```

You can see that all the functionality for playing sounds is now the responsibility of the `SoundController` helper class. The main `Controller` class doesn't need to know anything about how to actually play sounds or what those sounds are.

If the main `Controller` class wants to play a sound, all it needs to do is this:

```
_sound.smallExplosion();
```

Figure 7-15 illustrates the relationship between the two classes. As you can see, there's nothing complex about creating a helper class like this. It's very similar to how we created and used the `ExplosionManager` class in the previous chapter. It's basic OOP, but it neatly solves the problem of needing to delegate responsibilities to other classes while still maintaining a clear structure. You can pile on as many of these helper classes as you need—even hundreds—without breaking the essential elegance of the underlying MVC system.

GameController
_sound = new SoundController(gameModel);
_sound.explosion;
SoundController
public function explosion():void
{
_soundChannel= _explosion.play();
}

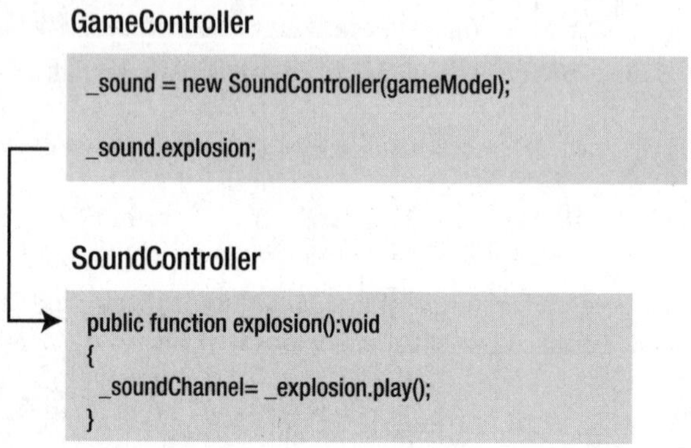

Figure 7-15. Offload responsibilities to helper classes

> *From a technical MVC standpoint, the `SoundController` class in this example is actually a combined **view/controller**. It imports sounds, which are a type of view, but also contains the logic to play them. It's very common to have combination view/controller classes if the view and controller are very closely linked. View/controller classes are also often used for classes that contain buttons. If you don't need to separate the view and controller, keep them together.*

In this example, the classes communicate using public methods, but you could just as effectively dispatch events to communicate if you prefer.

Structuring Escape!

Escape! is structured using the basic MVC game template from Chapter 4, and then creating helper classes as needed for each of the three main classes. Figure 7-16 shows the classes used and how they relate to each other. (In addition to these classes, the game uses classes in the `com.friendsofed.gameElements` folder to create the enemy turrets, UFO, and the explosions.)

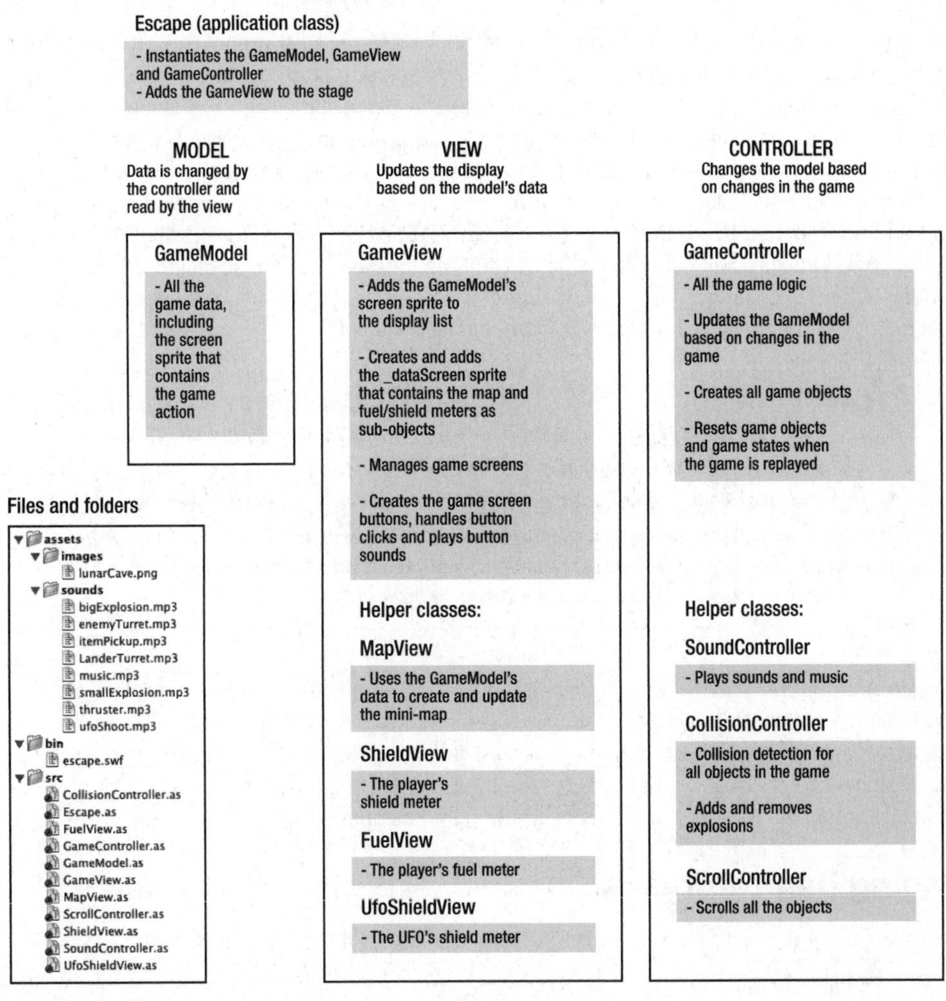

Figure 7-16. Classes, files, and folders used to structure Escape!

If someone had shown me Figure 7-16 before I started coding the game and said, "Make your game like this," I would have burst into tears. It looks complex, and that's because it is complex. But you'll be happy to know that I didn't plan any of this before I started building the game. In fact, I had no idea how the final structure was going to turn out until I was finished with it. I just added new classes as I thought I needed them, testing things as I went, and this is the end result.

But if you wipe away your tears for a moment and take a closer look at Figure 7-16, you'll notice that it's really nothing more than a very straightforward and strict implementation of the MVC. It's exactly the same structure that we've been using since Chapter 1. The only difference is that responsibilities have been distributed to additional helper classes.

This diagram only makes sense to me now, after I've finished the game. This is good news! It means you can do the same with your games. As long as you understand the MVC structure and how to build helper classes, just start coding. Use the game template from Chapter 4 and start from there. Experiment with new game ideas as you go, and keep what you like. You don't need to plan anything, think about the final structure, or draw any diagrams. Just begin with something very simple and add helper classes as you need them, for whatever seems appropriate. You might end up with a structure that looks like Figure 7-16, or it might look very different. However it turns out, the structure will naturally fall into place, as long as you're disciplined about sticking to the rules of the MVC pattern. This makes creating games organic and spontaneous, like writing a novel or composing music. You'll find your own individual style.

> *Many programmers use Unified Modeling Language (UML) models to help them plan complex programs. UML is a standard way of visually drawing your program as a flowchart of interconnected classes. It's a great way of getting a complete overview map of your entire program on one page. If you're working on a very complex project, taking a bit of time to learn UML will help you from getting lost in your own code. A simple web search will bring up many helpful resources to help you learn how to make UML diagrams.*

It's quite normal that your view classes will be among your most complex, and this game is a good example of this. Not only does the `GameView` need to manage three different game screens, but it also contains an intricate mini-map as well as level meters for the shields and fuel. These are all the responsibility of the `GameView`, and there's a lot that it needs to keep track of. So let's take a closer look at how the `GameView` is creating this complex display.

Managing game screens

Escape! uses three main game screens to control the flow of the game, as shown in Figure 7-17:

- The start screen, with the **`Play Game`** button
- The main game screen, including the game level, map, fuel, and shield displays
- The game-over screen, with the **`Play Again`** button (this displays either "You won!" or "You lost!" depending on the outcome of the game)

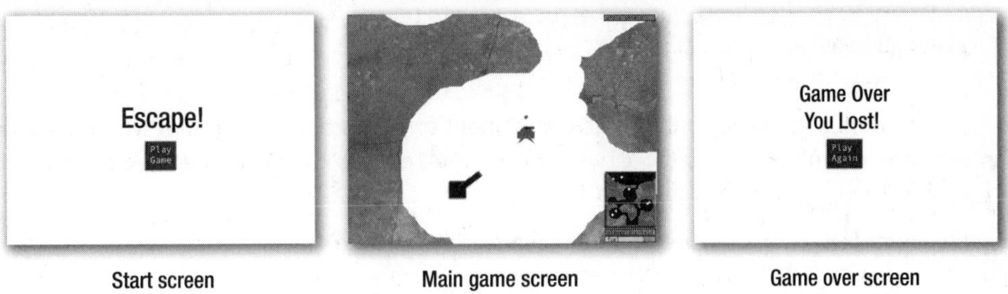

Figure 7-17. The three game screens

All three screens are sprites that are created and managed *inside* the GameView class. Remember that the GameView class is the only object that has been instantiated on the stage, so it is in the privileged position to be able to decide what is displayed on the stage and when. Figure 7-18 illustrates how all these display relationships fit together.

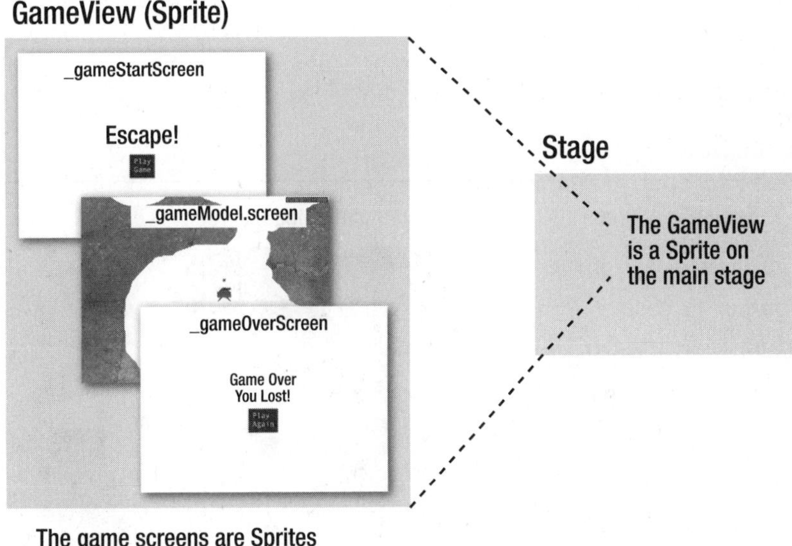

Figure 7-18. The GameView is a Sprite object on the stage, but the game screens are Sprite objects in the GameView. The GameView switches the game screens as needed, depending on the status of the game.

When the game starts, the GameView creates these three screens as sprites. It then adds the start screen and game screen to the display list:

```
//1. Add the start screen
addChild(_gameStartScreen);
```

```
//2. Add the game screen, but make it invisible
addChild(_gameModel.screen);
_gameModel.screen.visible = false;
```

The game screen is invisible so that it has a moment to initialize. It means that when the **Play Game** button is clicked and calls the `displayGameHandler`, the `GameView` just needs to set the main game screen's `visible` property to `true`.

```
private function displayGameHandler(event:Event):void
{
  //Remove the game start screen
  removeChild(_gameStartScreen);

  //Make the main game screen visible
  _gameModel.screen.visible = true;

  //...

  //Return focus to the stage
  stage.focus = stage;
}
```

It also removes the start screen. Figure 7-19 illustrates this.

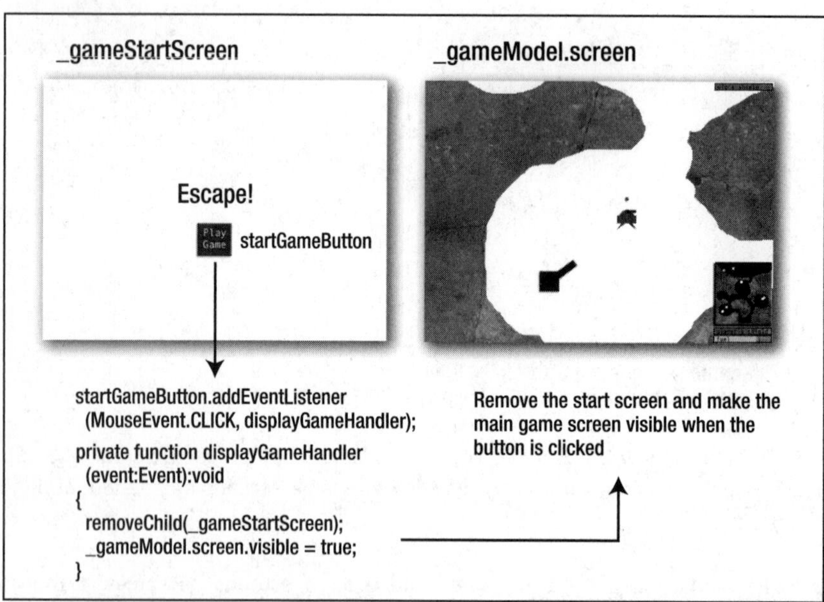

Figure 7-19. Clicking the button removes the start screen and displays the main game screen.

A little technical detail to take care of is that the code also needs to return **focus** to the main stage.

```
stage.focus = stage;
```

When an object has `focus`, it's sensitive to mouse and keyboard input. Whenever you click something, like a button, AS3.0 automatically gives it focus. But when the game screen is displayed, the new screen doesn't have focus because it hasn't been clicked yet. That means you won't be able to fly the lander around the cave without first clicking the stage. The preceding code gives the game screen the focus it needs. It means that the game screen will immediately be sensitive to the mouse and keyboard, without the player needing to click it first.

At the end of the game, the game screens are switched in a similar way. After the final showdown with the UFO mother ship, the game-over screen is displayed. How does the `GameView` know that the game is over?

Remember that the `GameView` is always listening for `CHANGE` events in the `GameModel`. If the `GameModel` sets its `gameOver` property to `true`, the `GameView` knows that it can display the game-over screen.

```
private function changeHandler(event:Event):void
{
  if(_gameModel.gameOver)
{
    //Make the game screen invisible
    _gameModel.screen.visible = false;

    //Add the game over screen
    addChild(_gameOverScreen);
}
}
```

It very simply makes the game screen invisible and adds the game-over screen, as shown in Figure 7-20.

The main game screen isn't removed or destroyed, because it might still be needed if the player wants to play again. If you know that an object is going to be used again in a game, find other ways of taking it out of the game without using `removeChild`. This makes it easier to reuse the object, and saves a bit of CPU power and memory, because the object doesn't need to be destroyed and re-created.

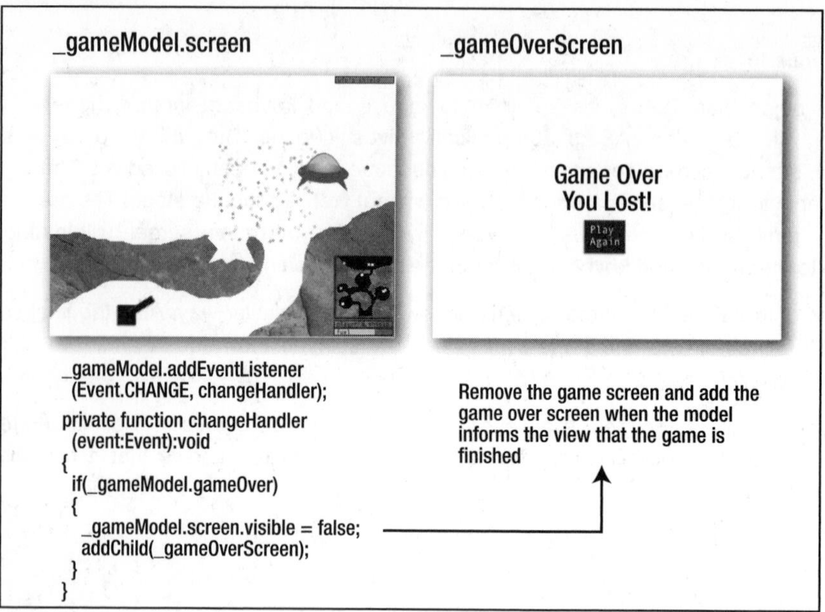
GameView
_gameModel.screen
_gameOverScreen
Game Over
You Lost!
Play Again
_gameModel.addEventListener
(Event.CHANGE, changeHandler);
private function changeHandler
(event:Event):void
{
if(_gameModel.gameOver)
{
_gameModel.screen.visible = false;
addChild(_gameOverScreen);
}
}
Remove the game screen and add the game over screen when the model informs the view that the game is finished

Figure 7-20. When the game finishes, the main game screen is made invisible and the game over screen is displayed.

When the player clicks the **Play Again** button, the game-over screen is removed, and the main game screen is made visible again. The `GameView` also calls the `GameController's resetGame` method, which resets the game values to their initial states.

Delaying the game-over screen

I actually oversimplified the explanation of how the game-over screen is displayed in the previous section. When you play the game, you'll notice that the game-over screen appears 2 seconds after the game finishes. This gives the player a chance to watch the final explosion before the screens are switched.

It's very common for games to delay displaying the game-over screen so that final animations or sounds have a chance to play to completion. In Escape!, the delay is handled in the `GameView` with a simple `Timer` event. The timer is initialized to 2 seconds

```
private var _timer:Timer = new Timer(2000);
```

When the `GameModel` sends a `CHANGE` event, the `GameView` adds a listener to the timer and starts it.

```
private function changeHandler(event:Event):void
{
  if(_gameModel.gameOver)
  {
    _timer.addEventListener
      (TimerEvent.TIMER, displayGameOverHandler);
    _timer.start();
  }
}
```

After a pause of 2 seconds, the `displayGameOverHandler` is called. It tells the `GameController` to display the game-over screen, reset the timer to zero so that it can be used again, and remove the timer's event listener.

```
private function displayGameOverHandler(event:TimerEvent):void
{
  _gameModel.screen.visible = false;
  addChild(_gameOverScreen);

  _timer.removeEventListener
    (TimerEvent.TIMER, displayGameOverHandler);
  _timer.reset();
}
```

There's nothing technically difficult about any of this; it's very basic programming and logic. You should find it quite easy to implement multiple game screens like this in your own games. Keep this basic structure in mind, and you can't go wrong.

Multiple views of the game data

The great strength of the MVC framework is that the data is completely separate from the display. You can display the same data in many different ways, without changing or corrupting that underlying data. What you see on the stage is just a visual interpretation of data.

The main game screen of Escape! displays a lot of data. Not only does it display the action in the game, but it shows the mini-map and the shield and fuel meters. All of this is displayed by the `GameView`.

Remember that the job of a view class is to mindlessly read data from the model. The mini-map, the meters, and the game itself are just based on the model's data. As long as the `GameView` class has access to the `GameModel`, it can use that data to create the display. The only logic in the `GameView` is the logic it needs to create and manage these different displays.

All of these displays are quite complex. It would be impractical to cram them into one big class. So Escape! distributes the work among a few different helper classes. Figure 7-21 shows which components of the `GameView` are handled by helper classes.

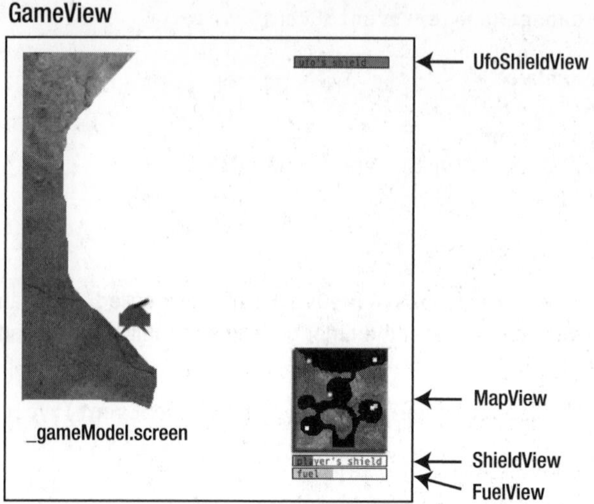

Figure 7-21. The GameView has helper view classes that display the GameModel's data in different ways.

Because the helper classes are themselves views, they all need a reference to the `GameModel`. So when the `GameView` creates a helper class, it sends it a reference to the `GameModel` in the constructor arguments.

```
var mapView:MapView = new MapView(_gameModel, _stage);
```

Some of the helper views also need a reference to the stage so that they can work out their sizes and positions using the stage's `stageHeight` and `stageWidth` properties.

> *If you browse through the `GameView` class in the source files, you'll notice that all the helper views are contained within a sprite called `_dataDisplay`. Keeping them all together in one sprite makes it easier to add and remove them from the display as a single unit. This is entirely optional.*

Again, this is basic OOP and basic MVC. You can break down each visual component into a helper class so that you declutter the main `GameView` class. This keeps everything organized and more readable, because you won't need to hunt through reams and reams of code to find the section of code relating to the mini-map or fuel meter, for example. If you delegate tasks to helper classes logically and use consistent naming conventions, you'll make it easy to find the relevant sections of code.

This structure is a good place to start for building views that need to display a lot of data, such as for a fantasy role-playing game. In a classic role-playing game, you might need a large number of view classes to display the game data, as well as an equally large number of game screens.

You'll probably need to keep track of these data display screens in arrays, and build a little mini-application to help you to display them when needed. But the basic format for reading and displaying that data, as well as keeping your classes organized, will be the same as in this example.

New enemy AI techniques

The other new feature of Escape! is the twist it takes on enemy AI:

- The enemy gun turrets wait until the player is within range, and then fires.
- The UFO mother ship follows a fixed elliptical path across the planet surface. It also fires only when the player comes within range.

You'll find all the code for these enemies in the `turret` and `ufo` folders in the `com.friendsofed.gamelements` package. I'll walk you through how these enemy AI systems work and communicate with the rest of the game.

Lying in wait

The enemy turrets lie in wait until the lander comes to within a radius of 300 pixels.

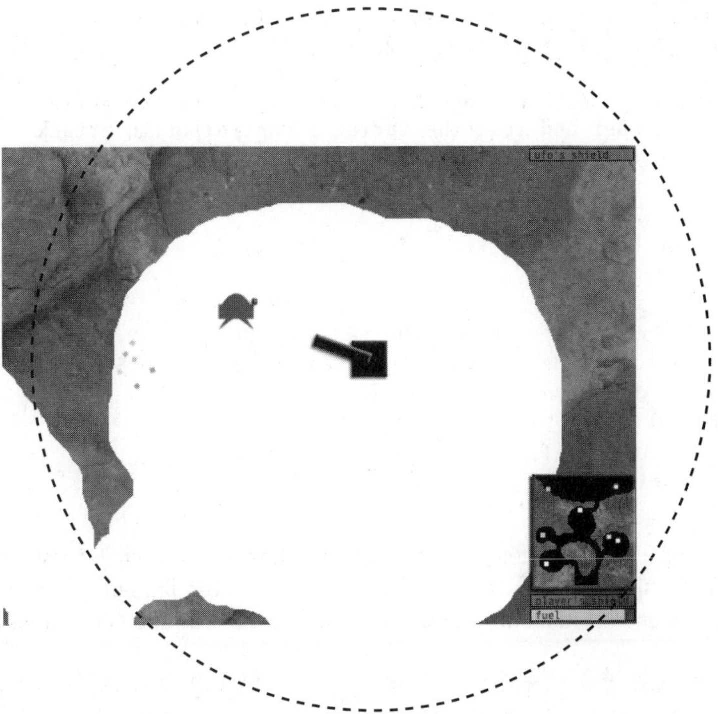

Figure 7-22. The enemy turrets attack when the lander comes within a 300-pixel radius.

The enemy turrets are an MVC system. The turret models have two important properties that indicate the enemy (the lander) and attack range (300 pixels).

```
public var enemy:Object;
public var attackRange:int = 300;
```

The turret's `enemy` property is assigned when the turret is created by the `GameController`.

The turret's view listens for `CHANGE` events from its `enemy` property (the lander).

```
_turretModel.enemy.addEventListener
  (Event.CHANGE, changeHandler);
```

When it detects a change in the lander's position, it uses a basic distance calculation to check whether the lander is within range.

```
private function changeHandler(event:Event):void
{
  var enemy:Object = _turretModel.enemy;

  //Create the vector
  var vx:Number = enemy.xPos - _turretModel.xPos;
  var vy:Number = enemy.yPos - _turretModel.yPos;

  //Calculate the distance (the vector's magnitude)
  var distance:int = Math.sqrt(vx * vx + vy * vy);

  //If the lander is within range and visible, rotate the turret
  //toward the lander and tell the turret's controller to attack
  if(distance < _turretModel.attackRange
  && enemy.visible)
  {
    var angle:Number
      = Math.atan2
      (
        _turretModel.yPos - enemy.yPos - enemy.height * 0.5,
        _turretModel.xPos - enemy.xPos - enemy.width * 0.5
      );
    _turretModel.angle = angle;
    _controller.attack();
  }
}
```

The turret's controller doesn't actually fire any bullets. The turret's controller just "arms" the turret so that it's ready to fire, and sets the turret model's `fireBullet` property `true`. To add a bit of variation, a timer is used to randomly set the fire time between 200 and 1000 milliseconds.

Here's the important section of the code that sets the `fireBullet` property to `true`:

```
internal function attack():void
{
  var fireTime:Number;

  if(!_turretArmed)
  {
    if(_turretModel.randomFire)
    {
      //Figure out the random fire time, which will be
      //a number between 200 and 1000 milliseconds.
      //(The _turretModel.fireFrequency propery has a
      //default value of 1000 milliseconds)
      fireTime
        = Math.round(Math.random() * turretModel.fireFrequency) + 200;
      }
      _timer = new Timer(fireTime);
           _timer.addEventListener
        (TimerEvent.TIMER, timerEventHandler);
      _timer.start();
    }
    _turretArmed = true;
  }
  private function timerEventHandler(event:TimerEvent):void
  {
    //When the timer finishes, set the turret model's
    //fireBullets property to true.
    //This gives the GameController permission
    //to add bullets to the stage. The turret itself
    //doesn't fire any bullets.
    //The GameController does the actual job of adding,
    //managing and removing the bullets in the game.

    _turretModel.fireBullet = true;
    _turretArmed = false;
    _timer.removeEventListener(TimerEvent.TIMER, timerEventHandler);
  }
```

The turret's model dispatches a `CHANGE` event when the value of `fireBullet` becomes `true`.

```
public function set fireBullet(value:Boolean):void
{
  _fireBullet = value;
  dispatchEvent(new Event(Event.CHANGE));
}
```

The `GameController` is listening for this `CHANGE` event. It adds a bullet to the stage and positions it at the end point of the turret. The `Game Controller` is the only object that adds and removes objects in the game.

```
private function turretChangeHandler(event:Event):void
{
  for(var i:int = 0; i < _gameModel.turretModels.length; i++)
  {
    if(event.target == _gameModel.turretModels[i])
    {
      var turret:TurretAIModel = _gameModel.turretModels[i];

      if(turret.fireBullet
      && turret.visible)
      {
          //Create the bullet model and push
          //it into the GameModel's bulletModels array
          var bulletModel:CircleModel = new CircleModel(2);
          _gameModel.bulletModels.push(bulletModel);

          //Position the bullet model at the end of the turret
          //and give it an initial velocity
          bulletModel.setX
             = turret.xPos - turret.width * Math.cos(turret.angle);
          bulletModel.setY
             = turret.yPos - turret.width * Math.sin(turret.angle);
          bulletModel.vx = Math.cos(turret.angle) * -5;
          bulletModel.vy = Math.sin(turret.angle) * -5;
          bulletModel.friction = 1;

          //Add the bullet view and push it
          //into the GameModel's bulletViews array
          var bulletView:CircleBlockView
             = new CircleBlockView(bulletModel);
          _gameModel.screen.addChild(bulletView);
          _gameModel.bulletViews.push(bulletView);

          //Play the sound
          _sound.enemyTurret();

          //Reset the turret so that it can fire again
          turret.fireBullet = false;
      }
    }
  }
}
```

The last thing the `GameController` does is to set the turret's `fireBullet` property to `false`. This allows the turret to fire again.

You can find all the classes for the enemy turret MVC system in the `com.friendsofed.gameElements.turret` package. It's composed of these three classes: `TurretAIModel`, `TurretAIView`, and `TurretAIController`.

Figure 7-23 illustrates how all these classes work together to help the enemy turrets fire bullets. The enemy turrets are self-contained MVC systems. The game itself is also a self-contained MVC system. These two systems communicate by using events and public properties. There is some dependency, but it's well defined by the mechanics of the MVC structure.

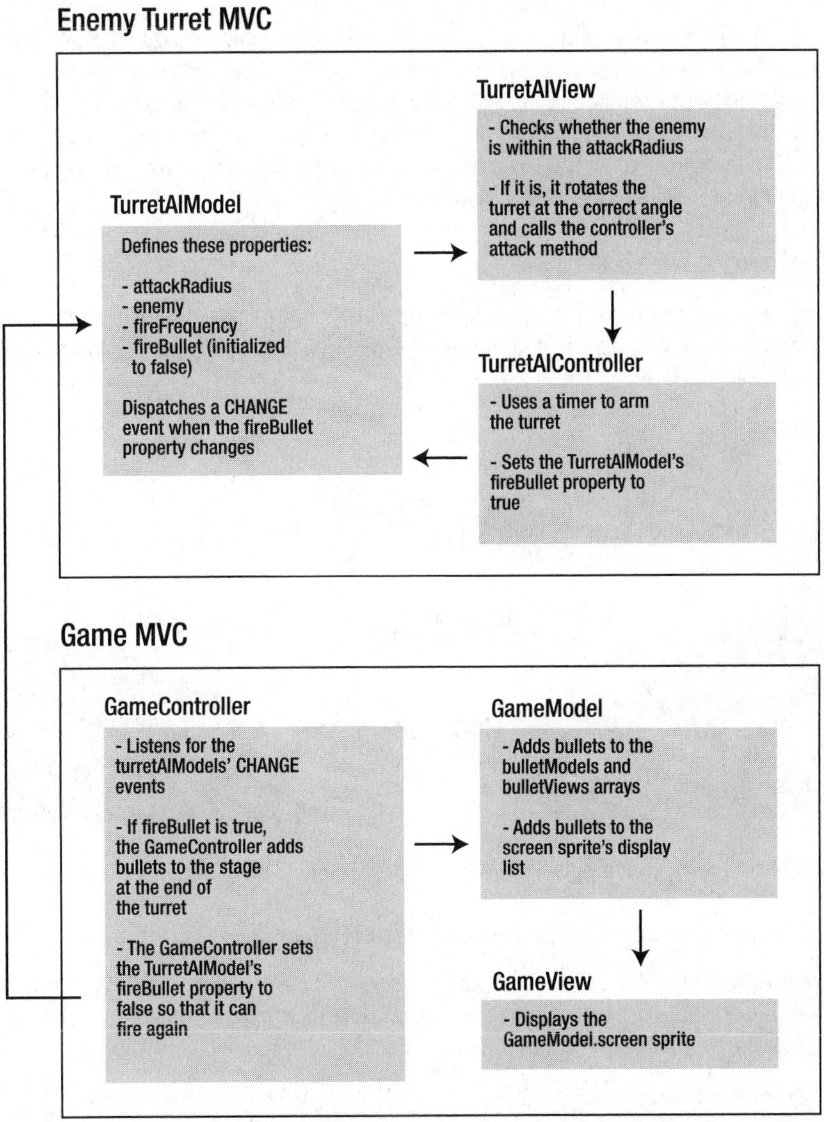

Enemy Turret MVC
TurretAIView
- Checks whether the enemy is within the attackRadius
- If it is, it rotates the turret at the correct angle and calls the controller's attack method
TurretAIModel
Defines these properties:
- attackRadius
- enemy
- fireFrequency
- fireBullet (initialized to false)
Dispatches a CHANGE event when the fireBullet property changes
TurretAIController
- Uses a timer to arm the turret
- Sets the TurretAIModel's fireBullet property to true
Game MVC
GameController
- Listens for the turretAIModels' CHANGE events
- If fireBullet is true, the GameController adds bullets to the stage at the end of the turret
- The GameController sets the TurretAIModel's fireBullet property to false so that it can fire again
GameModel
- Adds bullets to the bulletModels and bulletViews arrays
- Adds bullets to the screen sprite's display list
GameView
- Displays the GameModel.screen sprite

Figure 7-23. The enemy turret MVC system figures out whether it should fire bullets. The GameController does the job of adding the bullets to the game.

As you know, only a controller should change a model's properties. If you look again at Figure 7-23, you'll notice that the turret actually has *two controllers*: its own `TurretAIController` and the `GameController`. It's quite acceptable for a model to have more than one controller. What's slightly unusual is that the controller is listening for a model's `CHANGE` events. In an MVC system, shouldn't it just be the view that listens for model events?

Yes, but the difference here is that the `GameController` is listening for events in a model *from an MVC system that it created itself*. The enemy turret's model, view, and controller are all objects that the `GameController` instantiates when it initializes the game. The turrets exist within the `GameController` alone as subobjects. It's not listening for events in the `GameModel`. Using events like this to allow sub-MVC systems to communicate with a parent controller is very efficient and helps reduce dependencies between them.

Traveling along a fixed path

The UFO mother ship uses the same system as the enemy turrets to fire bullets at the lander. However, unlike the turrets, it's moving. It flies in a fixed elliptical path across the planet surface, as shown in Figure 7-24.

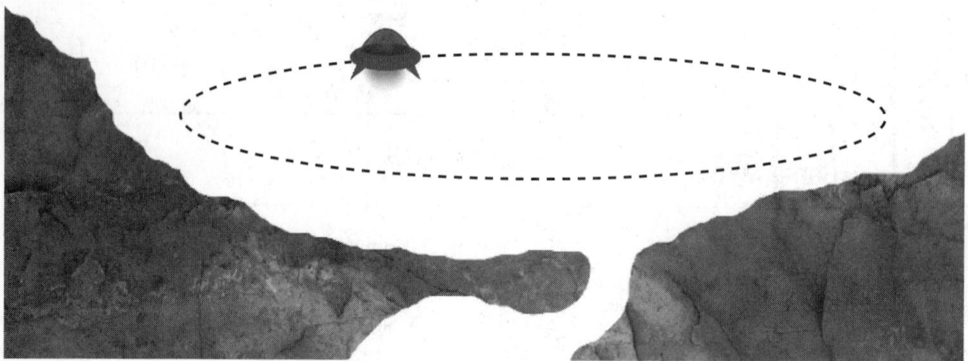

Figure 7-24. The enemy mother ship travels in a fixed elliptical path above the planet surface.

Two pairs of values determine the position and shape of the ellipse:

- `centerX`/`centerY`: You need to know where on the stage the center of the ellipse will be—the `centerX` and `centerY` values. For example, to place the center of the ellipse in the center of the stage, use these two values:

```
centerX = 275;
centerY = 200;
```

- `rangeX/rangeY`: You need to know how wide and how high the ellipse will be. I call this `rangeX` and `rangeY`. For example, if you want the ellipse to be 400 pixels wide and 200 pixels high, use these two values:

  ```
  rangeX = 200;
  rangeY = 100;
  ```

  This is similar to a radius, but unlike a circle's radius, the width and height are not the same.

Figure 7-25 shows what kind of ellipse you would end up with if you used these values.

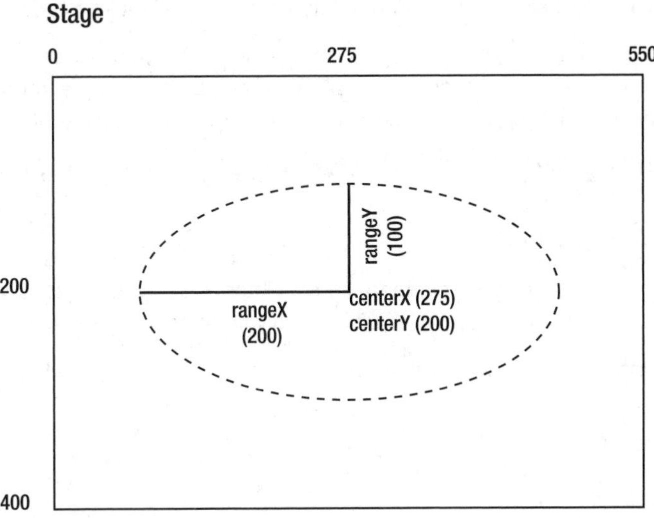

Figure 7-25. An ellipse positioned at the center of the stage.

These four values are properties of the UFO model. The `GameController` sets them when the game initializes.

```
//Set the center point for the UFO's elliptical flight path
_ufoModel.centerX = _caveBitmap.x + 800;
_ufoModel.centerY = _caveBitmap.y + 200;

//Set the range of the UFO's elliptical flight path
_ufoModel.rangeX = 500;
_ufoModel.rangeY = 50;
```

This places the center of the ellipse near the top of the scrolling background, above the planet surface. The ellipse is long and narrow, so the UFO traverses a complete flight path of 1000 pixels from left to right.

The UFO's model has a method called fly that moves the UFO along this ellipse. The GameController calls this fly method every frame to make the UFO move.

```
public function fly():void
{
  xPos = centerX + Math.sin(_angle) * rangeX;
  yPos = centerY + Math.cos(_angle) * rangeY;
  _angle += 0.01;
}
```

This is bit of very simple trigonometry that calculates the ellipse. By changing the amount by which the _angle value is incremented, you can alter the speed of the UFO. A lower number, like 0.005, will make it fly more slowly. A larger number, like 0.02, will make it move more quickly.

This is a useful bit of code that you can use whenever you want to make an object fly on a fixed orbit. You can also dynamically change the ellipse's center and range properties based on changing game conditions. This will give the object a very organic, natural-looking motion.

You'll find all the code for the UFO in the com.friendsofed.gameElements.ufo package.

Managing game states

There is a widely used system to manage game states that, while not used in Escape!, is something that you should know about it. You'll probably find a use for it at some point.

What is a **game state**? It's what the game is currently busy doing. Escape! has three main game states:

- Waiting to start
- Game running
- Game over

It could be important that objects in your game know about these game states. And you might want to run certain blocks of code only during a specific state.

You can define any game states you think you might need as constants in the GameModel.

```
public const STATE_WAITING:uint = 1;
public const STATE_RUNNING:uint = 2;
public const STATE_OVER:uint = 3;
//Initialize the first game state
public var state:uint = STATE_WAITING;
```

After the player clicks the start button, the GameController can change the state to show that the actual game is now running.

```
_gameModel.state = _gameModel.STATE_RUNNING;
```

The GameController can then use those states to figure out what code the game should run, depending on the current state. This typically happens in an enterFrameHandler. A switch statement figures out what the current state is and calls the appropriate method for that state.

```
private function enterFrameHandler(event:Event):void
{
  switch(_gameModel.state)
  {
    case _gameModel.STATE_WAITING:
      wait();
      break;

    case _gameModel.STATE_RUNNING:
      runGame();
      break;

    case _gameModel.STATE_OVER:
      gameOver();
      break;
  }
}
```

Each of those methods has a specialized task in the game. The enterFrameHandler will call the correct method every frame.

```
internal function wait():void
{
  //Code you want to run before the game starts
}

internal function runGame():void
{
  //All the game logic and animation
}

internal function gameOver():void
{
  //Code you want to run at the end of the game
}
```

The alternative would be to put all the code into one big enterFrameHandler and use if statements to make sure blocks of code run at the correct time, only when certain conditions are true. However, by using defined states, you put a firewall between code that should and shouldn't run at given time. It can lead to fewer errors and code that is easier to manage.

Now make your own game!

I'm actually going to suggest that you *don't* look at the complete source code for Escape! right now. It will just confuse you. It's a specific solution to a specific problem, and we've covered all the techniques it uses, with one exception: the game logic, which encompasses the conditions for winning and losing the game. But that amounts to no more than a few simple `if` statements in the `GameModel update` method. it checks the fuel and shield levels and sets the `GameModel`'s `gameOver` property to `true` if it finds the game is finished.

```
public function update():void
{
  //The game is over if the player or
  //UFO's fuel or shield
  //values drop below zero
  if(playerModel.fuel <= 0
  || playerModel.shield <= 0
  || ufoModel.shield <= 0)
  {
    gameOver = true;

    if(ufoModel.shield <= 0)
    {
      winner = "player";
    }
    else
    {
      winner = "ufo";
    }

    //Let the GameView know by dispatching a CHANGE event
    dispatchEvent(new Event(Event.CHANGE));
  }
}
```

The best way to learn how Escape! works is to build a similar game, using your own code, your own art, and your own ideas. Instead of a sci-fi action game, how about building a fantasy role-playing game or dungeon crawler? Or how about a children's action adventure game set in a garden, starring insects, flowers, and trees? The process, structure, and techniques will be the same. If you get stuck, you now have a model of a very complex game that you can use to help you detangle and organize your code.

By solving problems as you encounter them in your own game design, you'll begin to see how the solutions that I came up with for Escape! make sense. You can think of this little tour of how the game was made as a scrapbook of holiday snapshots. You can use them to help plan your own trip, but don't be afraid to find your own routes and make your own maps.

If you do have more specific questions about Escape!, you'll find the source code liberally commented and quite linear. I've erred on the side of having redundant code and keeping the methods very concrete, so that it will be easy for you to see how everything works.

Summary

Fun doesn't need to be complex or difficult. Fun just has to be fun. That's an obvious statement, of course, but fun is often the first thing that you can lose sight of in the middle of a big, technically challenging game project.

The art of video-game design is all about making the player feel in control of an alternate reality just on the other side of the screen. Our job as game designers is to build a living, breathing world that responds with relentless feedback to even the slightest user input. Noises, flashes of light, bubbling, and bursting fluffy things that cascade and ripple in patterns of color around the player—all of that makes the world come alive and make it feel like a real place. Immediate and complex responses from the game using multiple senses can instruct the player how to play the game and indicate how well they are doing. Give players enough tactile feedback, and they won't need to read any rules or keep track of their score. It all adds to that warm and tingly sense of wonder and escape that, like a good novel or film, makes games such a pleasure to play.

In this chapter, we've taken a detailed look at some of the things that make games fun to play: sound effects, music, and AI. You've seen how they can all work together in a big, very complex game project. Yes, it's possible to make fun games and have fun making them at the same time.

In the next chapter, we're going to look at a completely different game-design approach, called tile-based design. This approach lets you create game levels quickly using compact code that makes efficient use of system resources. It's an essential skill you need.

Chapter 8

Tile-Based Game Design

The game Escape! from the previous chapter was a good example of how to manage a very complex game project. However, it was a not a good example of how to avoid all that complexity in the first place. Escape! is fine as a prototype, but the code is far too specific to the particular game level for you to easily build new levels. What if you decided that you liked the idea of the game, but wanted 50 more levels of increasing complexity to add depth and replay value? You couldn't just quickly build a new level, snap it on somehow, and expect it to work. As is, the Escape! game engine just isn't flexible enough. You would need to spend a lot of time thinking about how to generalize the code to have new levels and game elements fit together like clockwork.

A far better approach to building a game prototype is to plan from the beginning that the prototype will become the final product. In fact, that almost always turns out to be the case. It's important to build prototypes and mini-test cases so that you can test how certain components of your game are working in isolation. But if you can keep one eye open for the final form that you hope your game will take, you'll save yourself a great deal of extra work and frustration.

Fortunately, the short history of video-game development has provided us with an extremely efficient and widely used system for building games: **tile-based game design** (sometimes referred to as **grid-based** game design).

In this chapter, I'm going to walk you through the process of building a tile-based game engine from scratch. I'll show you some focused examples that document each important step in building the game world. We're going to build a classic tile-based platform game, and then use those same techniques to build a car-racing game prototype with the same engine. In addition, I'll show you how to create a dynamic collision map for broad-phase collision detection.

I'm also going to use this chapter as an opportunity to demonstrate how to create a game entirely using the blit technique, which is the fastest game-display method. Blitting combined with a tile-based game engine is a match made in heaven. If you're a bit hazy about how blitting works, review the coverage of it in Chapter 6 before continuing here.

Tile-based game advantages

Tile-based systems for building games are so widely used that they've become the de facto standard approach for building games not just with Flash, but most other game-design technologies. This is true not only for 2D games, but 3D as well. Odds are that any professional games you've played have used a tile-based system, and by the time you've finished reading this chapter, you might find that most of the games you make will, too.

The tile-based system is popular because it automatically solves a number of problems that are very complex to solve by other means. Here are some of its advantages:

- **Array storage**: In tile-based games, game levels are stored in arrays. Once your tile-based engine is in place, you can add limitless numbers of new game levels quickly, just by creating new arrays to describe the levels. You can test and tweak your level design without touching the underlying game engine code, and also create visual tools for players to create their own levels.

- **Extremely efficient collision detection**: Objects check for collisions only with other objects in their immediate vicinity. This means that there's very little unnecessary checking going on, and that's a big performance savings.

- **Simplified AI**: In a tile-based world, game objects are aware of their surroundings. They can make decisions based on simple rules about what to do when their environment changes. Intricate AI behavior can often be created with code that is no more complex than one `if` statement. Pathfinding (the subject of the next chapter) is also a breeze to implement in a tile-based game world.

- **Efficient use of graphics**: Tile-based games make very efficient use of graphics by reusing as much artwork as possible. This results in small file sizes, low memory usage, and quick processing.

The concepts involved for making tile-based action games are the same as the concepts for making logic and board games. Once you understand the basic theory and techniques for building tile-based games, game projects that seem very complicated suddenly won't seem so complex anymore.

Building the game world

You'll be happy to know that in this chapter, we're going to diverge from the dark and brooding universe of sci-fi games and enter the bubbly, Technicolor world of platform and racing games.

Unsurprisingly, for a tile-based game, the first step is creating some tiles.

Making tiles

Tiles are rectangles that contain the graphics that you want to use in your game. The rectangles can be any height or width, but their size will place certain constraints on the dimensions of the stage. It's important to decide right from the beginning what size your tiles will be.

You can create tiles using any image-editing software you like, including the free GIMP image editor or Aviary, the online, Flash-based image and sound-editing suite.

All the tiles for the examples in this chapter are bitmaps that are 64 by 64 pixels. As noted in Chapter 6, computers handle bitmap sizes that are multiples of 2 very efficiently. Because of this, tile dimensions of 16 by 16, 32 by 32, and 64 by 64 are popular choices. But if you need tiles that are unusual sizes, like 23 by 77, go for it!

The tile sheet

The tiles for all the examples in this chapter are stored in a single 256-by-256 square bitmap image—the tile sheet—as shown in Figure 8-1. You'll find this in the `images` folder of the chapter's source files. I created all these game characters and objects individually using Adobe Illustrator, and then used Adobe Fireworks to scale them down to size and put together the single composite PNG file.

> *When working in Fireworks, I selected **`Show grid`** from the **`View`** menu and edited the grid settings so that each cell was 64 by 64 pixels. This made it easy to position each tile in the correct place. I also made sure that the background was transparent.*

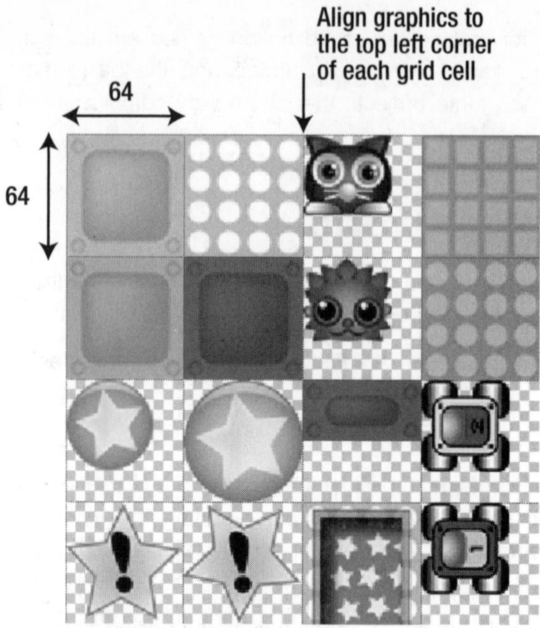

Figure 8-1. The tile sheet in Adobe Fireworks. All the game objects and environment graphics are contained in the cells of a single bitmap image called a tile sheet.

You can also see from Figure 8-1 that the images in the tiles are all different shapes and sizes. The 64-by-64 dimension is only the *maximum size* that a tile should be. Notice that images in the tiles that are smaller than the maximum size are aligned to the top-left corner of the cell they occupy. This will become a very important detail when we look at how tiles are copied from the tile sheet into the game.

There's no particular order to how these tiles are organized on the tile sheet. And the tile sheet itself can be any dimension you choose. You don't even need to decide how many tiles you need before you start coding a game—just add them to the tile sheet as you need them.

All of the games in this chapter were made using just this one tile sheet. Can you see how convenient this is? With just one small PNG file in your back pocket and a little code, you have a surprisingly large number of options available to make a wide variety of games.

Also, you can completely change the graphic style of a game by keeping all the code the same, and just swapping out the tile sheet for another one. This is great for prototyping. It means that even if you don't think you have any art or illustration skills, you can design and test a game with a tile sheet using simple images, and then hire an illustrator to create flashy graphics for you. All you need to do is drop in the illustrator's tile sheet—a single bitmap file—and you have a game that looks completely different.

Tile sheet coordinates

In the game code, we need a way to refer to each of these tiles individually. A simple way to do this is to assign each tile a unique ID number.

As shown in Figure 8-2, you can think of the tile sheet as a grid of columns and rows. Each tile has a unique column/row coordinate position. By putting the column number first and the row number second, you can give each tile a unique number. For example, in Figure 8-2, the cat has been assigned the number 20. The cat is in column 2, row 0.

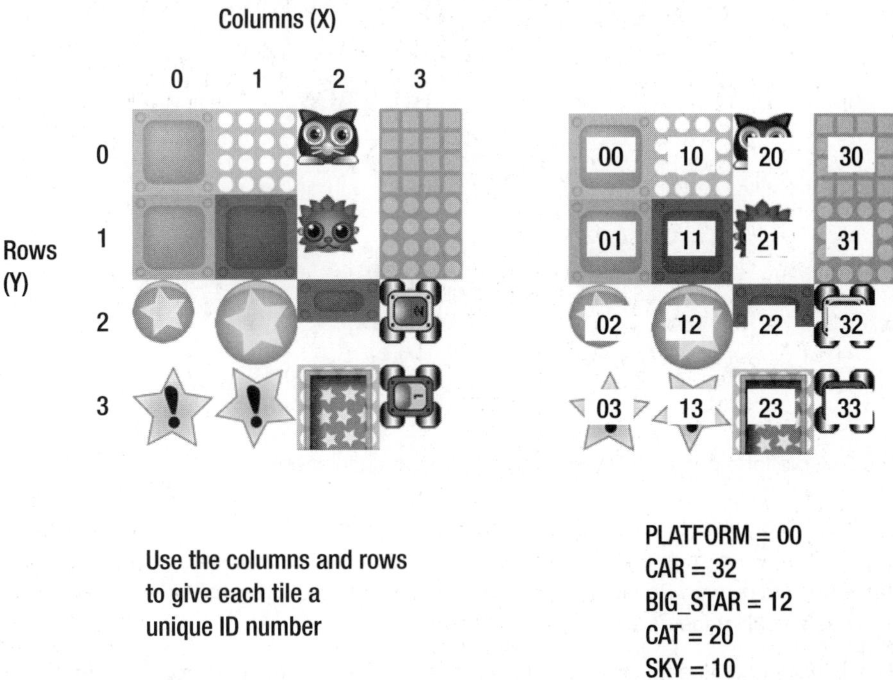

Figure 8-2. A unique ID number can tell your game what kind of thing the tile is as well as its position on the tile sheet.

This system is useful because it not only gives every tile a unique number, but its number tells the game where to find it on the tile sheet. Knowing these coordinates will be essential to copying the tile from the tile sheet into the game.

It's a little awkward to refer to every tile by a number, so it's good idea to define these numbers as constants at the start of the program. For example, these three constants define the ID numbers for the platform, sky, and cat tiles:

```
private const PLATFORM:uint = 00;
private const SKY:uint = 10;
private const CAT:uint = 20;
```

Now we just need to use the name PLATFORM whenever we want to refer to a platform tile.

Making a map

Now that we have tiles, we can use those tiles to build a game world. Let's create some platforms and a sky backdrop. Run the SWF file in the Map folder in the chapter's source files, and you'll see something that looks like Figure 8-3.

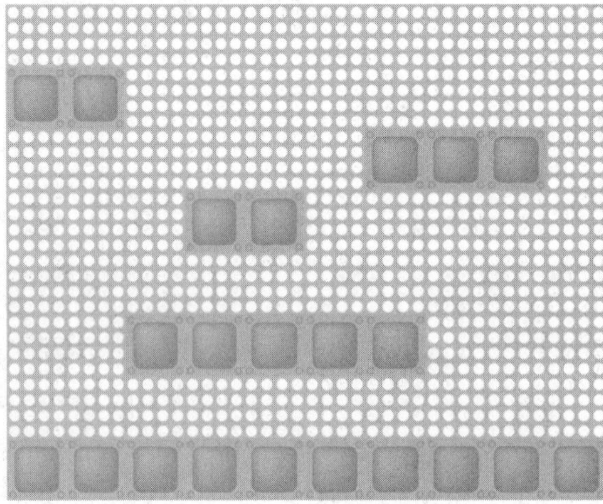

Figure 8-3. A platform game environment made from the tile sheet

Two of the tiles from the tile sheet have been used to make this game environment, as shown in Figure 8-4. They were copied from the tile sheet and plotted on the stage. The two tiles were repeated many times over. Because of the way the tiles are designed, the finished layout cleverly looks like one single image. But how was this scene made?

First, let's consider some of the constraints we face. It should be obvious from Figures 8-3 and 8-4 that the size of the game world will be partially determined by the size of the tiles. If you look carefully, you'll see that the finished game world is composed of ten columns and eight rows of tiles, as shown in Figure 8-5.

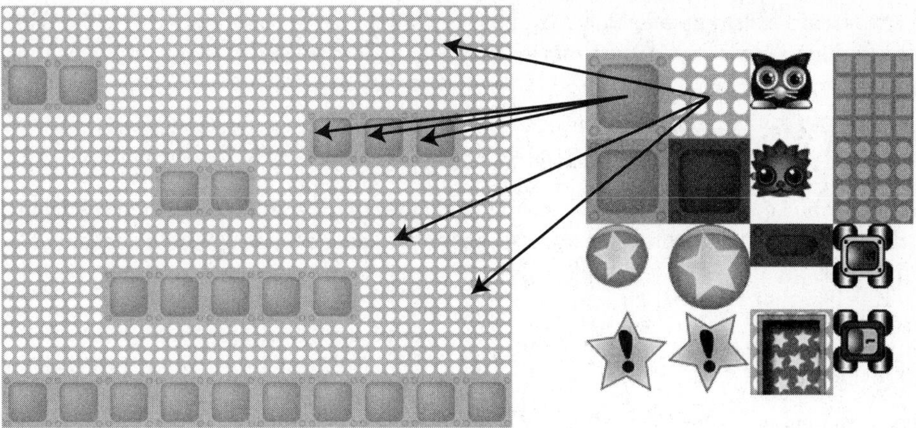

Figure 8-4. Only two tiles from the tile sheet were used to create this entire scene.

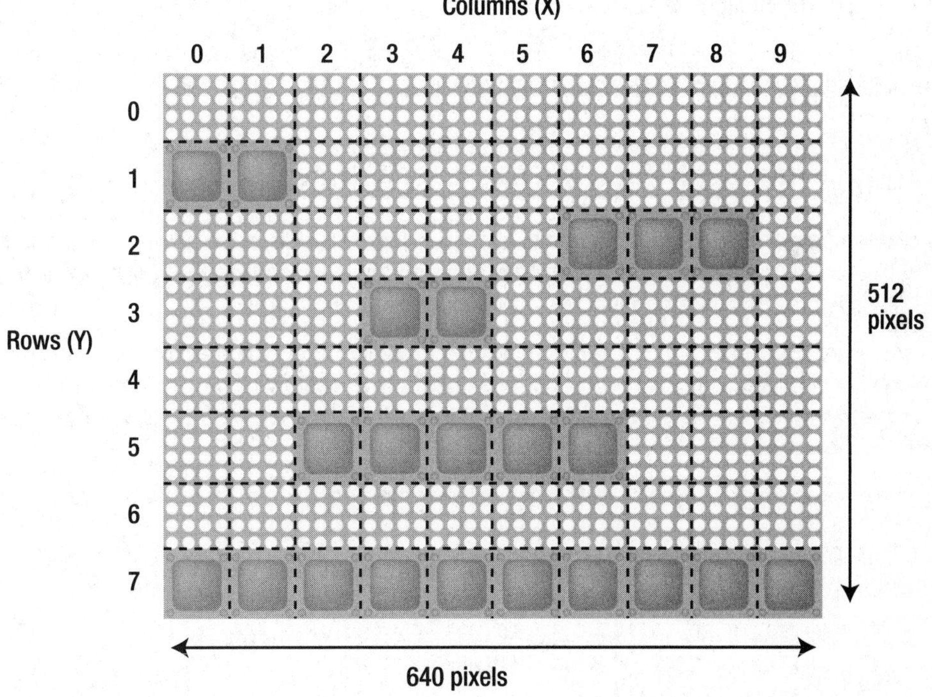

Figure 8-5. The game world is made up of ten columns (the x axis) and eight rows (the y axis).

If each tile is 64 pixels wide and high, the game world will be 640 pixels wide (64 * 10 = 640) and 512 pixels high (64 * 8 = 512). It makes sense to create a SWF file to match those same dimensions.

```
[SWF(width="640", height="512",
backgroundColor="#FFFFFF", frameRate="60")]
```

As you will soon see, the size of the tiles and the number of rows and columns are crucial to most aspects of a tile-based game engine. So it's important to define these values as constants at the start of the program.

```
private const MAX_TILE_SIZE:uint = 64;
private const MAP_COLUMNS:uint = 10;
private const MAP_ROWS:uint = 8;
```

To keep your head straight around some of the number juggling we'll be doing in a moment, make sure to keep this fact in mind:

- Columns refer to the stage's x axis coordinates.
- Rows refer to the stage's y axis coordinates.

This may seem obvious when it's printed in black and white on a page, but be careful. If you mix these up, it can lead to some dizzying confusion while you're still getting used to a tile-based view of the world.

Describing the map with a two-dimensional array

You can see from Figure 8-5 that the game world is a grid. The cells in the grid are the same size as the tiles on the tile sheet. But how will the program know which tiles to copy into which grid cells? We can provide this information by using a two-dimensional array.

You'll recall from Chapter 5 that a two-dimensional array is an array containing other arrays. It's often used to describe a grid of information. The inner arrays describe the rows, and the elements of those arrays describe the columns. It turns out that a two-dimensional array is the perfect way to describe how we want our game map to look.

The game map in Figure 8-5 was made using a two-dimensional array that looks like this:

```
private var _platformMap:Array
  = [
      [10,10,10,10,10,10,10,10,10,10],
      [00,00,10,10,10,10,10,10,10,10],
      [10,10,10,10,10,10,00,00,00,10],
      [10,10,10,00,00,10,10,10,10,10],
      [10,10,10,10,10,10,10,10,10,10],
      [10,10,00,00,00,00,00,10,10,10],
      [10,10,10,10,10,10,10,10,10,10],
      [00,00,00,00,00,00,00,00,00,00]
    ];
```

The columns and rows of the array match the columns and rows of our game world: ten by eight. But look closely at the numbers that the array contains. What do you see?

Remember that we've given each of our tiles a unique ID number. Here we use two tiles: `10` is the ID for the sky tile, and `00` is the ID for the platform tile. If you hold this book at arms length and squint a bit, it should all snap into focus—see Figure 8-6.

```
private var _platformMap:Array
  = [
     [10, 10, 10, 10, 10, 10, 10, 10, 10, 10],
     [00, 00, 10, 10, 10, 10, 10, 10, 10, 10],
     [10, 10, 10, 10, 10, 10, 00, 00, 00, 10],
     [10, 10, 10, 00, 00, 10, 10, 10, 10, 10],
     [10, 10, 10, 10, 10, 10, 10, 10, 10, 10],
     [10, 10, 00, 00, 00, 00, 00, 10, 10, 10],
     [10, 10, 10, 10, 10, 10, 10, 10, 10, 10],
     [00, 00, 00, 00, 00, 00, 00, 00, 00, 00],
    ]
```

Figure 8-6. Enter the matrix! The entire game world described by numbers.

What looks at first like abstract data turns out to be a perfect visual representation of the game world. This is one of the great benefits of making tile-based games. You have complete control of your game layout just by changing the tile ID numbers in the array. It's an extremely quick, fun, and precise way to build game levels. As long as the rows and columns of the two-dimensional array match the rows and columns you've decided on for your game, you have free rein to layout your game however you choose. Modifying the map is as simple as changing one number in the array.

We now know where to find our tiles and where to place them on the game map.

There's a lot of useful information here, which we might be able to store and use in our game. Before we go any further, let me introduce you to the `TileModel` class.

In this book, I've chosen to use `Array` objects to store game map data, mainly because 2D `Array` syntax is very easy to understand. However, you may want to consider using the `Vector` class for this in your own games. AS3.0 processes numbers stored in `Vector` objects faster than numbers stored in `Array` objects. Here is the syntax for a two-dimensional vector tile map.

```
var map:Vector.<Vector.<int>>
  = Vector.<Vector.<int>>
  (
    [
      Vector.<int>([10,10,10,10,10,10,10,10,10,10]),
      Vector.<int>([00,00,10,10,10,10,10,10,10,10]),
      Vector.<int>([10,10,10,10,10,10,00,00,00,10]),
      Vector.<int>([10,10,10,00,00,10,10,10,10,10]),
      Vector.<int>([10,10,10,10,10,10,10,10,10,10]),
      Vector.<int>([10,10,00,00,00,00,00,10,10,10]),
      Vector.<int>([10,10,10,10,10,10,10,10,10,10]),
      Vector.<int>([00,00,00,00,00,00,00,00,00,00])
    ]
  );
```

Two-dimensional vectors should be faster in theory, but in practice, they might not be any faster than two-dimensional arrays, and could even be slower, depending on which version of Flash Player you're using. You will need to test this in your own games with the latest version of Flash Player.

Creating the tile model

As you can see, we need to know a lot information about each tile: the tile sheet it's on; where on the game map to plot it; and its height, width, and x and y stage positions. It makes a lot of sense to create a class to store this information for every tile in our game. If you need to access this information quickly, it will be easy to find.

The custom `TileModel` class stores all of these properties. You'll find it in the `com.friendsofed.gameElements.primitives` package. It extends the `AVerletModel` class, so it inherits all the other properties you know so well, like `xPos` and `yPos`. `TileModel` adds a few more properties that are specific to tile-based games. It also adds some interesting new `get` methods, which you'll see near the end of the class. They won't make much sense to you now, but I will explain how they work in detail when we discuss tile-based collision detection later in this chapter. Two of the properties, `jumping` and `coordinateSpace`, are specific to a few examples that we will look at soon. You can ignore them for now. One property, `direction`, is used only for the tile-based maze game in the next chapter.

Here's the entire `TileModel` class for your reference:

```
package com.friendsofed.gameElements.primitives
{
  import flash.events.Event;
  import flash.events.EventDispatcher;
  import flash.display.*;

  public class TileModel extends AVerletModel
  {
    public var tileSheetRow:uint;
    public var tileSheetColumn:uint;
    private var _mapRow:uint;
    private var _mapColumn:uint;
    private var _currentTile:uint;
    private var _maxTileSize:uint;

    //Optional properties for platform
    //game characters
    public var jumping:Boolean = false;
    public var coordinateSpace:DisplayObject;

    //Optional property for maze game characters
    //(This is only used in Chapter 9)
    public var direction:String = "";

    public function TileModel
      (
        maxTileSize:uint = 64,
        tileSheetColumn:uint = 0,
        tileSheetRow:uint = 0,
        mapRow:uint = 0,
        mapColumn:uint = 0,
        width:uint = 0,
        height:uint = 0,
        setX:Number = 0
      ):void
    {
      this._maxTileSize = maxTileSize;
      this.tileSheetColumn = tileSheetColumn;
      this.tileSheetRow = tileSheetRow;
      this._mapRow = mapRow;
      this._mapColumn = mapColumn;
      this.width = width;
      this.height = height;
      this.setX = mapColumn * maxTileSize;
      this.setY = mapRow * maxTileSize;
    }
```

```
//Rows and column that the object occupies
public function get mapColumn():uint
{
   _mapColumn = uint((xPos + width * 0.5) / _maxTileSize);
   return _mapColumn;
}
public function set mapColumn(value:uint):void
{
   _mapColumn = value;
}
public function get mapRow():uint
{
   _mapRow = uint((yPos + height * 0.5) / _maxTileSize);
   return _mapRow;
}
public function set mapRow(value:uint):void
{
   _mapRow = value;
}
//Quick access to the tile's ID number if you need it
public function get id():uint
{
  var id:uint = tileSheetColumn * 10 + tileSheetRow;
  return id;
     }
//Top, bottom, left and right sides
public function get top():uint
{
   var top:uint = uint(yPos / _maxTileSize);
   return top;
}
public function get bottom():uint
{
   var bottom:uint = uint((yPos + height) / _maxTileSize);
   return bottom;
}
public function get left():uint
{
   var left:uint = uint(xPos / _maxTileSize);
   return left;
}
public function get right():uint
{
   var right:uint = uint((xPos + width) / _maxTileSize);
   return right;
}
```

```
    public function get centerX():uint
    {
      var centerX:uint = uint((xPos + width * 0.5) / _maxTileSize);
      return centerX;
    }
    public function get centerY():uint
    {
      var centerY:uint = uint((yPos + height * 0.5) / _maxTileSize);
      return centerY;
    }
  }
}
```

Now we have enough information to start making a tile-based game.

Putting the map in the game

To build the game world, create a nested `for` loop that simulates the game map's grid. This is the same nested `for` loop that we've used in other examples in this book to loop through grid data. The outer loop handles the columns, and the inner loop handles the rows. This means that the grid cells are read column by column, starting from the top left of the game world map. It reads the first cell in the column, works its way down each row, and then returns to the top of the next column.

```
for(var mapColumn:int = 0; mapColumn < MAP_COLUMNS; mapColumn++)
{
  for(var mapRow:int = 0; mapRow < MAP_ROWS; mapRow++)
  {
    //The tile ID number of the current cell in the game world
    var currentTile:int = _platformMap[mapRow][mapColumn];
  }
}
```

If you `trace` the value of `currentTile`, you'll see that it matches the value of the tile ID number in the `_platformMap` array. This is what the first two columns of `trace` data would look like after the outer loop has repeated once and the inner loop has run through twice:

```
10
0
10
10
10
10
10
0
10
0
10
10
```

```
10
10
10
0
```

You can see how these numbers match up with the actual game map in Figure 8-7. (The numbers in the trace have their leading zeros removed because a double zero is mathematically meaningless.)

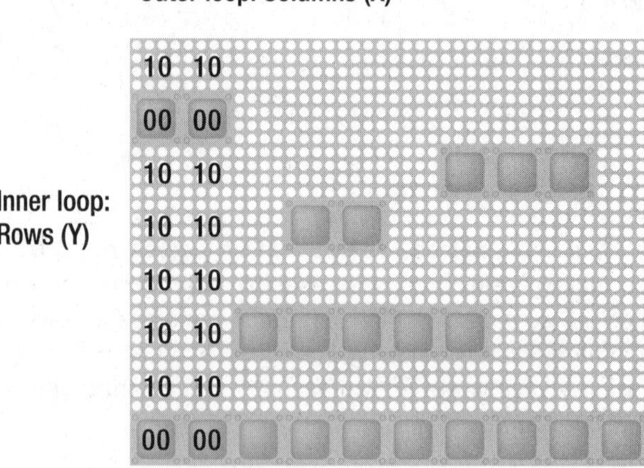

Figure 8-7. The value of currentTile after the outer loop has repeated twice and the inner loop has run twice

In total, the outer loop (the columns) will run once and repeat ten times. The inner loop (the rows) will run eight times. This covers all 80 cells in the game world's grid.

Now we have a way to figure out which tiles should be in which cells. The next step is to blit the tiles from the tile sheet onto their correct positions on the stage. You'll remember from Chapter 6 that to do this, we need to know two things:

- The x and y position of the tile we want to use from the tile sheet
- The x and y position on the destination bitmap that we want to copy it to.

We're on the verge of having that information. Our code now needs to do the following:

- Convert the tile's ID number into real x and y coordinates on the tile sheet.
- Use the nested `for` loop's current column and row numbers to find the real x and y positions on the stage to plot the tile.

The `Map` example source file uses a method called `buildMap` to do this. The `buildMap` method takes one argument, which is the name of the map array to build. To build the `_platformMap` array, use a line of code that looks like this:

```
buildMap(_platformMap);
```

Here's the entire buildMap method:

```
private function buildMap(map:Array):void
{

  //Loop through all the cells in the game map
  for(var mapColumn:int = 0; mapColumn < MAP_COLUMNS; mapColumn++)
  {
        for(var mapRow:int = 0; mapRow < MAP_ROWS; mapRow++)
        {
           //Find out which tile ID number is in
           //the current cell. This will be either
           //"00" (a platform) or "01" (sky)
           var currentTile:int = map[mapRow][mapColumn];

           //"-1" means that the tile destination grid will be blank
           //(This example doesn't use any blank tiles)
           if(currentTile > -1)
           {
              //Find the tile's column and row position
              //on the tile sheet
              var tileSheetColumn:uint = uint(currentTile / 10);
              var tileSheetRow:uint = uint(currentTile % 10);

              //Now the code checks what type of tile
              //the ID numbers says should be in the
              //game map's grid cell
              switch (currentTile)
              {
                case PLATFORM:
                  //If it finds a match, it creates
                  //a TileModel object
                  var platform:TileModel = new TileModel();
                  platform.tileSheetColumn = tileSheetColumn;
                  platform.tileSheetRow = tileSheetRow;
                  platform.mapRow = mapRow;
                  platform.mapColumn = mapColumn;
                  platform.width = MAX_TILE_SIZE;
                  platform.height = MAX_TILE_SIZE;
                  platform.setX = mapColumn * MAX_TILE_SIZE;
                  platform.setY = mapRow * MAX_TILE_SIZE;

                  //Blit the tile from the tile sheet onto the
                  //background bitmap using the
                  //drawGameObject method (discussed ahead)
                  drawGameObject(platform, _backgroundBitmapData);
                  break;
```

```
                    case SKY:
                      //Create a TileModel object
                      var sky:TileModel = new TileModel();
                      sky.tileSheetColumn = tileSheetColumn;
                      sky.tileSheetRow = tileSheetRow;
                      sky.mapRow = mapRow;
                      sky.mapColumn = mapColumn;
                      sky.width = MAX_TILE_SIZE;
                      sky.height = MAX_TILE_SIZE;
                      sky.setX = mapColumn * MAX_TILE_SIZE;
                      sky.setY = mapRow * MAX_TILE_SIZE;

                     //Blit the tile from the tile sheet onto the
                     //background bitmap
                     drawGameObject(sky, _backgroundBitmapData);
                      break;
              }
            }
          }
        }
      }
```

The code first checks to see if the value of `_platformMap[row][column]` is greater than -1. In the system I've used for this chapter, `-1` means a blank tile without any graphics.

```
if(currentTile > -1)
{…
```

This `Map` example doesn't use any blank tiles, so this first check is passed. (In later examples, you'll see how blank tiles are used to create empty spaces in the game world.)

Next, the code needs to extract the x and y coordinates of the tile on the tile sheet from its ID number. To do this, each digit in the ID must be read individually. This is done with a little bit of help from the **modulus operator** (%).

```
var tileSheetColumn:uint = uint(currentTile / 10);
var tileSheetRow:uint = uint(currentTile % 10);
```

The modulus operator is used to get the remainder of a division calculation. For example, 13 divided by 10 is 1 with a remainder of 3, which is the value returned by the modulus operator.

A concrete example will give you a better idea of how this works. Let's say that the tile ID is `24`. The `2` represents the tile sheet column, and the `4` represents the tile sheet row. But there's a problem: we need to extract the column number and row number, and store them as separate variables.

Finding the column number is easy enough. Just divide the ID number by 10:

```
24 / 10 = 2
```

As you can see, that's absolutely correct. The first digit of the ID `24` *is* `2`. That's how the `tileSheetColumn` value is found.

But how can we find the row number? That's where the modulus operator can help us. It will tell us the remainder:

```
24 % 10 = 4
```

24 divided by 10 is 2, but the remainder is 4. That's perfect! The second digit of the ID `24` *is* `4`. That exactly matches the tile sheet row number.

The `tileSheetColumn` and `tileSheetRow` variables find the column and row numbers in the same way. Do these two lines of code make more sense to you now?

```
var tileSheetColumn:uint = uint(currentTile / 10);
var tileSheetRow:uint = uint(currentTile % 10);
```

Next, the code checks to see whether the `currentTile` ID number matches any of the ID numbers that it knows about. In this example, it knows that `PLATFORM` tiles equal `00` and `SKY` tiles equal `01`. A `switch` statement checks for these. If it finds either of them, it creates a `TileModel` object. The following section looks for a `PLATFORM` ID number and creates the `platform` `TileModel` object. It also sets all the important properties on the `TileModel` object.

```
switch (currentTile)
{
  case PLATFORM:

    //Create the TileModel object
    var platform:TileModel = new TileModel();

    ///Set the tile sheet coordinates
    platform.tileSheetColumn = tileSheetColumn;
    platform.tileSheetRow = tileSheetRow;

    //Set the column and row coordinates where
    //the tile will be displayed on the game map
    platform.mapRow = mapRow;
    platform.mapColumn = mapColumn;

    //Set the size of the tile to match the game's
    //maximum tile size value
    platform.width = MAX_TILE_SIZE;
    platform.height = MAX_TILE_SIZE;

    //Set the actual x and y position values of the tile on the stage
    platform.setX = mapColumn * MAX_TILE_SIZE;
    platform.setY = mapRow * MAX_TILE_SIZE;
```

```
    //Blit the tile from the tile sheet onto the
    //background bitmap using the
    //drawGameObject method (discussed ahead)
    drawGameObject(platform, _backgroundBitmapData);
    break;

    //...
}
```

This code creates a `TileModel` object called `platform`, and sets some of its initial properties

- It assigns the `tileSheetColumn` and `tileSheetRow` values that we figured out earlier:

```
platform.tileSheetColumn = tileSheetColumn;
platform.tileSheetRow = tileSheetRow;
```

- It assigns its `mapRow` and `mapColumn` properties to the loop's current `mapRow` and `mapColumn` properties:

```
platform.mapRow = mapRow;
platform.mapColumn = mapColumn;
```

- It assigns its `height` and `width` values to the maximum height and width of tiles in the game:

```
platform.width = MAX_TILE_SIZE;
platform.height = MAX_TILE_SIZE;
```

The code then sets the tile's actual x and y stage position:

```
platform.setX = mapColumn * MAX_TILE_SIZE;
platform.setY = mapRow * MAX_TILE_SIZE;
```

This bit of code highlights a very important calculation. If you multiply the size of the tile by the current column or row number, you can find its x and y positions on the stage. For example, we know that the tile size is 64. If the tile is at column number 6 and row number 3, you can find its x and y positions like this:

```
x = 6 * 64
x = 384

y = 3 * 64
y = 192
```

That turns out to be a very important fact, as you shall soon see.

But there's also a flip side to this. If you know an object's x and y positions, you can also find out which map column and map row it's in. Just divide the x and y positions by the tile size. For example, let's take the x and y values we just looked at.

```
x = 384
y = 192
```

Divide these numbers by the tile size, which is 64.

```
mapColumn = 384 / 64
mapColumn = 6

mapRow = 192 / 64
mapRow = 3
```

That gives us the column and row that the tile occupies.

This works out neatly if the x and y positions are evenly divisible by 64. But what if you have a free roaming object in your game that could be at any x or y position? To figure this out, do the same calculation, but *round the resulting value down*. For example, let's say you have a game character jumping between platforms at these x and y positions:

```
x = 341
y = 287
```

Divide those numbers by 64 to find out which column and row it's in

```
mapColumn = 341 / 64
mapColumn = 5.3

mapRow = 287 / 64
mapRow = 4.4
```

That's very accurate, but we need to truncate those pesky decimal values. We can do this by using `Math.floor`. Or, better yet, we can cast the result as a `uint`. Here's an example:

```
mapColumn = uint(341 / 64)
mapColumn = 5

mapRow = uint(287 / 64)
mapRow = 4
```

Using `uint` is a faster alternative to `Math.floor` and has the same effect of rounding the numbers down.

Being able to convert from x and y positions to column and row positions is an important skill for tile-based game engines. You'll see just how useful this is in the upcoming examples.

Blitting tiles

The very last thing that the code in the previous section did was to display the tile on the stage using the `drawGameObject` method.

```
drawGameObject(platform, _backgroundBitmapData);
```

Let's take a close look at exactly how it does this.

You'll recall from Chapter 6 that to blit objects, you need two things:

- A source `BitmapData` object. That's the tile sheet.
- A destination `BitmapData` object. That's the stage bitmap.

In the Map example file, the tile sheet is embedded and its BitmapData created like this:

```
[Embed(source="../../images/tileSheet.png")]
private var TileSheet:Class;
private var _tileSheetImage:DisplayObject = new TileSheet();
private var _tileSheetBitmapData:BitmapData
  = new BitmapData
  (
    _tileSheetImage.width,
    _tileSheetImage.height,
    true,
    0
  );
```

When the application class initializes, it draws the _tileSheetImage into the _tileSheetBitmapData using the draw method.

```
_tileSheetBitmapData.draw(_tileSheetImage);
```

We need another bitmap on which to display the tiles. _backgroundBitmap is a bitmap that is the same size as the stage. We can blit the tiles onto it.

```
private var _backgroundBitmapData:BitmapData
  = new BitmapData(stage.stageWidth, stage.stageHeight, true, 0);
private var _backgroundBitmap:Bitmap
  = new Bitmap(_backgroundBitmapData);
```

It needs to be added to the stage so that we can see the game world.

```
addChild(_backgroundBitmap);
```

The custom drawGameObject method does the work of blitting from the tile sheet to the backgroundBitmap. It takes two parameters: a TileModel object and the destination BitmapData.

```
drawGameObject(tileModelObject, destinationBitmapData);
```

Remember that the TileModel class contains the coordinates of where on the tile sheet to find the correct tile. It also contains the coordinates of where on the game map the tile should be placed. This information and the name of the destination BitmapData are all we need to blit the tile.

Here's the drawGameObject method that copies the tile from the tile sheet onto the correct place on the backgroundBitmap:

```
private function drawGameObject
  (
    tileModel:TileModel,
    screen:BitmapData
  ):void
```

```
{
  var sourceRectangle:Rectangle
    = new Rectangle
    (
      tileModel.tileSheetColumn * MAX_TILE_SIZE,
      tileModel.tileSheetRow * MAX_TILE_SIZE,
      tileModel.width,
      tileModel.height
    );

  var destinationPoint:Point
    = new Point
    (
      tileModel.xPos,
      tileModel.yPos
    );

  screen.copyPixels
    (
      _tileSheetBitmapData,
      sourceRectangle,
      destinationPoint,
      null, null, true
    );
}
```

As you can see, this is identical to the system we used to blit the particle explosions in Chapter 6.

A `Rectangle` object defines where on the tile sheet the tile is located. It gets this information from the `TileModel` object that we initialized earlier. Notice how the x and y positions are found by multiplying the tile sheet column and row numbers by the maximum tile size.

```
var sourceRectangle:Rectangle
  = new Rectangle
  (
    tileModel.tileSheetColumn * MAX_TILE_SIZE,
    tileModel.tileSheetRow * MAX_TILE_SIZE,
    tileModel.width,
    tileModel.height
  );
```

Next, we find the destination point on the bitmap where we want to blit the tile. This will be whatever the `TileModel` object's `xPos` and `yPos` values are.

```
var destinationPoint:Point
  = new Point
  (
    tileModel.xPos,
    tileModel.yPos
  );
```

Finally, we copy the tile onto the bitmap using the BitmapData's copyPixels method.

```
screen.copyPixels
  (
    _tileSheetBitmapData,
    sourceRectangle,
    destinationPoint,
    null, null, true
  );
```

This is an all-purpose blit method that will be used, unchanged, for the blitting we'll be doing for all the examples in this chapter and the next.

Reviewing the Map application class

All the code that we've looked at so far in this chapter is from the Map.as application class. It forms the core of our tile-based game engine, so it's very important that you see all the code in its full context.

```
package
{
  import flash.events.Event;
  import flash.display.*;
  import flash.geom.Point;
  import flash.geom.Rectangle;
  import com.friendsofed.utils.*;
  import com.friendsofed.gameElements.primitives.*;

  [SWF(width="640", height="512",
  backgroundColor="#FFFFFF", frameRate="60")]

  public class Map extends Sprite
  {
    private const MAX_TILE_SIZE:uint = 64;
    private const MAP_COLUMNS:uint = 10;
    private const MAP_ROWS:uint = 8;

    //The PLATFORM and SKY constants define
    //the position of tile images in the tile sheet
    private const PLATFORM:uint = 00;
    private const SKY:uint = 10;

    private var _platformMap:Array
      = [
          [10,10,10,10,10,10,10,10,10,10],
          [00,00,10,10,10,10,10,10,10,10],
          [10,10,10,10,10,10,00,00,00,10],
          [10,10,10,00,00,10,10,10,10,10],
          [10,10,10,10,10,10,10,10,10,10],
```

```
      [10,10,00,00,00,00,00,10,10,10],
      [10,10,10,10,10,10,10,10,10,10],
      [00,00,00,00,00,00,00,00,00,00]
    ];

//Create a blank BitmapData object as the canvas for this bitmap
private var _backgroundBitmapData:BitmapData
  = new BitmapData(stage.stageWidth, stage.stageHeight, true, 0);
private var _backgroundBitmap:Bitmap
  = new Bitmap(_backgroundBitmapData);

//Tile sheet
//Variables required to display the tile sheet bitmap
[Embed(source="../../images/tileSheet.png")]
private var TileSheet:Class;
private var _tileSheetImage:DisplayObject = new TileSheet();
private var _tileSheetBitmapData:BitmapData
  = new BitmapData
  (
    _tileSheetImage.width,
    _tileSheetImage.height,
    true,
    0
  );

//Status box
private var _statusBox:StatusBox = new StatusBox;

public function Map():void
{
  //Draw the tile sheet
  _tileSheetBitmapData.draw(_tileSheetImage);

  //Add the stage bitmap.
  //This displays the contents of the _backgroundBitmapData.
  //It will be updated automatically when
  //the _backgroundBitmapData is changed
  addChild(_backgroundBitmap);

  //Run the buildMap method to convert the
  //map's array data into a visual display
  buildMap(_platformMap);

  //Display the status box
  addChild(_statusBox);
  _statusBox.text = "MAP:";
  _statusBox.text += "\n" + "TILE SIZE: " + MAX_TILE_SIZE;
  _statusBox.text += "\n" + "MAP_ROWS: " + MAP_ROWS;
  _statusBox.text += "\n" + "MAP_COLUMNS: " + MAP_COLUMNS;
}
```

```
//Create tile models and map them to the
//correct positions on the tile sheet
private function buildMap(map:Array):void
{

  //Loop through all the cells in the game map
  for(var mapColumn:int = 0; mapColumn < MAP_COLUMNS; mapColumn++)
  {
    for(var mapRow:int = 0; mapRow < MAP_ROWS; mapRow++)
    {
      //Find out which tile ID number is in
      //the current cell. This will be either
      //"00" (a platform) or "01" (sky)
      var currentTile:int = map[mapRow][mapColumn];

      //"-1" means that the tile destination grid will be blank
      //This example doesn't use any blank tiles
      if(currentTile > -1)
      {
        //Find the tile's column and row position
        //on the tile sheet
        var tileSheetColumn:uint = uint(currentTile / 10);
        var tileSheetRow:uint = uint(currentTile % 10);

        //Now the code checks what type of tile
        //the ID number says should be in the
        //game map's grid cell
        switch (currentTile)
        {
          case PLATFORM:
            //If it finds a match, it creates
            //a TileModel object
            var platform:TileModel = new TileModel();
            platform.tileSheetColumn = tileSheetColumn;
            platform.tileSheetRow = tileSheetRow;
            platform.mapRow = mapRow;
            platform.mapColumn = mapColumn;
            platform.width = MAX_TILE_SIZE;
            platform.height = MAX_TILE_SIZE;
            platform.setX = mapColumn * MAX_TILE_SIZE;
            platform.setY = mapRow * MAX_TILE_SIZE;

            //Blit the tile from the tile sheet onto the
            //background bitmap using the
            //drawGameObject method
            drawGameObject(platform, _backgroundBitmapData);
            break;
```

```
            case SKY:
             //Create a TileModel object
             var sky:TileModel = new TileModel();
             sky.tileSheetColumn = tileSheetColumn;
             sky.tileSheetRow = tileSheetRow;
             sky.mapRow = mapRow;
             sky.mapColumn = mapColumn;
             sky.width = MAX_TILE_SIZE;
             sky.height = MAX_TILE_SIZE;
             sky.setX = mapColumn * MAX_TILE_SIZE;
             sky.setY = mapRow * MAX_TILE_SIZE;

             //Blit the tile from the tile sheet onto the
             //background bitmap
             drawGameObject(sky, _backgroundBitmapData);
             break;
          }
        }
      }
    }
  }

  //Basic blit method
  private function drawGameObject
   (
     tileModel:TileModel,
     screen:BitmapData
   ):void
  {
    var sourceRectangle:Rectangle
       = new Rectangle
       (
         tileModel.tileSheetColumn * MAX_TILE_SIZE,
         tileModel.tileSheetRow * MAX_TILE_SIZE,
         tileModel.width,
         tileModel.height
       );

    var destinationPoint:Point
       = new Point
       (
         tileModel.xPos,
         tileModel.yPos
       );
```

```
        screen.copyPixels
          (
            _tileSheetBitmapData,
            sourceRectangle,
            destinationPoint,
            null, null, true
          );
    }
  }
}
```

Spend as much time as you need to understand how the Map example works before moving on to the more complex examples ahead. It's the heart of the tile-based game engine we're using in this chapter. If you're thinking of making your own tile-based game, now might be a good time to take a short break from reading to see if you can create your own game world map using these techniques.

Adding a game character

Now that we have a game world, we can start to add characters and objects. Run the SWF file in the Character folder, and you'll see something that looks like Figure 8-8.

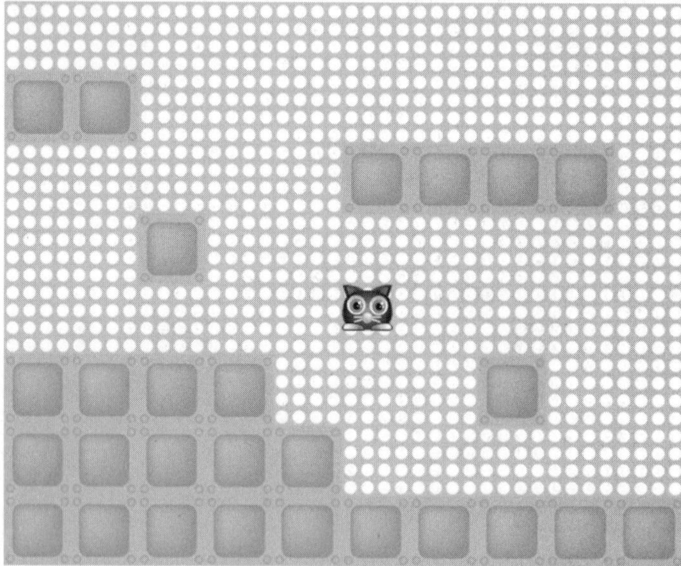

Figure 8-8. A character is added to the game world.

The character doesn't move yet; it just hangs in space. Before we make it run and jump around the screen, let's take a close look at how it was added to the game.

Layering maps

The cat character is quite a different kind of thing than the platforms or the sky. The platforms and sky are very much in the background; the cat is in the foreground. You can see from Figure 8-8 that the cat is in front of one of the sky tiles. The cat's alpha transparency is allowing the sky tile to show through from behind. This is thanks to the PNG file that represents the tile sheet. It has a transparent background and was exported with 32-bit alpha, which preserves transparency.

If you look at the `Character.as` application class, you'll see that the cat has been assigned a constant that matches its tile ID of `20`.

```
private const CAT:uint = 20;
```

That's the cat's column and row number on the tile sheet. You can use the ID `20` to add the cat to the game world in the map array.

But we have a small problem. The map array is already full of sky and platform tiles. We want the cat to appear in a cell that is already occupied by a sky tile. How can we solve this problem?

A common strategy in tile-based games is to create different maps for different types of objects. You can then layer the maps. This allows you to easily place more than one tile in the same map grid cell, and also simplifies depth management.

For the examples in this chapter, there is one map for platform and sky objects, and another map for foreground game objects, like the cat. The maps have the same number of columns and rows, but they contain different kinds of objects.

In the `Character` document class, you'll see that two map arrays are being used to describe the game world.

```
private var _platformMap:Array
  = [
      [10,10,10,10,10,10,10,10,10,10],
      [00,00,10,10,10,10,10,10,10,10],
      [10,10,10,10,10,00,00,00,00,10],
      [10,10,00,10,10,10,10,10,10,10],
      [10,10,10,10,10,10,10,10,10,10],
      [00,00,00,00,10,10,10,00,10,10],
      [00,00,00,00,00,10,10,10,10,10],
      [00,00,00,00,00,00,00,00,00,00]
    ];

private var _gameObjectMap:Array
  = [
      [-1,-1,-1,-1,-1,-1,-1,-1,-1,-1],
      [-1,-1,-1,-1,-1,-1,-1,-1,-1,-1],
      [-1,-1,-1,-1,-1,-1,-1,-1,-1,-1],
      [-1,-1,-1,-1,-1,-1,-1,-1,-1,-1],
```

```
    [-1,-1,-1,-1,-1,20,-1,-1,-1,-1],
    [-1,-1,-1,-1,-1,-1,-1,-1,-1,-1],
    [-1,-1,-1,-1,-1,-1,-1,-1,-1,-1],
    [-1,-1,-1,-1,-1,-1,-1,-1,-1,-1],
  ];
```

The `_platformMap` follows the same format as our first example, but the `_gameObjectMap` is new. Can you see where the cat has been positioned? It should be obvious!

As noted earlier, `-1` means that a cell contains a blank tile. In fact, the `_gameObjectMap` is blank except for the cat, which has an ID of `20`. However, as we add more game objects in later examples, you'll see how it starts to fill up with more image tiles.

You may recall from the discussion on blitting in Chapter 6 that, in a blit display environment, you need to handle all the depth management yourself. Fortunately, this is not difficult. The basic principle is this: tiles that are drawn last appear above those that are drawn earlier. If you want an object to appear above other objects, draw it later.

You can make your depth management easier by creating two or more display bitmaps. In a blit display system, there's always a "stage bitmap" onto which tiles are copied. Instead of having just one of these stage bitmaps, use two: one for background objects and the other for foreground objects. It's logical that certain types of objects will occupy similar planes in your game world. This is the same concept as using drawing layers in Photoshop to help manage the stacking order of images.

It's easy enough to do this in a tile-based game that uses blitting. You'll see in the `Character` source file that there are two bitmaps.

```
//Background bitmap
private var _backgroundBitmapData:BitmapData
  = new BitmapData(stage.stageWidth, stage.stageHeight, true, 0);
private var _backgroundBitmap:Bitmap
  = new Bitmap(_backgroundBitmapData);

//Foreground bitmap
private var _foregroundBitmapData:BitmapData
  = new BitmapData(stage.stageWidth, stage.stageHeight, true, 0);
private var _foregroundBitmap:Bitmap
  = new Bitmap(_foregroundBitmapData);
```

These are then added to the stage in the order that you want them to appear.

```
addChild(_backgroundBitmap);
addChild(_foregroundBitmap);
```

To create these two game maps and display them on the correct bitmap layer, run the `buildMap` method twice. Supply the name of the map you want to build in the argument.

```
buildMap(_platformMap);
buildMap(_gameObjectMap);
```

(The order that you run these in doesn't matter. The only thing that affects the stacking order is the order that they're added to the stage by addChild.)

This is good so far, but we haven't yet told the program whether we want to blit the cat character on the foreground or background bitmap. This is handled by the specific code in the buildMap method.

The buildMap method in the Character class is identical to our first example, except that it has an additional check to see whether any of the tiles match the value of CAT (20). If it finds a match, it creates a cat TileModel object, and tells the drawGameObject method to blit the cat onto the foreground. Here's the code that does this (with the line that blits the cat onto the correct bitmap layer highlighted):

```
case CAT:
  _catModel
    = new TileModel
    (
      MAX_TILE_SIZE,
      tileSheetColumn, tileSheetRow,
      mapRow, mapColumn,
      48, 42
    );

    drawGameObject(_catModel, _foregroundBitmapData);
    break;
```

The only other new thing here is that all the cat's initial properties are set in the TileModel constructor. This saves a bit of space and is a little more efficient than initializing each property line by line, as in the previous example. Here's the format for initializing TileModel objects in the constructor:

```
_tileModelObject
  = new TileModel
  (
    Maximum tile size,
    tileSheetColumn,
    tileSheetRow,
    game mapRow,
    game mapColumn,
    width,
    height
  );
```

Notice that the cat's width is 48 pixels and its height is 42 pixels. This shows that you can use any size tile. You're not limited to a 64-by-64 tile size. You can also see that tiles can be any shape. They don't need to be rectangular.

> *It's also possible to use tiles that are larger than the maximum tile size. You'll need to make a second tile sheet for big objects, and modify the tile game engine a bit to handle them. By the end of this chapter, you'll understand the concepts of tile-based games well enough that this shouldn't pose too big a challenge.*

The `Character` application class is identical to the first example except for these modifications. Our next step is to make the cat run and jump around the stage.

Making the game character move

Run the SWF in the `MovingCharacter` folder. You can use the mouse to make the cat run and jump, as shown in Figure 8-9. It can't jump on the platforms yet, but it does stop at the stage boundaries, like the bottom of the stage.

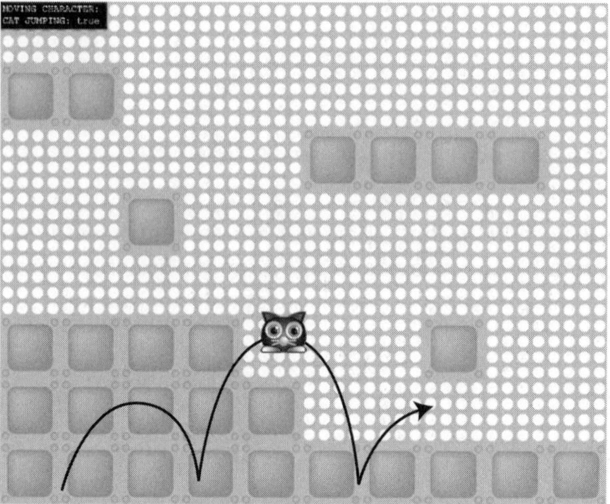

Figure 8-9. Use the mouse to make the cat jump.

Because the `TileModel` class extends the `AVerletModel` class, we can use the same physics system we've been using in all the other chapters in this book. And because our data is completely separate from the display, the physics code in a tile-based blit environment is identical to the physics code for sprites or movie clips. All we need to do is create a `UIView` and `UIController` to create the platform game control.

`UIPlatformView` and `UIPlatformController` handle the cat's jump physics. You'll find these classes in the `com.friendsofed.gameElements.primitives` package. The `UIPlatformView` captures the mouse input and sends it to the `UIPlatformController` to process. Both of these classes are instantiated in the `buildMap` method at the same time as the cat's `TileModel` class.

```
case CAT:
  _catModel
    = new TileModel
    (
      MAX_TILE_SIZE,
      tileSheetColumn, tileSheetRow,
      mapRow, mapColumn,
      48, 42
    );

    //Add some gravity
    _catModel.gravity_Vy = 0.98;

    //Add the UIView and UIController
    _UIPlatformController
      = new UIPlatformController(_catModel);
    _UIPlatformView
      = new UIPlatformView
      (_catModel, _UIPlatformController, stage);

    drawGameObject(_catModel, _foregroundBitmapData);
    break;
```

The cat's gravity is set at the same time. This is the standard MVC system that you should know quite well by now.

Jumping

The `TileModel` has a property called `jumping`. It's a Boolean variable that can be used to tell the game whether the cat is jumping or is on the ground. In this example, it's set to `true` in the `enterFrameHandler` whenever the cat is at the bottom of the stage.

```
if(_catModel.yPos + _catModel.height >= stage.stageHeight)
{
  _catModel.jumping = false;
}
```

When the `UIView` detects that the mouse button is pressed, it contacts the controller's `processMouseDown` method. The controller has a constant called `JUMP_FORCE`, which determines with how much force the cat should jump.

```
private const JUMP_FORCE:Number = -25;
```

If the cat is not already jumping, it adds the `JUMP_FORCE` to the cat's `vy`, and sets its `jumping` property to `true`. (`JUMP_FORCE` is a negative number because "moving up the stage" means subtracting values from an object's y position.)

```
internal function processMouseDown
  (event:MouseEvent):void
{
  jump();
}

internal function jump():void
{
  if(!_model.jumping)
  {
    _model.jumping = true;
    _model.vy += JUMP_FORCE;
  }
}
```

`jumping` is set to `false` again by the `MovingCharacter` application class's `enterFrameHandler` when the cat hits the ground.

```
if(_catModel.yPos + _catModel.height >= stage.stageHeight)
{
  _catModel.jumping = false;
}
```

This prevents the player from making the cat jump while it's still in the air.

In later examples, you'll see how this code works just as well with platforms without any other modification.

Moving with the mouse

You can make the cat move left and right by moving the mouse. There are a few unexpected pitfalls that you need to be aware of, so let's take a closer look at how this works.

The cat follows the mouse using a simple easing formula that you've probably used before at some point. At its most basic, it looks like this:

```
var vx:Number = stage.mouseX - (_model.xPos + _model.width * 0.5);
_model.vx = vx * 0.2;
```

The code measures the distance between the mouse and the center of the cat. That distance is then multiplied by an easing value, 0.2, and the result is assigned to the cat's velocity.

These two lines of code are at the heart of the cat's motion system. But how does the cat's controller know when to run this code? To be accurate, it must run every frame. Somehow, the code must connect the cat's controller to the game's frame rate.

To do this, first the application class calls the `_catModel`'s `update` method in the `enterFrameHandler`.

```
private function enterFrameHandler(event:Event):void
{
  //Update the cat's model
  _catModel.update();

  //...
}
```

AVerletModel, the cat's superclass, has an update method. The update method dispatches a custom "update" event every time it's called.

```
public function update():void
{
  //Verlet motion code...

  dispatchEvent(new Event("update"));
}
```

Because this event is dispatched each frame, it is the perfect event to listen for if you want to synchronize an object's controller with the game's frame rate. The cat's UIPlatformView listens for this event.

```
_model.addEventListener("update", updateHandler);
```

Its updateHandler calls the UIPlatformController's processUpdate method and sends it a reference to the stage.

```
private function updateHandler(event:Event):void
{
  _controller.processUpdate(_stage);
}
```

The UIPlatformController's processUpdate method implements the easing formula. But it also does two checks:

- Whether the cat's velocity is within the allowed speed limit. The SPEED_LIMIT constant is set to 100. This is needed to prevent the cat from moving around the stage too quickly.
- From which **coordinate space** to read the mouse position. I'll explain in detail how this works when we discuss scrolling later in this chapter. For now, know that the cat's default coordinateSpace property is set to null. This means that the code will use the stage's mouseX value to calculate velocity.

Here's the complete processUpdate method that runs these checks and implements the easing.

```
internal function processUpdate(stage:Object):void
{
  var vx:Number;

  //If the TileModel has no coordinateSpace
  //value, then assume that the stage's
```

```
  //coordinate space will be used to read
  //the mouseX value
  if(_model.coordinateSpace == null)
  {
    vx = stage.mouseX - (_model.xPos + _model.width * 0.5);
  }

  //If coordinateSpace isn't null, use that
  //space to calculate the mouseX value
  else
  {
    vx
      = _model.coordinateSpace.mouseX
      - (_model.xPos + _model.width * 0.5);
  }

  //Limit the velocity to the speed limit
  if(vx < -SPEED_LIMIT)
  {
    vx = -SPEED_LIMIT
  }
  if(vx > SPEED_LIMIT)
  {
    vx = SPEED_LIMIT
  }

  //Apply the easing formula to the model's velocity
  _model.vx = vx * EASING;
}
```

Figure 8-10 is a diagram of this entire process.

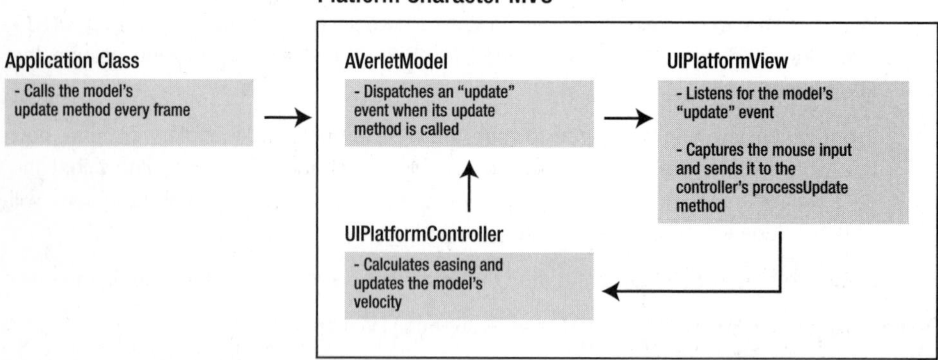

Figure 8-10. The mouse's new position needs to be captured each frame for accurate easing.

> *If you would prefer to create a platform game character that can be moved using the keyboard, take a look at the comments in the `UIPlatformView` and `UIPlatformController` classes. They include methods that will you help implement this quickly.*

This is an example of a fairly advanced character control system. It's not essential to implement something like this to create a tile-based game. For your first tile-based game or experiment, I suggest using a very basic character control system without any physics, such as the keyboard control system we looked at in Chapter 1. That will be a good learning step. When you feel more confident, look over the cat's control system and see if it can help you with your own physics-based character control system.

Blitting a moving character in a tile-based world

As you can see, even though we're now working in a tile-based world, all of our old physics skills still apply. We can use our whole bag of tricks. The only really big difference is the way in which the images are displayed on the stage.

You'll recall from Chapter 6 that to blit a moving object you need to do two things each frame:

- Every frame needs to start with a blank canvas. You need to completely clear the bitmap that you're blitting the tile onto using the `fillRect` method. In this example, the cat tile is being blitted onto the `_foregroundBitmap`. You can clear the `_foregroundBitmap` like this:
  ```
  _foregroundBitmapData.fillRect(_foregroundBitmapData.rect, 0);
  ```
- Copy the moving object's tile to its new place on the bitmap. In this example, that cat `TileModel` stores all of its position information. That means we can just reuse the same `drawGameObject` method we discussed in the previous section.
  ```
  drawGameObject(_catModel, _foregroundBitmapData);
  ```

Yes, those two lines are all you need to blit a moving tile!

All of this happens inside the `enterFrameHandler`. To keep your positions and collision detection accurate, make sure you add code to the `enterFrameHandler` in the following order:

1. Update the models.
2. Check for collisions.
3. Blit the objects.

If you follow that order, everything will be peachy!

Here's the enterFrameHandler from the MovingCharacter application class:

```
private function enterFrameHandler(event:Event):void
{
  //1. UPDATE THE MODELS

  //Update the cat's model
  _catModel.update();

  //2. CHECK FOR COLLISIONS

  //Stop the cat at the stage boundaries
  StageBoundaries.stopBitmap(_catModel, stage);

  if(_catModel.yPos + _catModel.height >= stage.stageHeight)
  {
    _catModel.jumping = false;
  }

  //3. BLIT THE OBJECTS

  //Clear the stage bitmap from the previous frame so that it's
  //blank when you add the new tile positions
  _foregroundBitmapData.fillRect(_foregroundBitmapData.rect, 0);

  //Blit the cat on the foreground bitmap
  drawGameObject(_catModel, _foregroundBitmapData);

}
```

Be sure to take a look at the complete MovingCharacter application class in the chapter's source files to see all the code in its proper context.

We have a game world and a game character. Now, let's add some real interactivity!

> *Objects that are displayed using blitting are called* ***blit objects****, which is sometimes shortened to* ***bob****. If you overhear some game designers casually discussing their "bobs," you now know what they're talking about!*

Platform collision

Efficient collision detection is one of the big strengths of a tile-based game engine. An inefficiency with all the collision-detection strategies in the book so far is that they check for collisions with objects that have no chance of ever colliding. For example, a ball at the top-left corner of the stage has no hope of ever colliding with a ball in the bottom-right corner of the stage in the current frame, or even in the next frame. This may not have any noticeable performance impact on a small game, but it's nonetheless an irksome and wasteful inefficiency. For a complex game with hundreds of moving objects, it could be a deal-breaker.

In Chapter 4, I explained the difference between broad-phase and narrow-phase collision detection. Here's a quick refresher.

- **Broad-phase**: Checking for objects that are in the immediate vicinity of one another. It tells you which objects are most likely to collide.
- **Narrow-phase**: Checking for actual collisions between those objects. This is most commonly a distance-based check.

All the collision detection that we've done in the book so far has been narrow-phase. With a tile-based game engine, we have a fantastically efficient system for implementing broad-phase collision detection. Specifically, it's a type of broad-phase collision detection called a **spatial grid** (also referred to as a **uniform grid**).

You'll find an example of spatial-grid broad-phase collision detection in the `PlatformCollision` folder. Now the cat can jump from platform to platform, as shown in Figure 8-11.

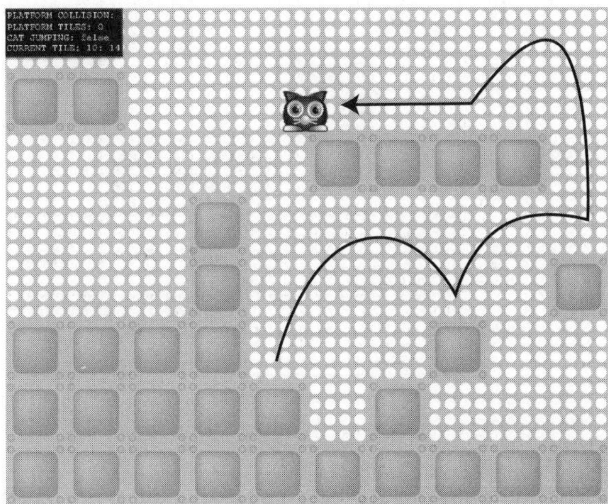

Figure 8-11. Accurate tile-based platform collision detection

The collision detection is clean and accurate, but the cat is only checking for collisions with platforms within its immediate vicinity. Let's take a close look at how this works

Understanding spatial grid collision

We know that our game world is a grid of cells. All the objects in the game, moving or stationary, occupy a cell.

The cat can collide only with objects that are in adjacent cells, so we just need to check the contents of those cells. If any of them contain objects that the cat needs to collide with, we will run a collision check on those objects.

To get you started thinking about this problem, I have a puzzle for you. Figure 8-12 is an illustration of a simple game world grid. The cat is in a cell at the center of the grid. Looking at that grid, can you tell which cells you need to check for collisions? Take a moment to think about it, and try not to peek at the answer.

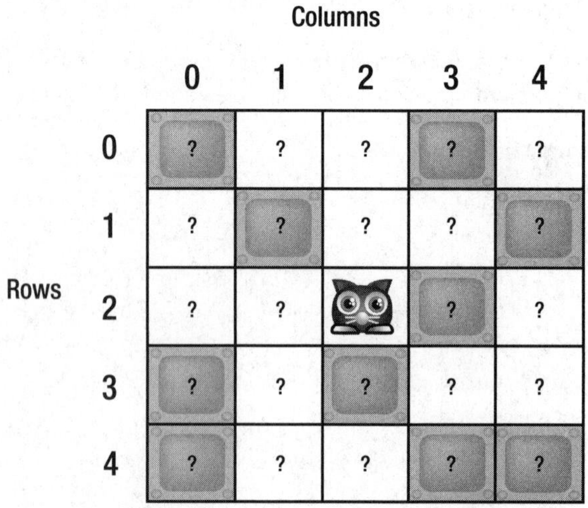

Figure 8-12. Puzzle 1: Which grid cells do you need to check for collisions?

Now I feel bad ... it was a trick question! The only cell that needs to be checked is the center cell that the cat occupies, 2-2. The cat is completely inside a single cell, so there's no likelihood that it will come into contact with any object from an adjacent cell.

But as you can see from the `PlatformCollision` SWF, the cat is hardly ever neatly contained within a single cell. It runs and jumps freely all over the stage, and is usually *between* cells. It's very likely that the cat will overlap more than one cell.

Figure 8-13 shows the second puzzle. The cat is overlapping four cells. Can you figure out which cells need to be checked for a collision?

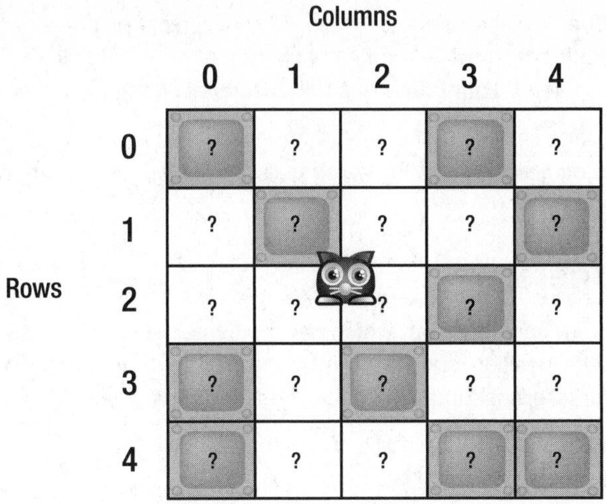

Figure 8-13. Puzzle 2: If the cat is overlapping more than one cell, which cells do you need to check for a collision?

The answer is that you must check every cell that the cat's four corners occupy. As shown in Figure 8-14, these are cells 1-1, 2-1, 1-2, and 2-2. By "the cat's four corners," I mean the tips of the cat's left and right ears, and the ends of its left and right paws.

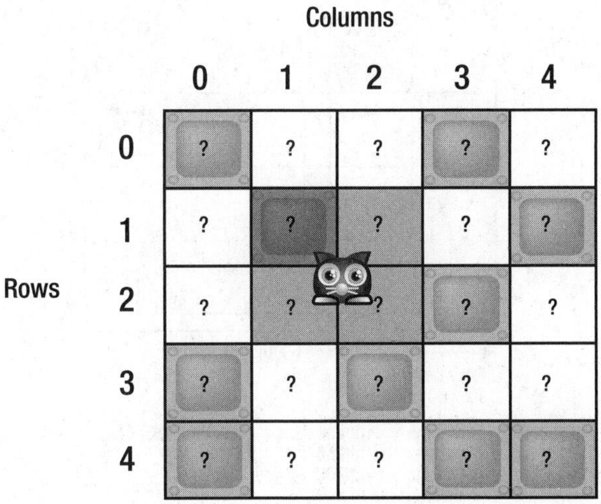

Figure 8-14. Find out which cells the four corners of the cat are in, and check those cells for collisions.

There are ten platforms on that grid. You don't need to do a collision check with all ten of them. Instead, you check the cat's four corners, and if any of those corners are in a cell that is occupied by a platform, you do a collision check on that cell. In a typical platform game where you might have hundreds of platforms, this is a huge savings. At most, you'll need to check for four platforms each frame. Even if your game has a thousand platforms, you'll never need to do more than those four checks.

But of course, this all hinges on knowing which cells the cat's four corners occupy. How can we figure this out?

Finding the corners

Let's first look at how we can figure out which cell the center of the cat occupies. To do this, find its center x and y stage position and divide it by the maximum tile size (64). Round it down to truncate the remainder. (This assumes the cat's `xPos` and `yPos` position is its top-left corner).

```
column = uint((cat.xPos + cat.width * 0.5) / 64);
row = uint((cat.yPos + cat.height * 0.5) / 64);
```

This is the same formula we looked at earlier in the chapter. Figure 8-15 illustrates how to find the cat's position.

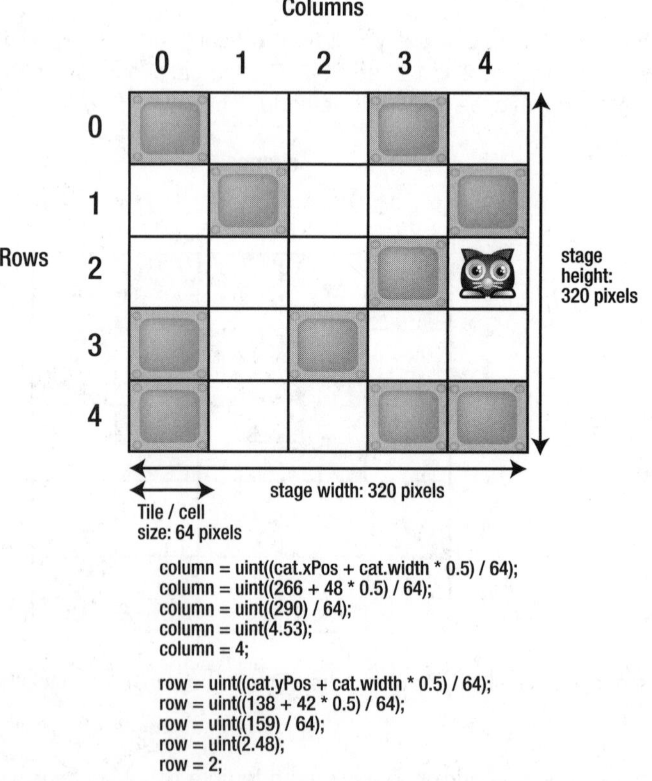

Figure 8-15. Find out in which column and row the cat is hiding.

Now we know the column and row of the cat's center point. To find its corner points, all we need to do is apply the same formula to the cat's corner points: top left, top right, bottom left, and bottom right, as shown in Figure 8-16.

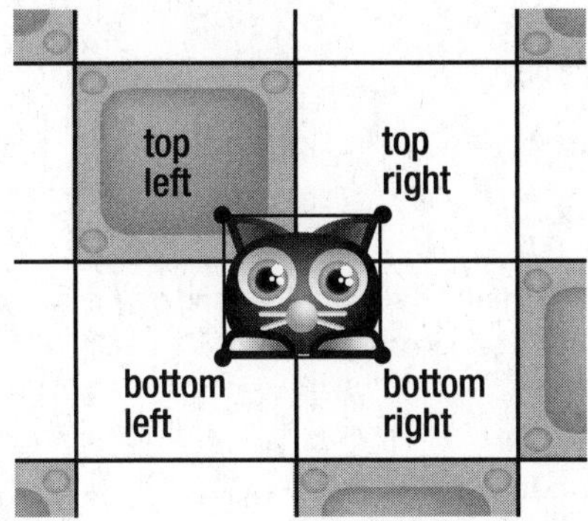

Figure 8-16. Apply the same formula to the cat's four corner points to find out which cells you need to check for collisions.

Calculating these points is basic to tile-based games, and the custom `TileModel` class introduced earlier in this chapter does this for us automatically. Remember that after the listing of that class, I told you to ignore the `get` methods at that time, because they wouldn't make sense to you yet. Now they certainly should make sense. Here are the getters from the `TileModel` class:

```
public function get top():uint
{
   var top:uint = uint(yPos / _maxTileSize);
   return top;
}
public function get bottom():uint
{
   var bottom:uint = uint((yPos + height) / _maxTileSize);
   return bottom;
}
public function get left():uint
{
   var left:uint = uint(xPos / _maxTileSize);
   return left;
}
public function get right():uint
{
   var right:uint = uint((xPos + width) / _maxTileSize);
   return right;
}
```

```
public function get centerX():uint
{
   var centerX:uint = uint((xPos + width * 0.5) / _maxTileSize);
   return centerX;
}
public function get centerY():uint
{
   var centerY:uint = uint((yPos + height * 0.5) / _maxTileSize);
   return centerY;
}
```

You can use these six values to find the columns and rows for all the corner points plus the object's center point. Here's what's you need to do this:

- A `TileModel` object
- A platform map array that contains the tile ID numbers of the platforms
- The ID numbers for the platform tiles, such as `00`

On each frame, you check which cells on the map the `TileModel` object's four corners are overlapping.

Here's a simplified, pseudo code version of how this all works:

```
var _platformMap:Array
  = [
      [10,10,10,10,10,10,10,10,10,10],
      [00,00,10,10,10,10,10,10,10,10],
      [10,10,10,10,10,00,00,00,00,10],
      [10,10,00,10,10,10,10,10,10,10],
      [10,10,10,10,10,10,10,10,10,10],
      [00,00,00,00,10,10,10,00,10,10],
      [00,00,00,00,00,10,10,10,10,10],
      [00,00,00,00,00,00,00,00,00,00]
    ];

var platform = 00;
var tileModel = new TileModel(MAX_TILE_SIZE, etc…);

enterFrameHandler
{
  //Move the tile model around the stage

  //Start the spatial grid, broad-phase collision check:

  //1. Check the top-left corner
  if(platformMap[tileModel.top][tileModel.left] == platform)
  {
    //Perform a narrow-phase collision check…
  }
```

```
  //2. Check the top-right corner
  if(platformMap[tileModel.top][tileModel.right] == platform)
  {
    //Perform a narrow-phase collision check…
  }

  //3. Check the bottom-left corner
  if(platformMap[tileModel.bottom][tileModel.left] == platform)
  {
    //Perform a narrow-phase collision check…
  }

  //4. Check the bottom-right corner
  if(platformMap[tileModel.bottom][tileModel.right] == platform)
  {
    //Perform a narrow-phase collision check…
  }
}
```

If your game objects are moving in only one direction at a time and not employing any physics, your collision methods could be as simple as just four `if` statements. As you will see, it becomes a little more complex in a practical application, but in essence, this is really all there is to it.

Remember that broad-phase collision can tell you only which objects are *likely to be colliding*. Its job is to weed out objects that will never collide, and tell you which objects you should probably check for a collision. It can't tell you if those objects actually are colliding or how you should handle those collisions. For that, you need to use any of these narrow-phase collision techniques:

- Particle versus line
- Circle versus line
- SAT
- Circle versus circle
- Bitmap collision

These are the same delightful little techniques we've spent much of this book discussing. The technique you use depends on the kinds of objects that are colliding. They're all completely compatible with a tile-based game engine.

Conveniently enough, the platforms in these examples are squares. That means that once we know that a collision is likely, we can use the SAT AABB collision technique discussed in Chapter 4 to resolve it.

Applying a spatial grid to platform collision

Now that you understand the concept, let's look at how the spatial grid is used in the example file.

We will be using many different collision methods in this chapter. To keep things organized, you'll find all of them in the TileCollisionController class in the com.friendsofed.utils package. The method in that class that checks for platform collisions is called platformCollision.

To use platformCollision, first create a new instance of the TileCollisionController class.

```
private var _collisionController:TileCollisionController
  = new TileCollisionController();
```

Then call its platformCollision method each frame.

```
private function enterFrameHandler(event:Event):void
{
  //...

  _collisionController.platformCollision
    (_catModel, _platformMap, MAX_TILE_SIZE, PLATFORM);

  //...
}
```

The platformCollision method takes four arguments:

- A TileModel object
- The array that stores the platform map
- The maximum tile size
- The ID number for the platform tiles (in this example, 00 or the value of PLATFORM)

The platformCollision method checks all four corners of the TileModel object to find out whether any of them are in a cell containing a platform tile. If this is true, it does a SAT-based collision check and moves the object out of the collision. And, because this is a platform game, the object's jumping property also must be set to false when it hits the bottom side of a platform. (Why? If you jump too high and bump your head on the ceiling, you usually stop jumping!)

The following is the full platformCollision method. Apart from a shortcut to simplify the SAT collision using the modulus operator (which I'll explain after the listing), it should be quite self-explanatory. It's a version of the code we discussed in detail in Chapter 4.

```
public function platformCollision
  (
    gameObject:TileModel,
    platformMap:Array,
    maxTileSize:uint,
    platform:uint
  ):void
{
  //Variables needed to figure out by how much the object
  //is overlapping the tile on the x and y axes
  //The axis with the most overlap is the axis on which
  //the collision is occurring. This is an inverted SAT system
  var overlapX:Number;
  var overlapY:Number;

  //If the object's top-left corner is overlapping the cell
  //on its upper left side...
  if(platformMap[gameObject.top][gameObject.left] == platform)
  {
    //Figure out by how much the object's top-left corner
    //point is overlapping the cell on both the x and y
    //axes
    overlapX = gameObject.xPos % maxTileSize;
    overlapY = gameObject.yPos % maxTileSize;

    if(overlapY >= overlapX)
    {
      //Extra check to see whether the object is moving up
      //and that its bottom-left corner isn't also touching a platform
      if(gameObject.vy < 0
      && platformMap[gameObject.bottom][gameObject.left] != platform)
      {
        //Collision on top side of the object
        //Position the object to the bottom
        //edge of the platform cell
        //which it is overlapping and set its vy to zero
        gameObject.setY = (gameObject.mapRow * maxTileSize);
        gameObject.vy = 0;
      }

    }
    else
    {
      //Collision on left side of the object
      //Position the object to the right
      //edge of the platform cell and set its vx to zero
      gameObject.setX
        = gameObject.mapColumn * maxTileSize;
      gameObject.vx = 0;
    }
  }
```

```
//If the object's bottom-left corner is overlapping the cell
//on its lower left side...
if(platformMap[gameObject.bottom][gameObject.left] == platform)
{
  overlapX = gameObject.xPos % maxTileSize;

  //Measure the y overlap from the far left side of the tile
  //and compensate for the object's height
  overlapY
    = maxTileSize
    - ((gameObject.yPos + gameObject.height) % maxTileSize);

  if(overlapY >= overlapX)
  {
    //Extra check to see whether the object is moving down
    //and that its top-left corner isn't also touching a platform
    if(gameObject.vy > 0
    && platformMap[gameObject.top][gameObject.left] != platform)
    {
      //Collision on bottom
      gameObject.setY
        = (gameObject.mapRow * maxTileSize)
        + (maxTileSize - gameObject.height);
      gameObject.vy = 0;
      gameObject.jumping = false;
    }
  }
  else
  {
    //Collision on left
    gameObject.setX
       = gameObject.mapColumn * maxTileSize;
    gameObject.vx = 0;
  }
}

//If the object's bottom-right corner is overlapping the cell
//on its lower right side...
if(platformMap[gameObject.bottom][gameObject.right] == platform)
{
  //Measure the x and y overlap from the far right and bottom
  //side of the tile and compensate for the object's
  //height and width
  overlapX
   = maxTileSize
   - ((gameObject.xPos + gameObject.width) % maxTileSize);
  overlapY
   = maxTileSize
   - ((gameObject.yPos + gameObject.height) % maxTileSize);
```

```
    if(overlapY >= overlapX)
    {
      //Extra check to see whether the object is moving up
      //and that its top-right corner isn't also touching a platform
      if(gameObject.vy > 0
      && platformMap[gameObject.top][gameObject.right] != platform)
      {
        //Collision on bottom
        gameObject.setY
          = (gameObject.mapRow * maxTileSize)
          + (maxTileSize - gameObject.height);
        gameObject.vy = 0;
        gameObject.jumping = false;
      }
    }
    else
    {
      //Collision on right
      gameObject.setX
        = (gameObject.mapColumn * maxTileSize)
        + ((maxTileSize - gameObject.width) - 1);
      gameObject.vx = 0;
    }
  }
  //If the object's top-right corner is overlapping the cell
  //on its upper right side...
  if(platformMap[gameObject.top][gameObject.right]  == platform)
  {
    //Measure the x overlap from the far right side of the
    //tile and compensate for the object's width
    overlapX
      = maxTileSize
      - ((gameObject.xPos + gameObject.width) % maxTileSize);
    overlapY = gameObject.yPos % maxTileSize;

    if(overlapY >= overlapX)
    {
      //Extra check to see whether the object is moving down
      //and that its bottom-right corner isn't also touching a platform
      if(gameObject.vy < 0
      && platformMap[gameObject.bottom][gameObject.right]
      != platform)
```

```
        {
          gameObject.setY = (gameObject.mapRow * maxTileSize);
          gameObject.vy = 0;
        }
      }
      else
      {
        //Collision on right
        gameObject.setX
          = (gameObject.mapColumn * maxTileSize)
          + ((maxTileSize - gameObject.width) - 1);
        gameObject.vx = 0;
      }
    }
}
```

The narrow-phase collision detection between the cat and platforms is handled using SAT. It's a standard rectangle-versus-rectangle (AABB) collision test. It just so happens that in this platform collision system, the platforms are the same size as the maximum tile size. We can use this to our advantage to take a sneaky shortcut in the SAT calculations to avoid needing to calculate any vectors.

All four sides of the platform are checked for a collision using the cat's four corner points. The top-left corner is the easiest to calculate. Let's look at how that works.

First, check whether the cat's top-left corner is inside a platform tile.

```
if(platformMap[gameObject.top][gameObject.left] == platform)
{...
```

If this is `true`, calculate the amount of overlap. All we need to do is find the *remainder* of the object's position divided by the maximum tile size. Finding the remainder means using the modulus operator (`%`).

```
overlapX = gameObject.xPos % maxTileSize;
overlapY = gameObject.yPos % maxTileSize;
```

This will tell us the distance of the point to the cell's top-left corner. It works no matter which cell in the grid we need to check. We don't need to know the column or row number, because all the cells are the same size. Figure 8-17 illustrates how the overlap value is found.

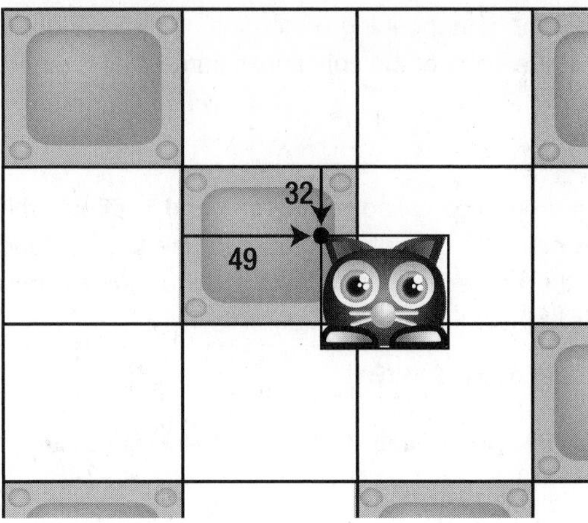

cat.xPos = 113
cat.yPos = 96
maxTileSize = 64

Calculate the overlap:

overlapX = cat.xPos % maxTileSize
overlapX = 113 % 64
overlapX = 49

overlapY = cat.xPos % maxTileSize
overlapY = 96 % 64
overlapY = 32

The overlap occurs on the axis with
the largest overlap value

Figure 8-17. Use the modulus operator to help calculate the amount of overlap on the x and y axes.

You can see in Figure 8-17 that the cat is colliding with the platform on the x axis, from the left. Because we are measuring the overlap based on the distance between the top-left corner of both the cat and the cell, it's the axis with the *largest* overlap that indicates the collision axis. This is an inversion of the usual SAT system, but the principle is exactly the same.

Now that we know the collision is happening on the left side of the platform, we can position the cat so that it's flush against the edge of the column it's currently occupying.

```
cat.setX = cat.mapColumn * maxTileSize;
cat.vx = 0;
```

The TileModel class has properties called mapColumn and mapRow, which tell you which column and row the center of the object is occupying. You can use these properties to move the object out of the collision, as in the preceding code. Here are the mapColumn and mapRow getters and setters from the TileModel class:

```
public function get mapColumn():uint
{
   _mapColumn = uint((xPos + width * 0.5) / _maxTileSize);
   return _mapColumn;
}
public function set mapColumn(value:uint):void
{
   _mapColumn = value;
}
public function get mapRow():uint
{
   _mapRow = uint((yPos + height * 0.5) / _maxTileSize);
   return _mapRow;
}
public function set mapRow(value:uint):void
{
   _mapRow = value;
}
```

The other three corners of the object are checked in the same way. However, the overlap is a bit trickier to calculate. For example, here's how to find the amount of overlap for the bottom-right corner:

```
overlapX
  = maxTileSize
  - ((gameObject.xPos + gameObject.width) % maxTileSize);
overlapY
  = maxTileSize
  - ((gameObject.yPos + gameObject.height) % maxTileSize);
```

We need to find the distance from the cat's bottom-right corner to the bottom-right corner of the cell.

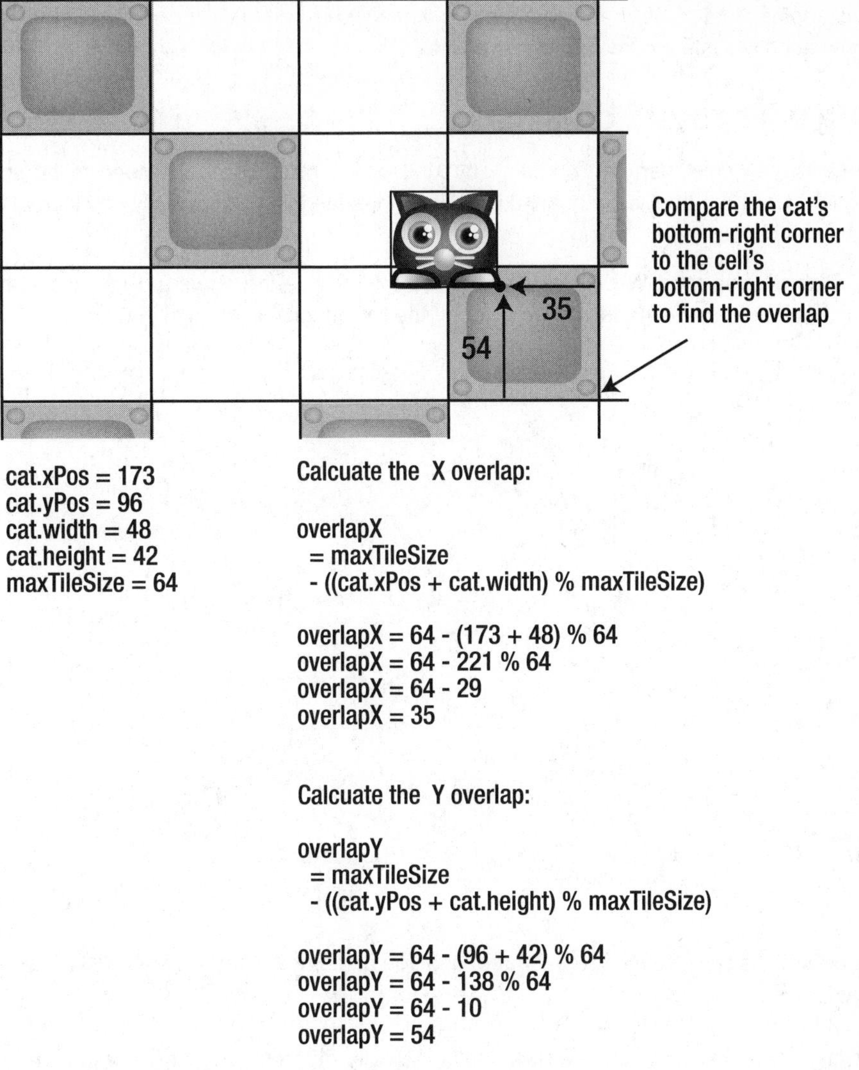
Compare the cat's
bottom-right corner
to the cell's
bottom-right corner
to find the overlap
35
54
cat.xPos = 173
cat.yPos = 96
cat.width = 48
cat.height = 42
maxTileSize = 64
Calcuate the X overlap:
overlapX
= maxTileSize
- ((cat.xPos + cat.width) % maxTileSize)
overlapX = 64 - (173 + 48) % 64
overlapX = 64 - 221 % 64
overlapX = 64 - 29
overlapX = 35
Calcuate the Y overlap:
overlapY
= maxTileSize
- ((cat.yPos + cat.height) % maxTileSize)
overlapY = 64 - (96 + 42) % 64
overlapY = 64 - 138 % 64
overlapY = 64 - 10
overlapY = 54

Figure 8-18. To calculate the overlap on the bottom-right corner, take the object's width and height into account.

The bottom-left and top-right corners are checked in a similar way. Again, because all the cells are exactly the same size, you don't need to know the actual stage position of the cell. It could be any cell; the formula will work the same for all of them.

This platform collision-detection system is one approach that solved the problem for the examples in this chapter, but it is certainly not a one-size-fits-all solution. You'll almost certainly need to tailor your collision-detection methods to suit the particular problems of your games. If you understand the basic principle of how to check which cells the four corners of your game objects are overlapping, that's really all you need to know. You can build on and adapt any of the collision-detection systems presented in this book.

Working with round tiles

The cells of the game map can contain any kind of objects. They don't need to be square or rectangular. They can be filled with any kinds of shapes, and you can employ any kind of collision strategy you choose.

For an example, run the SWF in the `RoundTiles` folder. Use the mouse to make the small star button bounce around the stage and ricochet off the big buttons, as shown in Figure 8-19.

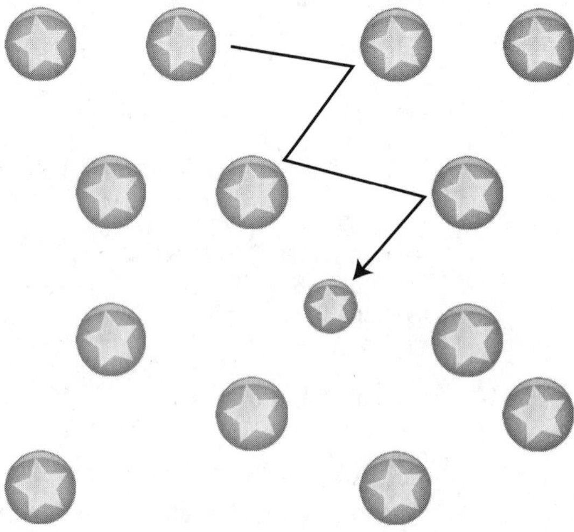

Figure 8-19. Tiles can be any size or shape, and you can employ any kind of collision-detection strategy.

At first glance, this seems like it would use a radically different kind of game engine than the platform game example. But the tile-based game engine is *exactly the same*.

The only difference is in the narrow-phase collision, which uses a circle-versus-circle collision-detection strategy. It's really just one line of code:

```
_collisionController.roundPlatformCollision
    (_playerModel, _platformMap, MAX_TILE_SIZE, ROUND_TILE);
```

You'll find specifics of this method in the `TileCollisionController` class. These two methods do all the work:

- *roundPlatformCollision* checks the four corners of the small star and calls the roundTileCollision method if it suspects a collision might be occurring.
- *roundTileCollision* performs a standard circle-versus-circle collision check. The code is almost identical to the code that we looked at in Chapter 3.

Make sure to check out the specifics of the code in the TileCollisionController class. You won't find any surprises, and the code is actually simpler than the code we've just looked at for platform collisions.

> *If your tile objects travel to the bottom or far right of the stage, there's a chance that they might check for a row or column that doesn't exist. For example, let's say your game map has eight rows. If your tile object is on the bottom row, it might check for objects in row 9, the next one down. But row 9 doesn't exist, and you'll get this nasty runtime error:*
>
> ```
> TypeError: Error #1010: A term is undefined and has no
> properties.
> ```
>
> *To avoid this, limit the cells that the tile object checks to the maximum numbers of columns and rows.*
>
> ```
> if(tileModelObject.bottom < platformMap.length
> && tileModelObject.right < platformMap[0].length)
> {…
> ```
>
> *This will constrain the search to the dimensions of the game map.*

From the RoundTiles example, you can see how a tile-based game engine would be great for quickly building a game like Peggle or Pinball.

Adding more interaction

Now that we have a game world, it's time to make it more interactive. We'll add ways to move around and explore, objects to collect, and enemies to overcome.

Adding soft platforms

Platform games usually feature a very common type of platform that I call a **soft platform**. A soft platform is like a one-way door. It's a platform that allows the player to jump up through it from below, onto its top surface. But when the player is on top of the platform, it stops the player from falling through. This gives the game a sense of shallow depth, as if the platforms were layered ledges or steps.

Soft platforms are a good example of how a tile-based game engine can help you easily solve what would otherwise be a complex logic problem.

You'll find an example of soft platforms at work in the SoftPlatform folder. Run the SWF, and you'll see the cat can jump up through the pink platforms, as shown in Figure 8-20.

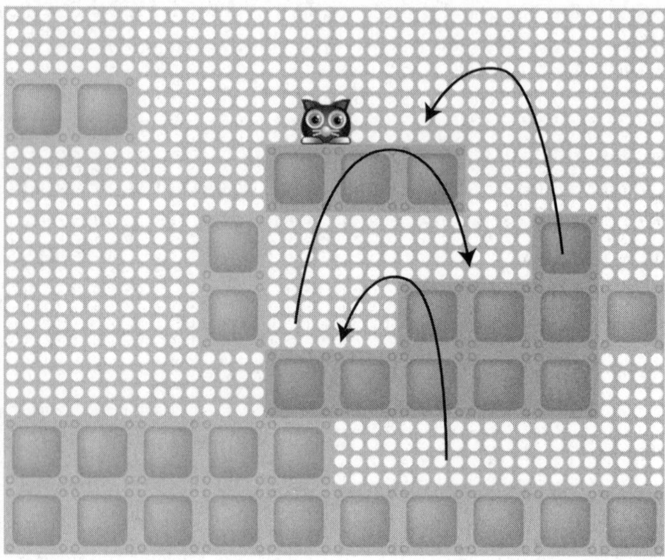

Figure 8-20. Soft platforms allow the cat to jump up onto them, but prevent it from falling through.

Take a look at the SoftPlatform application class, and you'll see that platform tiles are added to the game world just like all the other tiles, using the buildMap method. The enterFrameHandler checks for collisions with soft platforms each frame by calling the collision controller's softPlatformCollision method.

```
_collisionController.softPlatformCollision
   (_catModel, _platformMap, MAX_TILE_SIZE, SOFT_PLATFORM);
```

The _collisionController has a Boolean variable called _softPlatformOpen, which is initialized to true when the game first starts. As soon as the cat jumps up through the platform, it sets it to false. This locks the platform and prevents the cat from falling through it. _softPlatformOpen is set back to true when the cat jumps off the platform.

The code that does all this has a very interesting feature. It needs to know when the bottom of the cat has cleared the top of the platform so that the platform can be closed. It does this by checking what kind of tile the bottom of the cat occupied *in the previous frame*. The only reason for the previous tile being different from the current tile is that the cat has cleared the top of the platform.

This check acts as a tripwire to close the platform. Because we're using Verlet integration, we already know what the cat's previous position was. It's stored in the cat's previousY property that it inherited from the AVerletModel class. And because we're using a tile-based engine, we can easily analyze which tile the bottom of the cat occupied in both the current frame and the previous one. All this comes together in a few lines of surprisingly simple code.

Here's the `softPlatformCollision` method that achieves this effect:

```
public function softPlatformCollision
  (
    gameObject:TileModel,
    platformMap:Array,
    maxTileSize:uint,
    softPlatform:uint
  ):void
{
  //Check whether the object is moving down
  if(gameObject.vy > 0)
  {
    //If the object's bottom-left corner is overlapping the
    //soft platform cell
    //on its lower-left side or right side...
    if(platformMap[gameObject.bottom][gameObject.left]
      == softPlatform
    || platformMap[gameObject.bottom][gameObject.right]
      == softPlatform)
    {
      //Find out which cell the bottom of the object
      //was in on the previous frame
      var previousTile:uint
        = uint((gameObject.previousY
        + gameObject.height) / maxTileSize);

      //Compare the current tile to the previous tile.
      //If they're not the same, then you know that the
      //object has crossed above the top of the tile
      if(gameObject.bottom != previousTile
      || !_softPlatformOpen)
      {
        //Collision on bottom
        gameObject.setY
          = (gameObject.mapRow * maxTileSize)
          + (maxTileSize - gameObject.height);
        gameObject.vy = 0;
        gameObject.jumping = false;

        //Close the platform so that the object
        //can't fall through
        _softPlatformOpen = false;
      }
    }
  }
```

```
    //Open the platform if the object is
    //moving upwards again
    if(gameObject.vy < 0)
    {
      _softPlatformOpen = true;
    }
}
```

You can use this same technique for any kind of door or passageway where you want to permit the player to move in only one direction.

Adding elevators

So far, all the platforms in our tile-based game engine have been stationary. Let's give the cat a bit of a challenge: a moving elevator to jump on, as shown in Figure 8-21. You'll find this in the `Elevator` folder

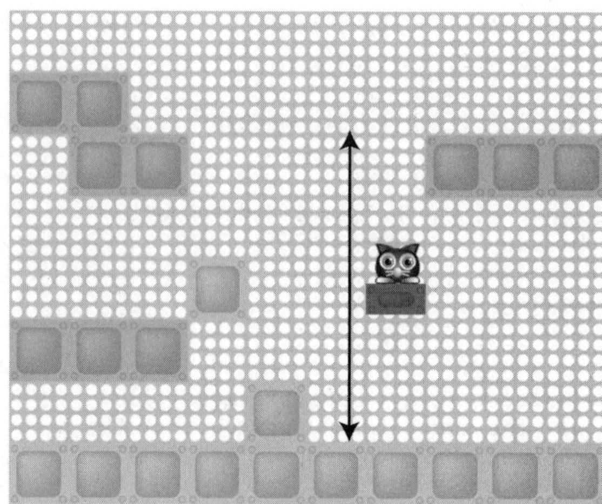

Figure 8-21. Take a ride on an elevator.

The elevator moves from the ground up to the platforms on the third row, and back down again. The cat can jump onto it at any point and take a ride to the top or bottom. The cat can also jump up through the elevator from the bottom, just as it can jump through soft platforms.

The concepts behind the elevator are quite simple. The game reverses the elevator's velocity when it detects that it's moving too far up or down. When the cat is on top of the elevator, its velocity is set to the velocity of the elevator.

Let's look at a few of the specifics in greater detail.

The elevator is added to the `_gameObjectMap`.

```
private const ELEVATOR:uint = 22;

private var _gameObjectMap:Array
   = [
        [-1,-1,-1,-1,-1,-1,-1,-1,-1,-1],
        [-1,-1,-1,-1,-1,-1,-1,-1,-1,-1],
        [-1,20,-1,-1,-1,-1,-1,-1,-1,-1],
        [-1,-1,-1,-1,-1,-1,-1,-1,-1,-1],
        [-1,-1,-1,-1,-1,-1,-1,-1,-1,-1],
        [-1,-1,-1,-1,-1,-1,-1,-1,-1,-1],
        [-1,-1,-1,-1,-1,-1,22,-1,-1,-1],
        [-1,-1,-1,-1,-1,-1,-1,-1,-1,-1],
     ];
```

Its location is its start position on row 7 near the bottom of the map.

It's added to the game world by the `buildMap` method.

```
case ELEVATOR:
  _elevatorModel
    = new TileModel
    (
      MAX_TILE_SIZE,
      tileSheetColumn, tileSheetRow,
      mapRow, mapColumn,
      64, 32
    );
  _elevatorModel.friction = 1;
  _elevatorModel.vy = -2;
  drawGameObject
    (_elevatorModel, _foregroundBitmapData);
  break;
```

It's given a velocity of `-2`, which causes it to start moving toward the top of the stage when the game first starts.

The `enterFrameHandler` updates the elevator's model. It also checks to see which row on the game map the elevator is currently occupying. If the top of the elevator reaches row 1 or its bottom reaches row 7, the elevator's velocity is reversed.

```
_elevatorModel.update();

if(_elevatorModel.top == 1
|| _elevatorModel.bottom == 7)
{
  _elevatorModel.vy = -_elevatorModel.vy;
}
```

The `enterFrameHandler` also blits the elevator to the foreground bitmap each frame.

```
drawGameObject(_elevatorModel, _foregroundBitmapData);
```

A collision check between the cat and the elevator is also done each frame.

```
_collisionController.elevatorCollision
    (_catModel, _elevatorModel);
```

This method runs a standard SAT collision check, which tests for overlapping rectangles. The one modification to the code we looked at in Chapter 4 is that it blocks the player only when the player is striking it from the top. This is the same soft platform effect described in the previous section. It allows the player to jump up through the elevator from the bottom and come to rest on its top side for a very natural-looking effect.

The following is the complete `elevatorCollision` method from the `TileModelController` class. This is an ordinary distance-based collision check using vectors, and doesn't use a spatial grid.

```
public function elevatorCollision
  (gameObject:TileModel, elevator:TileModel):void
{
 var v0:VectorModel
    = new VectorModel
    (
      gameObject.xPos + gameObject.width * 0.5,
      gameObject.yPos + gameObject.height * 0.5,
      elevator.xPos + elevator.width * 0.5,
      elevator.yPos + elevator.height * 0.5
    );

  if(Math.abs(v0.vy) < gameObject.height * 0.5 + elevator.height * 0.5)
  {
     //A collision has occurred!
     //Find out the size of the overlap on both the x and y axes
     var overlap_X:Number
       = gameObject.width * 0.5
       + elevator.width * 0.5 - Math.abs(v0.vx);
     var overlap_Y:Number
       = gameObject.height * 0.5
       + elevator.height * 0.5 - Math.abs(v0.vy);

     //The collision has occurred on the axis with the
     //smallest amount of overlap. Let's figure out which axis that is
     if(overlap_X >=  overlap_Y)
     {
       //The collision is happening on the x axis
       //But on which side? (top or bottom?)
       //v0's vy can tell us
       if(v0.vy > 0)
         {
           //Collision on top
           //Check whether the gameObject is completely
           //above the platform.
```

```
            //"-2" is added to provide a bit of
            //tolerance that might be needed if the
            //downward velocities of the gameObject and
            //platform are very similar.

            if
              (
                gameObject.previousY - 2
                  < elevator.yPos - gameObject.height
                || !_elevatorOpen
                || (uint(gameObject.vy) == 0 && elevator.vy < 0)
              )
           {
            //Move the gameObject out of the collision
            gameObject.setY = elevator.yPos - gameObject.height;

            //Set the gameObject's vy to the elevator's vy
            gameObject.vy = elevator.vy;
            gameObject.jumping = false;

            //Close the elevator so that the object
            //can't fall through
            _elevatorOpen = false;
           }
         }
       }
     }
     else
     {
        //No collision
     }
     //Open the elevator if the gameObject is
     //moving upwards again and its velocity
     //isn't exactly the same as the elevator's
     if(gameObject.vy < 0
     && gameObject.vy != elevator.vy)
     {
        _elevatorOpen = true;
     }
}
```

The elevator uses a different tripwire from the soft platforms we looked at earlier to prevent the cat from falling through. It checks whether the bottom of the cat was above the platform in the previous frame.

```
if
   (
      gameObject.previousY - 2
        < elevator.yPos - gameObject.height
      || !_elevatorOpen
      || gameObject.vy == 0 && elevator.vy < 0
   )
{
  //… stop the object on the surface of the elevator
```

The -2 value is a bit of tolerance that I added while testing the example. I found that if the vertical velocity of the elevator and the cat are too close, the cat will sometimes appear to unnaturally miss a collision with the top of the elevator.

If this wire is tripped, the code sets the cat's vertical velocity to the elevator's vertical velocity, and closes the elevator to prevent the cat from falling through. It does this by setting the _elevatorOpen variable to false. _elevatorOpen is set to true again when the cat moves upward at a velocity that doesn't equal the elevator's velocity. In other words, when it jumps off the elevator.

```
if(gameObject.vy < 0
&& gameObject.vy != elevator.vy)
{
  _elevatorOpen = true;
}
```

This can only mean that the cat is jumping off the elevator.

There's another check that the code needs to make:

```
|| gameObject.vy == 0 && elevator.vy < 0
```

This means "If the object isn't moving and the elevator is moving up …." This allows the cat to hop on an elevator when it's standing on the edge of platform and one of its bottom corners catches the lip of elevator as the elevator is moving up. It won't be apparent in this example how it works, but you'll see it in action in the Enemies example coming up soon.

Collecting objects

Run the SWF in the CollectingObjects folder for an example of how to make objects that can be collected in a tile-based blit environment. Ride the elevator up to the platform and collect the star. The star disappears when the cat touches it, as shown in Figure 8-22.

Figure 8-22. When the cat touches the star, it disappears.

It's easy to achieve this effect using `Sprite` or `MovieClip` objects, because you just need to set the object's `visible` property to `false` to make it disappear. But in a blit display environment, we don't have that option. Things become invisible when they stop being drawn to the stage. This means that the logic for making things invisible in a blit environment looks something like this:

```
if(the object exists)
{
  blit the object to the stage bitmap
}
```

As soon as you stop blitting the object, it disappears.

This is an extra little consideration in a blit display environment, but it's not difficult to implement.

The cat-versus-star collision detection uses a spatial grid. That means it first checks to see whether one of the cat's corner points is in the same cell as the star. If that turns out to be true, a distance check tests whether the cat and star are overlapping. If they are, the collision method returns `true` to the application class.

Here's the `starCollision` method from the `TileCollisionController` class that handles both this broad-phase and narrow-phase collision check:

```
public function starCollision
   (
     gameObject:TileModel,
     starTileObject:TileModel,
     platformMap:Array,
     maxTileSize:uint,
     star:uint
   ):Boolean
{
  var collision:Boolean = false;

  //Make sure that the code doesn't check for rows that
  //are greater than the number of rows and columns on the map
  if(gameObject.bottom < platformMap.length
  && gameObject.right < platformMap[0].length)
  {
     //If the object's corners are overlapping a tile
     //that contains a star...
     if(platformMap[gameObject.top][gameObject.left] == star
     || platformMap[gameObject.top][gameObject.right] == star
     || platformMap[gameObject.bottom][gameObject.left]  == star
     || platformMap[gameObject.bottom][gameObject.right] == star)
     {
        //Plot a vector between the gameObject's center point and the star
        var v0:VectorModel
          = new VectorModel
          (
            gameObject.xPos + (gameObject.width * 0.5),
            gameObject.yPos + (gameObject.height * 0.5),
            starTileObject.xPos + (starTileObject.width * 0.5),
            starTileObject.yPos + (starTileObject.height * 0.5)
          );

        //Calculate the the combined widths of the objects
        var totalRadii:Number
          = gameObject.width * 0.5
          + starTileObject.width * 0.5;

        if(v0.m < totalRadii)
        {
           //There's a collision if the distance between the objects
           //is less than their combined widths
           collision = true;
        }
     }
  }
```

```
  //Return the true or false value of "collision"
  //back to the application class
  return collision;
}
```

All this method really does is return a `true` or `false` value. The application class must decide what to do with this information. This is what it needs to consider:

```
if(the star exists…)
{
  Blit the star to the foreground bitmap.
  Check for a collision between the cat and the star…
  If(the collision method returns "true")
  {
    … set the star to null. It no longer exists.
  }
}
```

The actual code in the `CollectingObjects` application class that does this is not much different from the pseudo code.

```
_foregroundBitmapData.fillRect(_foregroundBitmapData.rect, 0);

//If the star exists...
if(_starModel != null)
{
  //Blit the star on the stage
  drawGameObject(_starModel, _foregroundBitmapData);

  //Check for a collision with the cat.
  //(This will be either "true" or "false")
  var collisionIsHappening:Boolean
    = _collisionController.starCollision
      (
        _catModel, _starModel,
        _gameObjectMap, MAX_TILE_SIZE, STAR
      );

  //Set the _starModel to null if a collision is happening.
  //This will prevent it from being displayed
  //in the next frame, which makes it "invisible"
  if(collisionIsHappening)
  {
    _starModel = null;
  }
}
```

It's very important to remember to add this code *after* the `foregroundBitmapData` is cleared, because the code blits the star to the stage.

```
_foregroundBitmapData.fillRect(_foregroundBitmapData.rect, 0);
```

If you accidentally add it before this line of code, the star will be cleared as soon as it's added, and you won't see it on the stage.

Wind them up and let them loose!

Objects in tile-based games are aware of their environment. They know whether they're on a platform, in the sky, or next to a wall. This means that you can create general rules about how enemies behave. You can program objects to always change direction when they hit a wall, to jump over lava pits, or take to the air if they reach the edge of a cliff. If you program your objects carefully, they will be able to make autonomous decisions about how to behave depending on the kinds of environmental obstacles that are in their way. You can create completely new game maps and drop your objects in to watch how they behave.

A simple example of this "wind them up and let them loose" effect is in the `Enemies` folder. A hedgehog enemy moves back and forth across the platform, and the elevator moves up and down between two levels of platforms, as shown in Figure 8-23.

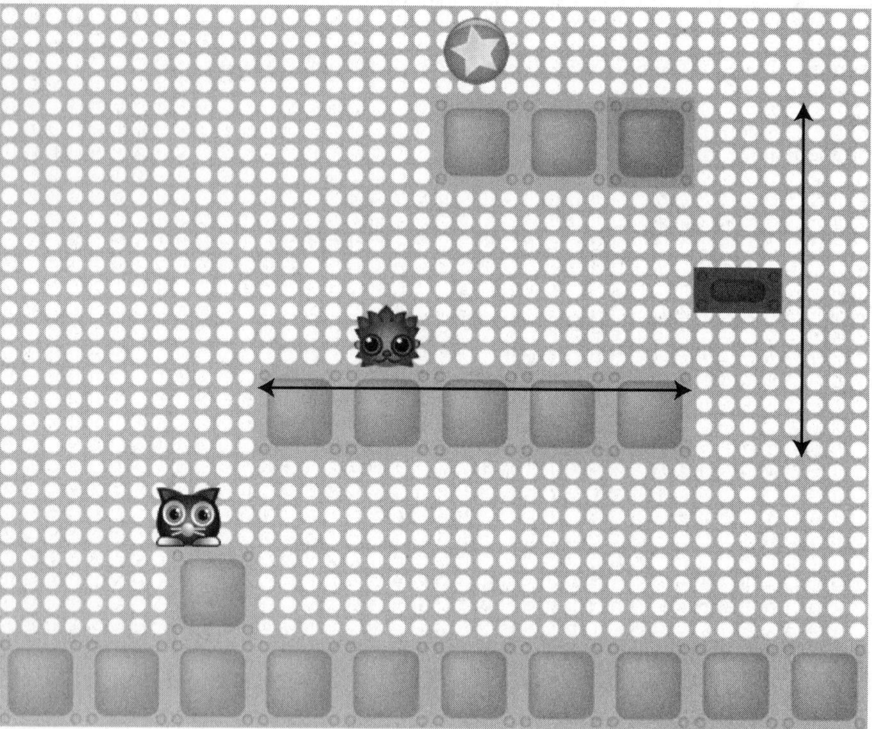

Figure 8-23. The hedgehog and elevator make decisions about where to move based on their changing environment.

Neither object has been preprogrammed to move between specific map cells. Instead, they're sensing where they are in the world and making a decision to act when their environment changes.

The hedgehog doesn't like heights. Whenever it reaches the edge of a platform, it gets spooked and reverses direction. But how does it know it's on "the edge of a platform"? Our code needs to find some way of describing this boundary. Look carefully at Figure 8-23, and you'll notice that this isn't too hard to figure out. When the tile in the row *below* the hedgehog becomes SKY, we know the hedgehog has reached the end of the platform. Check this for both the hedgehog's left and right side, and reverse the velocity if this turns out to be true. Figure 8-24 illustrates this logic.

Figure 8-24. The hedgehog changes direction if it detects that the tile below it is sky.

You can find the cell in the row below the hedgehog like this:

```
_platformMap[_hedgehogModel.centerY + 1][_hedgehogModel.centerX]
```

This will tell you what kind of tile is in the cell directly below the center of the hedgehog. The + 1 means "one greater than the current row." So, if the hedgehog is currently on row 6, adding +1 will refer to row 7.

The preceding line of code uses the hedgehog's center point to find the cell below it. If we used this line of code in the game, it would work, but the hedgehog would move halfway over the edge of the platform before it noticed that the bottom tile had changed to SKY. In this example, we want the hedgehog to change direction as soon as its extreme left and right edges sense that the lower tile has changed. To do this, we can use the TileModel's left and right properties.

Here's how to find the tile at the bottom left:

```
_platformMap[_hedgehogModel.centerY + 1][_hedgehogModel.left]
```

And here's how to find the tile at the bottom right:

```
_platformMap[_hedgehogModel.centerY + 1][_hedgehogModel.right]
```

All you need to do is use these in an if statement and check whether they equal the value of SKY. If they do, reverse the hedgehog's vx.

```
if
  (
```

```
    _platformMap
      [_hedgehogModel.centerY + 1]
      [_hedgehogModel.left]
      == SKY
    ||
    _platformMap
      [_hedgehogModel.centerY + 1]
      [_hedgehogModel.right]
      == SKY
  )
{
  _hedgehogModel.vx = -_hedgehogModel.vx;
}
```

The hedgehog's entire AI is this one simple `if` statement. And because it's based on a very general rule, it will work no matter how long the platform is or where on the map the hedgehog is placed. This means you can make maps with platforms and hedgehogs, place them anywhere, and they will work as expected, without changing a single line of code. It's a feature of the game engine.

The elevator follows the same logic, but needs to check for more conditions, as shown in Figure 8-25.

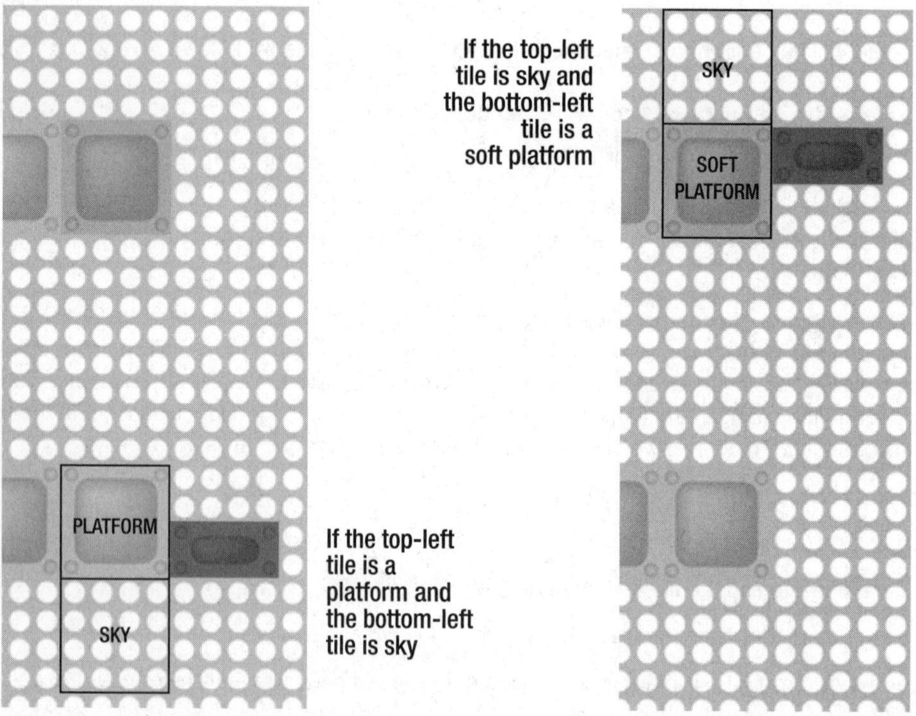

Figure 8-25. The elevator reverses direction when these specific environmental conditions are met.

If you can conceptualize this problem logically, it's a small step to turn it into working code. Here's the code from the `Enemies` application class that does this:

```
//If the elevator is going down...
if(_elevatorModel.vy > 0)
{
  if
    (
      _platformMap
         [_elevatorModel.bottom]
         [_elevatorModel.centerX - 1]
         == SKY
      &&
      _platformMap
         [_elevatorModel.top]
         [_elevatorModel.centerX - 1]
         == PLATFORM
    )
  {
    _elevatorModel.vy = -_elevatorModel.vy;
  }
}
//If the elevator is going up...
else
{
  if
    (
      _platformMap
         [_elevatorModel.top]
         [_elevatorModel.centerX - 1]
         == SKY
      &&
      _platformMap
         [_elevatorModel.bottom]
         [_elevatorModel.centerX - 1]
         == SOFT_PLATFORM
    )
  {
    _elevatorModel.vy = -_elevatorModel.vy;
  }
}
```

Complex conditional checks like this are possible because we can check the object's top and bottom corners simultaneously. This is a simple example, but using the same technique could result in sophisticated AI if you program your objects to react to changing game and environmental conditions.

Squashing enemies

In this next example, I'll show you how to vanquish an enemy in the time-honored tradition of jumping on its head. Run the SquashEnemy SWF, and you'll see that you can now make the hedgehog disappear by jumping on it. The collision will also cause the cat to bounce. Figure 8-26 shows the action.

Figure 8-26. Squash and bounce

This effect is much easier to implement than it might at first appear. For collision-detection purposes, the cat and the hedgehog are circles. This is a basic circle-versus-circle collision-detection system. The object's half widths are the collision circles' radii. A tweak is that a collision is checked only if the cat is above the hedgehog. The bounce effect is the standard circle bounce effect that we covered in Chapter 3.

As with the star object, the hedgehog needs to disappear from the stage when a collision is detected. This means setting its value to `null` after the collision. To ensure that the code doesn't try to access any `null` objects, we need to wrap the hedgehog's update, movement, collision, and blit code in a single `if` statement block.

```
if(_hedgehogModel != null)
{
  //1. Update the model
  _hedgehogModel.update();

  //2. Check platform boundaries
  if
  (
    _platformMap
      [_hedgehogModel.centerY + 1]
      [_hedgehogModel.left]
      == SKY
```

```
      ||
      _platformMap
         [_hedgehogModel.centerY + 1]
         [_hedgehogModel.right]
         == SKY
    )
  {
    _hedgehogModel.vx = -_hedgehogModel.vx;
  }

  //3. Collision check.
  //Set the _hedgehogModel to "null" if the
  //enemyCollision method returns "true"
  if
    (
      _collisionController.enemyCollision
         (_catModel, _hedgehogModel)
    )
  {
    _hedgehogModel = null;
  }

  //4. Blit the hedgehog if enemyCollision returns "false"
  else
  {
    drawGameObject(_hedgehogModel, _foregroundBitmapData);
  }
}
```

This `if` statement does the job of deciding whether or not to set the `_hedgehogModel` to `null` while also running the actual collision method:

```
if
  (
    _collisionController.enemyCollision
       (_catModel, _hedgehogModel)
  )
{
  _hedgehogModel = null;
}
```

Note that the `enemyCollision` method is run directly in the conditional statement. This will work because the `enemyCollision` method returns either `true` or `false`, which are the values that conditional statements check for.

Here's the enemyCollision method from the TileCollisionController class:

```
public function enemyCollision
  (gameObject:TileModel, enemy:TileModel):Boolean
{
  var gameObject_Radius:Number = gameObject.width * 0.5;
  var enemy_Radius:Number = enemy.width * 0.5;
  var enemySquashed:Boolean = false;

  //Vector between circles
  //Measure from the center points
  var v0:VectorModel
    = new VectorModel
    (
      gameObject.xPos + gameObject_Radius,
      gameObject.yPos + gameObject_Radius,
      enemy.xPos + enemy_Radius,
      enemy.yPos + enemy_Radius
    );

  //Calculate the radii of both circles combined
  var totalRadii:Number = gameObject_Radius + enemy_Radius;

  //If the totalRadii is less than the distance
  //between the objects and the cat is above the enemy…
  if(v0.m < totalRadii
  && gameObject.yPos + enemy_Radius < enemy.yPos)
  {
    //A collision is happening.
    //Find the amount of overlap between circles
    var overlap:Number = totalRadii - v0.m;

    gameObject.setX = gameObject.xPos - (overlap * v0.dx);
    gameObject.setY = gameObject.yPos - (overlap * v0.dy);

    //The cat's motion vector
    var v1:VectorModel
      = new VectorModel
      (
        gameObject.xPos, gameObject.yPos,
        gameObject.xPos + gameObject.vx,
        gameObject.yPos + gameObject.vy
      );
```

```
    //Create the cat's bounce vector
    var bounce_Player:VectorModel = VectorMath.bounce(v1, v0.ln);

    //Bounce the cat
    gameObject.vx = bounce_Player.vx;
    gameObject.vy = bounce_Player.vy;

    enemySquashed = true;
  }
  else
  {
    //No collision
  }
  return enemySquashed;
}
```

This is a distance-based collision check. If the method returns `true`, `_enemySquashed` is set to `true`, and the application class stops blitting the hedgehog and stops checking for a collision.

Blit animations

The squashing effect can be improved with a little explosion when the cat hits the hedgehog. Run the `PlayAnimation` SWF and squash the hedgehog. You'll see a quick, two-frame cartoon explosion, as shown in Figure 8-27.

Figure 8-27. A cartoon explosion animation made by blitting successive tiles in sequence

The animation is made up of two tiles from the tile sheet. A timer is used to display the tiles 200 milliseconds apart. Each frame of the animation is blitted to the stage, much as we've been blitting all the other game objects. However, because the animation frames must be displayed persistently on the stage between clicks of the timer, we need to employ a little programming gymnastics. Let's see how it all works.

When the code detects a collision between the cat and the hedgehog, it does the following:

- Captures the hedgehog's `x` and `y` positions in `explosion_X` and `explosion_Y` variables
- Starts the `_animationTimer`, which is set to fire every 200 milliseconds
- Sends the explosion's x and y values to the `playExplosion` method
- Sets the `_hedgehogModel` to `null`.

```
if
  (
    _collisionController.enemyCollision
      (_catModel, _hedgehogModel)
  )
{
  //Capture the hedgehog's position
  _explosion_X = _hedgehogModel.xPos;
  _explosion_Y = _hedgehogModel.yPos;

  //Start the timer
  _animationTimer = new Timer(200);
  _animationTimer.start();

  //Send the explosion's x and y values to the
  //playExplosion method
  playExplosion(_explosion_X, _explosion_Y);

  //Null the hedgehog
  _hedgehogModel = null;
}
```

The `playExplosion` method blits each frame of the animation from the tile sheet. It does so while the timer's `currentCount` property is less than the number of animation frames. `currentCount` is a built-in property of the `Timer` class that tells you how many times the timer has fired. It counts each tick of the clock. When the `currentCount` property is greater than the number of animation frames, it stops the timer and sets the `_explosion` flag to `false`.

```
private function playExplosion(x:Number, y:Number):void
{
  //The number of frames in the animation
  var animationFrames:uint = 2;
```

```
//Animate while the _animationTimer's currentCount
//is less than the number of frames in the animation. The first
//frame will be "0", the second will be "1"
if(_animationTimer.currentCount < animationFrames)
{
  //Find the tiles on the third row of the tile sheet
  var sourceRectangle:Rectangle
     = new Rectangle
       (
         _animationTimer.currentCount * MAX_TILE_SIZE,
         3 * MAX_TILE_SIZE,
         MAX_TILE_SIZE,
         MAX_TILE_SIZE
       );

  //The point on the stage where the animation should
  //be displayed. This will be the same as the
  //hedgehog's original position
  var destinationPoint:Point = new Point(x, y);

  _foregroundBitmapData.copyPixels
    (
      _tileSheetBitmapData,
      sourceRectangle,
      destinationPoint,
      null, null, true
    );
}

//If the maximum number of animation frames
//has been reached, stop the _animationTimer
//and set the _explosion variable to false
else
{
  //Stop and reset the timer
  _animationTimer.stop();
}
}
```

This is a pretty straightforward blit display system, but how does it know which tiles to use for the animation?

Figure 8-28 shows the two tiles in the tile sheet that are used as frames in the animation. They're both on row 3, and the first one is at column 0. This is important, so keep it in mind as I explain how these tiles are found.

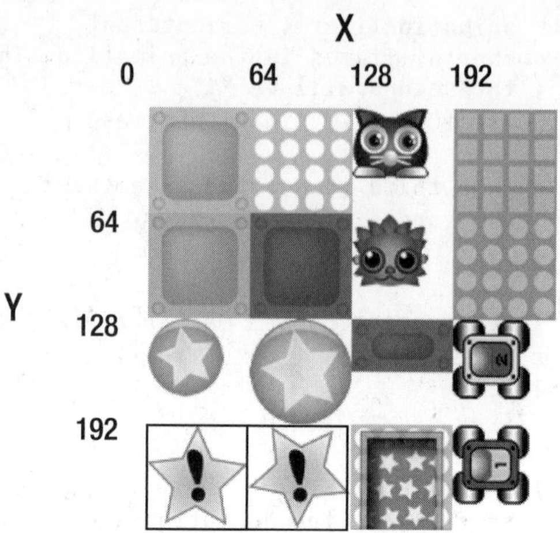

Figure 8-28. The animation frames start at column 0, row 3.

Here's the section of code that finds the correct position on the tile sheet:

```
var sourceRectangle:Rectangle
  = new Rectangle
  (
    _animationTimer.currentCount * MAX_TILE_SIZE,
    3 * MAX_TILE_SIZE,
    MAX_TILE_SIZE,
    MAX_TILE_SIZE
  );
```

Remember that a `Rectangle` object's constructor arguments are as follows:

```
(
  x position,
  y position,
  width,
  height
);
```

The x position in this case refers to the position of the tile on the tile sheet:

```
_animationTimer.currentCount * MAX_TILE_SIZE
```

The value of `currentCount` will be zero when the timer first starts. That means you can read the preceding line of code like this:

```
0 * 64
```

Of course, that just equals zero.

```
0
```

Why is that important? Because that's the x value of the first tile in the animation. Look back at Figure 8-28. The top-left corner of the first tile in the animation has an x position value of 0.

So we now know the x position, but we still need to find the y position:

```
3 * MAX_TILE_SIZE
```

You can read that as follows:

```
3 * 64
```

Or more simply, like this:

```
192
```

That's the y position of the tile on the tile sheet.

All this means is that on the first tick of the animation timer, the x position will be 0, and the y position will be 192. Those are exactly the coordinates of the first tile in the animation.

What happens when the second tick of the animation timer fires? This section of code is run again:

```
_animationTimer.currentCount * MAX_TILE_SIZE
```

But now `currentCount` equals 1. That means you can read this as follows:

```
1 * 64
```

(The y value is unchanged.) You can see from Figure 8-28 that the second tile has an x position of 64 and a y value of 192. In this way, the second tile is accurately selected. The `animationFrames` variable sets a limit of 2, so the timer is stopped after the second tile has been displayed.

The `playExplosion` method must be called on every frame so that the animation tiles persist on the stage between ticks of the timer. In other words, you need to play the explosion animation while the timer is running.

`Timer` objects have a property called `running` that returns `true` if the timer is currently running. The application class uses that property to call the `playExplosion` method while the timer is busy counting.

```
if(_animationTimer
&& _animationTimer.running)
{
  playExplosion(_explosion_X, _explosion_Y);
}
```

It first checks to make sure that `_animationTimer` isn't `null`, and checks to see if it's running. This will make the animation run until the timer is stopped.

Longer blit animations

The PlayAnimation example is a very simple blit animation system, but you can build a more sophisticated and flexible animation engine to suit your own game. You can think of this system as film projector, and the tile sheet as a strip of film. For longer or more complex animations, just increase the number of tiles in the animation. You may want to dedicate a single tile sheet to a very lengthy animation.

It's easier to manage animations if all the frames of the animation are on one row of the tile sheet. But if you have an animation that spans multiple rows, you'll need some way of figuring out when you need to jump to the next row down. You can do this with the help of the modulus operator (%).

Let's say that your tile sheet is five columns wide. If you can divide currentCount by 5 and there's no remainder, then you know that you've exceeded the last column and need to start a new row. Here's what your code might look like:

```
if(currentCount % 5 == 0)
{
  //Start a new row...
  row += 1;
}
```

Why does this work?

First, because the column numbering starts at 0, the fifth column is actually numbered as 4 (These are the five column numbers: 0, 1, 2, 3, 4.) Column 4 is the last column of any row. Keep that in mind!

That means when currentCount becomes 5, it's actually referring to the sixth column, But of course, our imaginary tile sheet is only five columns wide, so there is no sixth column! This can mean only one thing: you need to start a new row.

This formula currentCount % 5 will always return a remainder of 0 if currentCount is evenly divisible by 5. That means it will work just as well when currentCount becomes 10, 15, or 20. Each of those numbers can tell the code that you need to jump to a new row.

Movie clips vs. blitting for animation

If coding our cartoon explosion seems like an awful lot of work for two simple frames of animation, you're right—it is! Because we're using a blit display system, we don't have the luxury of the MovieClip object's play and stop methods.

If you're doing a lot of animation, you will probably want to use movie clips for them. It's the natural choice and much more manageable. MovieClip objects are designed for exactly such a job, so there's no need to reinvent the wheel. You can use MovieClip and Sprite objects in a blit environment for the best of both worlds. In the racing car examples at the end of the chapter, I'll show you how to blit tiles into sprites so that you can use all the sprite properties like scaling and rotation.

However, blitting your animation does have one big advantage: it's always going to be less CPU-intensive than playing movie clip animations.

Is there some way to combine the speed of blitting and the convenience of movie clip animation? There is! Even though you may not prefer it for writing code, Flash Professional is great for doing animation. It's possible for you to create all your animations as movie clips in Flash Professional, embed those clips into your code, and then cache each frame of the animation as a bitmap in an array when your game initializes. You can then use a custom method to loop through each bitmap in the array to re-create the movie clip animation as a blit animation. Adobe has published an excellent article by Michael James Williams that explains how to do just that. You can find it at the Adobe Developer Connection web site: `http://www.adobe.com/devnet/flash/articles/blitting_mc.html`.

> *We've been importing all sorts of assets into our code, like sounds and images. But did you know that you can just as easily import `Sprite` and `MovieClip` objects directly from SWF files and access all their content and properties? Here's how:*
>
> 1. *In Flash Professional, select **`Export for ActionScript`** for any objects you need to access with code.*
> 2. *Embed the SWF file into your code.*
>
> ```
> [Embed(source="FlashMovie.swf",
> symbol="AnyMovieClipSymbol")]
> var MovieClipObject:Class;
> ```
>
> 3. *Create an instance of `AnyMovieClipSymbol` and access its methods and properties like this:*
>
> ```
> theEmbeddedSymbol = new MovieClipObject();
> addChild(theEmbeddedSymbol);
> theEmbeddedSymbol.x = 100;
> theEmbeddedSymbol.y = 200;
> ```
>
> *By embedding objects from SWF files in this way, you have the freedom to work in any IDE you choose, but still take advantage of Flash Professional's strength as an excellent animation tool.*

Switching levels

A big advantage of tile-based games is how easy it is to create new game levels. You'll find an example of a game prototype with three levels in the `SwitchingLevels` folder. Each level has a door. When the cat reaches the door, a new game level is displayed, as shown in Figure 8-29. When the cat goes through the last door, the first level is displayed again. An infinite loop of levels!

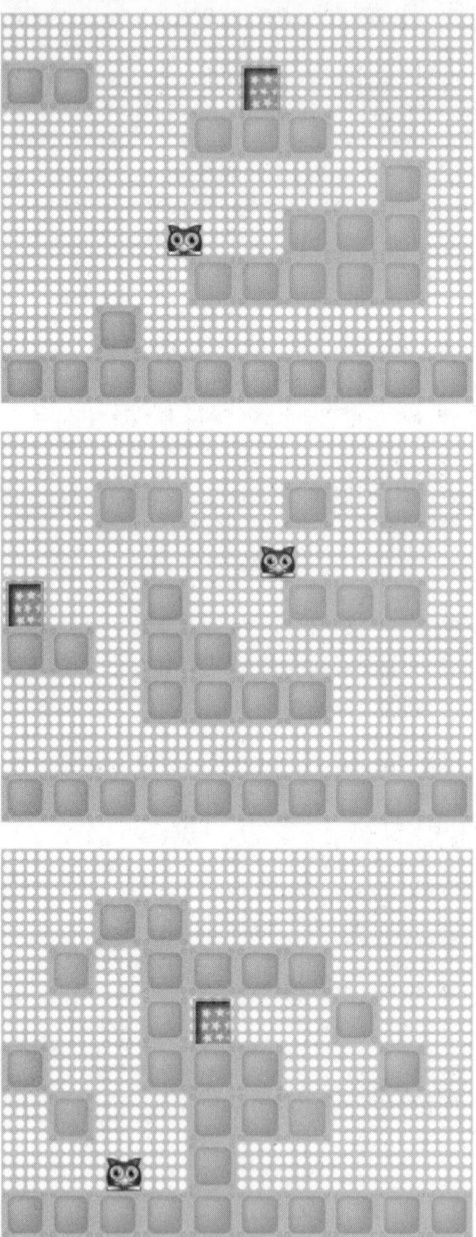

Figure 8-29. The game levels switch when the cat enters the door.

It takes only a few minutes to create these new game levels, and adding them does not require any changes to the tile game engine that we've been using since the beginning of the chapter. What's new is a method that initializes all these levels and adds them to level arrays when the game first starts.

For the levels, we need a few more variables to store the current platform map, the current game object map, and the current level number.

```
private var _currentPlatformMap:Array = [];
private var _currentObjectMap:Array = [];
private var _currentLevel:uint = 0;
```

We also need two more arrays that will store *all* the game maps.

```
private var _platformMaps:Array = [];
private var _gameObjectMaps:Array = [];
```

These arrays will hold the game map arrays that we'll make in the next step.

When the game is initialized, a method is called that creates all the game maps.

```
createMaps();
```

This method creates the maps for the three levels, and pushes them into the `_platformMaps` and `gameObjectMaps` arrays.

```
public function createMaps():void
{
  //Level 1
  var platformMap_1:Array
    = [
        [10,10,10,10,10,10,10,10,10,10],
        [00,00,10,10,10,23,10,10,10,10],
        [10,10,10,10,01,01,01,10,10,10],
        [10,10,10,10,10,10,10,10,01,10],
        [10,10,10,10,10,10,01,01,01,10],
        [10,10,10,10,01,01,01,01,01,10],
        [10,10,00,10,10,10,10,10,10,10],
        [00,00,00,00,00,00,00,00,00,00]
      ];

  var gameObjectMap_1:Array
    = [
        [-1,-1,-1,-1,-1,-1,-1,-1,-1,-1],
        [-1,-1,-1,-1,-1,-1,-1,-1,-1,-1],
        [-1,-1,-1,-1,-1,-1,-1,-1,-1,-1],
        [-1,-1,-1,-1,-1,-1,-1,-1,-1,-1],
        [-1,-1,-1,-1,-1,-1,-1,-1,-1,-1],
        [-1,-1,-1,-1,-1,-1,-1,-1,-1,-1],
```

```
          [-1,20,-1,-1,-1,-1,-1,-1,-1,-1],
          [-1,-1,-1,-1,-1,-1,-1,-1,-1,-1]
        ];

    _platformMaps.push(platformMap_1);
    _gameObjectMaps.push(gameObjectMap_1);

    //Level 2
    var platformMap_2:Array
      = [
          [10,10,10,10,10,10,10,10,10,10],
          [10,10,01,01,10,10,01,10,01,10],
          [10,10,10,10,10,10,10,10,10,10],
          [23,10,10,00,10,10,01,01,01,10],
          [00,00,10,00,00,10,10,10,10,10],
          [10,10,10,00,00,00,00,10,10,10],
          [10,10,10,10,10,10,10,10,10,10],
          [00,00,00,00,00,00,00,00,00,00]
        ];

    var gameObjectMap_2:Array
      = [
          [-1,-1,-1,-1,-1,-1,-1,-1,-1,-1],
          [-1,-1,-1,-1,-1,-1,-1,-1,-1,-1],
          [-1,-1,-1,-1,-1,-1,-1,-1,-1,-1],
          [-1,-1,-1,-1,-1,-1,-1,-1,-1,-1],
          [-1,-1,-1,-1,-1,-1,-1,-1,-1,-1],
          [-1,-1,-1,-1,-1,-1,-1,-1,-1,-1],
          [-1,-1,-1,-1,-1,-1,-1,-1,-1,20],
          [-1,-1,-1,-1,-1,-1,-1,-1,-1,-1]
        ];

    _platformMaps.push(platformMap_2);
    _gameObjectMaps.push(gameObjectMap_2);

    //Level 3
    var platformMap_3:Array
      = [
          [10,10,10,10,10,10,10,10,10,10],
          [10,10,00,00,10,10,10,10,10,10],
          [10,01,10,00,00,00,00,10,10,10],
          [10,10,10,00,23,10,10,00,10,10],
          [00,10,10,00,00,00,10,10,00,10],
          [10,01,10,10,00,00,01,10,10,10],
          [10,10,10,10,00,10,10,10,10,10],
          [00,00,00,00,00,00,00,00,00,00]
        ];
```

```
  var gameObjectMap_3:Array
    = [
        [-1,-1,-1,-1,-1,-1,-1,-1,-1,-1],
        [-1,-1,-1,-1,-1,-1,-1,-1,-1,-1],
        [-1,-1,-1,-1,-1,-1,-1,-1,-1,-1],
        [-1,-1,-1,-1,-1,-1,-1,-1,-1,-1],
        [-1,-1,-1,-1,-1,-1,-1,-1,-1,-1],
        [-1,-1,-1,-1,-1,-1,-1,-1,-1,-1],
        [-1,-1,20,-1,-1,-1,-1,-1,-1,-1],
        [-1,-1,-1,-1,-1,-1,-1,-1,-1,-1]
      ];

  _platformMaps.push(platformMap_3);
  _gameObjectMaps.push(gameObjectMap_3);

  _currentPlatformMap = _platformMaps[_currentLevel];
  _currentObjectMap = _gameObjectMaps[_currentLevel];
}
```

The last two lines are quite important. They set the first level of the game. They set the current maps to the value of `_currentLevel`. `_currentLevel` is initialized to `0` when the game starts. That means you can read those two lines like this:

```
_currentPlatformMap = _platformMaps[0];
_currentObjectMap = _gameObjectMaps[0];
```

This sets the current maps to the first maps that were pushed in to the `_platformMaps` and `_gameObjectMaps` arrays. This will be the first map you'll see when the game starts.

When that's done, we can run the usual `buildMap` method. But this time, we're sending it the values of `_currentPlatformMap` and `_currentObjectMap`.

```
buildMap(_currentPlatformMap);
buildMap(_currentObjectMap);
```

The `buildMap` method is basically unchanged since the first example in this chapter. The only difference is that it has been modified to understand what `DOOR` tiles are (tile ID `23`).

```
case DOOR:
   var door:TileModel
     = new TileModel
     (
       MAX_TILE_SIZE,
       tileSheetColumn, tileSheetRow,
       mapRow, mapColumn,
       MAX_TILE_SIZE, MAX_TILE_SIZE
     );
  drawGameObject(door, _backgroundBitmapData);
  break;
```

Now that the game has been initialized, we can use all the same tile-based game techniques that we've covered in this chapter. The game engine is completely agnostic to what level is currently loaded. It doesn't care. Because the game rules are general, they apply to all levels.

One new thing we need to do is to check for a collision with a `DOOR` tile, as shown in Figure 8-30.

Figure 8-30. A door collision triggers the level switch.

That will switch the level. The door collision uses a very basic spatial grid collision check.

```
if(_currentPlatformMap[_catModel.mapRow][_catModel.mapColumn]
    == DOOR)
{…
```

It checks whether the cat's center point is on a `DOOR` tile. If it is, it adds 1 to the value of `_currentLevel`, loads the new maps, and builds them.

```
//Check for a collision with the door
if(_currentPlatformMap[_catModel.mapRow][_catModel.mapColumn]
  == DOOR)
{
  //Add "1" to the current level
   _currentLevel++;

  //Optionally, loop the game levels by setting _currentLevel
  //back to "0" when the last level of the game is reached
  if(_currentLevel >= _platformMaps.length)
  {
    _currentLevel = 0;
  }
```

```
  //Use the new value of _currentLevel to load the new level maps
  _currentPlatformMap = _platformMaps[_currentLevel];
  _currentObjectMap = _gameObjectMaps[_currentLevel];

  //Build the maps using the usual buildMap method
  buildMap(_currentPlatformMap);
  buildMap(_currentObjectMap);
}
```

This code also sets the value of `_currentLevel` back to `0` if the number of game maps is exceeded. This is what loops the levels infinitely.

These few lines of code are all you need to extend a 1-level game to a 100-level or even 1000-level game. Can you see now how much easier it is to create new levels in a tile-based game engine than it is in a game like Escape!, where most of the level specifics were hardwired into the game engine?

I've kept this example simple so that you can clearly see the mechanics of switching and building new game levels. When you build your own game using this technique, you'll need to carefully consider the rules of the game, and make sure that they will apply no matter which level is loaded. Depending on your game, these rules could become quite complex. You may also find that it's useful to store specific level rules in an array of objects, and load those into the game when you load the new levels. In the race car examples later in this chapter, I'll show you one way you can store and load level rules in arrays along with your maps. In Chapter 10, you'll learn how to load levels and other game data from external XML files.

Blit scrolling

Scrolling a big environment is greatly simplified if you're using a blit display system in a tile-based game world. Because all the game objects are being projected onto single bitmaps, we can use the `Bitmap` class's ultra-fast `scrollRect` property. It's an optimized property designed exclusively for scrolling bitmaps, and it's perfect for scrolling game environments.

You'll find an example of a big, scrolling tile-based game environment using `scrollRect` in the `Scrolling` folder. The cat now has a huge playground to jump around in, and the game world camera follows it all the way. Figure 8-31 shows this version.

The tile-based game engine is essentially unchanged. We can drop the scrolling system directly onto the existing engine. The only small modifications we need to make are to account for the larger game world.

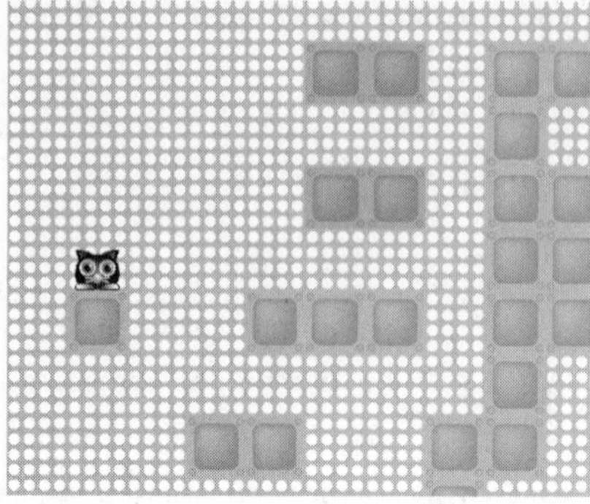

Area visible on stage

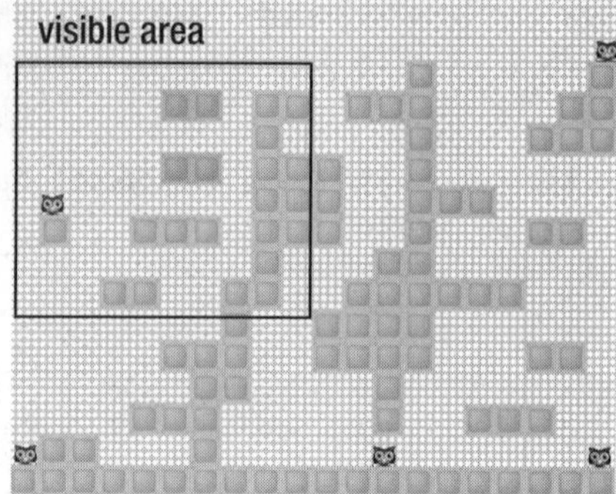

The entire scrollable game world

Figure 8-31. The scrolling game world

The map arrays are twice the size: 20 columns by 16 rows.

```
private var _platformMap:Array
    = [
        [10,10,10,10,10,10,10,10,10,10,10,10,10,10,10,10,10,10,10,10],
        [10,10,10,10,10,10,10,10,10,10,10,10,10,10,10,10,10,10,10,10],
        [10,10,10,10,10,10,10,10,10,10,10,10,10,00,10,10,10,10,10,00],
        [10,10,10,10,10,01,01,10,00,00,10,00,00,00,10,10,10,10,00,00],
        [10,10,10,10,10,10,10,10,00,10,10,10,10,00,10,10,10,00,00,00],
        [10,10,10,10,10,01,01,10,00,00,00,10,10,00,10,10,10,10,10,10],
        [10,10,10,10,10,10,10,10,00,00,00,10,10,00,00,00,10,10,10,10],
        [10,00,10,10,00,00,00,10,00,00,00,10,10,00,10,10,10,00,00,10],
        [10,10,10,10,10,10,10,10,00,10,10,10,00,00,10,10,10,10,10,10],
        [10,10,10,00,00,10,10,00,00,10,10,00,00,00,00,00,00,10,10,10],
        [10,10,10,10,10,10,10,00,10,10,00,00,00,00,10,10,10,10,10,10],
        [10,10,10,10,10,00,00,00,10,10,00,00,00,00,10,10,10,00,00,10],
        [10,10,10,10,10,10,00,00,10,10,10,10,00,10,10,10,10,10,10,10],
        [10,10,10,10,00,00,00,10,10,10,10,10,00,10,10,00,00,00,10,10],
        [10,00,00,10,10,10,00,10,10,10,10,10,10,10,10,10,10,10,10,10],
        [00,00,00,00,00,00,00,00,00,00,00,00,00,00,00,00,00,00,00,00]
    ];
```

The `_gameObjectMap` is equally large.

However, it doesn't matter how large these maps are; they can be any size. The `BitmapData` that contains them will automatically expand to fit the size of the array. This is because it finds the correct size by multiplying the number of rows and columns by the tile size.

```
private var _backgroundBitmapData:BitmapData
  = new BitmapData
    (
      MAP_COLUMNS * MAX_TILE_SIZE,
      MAP_ROWS * MAX_TILE_SIZE,
      true, 0
    );

private var _backgroundBitmap:Bitmap
  = new Bitmap(_backgroundBitmapData);

private var _foregroundBitmapData:BitmapData
  = new BitmapData
    (
      MAP_COLUMNS * MAX_TILE_SIZE,
      MAP_ROWS * MAX_TILE_SIZE,
      true, 0
    );
private var _foregroundBitmap:Bitmap
  = new Bitmap(_foregroundBitmapData);
```

You can design the game maps in the same ways as you design smaller maps. The same rules apply. However, if you use maps of different sizes, you'll need to make sure that the bitmaps are sized correctly. In Chapter 10, you'll learn how you can store this information in XML as metadata that you can load with the map.

Adding a camera

The maps are built using the same `buildMap` method, and there's nothing else that needs to be altered about the game engine. There's just one addition: a **camera**.

You can think of the camera as a rectangle that follows the cat around the world and selects which parts of the foreground and background bitmaps to display. It's your view onto the game world.

The camera is a `Rectangle` object. It's the same size as the stage.

```
private var _camera:Rectangle = new Rectangle
 (0, 0, stage.stageWidth, stage.stageHeight);
```

It's positioned so that it's always centered over the cat. These two lines of code in the `enterFrameHandler` will make the camera follow the cat all over the game world:

```
_camera.x = _catModel.xPos - stage.stageWidth * 0.5;
_camera.y = _catModel.yPos - stage.stageHeight * 0.5;
```

The camera should also be contained within the limits of the game world. It shouldn't expose what lies beyond the edges of the world. This section of code in the `enterFrameHandler` makes sure that it doesn't move outside the game world boundaries:

```
//Check the camera's game world boundaries
//Left
if(_camera.x < 0)
{
  _camera.x = 0;
}

//Right
if(_camera.x > (MAP_COLUMNS * MAX_TILE_SIZE)
  - stage.stageWidth)
{
  _camera.x = (MAP_COLUMNS * MAX_TILE_SIZE) - stage.stageWidth;
}

//Bottom
if(_camera.y > (MAP_ROWS * MAX_TILE_SIZE) - stage.stageHeight)
{
  _camera.y = (MAP_ROWS * MAX_TILE_SIZE) - stage.stageHeight;
}

//Top
if(_camera.y < 0)
{
  _camera.y = 0;
}
```

After the objects have been blitted to the foreground and background bitmaps, the game can be scrolled. This is done by assigning the bitmaps' `scrollRect` property to the value of `camera`. These two lines are also in the `enterFrameHandler`:

```
_foregroundBitmap.scrollRect = _camera;
_backgroundBitmap.scrollRect = _camera;
```

The bitmaps are cropped to the size of the `camera` rectangle. When the `camera`'s x and y values change, the bitmaps scroll within the `camera`'s rectangle.

And that's all there is to it! The scrolling is handled for you automatically. As you can see when you run the SWF, it's a very natural, classic video game scrolling effect.

Establishing game world coordinates

There is one small change to the way in which the cat responds to the movements of the mouse in this scrolling environment. In previous examples, the cat's easing was based on the difference between the cat's position and the position of the mouse on the stage. Now that our game world is much bigger than the stage, this won't work. We can't use the coordinate space of the stage. We need to use the coordinate space of the entire `_foregroundBitmap`.

The `TileModel` class has a property called `coordinateSpace` that we can use to take account of just such a situation. It can accept any `DisplayObject`, like a `Bitmap`.

The cat's coordinateSpace property is set when the _catModel is created by the buildMap method. I've highlighted it in the following code. (The rest of the code is identical to previous examples.)

```
case CAT:
  _catModel
    = new TileModel
    (
      MAX_TILE_SIZE,
      tileSheetColumn, tileSheetRow,
      mapRow, mapColumn,
      48, 42
    );

  _catModel.gravity_Vy = 0.98;
  _catModel.coordinateSpace = _foregroundBitmap;

  _UIPlatformController
    = new UIPlatformController(_catModel);
  _UIPlatformView
    = new UIPlatformView
    (_catModel, _UIPlatformController, stage);

  drawGameObject(_catModel, _foregroundBitmapData);
  break;
```

Setting that coordinateSpace property isn't much help unless you use it in some way. In this case, the cat's UIPlatformController uses it to find whether or not it should use the stage or some other DisplayObject to calculate the mouse's x and y coordinates.

```
var vx:Number

if(_model.coordinateSpace == null)
{
  vx
    = stage.mouseX
    - (_model.xPos + _model.width * 0.5);
}
else
{
  vx
    = _model.coordinateSpace.mouseX
    - (_model.xPos + _model.width * 0.5);
}
```

In this case, it chooses the second option. The code will calculate easing based on the position of the mouse on the _foregroundBitmap. This results in the accurate mouse-follow effect you can see in the SWF.

If you're making a game in a scrolling environment where you need to calculate the "bottom of the game world," you must also use the world's bitmap dimensions to help you find out where this is.

For example, let's say we want to set the cat's `jumping` property to `false` if the cats lands at the very bottom of the stage, at the bottom of the world. We can do this by checking whether the bottom of the cat is at a position that is at or greater than the height of the foreground bitmap:

```
if(_catModel.yPos + _catModel.height
  >= _foregroundBitmapData.height)
{
  _catModel.jumping = false;
}
```

This is the same as checking for the bottom of the stage in a nonscrolling environment.

As you can see, scrolling in a tile-based, blit display environment is quite painless. You'll probably find this the preferred way to do scrolling from now on.

Using sprites in a tile-based world

The drawback to using blit objects in games is that it's difficult to scale or rotate them. If you have an object that you want to rotate, you need to create individual tiles that represent every single stage in the rotation. That means for a full 360-degree rotation, you'll need 360 tile images, each of which will be one degree of rotation different than the rest. Not only will you end up with a huge tile sheet, but you'll need to create your own custom methods to handle and display the rotation. This will be a lot of work to create, manage, and maintain, and except for the most performance-intensive games, it's just not worth it.

Sprites and movie clips do scaling and rotation beautifully. It's also quite possible to use them in combination with a tile-based game environment. In fact, you can mix and match sprites, movie clips, and blit objects as much as you like, and still keep the same game engine intact. In this next example, I'll show you how.

Run the `DrivingGame` SWF in the chapter's source files. This is simple prototype for a tile-based car driving game. Use the arrow keys to drive the car around the track, as shown in Figure 8-32. If you run into the grass, you'll slow down until you're back on the road.

This may seem like a radically different type of game than the platform game examples we've been looking at, but the tile-based engine is identical. What's different here is that the car is a sprite. The car tile is being projected from the tile sheet into a containing sprite. Figure 8-33 is a simplified illustration of how this works.

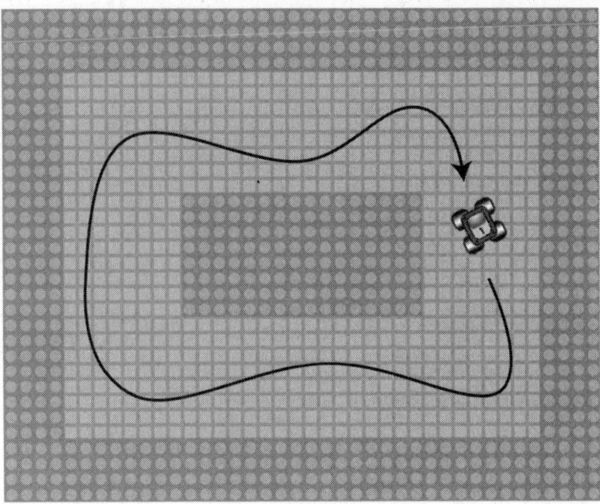

Figure 8-32. Drive the car around the track, but don't get stuck in the the grass!

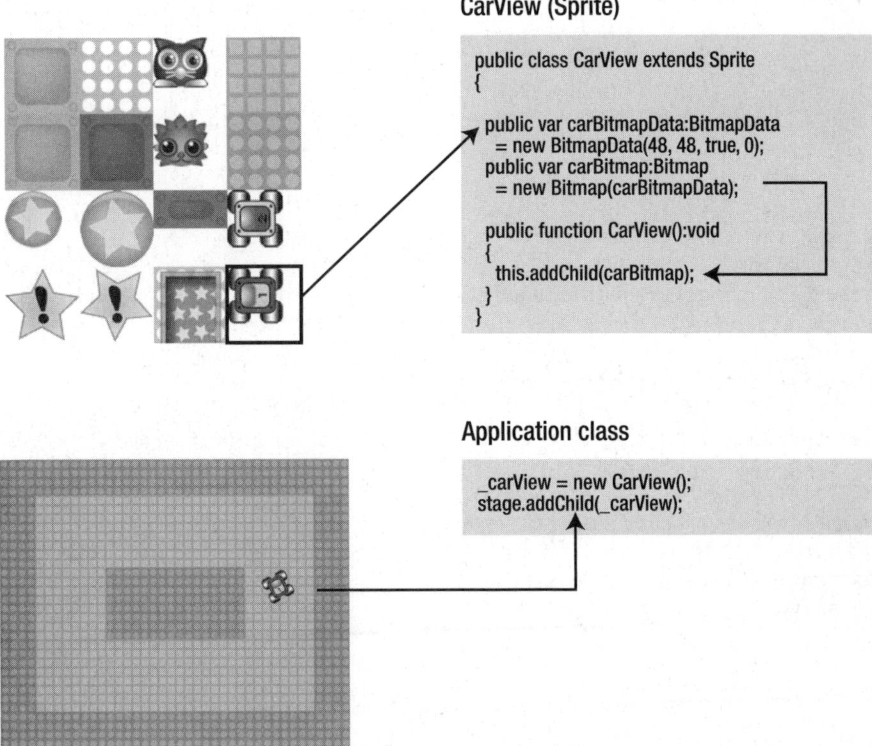

CarView (Sprite)
public class CarView extends Sprite
{
public var carBitmapData:BitmapData
= new BitmapData(48, 48, true, 0);
public var carBitmap:Bitmap
= new Bitmap(carBitmapData);
public function CarView():void
{
this.addChild(carBitmap);
}
}
Application class
_carView = new CarView();
stage.addChild(_carView);

Figure 8-33. Load the tile into a containing sprite, and then add that sprite to the stage.

Here's an overview of the process:

1. The car tile is read from the tile sheet.
2. It's assigned to the CarView sprite's carBitmapData. carBitmapData is the same size as the car tile.
3. The CarView adds the carBitmap to its own display list.
4. The application class adds the carView sprite to the stage.

Now we'll look at the details of how this works.

Blitting the tile into a sprite

The buildMap method creates all the tiles in the game. When it creates the CAR tile, it also creates the car's model, view, and controller. The view is a sprite, and the buildMap method adds it to the stage.

```
case CAR:
  _carTileModel
    = new CarTileModel
    (
      MAX_TILE_SIZE,
      tileSheetColumn, tileSheetRow,
      mapRow, mapColumn,
      48, 48
    );

  //Add the view and controller
  _carController
    = new CarController(_carTileModel);
  _carView
    = new CarView
    (_carTileModel, _carController, stage);

  //Load the tile from the tile sheet into the
  //car's containing Sprite
  loadTileIntoView
    (_carTileModel, _carView.carBitmapData);

  //Add the car's view to the stage
  stage.addChild(_carView);
  break;
```

Before the view is added to the stage, the car tile is loaded into it with this line of code:

```
loadTileIntoView
  (_carTileModel, _carView.carBitmapData);
```

Notice that it sends the car's `carBitmapData` property as an argument. The `loadTileIntoView` method is going to blit the car tile from the tile sheet directly into the `carBitmapData`.

The `loadTileIntoView` method in the application class is responsible for reading the tile sheet and copying the car tile into the `carView`'s `carBitmapData` property.

```
private function loadTileIntoView
  (tileModel:TileModel, bitmapData:BitmapData):void
{
  var sourceRectangle:Rectangle
    = new Rectangle
    (
      tileModel.tileSheetColumn * MAX_TILE_SIZE,
      tileModel.tileSheetRow * MAX_TILE_SIZE,
      tileModel.width,
      tileModel.height
    );

  var destinationPoint:Point = new Point(0, 0);

  bitmapData.copyPixels
    (
      _tileSheetBitmapData,
      sourceRectangle,
      destinationPoint,
      null, null, true
    );
}
```

This is a standard blit method. But instead of blitting the tile onto one of the stage bitmaps, it blits it into the `carView` sprite's `carBitmapData` property. This needs to happen only once, when the `carView` is initialized.

The `CarView` class contains the car tile bitmap and centers it in its own display. It needs to be centered so that the rotation happens around the car's center axis. Here's the complete `CarView` class.

```
package com.friendsofed.gameElements.car
{
  import flash.display.*;
  import flash.events.Event;
  import flash.events.KeyboardEvent;
  import flash.ui.Keyboard;
  import com.friendsofed.gameElements.primitives.*;
```

```
public class CarView extends Sprite
{
  private var _model:Object;
  private var _controller:Object;
  private var _stage:Object;
  public var carBitmapData:BitmapData
    = new BitmapData(48, 48, true, 0);
  public var carBitmap:Bitmap
    = new Bitmap(carBitmapData);

  public function CarView
    (
      model:AVerletModel,
      controller:CarController,
      stage:Object
    ):void
  {
    this._model = model;
    this._controller = controller;
    this._stage = stage;

    //Center this sprite
    this.x = _model.xPos + 24;
    this.y = _model.yPos + 24;

    this.addChild(carBitmap);

    //Center the carBitmap in this Sprite
    carBitmap.x = -24;
    carBitmap.y = -24;

    _model.addEventListener(Event.CHANGE, changeHandler);
    _stage.addEventListener
      (KeyboardEvent.KEY_DOWN, keyDownHandler);
    _stage.addEventListener
      (KeyboardEvent.KEY_UP, keyUpHandler);
  }

  private function keyDownHandler(event:KeyboardEvent):void
  {
    _controller.processKeyDown(event);
  }
  private function keyUpHandler(event:KeyboardEvent):void
  {
    _controller.processKeyUp(event);
  }
```

```
    private function changeHandler(event:Event):void
    {
      this.x = _model.xPos + 24;
      this.y = _model.yPos + 24;
      this.rotation = _model.rotationValue;
    }
  }
}
```

You'll find all this code in the `com.friendsofed.gameElements.car` package.

Creating the car's control system

The car's control system is very similar to the spaceship's control system that we looked at in Chapter 1, but has a few new twists. Unlike the spaceship, the car is able to nimbly change direction whenever the direction keys are pressed, even while it's not accelerating.

The car's control system is divided between two classes: `CarTileModel` and `CarController`. (You'll find both of these classes in the `com.friendsofed.gameElements.car` package.)

`CarTileModel` has two new public properties to help the car move:

```
public var accelerate:Boolean = false;
public var speed:Number = 0;
```

Here's the role they play in this system:

- `accelerate` is a Boolean variable that's set to `true` when the up arrow key is pressed, and `false` when it's not being pressed. It's the car's accelerator (gas pedal).
- `speed` is how fast the car is going.

These are two common-sense properties that you ordinarily associate with cars. Let's look at how they work together to make the car move.

The `CarController` handles key presses that the `CarView` sends it. Its two important methods are `processKeyDown` and `processKeyUp`. They set the car's rotation and tell it whether or not it should accelerate.

```
public function processKeyDown(event:KeyboardEvent):void
{
  switch (event.keyCode)
  {
    case Keyboard.LEFT:
      _model.rotationSpeed = -3;
      break;

    case Keyboard.RIGHT:
      _model.rotationSpeed = 3;
      break;
```

```
    case Keyboard.UP:
      _model.accelerate = true;
      break;
  }
}

public function processKeyUp(event:KeyboardEvent):void
{
  switch (event.keyCode)
  {
    case Keyboard.LEFT:
      _model.rotationSpeed = 0;
      break;

    case Keyboard.RIGHT:
      _model.rotationSpeed = 0;
      break;

    case Keyboard.UP:
      _model.accelerate = false;
      break;
  }
}
```

When the player presses the up arrow key, the car model's `accelerate` property is set to `true`.

```
case Keyboard.UP:
  _model.accelerate = true;
  break;
```

This is important because the car model uses `accelerate` to figure out whether it should move the car.

The `CarTileModel`'s `update` method moves the car using the standard Verlet integration system.

```
override public function update():void
{
  temporaryX = xPos;
  temporaryY = yPos;

  //Calculate the rotationValue
  rotationValue += rotationSpeed;

  //Calculate the angle and acceleration
  angle = rotationValue * (Math.PI / 180);
```

```
  //Increase the car's speed if the controller
  //tells it to accelerate
  if(accelerate)
  {
    speed += 0.1;

    //Add some optional drag
    speed *= friction;
  }
  //Add friction to the speed if the car is
  //not accelerating
  else
  {
    speed *= friction;
  }

  //Calculate the acceleration based on the angle of rotation
  acceleration_X = speed * Math.cos(angle);
  acceleration_Y = speed * Math.sin(angle);

  //Update the position
  xPos += acceleration_X;
  yPos += acceleration_Y;

  previousX = temporaryX;
  previousY = temporaryY;
}
```

If accelerate is true, then the value of speed is increased. If accelerate is false, speed is multiplied by the friction value to slow down the car.

```
if(accelerate)
{
  speed += 0.1;
  speed *= friction; //This line is optional
}
else
{
  speed *= friction;
}
```

speed is then multiplied by the angle of rotation to obtain the car's final acceleration values.

```
acceleration_X = speed * Math.cos(angle);
acceleration_Y = speed * Math.sin(angle);
```

These are then added to the car's position to move the car in the correct direction and at the correct speed.

```
xPos += acceleration_X;
yPos += acceleration_Y;
```

Notice that the update method in the CarTileModel begins with the keyword override.

```
override public function update():void
{…
```

Why is this?

CarTileModel extends TileModel. TileModel in turn extends AVerletModel. That means that CarTileModel also inherits all of AVerletModel's properties. This is very convenient because it means that the CarTileModel class has much less code than it would if it also had to contain all of AVerletModel's and TileModel's code. It can just extend TileModel and inherit all of AVerletModel's properties and methods as well—all for free. This is great, except that AVerletModel already contains a method called update. And its update method happens to be radically different from CarTileModel's update method. Using the keyword override tells AS3.0's compiler that it should ignore AVerletModel's update method and use this new one instead.

As you've seen, using the basic control system introduced in Chapter 1, you can achieve markedly different control styles by juggling the numbers in slightly different ways.

Stuck in the grass

The DrivingGame example also illustrates how a tile-based game engine can elegantly solve some otherwise tricky game design problems. A feature of the DrivingGame is that the car slows down when it runs into the grass, as shown in Figure 8-34. This is the single most annoying feature of driving games in general, so I had to include it!

Figure 8-34. Stuck in the grass, again!

The game does this by checking if the car is on a GRASS tile. If it is, it sets the car's friction to 0.85 to slow it down. The game sets it back to the usual 0.98 if it's not on the grass. This is the section of code in the DrivingGame application class that does this:

```
if(_raceTrackMap[_carTileModel.mapRow][_carTileModel.mapColumn]
  == GRASS)
{
  //Lots of friction if the car is on the grass
  _carTileModel.friction = 0.85;
}
else
{
  //Otherwise, normal friction
  _carTileModel.friction = 0.98;
}
```

Game design doesn't get much simpler than this. No creating of a lot of grass objects, no looping through arrays, no complex collision detection. Yay, tile-based games!

Storing extra game data in arrays

You've seen how map arrays are not just used for plotting tiles, but also to help interpret the game world. The enemy in the platform game could use that information to figure out that it was close to a ledge and needed to turn back. The elevator could use it to figure out how high or low it needed to travel. In the `DrivingGame` example, the `GRASS` data in the array not only helped plot the grass tile on the stage, but also played a crucial role in the game logic. The power of tile-based games is that map array data holds meaningful information, which can be used in the game for everything from the display to the AI system.

You can take this one step further. What if you stored data in the arrays that contained more information about the game world other than just what you can see on the stage?

Imagine that you're creating a fantasy role-playing game where players can cast spells that affect part of the game world. The Bard character casts a spell of Discordant Cacophony that makes all the enemies run away from the area of the game map where the spell is cast. How will you describe this information to the game?

You could create a "spell map" that matches the size of the game world. You could mark all the parts of the world that are affected by Discordant Cacophony with some kind of code, like `99`.

```
private var _spellMap:Array
  = [
      [-1,-1,-1,-1,-1,-1,-1,-1,-1,-1],
      [-1,-1,-1,-1,-1,-1,-1,-1,-1,-1],
      [-1,-1,-1,-1,99,-1,-1,-1,-1,-1],
      [-1,-1,-1,99,99,99,-1,-1,-1,-1],
      [-1,-1,-1,99,99,99,-1,-1,-1,-1],
      [-1,-1,-1,-1,99,-1,-1,-1,-1,-1],
      [-1,-1,-1,-1,-1,-1,-1,-1,-1,-1],
      [-1,-1,-1,-1,-1,-1,-1,-1,-1,-1]
    ];
```

Enemies could then take this information into account and decide whether or not they want to risk ruptured eardrums by entering any of those tiles.

This information isn't visual; it's just used by the logic of the game. When you start becoming comfortable thinking in a tile-based way about your games, you'll find that many otherwise complex problems can be solved easily with arrays of game data like this.

As an example, take a look at the `AIDrivingGame` in the chapter's source files. Now you have an opponent to play against: an AI-controlled robot car that does its best to race you around the track, as shown in Figure 8-35. It will give you a good run for your money until you get the knack of driving.

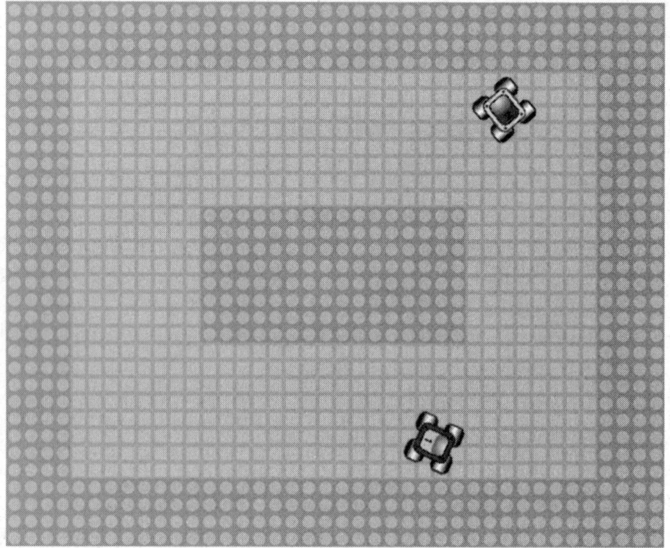

Figure 8-35. Race an AI opponent car around the track.

But here's the interesting part: the AI car isn't following a prescripted animation, and it doesn't have a dedicated AI controller. Instead, it's reading an array of numbers that tells it how it should try to angle itself depending on which cell it's in. It's following an invisible "angle map."

To give you a clearer sense of what's going on, here are the three maps used in the game:

```
private const ROAD:uint = 30;
private const GRASS:uint = 31;
private const CAR:uint = 33;
private const AI_CAR:uint = 32;
```

```
private var _raceTrackMap:Array
  = [
      [31,31,31,31,31,31,31,31,31,31],
      [31,30,30,30,30,30,30,30,30,31],
      [31,30,30,30,30,30,30,30,30,31],
      [31,30,30,31,31,31,31,30,30,31],
      [31,30,30,31,31,31,31,30,30,31],
      [31,30,30,30,30,30,30,30,30,31],
      [31,30,30,30,30,30,30,30,30,31],
      [31,31,31,31,31,31,31,31,31,31]
    ];

private var _gameObjectMap:Array
  = [
      [-1,-1,-1,-1,-1,-1,-1,-1,-1,-1],
      [-1,-1,32,-1,-1,-1,-1,-1,-1,-1],
      [-1,-1,33,-1,-1,-1,-1,-1,-1,-1],
      [-1,-1,-1,-1,-1,-1,-1,-1,-1,-1],
      [-1,-1,-1,-1,-1,-1,-1,-1,-1,-1],
      [-1,-1,-1,-1,-1,-1,-1,-1,-1,-1],
      [-1,-1,-1,-1,-1,-1,-1,-1,-1,-1],
      [-1,-1,-1,-1,-1,-1,-1,-1,-1,-1]
    ];

private var _angles:Array
  = [
      [045,045,045,045,045,045,045,045,045,045],
      [315,000,000,000,000,000,000,090,135,135],
      [315,000,000,000,000,000,000,090,135,135],
      [315,315,270,315,315,315,315,090,090,135],
      [315,315,270,135,135,135,135,090,090,135],
      [315,315,270,180,180,180,180,180,225,135],
      [315,315,315,180,180,180,180,180,225,135],
      [225,225,225,225,225,225,225,225,225,225]
    ];
```

The `_angles` array is the important one. It tells the opponent car what its target angle should be depending on where it is on the track.

Figure 8-36 illustrates how the angle map works. When the game first starts, the AI car will cruise along at an angle of 0—straight ahead. The first new angle number it hits is 90 (illustrated). The game thinks to itself, "Hmm... the AI car needs to be at a target angle of 90 at this spot. Its current angle is less than 90 at the moment, so I'll turn the car to the right." This logic is mirrored in the code that does the actual work. You'll find it in the `enterFrameHandler`.

```
private var _angles:Array

  = [

      [045, 045, 045, 045, 045, 045, 045, 045, 045, 045],

      [315, 000, 000, 000, 000, 000, 000, 090, 135, 135],

      [315, 000, 000, 000, 000, 000, 000, 090, 135, 135],

      [315, 315, 270, 315, 315, 315, 315, 090, 090, 135],

      [315, 315, 270, 135, 135, 135, 135, 090, 090, 135],

      [315, 315, 270, 180, 180, 180, 180, 180, 225, 135],

      [315, 315, 315, 180, 180, 180, 180, 180, 225, 135],

      [225, 225, 225, 225, 225, 225, 225, 225, 225, 225],

    ];
```

Figure 8-36. The game tries to make the AI car match the target angle in the array.

```
//Find the AI car's current angle
var currentAngle:Number = _aiCarTileModel.rotationValue;

//Get the target angle from the _angles array based on the
//cell the AI car is currently occupying
var targetAngle:Number
  = _angles[_aiCarTileModel.mapRow][_aiCarTileModel.mapColumn]

//Calculate the difference between the current
//angle and the target angle
var difference:Number = currentAngle - targetAngle;

//Figure out whether to turn the car left or right
if(difference > 0
&& difference < 180)
```

```
{
  //Turn left
   _aiCarTileModel.rotationSpeed = -2;
}
else
{
  //Turn right
  _aiCarTileModel.rotationSpeed = 2;
}
```

The code is trivial, but the results are almost spooky in their realism. No complex AI is required. It's done with just simple data in an array and the intuitive logic of the tile-based game engine. Be sure to check out the full code in the `AIDrivingGame` folder.

Creating the AI car

The AI car shares exactly the same model, `CarTileModel`, as the player's car. The code is identical, including the `update` method that we looked at earlier. It doesn't have a controller class; all its logic is entirely in the code from the application class. The only new class is the AI car's view, `AICarView`, which you'll find in the `com.friendsofed.gameElements.car` package. It's merely a simpler version of the player's car's view class that doesn't check for key presses.

Our good old friend the `buildMap` method in the application class does the job of creating the AI car and adding it to the stage.

```
case AI_CAR:
  _aiCarTileModel
    = new CarTileModel
    (
      MAX_TILE_SIZE,
      tileSheetColumn, tileSheetRow,
      mapRow, mapColumn,
      48, 48
    );
  _aiCarView
    = new AICarView
    (_aiCarTileModel, stage);

  loadTileIntoView
    (_aiCarTileModel, _aiCarView.carBitmapData);
  stage.addChild(_aiCarView);

  //Start the car moving by setting its
  //accelerate property to true
  CarTileModel(_aiCarTileModel).accelerate = true;

  break;
```

When the car is added to the stage, its accelerate property is set to true. This is what starts the car moving.

```
CarTileModel(_aiCarTileModel).accelerate = true;
```

But take a close look at the syntax in the preceding line. _aiCarTileModel needs to be cast as a CarTileModel type. Why is this? accelerate is not a property of the TileModel class, which is the class that CarTileModel extends. accelerate is a property of TileModel's *subclass*. The subclass is CarTileModel.

The short story of all this is that we need to force the compiler to look in the CarTileModel class if it wants to find the accelerate property. This is an odd quirk in AS3.0 and extremely important to keep in mind. You'll experience this a lot if you frequently extend classes to make new ones. So, you might see this error message:

```
Error: Access of possibly undefined property _____ through a reference with
static type ______
```

The problem could be that you need to cast an object as the correct type to keep the compiler happy.

Controlling the AI car

When you run the example SWF, you'll notice that the AI car also gets stuck in the grass quite often when it doesn't quite make the track corners. This is nice feature that makes the AI car seem like it's being driven by a human player. The code that slows it down in the grass is identical to the code that slows down the player's car.

```
if(_raceTrackMap
  [_aiCarTileModel.mapRow][_aiCarTileModel.mapColumn]
  == GRASS)
{
  _aiCarTileModel.friction = 0.85;
}
else
{
  _aiCarTileModel.friction = 0.98;
}
```

The single biggest thing that affects the behavior of the AI car is the value that you assign for its rotationSpeed. In the code we looked at earlier, this value was -2 to make the car turn left and 2 to make it turn right. Here's the section of code that does this:

```
if(difference > 0
&& difference < 180)
{
   //Turn left
   _aiCarTileModel.rotationSpeed = -2;
}
```

```
else
{
  //Turn right
  _aiCarTileModel.rotationSpeed = 2;
}
```

You can give the AI car a radically different driving style by changing these values. If you set `rotationSpeed` to `-5` and `5`, the AI car will drive with extreme precision. If you set it to `-1` and `1`, it will run into the grass with alarming frequency.

Here are some ways you could expand this example to a more fully developed racing game:

- Make a variety of AI cars at different skill levels just by varying the `rotationSpeed` number.
- Randomize the `rotationSpeed` value within a certain range to produce very organic and unpredictable driving styles.
- Have different AI cars using different angle maps to vary the difficulty.
- Make some cars fast and give them precise angle maps.
- Make other cars slower and give them maps that are less accurate.
- Analyze how well human players did after each race, and make the game more or less difficult to keep it challenging and unpredictable.

You'll surely find countless more solutions to tricky problems once you start thinking about storing and using game data in this way.

Collision maps

All the tile-based collisions in the examples so far have involved collisions with stationary objects. Although the enemy and elevator in the platform examples were moving, the collision detection between them and the cat didn't depend on knowing where they were on the maps. The examples used ordinarily distance-based collision detection, which was covered in the first few chapters of this book.

Yes, I sort of cheated! Why did I used distance-based collision on those moving objects, while at the same time I used spatial grid collision on the stationary platforms, like the doors and stars?

To use spatial grid collision detection on a moving game object requires updating the `_gameObject` map array each time the object moves. If the object enters a new map cell, the array must be updated to match it. I'm going to show you how to do that next, using a **collision map**. A collision map is a two-dimensional array that matches the game world maps, but tracks the locations of moving objects.

Plain-vanilla, distance-based collision is often the best method to use for moving objects, even for tile-based games. If you're checking for collisions with a relatively small number of objects, it's fast and simple. For small-scale games with a static game environment, it's the method of choice. But sometimes distance-based collision just won't cut it. Here are the two big scenarios where a different collision strategy makes sense:

- **A changing game environment**: All the platforms in the earlier examples were stationary. But what if you want to create a game where the platforms change interactively over the course of the game? The platform map array would need to be changed dynamically to match these new platform positions. This would also be the case if, instead of an action game, you were making a board game, like checkers. The map (game board) would need to be updated with new piece locations each time a player made a move. As you've seen in previous examples, if you know where different kinds of tiles are in relation to others in your game world, you can make intelligent decisions about what to do with them. In the next chapter, you'll see a practical example of this when we look at pathfinding.
- **Many moving objects**: With a lot of objects, distance-based collision starts to become inefficient because you're checking for collisions between objects that have no hope of ever colliding. You can cut down on a lot of unnecessary work by just checking for collisions between objects that are close to one another. This is an extra broad-phase check. How many moving objects is enough to justify implementing this extra step? The unscientific rule of thumb is more than 100, which is about the point where Flash Player 10 starts to slow down. You wouldn't want to use an additional broad-phase check with fewer objects because there can be quite a bit of overhead associated with updating and maintaining a dynamic array.

Let's look at how to implement a dynamic spatial grid to do tile-based collision checks on moving objects.

Understanding dynamic spatial grids

These are the essential concepts to creating collision maps:

- When game objects move, update their position in a two-dimensional array that describes their position in the game world.
- Use that new, updated array to check for collisions with objects.

There are many different ways that you can code a dynamic grid, and no one definitively right way. However, there are two main approaches that you can take: use a persistent array or rebuild the array for each frame.

When you use an array that persists across multiple frames, you have a single game object array that's initialized with your game and lasts until the end of the game. When game objects change their positions, they're removed from their old position in the array and added to the new position. To create this kind of dynamic grid, you need the following:

- To inform the game that an object's position has changed
- A system for adding new positions and removing old positions
- For collision detection, a system to make sure that objects don't do any redundant checking against one another or against themselves

The alternative is to create a new, blank array each frame and add objects to it. Instead on maintaining a persistent array, rebuild the array from scratch each frame. When you add objects to the array, their positions in the grid will match their positions on the current frame. The examples in this book use this method, for the following reasons:

- The code is simple to understand and implement.
- You can check for collisions while adding objects to the array, which avoids the problem of needing to account for double or redundant checking of objects.
- It uses less memory, and depending on the context, can have a lower CPU overhead. This is especially true if you have a lot of moving objects.
- You don't need to build additional systems to register and deregister objects with the array. This results in much simpler code and low overhead.

This isn't to say that this is always the best method, but it's a good place to start getting your feet wet with collision maps.

Updating a dynamic grid

Let's start by looking at how to add a single object to a dynamic grid and update its position each frame. You'll find an example in the `DynamicSpatialGrid` folder. Run the SWF, and you'll find a circle on the stage that you can control with the mouse or keyboard. The status box displays the position of the circle in the grid (which is the two-dimensional dynamic array). As you move the circle across the stage, watch how its array position changes in lockstep with its stage position. The `2` is its tile ID number. The array is being updated each frame with the circle's new position. You can see this illustrated in Figure 8-37.

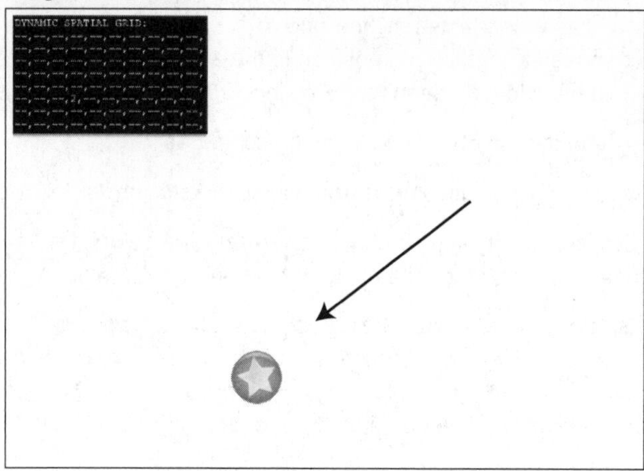

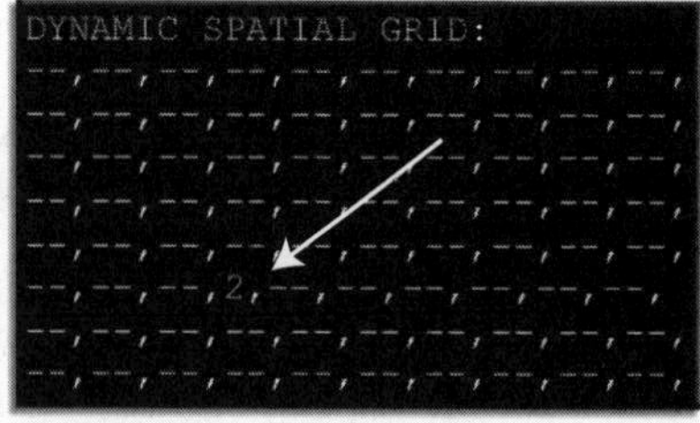

Figure 8-37. When the circle's position changes, a two-dimensional array is updated to mark its cell position in the game world.

The `com.friendsofed.utils` package includes a class called `GridDisplay` that visually displays the grid on the stage. It can help you debug or better understand what's going on. To use `GridDisplay`, instantiate it with the following parameters:

```
private var _grid:GridDisplay
   = new GridDisplay
   (
      MAX_TILE_SIZE, stage.stageWidth, stage.stageHeight
   );
```

Then add it to the stage.

```
addChild(_grid);
```

Figure 8-38 shows what this example looks like using a `GridDisplay` object.

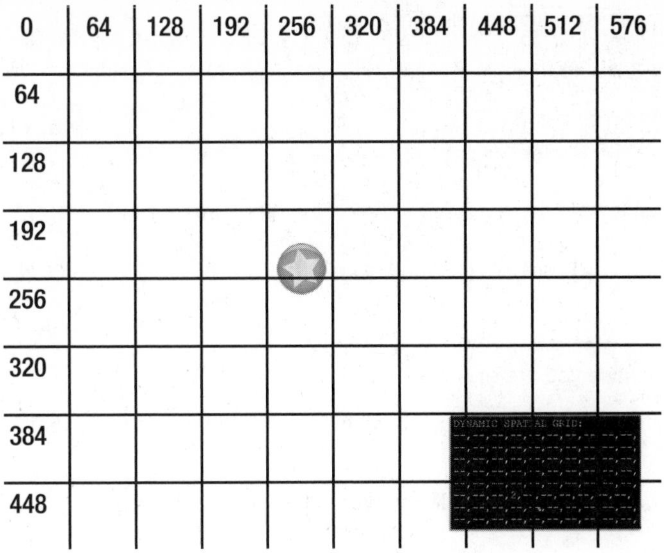

Figure 8-38. Use the optional GridDisplay utility to see the grid on the stage.

There haven't been any changes made to the tile-based engine. What's new is a two-dimensional array called `collisionMap`. Each element in the array is itself an array. If you like, you can think of this as a **three-dimensional array**, but it works like any other two-dimensional array. Instead of each array element containing some data, it contains another array (represented by the empty square brackets).

```
var collisionMap:Array
  = [
      [[],[],[],[],[],[],[],[],[],[]],
      [[],[],[],[],[],[],[],[],[],[]],
      [[],[],[],[],[],[],[],[],[],[]],
      [[],[],[],[],[],[],[],[],[],[]],
      [[],[],[],[],[],[],[],[],[],[]],
      [[],[],[],[],[],[],[],[],[],[]],
      [[],[],[],[],[],[],[],[],[],[]],
      [[],[],[],[],[],[],[],[],[],[]]
    ];
```

This array has exactly the same number of cells as the `_gameObjectMap`. You can think of it as another map layer. But unlike the other maps, it's initialized with `null` values. All the arrays are empty. It contains no information when it's created; it's just an empty skeleton.

If you prefer, you can also initialize this array like this:

```
var collisionMap:Array = new Array();
for(var row:int = 0; row < MAP_ROWS; row++)
{
  collisionMap[row] = new Array();

  for(var column:int = 0; column < MAP_COLUMNS; column++)
  {
    collisionMap[row][column] = new Array();
  }
}
```

It's up to you which style you prefer.

Unlike the other game maps, the `collisionMap` is initialized *inside* the `enterFrameHandler` as a local property.

```
private function enterFrameHandler(event:Event):void
{
  //...

  var collisionMap:Array
    = [
        [[],[],[],[],[],[],[],[],[],[]],
        [[],[],[],[],[],[],[],[],[],[]],
        [[],[],[],[],[],[],[],[],[],[]],
        [[],[],[],[],[],[],[],[],[],[]],
        [[],[],[],[],[],[],[],[],[],[]],
        [[],[],[],[],[],[],[],[],[],[]],
        [[],[],[],[],[],[],[],[],[],[]],
        [[],[],[],[],[],[],[],[],[],[]],
      ];

   //...
}
```

Because it's created in the `enterFrameHandler`, it means that it's built completely new each frame.

The next step is to copy the moving object's cell position on the stage into this grid.

The circle on the stage is a `TileModel` object called `_playerModel`. As you've seen, `TileModel` objects have properties called `mapColumn` and `mapRow` that tell you in which cell on the game world map the object currently is located. Just `push` the `_playerModel` into the dynamic grid at these same locations on every frame.

```
collisionMap
  [_playerModel.mapRow]
  [_playerModel.mapColumn]
  .push(_playerModel);
```

And that's it! The `_playerModel` has now been assigned to the correct cell in the dynamic grid. The result is exactly as you see it in the status box in Figure 8-37. Because the dynamic grid is created fresh each frame, it will always contain the `_playerModel`'s correct position. That's not bad for what's essentially just two lines of code!

For your reference, here's the code that plots the `collisionMap` array and displays it in the status box:

```
_statusBox.text = "DYNAMIC SPATIAL GRID:" + "\n";
for(var mapRow:int = 0; mapRow < MAP_ROWS; mapRow++)
{
  for(var mapColumn:int = 0; mapColumn < MAP_COLUMNS; mapColumn++)
  {
    if(collisionMap[mapRow][mapColumn][0] is TileModel)
    {
      _statusBox.text
        += collisionMap[mapRow][mapColumn][0].id + ",";
    }
    else
    {
      _statusBox.text += "--,"
    }
    if(mapColumn == collisionMap[mapRow].length -1)
    {
      _statusBox.text += "\n";
    }
  }
}
```

This is purely optional and may just help you in testing and debugging.

That's how to dynamically map one object. Of course, the usefulness of this system is in tracking many objects simultaneously and using it for something useful—like collision detection. Let's take a look at how to do that next.

Creating a collision map

With a lot of objects in the grid, you can implement the same kind of spatial grid collision detection that we used to check the cat against the platforms. If they pass that first broad-phase test, you can perform a narrow-phase, distance-based check.

You can see such a system at work in the `CollisionMap` example, as shown in Figure 8-39. It's a simple billiard-ball physics simulation like the one we looked at in Chapter 3. The difference here is that each circle is first performing a spatial grid collision check before it does a distance check. The status box displays the changing values of the dynamic grid in real time, and you can see that they match the stage positions of the circles.

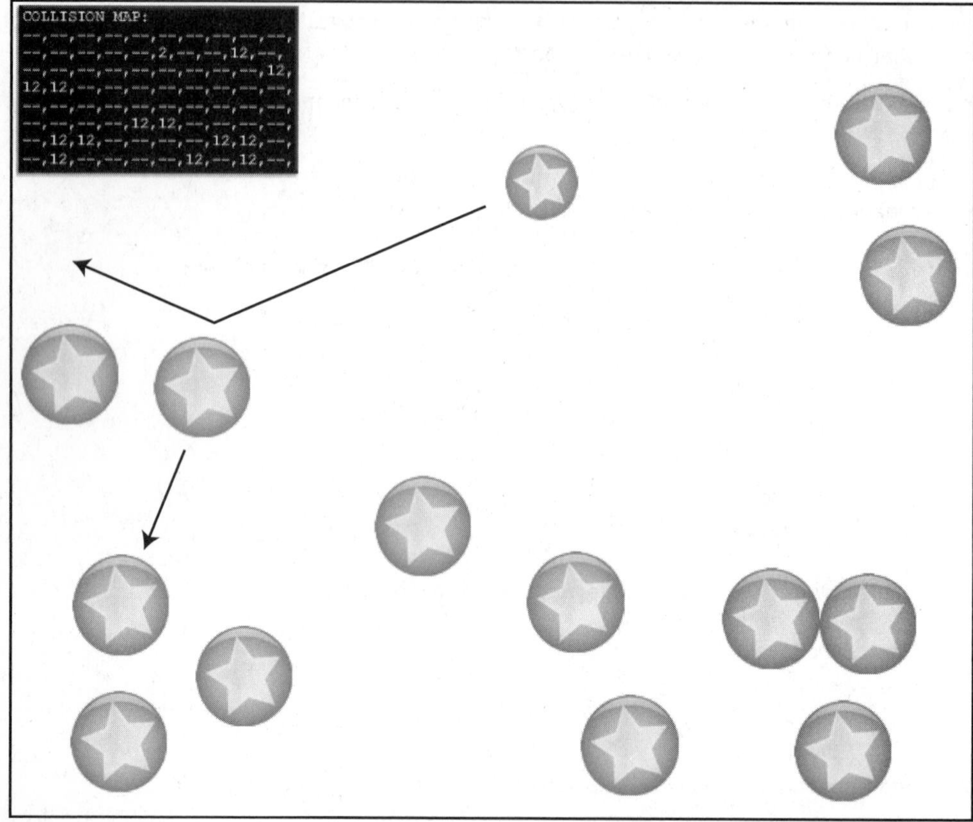

Figure 8-39. The circles first do a spatial grid check before they do a distance-based check.

Here are the general steps for making this collision detection work:

1. Push all the circle `TileModel` objects into an array called `_circles` when they're first created by the `buildMap` method.
5. Create a new, blank `collisionMap` array each frame in the `enterFrameHandler`.

6. The enterFrameHandler loops through all the circles in the _circles array and does the following:
   - Updates the models and checks stage boundaries.
   - Checks all eight cells surrounding the circle, as well as the cell it currently occupies, for any neighboring circles.
   - If it finds a neighboring circle, it does a distance-based collision check. This is the same moving circle-versus-moving circle code we looked at in Chapter 3.
   - Finally, the code adds the current circle being checked to the collisionMap array so that the next circle in line can check it for a collision.

Let's take a detailed look at the code that does this.

An array called _circles holds a reference to all the circles in the game.

```
private var _circles:Array = new Array();
```

There are two tiles in this game:

- PLAYER (the small circle), which has tile ID 02
- BIG_CIRCLE (the big circle, of course), which has tile ID 12

When the TileModel objects are created by the buildMap method, they're added to the _circles array.

```
switch(currentTile)
{
   case PLAYER:
      _playerModel
         = new TileModel
         (
            MAX_TILE_SIZE,
            tileSheetColumn, tileSheetRow,
            mapRow, mapColumn,
            48, 48
         );

      _UIController
         = new UIController(_playerModel);
      _UIView
         = new UIView(_playerModel, _UIController, stage);

      //Push the tile into the _circles array
      _circles.push(_playerModel);

      drawGameObject(_playerModel, _stageBitmapData);
      break;
```

```
    case BIG_CIRCLE:
      var bigCircle:TileModel
        = new TileModel
        (
          MAX_TILE_SIZE,
          tileSheetColumn, tileSheetRow,
          mapRow, mapColumn,
          MAX_TILE_SIZE, MAX_TILE_SIZE
        );

      //Push the tile into the _circles array
      _circles.push(bigCircle);

      drawGameObject(bigCircle, _stageBitmapData);
      break;
  }
```

This is pretty straightforward stuff. All the important code is in the `enterFrameHandler`.

```
private function enterFrameHandler(event:Event):void
{
  //Clear the stage bitmap from the previous frame
  _stageBitmapData.fillRect(_stageBitmapData.rect, 0);

  //Initialize a blank collision map
  var collisionMap:Array
    = [
        [[],[],[],[],[],[],[],[],[],[]],
        [[],[],[],[],[],[],[],[],[],[]],
        [[],[],[],[],[],[],[],[],[],[]],
        [[],[],[],[],[],[],[],[],[],[]],
        [[],[],[],[],[],[],[],[],[],[]],
        [[],[],[],[],[],[],[],[],[],[]],
        [[],[],[],[],[],[],[],[],[],[]],
        [[],[],[],[],[],[],[],[],[],[]]
      ];

  //Loop through all the circles.
  //Add them to the collision map
  //and check neighboring cells for other circles
  for(var i:int = 0; i < _circles.length; i++)
  {
    //Get a reference to the current circle in the loop
    var circle:TileModel = _circles[i];

    //Update the circle and check stage bounds
    circle.update();
    StageBoundaries.bounceBitmap(circle, stage);
```

```
//If this is the *first* circle, add it to the
//collision map, but don't bother checking
//for collisions because there won't yet be any other
//objects in the collision map to check for
if(i == 0)
{
   collisionMap[circle.mapRow][circle.mapColumn].push(circle);
}
//If this is the not the first circle…
else
{
   //Check the 8 cells surrounding this circle
   //as well as the cell it currently occupies
   //(9 cells in total)
   for(var column:int = -1; column < 2; column++)
   {
      for(var row:int = -1; row < 2; row++)
      {
         //Make sure that the code doesn't
         //check for rows that
         //are greater than the number of rows
         //and columns on the map
         if(circle.mapRow + row < collisionMap.length
         && circle.mapRow + row >= 0
         && circle.mapColumn + column < collisionMap[0].length
         && circle.mapColumn + column >= 0)
         {
            //Get a reference to the current cell being checked
            //and cast it as an Array using the "as" keyword
            //(the compiler needs that reassurance)
            var cell:Array
               = collisionMap
               [circle.mapRow + row]
               [circle.mapColumn + column]
               as Array;

             //If this cell isn't null, it must contain objects
             if(cell != null)
             {
               //Loop through all the elements in the cell
               //(It will usually just contain one object,
               //but you never know...)
               for
                 (
                   var element:int = 0;
                   element < cell.length;
                   element++
                 )
```

```
                    {
                        //Check whether the current element is
                        //a tile that we're interested in.
                        //(You don't need to check for the existence
                        //of the object that's performing the check
                        //because it hasn't been added to the array yet)
                        if(cell[element].id == BIG_CIRCLE
                        || cell[element].id == PLAYER)
                        {
                            //A possible collision!
                            //Get a reference to the object that
                            //might be involved in a collision
                            var circle2:TileModel = cell[element];

                            //Do a narrow-phase, distance-based
                            //collision check against the two circles.
                            //The _collisionController object does this
                            _collisionController.movingCircleCollision
                              (circle, circle2);
                        }
                    }
                }
            }
        }
      }
    }
    //Add the circle to the collision map
    //in the same position as its current
    //game map position. This has to happen last
    collisionMap[circle.mapRow][circle.mapColumn].push(circle);
  }

  //The last step is to update the display.
  //Blit all the circles to the stage bitmap
  //using the familiar drawGameObject method
  for(var j:int = 0; j < _circles.length; j++)
  {
    drawGameObject(_circles[j], _stageBitmapData);
  }
}
```

Let's look at how this code works.

After the loop updates the model and checks the stage boundaries, the code checks whether this is the first loop. If so, it adds the object to the `collisionMap`, but doesn't run any other code.

```
if(i == 0)
{
   collisionMap[circle.mapRow][circle.mapColumn].push(circle);
}
else
{... check for collisions…
```

Why doesn't the first object check any for collisions? Because if it's the first object, the map will be blank. There can't possibly be any other objects on the map. Obviously, it makes sense to check for collisions only if the map contains more than one object.

The code then runs a nested `for` loop that scans all adjacent cells around the object. It includes the eight surrounding cells as well as the cell that the object occupies.

```
for(var column:int = -1; column < 2; column++)
{
   for(var row:int = -1; row < 2; row++)
   {
      //Make sure that the code doesn't check for rows that
      //are greater than the number of rows and columns on the map

      //...

      //Get a reference to the current cell being checked
      var cell:Array
         = collisionMap
         [circle.mapRow + row]
         [circle.mapColumn + column]
         as Array;
```

The loop produces the numbers -1, 0, and 1 in three sets. If you add those numbers to the circle's current column and row position, the numbers will match all the circle's adjacent cells. Figure 8-40 illustrates how this works.

In previous examples, it was enough to just check the cells containing the object's four corner points. Why didn't we just do that in this case?

If all the objects are moving, you could miss certain types of collisions. Figure 8-41 illustrates one of these situations. The first circle is added by the loop, but can't find the second circle because the second circle hasn't been added to the collision map yet. When the loop eventually adds the second circle to the map, none of its corner points overlap the first circle's center cell. Therefore, it can't find the small circle, and the obvious collision is missed. To avoid this problem, check every cell surrounding the object.

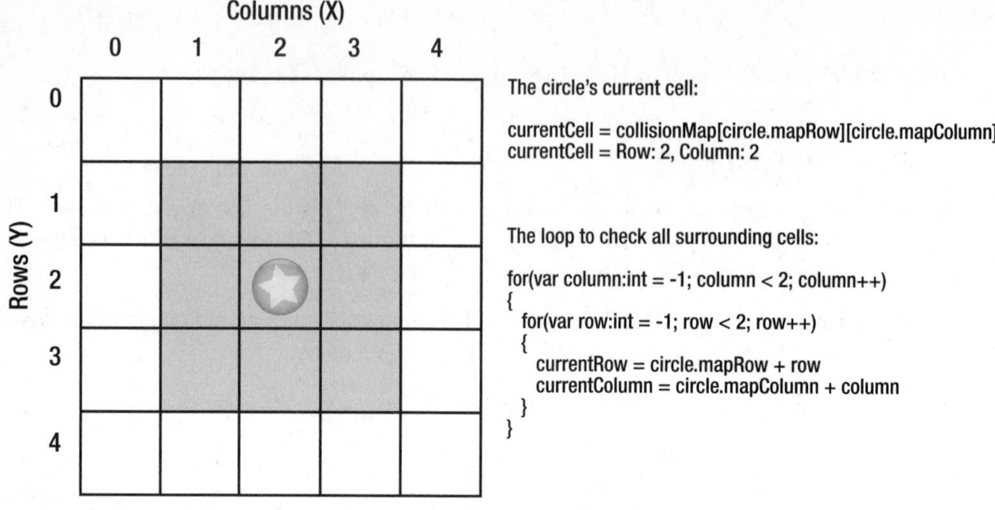
Columns (X)
0
1
2
3
4
Rows (Y)
0
1
2
3
4
The circle's current cell:
currentCell = collisionMap[circle.mapRow][circle.mapColumn]
currentCell = Row: 2, Column: 2
The loop to check all surrounding cells:
for(var column:int = -1; column < 2; column++)
{
for(var row:int = -1; row < 2; row++)
{
currentRow = circle.mapRow + row
currentColumn = circle.mapColumn + column
}
}

The loop produces nine results that correspond to all the adjacent cells, including the current cell:

Column: 1, Row: 1
Column: 1, Row: 2
Column: 1, Row: 3

Column: 2, Row: 1
Column: 2, Row: 2
Column: 2, Row: 3

Column: 3, Row: 1
Column: 3, Row: 2
Column: 3, Row: 3

Figure 8-40. Check all the cells around the object.

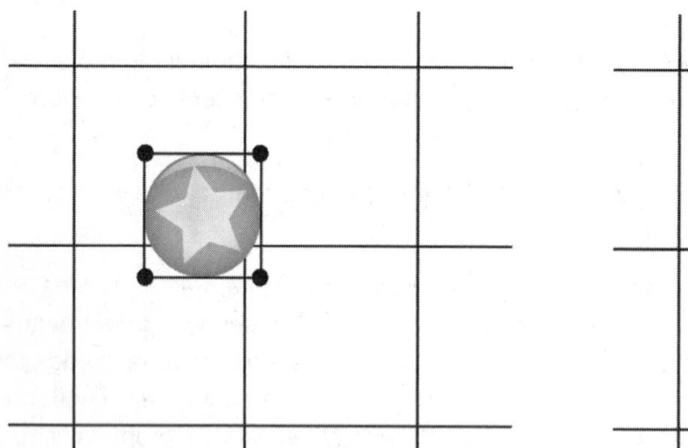

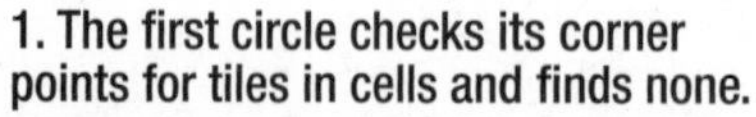
1. The first circle checks its corner points for tiles in cells and finds none.

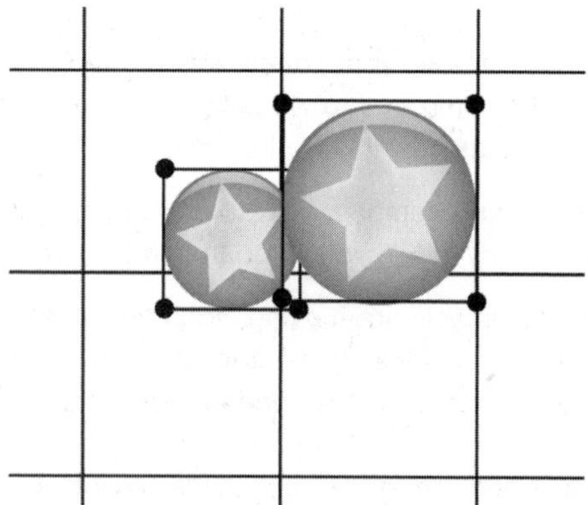

2. The second circle checks its corner points for tiles in cells and also finds none.

Figure 8-41. The reason it's not enough to check only corner points

The code also must make sure that it's checking for cells that actually exist in the array.

```
if(circle.mapRow + row < collisionMap.length
&& circle.mapRow + row >= 0
&& circle.mapColumn + column < collisionMap[0].length
&& circle.mapColumn + column >= 0)
{…
```

This needs to be done because if the circles are at the edges of the map, they could check for cells that don't correspond to elements in the `collisionMap` array. If that happens, you'll get a nasty runtime error. The additional check prevents this problem.

After all that, the code produces an `Array` object called `cell`:

```
var cell:Array
   = collisionMap
   [circle.mapRow + row]
   [circle.mapColumn + column]
   as Array;
```

This refers to any of the nine cells being checked, at any given point in the loop. (It must be cast `as Array` to keep the compiler happy.)

Because it's an array, it might be empty. We need to check for that as well.

```
if(cell != null)
{…
```

If the cell isn't empty … bingo! It means that it contains at least one tile. But how many of them? It doesn't really matter. We can run a `for` loop that will catch 1 or 100 objects in the cell.

```
for(var element:int = 0; element < cell.length; element++)
{…
```

In this example, there will almost certainly be only one object per cell, so this loop is a bit of overkill. However, in most of your games, many objects could occupy the same cell, especially if any of your tiles are smaller than the map cell. In this specific example, that will be very unlikely because the circles are large enough to push each other out of the map cells. But it could happen if your game has many small objects moving around.

The loop next checks the cell for the kinds of tiles that it's interested in. In this example, there are two kinds of tiles that could be colliding, and both can be handled in the same way.

```
if(cell[element].id == BIG_CIRCLE
|| cell[element].id == PLAYER)
{
```

If the loop finds any of these tiles, it switches to the narrow-phase of the collision-detection system. It does a moving circle-versus-moving circle collision check.

```
if(cell[element].id == BIG_CIRCLE
|| cell[element].id == PLAYER)
{
```

```
    //A possible collision!
    //Get a reference to the object that
    //might be involved in a collision
    var circle2:TileModel = cell[element];

    //Do a narrow-phase, distance-based
    //collision check against the two circles
    _collisionController.movingCircleCollision(circle, circle2);
}
```

You'll find the `movingCircleCollision` method in the `TileCollisionController` class in the `com.friendsofed.utils` package. It's identical to the code we looked at in detail in Chapter 3.

Finally, the code adds the current circle to the collision map.

```
collisionMap[circle.mapRow][circle.mapColumn].push(circle);
```

This allows the next circle in line for the collision check to be able to find it in the `collisionMap`.

This may seem a bit overwhelming at first, but don't let it intimidate you. Much of the code is just error prevention that, as grown-ups, is unfortunately something we just have to do. At its core, it doesn't contain anything new. You're looping through a 9-by-9 grid, and then looping through the objects in the arrays that each grid cell contains.

This is one way to create a collision map of moving objects. There are many other ways, and I'm sure you'll come up with some clever ideas for your own games.

Other broad-phase collision strategies

A spatial grid is an excellent all-purpose broad-phase collision-detection system that is a game designer's staple. It's hard to be beat for simplicity, speed, and low overhead. However, there are many other broad-phase collision strategies that each has its unique take on the problem. Here are the four most popular:

- **Hierarchical grid**: In a fixed-sized spatial grid such as the one we've been using in this chapter, the cell size must be as large as the largest object. But what if you have a game with a few very big objects and a lot of very small objects? The cell size will need to be big enough to accommodate those large objects, even if there aren't very many of them. You'll end up with a situation where each cell is full of many small objects, each doing expensive distance checks against one another.

  A hierarchical grid solves this problem by creating two or more grids of different-sized cells. It creates a grid with big cells for the big objects, and another one for the small objects, and any range of differing cell size grids in between. Collision checks between small objects are handled in the small-cell grid, and collisions between big objects are handled in the big-cell grid. If a small object needs to check for a collision with a big object, the system checks the cells that correspond to both grids.

- **Quadtree**: A specific type of hierarchical grid. The game world is divided into 4 rectangles, which are in turn divided into 4 more rectangles, resulting in 16. Each of those 16 rectangles are again split into 4 smaller rectangles, and this continues depending on how much detail you need. Each of the smaller rectangles is a child of the larger parents. The quadtree system figures out which objects to test for collisions depending on their level in their hierarchy. The 3D version of the quadtree is called an **octree**.
- **Sort and sweep**: Sort the objects in arrays based on their x and y positions. Check for overlaps on the x and y axes and, if found, do a more precise distance check. Because the objects are spatially sorted first, likely collision candidates come to the forefront first.
- **BSP tree**: Space is partitioned in a way that closely matches the geometry of the game objects. It's useful because it means that the partitions can be used both for collisions and to define environmental boundaries. Binary space partitioning (BSP) trees are closely related to quadtrees, but they're more versatile. BSP trees are widely used in collision detection for 3D games.

I suggest that you spend some time researching these other broad-phase collision strategies. You may find one of them holds a particularly good solution to a complex collision problem you might be facing.

Summary

Tile-based games solve many complex game-design problems in a very compact and efficient way. It should therefore be no surprise that most professionally designed games use an underlying tile-based engine. This is as true for 2D games as it is for 3D. You'll probably consider using a tile-based game engine for all your games from now on.

Although the focus of this book is on action video games, tile-based game engines are at the heart of puzzle, strategy, role-playing, and board games. Games like Tetris, Bejeweled, Age of Empires, and Chess are essentially tile-based games that use many of the techniques covered in this chapter.

This chapter has been an introduction to tile-based game design, but there's a lot more that you can learn. *AdvancED ActionScript 3.0 Animation* by Keith Peters (friends of ED, 2008) covers isometric and hexagonal tile engines, as well as some advanced pathfinding strategies.

If you're designing large or complex maps for your games, consider using specialized software to help you create your map arrays. Mappy (Windows) and Tiled (Mac OS X and Windows) allow you to visually create game maps from your tile sheets. They output XML or array data that you can use with your games.

In the next chapter, we're going to look at one of the most useful features of tile-based games: pathfinding.

Chapter 9

Pathfinding

An essential skill for any ambitious video-game enemy is being able to find its way around your game world. Remember the hedgehog from the platform game in the previous chapter? It was cute, but dumb! It couldn't do much more than run from one ledge to the other in a never-ending, vertigo-induced panic. It didn't know how to navigate the game world, find the player, or react to a changing game environment. These are things that all self-respecting game characters should be able to do.

In this chapter, we're going to take a close look at some essential techniques in an area of video-game design called **pathfinding**:

- Randomly moving through a maze
- Chasing a player character
- Using line of sight in a tile-based game world
- Finding the shortest path through an environment using the A* algorithm

But first, let's set up a game environment that's easy for your characters to move through.

Moving through a maze

One of the advantages of tile-based games is their predictable symmetry. The entire game world is composed of tiles that are the same size. You can leverage those fixed sizes to help simplify your game engine. This makes game design much easier, and the end result for players is that your game looks precise with clean mechanics.

In the platform game examples in the previous chapter, the cat's dimensions didn't match the tile dimensions. It could run and jump freely between tiles however it pleased. That was the effect we wanted to achieve, but we paid for it with complex physics and collision code. If you're willing to forgo some of the fancy physics and work within the limitations imposed by the underlying math of the tile-based engine, things become much simpler—and possibly even better.

For an example of this theory in action, take a look at the `MoveAroundMaze` example in the chapter's source files. It features the heroic return of Button Fairy in an underground dungeon maze, as shown in Figure 9-1. Use the arrow keys to move her around the maze.

Figure 9-1. Use the arrow keys to steer Button Fairy around the maze.

Notice how Button Fairy behaves in this example:

- She is neatly centered within in each tile cell.
- She changes direction only when she's precisely centered within a cell.
- She moves smoothly into new corridors without catching on the corners of the walls.

These features of the control system were planned to take advantage of some convenient side effects of the tile-based engine.

Centering game objects

All the examples in this chapter use a simple tile sheet that you'll find in the `images` folder in the chapter's source files. As shown in Figure 9-2, it's a 128-by-128 PNG file that contains four tiles: Button Fairy, a monster, a wall tile, and a floor tile.

Figure 9-2. The tile sheet used in this chapter

Take a close look at the fairy and monster tiles. They're smaller than the maximum tile size, but they're *not* aligned to the top-left corner. Instead, they're centered in the tile, as shown in Figure 9-3. Because of this, we can just blit the tile at full size, and we don't need to worry about centering it in the game engine.

Figure 9-3. The game characters are smaller than the maximum tile size and are centered in the tile sheet.

Button Fairy's actual character size is 64 (width) by 53 (height). But the `buildMap` method blits her to the stage as a full 64-by-64 tile. (The value of `MAX_TILE_SIZE` is `64`. The maze game examples in this chapter use the same tile engine as the previous chapter.)

```
_fairyModel
  = new TileModel
  (
    MAX_TILE_SIZE,
    tileSheetColumn, tileSheetRow,
    mapRow, mapColumn,
    MAX_TILE_SIZE, MAX_TILE_SIZE
  );
```

This gives her a bit of space on the top and bottom. That space is part of the tile.

So, even though she looks smaller, Button Fairy is a 64-by-64-pixel tile. That exactly matches the tile sizes of the walls and floors. Can we use this happy coincidence to our advantage?

Moving and changing direction

You can steer Button Fairy using the arrow keys. If you press the right arrow key, she'll move right until she hits a wall.

But if she's already moving right and you press the down key, she won't move down immediately. Instead, she'll move down only when she reaches an intersection. Even if you press the down key five tiles before she reaches that intersection, she won't attempt to move down until she is exactly centered over the intersection. This results in a very accurate movement system that feels precise and solid. Figure 9-4 illustrates Button Fairy's movements.

Here's a summary of the logic behind Button Fairy's control system:

- When the user presses an arrow key, keep that new direction in memory.
- When Button Fairy reaches an intersection, move her in that new direction.

Clever and interesting! But it also implies something a little more complex going on behind the scenes. How can we track the player's direction choices? And how do we know when Button Fairy reaches an intersection?

Let's take a closer look at the mechanics behind this system.

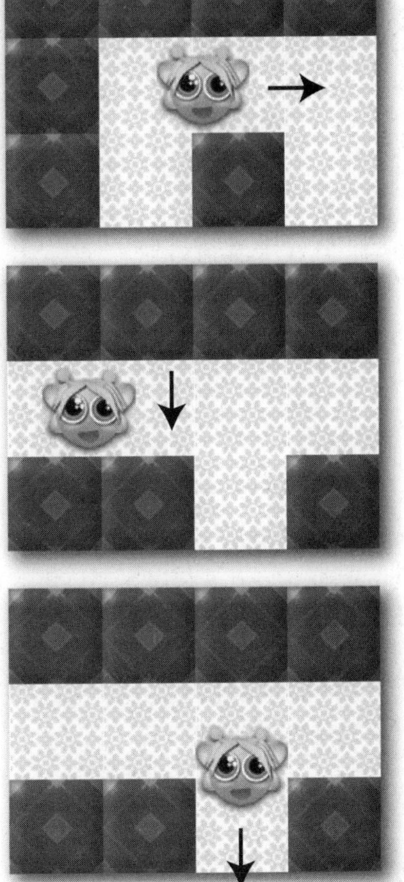

Press the right arrow key,
and Button Fairy moves right.
If you press the down arrow
key, Button Fairy will
continue to move right
if she isn't at an intersection.
When Button Fairy is centered
directly over the intersection,
she moves down.

Figure 9-4. Button Fairy changes direction only at an intersection.

Moving Button Fairy

When the `buildMap` method creates the `_fairyModel`, it also creates the `_UIMazeController` and `_UIMazeView` objects that control it.

```
_fairyModel
  = new TileModel
    (
      MAX_TILE_SIZE,
      tileSheetColumn, tileSheetRow,
```

```
      mapRow, mapColumn,
      MAX_TILE_SIZE, MAX_TILE_SIZE
    );

  //Add the UIView and UIController
  _UIMazeController
    = new UIMazeController(_fairyModel);
  _UIMazeView
    = new UIMazeView
    (_fairyModel, _UIMazeController, stage);

  //Disable friction (it's not needed in this example)
  _fairyModel.friction = 1;

  //Set the initial direction. "direction" is a
  //property of the TileModel class
  _fairyModel.direction = "right";

  //Blit the object to the stage
  drawGameObject(_fairyModel, _foregroundBitmapData);
```

It sets the initial direction to `"right"`. `direction` is a property of the `TileModel` class. It's used to set and track the direction of maze game characters.

`_UIMazeView` captures keyboard input and sends it to `_UIMazeController` for processing. `_UIMazeController` has a very simple job. It checks the key being pressed and assigns `"left"`, `"right"`, `"up"`, or `"down"` to the model's `direction` property.

```
internal function processKeyDown(event:KeyboardEvent):void
{
  if(event.keyCode == Keyboard.LEFT)
  {
    _model.direction = "left";
  }
  if(event.keyCode == Keyboard.RIGHT)
  {
    _model.direction = "right";
  }
  if(event.keyCode == Keyboard.DOWN)
  {
    _model.direction = "down";
  }
  if(event.keyCode == Keyboard.UP)
  {
    _model.direction = "up";
  }
}
```

The game can now use that information to find out if and when Button Fairy should move.

This happens in the application class's `enterFrameHandler`. It checks to see if Button Fairy is exactly at the corner of a tile. If she is, it moves her in the correct direction.

```
if(atCornerOfTile(_fairyModel))
{
  //Move in a new direction if there is no wall...
```

A method called `atCornerOfTile` checks whether `_fairyModel`'s top-left corner is precisely at the corner of a tile. `atCornerOfTile` returns `true` if she is. This prevents Button Fairy from changing direction until she is exactly aligned with the center of a new corridor.

Here's the `atCornerOfTile` method that performs this check:

```
public function atCornerOfTile(gameObject:TileModel):Boolean
{
  var objectIsAtCorner:Boolean = false;

  var tileCorner_X:uint
    = gameObject.mapColumn * MAX_TILE_SIZE;
  var tileCorner_Y:uint
    = gameObject.mapRow * MAX_TILE_SIZE;

  if(uint(gameObject.xPos) == tileCorner_X
  && uint(gameObject.yPos) == tileCorner_Y)
  {
    objectIsAtCorner = true;
  }
  else
  {
    objectIsAtCorner = false;
  }

  return objectIsAtCorner;
}
```

The method first finds the x and y positions of the tile that the `_fairyModel` currently occupies.

```
var tileCorner_X:uint
  = gameObject.mapColumn * MAX_TILE_SIZE;
var tileCorner_Y:uint
  = gameObject.mapRow * MAX_TILE_SIZE;
```

Let's say the `_fairyModel` is at column 10 and row 5. That would mean the tile's x position is 640 and its y position is 320. If the `_fairyModel`'s own x and y positions match those numbers, then we know that Button Fairy is exactly at the top-left corner of the tile.

```
if(uint(gameObject.xPos) == tileCorner_X
&& uint(gameObject.yPos) == tileCorner_Y)
{
  objectIsAtCorner = true;
}
else
{
  objectIsAtCorner = false;
}
```

Figure 9-5 illustrates this check.

Button Fairy's top-left corner matches the top-left corner of the tile she currently occupies.

Figure 9-5. If Button Fairy's top-left corner matches the tile's top-left corner, we know that she is centered exactly over the tile.

This sounds good, but there's a potential problem with this system. It will work only if we can *guarantee* that `_fairyModel`'s top-left x and y positions will at some point match the tile's top-left x and y positions. How will we know that Button Fairy will land exactly at those coordinates?

The solution is to limit Button Fairy's velocity to a number that divides the tile size evenly. That means we can use a velocity of 2, 4, 8, 16, 32, or 64. Any of those numbers will guarantee that Button Fairy's top-left corner will at some point match the tile's top-left corner, as shown in Figure 9-6.

This is what I was talking about at the beginning of the chapter when I mentioned working within the constraints of the tile-based engine. Can you live with a velocity of 2, 4, 8, 16, 32, or 64? If you can, sticking to this constraint will save you a lot of trouble, simplify your code, and be very light on the CPU. That sounds good enough for me … I'll take it!

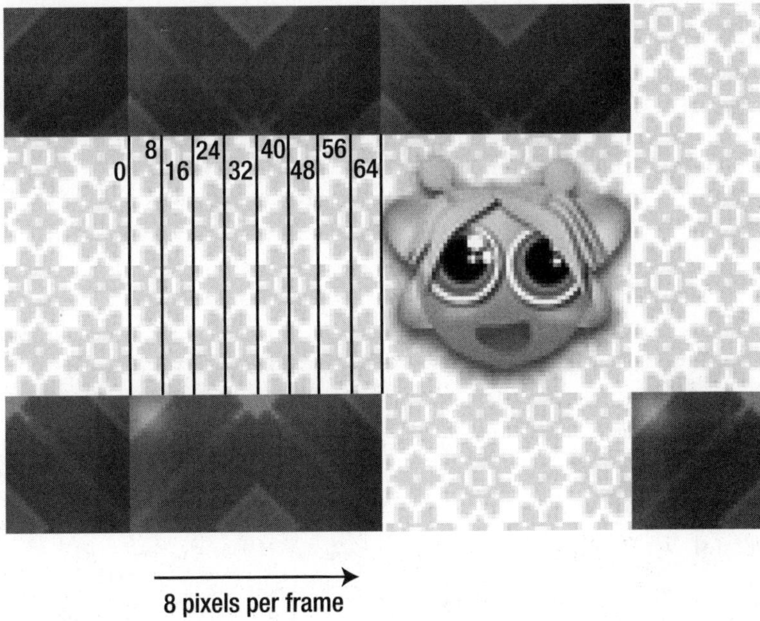

Figure 9-6. If Button Fairy moves 8 pixels each frame, her position will eventually match the tile's top-left corner.

Changing direction

We now know *when* Button Fairy can change direction: when she is at a tile's corner.

Next, we need to find out *if* she can move.

Maybe Button Fairy wants to move down, but can she? If the tile she wants to move into is a `FLOOR` tile, she can. Otherwise, she will need to continue moving in her current direction until a `FLOOR` tile is found.

The `enterFrameHandler` checks for this. If it finds an adjacent `FLOOR` tile, it assigns a new velocity of `8` in the direction Button Fairy wants to move. But if there's a `WALL` tile in the direction she is currently moving, it stops her.

```
if(atCornerOfTile(_fairyModel))
{
  //Move in a new direction if there is no wall
  if(_fairyModel.direction == "left"
  && _mazeMap[_fairyModel.mapRow][_fairyModel.mapColumn - 1]
    == FLOOR)
```

```
{
  _fairyModel.vx = -8;
  _fairyModel.vy = 0;
}

else if(_fairyModel.direction == "right"
&& _mazeMap[_fairyModel.mapRow][_fairyModel.mapColumn + 1]
  == FLOOR)
{
  _fairyModel.vx = 8;
  _fairyModel.vy = 0;
}

else if(_fairyModel.direction == "up"
&& _mazeMap[_fairyModel.mapRow - 1][_fairyModel.mapColumn]
  == FLOOR)
{
  _fairyModel.vx = 0;
  _fairyModel.vy = -8;
}

else if(_fairyModel.direction == "down"
&& _mazeMap[_fairyModel.mapRow + 1][_fairyModel.mapColumn]
  == FLOOR)
{
  _fairyModel.vx = 0;
  _fairyModel.vy = 8;
}

//Stop if there is a wall in the current direction
if(_fairyModel.vx > 0
&& _mazeMap[_fairyModel.mapRow][_fairyModel.mapColumn + 1]
  == WALL)
{
   _fairyModel.vx = 0
}
else if(_fairyModel.vx < 0
&& _mazeMap[_fairyModel.mapRow][_fairyModel.mapColumn - 1]
  == WALL)
{
   _fairyModel.vx = 0
}
if(_fairyModel.vy > 0
&& _mazeMap[_fairyModel.mapRow + 1][_fairyModel.mapColumn]
  == WALL)
{
   _fairyModel.vy = 0
}
```

```
    else if(_fairyModel.vy < 0
    && _mazeMap[_fairyModel.mapRow - 1][_fairyModel.mapColumn]
      == WALL)
    {
       _fairyModel.vy = 0
    }
}
```

It's simple, refreshingly physics-free, and very precise. Be sure to check out the complete `MoveAroundMaze` source file so that you can see all this code in its proper context.

Now let's raise the stakes a bit, and add the monster to the maze.

Random movement in a maze

Run the `RandomDirection` SWF, and you'll see that the maze is now also occupied by a monster that changes direction at each intersection, as shown in Figure 9-7.

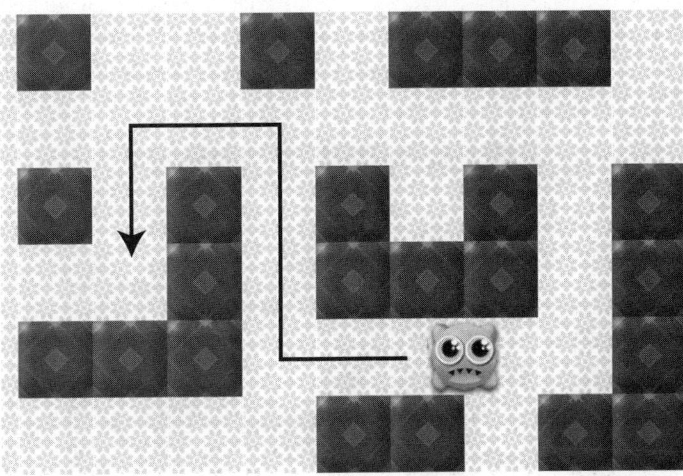

Figure 9-7. What's a maze without a monster? The monster selects a random direction at each intersection.

The monster chooses a new random direction whenever it reaches an intersection. "Random direction? Kid stuff!" I hear you say. if it were just a matter of assigning a random direction, we could simply pick a number between 1 and 4 and be done with it, right?

On closer inspection, this problem is a little more complex. The monster's path through the maze *looks* completely random, but it's not entirely so. Two issues arise:

- The monster changes direction only when he reaches an intersection. This poses a problem: how do we define what an intersection is?

- The monster doesn't choose just any route when he reaches an intersection. He tends to choose a vertical path if he has been traveling horizontally or a horizontal path if he has been traveling vertically. This feature forces the monster to explore more of the maze sooner, and makes his path seem more natural than if he chose a purely random direction.

Let's find out how these two issues are solved.

Finding an intersection

Navigating Button Fairy around the maze is easy. We can see when an intersection is approaching and change her direction to move her into a new corridor. But the monster can't "see" anything. He is as blind as a bat, groping along the corridors with no idea of where to turn or when. We need to come up with some sort of logical way to explain to the monster that he needs to change direction at an intersection. But even before that, we need to describe to the monster what an intersection looks like. Fortunately, this is exactly what a tile-based game engine is good at doing.

Figure 9-8 marks all the intersections in the maze with an X. Take a close look at these intersections. Is there any common pattern associated with the tiles surrounding an intersection? If you find a pattern, you could use that pattern to help you define what an intersection is.

Figure 9-8. All the intersections in the maze. When the monster reaches an intersection, he must choose a new random direction.

It turns out that there is a pattern. All of the intersections in the maze are surrounded by at least one adjacent vertical `FLOOR` tile and one adjacent horizontal `FLOOR` tile. If you find a tile that is surrounded by any combination of the following `FLOOR` tiles, you *must* be at an intersection.

- Left and up
- Left and down
- Right and up
- Right and down.

Figure 9-9 illustrates this pattern. (Cul-de-sacs are a special case, and you'll see how to deal with them shortly.)

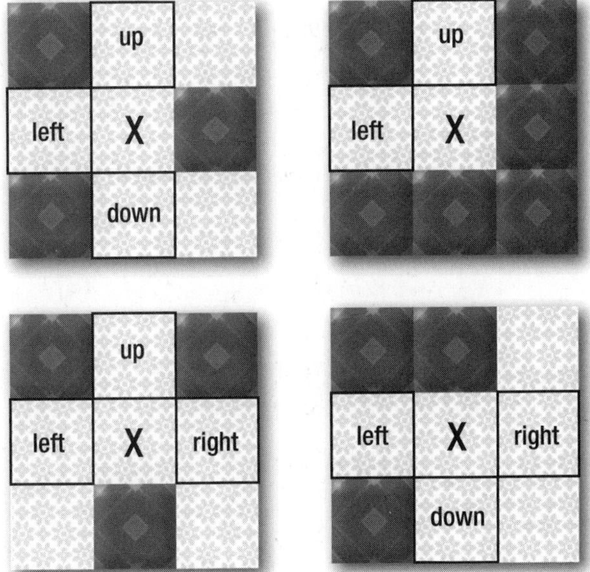

Figure 9-9. All intersections have at least one adjacent vertical `FLOOR` tile and one adjacent horizontal `FLOOR` tile.

The monster moves at 8 pixels per frame, just like Button Fairy. Each time he reaches a tile corner, the code checks whether he is at an intersection by calling the `atIntersection` method.

```
if(atCornerOfTile(_monsterModel)
&& atIntersection(_monsterModel))
{
  findNewDirection(_monsterModel);
}
```

The `atIntersection` method returns `true` if it finds that the monster is at an intersection. It uses the logic I've just explained. If it finds both a vertical and horizontal passage, then the monster must be at an intersection. It runs an additional check to find out if the monster is in a cul-de-sac, and returns `true` if it is.

```
public function atIntersection(gameObject:TileModel):Boolean
{
  var horizontalPassage:Boolean = false;
  var verticalPassage:Boolean = false;
  var objectIsAtIntersection:Boolean = false;

  //An intersection is defined in this game as a place
  //where there is at least one horizontal and one
  //vertical passage open
  if(_mazeMap[gameObject.mapRow][gameObject.mapColumn + 1]
    == FLOOR
  || _mazeMap[gameObject.mapRow][gameObject.mapColumn - 1]
    == FLOOR)
  {
    horizontalPassage = true;
  }
  if(_mazeMap[gameObject.mapRow + 1][gameObject.mapColumn]
    == FLOOR
  || _mazeMap[gameObject.mapRow - 1][gameObject.mapColumn]
    == FLOOR)
  {
    verticalPassage = true;
  }

  //If both vertical and horizontal passages are open,
  //we've found an intersection
  if(horizontalPassage && verticalPassage)
  {
    objectIsAtIntersection = true;
  }

  //Check whether the object is in a
  //cul-de-sac (surrounded by walls on 3 sides)

  //Create a counter variable to count the number of walls
  var wallCounter:uint = 0;

  //Check the four surrounding tiles for walls
  if(_mazeMap[gameObject.mapRow][gameObject.mapColumn + 1]
    == WALL)
  {
    //Add one to the counter if a wall is found
    wallCounter++;
  }
  if(_mazeMap[gameObject.mapRow][gameObject.mapColumn - 1]
    == WALL)
  {
    wallCounter++;
  }
```

```
  if(_mazeMap[gameObject.mapRow + 1][gameObject.mapColumn]
    == WALL)
  {
    wallCounter++;
  }
  if(_mazeMap[gameObject.mapRow - 1][gameObject.mapColumn]
    == WALL)
  {
    wallCounter++;
  }

  //If there are more than two walls, the object must be in
  //a cul-de-sac. This is also a type of intersection, so the
  //same rules apply.
  if(wallCounter > 2)
  {
    objectIsAtIntersection = true;
  }

  return objectIsAtIntersection;
}
```

To find out whether the monster is in a cul-de-sac, the code counts the number of surrounding walls. If it finds more than two, the he must be in a cul-de-sac, as shown in Figure 9-10. The monster's behavior in a cul-de-sac is the same as for a normal intersection, so the method returns `true`.

Figure 9-10. A cul-de-sac is defined by the game as a tile surrounded by three walls.

Changing direction

If an intersection is found, the monster needs to figure out what to do. This is handled by the `findNewDirection` method.

```
if(atCornerOfTile(_monsterModel)
&& atIntersection(_monsterModel))
```

```
{
  findNewDirection(_monsterModel);
}
```

findNewDirection randomly selects a new direction for the monster to travel. If that new direction is blocked by a wall, the method calls itself recursively until it finds a direction that isn't blocked.

> ***Recursion** is when a method calls itself. Here's a simple example of a recursive method.*
>
> ```
> function recursiveMethod():void
> {
>   recursiveMethod();
> }
> ```
>
> *Obviously, the code above will result in an infinite loop, so you need to use care when using recursion. It's useful for testing things using trial and error. If the method returns false, just keep trying with different values until you get it right.*

The direction that findNewDirection chooses isn't entirely random. If the monster has been moving left or right, it will choose up or down as a first choice. This has the effect of making the monster look like he is actively exploring the maze, rather than just blindly stumbling through it.

Here's the entire findNewDirection method:

```
public function findNewDirection(gameObject:TileModel):void
{
  var newDirection:String = "";

  //Choose a random number between 1 and 4
  var randomDirection:int = Math.ceil(Math.random() * 4);

  //Encourage the monster to choose up or down if
  //it's currently moving left or right
  if(gameObject.direction == "left"
  || gameObject.direction == "right")
  {
    if(randomDirection <= 2)
    {
      newDirection = "up";
    }
    else
    {
      newDirection = "down";
    }
  }
```

```
//...if the monster is currently moving up or down, make
//it move left or right
else
{
  if(randomDirection <= 2)
  {
    newDirection = "left";
  }
  else
  {
    newDirection = "right";
  }
}

//Test the new direction and call this method recursively
//if the direction runs the object into a wall

switch(newDirection)
{
  case "left":
    if(_mazeMap[gameObject.mapRow][gameObject.mapColumn - 1]
      == FLOOR)
    {
      gameObject.direction = newDirection;
      gameObject.vx = -8;
      gameObject.vy = 0;
    }
    else
    {
      //If the test hits a wall, assign this direction as
      //the object's new direction and test again.
      //(Assigning the new direction prevents the object
      //from accidentally getting stuck in cul-de-sacs)
      gameObject.direction = newDirection;
      findNewDirection(gameObject);
    }
    break;

    case "right":
      if(_mazeMap[gameObject.mapRow][gameObject.mapColumn + 1]
        == FLOOR)
      {
        gameObject.direction = newDirection;
        gameObject.vx = 8;
        gameObject.vy = 0;
      }
```

```
        else
        {
          gameObject.direction = newDirection;
          findNewDirection(gameObject);
        }
        break;

      case "up":
        if(_mazeMap[gameObject.mapRow - 1][gameObject.mapColumn]
          == FLOOR)
        {
          gameObject.direction = newDirection;
          gameObject.vx = 0;
          gameObject.vy = -8;
        }
        else
        {
          gameObject.direction = newDirection;
          findNewDirection(gameObject);
        }
        break;

        case "down":
          if(_mazeMap[gameObject.mapRow + 1][gameObject.mapColumn]
            == FLOOR)
          {
            gameObject.direction = newDirection;
            gameObject.vx = 0;
            gameObject.vy = 8;
          }
          else
          {
            gameObject.direction = newDirection;
            findNewDirection(gameObject);
          }
          break;
        }
    }
```

The method first chooses a random number between 1 and 4.

```
var randomDirection:int = Math.ceil(Math.random() * 4);
```

The code then takes a look at the monster's current direction. If it's "left" or "right", it attempts to assign a new direction of "up" or "down". If the random number is 1 or 2, it chooses "up". If it's 3 or 4, it will choose "down".

```
if(gameObject.direction == "left"
|| gameObject.direction == "right")
{
  if(randomDirection <= 2)
  {
    newDirection = "up";
  }
  else
  {
    newDirection = "down";
  }
}
```

The code runs this same directional flip on the other axis if the monster is currently moving down or up.

The method now has a new direction for the monster. But is it a valid direction? We don't yet know whether the new direction is blocked by a wall, so the code needs to test this.

A `switch` statement tests all four possible new directions. If it doesn't find a wall, the new direction is assigned to the monster's `direction` property, and he will start to travel in that direction. If it finds a `WALL` tile, it calls the `findNewDirection` method again, until it finds a direction that isn't blocked. Here's how it tests the `"left"` direction:

```
switch(newDirection)
{
  case "left":
     if(_mazeMap[gameObject.mapRow][gameObject.mapColumn - 1]
       == FLOOR)
    {
      gameObject.direction = newDirection;
      gameObject.vx = -8;
      gameObject.vy = 0;
    }
    else
    {
      //Call the findNewDirection method recursively if the test hits a wall
      gameObject.direction = newDirection;
      findNewDirection(gameObject);
    }
    break;

  //... test the other three directions…
}
```

The only other important detail is that if the test finds a wall, it assigns the tested `newDirection` value back to the monster's `direction` property.

```
gameObject.direction = newDirection;
```

This means that when a new random direction is tried again, it will try the alternate axis first. This prevents the monster from endlessly ping-ponging back and forth between walls in a cul-de-sac.

And there we have not-really-random random movement! But now let's boost the monsters IQ a bit and give Button Fairy a run for her money.

Chasing

Run the `chasing` SWF in the chapter's source files, and you'll see that the monster is now able to aggressively chase Button Fairly around the maze, as shown in Figure 9-11. Button Fairy can't outrun the monster, but sometimes, if she is persistent, the monster gives up and tries a different route.

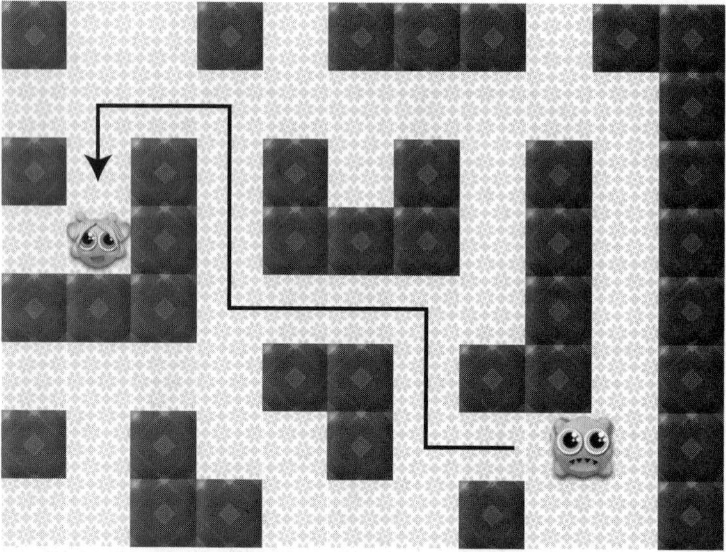

Figure 9-11. The monster chases Button Fairy around the maze.

This behavior is not that difficult to create. The code plots a vector between Button Fairy and the monster. It uses that information to tell the monster to move left, right, up, or down, depending on which direction is closer to Button Fairy. It tries that direction, and if that path is not blocked by a wall, the monster goes that way.

The enterFrameHandler in the Chasing application class gets the ball rolling. It checks whether the monster is at an intersection, and if he is, it calls the chasePlayer method.

```
if(atCornerOfTile(_monsterModel)
&& atIntersection(_monsterModel))
{
  chasePlayer(_monsterModel, _fairyModel);
}
```

chasePlayer uses _monsterModel and _fairyModel to calculate the vector between the characters. Here's the entire chasePlayer method. Take a careful look at it; you'll soon see that it's made up of bits of familiar code that you should know quite well by now.

```
public function chasePlayer
  (
    chasingObject:TileModel,
    targetObject:TileModel
  ):void
{
  //Find the distance between the objects
  var vx:Number = targetObject.xPos - chasingObject.xPos;
  var vy:Number = targetObject.yPos - chasingObject.yPos;

  //If the distance is greater on the x axis...
  if(Math.abs(vx) > Math.abs(vy))
  {
    //Check whether to go left or right
    if(vx < 0)
    {
      //Try to go left
      if
        (
          _mazeMap[chasingObject.mapRow]
          [chasingObject.mapColumn - 1]
          == FLOOR
        )
      {
        chasingObject.direction = "left";
        chasingObject.vx = -8;
        chasingObject.vy = 0;
      }
```

```
      //If the left is blocked, try another random direction.
      //You can make this algorithm more precise by checking
      //the next most likely vertical direction. This less
      //precise version gives the AI a bit of extra randomness
      //which makes it look more natural. It means the player
      //can appear to throw the monster off by
      //ducking behind walls

      else
      {
        findNewDirection(chasingObject);
      }
    }
    else
    {
      //Try to go right
      if
        (
          _mazeMap[chasingObject.mapRow]
          [chasingObject.mapColumn + 1]
          == FLOOR
        )
      {
        chasingObject.direction = "right";
        chasingObject.vx = 8;
        chasingObject.vy = 0;
      }
      else
      {
        findNewDirection(chasingObject);
      }
    }
  }

  //If the distance is greater on the y axis...
  else
  {
    if(vy < 0)
    {
      //Try to go up
      if
        (
          _mazeMap[chasingObject.mapRow - 1]
          [chasingObject.mapColumn]
           == FLOOR
        )
```

```
        {
          chasingObject.direction = "up";
          chasingObject.vx = 0;
          chasingObject.vy = -8;
        }
        else
        {
          findNewDirection(chasingObject);
        }
      }
      else
      {
        //Try to go down
        if
          (
            _mazeMap[chasingObject.mapRow + 1]
            [chasingObject.mapColumn]
            == FLOOR
          )
        {
          chasingObject.direction = "down";
          chasingObject.vx = 0;
          chasingObject.vy = 8;
        }
        else
        {
          findNewDirection(chasingObject);
        }
      }
    }
  }
```

The code finds out which direction will bring the monster closer to the fairy and chooses it. If that direction is blocked by a wall, it chooses another, completely random direction, by calling the `findNewDirection` method that we looked at in the previous section.

```
findNewDirection(chasingObject);
```

Why does it choose a random direction? Shouldn't it try the next most likely one? For example, if the left is blocked, couldn't it try moving up so that it would bring the monster closer to his target?

Yes, if you wanted deadly accurate precision, that's exactly the strategy you would take. However, too much accuracy could prevent the game from being fun if there is no way to eventually evade the monster. Far from seeming less accurate, this element of randomness actually makes the monster look more intelligent. When the monster suddenly changes direction unexpectedly after a long pursuit, it appears as though he came up with a clever plan to cut the fairy off at the next intersection. Or, it can look like the monster has become fatigued and wants to try some other tactic.

You'll also notice that when the monster is only a few tiles away from the fairy, he follows her very persistently and never chooses a random direction. That's because if he is right behind her, he will never hit a wall, so the first direction choice will always be correct. You can see this illustrated in Figure 9-12.

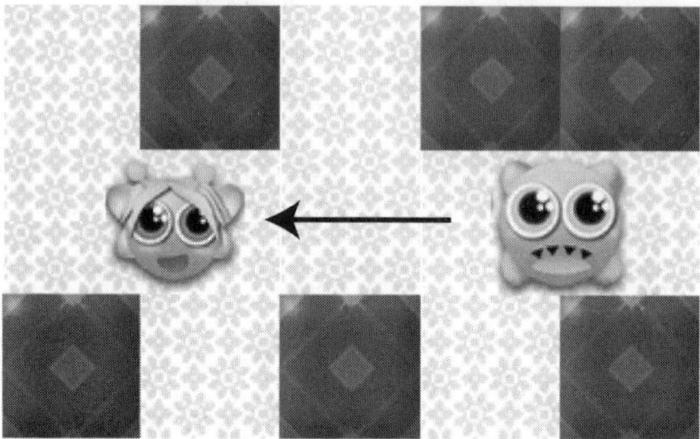

Figure 9-12. If there are no walls between the objects, the best route will always be chosen first.

It's quite hard to evade the monster. And the impression you get when you're playing the game is that the monster becomes more accurate as he gets closer, which is indeed what's happening! Still, if the monster isn't too close, Button Fairy can throw him off by quickly darting around a corner. This forces the monster to make a new direction choice, which will result in a random direction if a wall is blocking the shortest route, as shown in Figure 9-13. This makes the chase seem fair and realistic.

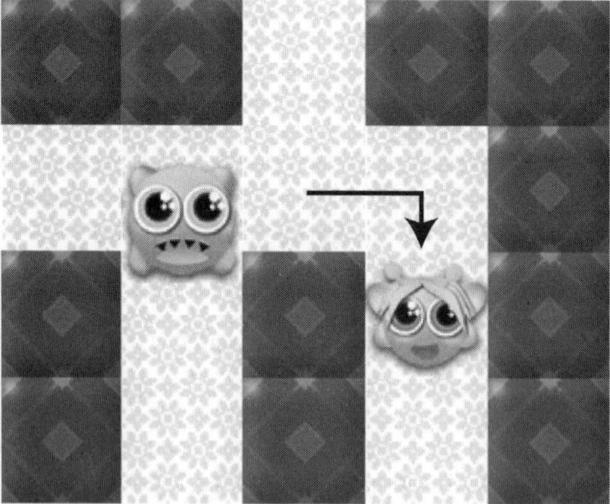

Figure 9-13. Try to confuse the monster by darting around a corner.

It appears that the monster has some sort of intelligence, but of course, it's an illusion created with just a few `if` statements and a random number.

Using this chase algorithm in a game would make the game quite it hard. You can moderate the difficulty by making the monster alternate between random roaming and aggressive attack. One option is to make the monster's movements random until he is within a certain radius of the target. He could then switch to a more aggressive chase. To give the player a fighting chance, the chase could be limited to a certain time or a certain number of direction changes. For example, the monster might decide to give up the chase after five intersections. This will keep things exciting, challenging, and unexpected for the player.

Another option is to move the monster randomly until he can see the player. Our next example demonstrates how this approach works.

Tile-based line of sight

Line of sight is a very common enemy AI strategy used by maze game enemies, most famously in Pac-Man. It offers a well-balanced level of difficulty and allows the player to plan a strategy based on this behavior. You could also add a few more monsters to the maze, and it still wouldn't be too hard to play.

You'll find an example of this in the `LineOfSight` of folder. When the monster can't see Button Fairy, he wanders the maze randomly. If he spots her down a corridor, he gives chase. Figure 9-14 illustrates this behavior.

Figure 9-14. The monster can chase Button Fairy only if he can see her.

This behavior depends on the game being able to determine whether the monster has line of sight. The game needs to know if there's a wall between the monster and the target.

In Chapter 7, we took a detailed look at how to determine line of sight using vectors. Finding line of sight in a tile-based game is easier, because you can take some shortcuts to calculate the vectors. This is thanks to the predictably symmetrical logic of tile-based math. However, the same basic concept applies: choose a direction and check each tile along a row or column for any obstructing walls.

The `enterFrameHandler` in the `LineOfSight` application class calls the `checkLineOfSight` method to help figure this out.

```
if(atCornerOfTile(_monsterModel)
&& atIntersection(_monsterModel))
{
  checkLineOfSight(_monsterModel, _fairyModel);
}
```

The `checkLineOfSight` method first checks whether the objects are on the same row or column. If they are, it figures out how many tile spaces are between them. It then runs a `while` loop to check whether any of the tiles between them are walls. If it doesn't find a wall, it moves the monster in the direction of the target. If it finds a wall, it chooses another random direction.

Here's the complete `checkLineOfSight` method:

```
public function checkLineOfSight
  (
    chasingObject:TileModel,
    targetObject:TileModel
  ):void
{
  //A variable to help track whether any obstructing walls are found
  var wallFound:Boolean = false;

  //While loop counter variable
  var counter:uint;

  //A variable to help determine whether the direction is
  //left, right, up or down
  var direction:int = 1;

  //Check whether the objects are on the same row
  //but not in the same column
  if(chasingObject.mapRow == targetObject.mapRow
  && chasingObject.mapColumn != targetObject.mapColumn)
  {
    //If they are, find out whether the targetObject is
    //to the left or right of the chasingObject
    var vx:Number = targetObject.xPos - chasingObject.xPos;

    //Set the direction variable to "-1" if the targetObject
    //is to the left, or set it to "1" if it's to the right
    if(vx < 0)
```

```
{
  direction = -1;
}
else
{
  direction = 1;
}

//The counter is initialized to the number of tiles
//between the chasingObject and the targetObject
counter = uint(Math.abs(vx) / MAX_TILE_SIZE);

while(counter-- != 0)
{
  //Multiply the counter by the direction value to
  //find the correct number of cells to the left or right
  if
    (
      _mazeMap
        [chasingObject.mapRow]
        [chasingObject.mapColumn + (counter * direction)]
        == WALL
    )
  {
    wallFound = true;
    break;
  }
}

//Find a new random direction if a wall is found,
//otherwise move in the direction of the targetObject

if(wallFound)
{
  findNewDirection(chasingObject);
}
else
{
  if(direction == -1)
  {
    chasingObject.direction = "left";
    chasingObject.vx = -8;
    chasingObject.vy = 0;
  }
```

```
      else
      {
        chasingObject.direction = "right";
        chasingObject.vx = 8;
        chasingObject.vy = 0;
      }
    }
  }

  //Check whether the objects are in the same column
  //but not the same row
  if(chasingObject.mapColumn == targetObject.mapColumn
  && chasingObject.mapRow != targetObject.mapRow)
  {
    var vy:Number = targetObject.yPos - chasingObject.yPos;

    //Set the direction
    if(vy < 0)
    {
      direction = -1;
    }
    else
    {
      direction = 1;
    }

    //Check for walls
    counter = uint(Math.abs(vy) / MAX_TILE_SIZE);
    while(counter-- != 0)
    {
      if
        (
          _mazeMap
            [chasingObject.mapRow + (counter * direction)]
            [chasingObject.mapColumn]
            == WALL
        )
      {
        wallFound = true;
        break;
      }
    }
```

```
    //Find a new random direction if a wall is found,
    //otherwise follow the targetObject
    if(wallFound)
    {
      findNewDirection(chasingObject);
    }
    else
    {
      if(direction == -1)
      {
        chasingObject.direction = "up";
        chasingObject.vx = 0;
        chasingObject.vy = -8;
      }
      else
      {
        chasingObject.direction = "down";
        chasingObject.vx = 0;
        chasingObject.vy = 8;
      }
    }
  }

  //If the objects are in completely different rows and columns,
  //or they occupy exactly the same tile cell, the chasingObject
  //should find a new random direction
  if
    (
      (chasingObject.mapColumn != targetObject.mapColumn
        && chasingObject.mapRow != targetObject.mapRow)
      ||(chasingObject.mapColumn == targetObject.mapColumn
        && chasingObject.mapRow == targetObject.mapRow)
    )
  {
    findNewDirection(chasingObject);
  }
}
```

This code checks for three important conditions:

- Whether the objects are in the same row but different columns. This means the target will be to the left or right of the monster.
- Whether the objects are in the same column but different rows. This means the target will be above or below the monster.
- Whether they occupy the same row *and* column. This can only mean that they're in the same cell together.

Figure 9-15 illustrates these three conditions. When you know which condition you're dealing with, you then need to decide which action to take.

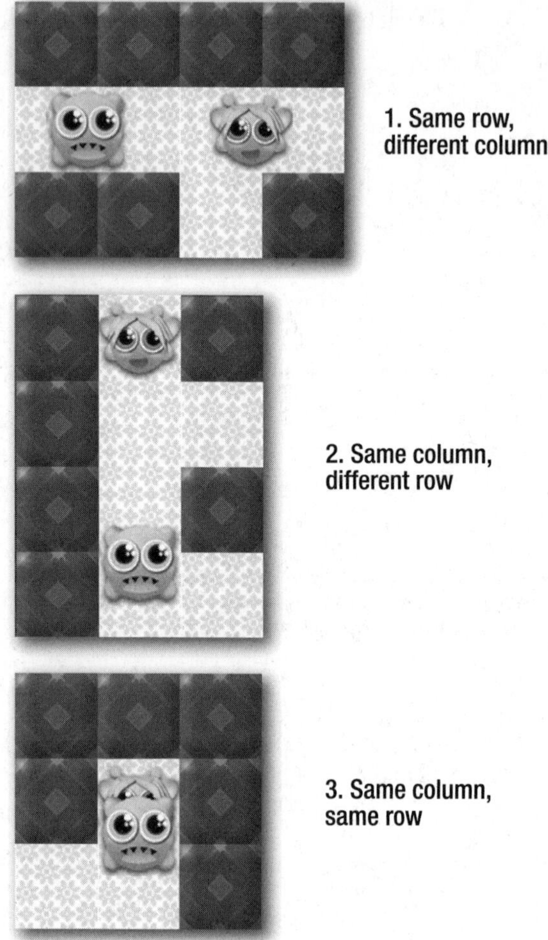

Figure 9-15. The three line-of-sight conditions to check

Let's look at the "same row different column" condition as an example.

```
if(chasingObject.mapRow == targetObject.mapRow
&& chasingObject.mapColumn != targetObject.mapColumn)
{...
```

When the code has determined that the objects are on the same row, it needs to decide whether to check the line of sight on the left or right. It does this by measuring the distance between the objects on the x axis.

```
var vx:Number = targetObject.xPos - chasingObject.xPos;
```

If the `targetObject` is to the left, it assigns `-1` to the local `direction` variable. If the target is to the right, it assigns `1`.

```
if(vx < 0)
{
  direction = -1;
}
else
{
  direction = 1;
}
```

The code then needs to figure out how many tiles are between the two objects. Is does this by dividing the distance by `MAX_TILE_SIZE`. It uses that value as the loop counter.

```
counter = uint(Math.abs(vx) / MAX_TILE_SIZE);
```

For example, let's say that there are 134 pixels between the two objects. If you divide 134 by 64 (the value of `MAX_TILE_SIZE`), you end up with a rounded-down value of 2.

```
134 / 64 = 2;
```

`2` will be the number of tiles between the objects. The code can now use that number, stored in the counter variable, to run a loop twice and check for `WALL` tiles between the objects.

```
while(counter-- != 0)
{
  if
    (
      _mazeMap
        [chasingObject.mapRow]
        [chasingObject.mapColumn + (counter * direction)]
        == WALL
    )
  {
    wallFound = true;
    break;
  }
}
```

The important bit of code checks the column cell:

```
[chasingObject.mapColumn + (counter * direction)]
```

Remember that `direction` can be either `-1` or (positive) `1`, depending on whether we're checking to the left or right. Let's say that the monster is currently at column `8`, the loop counter is at `2`, and direction is `1`. We could interpret the preceding code like this:

```
[8 + (2 * 1)]
```

This is equal to:

```
10
```

So, the tenth column is being checked for a `WALL` tile.

On the second loop, the value of `counter` is reduced by one.

```
while(counter-- != 0)
{...
```

That means it now has a value of `1`. The section of code that checks the columns for walls now looks like this:

```
[8 + (1 * 1)]
```

This is equal to:

```
9
```

This means that the ninth column is being checked for a `WALL` tile.

The monster is already at column 8, so he doesn't need to check his own position for a wall. The `while` loop will quit when counter reaches zero at the next loop.

```
while(counter-- != 0)
{...
```

`counter` is now zero, so the loop doesn't continue. The counter is decremented directly in the conditional statement, so the body of the `while` loop doesn't execute.

If the code finds a wall, it calls the `findNewDirection` method that we covered earlier to assign a random direction. Otherwise, it tells the monster to move left or right depending on the value of the `direction` variable.

```
if(wallFound)
{
  findNewDirection(chasingObject);
}
else
{
  if(direction == -1)
  {
    chasingObject.direction = "left";
    chasingObject.vx = -8;
    chasingObject.vy = 0;
  }
```

```
  else
  {
    chasingObject.direction = "right";
    chasingObject.vx = 8;
    chasingObject.vy = 0;
  }
}
```

The `checkLineOfSight` method performs the same kind of check on the y axis if the objects occupy the same column.

The one special case is if the objects occupy exactly the same cell. In that case, the monster is simply assigned a new random direction using the same `findNewDirection` method.

```
if
  (
    (chasingObject.mapColumn != targetObject.mapColumn
      && chasingObject.mapRow != targetObject.mapRow)
    || (chasingObject.mapColumn == targetObject.mapColumn
      && chasingObject.mapRow == targetObject.mapRow)
  )
{
  findNewDirection(chasingObject);
}
```

The effect of this is very natural when you see it in action.

You now have a quite a few strategies to help you design the AI for maze monsters in your own games. It's at least enough to get you started thinking about the problems you'll face, but you'll almost certainly need to tailor the solutions to your own games.

Finding the shortest path

There is one last major area of pathfinding we need to tackle: finding the shortest path through a maze. As it turns out, this is not just an interesting aside, but one of the most important game-design skills you need to know.

All the player control systems that we've covered in the book so far have involved moving the player around the stage with the keyboard or the mouse. But games often employ a point-and-click control scheme. Point the mouse to some place on the map and click. The character will walk there and magically seem to find the shortest path to the destination while cleverly sidestepping any obstacles. Graphical adventure games use this control system, as do almost all strategy and turn-based games.

Moving a character along the shortest path is really a two-part process:

1. **Find the shortest path**: This involves testing all the most likely tiles between the start point and the destination. You need to figure out which tiles will get you to the destination sooner, and which contain obstacles to avoid. At the end of this testing, you end up with an array of tiles that tell you the shortest path.
2. **Follow the tiles in the path**: The array of tiles you end up with are like breadcrumbs that the game character can follow. Tell the character to follow these crumbs from its start position to the destination.

If the first step seems like it might be rather complex, it is! But the good news is that excellent solutions have been found already. That means you don't need to worry about coming up with your own solution—you can just choose a ready-made one and implement it in your game.

There are a number of different pathfinding algorithms you can use, including **best-first**, **breadth-first**, and **Dijkstra's algorithm**. All will do a reasonable job of solving the problem. But the best is generally regarded to be **A*** (A star). The A* algorithm has the overall best performance, and it is extremely flexible. If there's only one pathfinding algorithm you should learn, A* is it.

> *A* was developed in the 1960s by Peter Hart, Nils Nilsson, and Bertram Raphael. It's an improvement to Dijkstra's algorithm, a pathfinding algorithm that was postulated in the 1950s by pioneering computer scientist Edsger Dijkstra.*

Before I show you how to use A* in a game, let's take detailed a look at how the algorithm works.

Understanding A*

We can be proud of our evolutionary ancestors. Thanks to good pathfinding ability, they all successfully evaded larger protozoa, sidestepped gnashing dinosaur teeth, and avoided ending up as fossilized remains at the bottom of the Sterkfontein caves. Pathfinding is a skill that is as essential to being able to survive as a tree frog in the Amazon as it is to being able to catch the bus in the morning. It's a survival skill that allows you to automatically figure out the shortest path from point A to point B without being eaten, dying of starvation, or being late for work. One glance at Figure 9-16, and you'll immediately be able to see the shortest path between point A and point B.

Computers, on the other hand, are like, pampered, prize-winning, Persian lap cats. They sit around all day, spend far too much time on the Internet, and sleep a lot. They haven't had their skills honed through countless millennia of fighting it out in the primordial soup as we have. We need to tell them in the bluntest growl possible, "This path good!" or "This path not good!" and practically threaten them with a gnarled club.

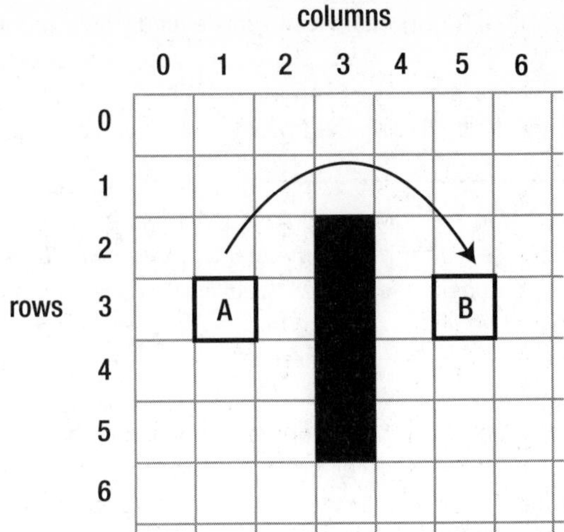

Figure 9-16. What's the shortest path between point A and point B? It's obvious to us humans, but how do you explain it to a computer?

But what is a "good path"? In the case of finding the *shortest* path, it's the one that gets you to your destination sooner. The problem is that computers can't see the big picture. They can see only one small step at a time. So the strategy for telling a computer how to find the shortest path goes something like this:

- Break the entire path into many small steps.
- For each step, figure out which step to take next.
- Take that step, and repeat the process until you get where you're supposed to be.

But the computer must still be able to tell the difference between a good path and a bad path. Let's see how to help it figure that out.

Calculating costs

Solve this riddle:

A newspaper is delivered to your front door every morning. What's the least expensive way of picking up it up?

A. Opening the front door.

B. Walking out the back door, jumping over your garden fence, running down the alley, hailing a taxicab, and riding around the block to your front door?

Option A was free, but option B cost you about $3.75 in cab fare. This means that option B is more **expensive**.

Expensive is the term that the A* algorithm uses to describe how much work it takes to travel between two points. A* figures out the *least expensive* routes to a destination. It does this by assigning a **cost** to every possible step you can take on the path. The step with the lowest cost is the better step to take. A* works by finding the lowest cost moves and the least expensive paths.

> *A* has its own set of terms and vocabulary.* Cost *and* expense *are two of those terms and, as you'll see, they're a convenient way to describe some of its core concepts. I'll be introducing a few other specific A* terms ahead. Keep a special lookout for* node *and* heuristic, *coming up soon!*

Figure 9-17 explains what I mean by cost. Imagine that you're a bacterium in a Petri dish, free-floating and minding your own business at point A. Suddenly, the shadow of a huge, hungry single-celled amoeba looms over you with the lone goal of subsuming your cellular matter. You know you're in trouble if you don't hide right away. There are only two places you can hide: point B or point C. You have a split second to decide which is the closest.

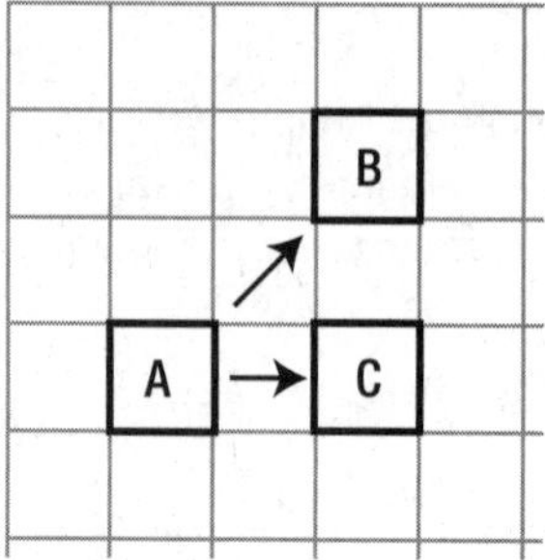

Figure 9-17. Which is closer, B or C?

In the example in Figure 9-17, traveling to point B takes about one-third longer than traveling to point C. In fact, it takes *exactly* 1.41 times longer to travel to point B from point A. That means that point C is where you need to swim to escape that amoeba. The value 1.41 is the *cost* of traveling diagonally.

In a rectangular grid-based game world, there are only two choices of movement, and each has a cost:

- **Diagonally**: The cost is 14.
- **Directly across**: Going horizontally or vertically, the cost is 10.

It doesn't really matter what those costs are, as long as they proportionately represent the amount of time it takes to move in those directions. So, 14 versus 10 is the same proportion as 1.4 versus 1, and we conveniently don't need to worry about decimal numbers. You can certainly use 1.4 and 1 in your own code if you prefer. Figure 9-18 shows the cost of movement between cells.

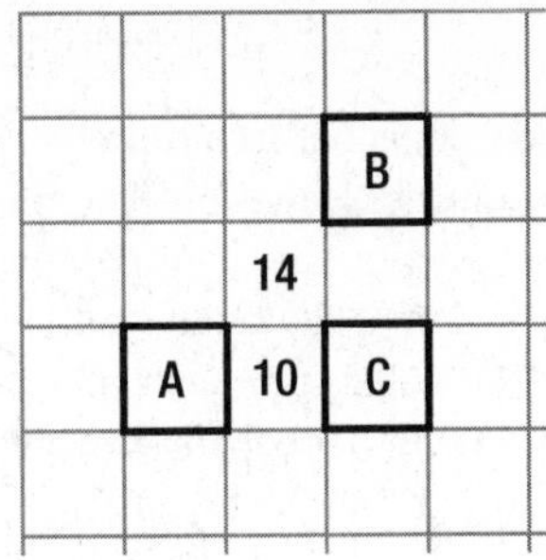

Figure 9-18. The costs of traveling through cells

Now we have a way of describing to the computer what a good path is: the one with the lowest cost.

Figure 9-19 shows two possible paths from A to B. Not only can you clearly see that path 1 is the shortest, but it also happens to be the least expensive.

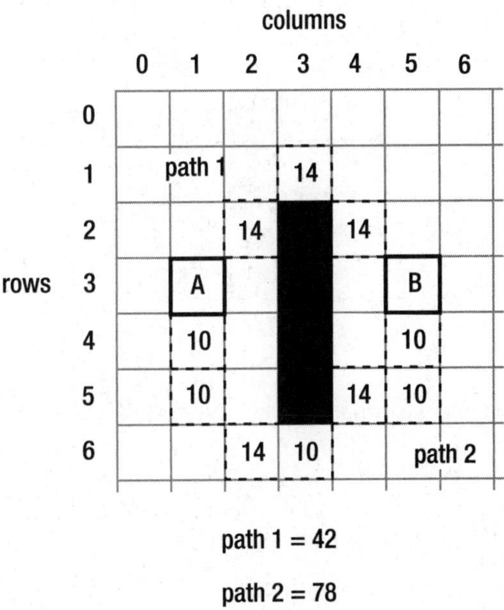

Figure 9-19. The shortest path is also the least expensive.

Earlier, I mentioned that computers can see only one step in the path at any given time. You can see from Figure 9-19 that each step is the least expensive step that could have been chosen to get to point B. But that's only obvious *after you already know the outcome of the path*. The computer doesn't know this before it starts building the path. How does it know which step to take next, directly from point A?

Finding the second step

In A*'s terminology, every step in the path is called a **node**. As far as we're concerned, nodes are just cells in a two-dimensional array or grid. However, I'm going to start calling them *nodes* from now on, just so that you get used to that term. You'll find it widely used in discussions of pathfinding in other texts. A* uses the term *node* because there's no reason why you can't divide your space in ways other than a rectangular grid, such as by using hexagons or circles. But for our purposes, when you hear me talk about nodes, just know that I mean grid cells.

A* starts searching for the shortest path at point A. Point A is the **parent node**. A parent node is a definite, confirmed step on the path. Obviously, we know that point A is going to be the first step, so it automatically becomes the first parent node.

If we know what the first step is, how do we find the second step? A* must check all eight cells surrounding the parent node to discover which of those is the next most likely candidate. Figure 9-20 shows point A as the parent node, and all the surrounding nodes that it needs to check. (If any of those nodes happen to be walls or impassable objects, it ignores them.)

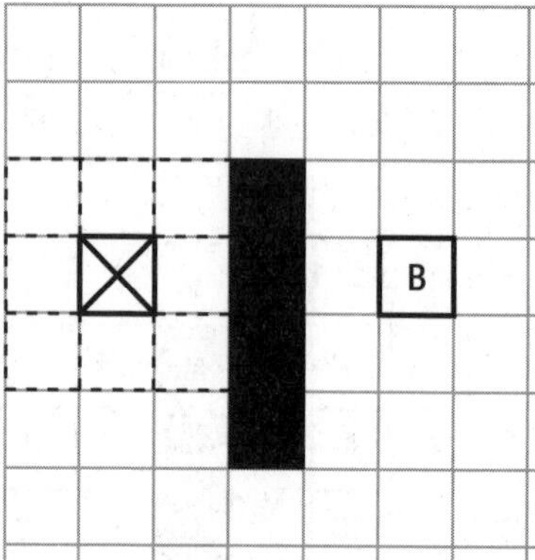

Figure 9-20. Check all the nodes surrounding the parent to see which might be the next most likely step in the path.

Each of these surrounding cells declares the current parent node as *its* parent. The code that does this in the A* algorithm will look something like this:

```
surroundingNode.parent = currentParent;
```

This is important because it means that A* can trace the best path to the destination by following the trail of parent nodes. Don't worry too much about this now, as you'll see how it works in the pages ahead. Just remember that each node has a `parent` property that keeps track of the node that it's linked to in the path.

A* then needs to find out what the cost will be to travel from the parent node to the surrounding child nodes. It turns out that this happens to be an important number, so A* refers to this cost as **G**. Figure 9-21 shows the G costs for all the surrounding nodes.

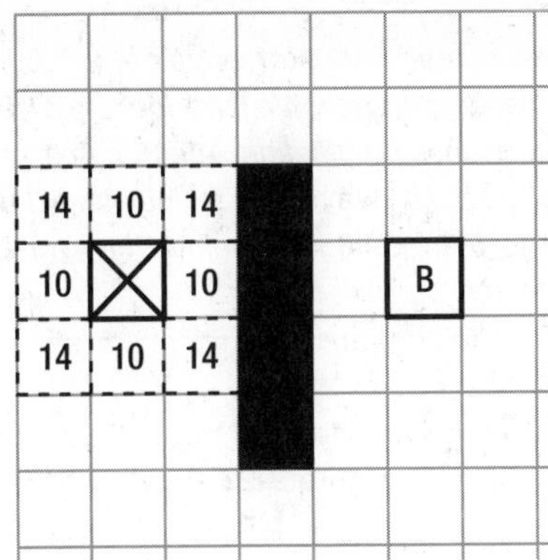

Figure 9-21. Each surrounding node is given a cost, referred to in A*'s terminology as G.

A* then figures out which surrounding node is closer to the destination, point B. It calculates the cost of traveling from point B to every surrounding node. (The wall standing in the way is treated as if it were not there for now, but as you'll see, this is compensated for by later tests.) Figure 9-22 shows the path from the first surrounding node to point B. You can see that it calculated the cost of the test path from that node as 54.

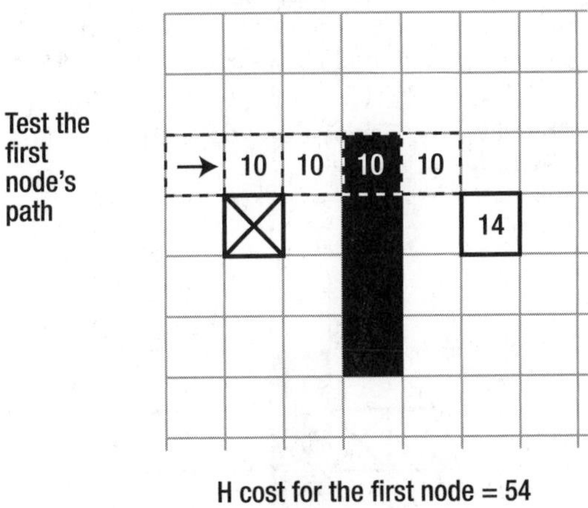

Figure 9-22. Figure out the cost of each path from every surrounding node to point B.

This distance test is called a **heuristic**. Heuristic simply means figuring something out by trial and error. (It's derived from the Greek work *heuriskein*, which means *find*.) Heuristic is not random trial and error, however. It's trial and error within a set of logical rules that are likely to produce the answer we're seeking. A* has no idea which of the surrounding child nodes will end up with the least expensive path, so it just tries all eight of them. The cost of each heuristic path also happens to be very important, so A* refers to this cost as **H**.

> *There are actually three commonly used ways of calculating the heuristic path: Manhattan, Euclidean, and diagonal. We'll be looking at each of these in detail in the "Understanding heuristics" section later in this chapter. For now, just know that these are specific ways for calculating the distance from the surrounding test node to the destination point. Figure 9-22 shows an example of the Manhattan heuristic.*

A* figures out the H cost for every surrounding child node. If you combine the H and G costs, you come up with a third, final cost, called **F**. Figure 9-23 shows what all the G, H, and F costs are for each node.

G:14 H:54 F:68	G:10 H:44 F:54	G:14 H:34 F:48			
G:10 H:50 F:60		G:10 H:30 F:40			B
G:14 H:54 F:68	G:10 H:44 F:54	G:14 H:34 F:48			

Figure 9-23. Find the final F cost of each node by adding the G and H costs together.

The winner is the node with the lowest F cost. Can you see it? It's the one directly to the right of the parent node, as shown in Figure 9-24.

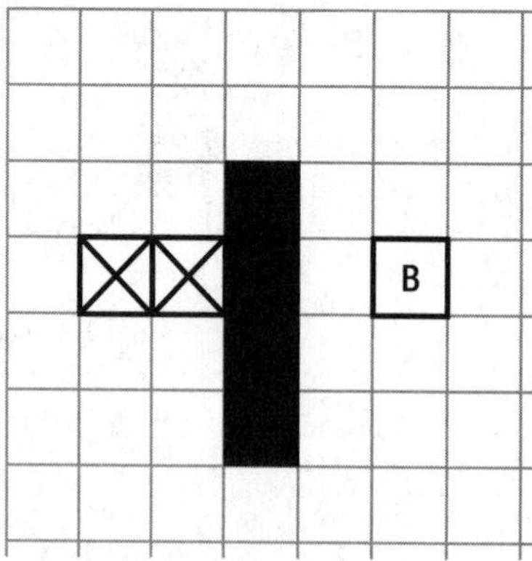

Figure 9-24. The node with the lowest F cost becomes the most likely next step in the path.

This node now becomes a potential new parent node. A* doesn't yet know for sure whether this will be the best second step to take, but as far as it can tell, it's a pretty good place to continue checking. (In fact, it's not the best second step, but A* will soon find this out, as you will see.)

You can see from Figure 9-24 that each parent node represents a potential step in the path to point B. I use the word *potential* because A* doesn't know for sure whether any given parent node is the best step until it does a little more checking. You can already see a problem occurring in Figure 9-24. The new parent node is *not* the best next step. It would be better to move diagonally up from point A. Figure 9-25 illustrates this.

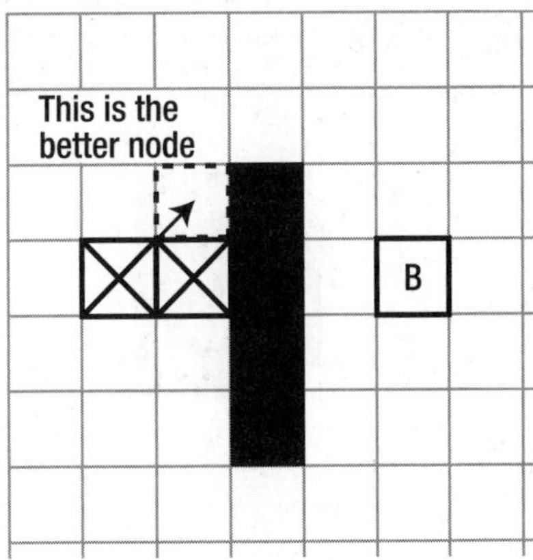

Figure 9-25. The obvious first choice isn't always the best one. How will A* figure out that it's better to move diagonally up from the start point?

Luckily, A* has a system for cross-checking nodes and weeding out inefficiencies like this.

A* keeps track of the possible best parent nodes to use for the route by keeping two lists:

- **Closed list**: This is a list of nodes that don't need to be checked. Whenever a new parent node is found, it's added to this list.
- **Open list**: This is a list of all the nodes surrounding each parent. They're the nodes that need to be checked.

When a new potential parent node checks all the surrounding nodes, it looks at each node's previous G cost on the open list. Figure 9-26 shows that the previous G cost for the node directly above it was 14.

Figure 9-26. The old G cost was 14. Will its new cost be more or less?

To find its new G cost, A* takes the current G value of the parent node and adds 10 more, which is the cost of traveling up one node. That brings the total new G cost to 20. Figure 9-27 illustrates this.

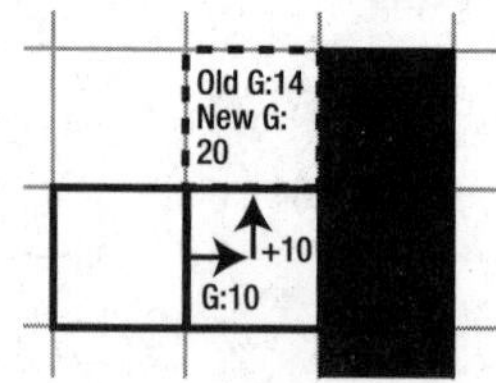

Figure 9-27. Add the parent node's G cost (10) to the cost of traveling up one node (10) to find the new G cost (20).

If it finds that the new cost is lower, A* changes the node's parent to the current parent:

```
if(newG < oldG)
{
  surroundingNode.parent = currentParent;
}
else
{
  don't change the surrounding node's parent
}
```

But if the new G cost is more expensive, the node's parent *doesn't change*. That's the case in this example. It will keep the same parent that it was assigned in the first step, which was the start node. The current parent node that we're checking is left out in the cold.

This is very important because A* creates the path by linking nodes together through their parents, like a chain.

A* runs this same check with all the other surrounding nodes, and calculates their new G costs based on what they will be if they need to run through the new parent, as shown in Figure 9-28.

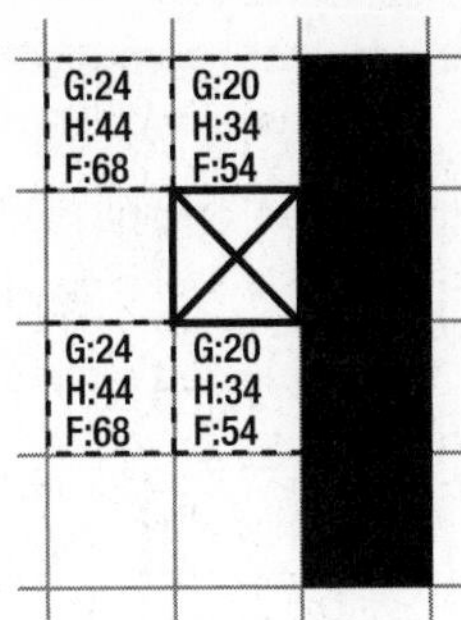

Figure 9-28. Find out if any of the G costs of the other nodes are less by routing the path through this current parent. They're not.

As you can see from Figure 9-28, the G costs of *all* the nodes will be higher by going through the current parent. That means that none of them will change their parent to the current parent. The current parent is toast! It has no children, so it's definitely not going to be part of the shortest path.

But A* still needs to figure out which node to test next. It ignores wall nodes and the previous parent node. It chooses the next node with the lowest F cost as the new parent node, as shown in Figure 9-29.

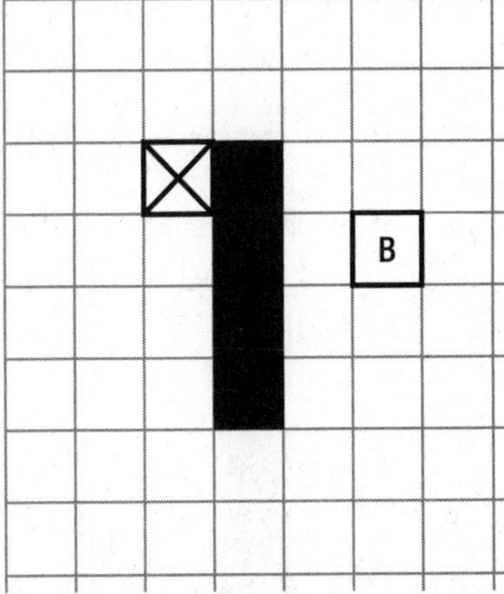

Figure 9-29. The surrounding node with the lowest F cost becomes the new parent node.

But what happens if some of the nodes have the same cost? You can see from Figure 9-28 that the nodes directly above and below the parent are tied for first place, each with the same low score of 54. In this case, A* chooses whichever node comes up first in the loop that runs this check. If it happens to be the wrong one, this will be corrected later by further checks. But by pure chance, this time the first node with the lowest score also happens to be the better choice. It's chosen as the new parent node, and A* continues checking.

It's also quite likely that there will be more than one possible shortest path. The one A* builds is determined by how it selects nodes whose costs are tied.

We've currently tested two nodes, and have selected a third, as you can see from Figure 9-30.

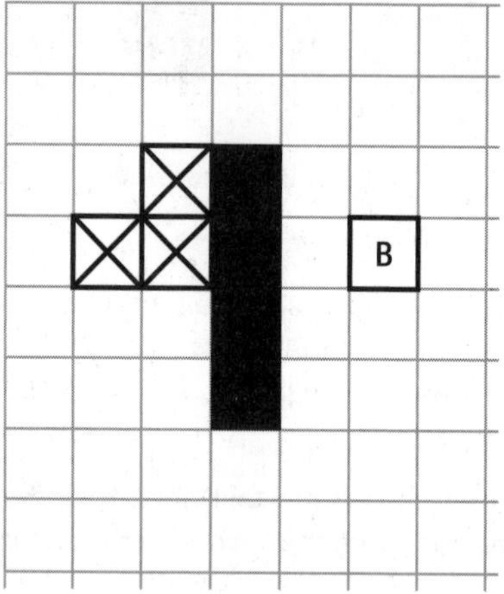

Figure 9-30. Three nodes are candidates for steps on the path, but which will make the final shakedown?

But only two of those nodes are part of the path. How do we know? *Because the node on the upper right has assigned the start node as its parent.* This is a relationship that chains the two nodes together, as shown in Figure 9-31. It forms the first two steps in the path.

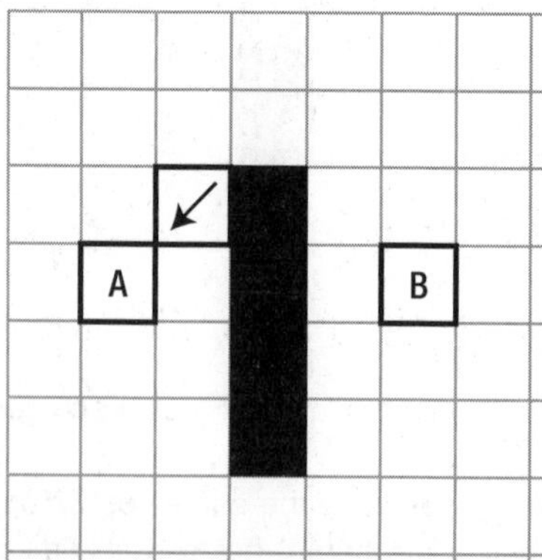

Figure 9-31. The start node is the parent of the upper-right node. This relationship chains the nodes together.

Linking the nodes through their parents

A* then continues following this same logic until it reaches the destination node, point B. In a very big game world, this could involve checking hundreds of nodes.

When A* finally builds the path, it traces the route from parent node to parent node to link the start and end points together. You can see this illustrated in Figure 9-32.

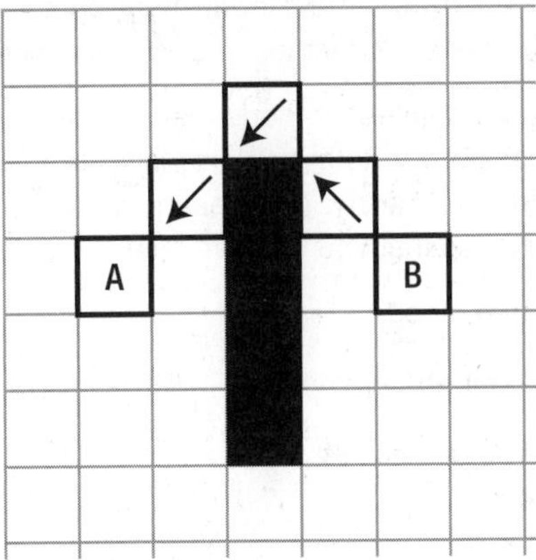

Figure 9-32. Each node in the final path has a reference to its parent.

When A* reaches the destination, point B, it stops checking. A* then just needs to work backward from point B, following the parent nodes, to construct the path. The A* algorithm produces an array that will tell you each node you need to walk through to find the shortest route from point A to point B.

Now that you understand the theory, let's have a look at the actual AS3.0 code.

A* in code

It should be pretty obvious by now that nodes are quite important things in the A* universe. Each node needs to store quite a bit of information:

- Its position (its row and column on the grid)
- Its G, H, and F costs
- Its parent node

It therefore makes sense to create a `Node` class or `node` objects to store this information. In the sample code ahead, I've decided to create them as simple objects for the sake of clarity.

The `com.friendsofed.utils` package includes a class called `AStar` that contains all the A* code for this example. We'll be looking at the entire class in detail, beginning with the section that creates a **node map**. It's the first bit of code that runs, and forms the structure for the rest of the A* algorithm, so you need to understand how it works.

Creating a node map

Before we can run the A* algorithm, we need to create a node map. The concept is identical to creating a collision map. The node map is a two-dimensional array that exactly matches the game's maze map. However, each cell of the node map contains a `node` object. These `node` objects will store all the important node properties and values we need.

The `initializeNodeMap` method creates the node map. It takes one argument, which will be the original maze map two-dimensional array that you're using in your game. It matches the maze map array cell for cell to create a new array. It fills each cell of the new array with a `node` object. All the `node` objects are initialized so that you can see they're blank when A* first starts working.

Here's the `initializeNodeMap` method:

```
private function initializeNodeMap(map:Array):Array
{
  //A blank array to store the nodes
  var nodeMap:Array = [];

  for(var row:int = 0; row < map.length; row++)
  {
    nodeMap[row] = new Array();

    for(var column:int = 0; column < map[0].length; column++)
    {
      //Create the node object and initialize the
      //values it will need to track
      var node:Object = new Object();
      node.f = 0;
      node.g = 0;
      node.h = 0;
      node.parent = null;

      //Assign the row and column
      node.row = row;
      node.column = column;

      //Assign the node's unique ID number
      node.id = (column * 100) + row;

      //Add the node object to this cell
      nodeMap[row][column] = node;
    }
  }
```

```
  //Return the nodeMap array
  return nodeMap;
}
```

The method returns a two-dimensional array containing all the initialized `node` objects.

An important detail is that each node is assigned a unique ID number.

```
node.id = (column * 100) + row;
```

This is the same ID numbering system used in Chapter 8. However, in this chapter, the map sizes are bigger. Using `100` allows the ID numbering system to account for map sizes of up to 100 rows by 100 columns.

Now that we have our node map, let's look at the complete `AStar` class.

The complete AStar class

First, we need to create an instance of the `AStar` class in our application class:

```
private var _aStar:AStar = new AStar();
```

The heart of the `AStar` class is the `findShortestPath` method. It returns an array that contains the shortest path from point A to point B. Here's an example of how to call it, including the arguments to include.

```
var shortestPath:Array
  = _aStar.findShortestPath
    (
      The start node ID number,
      The destination node ID number,
      The game's maze map,
      The names of unpassable tiles, like WALL,
      The kind of heuristic to use, such
        as "manhattan", "euclidean" or "diagonal",
      The cost of traveling directly across nodes (usually 10),
      The cost of traveling diagonally through nodes (usually 14)
    );
```

As you can see, the arguments match the kinds of information that we looked at earlier. The one thing we haven't discussed yet is the kind of heuristic to use. I'll explain the heuristic options and how they work in the "Understanding heuristics" section.

The following is the entire `AStar` class. Apart from a few additional checks that it needs to make sure that all the data is valid, it's doing pathfinding just as I explained in the description of how the A* algorithm works. Read through all the comments and try to match up the code to the earlier description.

```
package com.friendsofed.utils
{
  public class AStar
  {
    //An array to store the shortest path
    public var shortestPath:Array;

    //A 2D array of test nodes that matches the maze map
    public var nodeMap:Array;

    //The path's start and end nodes
    public var startNode_ID:uint = 0;
    public var destinationNode_ID:uint = 0;

    //How much it will cost to move between nodes?
    private var _straightCost:uint = 0;
    private var _diagonalCost:uint = 0;

    public function AStar()
    {
    }

    public function findShortestPath
      (
        startNode_ID:uint,
        destinationNode_ID:uint,
        map:Array,
        wall:uint,
        heuristic:String,
        straightCost:uint,
        diagonalCost:uint
      ):Array
  {
     this.startNode_ID = startNode_ID;
     this.destinationNode_ID = destinationNode_ID;
     _straightCost = straightCost;
     _diagonalCost = diagonalCost;

      //Initialize the shortestPath array
      shortestPath = [];

      //Initialize the node map
      nodeMap = initializeNodeMap(map);

      //Initialize the closed and open list arrays
      var closedList:Array = [];
      var openList:Array = [];
```

```
//Get the current center node. The first one will
//be the startNode_ID, which is the player's start
//position.
var centerNode:Object
  = nodeMap
  [uint(startNode_ID % 100)]
  [uint(startNode_ID / 100)];

//Get a reference to the destinationNode. It will
//match the destinationNode_ID
var destinationNode:Object
  = nodeMap
  [uint(destinationNode_ID % 100)]
  [uint(destinationNode_ID / 100)];

//Loop until the destination node is found
while(centerNode.id != destinationNode_ID)
{
  //Check all the 8 nodes surrounding the centerNode
  for(var column:int = -1; column < 2; column++)
  {
    for(var row:int = -1; row < 2; row++)
    {
      //Find the row and column to test
      var testRow:int = centerNode.row + row;
      var testColumn:int = centerNode.column + column;

      //Make sure that the row and column being tested are
      //valid array elements and aren't beyond the
      //edges of the map
      if(testRow > -1 && testRow <= nodeMap.length
      && testColumn > -1 && testColumn <= nodeMap[0].length)
      {
        //If the test node isn't the centerNode
        //and the mazeMap doesn't contain a wall tile...
        if(nodeMap[testRow][testColumn].id
          != centerNode.id
        && map[testRow][testColumn] != wall)
        {
          //Get a reference to the surrounding node
          var testNode:Object = nodeMap[testRow][testColumn];

          //Find out whether the node is on a straight axis or
          //a diagonal axis, and assign the appropriate cost

          //A. Declare the cost variable
          var cost:uint;
```

```
//B. Do they occupy the same row or column?
if(centerNode.row == testNode.row
|| centerNode.column == testNode.column)
{
  //... if they do, assign a cost of "10"
  cost = straightCost;
}
else
{
  //otherwise, assign a cost of "14"
  cost = diagonalCost;
}

//C. Calculate the costs (g, h and f)
//The node's current cost
var g:uint = centerNode.g + cost;

//The cost of travelling from this node to the
//destination node (the heuristic)
var h:uint
switch(heuristic)
{
  case "manhattan":
    h = manhattan(testNode, destinationNode);
    break;

  case "euclidean":
    h = euclidean(testNode, destinationNode);
    break;

  case "diagonal":
    h = diagonal(testNode, destinationNode);
    break;

  default:
    throw new Error
      ("Oops! You misspelled the heuristic");
}

//The final cost
var f:uint = g + h;

//Find out if the testNode is in either
//the openList or closedList array
var isOnOpenList:Boolean = false;
var isOnClosedList:Boolean = false;
```

```
            //Check the openList
            for(var i:int = 0; i < openList.length; i++)
            {
              if(testNode == openList[i])
              {
                isOnOpenList = true;
              }
            }

            //Check the closedList
            for(var j:int = 0; j < closedList.length; j++)
            {
              if(testNode == closedList[j])
              {
                isOnClosedList = true;
              }
            }

            //If it's on either of these lists, we can check
            //whether this route is a lower-cost alternative
            //to the previous cost calculation. The new G cost
            //will make the difference to the final F cost
            if(isOnOpenList || isOnClosedList)
            {
              if(testNode.f > f)
              {
                testNode.f = f;
                testNode.g = g;
                testNode.h = h;

                //Only change the parent if the new cost is lower
                testNode.parent = centerNode;
              }
            }

            //Otherwise, add the testNode to the open list
            else
            {
              testNode.f = f;
              testNode.g = g;
              testNode.h = h;
              testNode.parent = centerNode;
              openList.push(testNode);
            }
          }
        }
      }
    }
```

```
      //Push the current centerNode into the closed list
      closedList.push(centerNode);

      //Quit the loop if there's nothing on the open list.
      //This means that there is no path to the destination or the
      //destination is invalid, like a wall tile
      if(openList.length == 0)
      {
        //trace("No path found");
        return shortestPath;
      }
      //Sort the open list according to final cost
      openList.sortOn("f", Array.NUMERIC);

      //Set the node with the lowest final cost as the new
      //centerNode
      centerNode = openList.shift();
    }

    //Now that we have all the candidates, let's
    //find the shortest path!
    if(openList.length != 0)
    {
      //Start with the destination node
      var node:Object = destinationNode;
      shortestPath.push(node);

      //Work backwards through the node parents
      //until the start node is found
      while(node.id != startNode_ID)
      {
        //Step through the parents of each node,
        //starting with the destination node
        //and ending with the start node
        node = node.parent;

        //Add the node to the beginning of the array
        shortestPath.unshift(node);

        //...and then loop again to the next node's parent till you
        //reach the end of the path
      }
    }
    return shortestPath;
  }
```

```
  private function initializeNodeMap(map:Array):Array
  {
    //A blank array to store the nodes
    var nodeMap:Array = [];

    for(var row:int = 0; row < map.length; row++)
    {
      nodeMap[row] = new Array();

      for(var column:int = 0; column < map[0].length; column++)
      {
        //Create the node object and initialize the
        //values it will need to track
        var node:Object = new Object();
        node.f = 0;
        node.g = 0;
        node.h = 0;
        node.parent = null;

        //Assign the row and column
        node.row = row;
        node.column = column;

        //Assign the node's unique ID number
        node.id = (column * 100) + row;

        //Add the node object to this cell
        nodeMap[row][column] = node;
      }
    }

    //Return the nodeMap array
    return nodeMap;
  }

//Heuristic methods
//1. Manhattan
private function manhattan
  (testNode:Object, destinationNode:Object):uint
{
  var h:uint
      = Math.abs
        (testNode.row - destinationNode.row) * _straightCost
      + Math.abs
          (testNode.column - destinationNode.column) * _straightCost;

    return h;
}
```

```
    //2. Euclidean
    private function euclidean
      (testNode:Object, destinationNode:Object):uint
    {
      var vx:int = destinationNode.column - testNode.column;
      var vy:int = destinationNode.row - testNode.row;
      var h:uint = uint(Math.sqrt(vx * vx + vy * vy) * _straightCost);

      return h;
    }

    //3. Diagonal
    private function diagonal
      (testNode:Object, destinationNode:Object):uint
    {
      var vx:uint
        = Math.abs(destinationNode.column - testNode.column);
      var vy:uint
        = Math.abs(destinationNode.row - testNode.row);

      var h:uint;
      if(vx > vy)
      {
        h = uint(_diagonalCost * vy + _straightCost * (vx - vy));
      }
      else
      {
        h = uint(_diagonalCost * vx + _straightCost * (vy - vx));
      }

      return h;
    }
  }
}
```

Now let's see exactly what this produces.

Using the AStar class

In the chapter's source files, you'll find a folder called `ShortestPath`. Run the SWF, and you'll see Button Fairy sitting in simple maze environment, as shown in Figure 9-33.

Click anywhere, and the SWF will mark the shortest path from Button Fairy to the mouse's position, as shown in Figure 9-34.

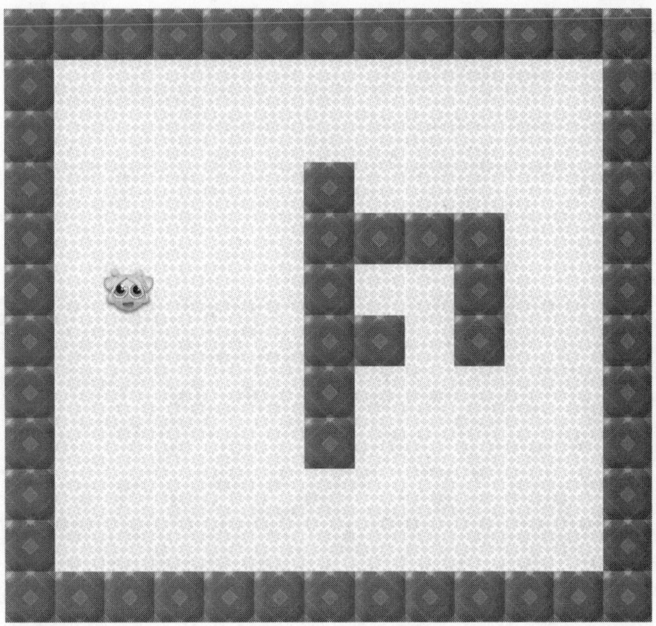

Figure 9-33. Click to draw a path from Button Fairy to the mouse's position.

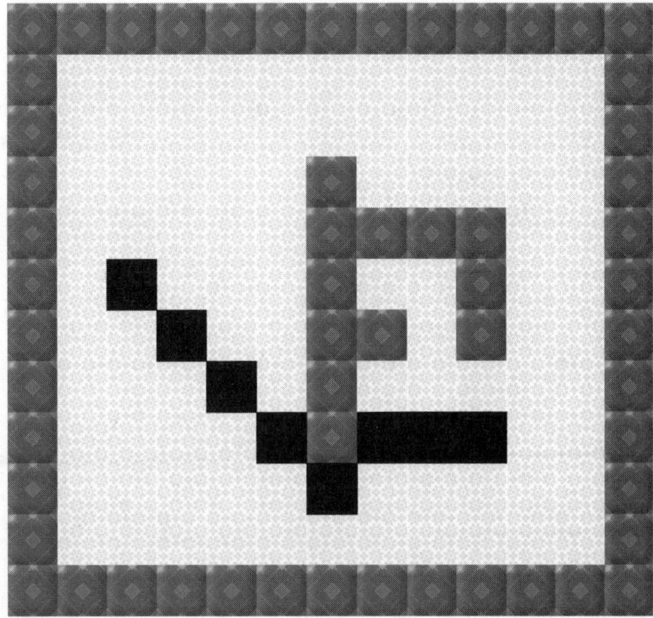

Figure 9-34. The shortest path

It also displays a status box that tells you some useful information:

- The path's start and end points
- The nodes that were chosen to build the shortest path
- A display of the entire node map that lists each node's unique ID number

Figure 9-35 shows this status box. This is information you can use if you need to debug your pathfinding.

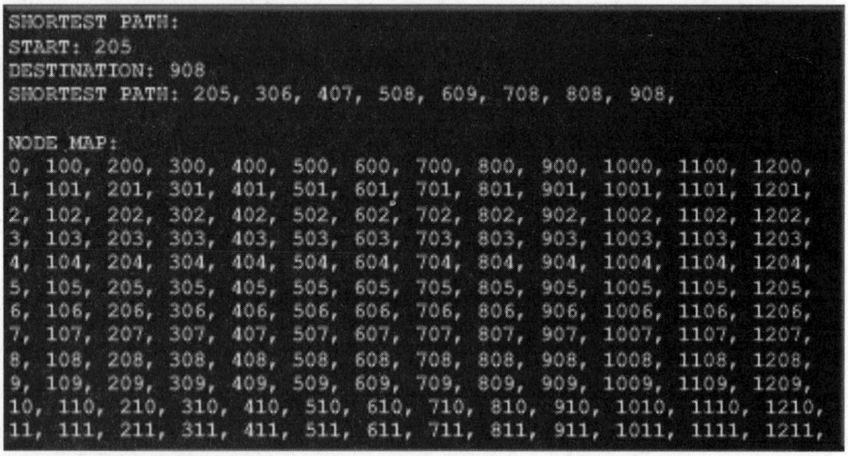

```
SHORTEST PATH:
START: 205
DESTINATION: 908
SHORTEST PATH: 205, 306, 407, 508, 609, 708, 808, 908,

NODE MAP:
0, 100, 200, 300, 400, 500, 600, 700, 800, 900, 1000, 1100, 1200,
1, 101, 201, 301, 401, 501, 601, 701, 801, 901, 1001, 1101, 1201,
2, 102, 202, 302, 402, 502, 602, 702, 802, 902, 1002, 1102, 1202,
3, 103, 203, 303, 403, 503, 603, 703, 803, 903, 1003, 1103, 1203,
4, 104, 204, 304, 404, 504, 604, 704, 804, 904, 1004, 1104, 1204,
5, 105, 205, 305, 405, 505, 605, 705, 805, 905, 1005, 1105, 1205,
6, 106, 206, 306, 406, 506, 606, 706, 806, 906, 1006, 1106, 1206,
7, 107, 207, 307, 407, 507, 607, 707, 807, 907, 1007, 1107, 1207,
8, 108, 208, 308, 408, 508, 608, 708, 808, 908, 1008, 1108, 1208,
9, 109, 209, 309, 409, 509, 609, 709, 809, 909, 1009, 1109, 1209,
10, 110, 210, 310, 410, 510, 610, 710, 810, 910, 1010, 1110, 1210,
11, 111, 211, 311, 411, 511, 611, 711, 811, 911, 1011, 1111, 1211,
```

Figure 9-35. The status box displays information about the path.

When you click with the mouse on the stage, the application class's `mouseDownHandler` is called. It finds the start and destination points, runs the `findShortestPath` method, and runs the `displayPath` method to display the path.

```
private function mouseDownHandler(event:MouseEvent):void
{
  //1. Find the startNode
  var playerColumn:uint = uint(_fairyModel.xPos / MAX_TILE_SIZE);
  var playerRow:uint = uint(_fairyModel.yPos / MAX_TILE_SIZE);
  var startNode_ID:uint = (playerColumn * 100) + playerRow;

  //2. Find the destinationNode
  var mouseColumn:uint = uint(stage.mouseX / MAX_TILE_SIZE);
  var mouseRow:uint = uint(stage.mouseY / MAX_TILE_SIZE);
  var destinationNode_ID:uint  = (mouseColumn * 100) + mouseRow;
```

```
  //3. Get the array containing the shortest path
  //from the _aStar object
  var shortestPath:Array
    = _aStar.findShortestPath
      (
        startNode_ID,
        destinationNode_ID,
        _mazeMap,
        WALL,
        "manhattan",
        10, 14
      );

  //4. Display the path that's found
  displayPath(shortestPath);
}
```

The path is displayed on the stage by drawing rectangles at the same position as each node in the `shortestPath` array. This is done by the `displayPath` method.

```
private function displayPath(shortestPath:Array):void
{
  //Clear any previous path that might be on the stage
  while(_pathMarkers.length != 0)
  {
    removeChild(_pathMarkers.shift());
  }

  for(var i:int = 0; i < shortestPath.length; i++)
  {
    //Create a square shape the size of a tile
    var shape:Shape = new Shape();
    shape.graphics.lineStyle(1);
    shape.graphics.beginFill(0x000000);
    shape.graphics.drawRect(0, 0, MAX_TILE_SIZE, MAX_TILE_SIZE);
    shape.graphics.endFill();
    addChild(shape);

    //Plot the shape on the correct path tile
    shape.x = uint(shortestPath[i].id / 100) * MAX_TILE_SIZE;
    shape.y = uint(shortestPath[i].id % 100) * MAX_TILE_SIZE;

    _pathMarkers.push(shape);
  }
}
```

One rectangle is drawn for every step in the path. An array called `_pathMarkers` stores all these rectangles. Each time a new path is found, the previous path is removed from the stage. This block of code loops through each rectangle in the array to simultaneously remove it from the stage and the array:

```
while(_pathMarkers.length != 0)
{
  removeChild(_pathMarkers.shift());
}
```

The shift method removes the first element from the array, but also returns it. The preceding code is a slightly more efficient way of writing this:

```
while(_pathMarkers.length != 0)
{
  var removedElement:Shape = _pathMarkers.shift();
  removeChild(removedElement);
}
```

You can see that as long as you have the shortestPath array, there's a lot that you can use it for. In the examples ahead, I'll show you how you can use it to make Button Fairy walk through the maze. But first, let's look at a topic that I've been strategically avoiding until now: heuristics.

Understanding heuristics

There will usually be more than one shortest path to a destination, as you can see in Figure 9-36. None of the paths is any better or worse than the other, and they all have the same cost. But each has a unique style. This style depends on the heuristic that A* uses to calculate the path.

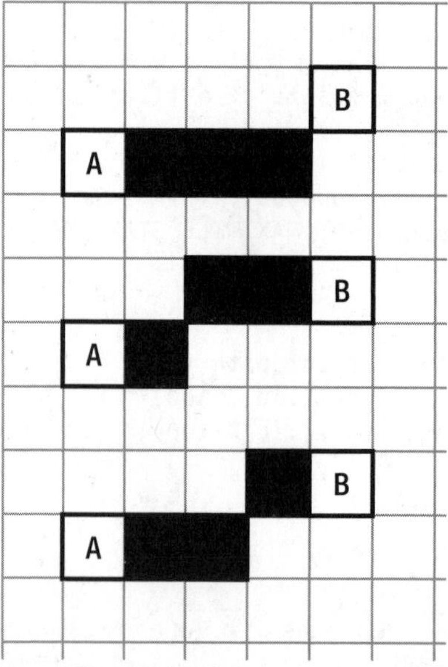

Figure 9-36. All threee paths are the same length, but the route they choose is different.

A **heuristic** is a mini-algorithm whose job is to work out distances based on a simple formula. Three famous heuristics are often used with A*: Manhattan, Euclidean, and diagonal. Figure 9-37 illustrates the different paths that each heuristic in the `AStar` class produces. Which do you prefer?

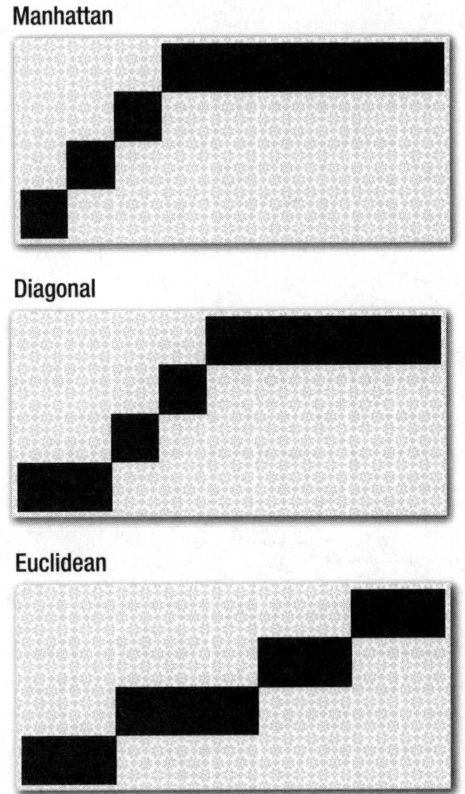

Figure 9-37. Different heuristics produce different paths.

The `AStar` class selects which heuristic to use based on the argument supplied to the `findShortestPath` method.

```
var shortestPath:Array
  = _aStar.findShortestPath
    (
      startNode_ID,
      destinationNode_ID,
      _mazeMap,
      WALL,
      "euclidean",
      10, 14
    );
```

A `switch` statement in the `findShortestPath` method finds the value of H by delegating the work to whichever heuristic method was specified.

```
var h:uint
switch(heuristic)
{
  case "manhattan":
    h = manhattan(testNode, destinationNode);
    break;

  case "euclidean":
    h = euclidean(testNode, destinationNode);
    break;

  case "diagonal":
    h = diagonal(testNode, destinationNode);
    break;

  default:
    throw new Error
      ("Oops! You misspelled the heuristic");
}
```

> *This bit of code also demonstrates how you can create error messages for yourself.*
>
> `throw new Error("Oops! You misspelled the heuristic");`
>
> *If you spell any of the heuristic names wrong, you'll get a runtime error that says, "Oops! You misspelled the heuristic." Creating your own error messages like this is useful if you're working on complex code and need to check that you're not accidentally making silly mistakes that might be hard to debug.*

Each heuristic method calculates the distance between the start and end point in different ways. The Manhattan method is simplest. It just adds together the rows and columns, and multiplies the sum by the cost. It ignores any possible diagonal shortcuts

```
private function manhattan
  (testNode:Object, destinationNode:Object):uint
{
  var h:uint
    = Math.abs
      (testNode.row - destinationNode.row) * _straightCost
    + Math.abs
      (testNode.column - destinationNode.column) * _straightCost;

  return h;
}
```

It's called Manhattan because if you were walking down the streets of New York City, you wouldn't be able to take a shortcut diagonally through any city block.

Ignoring possible diagonal routes makes the Manhattan heuristic fast to process. This is important because A* is an *extremely* CPU-hungry algorithm. If you need to do pathfinding for a lot of game characters each frame, Manhattan will save you some performance impact. However, because it doesn't account for diagonal routes, it may not always guarantee the absolute shortest path.

The Euclidean method uses the Pythagorean theorem to calculate the distance.

```
private function euclidean
  (testNode:Object, destinationNode:Object):uint
{
  var vx:int = destinationNode.column - testNode.column;
  var vy:int = destinationNode.row - testNode.row;
  var h:uint = uint(Math.sqrt(vx * vx + vy * vy) * _straightCost);

  return h;
}
```

The Euclidean method does account for diagonals, so it produces a very natural-looking path. However, it's a little slower to process than the Manhattan method because of that hungry `Math.sqrt` method.

The diagonal method compensates for the costs of moving straight across or diagonally, so it ends up with a very accurate cost estimate. This means that A* may need to do less searching and produce a faster result, and it will definitely produce the shortest possible path.

```
private function diagonal
  (testNode:Object, destinationNode:Object):uint
{
  var vx:uint
    = Math.abs(destinationNode.column - testNode.column);
  var vy:uint
    = Math.abs(destinationNode.row - testNode.row);

  var h:uint;
  if(vx > vy)
  {
    h = uint(_diagonalCost * vy + _straightCost * (vx - vy));
  }
  else
  {
     h = uint(_diagonalCost * vx + _straightCost * (vy - vx));
  }

  return h;
}
```

There's no one right heuristic to use. You just need to decide which produces the kind of path that seems the most natural for the game you're making.

Rounding corners

There's a potential problem with our current A* algorithm: it calculates the shortest path by taking a shortcut around the corners of walls. This is accurate, but it poses a problem for games. In most games, you'll want your characters to walk around the edges of walls. Figure 9-38 illustrates this dilemma.

Cut through the corner

Round the corner

Figure 9-38. Game characters will usually need to walk around walls, not cut through their corners.

Fortunately, we can fix this with only one very small rule change to the existing A* algorithm.

A* makes sure that it doesn't check any wall tiles in this bit of code:

```
if(nodeMap[testRow][testColumn].id
  != centerNode.id
&& map[testRow][testColumn] != wall)
{…
```

We can extend this check to help solve our problem. All we need to do is make sure that there isn't a wall in the same row or column as the current `centerNode` (the node in the center of the test).

```
if(nodeMap[testRow][testColumn].id
  != centerNode.id
&& map[testRow][testColumn] != wall
&& map[testRow][centerNode.column] != wall
&& map[centerNode.row][testColumn] != wall)
{…
```

And that's all there is to it!

Walking the path

Now that we know how to find a path, we need to teach our game characters how to walk along it. You'll find an example of this in the `WalkPath` folder. Click anywhere in the maze, and Button Fairy will take the shortest route to get there. The A* algorithm uses the modification we just looked at to allow the path to round corners, as shown in Figure 9-39.

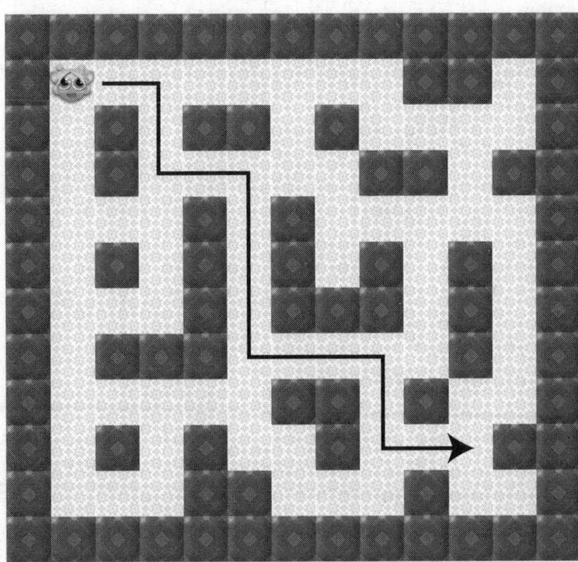

Figure 9-39. Click anywhere on the map, and Button Fairy will walk there.

The AStar class's findShortestPath method returns an array containing all the cells that Button Fairy will need to traverse to reach her destination. To make her walk this path, the enterFrameHandler moves her from the center of her current cell to the center of the next cell on the list. This is the logic it uses:

1. When Button Fairy is at a tile's corner, find the next node in the shortestPath array to move to.
2. Set Button Fairy's velocity so that she moves in the direction of the next node.
3. Remove the current node from the shortestPath array. This means the path will gradually get shorter and shorter.
4. Stop Button Fairy when there are no more node elements left in the shortestPath array.

Here's the important code from the enterFrameHandler in the WalkPath application class that does this:

```
private function enterFrameHandler(event:Event):void
{
  _fairyModel.update();

  //Make the _fairyModel move if it's at the corner of a tile
  //and if the shortestPath array isn't null
  if(atCornerOfTile(_fairyModel)
  && aStar.shortestPath != null)
  {
    //As long as there are elements in the shortestPath array,
    //make the _fairyModel move
    if(aStar.shortestPath.length != 0)
    {
      //Find the row and column in the path that the
      //_fairyModel has to walk to next
      var nextColumn:uint = uint(aStar.shortestPath[0].id / 100);
      var nextRow:uint = uint(aStar.shortestPath[0].id % 100);

      //If the _fairyModel is on the start node,
      //use the next node in the shortestPath array and remove the
      //first one
      if(_fairyModel.mapColumn == nextColumn
      && _fairyModel.mapRow == nextRow)
      {
        //Find the next column and row in the path
        nextColumn = uint(aStar.shortestPath[1].id / 100);
        nextRow = uint(aStar.shortestPath[1].id % 100);

        //Remove the current node
        aStar.shortestPath.shift();
      }
```

```
    //If the _fairyModel isn't standing on the next
    //column or row in the path, set her velocity
    //so that she starts walking in the right direction
    if(_fairyModel.mapColumn != nextColumn)
    {
      if(_fairyModel.mapColumn > nextColumn)
      {
        //Move left
        _fairyModel.vx = -8;
        _fairyModel.vy = 0;
      }
      else
      {
        //Move right
        _fairyModel.vx = 8;
        _fairyModel.vy = 0;
      }
    }
    else if(_fairyModel.mapRow != nextRow)
    {
      if(_fairyModel.mapRow > nextRow)
      {
        //Move up
        _fairyModel.vx = 0;
        _fairyModel.vy = -8;
      }
      else
      {
        //Move down
        _fairyModel.vx = 0;
        _fairyModel.vy = 8;
      }
    }

    //Remove the current node from the path.
    //This means that the path will gradually get shorter as
    //the _fairyModel moves along it
    aStar.shortestPath.shift();
  }

  //If there are no more elements left in the
  //shortestPath array, stop the _fairyModel
  else
  {
    _fairyModel.vx = 0;
    _fairyModel.vy = 0;
  }
}
```

```
  //...Blit the _fairyModel and update the status box
}
```

In the chapter's source files, you'll find a folder called `MonsterMaze` that adds the monster to this system. There are many different ways that you could make a game object walk a path, but this will be enough to get you started.

Extending and customizing A*

You will definitely need to invest a bit of time into getting comfortable using A* and understanding all its subtleties. But it's certainly worth the effort, as it's a cornerstone game-design technique that is used on all platforms in most game genres.

A big part of A*'s appeal is its flexibility. As you've seen, you can produce a different kind of path just by switching the heuristic. But it's not just the heuristics that make A* as flexible as it is. Let's look at few of the other possibilities the A* algorithm offers.

Variable terrain

In this chapter's examples, we've had only one type of obstacle: walls. However, you may have different kinds of obstacles in your games, not all of which are impenetrable.

What if you had a game with a mud pit? Characters could still move through the mud, but it would slow them down. You could modify A* so that nodes containing mud have a high costs. For example, give your G costs an extra 20 or 30 points when A* encounters a mud node. A* would then calculate whether it's faster to go around the mud or take the shortcut through it.

Strategy games use this technique all the time. Troops need to consider whether it's better to stick to the plains and travel fast, or take their time crossing mountains. This analysis is all done by A*'s cost analysis of different kinds of moves.

Influence map

Here's another interesting problem that's solvable with A*. Imagine that you have enemy AI characters that are using A* to find the best exit to a dungeon. The only problem is that you've discovered that you can easily rack up a high score by hiding near that exit and knocking off each enemy as it blindly stumbles by. The enemies have no way of warning their friends that this might be the shortest route but it's also extremely dangerous.

You can fix this by using what's called an **influence map**. If an area of the game world becomes particularly dangerous, make those nodes very high cost. When A* searches for a path, it will avoid those expensive, dangerous areas.

You can also extend this concept to solve the problem of many enemies following the same path. In many games, it will seem very unnatural if all the enemies choose the same shortest path. You can force enemies to take a different path by tracking the path that each chooses, and assigning high costs to those nodes. A* will then avoid nodes and paths that have already been chosen by other enemies.

Dijkstra's algorithm

Earlier, I mentioned that A* was an improvement over Dijkstra's algorithm. This is a bit misleading because, in fact, Dijkstra's algorithm is better to use when you don't know the final destination of the path.

The only difference between A* and Dijkstra's algorithm is that A* adds heuristics. In Dijkstra's algorithm, H always has a value of zero. The means that when Dijkstra's algorithm starts looking for a path, it doesn't know in which direction to start looking. It must do a lot more searching than A* to find the goal.

But what if you have a game where you're not sure where the character's final destination will be? Imagine that you're designing a strategy or resource management game and your villagers need to collect strawberries. There are four strawberry bushes around the town, but you don't know which bush is the closest. If you use Dijkstra's algorithm, it will search outward in all directions until it finds the first one. If you use A*, you will need to calculate four different paths to each bush and choose the shortest. Dijkstra's algorithm saves you from having to do this, so it would be a better choice in this case.

If you want to use Dijkstra's algorithm rather than A*, just assign 0 to all the H costs. The rest of the A* code will be the same.

Summary

This chapter has presented a brief introduction to pathfinding, which should get you thinking about what's possible for your own games. Adventure games, strategy games, and any games that require sophisticated AI will benefit from these techniques.

In Chapter 10, we'll finish the book by taking a look at how to work with external game data. Saving games, loading games, and using XML are coming up next.

Chapter 10

XML and External Data

You might be surprised to know this, but we've just about covered all the most essential topics in game design. We've left few stones unturned, and I hope you've been inspired to build a few new games along the way.

In this last chapter of the book, we're going to look at how to load and save game data using some of AS3.0's built-in tools. We'll cover these topics:

- Local shared objects
- Loading and saving files using `FileReference`
- Using XML to store and load game levels
- Loading files at runtime using `URLLoader`
- Flash Player security issues

These are very general techniques that have a wide application in games. You can use them along with any of the other techniques we've covered in this book.

At the end of this chapter, I'll give you a few suggestions on where to go from here to take your study of game design further.

Local shared objects

The simplest way to save game data with AS3.0 is in something called a **local shared object**. This is an AS3.0 `Object`, like any other object you've used in your code. The only difference is that a local shared object is stored outside the SWF, in a separate file on the user's hard drive. That means that even after the SWF is closed, the shared object still exists. When the user starts the game again, you can load the object and use its data to resume the game from where it was saved.

Creating and loading shared objects

Creating a local shared object is simple. First, import the `SharedObject` class from the `flash.net` package.

```
import flash.net.SharedObject;
```

Next, create the shared object with the `SharedObject` class.

```
var sharedObject:SharedObject =  SharedObject.getLocal("savedData");
```

The `getLocal` method creates a shared object on the user's hard drive called `savedData`. If `savedData` has already been created in a previous session, the code loads it into the program and stores its data in the new `sharedObject` variable.

The `sharedObject` that was created has a `data` object property.

```
sharedObject.data
```

You can assign any variables or values to the `data` object that you need. Do this by creating new properties on the `data` object, and assign values to those new properties.

```
sharedObject.data.name = "Player Name";
sharedObject.data.score = gameScore;
sharedObject.data.levelArray = mapArray;
```

These properties are dynamic. Any values that you assign to the `data` object will become your saved information.

The shared object will be saved to the user's local hard drive automatically when the user closes the SWF window. However, you can also force the shared object to be saved at any time by using the colorfully named `flush` method.

```
_sharedObject.flush();
```

Now the data is saved to the hard drive.

To load the shared object, use the `getLocal` method. The `getLocal` method takes one argument, which is the name of the shared object you want to load. It should be the same name that you supplied in `getLocal`'s argument when you created the shared object.

```
sharedObject = SharedObject.getLocal("savedData");
```

You can now access all the `data` properties that you created earlier.

```
sharedObject.data.name
sharedObject.data.score
sharedObject.data.levelArray
```

This is useful for resuming a game from a save point.

Where on the hard drive is the shared object actually saved? One limitation of using local shared objects is that the user or developer has no control over the save location. Flash Player saves the shared object in a folder that it knows can't be exploited to breach the operating system's security—someplace that Flash Player deems safe. The exact save location depends on the user's operating system and can change depending on whether the SWF file is being executed directly or run in a browser. Flash Player saves the file with the `.sol` file name extension, in a folder with a random name, so that a malicious SWF can't try to guess the folder name.

On Windows, you can look for `.sol` files here:

```
C:\Documents and Settings\username\Application Data\Macromedia\Flash Player
\#SharedObjects\[a folder with a random name]
```

On Mac OS X, look here:

```
/User/username/Library/Preferences/Macromedia/Flash Player/#SharedObject
\[a folder with a random name]
```

> *If you're building games for the Web, you'll almost certainly need to store game data online. With Adobe's Flash Media Server, you can also use a* ***remote shared object*** *to save data online. For more information about remote shared objects, see the SharedObjects entry in Adobe's online ActionScript 3.0 Language and Components Reference. Also, a great introduction to this topic is* Foundation Flex for Developers: Data-Driven Applications with PHP, ASP.NET, ColdFusion, and LCDS *by Sas Jacobs with Koen De Weggheleire (friends of ED, 2007).*

Let's look at a practical example of how to use local shared objects.

Using shared objects

In the chapter's source files, you'll find a folder called `LocalSharedObjects`, which contains a simple example of how to use a shared object to save and load game data. Run the SWF, and you'll see input and output text fields with **`Save`** and **`Load`** buttons. Type something into the input field and click the **`Save`** button, as shown in Figure 10-1.

Close the SWF, and then launch it again. Click the **`Load`** button, and you'll see the text that you saved has been copied into the output text field, as shown in Figure 10-2.

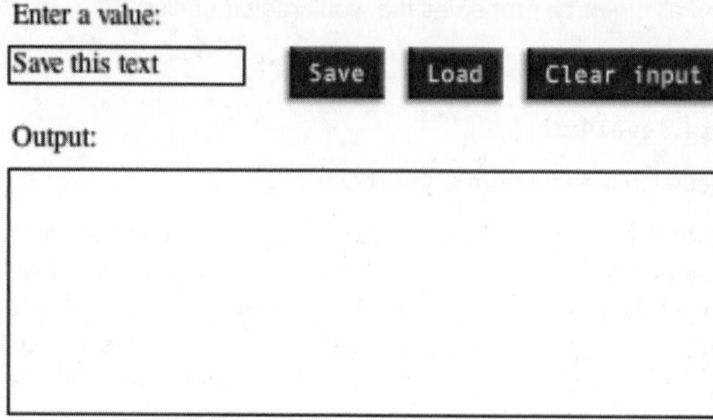

Figure 10-1. Enter some text and click the Save button to save it.

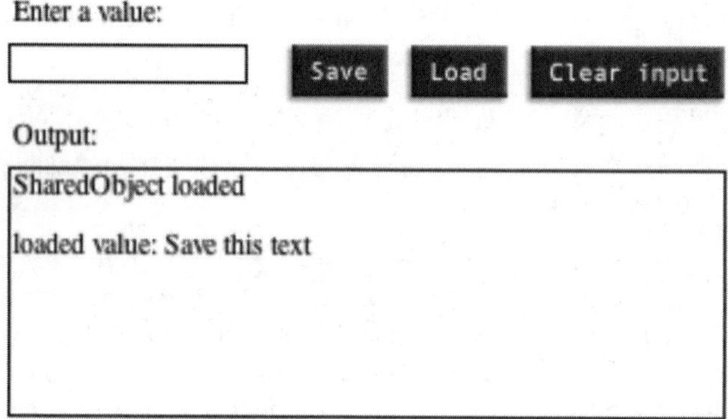

Figure 10-2. Click the Load button to load the text you saved previously.

The following is the entire application class that creates the buttons and text fields, and loads and saves the data. (You'll find the code for the `EasyButton` class that creates the buttons in the `com.friendsofed.utils` package.)

```
package
{
  import flash.net.SharedObject;
  import flash.text.*;
  import flash.display.Sprite;
  import flash.events.MouseEvent;
  import com.friendsofed.utils.StatusBox;
  import com.friendsofed.utils.EasyButton;

  [SWF(backgroundColor="0xFFFFFF", frameRate="30",
  width="550", height="400")]
```

```
public class LocalSharedObjects extends Sprite
{
  //Create the shared object.
  //This creates a "savedData" object that can
  //contain any saved values.
  private var _sharedObject:SharedObject
    = SharedObject.getLocal("savedData");

  //Text labels
  private var _inputLabel:TextField = new TextField();
  private var _outputLabel:TextField = new TextField();

  //Input and output text fields
  private var _input:TextField = new TextField();
  private var _output:TextField = new TextField();

  //Buttons
  private var _saveButton:EasyButton
    = new EasyButton("Save", 10, 40, 21);
  private var _loadButton:EasyButton
    = new EasyButton("Load", 10, 40, 21);
  private var _clearButton:EasyButton
    = new EasyButton("Clear input", 10, 80, 21);

  //Status box
  private var _status:StatusBox;

  public function LocalSharedObjects():void
  {
    _status = new StatusBox("LOCAL SHARED OBJECTS");
    addChild(_status);

    //Input label
    addChild(_inputLabel);
    _inputLabel.x = 10;
    _inputLabel.y = 50;
    _inputLabel.text = "Enter a value:";

    //Input text field
    addChild(_input);
    _input.x = 10;
    _input.y = 70;
    _input.width = 100;
    _input.height = 15;
    _input.border = true;
    _input.background = true;
    _input.type = TextFieldType.INPUT;
```

```
    //Output label
    addChild(_outputLabel);
    _outputLabel.x = 10;
    _outputLabel.y = _input.y + 30;
    _outputLabel.text = "Output:";

    //Output text field
    addChild(_output);
    _output.x = 10;
    _output.y = _outputLabel.y + 20;
    _output.width = 300;
    _output.height = 100;
    _output.multiline = true;
    _output.wordWrap = true;
    _output.border = true;
    _output.background = true;

    //Add and position the buttons
    addChild(_saveButton);
    _saveButton.y = _input.y;
    _saveButton.x = _input.x + _input.width + 20;

    addChild(_loadButton);
    _loadButton.y = _saveButton.y;
    _loadButton.x = _saveButton.x + _saveButton.width + 10;

    addChild(_clearButton);
    _clearButton.y = _loadButton.y;
    _clearButton.x = _loadButton.x + _loadButton.width + 10;

    //Button listeners
    _clearButton.addEventListener
      (MouseEvent.CLICK, clearHandler);
    _saveButton.addEventListener
      (MouseEvent.CLICK, saveHandler);
    _loadButton.addEventListener
      (MouseEvent.CLICK, loadHandler);
  }

  private function clearHandler(event:MouseEvent):void
  {
    _input.text = "";
  }

  private function saveHandler(event:MouseEvent):void
  {
    //Save the input text in the shared object
    _sharedObject.data.savedInput = _input.text;
```

```
      //Write the data to a local file
      _sharedObject.flush();

      //Confirm the save in the output box
      _output.appendText("Input text saved" + "\n");
    }

    private function loadHandler(event:MouseEvent):void
    {
      //Load the shared object. This loads a "savedData" object that can
      //contain any saved values.
      _sharedObject = SharedObject.getLocal("savedData");
      _output.appendText("SharedObject loaded" + "\n\n");
      _output.appendText
        ("loaded value: " + _sharedObject.data.savedInput + "\n\n");
    }
  }
}
```

When the class is initialized, the shared object is created.

```
private var _sharedObject:SharedObject
  = SharedObject.getLocal("savedData");
```

This creates an `.sol` file on the user's local drive called `savedData`. If there's already an existing SOL file called `savedData`, it loads it into the `_sharedObject` variable.

When the **Save** button is clicked, it calls the `saveHandler` that does the job of saving the text from the input field to the SOL file. First, it copies the value of the input field's `text` property to the shared object's `data` object.

```
_sharedObject.data.savedInput = _input.text;
```

It stores the value in a property called `savedInput`, which is a dynamic property that is created on the `data` object. The `data` object is dynamic, so you can create any new properties on it when you need to and give them any names you choose. You can save any kind of values in properties in the `data` object, including XML objects.

The shared object saves the SOL file containing the new data by calling its `flush` method.

```
_sharedObject.flush();
```

The data will now be saved to the user's hard drive.

Flash Player will automatically save the `.sol` file when the SWF is closed, so calling `flush` is optional in most cases. As long as the information you want to save has been copied to the shared object's `data` property, it will be saved when the SWF quits. Use `flush` only if you want to force the data to be saved at a particular time, such as with a button click.

The shared object loads the data with the getLocal method when the user clicks the **Load** button.

```
_sharedObject = SharedObject.getLocal("savedData");
```

The savedInput property that was saved previously is then displayed in the output text field using the TextField class's appendText method.

```
_output.appendText
  ("loaded value: " + _sharedObject.data.savedInput + "\n\n");
```

Using appendText is a faster way of adding text in a text field than by doing it with the increment operator, like this:

```
textFieldObject.text += "new text to add to the text field";
```

The SharedObject also has a clear method, which clears all the shared object's data and deletes the .sol file from the disk. Its size property tells you the size, in bytes, of the shared object.

> *SharedObject has a few more specialized properties, mostly relating to remote shared objects, that you'll find described in the SharedObject entry in Adobe's online ActionScript 3.0 Language and Component Reference.*

Limitations of local shared objects

Adobe gives SWF files very limited local file access. This is to maximize security, so that Flash developers can't use SWF files to write and distribute worms, viruses, and spyware. In addition to Flash Player determining the save location, there are a few more limitations to using shared objects:

- By default, Flash Player limits the maximum amount of storage for SOL files to 100KB. However, users can change this in the Flash Player settings to prevent any SOL files from being saved at all. This is something you have no control over.
- Flash Player manages SOL files, and it can delete them (without informing anyone) if the user runs out of allocated storage space.
- The user can choose to block SWF files from specific domains from saving SOL files by using the Flash Player Settings Manager.
- The SWF file needs to be at least 215 by 138 pixels so that Flash Player has enough room to display the dialog box that prompts users to increase their storage, if necessary.

You'll need to decide whether these limitations are a deal-breaker for the kind of game you're building. For many small, pick-up-and-play Flash games, local shared objects are a quick and efficient solution for saving noncritical persistent game data. However, because of these limitations, you should avoid using local shared objects for any mission-critical game data.

> *If you need more reliability, for storing data locally, consider designing your game using Adobe Integrated Runtime (AIR). AIR is a specialized framework for AS3.0 that allows you build desktop applications with deep access to the operating system. It requires the user to download and install the AIR runtime, but doesn't tie your hands as SWF files do when it comes to local storage. For more information about AIR, visit the website at* `http://www.adobe.com/products/air/`*.* The Essential Guide to Flash CS4 AIR Development *by Marco Casario (friends of ED, 2008) is an excellent book on the subject that will show you how to build desktop apps using AIR and AS3.0.*

There is one more option for local file storage. AS3.0 has a class called `FileReference` that makes it possible for a user to load and save a data file in any location in the local hard drive, without using AIR.

Loading and saving files to a specific location

`FileReference` opens a file browser window whenever a file needs to be loaded or saved. The file browser is launched by the operating system, so it isn't limited by Flash Player's security. Because the loading and saving is done by the operating system, and the user can choose which file to open, Flash Player can safely wash its hands of any responsibility for possible security breaches.

A disadvantage to this approach is that your game can't discreetly save data in the background to a directory of your choosing. The user will need to take the initiative to load and save the game data. Is that asking too much from the user? It might be, but you'll need to decide based on any given project requirements.

For example, you might find `FileReference` useful if you are making a puzzle game where users can upload their own images into the game. You could also use `FileReference` to create a game level editor, either for yourself to edit levels quickly or for users to make their own levels and save them.

In the chapter's source files, you'll find an example in a folder called `UsingFileReference`. Click the **`Load`** button, and a file browser window will open. Select the `map.xml` file from the `sampleFiles` folder. It will be loaded into a text field labeled **`XML Data`**, as shown in Figure 10-3. `map.xml` is game level map formatted as XML, which is a format that AS3.0 can easily read.

> *If you haven't used XML files before, for now, you can think of them as overachieving text files. We'll take a detailed look at XML and how to use it to create files like* `map.xml` *a little later in this chapter.*

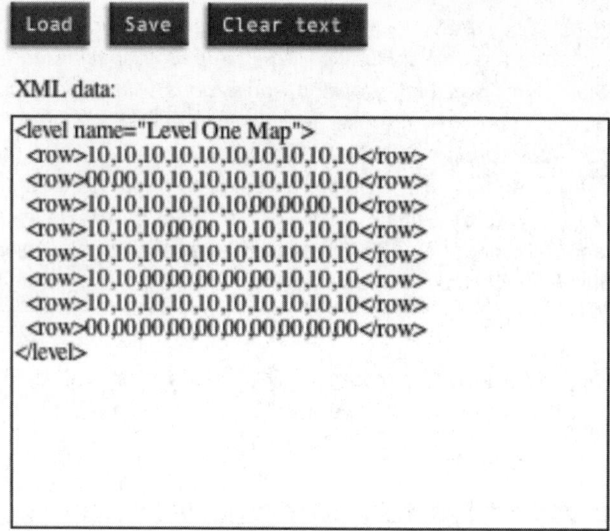

Figure 10-3. Load an XML file, make some changes to it, and save it to any location.

Make some changes to the level data, and then click the **Save** button. A file browser opens, and you're prompted to save the XML file in any location with any name you like. This demonstrates how, unlike with `SharedObject`, the user has control over exactly which file is opened, where it's saved, and what it's called.

The two new classes used to make this happen are `FileReference` and `FileFilter`, both of which are part of the `flash.net` package.

```
import flash.net.FileReference;
import flash.net.FileFilter;
```

The application class initializes a new `FileReference` object like this:

```
private var _fileReference:FileReference = new FileReference();
```

Let's look at how to use `FileReference` objects to load and save an XML file.

Loading the file

When you click the **Load** button, the `loadHandler` lets you browse for the data file. In this example, the file is an XML file.

```
private function loadHandler(event:MouseEvent):void
{
  //Create a FileFilter to prevent the user from
  //opening any file type except XML files
  var fileFilter:FileFilter
    = new FileFilter("XML Documents", "*.xml;");
```

```
  //Allow the user to browse for the new file.
  //Pass the fileFilter as an argument
  _fileReference.browse([fileFilter]);

  //FileReference SELECT listener. This is fired when the
  //user selects the correct file
  _fileReference.addEventListener(Event.SELECT, selectHandler);
}
```

You can make sure that the user can open only a specific type of file by using a `FileFilter` object. In this example, the `FileFilter` prevents the user from opening any files except XML files. All other types of files will be dimmed in the file browser.

```
var fileFilter:FileFilter
  = new FileFilter("XML Documents", "*.xml;");
```

The first argument, `"XML Documents"`, is just a description. This description is displayed in the title bar of Windows and Linux file browsers. The second argument, `"*.xml;"`, is the type of file you want to open. In this case, it's any file with an `.xml` extension. To allow the user to open more than one type of file, add more extension names and separate them with semicolons, like this:

```
var fileFilter:FileFilter = new FileFilter
  ("Documents", "*.xml; *.doc; *.txt; *.pdf");
```

Of course, your AS3.0 code will need to be able to interpret any file you open. AS3.0 can read XML files natively, which is why they're used in this example.

Next, the code calls the `_fileReference` object's `browse` method and passes the `fileFilter` as an argument.

```
_fileReference.browse([fileFilter]);
```

This is what launches the operating system's file browser and dims the names of all files except those with an `.xml` extension. The code then attaches a listener that calls the `selectHandler` when the file has been selected by the user in the file browser.

```
_fileReference.addEventListener(Event.SELECT, selectHandler);
```

The `selectHandler` does the job of loading the file into the SWF with `FileReference`'s `load` method. It calls the `loadCompleteHandler` when it's finished.

```
private function selectHandler(event:Event):void
{
  //Remove this listener
  _fileReference.removeEventListener(Event.SELECT, selectHandler);

  //Add a listener to check whether the file has
  //successfully loaded
  _fileReference.addEventListener
    (Event.COMPLETE, loadCompleteHandler);
```

```
    //Load the file
    _fileReference.load();
}
```

The loadCompleteHandler reads the loaded data, casts it as an XML object, and copies it into the text field so that the file data is visible on the stage

```
private function loadCompleteHandler(event:Event):void
{
  //Remove this listener
  _fileReference.removeEventListener
    (Event.COMPLETE, loadCompleteHandler);

  //Store the FileReference's data in the XML object
  var xmlData:XML = XML(_fileReference.data);

  //Display the XML object in the text field
  _textField.text = xmlData;
}
```

FileReference objects have a data property that contains the loaded data. The following directive reads the loaded data and interprets it as XML.

```
_xmlData = XML(_fileReference.data);
```

Finally, xmlData, the loaded XML file, is displayed in the text field on the stage.

```
_textField.text = xmlData;
```

> *This same technique works for images as well. In this chapter's source files, you'll find the `LoadingImages` folder. Run the SWF, and use the **Load** button to load any image file onto the stage. The code loads the images with the help of the `Loader` and `LoaderInfo` classes. Check the comments in the source code for more details.*

Saving the file

When the XML file is loaded into the text field, you can make any changes to it that you like. To allow editing directly in the text field, the text field's selectable property must be set to true, and its type needs to be set to INPUT.

```
_textField.selectable = true;
_textField.type = TextFieldType.INPUT;
```

Once you've made some changes, click the **Save** button. The **Save** button's listener calls the saveHandler. The saveHandler creates a new FileReference object that saves the data from the text field as an XML file. A file browser window prompts the user to choose a file name and the directory location to save the new file.

```
private function saveHandler(event:MouseEvent):void
{
  //Create a FileReference object for the save data
  var saveFile:FileReference = new FileReference();

  //Add an optional listener that confirms that the file has
  //been saved
  saveFile.addEventListener
    (Event.COMPLETE, saveCompleteHandler);

  //Create a new temporary XML object to store the
  //changed data in the text field
  var newXML:XML = XML(_textField.text);

  //Save the changed XML data with the name "newMap.xml"
  saveFile.save(newXML, "newMap.xml");
}

private function saveCompleteHandler(event:Event):void
{
  trace("Save completed");
}
```

First, a new FileReference object is created called saveFile. Its job will be to save the changed data in the text field.

```
var saveFile:FileReference = new FileReference();
```

The saveFile object adds an Event.COMPLETE listener that is called when the file is actually saved.

```
saveFile.addEventListener
    (Event.COMPLETE, saveCompleteHandler);
```

In this example, it just traces as "Save completed," but you could use it to trigger some other code. This is optional.

Next, we need to create a new temporary XML object that contains the text from the text field.

```
var newXML:XML = XML(_textField.text);
```

The saveFile object can then use its save method to initiate the file save.

```
saveFile.save(newXML, "newMap.xml");
```

This directive opens a new file browser window. The browser will allow you save a file called newMap.xml anywhere you like on your hard drive. You can also change the name of the file if you wish.

This is a simple example, but is the basis for creating something more complex, like a game level editor using XML data.

> *The basic technique described here can also be used to modify and save user-loaded images. Adobe has a detailed tutorial by H. Paul Robertson on how to crop and save such images at the Adobe Developer Connection website (`http://www.adobe.com/devnet/flash/quickstart/filereference_class_as3/`). It includes two specialized classes that will encode the final modified images as PNG or JPEG files.*

Understanding XML

In this chapter, we're going to take a detailed look at AS3.0's powerful built-in tools for reading and writing XML. When you become comfortable working with XML, you may find that it's the primary way in which you store and manage your game's data. Knowing how to work with XML is an essential skill for any game designer.

XML stands for Extensible Markup Language. This language is a way of describing data so that computers can understand it. XML is useful for game designers because it allows you to keep your game data file completely separate from the rest of your code.

You can load XML files into your game at runtime. This means you can tweak, change, and add to all of the game's data without needing to recompile the SWF file or change your AS3.0 code. You can load XML files into the game from a local directory or over a network from any server on Earth.

XML is a standardized data format that's used as a common interface for sharing data between virtually all software and database platforms. Even though AS3.0 might be a completely different language from PHP, C#, or Java, you can be sure that any data stored as XML can be read by all of them. Storing and sharing game data as XML ensures maximum compatibility. It's also easily readable by humans and fun to learn.

The building blocks of XML

Imagine that we're creating a multiple-choice quiz game that looks like Figure 10-4. The quiz presents three questions with three possible answers, one of which is the correct response. Wouldn't it be useful if our program could actually understand what all those sections of the quiz represent—the questions, the answers, and even which are the correct answers?

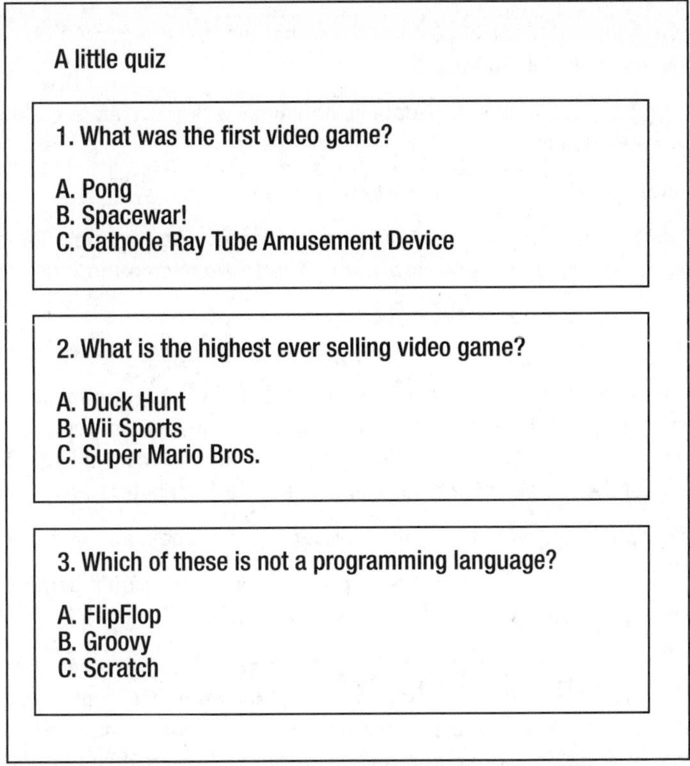

Figure 10-4. XML can be used to explain the meaning of data in a document.

XML can help you structure data so that's easily readable by a computer. The basic concept in XML is that every important item in your data is described by a **tag**. XML tags are just like HTML tags. They're descriptive words, surrounded by opening and closing angle brackets. You can use any tag names you like to describe your data.

Here's an XML tag that could be used to describe which part of the quiz is a question:

```
<question>
```

This tells the computer than anything that follows is part of the quiz's question.

Each tag must have a matching **closing tag**, so that the computer knows where the item ends. Closing tags have the same name as the opening tag, but are preceded by a forward slash, like this:

```
</question>
```

The opening and closing tags work together to describe the information they contain. Here's how we could format the first question of the quiz as XML:

```
<question>What was the first video game?</question>
```

Because the text is surrounded by opening and closing `question` tags, the computer will know that any data within them will be a question.

A matching pair of XML tags, and the data it contains, is known as an **element** in XML's terminology. This is an element:

```
<question>…</question>
```

Each individual part of the element is known as a **node**. For example, a single opening `<question>` tag can be called the **question node**. The text between the tags is called the **text node**.

```
<question>This text between the element tags is the text node</question>
```

XML can also contain extra information about the data that your program might need. This extra information is sometimes called **metadata**. For example, let's say that in our quiz game, we want to assign 10 points to the correct answer. We can do this by including an **attribute** in the tag. Here's what the tag for the answer might look like with this new attribute:

```
<answerC points="10">Cathode Ray Tube Amusement Device</answerC>
```

The attribute is part of the opening tag. The program that runs your quiz game could then read this attribute and assign the player 10 points for a correct guess.

> *Yes, the magnificently titled Cathode Ray Tube Amusement Device was indeed the world's first completely electronic game with a video output source (an oscilloscope). It was designed and built by Thomas T. Goldsmith, Jr. and Estle Ray Mann in 1947. It was a missile game that allowed the player to fire at targets. A celluloid screen overlay displayed the targets, and the player used knobs to adjust the trajectory of the missiles. It was never commercialized, and no prototypes appear to have survived.*

You can create as many different attributes with whatever names and values you need.

Elements, nodes, and attributes are XML's basic building blocks.

XML hierarchy

XML is hierarchical. That means that you can group elements inside other elements to keep related information together. Figure 10-5 shows how each question in the quiz and its three answers make up a single unit (which I've called "quiz items").

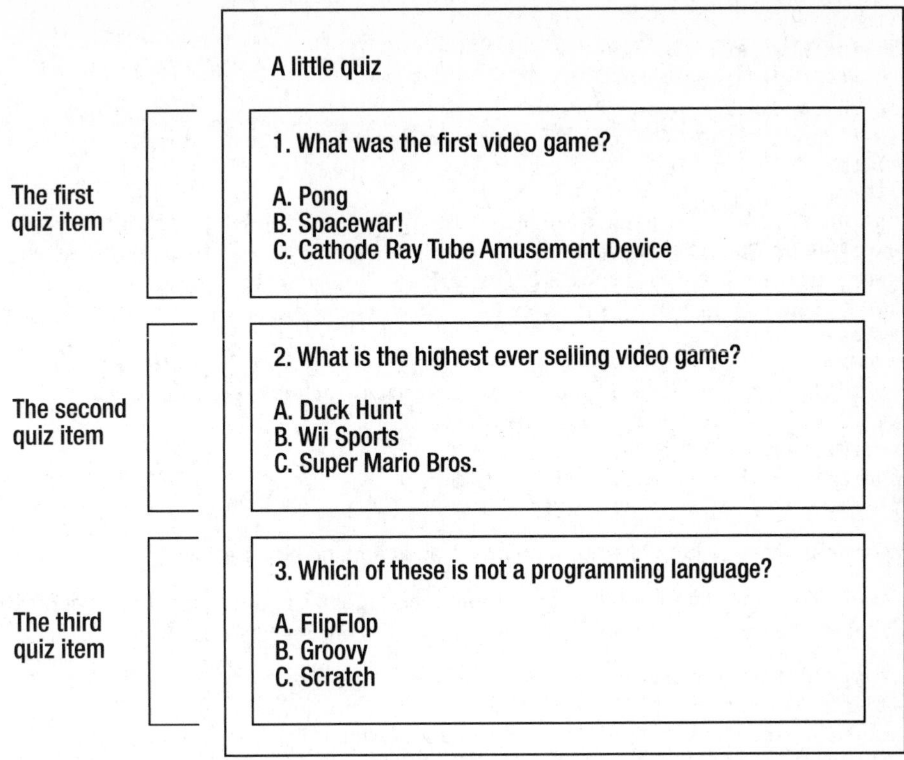

A little quiz
The first
quiz item
1. What was the first video game?
A. Pong
B. Spacewar!
C. Cathode Ray Tube Amusement Device
The second
quiz item
2. What is the highest ever selling video game?
A. Duck Hunt
B. Wii Sports
C. Super Mario Bros.
The third
quiz item
3. Which of these is not a programming language?
A. FlipFlop
B. Groovy
C. Scratch

Figure 10-5. XML can keep related data together.

You can box together bits of related data like this by surrounding the data with additional tags. For example, we could create a `<quizItem>` tag that keeps together each question and its three answers. Here's what the XML structure might look like:

```
<quizItem>
  <question>What was the first video game?</question>
  <answerA>Pong</answerA>
  <answerB>Spacewar!</answerB>
  <answerC points="10">Cathode Ray Tube Amusement Device</answerC>
</quizItem>
```

The `<quizItem>` and `</quizItem>` tags are used to bookend all the related information.

You can see from Figure 10-5 that there are three question-and-answer groups in this quiz. Each of them can be grouped inside `<quizItem>` tags to keep them separated from each other.

```
<quizItem>
  <question>What was the first video game?</question>
  <answerA>Pong</answerA>
  <answerB>Spacewar!</answerB>
  <answerC points="10">Cathode Ray Tube Amusement Device</answerC>
</quizItem>
<quizItem>
  <question>What is the highest ever selling video game?</question>
  <answerA>Duck Hunt</answerA>
  <answerB points="10">Wii Sports</answerB>
  <answerC>Super Mario Bros.</answerC>
</quizItem>
<quizItem>
  <question>Which of these is not a programming language?</question>
  <answerA points="10">FlipFlop</answerA>
  <answerB>Groovy</answerB>
  <answerC>Scratch</answerC>
</quizItem>
```

Now you can easily see where one question group ends and the next begins.

Figure 10-5 also shows that the entire quiz is grouped together in a single box that contains all the quiz items. We can create another tag called `<quiz>` to enclose the quiz.

```
<quiz name="A little quiz">
  <quizItem>
    <question>What was the first video game?</question>
    <answerA>Pong</answerA>
    <answerB>Spacewar!</answerB>
    <answerC points="10">Cathode Ray Tube Amusement Device</answerC>
  </quizItem>
  <quizItem>
    <question>What is the highest ever selling video game?</question>
    <answerA>Duck Hunt</answerA>
    <answerB points="10">Wii Sports</answerB>
    <answerC>Super Mario Bros.</answerC>
  </quizItem>
  <quizItem>
    <question>Which of these is not a programming language?</question>
    <answerA points="10">FlipFlop</answerA>
    <answerB>Groovy</answerB>
    <answerC>Scratch</answerC>
  </quizItem>
</quiz>
```

This type of hierarchical structure is called a `tree`. `<quiz>` is the **root element**, or `parent`, of all the other elements. Each `<quizItem>` is a **child** of the `<quiz>` element. This is a very basic hierarchical structure that you should be quite familiar with by now. XML structure makes this very clear. Figure 10-6 shows how the XML structure of the quiz matches the quiz diagram.

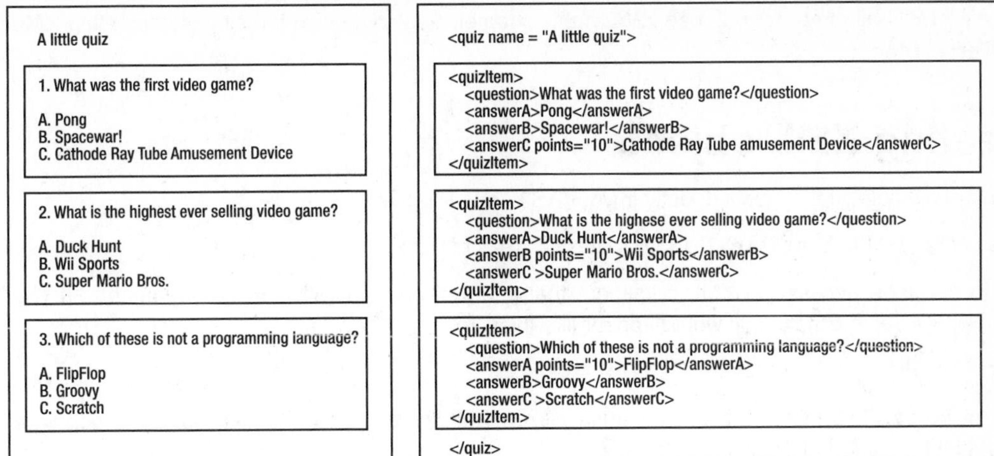

Figure 10-6. A simple quiz structured as XML

Now that the quiz is completely described by XML, let's see how we can use that information with AS3.0.

XML and ActionScript

AS3.0 has a special syntax for working with XML called ECMAScript for XML (E4X). E4X allows you access elements, nodes, and attributes in XML documents in much the same way that you access properties in objects.

> *In this chapter, I'm going to call XML files XML documents, just for the sake of simplicity. The official XML specification refers to XML applications. They're the same thing. From a programmer's point of view, XML doesn't contain the same kind of logic that we associate with software applications, and are more like plain text documents.*

You can use XML in your programs in three ways:

- Create XML objects directly in your code.
- Embed the XML file at compile time, with the `Embed` metatag, in the same way that we've embedded other files in this book's examples.
- Load the XML file at runtime. This allows a compiled SWF file to read an XML file when it loads. It means that if you want to change any data in your game, you just need to update the XML file, rather than recompile the SWF. This is probably the most common way that XML is used with Flash.

We'll look at all three ways to use XML in this chapter, beginning with the simplest: creating XML objects in code.

Creating XML objects

You can create XML objects directly in your AS3 code like this:

```
var title:XML = <title>This is the title</title>;
```

You can then access the XML document that you just created with the `title` variable. If you traced the value of `title`, it would appear like this:

```
<title>This is the title</title>
```

It might look like plain text, but because it's an XML object, you can access all its separate components individually. You'll soon see how.

Now let's see how we can create our little quiz as an XML object in AS3.0. Although it's not required, you'll make your code a little more readable if you give your XML object the same name as the root element. The root element is `<quiz>`, so a good name for the XML object is `quiz`.

```
var quiz:XML
=
<quiz name="A little quiz">
  <quizItem>
    <question>What was the first video game?</question>
    <answerA>Pong</answerA>
    <answerB>Spacewar!</answerB>
    <answerC points="10">Cathode Ray Tube Amusement Device</answerC>
  </quizItem>
  <quizItem>
    <question>What is the highest ever selling video game?</question>
    <answerA>Duck Hunt</answerA>
    <answerB points="10">Wii Sports</answerB>
    <answerC>Super Mario Bros.</answerC>
  </quizItem>
  <quizItem>
    <question>Which of these is not a programming language?</question>
    <answerA points="10">FlipFlop</answerA>
    <answerB>Groovy</answerB>
    <answerC>Scratch</answerC>
  </quizItem>
</quiz>
;
```

Yes, it's really long, but it works just fine. (Just don't forget that final semicolon!) If you trace the value of `xmlData`, you'll see the entire XML document, neatly formatted as it appears in the preceding code.

Now that we have an XML object, we need to access this information.

Reading elements, text nodes, and attributes

The quiz has nine possible answers to choose from: three answer As, three answer Bs, and three answer Cs. We can find all the `<answerA>` elements like this:

```
quiz.quizItem.answerA
```

Here's the result:

```
<answerA>Pong</answerA>
<answerA>Duck Hunt</answerA>
<answerA points="10">FlipFlop</answerA>
```

It might be more useful to just have access to the elements' text nodes, without the surrounding tags. We can use the `text` method to find them.

```
quiz.quizItem.answerA.text()
```

This will return all three of `<answerA>`'s text nodes. If you trace them, you'll see them all on one line, without spaces between them, like this.

```
PongDuck HuntFlipFlop
```

If you want to access an individual text node, you can do so by using an array index number. To retrieve the second text node, use `[1]`.

```
quiz.quizItem.answerA.text()[1]
```

This will return the second `<answerA>` text node.

```
Duck Hunt
```

The logic is exactly the same as working with arrays. (And, as with arrays, the first element will have an index number of 0.)

The `length()`method works like an array's `length` property. To find out how many questions are in this quiz, we can use the `length()` method to return the number of `<quizItem>` elements, like this:

```
quiz.quizItem.length()
```

This will return `3`.

If you're trying to target an element but are unsure of how deeply nested it is in the XML hierarchy, you can use the **double-dot** operator. For example, you can access `answerA` like this:

```
quiz..answerA
```

There are two dots between `quiz` and `answerA` to show that "there might be some other nodes between, but I have no idea what they might be." This syntax will target `answerA` without any problems.

Reading attributes

In the example XML, the name of the quiz is in the `<quiz>` tag's attribute, like this.

```
<quiz name="A little quiz">
```

It's important to access this attribute so that it can be displayed. The `attributes` method finds this information.

```
quiz.attributes()
```

This will return the values of all the attributes in the `<quiz>` element:

```
A little quiz
```

But what if any of your elements contain more than one attribute?

```
<quiz name="A little quiz" totalPoints="30" importance="not much">
```

Using `quiz.attributes()` will give you all of them. Here's how it would trace (again, without spaces or line breaks):

```
A little quiz30not much
```

You can also access these attributes individually by using an array index number. Here's how to find the third attribute:

```
quiz.attributes()[2]
```

This will return:

```
not much
```

You might also need to read the names of attributes. For example, the names of the three attributes in the `<quiz>` tag are `name`, `totalPoints`, and `importance`:

```
<quiz name="A little quiz" totalPoints="30" importance="not much">
```

You can access them with the `name` method. To find the name of the third attribute, use this syntax:

```
quiz.attributes()[2].name();
```

This will return:

```
importance
```

Unfortunately, this works with only one attribute at a time. You can't use `quiz.attributes().name()` to list all the names. To do that, use a `for each` loop, like this:

```
for each(var attribute:XML in quiz.attributes())
{
  trace(attribute.name());
}
```

This will trace as the following:

```
name
totalPoints
importance
```

It could be that you already know the name of an attribute and just need its value. You can use the `@` operator, followed by the attribute name, to find the value.

```
quiz.@totalPoints
```

This will return:

```
30
```

You can also use the `length()` method to find out how many attributes an element has.

```
quiz.attributes().length()
```

This will return `3`, based on the current example.

Looping through elements and attributes

Earlier, I showed you how you can access elements and text nodes directly, like this:

```
quiz.quizItem.answerA.text()
```

This will return all the text nodes within the `<answerA>` tags. You'll get all the information in one long line of text, like this:

```
PongDuck HuntFlipFlop
```

To make this usable, you'll almost certainly need to push this information into arrays. That means you'll need to loop through it.

AS3.0 has a special object called an `XMLList`, which is an array that contains a group of XML objects. In the preceding example, `Pong`, `Duck Hunt`, and `FlipFlop` are single XML objects. However, you can work with them together in an array as an `XMLList` of objects. Let's see how.

First, create an `XMLList` object that defines the array of XML objects of interest. Here's how we could create an array of `<answerA>` elements:

```
var answerAList:XMLList = quiz.quizItem.answerA;
```

`answerAList` is now an array that contains all three of the `<answerA>` elements. We can now loop through that array with a `for each` loop to find each item.

```
for each (var answerAElement:XML in answerAList)
{
  trace(answerAElement);
}
```

This code will trace as the following:

```
Pong
Duck Hunt
FlipFlop
```

Alternatively, we can produce the same result using a `for` loop and the `length()` method.

```
var answerAList:XMLList = quiz.quizItem.answerA;

for (var i:int = 0; i < answerAList.length(); i++)
{
  var answerAElement:XML = answerAList[i];
  trace(answerAElement);
}
```

It's entirely up to you which style you prefer.

You can loop through attributes in the same way. Let's imagine that we want to find out which of the `<answerA>` elements have `point` attributes. (In our example, we know that only one does, but let's pretend we're reading an XML document that we've never seen before.) We can use `XMLList` to help us loop through each `<answerA>` element and tell us the values of each of their `point` attributes.

```
var answerAPoints:XMLList = quiz.quizItem.answerA.attributes();

for each (var points:XML in answerAPoints)
{
   trace(points);
}
```

It loops through all three `<answerA>` elements looking for attributes called `points`. If it finds one, it will return the value. As expected, the preceding code will return `10`. That's because there's only one `<answerA>` element that has a `points` attribute, and its value is 10.

Finding all the child elements

Let's say we want to loop through all the `<answerA>`, `<answerB>`, and `<answerC>` elements to find the total number of points in the quiz. Those three elements are all child nodes of `<quizItem>`. Figure 10-7 illustrates this relationship.

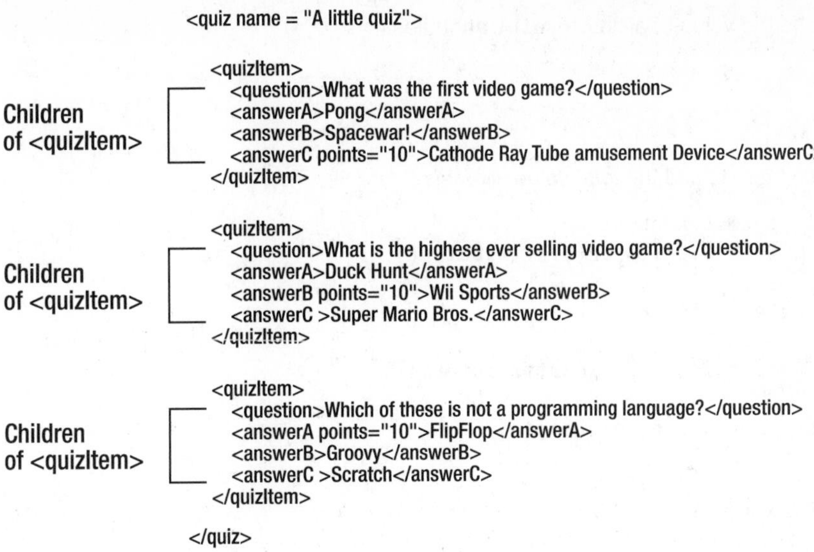

Figure 10-7. The answer nodes are all children of the <quizItem> parent node.

The `children` method will return all of the children of any node that you specify. Here's how to use it to find all the children of the `<quizItem>` nodes:

```
quiz.quizItem.children();
```

This will return all the child elements, which include the questions and answers.

```
<question>What was the first video game?</question>
<answerA>Pong</answerA>
<answerB>Spacewar!</answerB>
<answerC points="10">Cathode Ray Tube Amusement Device</answerC>
<question>What is the highest ever selling video game?</question>
<answerA>Duck Hunt</answerA>
<answerB points="10">Wii Sports</answerB>
<answerC>Super Mario Bros.</answerC>
<question>Which of these is not a programming language?</question>
<answerA points="10">FlipFlop</answerA>
<answerB>Groovy</answerB>
<answerC>Scratch</answerC>
```

To find all the `point` attributes in this data, use a `for each` loop. Here's how we can loop through them and add up all the points.

```
var attributeList:XMLList = quiz.quizItem.children().attributes();
for each (var points:XML in attributeList)
{
   trace(points);
}
```

This will trace the value of all three `point` attributes.

```
10
10
10
```

We can sum them to find the total value, like this:

```
var attributeList:XMLList
  = quiz.quizItem.children().attributes();

var totalPoints:uint = 0;

for each (var points:XML in attributeList)
{
  totalPoints += uint(points);
}

trace(totalPoints);
```

This will trace as `30`.

You can also use the `children` method to find the values of child element text nodes. The following bit of code will display all the text nodes that are children of `<quizItem>`.

```
var quizItemChildren:XMLList = quiz.quizItem.children();

for each (var quizItemChild:XML in quizItemChildren)
{
   trace(quizItemChild);
}
```

This will trace as the following:

```
What was the first video game?
Pong
Spacewar!
Cathode Ray Tube Amusement Device
What is the highest ever selling video game?
Duck Hunt
Wii Sports
Super Mario Bros.
Which of these is not a programming language?
FlipFlop
Groovy
Scratch
```

Perhaps we just want to find the names of those elements. We can do that by using the `name` method. The following code is identical to the code from the previous example, except that it traces `quizItemChild.name()`.

```
var quizItemChildren:XMLList = quiz.quizItem.children();
for each (var quizItemChild:XML in quizItemChildren)
{
   trace(quizItemChild.name());
}
```

It will trace only the names of the elements, not their text node values.

```
question
answerA
answerB
answerC
question
answerA
answerB
answerC
question
answerA
answerB
answerC
```

That's great, but how useful is it? It's very useful for filtering information so that you can find what you're looking for.

Let's say we just want to find the quiz's questions. We could use the `name()` method to display only the questions and ignore the answers. Here's the code that will do that:

```
var quizItemChildren:XMLList = quiz.quizItem.children();
for each (var quizItemChild:XML in quizItemChildren)
{
 if(quizItemChild.name() == "question")
 {
   trace(quizItemChild);
 }
}
```

This will trace as the following:

```
What was the first video game?
What is the highest ever selling video game?
Which of these is not a programming language?
```

The `name` method works for attributes as well, so you can use this same technique to filter any specific attributes that you want to find.

A better way to find what you're looking for

Looking for specific data in XML documents is such a common task that E4X has some specialized syntax to deal with it.

Let's imagine that we want to find out which quiz items contain the question "What was the first video game?" We can use this line of code to find out:

```
var questionList:XMLList
  = quiz.quizItem.(question == "What was the first video game?");
```

This will return the entire `<quizItem>` element that contains a question text node that matches the search term.

```
<quizItem>
  <question>What was the first video game?</question>
  <answerA>Pong</answerA>
  <answerB>Spacewar!</answerB>
  <answerC points="10">Cathode Ray Tube Amusement Device</answerC>
</quizItem>
```

If we happened to have more than one match, all matching `<quizItem>` elements would be returned. This is a very powerful database-style search feature that is built right into the syntax.

The previous example displayed all the XML information. To display the exact information we're looking for, we can append the element name to the end of the search directive, like this:

```
var questionList:XMLList
  = quiz.quizItem.(question == "What was the first video game?").question;
```

This will return:

```
What was the first video game?
```

That's interesting, but might in itself be rather useless. What could be useful is to determine the first possible answer to this question. We can do that by appending `answerA` to the search directive, like this:

```
var questionList:XMLList
  = quiz.quizItem.(question == "What was the first video game?").answerA;
```

This will return the first answer that matches that question: `Pong`. Again, if there's more than one match in the XML document, all the matches will be returned.

You can search for attributes in the same way by using the `@` operator to indicate that you're looking for an attribute. The following code will tell us which quiz item is the one that has answer A as the correct answer.

```
var pointsList:XMLList = quiz.quizItem.(answerA.@points == "10");
```

This will return the `<quizItem>` element in which `<answerA>`'s `point` attribute equals 10.

```
<quizItem>
  <question>Which of these is not a programming language?</question>
  <answerA points="10">FlipFlop</answerA>
  <answerB>Groovy</answerB>
  <answerC>Scratch</answerC>
</quizItem>
```

How can we use this to find out which answer equals 10 points? Just append the name of the element we want to find, like this:

```
var pointsList:XMLList
  = quiz.quizItem.(answerA.@points == "10").answerA;
```

This will return: `FlipFlop`.

As you can see, there are many ways to mix and match these techniques to help you find what you're seeking. The following code combines a few of the techniques to find the correct answer to a particular question.

```
var questionList:XMLList
  = quiz.quizItem.(question == "What was the first video game?");

var quizItemChildren:XMLList = questionList.children();
for each (var quizItemChild:XML in quizItemChildren)
{
 if(quizItemChild.@points == "10")
 {
   trace(quizItemChild);
 }
}
```

This will correctly trace as:

```
Cathode Ray Amusement Device
```

E4X syntax gives you very detailed access to XML data that you can use in your games however you wish. You'll find a working SWF called `XMLBasics` in the chapter's source files that illustrates all these examples using live code.

Changing XML data

It's very useful to be able store information about a game's current state in an XML document. You could create an XML document based on information such as a player's score and the current level, so that the game can be saved and resumed later. When the player resumes the game, you can load the custom XML document and feed the relevant data into the game engine. To do this, you need to be able to modify XML data and possibly add and remove nodes. E4X syntax gives you a number of tools to help you with this.

Adding new elements and attributes

Let's first start with an empty XML document called gameData.

```
var gameData:XML = <gameData></gameData>;
```

We can use this as a blank slate to add elements and attributes. Let's say that we need to add an element called <player>, which stores the player's name. We simply add the name of the new element to the XML object using dot notation, and assign an empty tag that matches the element name.

```
gameData.player = <player></player>;
```

If you now trace gameData, you'll see this:

```
<gameData>
  <player/>
</gameData>
```

We created a new, empty tag by using a single tag followed by a forward slash. You can also create a new empty tag with this line of code:

```
gameData.player = <player />;
```

This is preferable syntax to use when creating an empty element.

Now that we have a new, empty element, we can easily add a text node to it, like this:

```
gameData.player = "Player Name";
```

It's as simple as assigning a variable value. Our new XML document will now trace as follows:

```
<gameData>
  <player>Player Name</player>
</gameData>
```

But you can also create the element and text node together in a single step, like this:

```
gameData.player = <player>Player Name</player>;
```

This produces the same XML as the preceding trace.

You can just as easily create elements using existing variables. Simply assign the variable name to the new element. For example, if we have a variable called playerName that stores the player's name, we can assign its value to the <player> element as follows:

```
gameData.player = playerName;
```

This will also work with arrays or any other type of data.

Four specialized methods for adding elements are especially useful if you want to insert elements into an existing XML document: appendChild, prependChild, insertChildBefore, and insertChildAfter.

appendChild allows you add a new child element to any other element. Here's how we could add a new <score> element to our XML document:

```
gameData.appendChild(<score>50</score>);
```

Our XML document will now look like this:

```
<gameData>
  <player>Player Name</player>
  <score>50</score>
</gameData>
```

The new <score> element is added after the existing <player> element.

If we want to add a new element *before* the <player> element, we can do so using the prependChild method.

```
gameData.prependChild(<gameName>Cosmic Fluff Bubbles</gameName>);
```

prependChild will add this new element before all the others:

```
<gameData>
  <gameName>Cosmic Fluff Bubbles</gameName>
  <player>Player Name</player>
  <score>50</score>
</gameData>
```

You can specify exactly where in the order of elements you want to insert an element by using insertChildBefore and insertChildAfter. Let's insert a new element called <location> after the <player> element.

```
gameData.insertChildAfter
  (gameData.player, <location>Bangalore</location>);
```

This will trace as follows:

```
<gameData>
  <gameName>Cosmic Fluff Bubbles</gameName>
  <player>Player Name</player>
  <location>Bangalore</location>
  <score>50</score>
</gameData>
```

To insert a new element before another, use insertChildBefore rather than insertChildAfter.

You can add new attributes in the same way that you add new elements. Just include the @ operator in front of the name of the attribute you want to add. Here's how to add an attribute called bubblesPopped to the <score> element:

```
gameData.score.@bubblesPopped = 13;
```

This will trace as follows:

```
<score bubblesPopped="13">50</score>
```

The @ operator always indicates that you're referring to an attribute.

Building XML documents from existing variables

You can easily build XML documents from existing variables. Surround each variable with a pair of curly braces, { }, and insert it in each element's text node.

Let's suppose our game uses these four variables.

```
var gameName:String = "Cosmic Fluff Bubbles";
var player:String = "Player Name";
var location:String = "Bangalore";
var score:uint = 50;
```

We can use them to build our XML document by surrounding them in curly braces and inserting them into each element's text nodes:

```
var gameData:XML
  =
  <gameData>
    <gameName>{gameName}</gameName>
    <player>{player}</player>
    <location>{location}</location>
    <score>{score}</score>
  </gameData>
  ;
```

This traces just as you would expect:

```
<gameData>
  <gameName>Cosmic Fluff Bubbles</gameName>
  <player>Player Name</player>
  <location>Bangalore</location>
  <score>50</score>
</gameData>
```

You can use any variable names you like; they don't need to match the element names.

You can create attributes from variables in the same way. In the following example, the `timesPlayed` variable is used as an attribute in the `<score>` element.

```
var timesPlayed:uint = 3;

var gameData:XML
  =
  <gameData>
    <gameName>{gameName}</gameName>
    <player>{player}</player>
    <location>{location}</location>
    <score timesPlayed = {timesPlayed}>{score}</score>
  </gameData>
  ;
```

This will trace with the `timesPlayed` attribute having the value `3`:

```
<gameData>
  <gameName>Cosmic Fluff Bubbles</gameName>
  <player>Player Name</player>
  <location>Bangalore</location>
  <score timesPlayed="3">50</score>
</gameData>
```

Removing nodes from XML documents

You can remove any element, attribute or text node with the `delete` keyword. To remove the `<location>` element in our example XML document, use this line of code:

```
delete gameData.location;
```

Our document now looks like this:

```
<gameData>
  <gameName>Cosmic Fluff Bubbles</gameName>
  <player>Player Name</player>
  <score bubblesPopped="13">50</score>
</gameData>
```

You can use `delete` to remove attributes as well. Just remember to target an attribute name with the `@` operator. Here's how to delete the `bubblesPopped` attribute:

```
delete gameData.score.@bubblesPopped;
```

And now the XML looks like this:

```
<gameData>
  <gameName>Cosmic Fluff Bubbles</gameName>
  <player>Player Name</player>
  <score>50</score>
</gameData>
```

`delete` can also be used to remove text nodes. Let's use it to remove `Cosmic Fluff Bubbles` from the `<gameName>` element.

```
delete gameData.gameName.text()[0];
```

You also need to supply the index number of the text node, which will always be `0`. Our new XML document looks like this:

```
<gameData>
  <gameName/>
  <player>Player Name</player>
  <score>50</score>
</gameData>
```

The `<gameName>` element is now completely empty.

You'll find working examples of all this code in the `ChangingXML` folder.

This has been a long but important introduction to XML. These general techniques cover most of the ways that you can manipulate XML data.

> *The XML standard is maintained by the World Wide Web Consortium (W3C). For much more detail on XML, visit the official W3C site at `http://www.w3.org/TR/REC-xml/`. AS3.0's XML object also contains many more properties and methods than those covered here, some of which you might find useful. Be sure to check the XML entry in Adobe's ActionScript 3.0 Language and Components Reference for all the details.*

There are countless ways in which you can use XML data in your games. Next, we'll look at one of the most useful: to load game levels.

Loading game levels from XML data

The ideal use for XML in games is to use it to load game map levels and values that you need to initialize the game. You can load all the game's data from an external XML file, which you can keep separate from your AS3.0 source files and the SWF. The easiest way to do this is to embed an XML file into your AS3.0 code in the same way that you embed any other type of file—using the `Embed` metatag.

To embed an XML file, use this syntax:

```
[Embed(source = "anyXmlFile.xml",
mimeType = "application/octet-stream")]
private var XmlData:Class;
```

The XML file is now accessible in the `XmlData` class.

Next, create an object from the `XmlData` class:

```
var level:Object = new XmlData();
```

There are two things you need to keep in mind when creating this new object:

- Its name should preferably match the first element of the XML document. In this case, the first element of the XML document would be `<level>`.
- The object that you create from the `XmlData` class must be typed as `Object`. You can't type it as `XmlData`. This is because the `XmlData` class was created directly in the class, and the compiler won't yet have access to it when it tries to compile the code.

Finally, cast the new object as XML.

```
level = XML(level);
```

This tells the compiler that it should interpret the `level` object as an XML object. You can now work with the `level` object just as you would any ordinary XML object.

Now let's see how you can use an embedded XML file to create a game level map.

Creating a game level map

Run the SWF in the chapter's source files called `XMLMap`. The SWF displays a standard tile-based level map that's identical to the kind of maps you saw in Chapter 8, as shown in Figure 10-8.

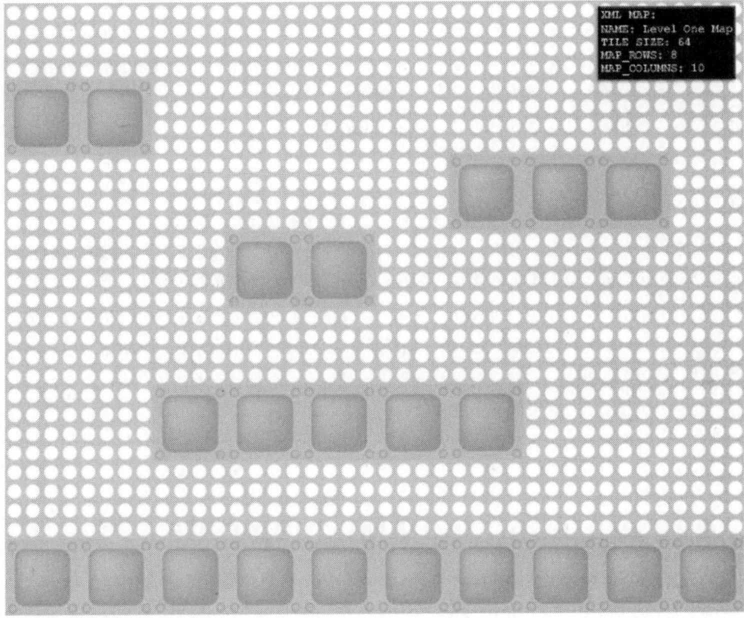

Figure 10-8. The map data is loaded from an external XML file.

It's nothing special to look at, but what is significant is that all the data for the level map is loaded from an external XML file. Additionally, the SWF displays the name of the map, "Level One Map," which is also stored in the XML file.

The XML file is in the `assets/xml` folder and is called `maps.xml`. Here's what it looks like:

```
<level name = "Level One Map">
  <row>10,10,10,10,10,10,10,10,10,10</row>
  <row>00,00,10,10,10,10,10,10,10,10</row>
  <row>10,10,10,10,10,10,00,00,00,10</row>
  <row>10,10,10,00,00,10,10,10,10,10</row>
```

```
  <row>10,10,10,10,10,10,10,10,10,10</row>
  <row>10,10,00,00,00,00,00,10,10,10</row>
  <row>10,10,10,10,10,10,10,10,10,10</row>
  <row>00,00,00,00,00,00,00,00,00,00</row>
</level>
```

You see the familiar two-dimensional array data that we've used to build all the tile-based maps in the book so far. But don't be fooled by this—it's not an array! It's XML data that has been structured so that it mimics two-dimensional array structure.

This XML file is going to be read by our AS3.0 code and eventually copied into a real two-dimensional array that's used to actually build the level. Structuring the XML data in an array-like format makes it easy for it to work with our existing tile-based game engine. You can format XML map data however you like, as long as your game engine has some way of interpreting it.

> *If you're going to share your XML document with other information systems like web servers outside your AS3.0 code, you might need to preface it with a header tag, called a Document Type Declaration (DTD). This is the standard DTD header recommended by W3C:*
>
> ```
> <?xml version="1.0" encoding="ISO-8859-1"?>
> ```
>
> *Its job is to describe how the XML has been encoded so that it can be properly interpreted by whatever system is reading it. It should be the first tag in the XML document. If you're sending and loading XML data to and from a server, find out if there are custom headers that you need to use so that the server can interpret the XML file correctly. DTDs like this are ignored by AS3.0, so you can safely use any header that you choose, or none at all.*

Loading and interpreting the XML map data

The `XMLMap` application loads the XML file that contains the map data and copies it into a two-dimensional array. The level that you see on the stage is actually being read and built from that two-dimensional array, using exactly the same `buildMap` method, unchanged, that we used in Chapter 8. What's important for you to know is how the XML file is loaded and how its data is copied into the two-dimensional array that's used to build the level.

This is the code from the `XMLMap` application class that embeds the file and creates the XML object called `level`:

```
//Embed the XML file
[Embed(source = "../assets/xml/maps.xml",
mimeType = "application/octet-stream")]
private var XmlData:Class;
```

```
public function XMLMap():void
{
  // Create the XmlData object
  var level:Object = new XmlData();

  //Cast it as an XML object. The name of the object
  //should preferably match the first XML element
  level = XML(level);
  //...
```

This is the same basic code that we looked at back at the start of this section. The `level` object contains the XML file, and we can now use it to build the two-dimensional array.

A blank array called `_platformMap` will be used to build the two-dimensional array. The code does this by looping through each `<row>` element and pushing the row's content into an array. There are eight rows in the XML files, so this results in eight row arrays. Each of those eight row arrays are then pushed into the `_platformMap` array. The result is that `_platformMap` becomes a two-dimensional array containing eight row arrays. Here's the section of code from the application class that does this:

```
//Create an XMLList object to help you loop through
//all the row elements
var rowList:XMLList = level.row;

//Loop through each row
for each(var row:XML in rowList)
{
  //Convert the row text node into a string
  var rowString:String = row.text();

  //Convert the string into an array.
  //Commas in the XML file are used to
  //separate each array element.
  //This array represents one <row> in the XML document
  var rowArray:Array = rowString.split(",");

  //Push the new rowArray into the _platformMap array.
  //This creates a 2D level map
  //which will contain all 8 rows by the time the loop quits
  _platformMap.push(rowArray);
}
```

The result of this is that the `_platformMap` array can now be used to build the game level in exactly the same way as in Chapter 8.

Let's take a closer look at how this loop works. We first need an `XMLList` object of all the `<row>` elements.

```
var rowList:XMLList = level.row;
```

We can now loop through each element in the rowList using a for each loop.

```
for each(var row:XML in rowList)
{…
```

This will loop eight times—once for each <row> element.

The first thing that the loop does is to extract the row's text node and store it in a String variable called rowString.

```
var rowString:String = row.text();
```

The row is now just a simple string of numbers, separated by commas. If you traced rowString, this is what you would see for the first row:

```
10,10,10,10,10,10,10,10,10,10
```

It's just a plain string of characters. And because it's a single string, those numbers cannot be read individually. As far as AS3.0 is concerned, the string is a solid block of meaningless characters. It might just as well be "abracadabra" or "Eyjafjallajokull"; AS3.0 can't read the individual numbers.

Our next job is to find a way to extract each of those numbers and load them as individual elements into an array. AS3.0's String object has a method called split, which is perfect for doing this. The split method separates each character or related group of characters in a string and returns them as an array of individual elements.

To use split, you need to tell it how it should define a single element. You can clearly see from the <row> elements that each number is separated by a comma. This means that we can tell the split method to use commas to separate each element. Here's how:

```
var rowArray:Array = rowString.split(",");
```

The comma character is supplied as split's argument. This means it will extract every character separated by a comma and return it as an individual array element. The result is a new array called rowArray. Each element in rowArray is one of the ten numbers from the <row> element.

Lastly, the loop pushes this new row array into the _platformMap array.

```
_platformMap.push(rowArray);
```

At the end of the loop, _platformMap will contain eight arrays, one for each row.

We now have a perfectly ordinary two-dimensional array that contains all the map data. We can use it with the buildMap method to build the level using exactly the same code that we used to build levels in Chapter 8.

```
buildMap(_platformMap);
```

The other thing this code does is to extract the name of the level from the XML file and display it in the status box. The level name is stored in the XML file in the name attribute of the <level> element.

```
<level name = "Level One Map">
```

The application class loads this into a variable called `_levelName`.

```
_levelName = level.@name;
```

It's then used to display the level name in the status box.

```
_statusBox.text += "\n" + "NAME: " + _levelName;
```

You can store as much metadata like this as you like in the same XML file that describes the map.

It's important for you to see all this code in its proper context, so here's most of `XMLMap`'s constructor method and the `Embed` code that does all this work:

```
//Embed the XML file
[Embed(source = "../assets/xml/maps.xml",
mimeType = "application/octet-stream")]
private var XmlData:Class;

public function XMLMap():void
{
  //Create the XmlData object
  var level:Object = new XmlData();

  //Cast it as an XML object. The name of the object
  //should preferably match the first XML element
  level = XML(level);

  //Create an XMLList object to help you loop through
  //all the row elements
  var rowList:XMLList = level.row;

  //Loop through each row
  for each(var row:XML in rowList)
  {
    //Convert the row text node into a string
    var rowString:String = row.text();

    //Convert the string into an array.
    //Commas in the XML file are used to
    //separate each array element.
    //This array represents one <row> in the XML document
    var rowArray:Array = rowString.split(",");
```

```
        //Push the row array into the _platformMap array.
        //This creates a 2D level map
        //which will contain all 8 rows by the time the loop quits
        _platformMap.push(rowArray);
    }

    //Capture the level "name" attribute like this:
    //and store it in the _levelName variable
    _levelName = level.@name;

    //Draw the tile sheet
    _tileSheetBitmapData.draw(_tileSheetImage);

    //Add the stage bitmap
    addChild(_backgroundBitmap);

    //Run the buildMap method to convert the
    //map's array data into a visual display
    buildMap(_platformMap);

    //Add the status box
    addChild(_statusBox);

    //Update status box
    _statusBox.text = "XML MAP:";
    _statusBox.text += "\n" + "NAME: " + _levelName;
    _statusBox.text += "\n" + "TILE SIZE: " + MAX_TILE_SIZE;
    _statusBox.text += "\n" + "MAP_ROWS: " + MAP_ROWS;
    _statusBox.text += "\n" + "MAP_COLUMNS: " + MAP_COLUMNS;
}
```

Refer to Chapter 8 if you have any questions about how the rest of the tile-based game engine works, including the `buildMap` method.

Now you've seen how to load one level map, but most games have many levels. You can use the same techniques to load multiple maps into the game, and switch levels as needed

Creating multiple game levels with XML

In the `MultipleXMLMaps` folder, you'll find an example of how to use XML to load multiple level maps into a game. Run the SWF, and you'll see that the result is the same as the `SwitchingLevels` example we looked at in Chapter 8, as shown in Figure 10-9. The underlying code that switches levels is identical. The difference is that all three game levels are loaded from a single XML file.

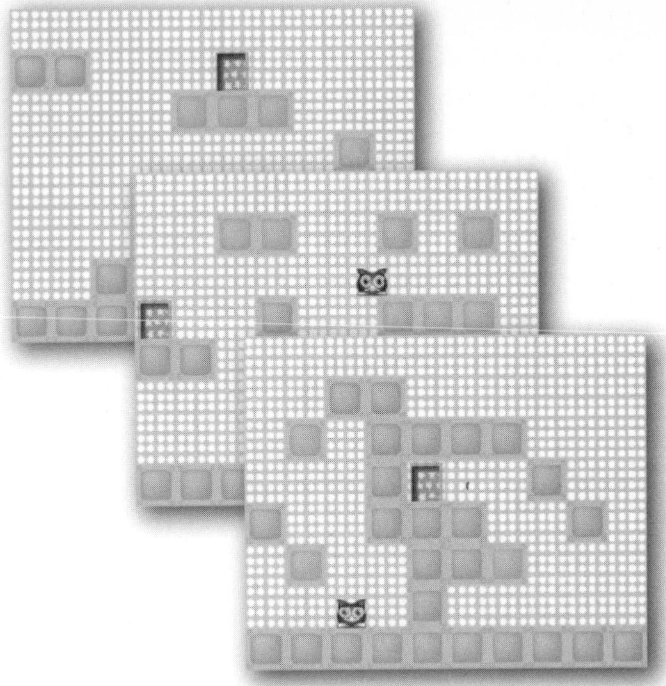

Figure 10-9. Multiple game levels made from a single XML file

You'll find the `maps.xml` file that stores these levels in the `assests/xml` folder. Recall from Chapter 8 that we needed two maps for each level:

- A map that contains the platforms
- A map that contains the game objects

You can see in the following code that each level contains these two types of maps.

```
<maps>
  <level>
    <name>Platform Pandemonium!</name>
    <platformMap>
      <row>10,10,10,10,10,10,10,10,10,10</row>
      <row>00,00,10,10,10,23,10,10,10,10</row>
      <row>10,10,10,10,01,01,01,10,10,10</row>
      <row>10,10,10,10,10,10,10,10,01,10</row>
      <row>10,10,10,10,10,10,01,01,01,10</row>
      <row>10,10,10,10,01,01,01,01,01,10</row>
      <row>10,10,00,10,10,10,10,10,10,10</row>
      <row>00,00,00,00,00,00,00,00,00,00</row>
    </platformMap>
```

```
    <gameObjectMap>
      <row>-1,-1,-1,-1,-1,-1,-1,-1,-1,-1</row>
      <row>-1,-1,-1,-1,-1,-1,-1,-1,-1,-1</row>
      <row>-1,-1,-1,-1,-1,-1,-1,-1,-1,-1</row>
      <row>-1,-1,-1,-1,-1,-1,-1,-1,-1,-1</row>
      <row>-1,-1,-1,-1,-1,-1,-1,-1,-1,-1</row>
      <row>-1,-1,-1,-1,-1,-1,-1,-1,-1,-1</row>
      <row>-1,20,-1,-1,-1,-1,-1,-1,-1,-1</row>
      <row>-1,-1,-1,-1,-1,-1,-1,-1,-1,-1</row>
    </gameObjectMap>
  </level>
  <level>
    <name>Extensible Mark-up Mayhem!</name>
    <platformMap>
      <row>10,10,10,10,10,10,10,10,10,10</row>
      <row>10,10,01,01,10,10,01,10,01,10</row>
      <row>10,10,10,10,10,10,10,10,10,10</row>
      <row>23,10,10,00,10,10,01,01,01,10</row>
      <row>00,00,10,00,00,10,10,10,10,10</row>
      <row>10,10,10,00,00,00,00,10,10,10</row>
      <row>10,10,10,10,10,10,10,10,10,10</row>
      <row>00,00,00,00,00,00,00,00,00,00</row>
    </platformMap>
    <gameObjectMap>
      <row>-1,-1,-1,-1,-1,-1,-1,-1,-1,-1</row>
      <row>-1,-1,-1,-1,-1,-1,-1,-1,-1,-1</row>
      <row>-1,-1,-1,-1,-1,-1,-1,-1,-1,-1</row>
      <row>-1,-1,-1,-1,-1,-1,-1,-1,-1,-1</row>
      <row>-1,-1,-1,-1,-1,-1,-1,-1,-1,-1</row>
      <row>-1,-1,-1,-1,-1,-1,-1,-1,-1,-1</row>
      <row>-1,-1,-1,-1,-1,-1,-1,-1,-1,20</row>
      <row>-1,-1,-1,-1,-1,-1,-1,-1,-1,-1</row>
    </gameObjectMap>
  </level>
  <level>
    <name>Kittykat Katastrophe!</name>
    <platformMap>
      <row>10,10,10,10,10,10,10,10,10,10</row>
      <row>10,10,00,00,10,10,10,10,10,10</row>
      <row>10,01,10,00,00,00,00,10,10,10</row>
      <row>10,10,10,00,23,10,10,00,10,10</row>
      <row>00,10,10,00,00,00,10,10,00,10</row>
      <row>10,01,10,10,00,00,01,10,10,10</row>
      <row>10,10,10,10,00,10,10,10,10,10</row>
      <row>00,00,00,00,00,00,00,00,00,00</row>
    </platformMap>
    <gameObjectMap>
      <row>-1,-1,-1,-1,-1,-1,-1,-1,-1,-1</row>
```

```
    <row>-1,-1,-1,-1,-1,-1,-1,-1,-1,-1</row>
    <row>-1,-1,-1,-1,-1,-1,-1,-1,-1,-1</row>
    <row>-1,-1,-1,-1,-1,-1,-1,-1,-1,-1</row>
    <row>-1,-1,-1,-1,-1,-1,-1,-1,-1,-1</row>
    <row>-1,-1,-1,-1,-1,-1,-1,-1,-1,-1</row>
    <row>-1,-1,20,-1,-1,-1,-1,-1,-1,-1</row>
    <row>-1,-1,-1,-1,-1,-1,-1,-1,-1,-1</row>
   </gameObjectMap>
  </level>
</maps>
```

Here's what our AS3.0 code needs to do to make sense out of all this data:

- **Two-dimensional arrays for each map**: Two types of maps are needed to create one game level: platform maps and game object maps. There are three of each type, for a total of six. Each of those six maps needs to be its own two-dimensional array. The code needs to loop through the XML data and create a two-dimensional array for each map.
- **Container arrays for each map type**: The code needs to separate the platform maps from the game object maps so that it can work with each type separately. This means it must create two more container arrays: one for each map type. The result is that there will be one array containing all the two-dimensional platform map arrays and another array containing all the two-dimensional game object map arrays.
- **The current maps for the game level to display**: The code needs to know which maps are current for the game level it will display.

If all this sounds a little confusing, take a look at Figure 10-10 which illustrates how all this data is organized. It's a bit like a row of Russian babushka dolls, with arrays inside bigger arrays, inside bigger arrays.

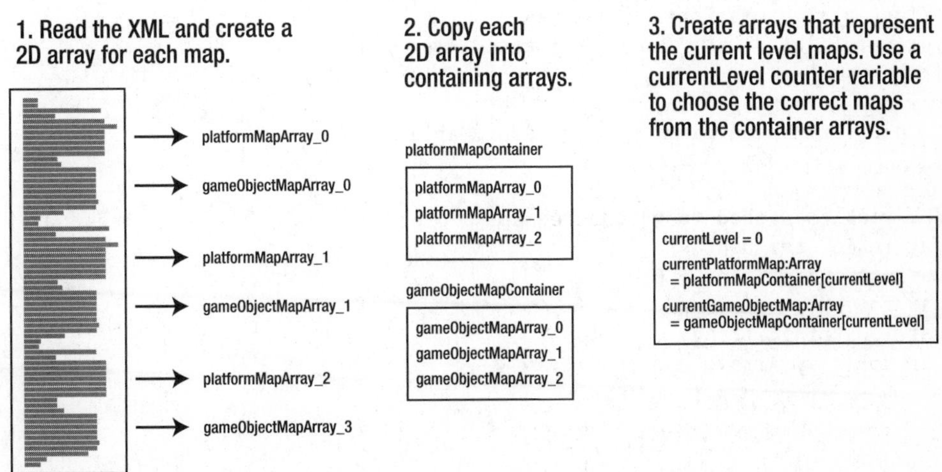

Figure 10-10. The process of converting the XML file into usable game level arrays

Let's put all our hard-won XML skills to work and take a look at the code that does this. Keep the diagram in Figure 10-10 close at hand as we walk though the code. It will make everything much easier to understand.

It all happens in a method called `createXMLMaps`. The method is long, but that's mostly because it repeats a lot of the same code twice: once for the platform maps and once for the game object maps. I've kept this repetitive code just to make everything a bit more understandable, but feel free to compact it.

Here's the entire `createXMLMaps` method so that you can see everything in context. I'll explain it in detail in the pages ahead.

```
//…Embed the XML file as in the previous examples

public function createXMLMaps():void
{
  //Load the XML file
  var maps:Object = new XmlData();

  //Cast it as an XML object
  maps = XML(maps);

  //Find out how many maps there are
  //and how many rows there are in each map
  var numberOfMaps:int = maps.level.platformMap.length();
  var numberOfRows:int = maps.level.platformMap.row.length();
  var rowsPerMap:int = numberOfRows / numberOfMaps;

  //Load the platform maps

  //Create empty map arrays for each map and store them in the
  //the _platformMapContainer array
  for(var i:int = 0; i < numberOfMaps; i++)
  {
    var platformMap:Array = [];
    _platformMapContainer.push(platformMap);
  }

  //Variables needed to build the maps
  var rowCounter:uint = 0;
  var mapCounter:uint = 0;
  var row:XML;
  var rowString:String;
  var rowArray:Array;
```

```
//Loop through each platformMap.row element
var platformRowList:XMLList = maps.level.platformMap.row;
for each(row in platformRowList)
{
  //Convert the row text node into a string
  rowString = row.toString();

  //Convert the string into an array.
  //Commas separate each array element
  rowArray = rowString.split(",");

  //Push the rowArray into one of the
  //platform map arrays
  _platformMapContainer[mapCounter].push(rowArray);

  //Add one to the row counter
  rowCounter++ ;

  //If the rowCounter is divisible
  //by 8 (the value of rowsPerMap)
  //then you know you've reached the first row of the next map.
  // Increase the mapCounter by one
  if(rowCounter % rowsPerMap == 0)
  {
     mapCounter++;
  }
}

//Load the game object maps.
//This code is almost identical to the code above that
//loaded the platform maps

//Create empty map arrays for each map and store them in the
//the _gameObjectMapContainer array
for(var j:int = 0; j < numberOfMaps; j++)
{
  var gameObjectMap:Array = [];
  _gameObjectMapContainer.push(gameObjectMap);
}

//Reset the row and map counters so they
//can be used again
rowCounter = 0;
mapCounter = 0;
```

```
    //Loop through each row element in the
    //game object maps
    var objectRowList:XMLList = maps.level.gameObjectMap.row;
    for each(row in objectRowList)
    {
      //Convert the row text node into a string
      rowString = row.toString();

      //Convert the string into an array.
      //Commas separate each array element
      rowArray = rowString.split(",");

      //Push the rowArray into one of the
      //game object map arrays
      _gameObjectMapContainer[mapCounter].push(rowArray);

      //Add one to the row counter
      rowCounter++

      //If the rowCounter is divisible
      //by 8 (the value of rowsPerMap)
      //then you know you've reached the first row of
      //the next map. Increase the mapCounter by one
      if(rowCounter % rowsPerMap == 0)
      {
         mapCounter++;
      }
    }

    //Load the names of each level
    //by looping through all the <name> elements
    //and pushing them into an array
    var nameList:XMLList = maps.level.name;
    for each (var name:XML in nameList)
    {
      _levelNames.push(name.toString());
    }

    //Set the current maps for the first level
    //that you want to be displayed
    _currentPlatformMap = _platformMapContainer[_currentLevel];
    _currentObjectMap = _gameObjectMapContainer[_currentLevel];
}
```

The code first creates a maps XML object in the same way that we created XML objects in previous examples.

```
var maps:Object = new XmlData();
maps = XML(maps);
```

Its name is maps because <maps> is the first element in the XML file.

We then need to figure out how many levels there are in the XML file. We can find this out by calling the length method of the <platformMap> element.

```
var numberOfMaps:int = maps.level.platformMap.length();
```

The length method will tell us how many <platformMap> elements there are in the XML file. There happen to be three. We can use this value for a few different things, such as allocating the number of arrays we'll need to make to store these maps. (The number of platform maps is the same as the number of game object maps, so we can use this value for both kinds of maps.)

Next, we need to determine how many rows the <platformMap> elements have. We can find this out by calling the <row> element's length method.

```
var numberOfRows:int = maps.level.platformMap.row.length();
```

This will tell us the number of rows that all the <platformMap> elements have combined. There are three <platformMap> elements, and each contains eight <row> elements. This results in 24, but that is a rather useless number. What we really need to know is how many rows each map has. We can easily find this out by dividing the numberOfRows by the numberOfMaps.

```
var rowsPerMap:int = numberOfRows / numberOfMaps;
```

Now we know that there are three platform maps and each has eight rows. (Again, these numbers apply to both of the game object maps, because their structure is the same.)

Next, the code starts building the platform map arrays. The first thing it does is to create three empty arrays inside the _platformMapContainer. Remember that the _platformMapContainer is a container array that holds the all the two-dimensional platform map arrays. Refer back to Figure 10-10, and you'll see it in step 2. The following code creates three empty arrays inside that container array.

```
for(var i:int = 0; i < numberOfMaps; i++)
{
  var platformMap:Array = [];
  _platformMapContainer.push(platformMap);
}
```

This gives us an empty structure to work with. We can now start building each of the three arrays inside this container.

The next bit of code is a for each loop. It loops through each <platformMap> element and builds the two-dimensional array for each map. It also needs to figure out where one map ends and the next one starts.

```
var rowCounter:uint = 0;
var mapCounter:uint = 0;
var row:XML;
var rowString:String;
var rowArray:Array;
```

```
//Loop through each row
var platformRowList:XMLList = maps.level.platformMap.row;
for each(row in platformRowList)
{
  //Convert the row text node into a string
  rowString = row.toString();

  //Convert the string into an array.
  //Commas separate each array element
  rowArray = rowString.split(",");

  //Push the rowArray into one of the
  //platform map arrays
  _platformMapContainer[mapCounter].push(rowArray);

  //Add one to the row counter
  rowCounter++

  //If the rowCounter is divisible
  //by 8 (the value of rowsPerMap)
  //then you know you've reached the first row of
  //the next map. Increase the mapCounter by one
  if(rowCounter % rowsPerMap == 0)
  {
     mapCounter++;
  }
}
```

The first part of this loop will be familiar to you from the earlier example. The text node in the <row> element is copied into a string, and then each number is copied into an array using the split method.

```
rowString = row.toString();
rowArray = rowString.split(",");
```

Next, the rowArray is copied into the platformMap array. But which platformMap array? Remember that there are three of them. They're all inside the _platformMapContainer. (See Figure 10-10 for a reminder.)

To keep track of which platformMap array to use, we have a variable called mapCounter. It's initialized to 0 before the loop starts.

```
var mapCounter:uint = 0;
```

mapCounter is used as an array index number for the _platformMapContainer. If _platformMapContainer has an array index of 0, then it refers to the first map, like this:

```
_platformMapContainer[0]
```

That means that if you want to push a row array into the first platformMap array, your code will look like this:

```
_platformMapContainer[0].push(rowArray)
```

This could be a bit confusing. Remember that you're not pushing the row into the _platformMapContainer—you're pushing it into *the first array that* _platformMapContainer *stores.*

The mapCounter variable is keeping track of what the current map is, so we can use its value to refer to the correct platformMap array.

```
_platformMapContainer[mapCounter].push(rowArray);
```

But hey, there's a problem! How do we know when to increase the value of mapCounter? How do we know when we've finished filling all the rows of one map and need to move on to the next one?

Remember that each map has eight rows. All we need to do is count the rows. If they exceed eight, then we know we can move on to the next map by increasing mapCounter by one. The code could look something like this:

```
if(rowCounter > 7)
{
  mapCounter++;
  rowCounter = 0;
}
```

In other words, "If we've counted more than eight rows (starting at zero), then increase the mapCounter by one and reset the rowCounter."

This code will work perfectly well. But, in the interest of showing you another use of the oh-so-talented modulus operator (%), this is the code I've actually used.

```
if(rowCounter % rowsPerMap == 0)
{
  mapCounter++;
}
```

Imagine that the loop has run eight times, so that rowCounter has a value of 8. It just so happens that rowsPerMap also has a value of 8. The code will look like this:

```
if(8 % 8 == 0)
{
  mapCounter++;
}
```

This is another way of saying, "If the remainder of 8 divided by 8 is 0, we're at the start of a new map. Increase mapCounter by one."

Here's the important part: *only the first row of each new map will ever be evenly divisible by eight.* That means that this will by true if the rowCounter is 16, 24, 32, or any multiple of 8.

At the first row of the second map, rowCounter will equal 16, and mapCounter will be increased by one again, and thus a different platform map array will be referenced. As long as all our maps have eight rows, this code will work.

And that's how our three platformMap arrays are built. At the end of the loop, all three are safely tucked away in the _platformMapContainer array.

The rest of the code builds the three gameObjectMap arrays in exactly the same way and copies them into the _gameObjectMapContainer array.

Next, the code needs to decide which maps from each container array will be used to build the first level. The maps that are currently displayed are stored in the _currentPlatformMap and _currentObjectMap arrays. Here are the two directives that do this:

```
_currentPlatformMap = _platformMapContainer[_currentLevel];
_currentObjectMap = _gameObjectMapContainer[_currentLevel];
```

_currentLevel is set to 0 when the game initializes. This means the first map arrays from both containing arrays will be displayed first. (Refer to Figure 10-10 to see how this fits into the bigger picture.) When the game engine switches levels, _currentLevel is increased by one, and the next maps in the container arrays are set as the current maps.

The last thing that this code does is to make an array to store all the level names. The XML file has an element called <name> that contains all the names of the levels.

```
<name>Platform Pandemonium!</name>
...
<name>Extensible Mark-up Mayhem!</name>
...
<name>Kittykat Katastrophe!</name>
```

> *Why didn't I create the level names as attributes, as I did in the previous examples? Just to show you that there are many different ways you can set up an XML file to store data, and no one right way. It makes no difference whether you store data as element text nodes or as attributes. The tendency is for attributes to be used to store metadata (extra information about the main data), but it's really just a matter of style, and it's completely up to you.*

The example SWF displays these names in the status box, and they match the currently displayed level. Here's the code that loops through the <name> elements and copies their text nodes into an array.

```
var nameList:XMLList = maps.level.name;
for each (var name:XML in nameList)
{
  _levelNames.push(name.text());
}
```

Because all the names are now in an array, we can use the same `_currentLevel` value that's used to switch levels to also display the correct level names. The level name index numbers will always match the correct map index numbers because they were pushed into their arrays in the same order. Here's how the status box uses this feature to display the correct level name:

```
_statusBox.text
  += "\n" + "LEVEL NAME: " + _levelNames[_currentLevel];
```

And now you know how to use XML to create game levels!

> *You might be wondering how XML fits into the MVC framework that we've used so often in this book. It's associated with the model. The model's job is to store game data. That means you should load an XML file into the model when the game initializes. The main application class could load the XML file, and pass the XML object to the model as an argument when it builds the game's MVC system.*

As you've seen, XML is very useful for storing game data. It's really the perfect data-storage solution for most games. I've shown you a few practical uses, but there are countless others. Jump right in and start using XML in your games whenever you can.

Next, let's look at one more way to load XML files.

Loading XML files at runtime

So far, I've shown you how to create XML data directly with AS3.0 code and how to embed an external XML file. These are actually the least common ways that XML is used in Flash games. Far and away the most common is to load the XML file at runtime. This is called **runtime loading**.

The problem with embedding an XML file with the `Embed` metatag is that whenever you make any changes in the XML, you need to recompile the SWF. Wouldn't it be far nicer if you could tinker with the game by just making changes to the XML, and have the SWF read the new XML data each time it runs? It would. This way, you could have a game running on a server and completely change the levels or any of the game data by just uploading a new XML file. You don't need to touch the rest of your code or recompile and re-upload the SWF.

Using URLLoader to load files

AS3.0 allows you to load files at runtime with the `URLLoader` class. You can use `URLLoader` to load any file, such as images or SWF files, not just XML files.

To load files at runtime, import the `URLLoader` and `URLRequest` class from the `flash.net` package.

```
import flash.net.URLLoader;
import flash.net.URLRequest;
```

First, create a URLRequest object.

```
var loader:URLLoader = new URLLoader();
```

Then use the loader object's load method and the URLRequest class to load the file.

```
loader.load(new URLRequest("fileName.xml"));
```

Because the file you're loading isn't part of the compiled SWF, your code shouldn't be dependent on it until the file has loaded. You can use the URLLoader's COMPLETE event to tell you when the file has loaded. To use it, add a COMPLETE event listener to an URLLoader object and a matching event handler.

```
loader.addEventListener(Event.COMPLETE, fileLoadedHandler);

private function fileLoadedHandler(event:Event):void
{
  //Create an XML object based on the event target's data property

  var xmlData:XML = new XML(event.target.data);
  trace("File loaded");

  //Run any code that depends on this data to initialize…
}
```

The loaded file will be in the event.target.data property.

You'll find a working example of a simple system to load XML files using URLLoader in the LoadingXML folder in the chapter's source files.

Runtime loading security issues

There's an inevitable issue that arises when you load files at runtime: Flash Player security. As I mentioned earlier, Flash Player locks down SWF files extremely tightly so that there's no chance that they could be used to distribute worms, viruses, or spyware. This tight security is one of Flash's strengths and why it is so widely used. However, it also means that Flash Player is extremely picky about which files it allows SWFs to load.

SWF files created by Flash Professional and Flash Builder will be able to load local files without any problems. That's because they assume developers can be trusted. (Oh, if only they knew!) However, if you create a SWF file using some other IDE or test the SWF in the environment that users will be accessing it, it's very likely that URLLoader won't be able to load external files. Instead, you'll get a "security sandbox violation" error.

Here, I'll point you to some resources to help you resolve sandbox violation errors if you get them.

Problems loading files locally

If you're not using Flash Builder or Flash Professional to create a SWF, you'll need to explicitly tell Flash Player that a particular SWF is "trusted" and has the right to load external files. You can do this in two different ways: with a CFG file or by setting Flash Player's global security settings.

The CFG file is a text file with a `.cfg` extension. All it contains is the path to the SWF that you want to trust to load local files. In Windows, the path from the hard drive root might look like this:

```
C:\Code\Flash\Game\bin\game.swf
```

In Mac OS X, you could use this format:

```
/Code/Flash/Game/bin/game.swf
```

If you want all SWF files in any given directory to be trusted, use the path to a general directory without specifying any SWF files. The following path will make *all* the SWF files in the `Flash` folder trusted and able to load local files:

```
C:\Code\Flash
```

After you create a CFG file, you need to save it in the `FlashPlayerTrust` directory, which will be in a different place depending on your operating system. In Windows, you'll find it here:

```
C:\WINDOWS\system32\Macromedia\Flash\FlashPlayerTrust
```

In Mac OS X, it will be here:

```
/Library/Application Support/Macromedia/FlashPlayerTrust
```

When you open the `FlashPlayerTrust` folder, you'll find a few other CFG files that were created by different applications.

As an alternative to creating a CFG file, you can adjust the Flash Player's security settings. The Flash Player's Settings Manager allows you specify trusted directories. Here's how:

1. Run Flash Player and select **`Settings ➤ Advanced`**. A web browser window will open with advanced settings that you can set for Flash Player.
2. Click the Global Security Settings panel.
3. Click the link that says **`Global security settings for content creators`**. This opens a new page with a Flash application running inside it. This Flash app is the actual advanced control panel for *your* Flash Player. Yes, it's the Flash Player program installed on your system. It's not an interface to anything on Adobe's website, even though it looks that way.
4. Click the **`Edit Locations`** drop-down menu and select **`Add Location.`**
5. A file browser will opening that allows you add local files or folders that your Flash Player should deem to be trusted.

Your SWF files should now be able to load local files at runtime with `URLLoader`.

Problems loading files remotely

If you're running a SWF on a server in one domain, and it tries to load a file from another server in another domain, you need to create a **cross-domain policy file**. This is an XML file that tells Flash Player which domains it can trust. Here's an example of a cross-domain policy file:

```
<?xml version="1.0"?>
<cross-domain-policy>
  <allow-access-from domain="www.anyDomainName.com" />
  <allow-access-from domain="www.anyOtherDomainName.com" />
</cross-domain-policy>
```

Files from any of the listed domains will be trusted.

Name your new policy file `crossdomain.xml`, and then upload it to your server's root directory. You should be able to see it if you browse for it. For example, browse to `www.anywebsite.com/crossdomain.xml`.

Flash Player will automatically look for a policy file with that name and in that location when the SWF loads.

You can also specify trusted domains directly within your AS3.0 code by using the `allowDomain` method, like this:

```
flash.system.Security.allowDomain("http://www.anyDomainName.com");
```

If it's a secure website (a site name with a URL that begins with `https://`), you need to use the `allowSecureDomain` method.

```
flash.system.Security.allowSecureDomain
  ("https://www.anyOtherDomainName.com");
```

This will also work for local files—just supply the path name to the local folder

```
flash.system.Security.allowSecureDomain("C:\Code\Flash ");
```

If you know in advance which domains should be trusted, using `allowDomain` and `allowSecureDomain` is a good solution. However, you often don't know the details of these until the time comes to deploy the SWF. That's why using an XML policy file is useful. It allows you to change trusted sites by uploading a new policy file at any time, without needing to recompile and re-upload the SWF.

> *Although voluminous tomes can (and have) been written about Flash Player security, the best place to start is the "Flash Player security" chapter in Adobe's online manual Programming ActionScript 3.0 for Flash (`http://help.adobe.com/en_US/ActionScript/3.0_ProgrammingAS3/`). Specifically, for more information about cross-domain policy files, see the "Website controls (policy files)" chapter. To get to this chapter, follow these links:* ***Flash Player security ➤ Permission controls ➤ Website controls (policy files)***.

The most important thing to remember regarding Flash Player security is to test the SWF in the same environment as users are going to be using it. Security issues often won't raise their head until you do this.

Are we there yet?

The ten chapters of this book have covered all the important topics that every Flash game designer needs to know. Is this the end of the road? Not by any means! What we've covered in this book will form the basis for a rich and creative career in game design, but it's nowhere near the end of the journey.

I have a few suggestions for where to go from here.

3D games

At the time of writing, if you want to make 3D games in Flash, you need to use a third-party API such as Alternativa3D, Away3D, or Papervision3D. This involves installing the API and learning how to use it. This is no small undertaking, so you'll need to commit to learning libraries of new methods, properties, events, and all the concepts and terminology that go along with it. You could also create your own 3D API from scratch, which would be a great learning experience, but a huge project.

You also need to be aware that the latest Flash Player at the time of this writing, 10.1, did not have true graphics processing unit (GPU) support. This means that all 3D Flash is software-rendered, which makes it quite low-tech and slow by modern standards. But if you moderate your expectations and don't expect next-gen 3D graphics, Flash can do a reasonable job. It's about on par with a Nintendo DS.

The good news is that you'll be able to apply all the general game design concepts that we've covered in this book to 3D games. You have just one more dimension to worry about. And the other good news is that there are some excellent books to help you get started:

- *The Essential Guide to 3D in Flash* by Rob Bateman and Richard Olsson (friends of ED, 2010) is a complete introduction to 3D in Flash using the Away3D engine.
- *The Essential Guide to Open Source Flash Development* by Chris Allen *et al.* (friends of ED, 2010) includes a chapter on Papervision3D.

However, watch this space! This is a very competitive, fast-changing industry, so make sure to check Adobe's website for the latest word on 3D for Flash Player (`http://www.adobe.com/products/flashplayer/`).

2D physics

Much of this book has been about physics (and thermodynamics, like friction) for games. For most general-purpose Flash games, what you've learned here will be all you'll need to know. You'll be able to apply the same formulae and concepts to other programming platforms as you broaden your repertoire of skills. And it has also laid the foundation for a much deeper exploration of game physics, if that's an area in which you want to specialize. But if you don't want to specialize in it and yet still take your game physics a few steps further, there's another option. You can use a physics API, like Box2D, Glaze, APE, or Fisix.

The advantage to using an API is that it will do all the math for you. Games like Angry Birds and Crush the Castle depend on detailed physics simulations of the real world. The physics are so complex that using a good API is really the only practical solution for a lone game developer or small team.

On the other hand, always consider writing as much original physics code as you can. As you've seen, most game physics can be boiled down to a few lines of fairly routine code. How many lines of code was our billiards game prototype? About 15 or 20. For most games, a big physics API is overkill and will unnecessarily eat up resources. The other problem with using an API is that you'll need to know it inside out to be able to debug easily, which can be a problem if you snag a bug in a complex project with deadlines looming. If you can't figure it out, your only hope might be for a leprechaun to whisper the answer in your ear. If you write your own physics code, you'll know it thoroughly, and debugging will be a snap.

Online multiplayer games

Creating multiplayer games are an important but vast and complex topic. This type of game development spans numerous technologies on many different platforms and requires a lot of knowledge about networking.

I strategically avoided multiplayer games in this book to put the focus on essential, core game-design techniques. However, you will inevitably want to start making online multiplayer games at some point—the temptation is just too compelling. So, let me help you out by pointing the way to some useful resources.

First, you'll need to install a multiplayer socket server. Here are some commercial servers that work especially well with Flash:

- ElectroServer (`http://www.electro-server.com`)
- SmartFoxServer (`http://www.smartfoxserver.com`)
- dimeRocker (`http://www.dimerocker.com`)
- Adobe Flash Media Server (`http://www.adobe.com/devnet/flashmediaserver`)

These servers are specialized for Flash games, but each has different strengths and weaknesses, so research them carefully before jumping in. They're all very powerful, robust products that can handle tens of thousands of simultaneous connections.

If you don't want or need to spend money on a commercial socket server and want to try something new, you can write your own. You'll need to learn a bit of Java, but as it's very closely related to AS3.0, that won't be a major hurdle. A good place to start is this Broculus.net tutorial (`http://www.broculos.net/tutorials/how_to_make_a_multi_client_flash_java_server/20080320/en`). It will show you how to write a Flash chat application using a Java socket server.

Further reading

There are many excellent books available to help inspire you further. Here are a few that I recommend:

- *The Essential Guide to Flash Games: Building Interactive Entertainment with ActionScript* by Jeff Fulton and Steve Fulton (friends of ED, 2010) provides a detailed and comprehensive look at the making of ten complete Flash games, from the ground up. It offers unparalleled insight into building professional Flash games, and is a perfect complement to this book.
- *Foundation ActionScript 3.0 Animation: Making Things Move* (friends of ED, 2007) and *AdvancED ActionScript 3.0 Animation* (friends of ED, 2008) by Keith Peters are both rich resources of scripted animation, math, and AI algorithms that are usable for all types of games. *AdvancED ActionScript 3.0 Animation* has a chapter on building isometric (pseudo 3D) environments for tile-based games and another on AI steering behaviors.
- *Real Time Collision Detection* by Christer Ericson (Morgan Kaufmann, 2005) is the final word on collision detection for 2D and 3D games. This textbook-style book is quite math-heavy, but oh, what wonderful math it is! The sample code is written in C++, but since it's a close cousin of ActionScript, you should have no difficultly comprehending it. If you just need to implement a BSP tree in your next game, you'll find out how to do it here.

Where to next?

Where you go from here is entirely up to you. You now have all the skills you need to start making some amazing Flash games. The rest is just practice, experimentation, and—most of all—imagination.

Flash game designers tend to be independent developers working alone or in a small team. How can a lone video game designer with a tiny budget compete with the likes of Electronic Arts, Activision, or Ubisoft, all of whom employ thousands and have Hollywood-sized budgets? The answer is that great game design is not about technology. It's about ideas. Just one original game idea can completely transform the industry.

Video games are such a relatively new medium that the best game ideas just haven't been thought of yet. What could they be, and who will come up with them? The Bachs, Picassos, and Shakespeares of the game world have yet to make their mark. But you can be sure that they will come from the ranks of independent game designers, and there's no reason why you can't be one of them.

Index

B

F

G

M

N

O

P